PENGUIN B

WODEHOUSE ON WOL

P. G. Wodehouse was born in Guildford in 1881 a
Dulwich College. After working for the Hong Kong a
Bank for two years, he left to earn his living as a journalist and
writer, writing the 'By the Way' column in the old *Globe*. He also
contributed a series of school stories to a magazine for boys, the
Captain, in one of which Psmith made his first appearance. Going to
America before the First World War, he sold a serial to the *Saturday
Evening Post* and for the next twenty-five years almost all his books
appeared first in this magazine. He was part author and writer of the
lyrics of eighteen musical comedies including *Kissing-Time* (with Guy
Bolton); he married in 1914 and in 1955 took American citizenship.
He wrote over ninety books and his work has won world-wide acclaim,
being translated into many languages. *The Times* hailed him as 'a
comic genius recognized in his lifetime as a classic and an old master
of farce'. P. G. Wodehouse said, 'I believe there are two ways of
writing novels. One is mine, making a sort of musical comedy without
music and ignoring real life altogether; the other is going right deep
down into life and not caring a damn . . .' He was created a Knight
of the British Empire in the New Year's Honours List in 1975. He
died on St Valentine's Day in 1975 at the age of ninety-three.

Guy Bolton was born in 1884 at Broxbourne in Hertfordshire and was
educated privately and at the École des Beaux Arts. He started life as
an architect, practising in New York City, but in 1913 began writing
for the stage and was the author of over fifty plays and musical
comedies. His stage successes include *Sally*, *The Dark Angel*, *Lady Be
Good* and *Swing Along*. Many of his musicals were written in collaboration with P. G. Wodehouse, the last being *Jeeves*, and in 1954 they
published a joint autobiography, *Bring on the Girls*, which is included
in this volume. Guy Bolton died in 1979.

P. G. Wodehouse

Wodehouse on Wodehouse

BRING ON THE GIRLS
(with Guy Bolton)

PERFORMING FLEA

OVER SEVENTY

Penguin Books

Penguin Books Ltd, Harmondsworth, Middlesex, England
Penguin Books, 625 Madison Avenue, New York, New York 10022, U.S.A.
Penguin Books Australia Ltd, Ringwood, Victoria, Australia
Penguin Books Canada Ltd, 2801 John Street, Markham, Ontario, Canada L3R 1B4
Penguin Books (N.Z.) Ltd, 182 190 Wairau Road, Auckland 10, New Zealand

Bring On the Girls first published by Herbert Jenkins 1954
Performing Flea first published by Herbert Jenkins 1953
Over Seventy first published by Herbert Jenkins 1957
This edition first published by Hutchinson 1980
Published in Penguin Books 1981

**Reproduced, printed and bound in Great Britain by
Hazell Watson & Viney Ltd, Aylesbury, Bucks**
Set in Baskerville

Contents

Publisher's Note

The three books contained in *Wodehouse on Wodehouse* comprise the only autobiographical account of P. G. Wodehouse's full life and long career. They were originally published in the UK by Herbert Jenkins between 1953 and 1957, and the text of *Wodehouse on Wodehouse* is based on these UK editions. The American versions of all three books differ from the British editions – quite substantially in the case of *Performing Flea* and of *Over Seventy*, which appeared under the changed titles of *Author! Author!* and *America, I Like You* in the States.

The minor revisions which Guy Bolton made to *Bring On the Girls* shortly before he died in September 1979, four and a half years after his old friend and contemporary 'Plum', have been included.

The books have been arranged here in the order in which they first appeared in the States. Wodehouse's 'autobiography' therefore starts with *Bring On the Girls*, the collaboration with Guy Bolton, described in the subtitle as 'The Improbable Story of Our Life in Musical Comedy'. Then comes *Performing Flea*, his 'Self-Portrait in Letters', and finally *Over Seventy*, 'An Autobiography with Digressions'. Not surprisingly a few landmarks in his life appear in each of the three books, but since they were first written over a period of several years and with no thought of their ever being brought together there is remarkably little duplication of material.

BRING ON THE GIRLS

*The Improbable Story of Our Life
in Musical Comedy*

P. G. Wodehouse

and

Guy Bolton

ONE

I

The scene is a smoke-filled room in a hotel in Boston or Philadelphia or New Haven or wherever else musical comedies are
tried out in preparation for their New York opening. Tonight's
performance of this new venture has revealed a dull spot in the
second act, what is technically known as a bug, and a conference has been called to debate methods of ironing it out.

Various proposals are made. The comedian thinks that, if
he were given another song there, all would be well. The
baritone feels that it is more the place for a baritone solo. The
author of the book. . . .

In an armchair in the corner there is sitting a man in shirt-
sleeves, chewing an enormous (unlighted) cigar. He is fifty-five
years old and for twenty-five of those years he has been an
impresario of musical comedy. Lending to the discussion the
authority of long experience and uttering the slogan which he
probably learned at his mother's knee, he says, 'Bring on the
girls!'

It is the panacea that never fails. It dates back, according to
the great Bert Williams, to the days of ancient Egypt.

'When one of those Pharaohs died,' he used to explain to his
partner Walker, 'they'd lay that ole Pharaoh out, and then,
just to make sure, they'd bring in wine – finest wine in the
country – and they'd put it beside him. Then they'd bring in
rich food that smelled just beautiful an' put that on the other
side of him. Then they'd bring on the girls, an' those girls
would do the veil-dance. An' if that ole Pharaoh didn't sit
right up and take notice then . . . brother, he was dead.'

The impresario has his way. The girls are brought on.

And how wonderful those girls always were. They did not spare themselves. You might get the impression that they were afflicted by some form of chorea, but the dullest eye could see that they were giving of their best. Actors might walk through their parts, singers save their voices, but the personnel of the ensemble never failed to go all out, full of pep, energy and the will to win. A hundred shows have been pushed by them over the thin line that divides the floperoo from the socko.

It is for this reason that Bolton (Guy) and Wodehouse (P.G.), looking back over their years of toil in the musical comedy salt-mines, raise their glasses and without hesitation or heel-taps drink this toast: To the Girls!

And they feel that the least they can do in gratitude for all their hard work is to honour them in the title of this book.

2

There was I and there were you three thousand miles apart:
    Who'd have thought that we would ever have met at the start?
But it's plain to see 'twas meant to be in spite of every bar,
    For I met you and you met me, you see, and here we are.

The above is the refrain (or 'burthen', as Jerry Kern always insisted on calling it) of a duet Carroll McComas and Harry Brown used to sing in the fourth of the series of Princess Theatre intimate musical comedies, *Oh, Lady, Lady*, the idea being that, having discovered that they were kindred souls, they were feeling how tragic it would have been if they had never met. The thought might apply with equal force to the authors of the play.

At the outset it would have seemed that conditions for an early meeting were just right. Wodehouse was born in Guildford, Surrey, England, and almost simultaneously Bolton was added to the strength of Broxbourne, Herts. As the crow flies, Guildford and Broxbourne are not much more than twenty miles apart, and it is quite possible that the two infants, destined to collaborate for forty years, may often have seen the same crow engaged in checking the distance. One would have said that it would have been a mere matter of weeks before they got together and started working on a show.

But it was not to be. Just as Wodehouse, who even then wanted to write musical comedy lyrics, heard that there was a baby over at Broxbourne who wanted to write musical comedy books and resolved to save his pocket money and look him up directly he had amassed enough for the fare, he was stunned by the news that the Bolton parents, who were American, were taking their issue back to New York. And at about the same time he had to return with his own parents to Hong Kong, where the elder, bread-winning Wodehouse won bread as a judge. Collaboration for the moment became, if not void, certainly null.

It remained null for a considerable number of years, during which Bolton ripened into an architect in New York and Wodehouse into a writer in London, and the odds against the two ever meeting were raised astronomically by the fact that the latter's principal means of support was the composition of a daily column, supposedly humorous, on the London *Globe*. It was a steady job – £3 a week, just like finding it – and in those days no Englishman ever dreamed of giving up a steady job. It seemed as though Fate had definitely arranged that the words 'Book and Lyrics by Guy Bolton and P. G. Wodehouse' should never appear on a theatre programme.

But what Fate had not allowed for was the latter's secret passion for America. From his earliest years America had been to this pie-faced young dreamer the land of romance, and came a day when he decided that he had got to see it, if only briefly. The *Globe* job carried with it a five weeks' holiday per annum, and in 1909 it suddenly struck Wodehouse, an able mathematician, that, allowing eight days for the voyage out and another eight days for the voyage back, he could manage nearly three weeks in sunny Manhattan. Packing a toothbrush and a couple of short stories, he set out.

A week after his arrival he had sold one of the stories to the *Cosmopolitan* and the other to *Collier's Weekly*, both on the same day and each for $300, and feeling that a good thing like this must certainly be pushed along – the London price at that time for a Wodehouse story was £7 10s. – he sent in his resignation to the *Globe* and settled down in Greenwich Village with a second-hand Monarch typewriter and plenty of paper.

It was not too difficult, he found, to make a living of a sort as a freelance writer in New York. He had hit the city at a time when magazines multiplied like rabbits there, and even if you failed to join the swells in George Horace Lorimer's *Saturday Evening Post*, there were plenty of other markets where you could pick up your $150 or $200 for a short story, and you could live an incredible time on $200 in those days. And if everything else failed, there was the Munsey group of more or less half-witted pulp-paper magazines, with Bob Davis, their editor, always ready to bury his head in his hands for a couple of minutes and come up with a plot, which he presented to you gratis, and bought, when worked into a story, for 50 of the best or sometimes even 75.

The gap between the future collaborators having thus shrunk to a few city blocks, their meeting could not be postponed much longer. For there was now a new link between them. Like the men in the Bab ballad who both knew Robinson, they both knew Jerome Kern. A few years before, Wodehouse had written some numbers with Jerry – then aged about eighteen – for a London production, while Bolton had just done a piece called *Ninety in the Shade* with Kern music, the first time Jerry had been entrusted with an extra score.

Wodehouse, moreover, had recently become dramatic critic for Frank Crowninshield's *Vanity Fair*, and in this capacity he attended the opening performance of *Very Good Eddie* – book by Bolton, music by Kern – the second of the 'intimate' musical comedies at the little Princess Theatre on 39th Street.

3

It was Elizabeth Marbury, dear, kindly, voluminous Bessie Marbury, who first thought of musical comedy on a miniature scale – musical comedy with not more than two sets, eight to twelve girls and an orchestra of eleven, a celeste to take the place of woodwind. It was one of those inspired ideas that used to come to her every hour, on the hour.

For Bessie was a brilliant woman, a dramatic agent who held the entire European market in her plump and capable hands.

Her clients relied on her not only to sell their work but to help them write it. If their second act seemed to have blown a fuse, she would tell them what to do about it. She would even suggest plots and characters. She was a sort of female Bob Davis.

She and Ray Comstock were running the little Princess Theatre on 39th Street at that time and not making much of a go at it. It was difficult to get the right sort of show for a house of that size. The last thing tried there had been an evening of one-act plays, and it had been a painful failure.

It was then that Bessie got her inspiration. Midget musical comedy!

The venture would have to be economically planned. The Princess, seating only 299, could not afford as author and composer any of the men with big names – the Henry Blossoms, the Otto Harbachs, the Victor Herberts and the Ivan Carylls, who, being established, had large views on the sort of money for which they were prepared to work. What was needed was young fellows who were on their way up the ladder but still climbing the lower rungs.

Jerry Kern was the obvious choice for composer. A much less knowledgeable woman than Bessie Marbury could have spotted him as a coming champ. In those days managers were importing large, heavy Viennese operettas with large, heavy scores, and it was always the gay, tuneful interpolated Kern numbers that put them over. She signed up Jerry at once. The question then arose: Who was to do the book? Jerry suggested Guy.

Bessie not only looked like a very charming and benign elephant, she had an elephant's memory. She remembered *Ninety in the Shade*, she remembered a divorce comedy by Bolton, *The Rule of Three*, and she remembered having heard his name mentioned by Charles Hanson Towne, the editor of the *Smart Set*, who had published some Bolton short stories.

'Yes, I know Bolton's work. He shows promise.'

'And now,' said Jerry, 'you're going to promise him shows.'

Nobody Home was the first of the series. It was enough of a success to encourage the management to feel that they were on the right lines, and Bolton and Kern were commissioned to write another. With this one, *Very Good Eddie*, intimate musical comedy – later to be known as the 'Princess Shows' – became definitely a New York institution.

4

Very Good Eddie took its title from a catchphrase which Fred Stone had made popular in his ventriloquist act in the latest Montgomery and Stone extravaganza at Charles Dillingham's Globe. It was a farce-comedy which would have been strong enough to stand on its own feet without the help of music, the first of its kind to rely on situation and character laughs instead of the clowning and cross-talk with which the large-scale musicals filled in between the romantic scenes. It was, in fact, intimate. It had no star part, the interest being distributed among a number of characters played by Ernest Truex, Jack Hazzard, John Willard (who later wrote *The Cat and the Canary*), Ada Lewis, Alice Dovey, who had made a success in that classic musical comedy, *The Pink Lady*, and a promising young beginner named Oscar Shaw.

On the opening night Jerry Kern came over to where Bolton stood leaning on the back-rail, his face pale, his lips moving as if in prayer.

'How do you think it's going?' he asked.

Guy came out of his trance.

'I'm too numb to tell. There's a man in large spectacles over there in the tenth row who seems to be enjoying it.'

Jerry glanced in the direction indicated.

'Wodehouse,' he said.

'I suppose it is,' said Guy, 'but that's only to be expected on an opening night. The question is, what's it going to be like tomorrow?'

'What on earth are you talking about?'

'You said it's a good house.'

'I didn't. I said Woodhouse.'

(For the benefit of the uninitiated, that is the way it is pronounced.)

'Oh, you mean his *name* is Woodhouse?'

'That's right. Plum Wodehouse.'

A gentleman in the last row, down whose neck Jerry was breathing, turned.

'I've no doubt what you two are saying is a lot funnier than what's going on on the stage,' he said, 'but I can't follow the two plots at once.'

'Sorry,' said Guy, cringing. 'Actually what's going on on the stage is very funny indeed.'

'Sez you,' said the man in the last row morosely.

The team-mates withdrew to the balcony stairs and sat down on them. A decent five or six feet now separated them from the audience.

> Any old night is a wonderful night
> If you're there with a wonderful girl. . . .

sang Oscar Shaw.

'Lousy lyric,' said Kern.

A standee turned to them.

'Look,' he said, 'if you don't like this show, why don't you get out?'

The pair withdrew to the lobby. If you applied an eye to the crack of the folding doors, the stage could still be seen. The doorman, who had been using this vantage-point to watch the proceedings, obligingly made way for them. Guy squinted through the crack.

'What has Ada Lewis done to her face?' he muttered anxiously. 'She looks most peculiar.'

'That isn't her face,' said the doorman. 'She's walking on her hands. Saving her face for the last act.'

Guy eyed the honest fellow with displeasure.

'We should have come to you for some gags,' he said coldly.

'Why didn't you?' said the doorman. 'I'd have been glad to help out if I'd known the show was supposed to be funny.'

'How's it going?' asked Jerry.

'It seems to be going all right.'

'Ever hear the one about the English author feller that had a show on over here with Charlie Dillingham?' broke in the doorman in his charming, friendly way. Neither Guy nor Jerry had ever seen a man so patently resolved to be the life of the party. 'He was in London, see, on account he couldn't get over for the opening, and he cabled Charlie "How's it going?" And C.B. [Dillingham] cabled back "It's gone." See what I mean? This feller asked "How's it going?" and Charlie cabled back "It's gone!" Get it?'

Guy drew a deep breath.

'I get it,' he said. 'Very droll.'

'Most amusing,' said Jerry. 'I'm convulsed. What's happening in there? Have the customers rushed the stage yet?'

'Not yet. And that chap with the spectacles is laughing again.'

'Probably overheard that story of mine,' said the doorman.

The lights on the stage dimmed for the *Babes in the Wood* number.

> Give me your hand:
> You'll understand
> We're off to slumberland. . . .

sang Ernie Truex in a cracked voice.

'God!' said Jerry. 'You never know what words are going to sound like till you hear them with a first-night audience. Why don't you get Plum to do your lyrics?'

'Does he write lyrics?'

'He certainly does. I did half a dozen numbers with him for a thing in London called *The Beauty of Bath*. One of them – "Mister Chamberlain" – used to get ten encores every night. As a lyric writer he's the cat's pyjamas.'

'Rather a dated expression,' said Guy coldly.

The audience began to stream into the tiny lobby. The man with the spectacles came up to them.

'Oh, hullo, Jerry,' he said.

'Hello,' said Kern. 'This is Bolton. You two fellows ought to know each other.'

Guy and Plum shook hands.

'I hope you liked the show,' said Guy.

'Best thing I ever saw in my life.'

'I wonder,' said Guy, 'if you would mind stepping over behind that man with the crumpled shirt-front and the rumpled hair? He is the *Tribune* critic.'

They moved to where Heywood Broun was chatting with Alexander Woollcott.

'What did you think of our little entertainment, Mr Wodehouse?' asked Guy in a clear, carrying voice.

'Not bad,' said Plum.

After the final curtain Jerry took them to his apartment on West 68th Street. There they were joined by a group of English friends who were appearing at Dillingham's Globe Theatre in *Tonight's the Night*. Fay Compton was there, and Lawrie Grossmith and his brother George, also Lawrie's brother-in-law, Vernon Castle, with his wife and dancing partner, Irene. They were all eager for news of *Very Good Eddie*.

The two interested parties had decided they would wait up for the notices. They were glad to have company for part of the night. Jerry took his place at the piano, Fay stood beside it and sang. Two or three of the girls were working away in the kitchen making sandwiches.

Plum and Guy gravitated to a corner. 'Do you think *Eddie* got over?' said Guy.

'I think it's a smash. I was listening to the audience as they came out. The woman ahead of me said it was the cat's pyjamas.'

'Really?' said Guy, beaming. 'The cat's pyjamas – one of my favourite expressions. Very clever and original. By the way Jerry Kern used it about you.'

'Me?'

'Yes, as a writer. He says you write good lyrics. Have you done any over here?'

'Not yet. But only the other day I missed landing a big job by a hairbreadth. Somebody gave me an introduction to Lee Shubert, and I raced round to his office. "Good morning, Mr Shubert," I said. "I write lyrics. Can I do some for you?" "No," said Lee Shubert. Just imagine if he had said "Yes." It was as near as that.'

'Would you like to join Jerry and me?'

'I'd love it.'

'Then let's get together.'

The Bolton diary of this date has the following entry:

Eddie opened. Excellent reception. All say hit. To Kerns for supper. Talked with P. G. Wodehouse, apparently known as Plum. Never heard of him, but Jerry says he writes lyrics, so, being slightly tight, suggested we might team up. W. so overcome couldn't answer for a minute, then grabbed my hand and stammered out his thanks.

Turning to the Wodehouse diary, we find:

Went to opening of *Very Good Eddie*. Enjoyed it in spite of lamentable lyrics. Bolton, evidently conscious of this weakness, offered partnership. Tried to hold back and weigh the suggestion, but his eagerness so pathetic that consented. Mem: Am I too impulsive? Fight against this tendency.

TWO

I

Eddie was an immediate success and not one of the Princess's 299 seats was ever empty, but neither Bolton nor Kern, drawing their infinitesimal royalties, was able as yet to feel that he had made any very noticeable impact on Broadway.

What they needed, to put them up among the Blossoms, the Harbachs, the Herberts and the Carylls, was an equally successful venture at one of those vast houses that could play, when full, to as much as $16,000 on the week – say, for instance, Erlanger's New Amsterdam.

Abraham Lincoln Erlanger was at that time the Czar of the New York theatre, though beginning to be a little worried by the competition of the up-and-coming Shuberts. All the big managers – Ziegfeld, Dillingham, Savage, Belasco, Cohan and Harris and the rest of them – were Erlanger men, booking their plays in his theatres.

One morning Plum had a telephone call from Guy.

'I've got a job for us,' said Guy. 'Come on down and I'll tell you about it.'

Plum found his partner looking awed, as if he had recently passed through some great spiritual experience.

'It's a Viennese operetta,' he said.

'Oh, my God!'

'It was a big hit in Vienna.'

'What wouldn't be?'

'And Erlanger wants a new story and new lyrics fitted into the score.'

Plum tottered.

'Did you say *Erlanger*?'

'Yes, it's a Klaw and Erlanger production.'

'And I was just going to advise you not to touch it! Why, they might put it on at the New Amsterdam.'

'That's where they're going to put it on.'

'But how did you manage to land a terrific job like that?'

'Apparently all the men up top had a go at it and couldn't satisfy the old boy, so he scraped the bottom of the barrel and found me. I did a scenario which he liked, thank goodness, and it's all settled. You are to do the lyrics and Jerry some interpolated numbers. You'll have a lot of work, I'm afraid. It's one of those shows where the finale starts half-way through each act.'

'That's all right. I love work. Tell me about Erlanger. He really exists, does he? You've actually seen him? What's he like? To look at, I mean.'

Guy considered.

'He's rather like a toad,' he said. 'Not that I have anything against toads.'

'Nor me. Many of my best friends are toads. I look forward to meeting him.'

'You'll be doing that in half an hour from now. He wants us at his office at eleven. Be careful not to say anything disrespectful about Napoleon.'

'I'll watch myself. But why?'

'Because he has a Napoleon complex. He not only admires Napoleon, he thinks he *is* Napoleon.'

'Reincarnated?'

'I suppose so.'

'What would happen if I kidded him about Moscow?'

'He would probably shoot you. He keeps a loaded revolver in his desk. They say he did shoot a man once.'

'Mistook him for the Duke of Wellington, no doubt. He sounds a bit of a Tartar.'

'That's our expression. The Tartars, meeting a particularly tough specimen, would say that he was a bit of an Erlanger. Still, he's said to be kind to authors and dumb animals, so let's go.'

2

The Erlanger office was large and picturesque. In one corner was a punching-bag, beside it a barber's chair. The barber who came each morning to shave the imperial face had been specially chosen for that high office because he could speak French. When called on to do so, he would take down one of the volumes of Napoleon's letters that filled a wall-bookcase over Erlanger's head and translate. One can picture the stream of small-fry managers and rural 'Opry House' owners who drifted in and out of the office being considerably impressed by this display of culture. A man must be quite something when even his barber can sight-read from French into English.

It being now eleven o'clock, the barber had done his work and departed (no doubt with a respectful *Vive l'Empereur!*), and A. L. Erlanger was seated behind the huge desk in one of the drawers of which, probably the open one so as to be handy, lay the celebrated loaded revolver. Lounging in a chair beside him was a small boy in knickerbockers, who gave the two collaborators a cold look as they entered, as if he did not think highly of book writers and lyrists.

'Who's the kid?' asked Plum out of the side of his mouth.

'I don't know,' said Guy.

'*L'Aiglon*, perhaps?'

'I shouldn't wonder.'

It turned out later that the stripling was some sort of a relation, a nephew or the son of a cousin or something, and he was a very valued and esteemed cog in the Erlanger organization. Aged twelve years, he had been selected by Erlanger as possessing exactly the intelligence of the average New York theatre audience. If he liked something, Erlanger reasoned, the public would like it, too. If he didn't, they wouldn't.

It was not immediately that A.L.E. was at liberty to attend to his book writer and lyrist, for he was engaged at the moment of their entry in what – on his side – appeared to be a heated argument with Jack Hazzard. It seemed that Jack had been offered the comedian's part in the Viennese show and was hesitating whether or not to accept it.

This was so perilously near to *lèse-majesté* that Napoleon was not unnaturally incensed.

'I don't know what you're wibble-wobbling about,' he was saying. 'You ought to be down on your knees thanking me for giving you such a chance. Eh, Plymouth?'

'You betcha,' said the knickerbockered child. 'I'm astounded.'

'I'm more than astounded, I'm surprised. It's not only incredible, it's unbelievable. You're nobody. No one ever heard of you. And here I am, offering you – '

Jack stirred uneasily. He was sitting on the edge of a hard chair immediately opposite the desk. Guy and Plum were side by side on a leather settee. The arrangement was faintly suggestive of a courtroom with judge, jury and criminal.

'Well, sir, Mr Erlanger,' said Jack, nervously revolving the hat that dangled between his knees, 'I'm in a hit, you see – '

'A hit? What hit? Where?'

'*Very Good Eddie*, Mr Erlanger. At the Princess.'

Erlanger exploded.

'The Princess? That broken-down little cheesebox under the Sixth Avenue EL?' (The 'Princess' was a Shubert house.) 'Do you realize I'm offering you a chance to appear on the stage of the *New Amsterdam*? And there you sit, humming and hawing – '

'He's crazy,' said Plymouth.

'It sure is a great opportunity,' Jack agreed. 'What's the character like that you want me to play, Guy?'

'He's very loquacious.'

'Yes,' said Erlanger, 'and another thing, he talks a lot.' He looked at his watch. 'Well, think it over,' he said. 'I've got to go down to the theatre to see a run-through of Georgie Cohan's new show. Come along, Plymouth.'

He bustled out, followed by *l'Aiglon*, followed by Bolton, followed by Wodehouse. No actual invitation had been extended to the last-named to join the party, but it seemed to them the prudent thing to do. The first rule a young author learns in the theatre is never to let the manager get out of his sight.

The Cohan show was in full swing when they arrived. They had come just in time for the entrance of the policemen, six chorus-boys in uniform who marched on to a special tune. It was one of those neat tricks in which Cohan specialized, and it should have been very effective. But unfortunately one of the six, a big, awkward young man with red hair, seemed incapable of moving in time to the music. He made the wrong turn, got out of line and generally ruined the thing.

This did not escape Plymouth's observant eye. His voice rang out like that of the daughter of the village Blacksmith.

'Hey!'

'Yes, Plymouth?'

'That one's no good.'

'Which one?'

'The one third from the end.'

Cohan nodded gloomily.

'I've been trying for five weeks to get that boy to march in time, but nothing I say makes any difference.'

Erlanger snorted.

'You're too soft with him. You're too easy. You don't know how to handle these guys. Let *me* talk to him!'

His remarks, filtered for family reading, ran about as follows:

'You filtered fool, what do you think you're doing? Can't you hear the beat of that music? Can't you pick up your feet, you filtered lummox? Don't stand there gaping at me like a filtered half-wit. Go back and make the entrance again.'

Instead of going back, the lummox came forward, right down to the footlights. His manner, if a little reserved, was extremely courteous. At least, it began by being extremely courteous.

'I regret exceedingly,' he said, 'that I have fallen short of the requirements of the part entrusted to me, Mr Erlanger. I am not a professional actor. I gave up a good job in a garage to join this production because I'm married to one of the ladies in the chorus, Miss Pansy LeBoeuf, and I didn't want us to be separated. I informed Mr Harris that I had a very poor ear for music, and he assured me that it did not greatly matter. If it does, you can of course dismiss me. *But what you can't do, you filtered son of a filter, is to talk to me that way in front of my wife, and if you do it again I'll come down there and knock your filtered block off, and that goes for Cohan too.*'

Erlanger had his coat half off, starting for the stage, but

George Cohan was ahead of him. He stuck his hand up to the boy.

'Put it there, kid!' he said. 'And let me tell you you're going to be one of our policemen as long as you want the job. Practise that walk and see if you can't get it, but if you can't, to hell with it.'

The performance continued. Erlanger had slumped back into his seat, baffled. His favourite Marshal had let him down. Guy was thinking how typical that generous gesture had been of George M. Cohan. Plum's mind was occupied with the name he had heard.

'Pansy LeBoeuf, did he say?'

'That's how I got it.'

'Quite a name.'

'Yes, almost as good as Pickles St Clair, who's with Dillingham. But we've got a girl in the *Eddie* chorus who tops them both – Dawn O'Day.'

A few minutes later Erlanger rose.

'It's okay, George,' he said. 'I've seen enough to satisfy me. You open at the Chestnut Street in Philly, and I'll route you west to the Grand in Chicago.'

Without waiting for a reply, he strode off up the aisle. He called over his shoulder to Guy and Plum as he passed them.

'Come upstairs, you two. I'll get Klaw to give you your contracts.'

Next morning Plum called at Guy's apartment.

'Yesterday inspired me,' he said. 'It gave me an idea for a lyric. I've only done a bit of it, but here's how it goes so far.'

> Napoleon was a little guy:
> They used to call him Shorty.
> He only stood about so high.
> His chest was under forty
> But when folks started talking mean,
> His pride it didn't injure:
> 'My queen,' he'd say to Josephine,
> 'The thing that counts is ginger.'

'And the refrain?'

'I haven't done the refrain yet. But here's another verse.'

He got too fat. We all know that
From portraits in the galleries.
He never seemed to learn the knack
Of laying off the calories.
But though his waist was large, he faced
And overcame all foemen.
He knew quite well it's brains that tell
And not a guy's abdomen.

'Erlanger's going to love it,' said Plum.

The song was destined for success, but not in an Erlanger production. Jerry Kern wrote a delightful tune and orchestrated it with toy trumpets, and it was sung by Billy B. Van in *Have a Heart*.

3

The new piece was to be called *Miss Springtime*. Guy's title had been *Little Miss Springtime*, but that was changed very promptly by Abraham Lincoln Erlanger.

'We don't have nothing little at the New Amsterdam,' said Abe.

By a great stroke of good fortune Plymouth had picked up a germ and gone down with the mumps, so was not on hand with his sympathy, encouragement and advice, and rehearsals proceeded smoothly. Everything connected with an Erlanger show always moved with the precision of a Napoleonic campaign. The boss kept an eye on things himself and stood no nonsense.

There was once an expensive foreign tenor who was engaged for a leading role in an Erlanger production, and on the night of the dress rehearsal Erlanger, seated in the stage-box, was puzzled and annoyed to note that all that was proceeding from the gifted artist was a faint sound like gas escaping out of a pipe. Stopping the performance and inquiring into this, he was informed by the tenor in a hushed whisper that he, the tenor, was saving his voice for tomorrow night.

Erlanger's eyes bulged slowly from his head. He swallowed once or twice.

'Sing,' he said.

The tenor went into a whispered explanation. When he said he was 'saving his voice', the voice was in fact saving itself.

'She is gone,' he said, alluding to his voice, as serious singers will, as if it were an independent entity. 'Tonight she is gone, but tomorrow she will be back.'

'Sing!' said Erlanger.

'But I'm telling you, Mr Erlanger' – the whisper was even fainter – 'the vo-chay, she is not there. She does this.' He pinched his throat between thumb and forefinger by way of illustration.

'Sing!' said Erlanger.

'Please,' the whisper was now scarcely audible. 'They are delicate, these great voices. They – '

Erlanger rose from his seat, removed his coat and sprang from box to stage. He placed one large hand on the tenor's left shoulder, another large hand on his right shoulder, got a good grip, and shook him backwards and forwards for some moments, then from side to side. He raised him in the air and brought him down with a bump that shook the New Amsterdam stage.

'*Sing!*' he said.

The tenor let out a note that could be heard as far down town as the Battery.

The Emperor had handed over the preparation of *Miss Springtime* to two of his most trusted Generals – Herbert Gresham for the book and Julian Mitchell for the dances. Martial law had been proclaimed on the first day of rehearsals, and Gresham readily adjusted himself to the military atmosphere. Whenever the Little Corporal of 42nd Street strode on to the stage, he would come smartly to attention, and it was clearly with an effort that he refrained from saluting.

Julian Mitchell was much less docile. He was a sort of Marshal Ney, an independent spirit who truckled to no one. He would fight manfully against any suggestion, even from the All Highest, that was in his opinion bad for the show. He knew his job, he did his job, and he was not going to have anyone telling him how to do it. He was fired oftener than a machine-gun, but whoever fired him always had to take him back again, for Julian stood alone. He was the real creator of the *Ziegfeld*

Follies, for two editions of which Flo Ziegfeld was merely the brilliant pressman.

It was amazing that he should have reached such a position, for he was very nearly stone deaf. His method of hearing a melody was to press his ear closely to the back of the piano. If the piano was in the pit, he would seat himself on top of it like a sort of Buddha. For some reason which aurists may be able to explain he could hear a little better in this position.

Miss Springtime – with Sari Petrass, George Macfarlane, Jack Hazzard, Georgie O'Ramey and Jed Prouty as its principals – opened at the old Forest Theatre in Philadelphia. It moved like clockwork, the beautiful Joseph Urban settings appearing and disappearing without a single hitch. Even the audience did what was asked of them.

As the orchestra struck up the 'play-out', the two authors pressed back through the outgoing crowd to the pass door. Erlanger was already on the stage, the department heads, directors, scene painters, stage carpenters, electricians, head props and costume designer assembled about him. The company stood in lines facing him. Napoleon, with his Marshals about him, preparing to address his troops.

His speech was a eulogy. He scattered medals like birdseed. It was plain that what had occurred tonight had been an Austerlitz. He was particularly enthusiastic about the chorus dancing, the precision and verve of which, he said, had been exceptional.

'The finest line of dancers I've watched in years,' he said and motioned to Julian to say a few graceful words.

Julian, who had not heard a syllable of the speech, stepped forward, a bundle of scribbled notes in his hand.

'I'm ashamed,' he said, brushing away a tear, 'I'm ashamed and mortified at the way you girls let me down tonight. The whole lot of you danced as if you were wearing snowshoes. No precision, no verve, the worst line of dancers I've ever watched.'

He would have spoken further, but at this point a justly incensed Czar of the New York Theatre, speaking carefully into his left ear, fired him. It was not till late on the following day that he was taken back again.

Guy summoned up courage to ask a timid question.

'Do you think it's a hit, Mr Erlanger?'

Plum, on his other side, made a similar query.

'It's a hit, don't you think, Mr Erlanger?'

The Emperor swelled portentously.

'A hit? Of course it's a hit. Do I ever put on anything that isn't a hit?'

'No, no, Mr Erlanger.'

'Certainly not, Mr Erlanger. Of course not, Mr Erlanger.'

'It will run at the New Amsterdam for a year, and as soon as I have the New York opening off my hands I shall organize a Western company.'

The two collaborators beamed at him. People said unkind things about old Abe, did they? He had ruined people, had he? Well, what of it? They probably thoroughly deserved to be ruined, and as for him shooting that man everybody said he had shot, why shouldn't a fellow shoot a chap from time to time if the situation seemed to call for it? What's the sense of having a loaded revolver if you never use it?

Those were the days. None of this modern nonsense about 'hoping they'll like us in New York,' and 'We'll have to wait and see what the critics think of us.' 'It will run at the New Amsterdam for a year, and as soon as I have the New York opening off my hands, I shall organize a Western company.' Just like that. And the West was the West then. A full season in Chicago, fifty-two one-week stands, a third season of three-nighters.

And, as a matter of record, Erlanger was right. *Miss Springtime* ran at the New Amsterdam for 230 performances – a very long run for those days – and was an even bigger success in Chicago. It went on touring for several years.

THREE

I

Guy and Plum were lunching at Armenonville, the charming grill-room of the Knickerbocker Hotel at the corner of 42nd Street and Broadway. This was a step up from their customary Childs', the New York equivalent of London's ABC shops, but they were doing well now and could afford to cut a modest dash. Guy had two hits running on Broadway, and Plum had just sold his novel, *Piccadilly Jim*, as a serial to the *Saturday Evening Post*.

'Tell me about last night,' said Plum, when they had finished the important business of ordering. 'How did you make out with Belasco?'

The question concerned a play called *Polly-With-a-Past*, a comedy which Guy had written with George Middleton.

'I don't quite know,' said Guy. 'It was hard to tell whether he liked it or not. He was hanging pictures.'

'Hanging pictures?'

'While George was reading the play to him. I must say my heart bled for poor old George.'

'Where did this take place? The famous studio?'

'Yes, as sinister a joint as I've ever been in. It looks like the scene of nameless orgies.'

'But this picture-hanging – ?'

'Apparently the Master is always tinkering, trying new effects with priest-robes, painted cassones, all that sort of junk. Now he was hanging pictures. Well, he told George to go ahead and read the play. George would read a couple of lines and then there'd be bang, bang, bang. He'd stop, and Belasco would call out, "Go on, I'm listening."'

'Pretty ghastly for George.'

'Yes, he seemed to be suffering. And that wasn't all. Belasco's secretary was there, the one they call Ginty, and the poor thing was suffering from neuralgia. It was in the left eye that it seemed to be troubling her most. She kept applying hot compresses to it and groaning "Oh, my God! This is terrible!" It made her sound like a dramatic critic. George would read a line, and there would be a yell of "Awful! Awful!" It jolted him quite a bit.

'But George is not a man to be lightly stayed in his appointed course. Pausing for but a moment, he ploughed manfully on. Another couple of comedy lines, and there would come a bang, bang, *bang*. ("Don't stop. I can hear you.") And Ginty would shriek "Ow! Ow! This is frightful!" '

Plum drew his breath in sharply, as if he had had a sudden twinge of neuralgia in the left eye.

'So that's reading a play to Belasco! How did this custom of reading plays to managers ever start, I wonder.'

'I believe it's a hangover from the days when most managers couldn't read.'

'Now that a fair proportion of them can, why not let them wrestle with the thing themselves?'

'Yes, if they would do it, that would be fine. The trouble is, the last thing managers want to do is read a play. They think it makes them look important having a great pile of unread scripts on their desks. The higher the pile, the bigger the manager.'

'Then what's the answer?'

'I know the answer, if you could always work it. I managed it once with Harry Frazee. It was one evening after office hours. His staff had gone home, and it seemed that there was nothing to interrupt us. I didn't know then, as I do now, that during the reading of a play a manager has to have something to do that will keep him usefully employed. I believe Arch Selwyn does fretwork, while Crosby Gaige catches up on his burnt-leather bookmarks. Harry Frazee, sticking more closely to business, uses such time for cleaning out the drawers of his desk, getting rid of empty whisky bottles, appeals for charity, cancelled summonses and so on.

'After I had read a couple of pages during which he was entirely invisible, dealing with the contents of his lower right-hand drawer, he suddenly bobbed up and told me to stop reading and leave the play with him. I pointed to the vast pile on his desk.

' "As fairness would demand my play going to the end of the queue, it wouldn't reach you for another two years."

' "All right", he conceded grudgingly. "Read a couple more pages. But those dialects! I can't make head or tail of them." He disappeared again on the left side of his desk.

'I must admit the play was rather rich in dialects, though I was surprised he'd noticed it. It was about a bunch of soldiers, an Italian, a German-American, a coloured boy etc. I read two more pages as soon as Harry had got back with a pair of galoshes, a bottle of glue and a girl's brassière. He again told me to stop reading. He said he couldn't understand a word I was saying, he hated plays with a lot of foreign accents in them and I was wasting his time.

' "But you've still got several drawers to sort," I said. "You might as well let me read a bit more."

' "I've just told you," he said. "I can't follow you when you do those dialects."

' "Look," I said – I'd had a sudden inspiration – "How about you reading the play to me? If you'd just read to the end of the first act, I bet you won't want to stop. I bet you five bucks!"

'A bet is something Harry can't resist. He grabbed the script and started to read.

' "Gosh," I said. "It's better than I thought it was. You're good, Mr Frazee. You were an actor once, of course?"

' "No, I was never an actor."

' "You should have been – that's all I've got to say." That encouraged him. He started to work harder.

'It went like a breeze. I may not be much of a reader, but I was right there as an audience. A first act by a budding playwright was never better received.

' "I can't wait," I said, "to hear what you're going to do with that second act twist. Gosh, I've got a treat coming to me there."

'From then on he was selling the play to me. He took off his coat and stood up so that he could really act. I went round and sat in his deck chair. I could rock better on the laughs.

'By the time he got to the end of the play he was all in. I had to pour him a stiff drink. I took one myself. We were buddies. He asked me to call him Harry.'

'He bought it?'

'I left the office with a cheque for $1000 in my pocket. The little masterpiece was never produced, because he subsequently came out of the ether, but it got me $1000 at a time when I most needed it. And if you can get $1000 out of Harry Frazee, you're good.'

'Yes, I've always heard he's a pretty hardboiled egg.'

'Most managers are!'

'But not all. There are shining exceptions. One points with pride, for instance, to Savage.'

'Colonel Henry W. Savage? Have you met him?'

'I was in his office yesterday, and he's very different from . . . well, somebody like Abe Erlanger. Mind you, I'm quite fond of Abe. He eats broken bottles and conducts human sacrifices at the time of the full moon, but he's a thoroughly good chap, heart of gold beneath a rugged exterior and all that sort of thing. All the same, you couldn't describe him as a *preux chevalier*. He lacks a certain something.'

'You don't often get a manager who's a Chesterfield.'

'Exactly. That is why I say that, when you do, you should grapple him to your soul with hoops of steel. This Savage, now, of whom I speak, is the answer to an author's prayer, a charming, refined, cultured gentlemen of the old school with delightful, courtly manners, frank blue eyes and a heart as far from fraud as heaven from earth. He radiates benevolence. He is without guile.'

'His heart is as the heart of a little child?'

'You put it in a nutshell. That gentle soul would not harm a fly.'

'How do you know?'

'I've seen him.'

'Seen him what?'

'Not harming flies. He is a sort of modern St Francis of Assisi, dripping with goodwill to all men and running his business in a spirit of pure altruism. By the way, he wants to see us after lunch.'

A man who had been sitting with his back to them turned in his chair.

'Excuse me, gentlemen,' he said. 'I could not help overhearing your conversation. You were speaking, if my ears did not deceive me, of that hornswoggling old pirate and premier louse of the world, Colonel Henry W. Savage.'

'That . . . *what* did you call him?'

' "Hornswoggling old pirate and premier louse of the world" was the expression I used. I could think of nothing stronger on the spur of the moment.'

Guy had recognized the man now. His was a face which since *The Merry Widow* had become a well-known one.

'You're Donald Brian, aren't you?'

'That's right. You're Guy Bolton, I think, and. . . .'

'This is P. G. Wodehouse.'

'How do you do? Mr Wodehouse,' said Donald Brian, 'I will address myself to you, for it was you who were describing Colonel Henry W. Savage as a gentle soul devoid of guile. I assure you, Mr Wodehouse,' said Donald Brian earnestly, 'that that man, that seemingly saintly Hank Savage, is so crooked that he could hide at will behind a spiral staircase. Let me tell you a little story. Some years ago this child of unmarried parents sent for me. He was casting a piece called *The Merry Widow*, of which you may have heard. He wished me to play the hero, a certain Prince Danilo.'

'You were terrific as Prince Danilo,' said Guy.

Donald Brian bowed.

'Thank you. I am a conscientious artist, and I spared no effort to earn my $75 a week.'

'Your *what*?'

'That was my salary throughout the run. I asked a somewhat higher figure. The Colonel refused, and we started arguing about it. "Look, Donny," he said at last – "I'll tell you what let's do. Let's toss for it. If you win, I'll give you what you're asking. If I win, you'll work for $75." Then he pulled a half-dollar from his pocket and said, "Heads or tails?" '

Donald Brian paused a moment. He seemed to be struggling with his feelings.

'Now, psychologists have established,' he resumed, 'that in seventy-seven cases out of a hundred the answer to that question is "heads". I saw no reason to be different, so I said "heads" like all the rest of the boys.'

'And it came tails?'

'It had to come tails, because, as I learned later, it was tails on both sides – one of those freak coins that the Mint has turned out occasionally. You see, the old boy knew all about that quirk of human nature that gives "heads" a big preference. And so through the whole run of the *Widow* I worked for $75 a week. And when the show had been running for a year to capacity business and he had made a fortune out of it, I asked for a rise. "Why, Donny, I'm surprised," the Colonel said. "I thought you were a good sport. That was your end of a bet – $75 a week. You're not going to welsh, are you?" '

Brian sighed, and turned back to his table.

2

It was a tale that provided food for thought, but Plum, as they walked over to the Savage office, was inclined to make light of it.

'These actors!' he said. 'Extraordinary how they love to invent yarns. Anything for a good story.'

'You think it was an invention?' said Guy, who seemed pensive.

'Of course. You aren't going to tell me that a man like Colonel Savage. . . .'

Plum broke off. They had paused in front of the George M. Cohan Theatre to look at the photographs in the entrance. Colonel Savage's star, Mitzi Hajos, was playing there in a piece called *Sari*.

'Someone over on the horizon seems to be trying to pass the time of day with you,' he said. 'He's waving, and I think I caught the word "Guy".'

Guy turned.

'Oh, that's Tom Cushing. He wrote the book and lyrics of

Sari. Hullo, Tom,' he said, as the other came up. 'Do you know P. G. Wodehouse?'

'We've never met. How are you, P.G.?'

'How do you do? Guy tells me you're the author of this outstanding success.'

'Well, I adapted it from the Hungarian original, and it was a hell of a job, let me tell you. You know what stinkers these Hungarian books are. I had to invent practically a new story. I also fitted new lyrics to all that endless music Kalman writes. It took me months.'

'Still, you must be making a packet out of it.'

A spasm of pain contorted Cushing's face, the same sort of spasm which had twisted the features of Donald Brian when he had been speaking of double-tailed half-dollars.

'Do you know Savage?' he asked.

'Slightly. Guy hasn't met him yet. We're on our way to his office now.'

'God help you,' said Tom Cushing. 'Forgive me if I seem to speak bitterly, but I have passed through the furnace. Do you know what the Colonel paid me for all the work I did on *Sari*? $500.'

'$500 *flat*?'

'That's what.'

'Good Lord!'

'I was to be paid in five monthly instalments, which were to cease if the play should close. That was to keep me up to the mark. Unless I did my damnedest, it might close in three months, and then I would only get $300.'

'It's been running a good twenty weeks, hasn't it?'

'Twenty-four, to capacity. Well, I got my five cheques, and then the generous old fellow sent me another. A darned graceful gesture, I thought, and so I told Madison Corey, the Colonel's manager, when I happened to run into him on the street. I said, "That was nice of Colonel Savage to keep on with those $100 payments because the show is such a success. I appreciated it greatly. What a dear old chap he is!" And next morning there came a letter from the dear old chap saying that his bookkeeping department had made a mistake and, unless the $100 was returned immediately, legal proceedings would be instituted.'

Guy had paled a little beneath his tan.

'I can't believe it.'

'It's true.'

'What did you do?'

'I sent him $98.50. I told him I was using the other dollar and a half to buy a frame for his letter. Oh, well,' said Cushing philosophically, 'it'll be something to tell my grandchildren about when they cluster round my knee.'

He passed on, and Guy eyed Plum fixedly.

'You and your answers to an author's prayer! You and your modern St Francises of Assisi! Thank goodness we haven't got to have anything to do with this old devil. What are we seeing him about, anyway? I suppose he has some frightful Hungarian thing he wants us to fix up for $50 paid in monthly instalments.'

Plum coughed.

'Well, not quite that. The fact is. . . .' He paused. He seemed embarrassed. 'You know that thing we roughed out, the one we thought of calling *Have a Heart*?'

'To follow *Eddie* at the Princess?'

'Yes, that was the idea, but I'm afraid I've promised it to Savage.'

'You've done *what*?'

'He's a very persuasive old gentleman. He talked me into it.'

'I wouldn't let him touch it with a ten-foot pole.'

Plum coughed again. His embarrassment had become more marked.

'The trouble is,' he said, 'I'm afraid I rather let myself be carried away and, to cut a long story short, he's got a verbal agreement, and there's no possible way we can get out of it.'

3

Colonel Savage was a man in the middle-fifties, tall and thin and benevolent, his open, candid face surmounted by a handsome mop of grey hair. He walked with a slight limp, having probably in the course of his career been bitten in the leg by some indignant author.

He received the visitors beamingly.

'I want to sign those *Have a Heart* contracts today,' he said, all heartiness and joviality, like something out of Dickens. 'Yes, Miss Stanchfield?'

Miss Stanchfield, his secretary, had entered.

'I've just spoken to the hospital, Colonel,' she said. 'Mr Scarborough seems a little better this morning. I thought you would like to know.'

'Yes, indeed,' said the Colonel. 'I take a fatherly interest in all my authors. Poor Scarborough,' he explained, 'had a breakdown when we were out on the road shaping up his play for New York. He was carried off the train on a stretcher. Well, well. These authors you get today seem very brittle. No stamina. No reserve force. Poor Cushing collapsed while we were trying out *Sari*. And look at poor Browne. There was a sad case.'

'Browne?' queried Plum, as Miss Stanchfield went out. He noted uneasily that all the Savage authors mentioned so far had been qualified by the ominous adjective 'poor'.

'Walter Browne, who wrote *Everywoman*, one of the greatest successes of my career. He died the night the play opened. That's the second one I've had die on me, though the other was only a composer. Ah, well, here today and gone tomorrow. All flesh is grass, I sometimes say. I see,' said the Colonel, following Guy's eye, which had become glassy and was fixed on a picture of a sailing vessel on the wall, 'you are looking at my grandfather's ship. What a beauty! He made a lot of money out of that boat. She was a real clipper. Cargo after cargo she carried.'

'Tea?'

'Slaves. And now,' the Colonel went on, dismissing the subject, 'about those contracts for *Have a Heart*. I like to get these business details off my mind before going ahead. What figure would you suggest? Some authors, I believe, prefer to take a flat sum down – '

'$500?' said Guy with an unpleasant tinkle in his voice.

'Yes, I wouldn't mind going as high as that.'

'We would prefer a royalty.'

'What royalty were you thinking of?'

'The usual 3 per cent.'

'3 per cent is not usual with *me*,' said the Colonel emphatically. 'Still, I'll tell you what I'll do,' he went on, drawing a coin from his pocket. 'I'll toss you for it. 3 per cent if you win, 1 if I win. Heads or tails?' he said, flickering the coin into the air.

'*Tails!*' shouted the authors in unison.

The Colonel picked up the half-dollar and put it in his pocket. He seemed to have aged quite a little in the last few moments. He looked at the authors in silence for a while.

Then he spoke.

'I suppose you boys know quite a few people in our business?' he said reflectively.

4

Have a Heart opened on a cold winter's night – 27th December 1916, to be exact – at the Opera House, Trenton, New Jersey – not quite the best spot for the presentation of a highly sophisticated divorce story in which a honeymooning couple are being pursued by a lawyer bearing the tidings that their marriage is not legal.

The hero was the proprietor of a department store where the heroine worked. When the century was in its teens, there was much talk of model employers and of making conditions luxurious for the workers, and there was a good deal of brilliant satire on the subject in *Have a Heart*.

The clientele of the Trenton Opera House found it all a bit exotic. Their response on the opening night was tepid, and it came as no surprise to the authors to be told by Miss Stanchfield after the final curtain had fallen – to applause of the kind known as sporadic – that Colonel Savage would like to see them in the dining-room of Teller's Hotel for a conference.

The personnel of the meeting, which began shortly after midnight, consisted of the manager, the authors and George Marion, a fine old character actor who, having yet some years to wait for 'Anna Christie' to bring him his best role, eked out a poorly paid living as book director for the Colonel's musical productions.

It needed but a glance at the big chief to tell the two partners that the proceedings were likely to take some time. All through the performance he had been dictating whispered notes to Miss

Stanchfield, and these, as he dumped them down on the table, looked like the manuscript of a three-volume novel.

'Let's get to work,' he said.

Line by line the script was gone through. Cuts were proposed, changes discussed. The hands of the big, fly-specked clock on the wall pointed to five past two.

'What do you think of that suggestion?' asked Savage, turning to George Marion as Guy proposed a major alteration.

'Let me ponder it,' said George. 'I would like to try to visualize it as it affects the entire dramatic structure.'

He folded his arms on the table in front of him, and rested his forehead on them. Several minutes passed while the authors waited politely for his opinion.

'Go on,' said the Colonel. 'We'll get on to something else while George is thinking.'

They got on to something else, and George continued thinking. He was still thinking when the Colonel rose and announced that he was going to bed.

'We old fellows have to take care of our health,' he said.

'You approve the change I suggested?' asked Guy.

'Certainly,' said the Colonel. It was plain by now that anything in the nature of a change was meat and drink to him. 'And of course there will be those two new lyrics I mentioned. Start on them at once. Miss Stanchfield will meet you at eight-thirty tomorrow morning to collect the material. She will have everything typed and parts extracted by ten. You will then go over the whole thing with George and Teddy Royce, which will give you time to rewrite anything they disapprove of before you get down to rehearsal.'

'May I ask a question?' said Plum.

'By all means.'

'When do we sleep?'

'Sleep?' said the Colonel reprovingly. 'You didn't come here to sleep. You came here to get a show ready for Broadway.'

Plum looked at Guy – Guy looked at Plum. Their thoughts had flashed to George Scarborough, carried off on a stretcher at the end of the pre-Broadway tour, to Walter Browne, dying on the opening night, and – yes, there was another, that unnamed composer who had expired at the close of one of these Savage tuning-up sessions.

'I love the theatre,' said Colonel Savage. 'I love the good old-fashioned show-people to whom the stage came first, whatever crisis might arise. I'd like to tell you boys a little story that will illustrate what I mean. I was a friend of Maurice Barrymore and I knew that in spite of all his peccadilloes he was devoted to Georgie, his wife. I went to see him the day after she died and found him, his eyes red from weeping, with the newspapers spread about the bed in which he was lying.

' "I've had a cruel loss, Hank," he said. "One I shall never get over. But I must say they've given the old girl some damn good notices." Good night, boys. Don't forget. Eight-thirty sharp.'

He left them. George Marion, still bent over the table, stirred slightly.

'Do you realize,' said Plum, regarding the bowed form sympathetically, 'that this pondering business of George's is the only way the poor devil can get any sleep.'

'Yes,' agreed Guy. 'We only have one tour to cope with. Poor old George goes on, from play to play.'

'Well, we'd better get upstairs and work, I suppose. What do you think we ought to do about George? Should we stir him, do you feel?'

The question was decided for them by George suddenly sitting up.

'Yes,' he said briskly, 'I've gone over the whole thing in my mind and I see no insurmountable obstacles. I therefore vote for the change, Colonel.'

'The Colonel has gone to bed.'

'Really?' said George. 'I was so absorbed in the problem I didn't notice him leaving. Gone to bed, eh? Well, well, I'm afraid the old boy's beginning to feel his age. He's not as wide-awake at these conferences as he was five or ten years ago.'

The two authors went up to their room and settled down to work. By a quarter to six it was done, and Plum stretched himself wearily.

'Have you ever reflected,' he said, 'that 40,000 people were killed in automobile accidents last year, and not one of them was Colonel Henry W. Savage? Looks to me like mismanagement somewhere. Do you believe in heredity?'

'Why?'

'I was only thinking of the Colonel's grandfather, the slaver. Still, I believe the show's a hit, don't you?'

'A hit? Of course it's a hit. Do we ever put on anything that isn't a hit?' said Guy, making use of A. L. Erlanger's non-copyright material.

'But I was disappointed in the way "Napoleon" went.'

'They've probably never heard of Napoleon in Trenton.'

'No, it wasn't the audience. It was the fellow who sang it.'

'Napoleon' had been sung by the principal comedian, who played a brash elevator-boy named Henry. It was Henry's boast that he had told more women where they could get off than any man in New York.

'He's too old. Too old and too large.'

'There aren't many comics who can look like boys of sixteen.'

'I know one who can. I've seen him in vaudeville. Billy B. Van. But would the Colonel engage him? He's expensive.'

'Well, what's money? You can't take it with you.'

'I know you can't, but nobody ever told that to Hank Savage.'

'Listen,' said Guy. 'Let's snatch forty minutes' refreshing sleep, which seems to be the most we shall ever get a night during this tour, then we'll be all rested and alert for taking it up with him before rehearsal.'

Colonel Savage, approached an hour or two later, agreed that Billy B. Van would be ideal for the part of Henry.

'But his salary!' he said, a look of pain coming into his fine eyes. 'I doubt if you could get him under $300.'

'$300 isn't much.'

'It is to me,' said the Colonel, who, having only $27 million tucked away in sound securities, had to be careful. 'But I'll tell you what I'll do. . . .'

'*Tails!!*' cried the two authors, speaking as one author.

The Colonel smiled faintly and very wryly. The old wound still troubled him.

'If you boys will pay half his salary for the first three months, it's a deal.'

Guy and Plum looked at one another. The same thought was in both their minds – viz. that for an author to pay out money to a manager instead of taking it off him was like rubbing velvet the wrong way. Then they thought of Billy B. Van singing 'Napoleon', and the sensation of nausea passed.

'I'm game,' said Guy.

'So am I,' said Plum.

So the matter was arranged. Billy B. Van was engaged and was an instantaneous success in New York, rolling the customers in the aisles with his comedy and singing 'Napoleon' like a linnet. And all through the first three months Guy and Plum duly paid up $75 per week per person, their contribution to his salary.

At the end of the third month the Colonel fired him.

FOUR

I

Have a Heart was one of those semi-successes in New York. It played to capacity for three months, but after Billy Van left business dropped. Old Hank didn't seem to mind. The fact that he had engaged a new comedian cheaper than Billy by $150 apparently compensated him for the loss of thousands at the box-office. He was not, as a matter of fact, very interested in a New York run. What he liked was the road. *Have a Heart*, which had done only five months and two weeks on Broadway, played for six years outside New York.

Shortly after it had opened at the Liberty Theatre on 42nd Street (now a second-run movie-house) its authors had a call from Ray Comstock, Bessie Marbury's partner, asking them to come to the Princess and confer with him about a show to follow *Very Good Eddie*, which had just passed its 200th performance.

Plum, as they started off for 39th Street, was at the top of his form. This business of being asked by managers to look in and confer about shows was still an exhilarating novelty to him. It pained him, accordingly, to see that his colleague was moody and preoccupied.

'Girl trouble,' said Guy briefly, in answer to a sympathetic query. 'I had a little girl trouble last night.'

'Who was the little girl?'

Guy stiffened. There came into his eyes that cold, stern look which had caused him to be known in the old regiment as Chilled-Steel Bolton.

'Does one bandy a woman's name in mess, old boy? If one does, Emily Post has been fooling me for years.'

Plum flushed. The rebuke had been a just one.

'Forgive me, old chap. I should not have said it. Call her X and tell me what happened.'

Guy was silent for a moment. His finely chiselled features twisted a little, as if the memory pained him. With men of the Guy Bolton type memories are like mulligatawny soup in a cheap restaurant. It is wiser not to stir them.

'I can't imagine what induced her to come to that elevator,' he said at length.

'She wished to go up . . . or possibly to go down?' hazarded Plum.

'True, we had parted in anger, but that was no reason why she should have come to the elevator. What happened was that we disagreed on the subject of her new hat and, one thing leading to another, she threw a vase – containing, if I remember correctly, roses – at my head, and I, thinking I might as well be going, walked out and rang for the elevator. It arrived, full of people, and I was just about to get aboard, when X came dashing down the hall, screaming loudly, and attached herself to my coat-tail.'

'Embarrassing.'

'Most. I disengaged myself and stepped in, she still screaming, and as we started to descend I was aware of a figure standing at my elbow, a grey-haired figure in a clerical collar.'

'Not – ?'

'Yes. Belasco. He was looking at me austerely, like a clergyman who had discovered schism in his flock.'

'Did he say anything?'

'He said – very coldly – "Good evening, Mr Middleton." '

'And what did you say?'

'I said, "Oh, good evening, Mr Belasco. I didn't think you would remember me." '

They arrived at the Princess, which for years now has ceased to be a theatre. Today it is not even a second-run movie-house, it is a television den, God help it! The lion and the lizard keep the courts where Comstock gloried and drank deep. They found Ray seated at his desk with a bottle of whisky beside him for purposes of reference.

'That must be powerful stuff you're drinking,' said Guy.

'You can smell the fumes as you come up the stairs.'

'It isn't this bottle,' said Comstock. 'It's the ceiling,' and they saw that it was covered by a dark stain on which beads of moisture had formed. 'Whisky,' said Comstock mournfully. 'The finest money can buy. I stacked it up in the loft, twenty-four cases. I forgot the steam-pipes run through there. The stuff got so hot it exploded.'

Ray Comstock was a thin, rangy individual who looked like a boy and had almost as much charm as Charlie Dillingham. He seemed to be perpetually telephoning and had a telephone receiver that he could balance on his shoulder, thus leaving his hands free for opening letters, pouring drinks and so forth.

His mind seemed equally detachable. He could listen on the telephone and talk to visitors simultaneously. There was never any clue as to who was on the other end of the wire. His part in the conversation was mostly monosyllabic, the other person evidently doing the major part of the talking. He addressed all these callers as 'Honey'.

He had sent for Guy and Plum, as he had hinted over the telephone, to tell them that the time had come to be thinking of something to follow *Very Good Eddie*. *Eddie* he proposed to move to the Casino, where there were 1500 seats. It would thus become available to a public that could not afford to pay the high scale of $1–$3 charged at the 'Princess'.

This was the policy adopted from now on with the Princess shows, and a very good one, too.

He then told them something else. Bessie Marbury was out. She had withdrawn from the partnership.

'She didn't like the play.'

'What play?'

'The play you boys are going to turn into a musical. Charlie Hoyt's *A Milk White Flag*.'

Plum remained calm – he had never heard of *A Milk White Flag* – but Guy nearly hit the dark patch on the ceiling.

'You're crazy, Ray. You can't be thinking of making that into a Princess musical.'

'Why not?' said Comstock. He spoke into the telephone. 'I said, "Why not?" to somebody else, honey. "Decidedly not," is what I say to you.'

Guy was still staring incredulously.

'I've read *A Milk White Flag*,' he said. 'It's about a man who pretends to be dead so as to evade his creditors and collect on his insurance. He's laid out on ice and catches cold.'

'That's right,' said Ray, laughing heartily. 'I had forgotten about him catching cold. I remember now it was terrific. Every now and then there would be a sneeze from the room where the body was laid out. The family were scared pop-eyed.' He laughed again at the recollection of this rich comedy, and spoke into the telephone. 'No, honey, you needn't get sore. I'm not laughing at you.'

'But listen, Ray. The thing that has made the Princess shows is charm. We must have charm.'

'Be as charming as you like. No one's stopping you.'

'Well, you can't say *A Milk White Flag* has charm, with a corpse that keeps coming on the stage without any trousers on.'

'Why would a corpse have trousers on? Only the upper half of the body would be on view. No, honey, I'm not talking about the party last night. This is in a play, the new Princess show.'

'And he makes a buffet dinner off the sandwiches set out for the mourners.'

'We'll change it to a sit-down dinner.'

'A *what*?'

'I was speaking on the telephone.'

'Perhaps we had better wait until Ray's finished phoning,' suggested Plum.

'He's never finished phoning,' said Guy. 'As soon as he hangs up on that call, there'll be another.'

'Look, Ray,' said Plum. 'Guy doesn't seem to like this *Milk White Flag* of yours. Why not do the piece we've been working on?'

He was referring to a fantasy which Guy had written called *The Little Thing*, a whimsical trifle about an orphan girl in a Greenwich Village boarding-house. Every young playwright has something of this sort tucked away in a drawer, and it is always something which managers refuse to consider. Shakespeare, as he sat listening to the audience at the Globe whistling and stamping its feet at the end of the 'To be or not to be' soliloquy, was probably not congratulating himself that

Hamlet was a sell-out and that if business kept up like this they would do fifteen ducats, eleven rose-nobles and four pieces of eight on the week. It is far more likely that he was thinking wistfully of his masterpiece, that *Tragedy of Alexander the Great* which he could never get Burbage to look at.

'What piece is that?' asked Comstock.

'It's called *The Little Thing*. It's a fantasy.'

'It's wonderful,' said Guy.

'Terrific,' said Plum. 'Strikes a new note.'

'Yes, honey,' said Comstock. 'No, honey,' said Comstock. 'Just as you say, honey. Good-bye, honey.' He hung up the receiver. 'I'm glad you like the idea, boys,' he said. 'A big hit in its day, the *Milk White Flag*.'

Guy clutched his forehead.

'But what about the numbers?'

'Oh, hello, honey,' said Comstock as the telephone tinkled. He tucked the receiver between ear and shoulder and poured himself a drink. There was nothing to indicate whether this was the previous honey, playing a return date, or another honey. 'What's your trouble?' he said. 'Not yours, honey. I have some authors with me.'

'Who does the numbers?'

'The corpse has two daughters, and they have beaux. What more do you want?'

'But the daughters think their father is lying dead on ice in the next room. They'll scarcely be in the mood to sing.'

'That's up to you. I'm not writing the show. Would you mind repeating that, honey, somebody was talking. No, I *can't* throw them out on their fannies, honey, this is business. I have to work, don't I, honey? If I didn't, where would you be? Oh, you would, would you? Oh, they do, do they? Begging you on their bended knees, are they? Well, why don't you? Darned good idea.' He seemed not in the least perturbed. His tone was mild, even affectionate. 'Go to hell, honey!' he concluded almost lovingly and, hanging up the receiver, turned to Bolton. 'What were you saying about a fantasy?'

'I was speaking about the show we've written, *The Little Thing*.'

'I don't like fantasies.'

'You'll like this fantasy.'

'Who says so?'

It seemed to Plum that it was a case for compromise.

'Well, if *The Little Thing* doesn't appeal to you, Ray, how about *Oh, Boy!*?'

'What's *Oh, Boy!*?'

'Another show we've been working on. It's not a good story, and Jerry and I have finished half the numbers. There's one called "Till the Clouds Roll By" – '

'Perfect for the *Milk White Flag*. One of the beaux is trying to cheer up one of the daughters. "Too bad your old man shuffled off," he says. "Yes, damned shame if you ask me," says the daughter. "Still, nothing to be done about it, of course," says the fellow. "No," says the girl. "Let's wait till the clouds roll by." And into number. Fits like the paper on the wall.'

Guy rose.

'The charm dissolves space,' he said. 'I quote Shakespeare.'

'That's the trouble with you,' said Comstock. 'You've been reading Shakespeare. You've gone highbrow on me. This *Oh, Boy!* What's it a musical version of?'

'It isn't a musical version of anything. It's original. Our own unaided work.'

Comstock shook his head.

'I don't want an original. I want something I've heard them laugh at. Then I know what I'm getting. Now, *A Milk White Flag* – '

'No,' said Guy firmly. 'Shoot, if you must, this old grey head, but don't ask me to make a Princess musical with half the numbers done by a corpse with no trousers on. I'm sorry.'

'I'm sorry, too,' said Comstock. The telephone tinkled. 'Oh, hello, honey,' he said. 'Haven't heard from you in some time.'

2

For some months after that a number of writers wrestled with *A Milk White Flag*. Otto Harbach made a start, but gave it up. Henry Blossom, Victor Herbert's writing-partner, had a go, and turned in his portfolio. It was finally taken on by a triumvirate consisting of John L. Golden, Anne Caldwell and Jack

Hazzard. The music was by Baldwin Sloane, and the piece had been called *Go To It*, one of those unfortunate titles which spell disaster from the outset. Offer a dramatic critic something called *Go To It*, and he is immediately struck by the happy thought of saying that it should have been called *Don't Go To It*, for these dramatic critics are as quick as lightning.

Bolton held his breath. Wodehouse held his breath. Kern, in his Bronxville home, was also holding his breath. They realized that this was a crisis. If *Go To It* was a hit, their hold on the Princess was gone, and the chance to put on an original anywhere would vanish for ever. The adapted farce would seem to every manager, as it seemed to Ray Comstock, a safer bet, and their *Oh, Boy!* (retitled *Oh Joy!* for its British production in 1919) would not have a hope of production.

They journeyed down to Atlantic City for the out-of-town opening, and were able to breathe again. The thing was awful, just as they had predicted it would be. Not even the corpse on its bed of ice was colder than the audience. It was with uplifted hearts that they returned to the Traymore. In the lobby they encountered Freddie Zimmerman, the son of the owner of a large chain of theatres in the provinces, who invited them to his suite for a nightcap. He had come over from Philadelphia as an emissary of his father to view the new Princess show and decide whether to accept it as tenant of one of the Zimmerman houses. After the first intermission he had phoned his old man and told him to let *Go To It* go elsewhere.

In Freddy's suite they found Joe Urban. Joe, who was making history with his stage settings and even more with his revolutionary stage lighting, had done a beautiful job with *Miss Springtime*. He eyed the trio with momentary anxiety.

'This *Go To It* – you boys did not write it?' he asked.

With considerable emphasis the boys assured him they did not.

'I am so glad,' he said. 'For me it is a very bad smell. It should be taken away by the grubbage collector to the city dumpings.'

Joe, a charming Austrian, spoke a language of his own. He couldn't drink milk because it curdled in his stomach; he promised that he would have his sketches ready at the drop of a bucket, and, when he grew emphatic, his favourite expression was 'just mock my words'. In those days people collected Urbanisms as they later collected the quaint sayings of Samuel Goldwyn.

Joe remarked that he loved Atlantic City. The air was so embracing.

'I can remember a time when it wasn't as embracing as you would have liked it to be,' laughed Freddy.

'No,' agreed Joe, 'I get a sock in the pants that time I shall never forget.'

It had happened during the war when Atlantic City was full of volunteer spy-chasers, dollar-a-year men, proud of the federal badge they carried under their lapels and all anxious to make a name for themselves by uncovering a trail of espionage. One of these had his eye on Joe. The *Follies* scenery had been damaged in transit and Joe had sent for his Austrian business manager, who had arrived with three Austrian scene-painters, and, while they worked, the manager would whisper to Joe asking how chances were for getting some money out of Ziegfeld, and Joe would whisper back that they were not good, explaining that, while fantastically generous about anything *h*e didn't owe, Ziegfeld had a constitutional objection for pay-*i*ng what he did.

It was these Teutonic whisperings that had aroused the suspicions of the spy-chaser, who was lurking in the background, but what really set him hot on the trail was the signalling.

'In the mornings,' said Joe, 'I do always my sitting-up exercises. We are staying at the Shelbourne that time and I open the window and breathe the invizerating sea's air while I go oop, down, out, back with the arms.'

'The sleuth-hound was down below,' supplemented Freddy, 'making notes.'

'What did he think you were doing – signalling to Germany?'

'To Germany, no. To someone in the Bellevue – Stratford. It is you know only a stone's jump from the Shelbourne. This dumkopf think when I go oop, down, out, back it is a code – a wag-wag.'

It seems that the thrill of sharing a hotel with the *Follies* beauties had been too much for Joe. He had fallen in love. What is more he had fallen in love with the gorgeous prize peach of the 1917 crop. And Joe's Austrian charm, his soft, vibrant voice breathing words of adoration, had found ready response from a heart which, like the US Navy, was 'open to all men from eighteen to forty'.

Joe, somewhat falteringly, had suggested that if she would come up to his suite he would show her a collection of his drawings and, at the same time, they could deal with another bottle of Bollinger non-vintage. She accepted on both counts, and they made their way to the Shelbourne. When they got in the elevator a man stepped in with them. When they got out he followed. As Joe was putting the key in the lock he felt a hand on his shoulder and a voice said, 'You are under arrest.'

'I think it is someone pushing my leg,' said Joe. 'I say to him in my most chalant manner, "This is no time for clown-making." He say it is no clown-making but honest-to-level and that I must come with him. I make pleadings. I say I do not know what I have done but can he not, for a little while, let bygones be hasbeens? All he does is say like a parrot, "You are under arrest."'

Ziegfeld was sent for and he explained who Joe was, adding that, while the United States was important, the *Ziegfeld Follies* wasn't to be kicked around either. He needed Joe to get his scenery right. Finally a compromise was effected. The Sleuth would give Joe a week before hauling him into court but, during that time, the artist must remain in his custody. Not for a single moment was he to be out of his sight.

'Everywhere I go,' said Joe, 'there he is dodging my feetsteps. Whenever my girl and me went chair-riding it must be one of those big for-three chairs. She has heard of a wonderful fish ghetto where they make special fine lobster-humidor. This lowlife goes with us to the ghetto. He also eats lobster-humidor.'

When the week was up Joe was carted over to Philadelphia, taken before a judge – and cleared. He returned to New York just in time for the *Follies* opening.

'So it all ended happily?'

'Not so much happily,' answered Joe. 'I ask my girl to have supper with me opening night, but she say she cannot. And then when I walk into Rector's after the show, what do I see? She is sitting handholding with the verdampte spychaser!'

3

Go To It duly opened at the Princess. All the critics – except one, who headed his review with the word 'Why?' – said that it should not have been called *Go To It* but *Don't Go To It*. Jerry Kern had a call from Comstock soon after breakfast, asking him to come at once to the office and bring Guy and Plum.

In the Comstock office there was a hushed, funeral atmosphere. The customary row of actors sat in the waiting-room, looking rather more animated than usual. One gathered that the newspaper each one held contained a message of hope for the artist who was resting. They would soon be casting again at the Princess.

Ray Comstock was at his desk, the receiver wedged against his ear.

'Come in, boys,' he said. 'Yes, honey, it's a flop. . . . So am I, honey. . . . Thanks, honey. . . . Good-bye, honey,' He hung up. 'Now, boys,' he said with, for him, a surprising briskness, 'we've taken a kick in the pants, as I'm sure you all know. I blame you fellows, partly. Oh, hello, honey. If you'd tackled the job as I asked you to, things might have been different. You've got something – maybe it's this "charm" you talk about. No, honey, I'm not talking to you, I'm talking to the boys. I saw *Miss Springtime* the other night. It's a swell show, a clever show, plenty of laughs, too.'

'It isn't in it with *Oh, Boy!*' said Guy.

'That's what I wanted to see you about. Get off this damned line, will you, honey. I'll give you a contract for *Oh, Boy!* right now.'

'But you haven't read it.'

'I don't need to. You fellows know what you are doing. I'll see it opening night. The only question is how soon can we get into rehearsal?'

Guy reflected.

'A month for writing, a couple of weeks for casting – we should be ready by December.'

'Okay, boys, go to it.' Comstock coughed apologetically. 'Sorry, it slipped out. I shall try never to use those words again.'

'You really mean that you'll buy the show without reading it or hearing a note of music?'

'That's right. Tell your agent to draw the contracts, 7 per cent, no more. You choose the directors and the cast. If they'll fit in the budget, you can have anyone you name.'

'I'd like Robert Milton to stage the book,' said Guy.

'Isn't that the red-headed Russian who talks about "pear-shaped tones"?'

'Yes, but he's clever just the same, and he's begging for a chance to do a musical.'

'That's what I like,' said Ray, 'people begging. It's when you got to beg *them* that things get expensive. Now run along. Don't waste time talking. Go to – ' He checked himself.

'Get busy,' he amended.

The three rose. Plum pulled a cigar from his pocket and held it out.

'Have a cigar, Ray,' he said. It was the first and perhaps the last time an author ever gave a cigar to a theatrical manager. Ray took it with a slightly dazed air.

'Thank you, honey,' he said mechanically.

FIVE

I

There were two small female roles in *Oh, Boy!* which still remained to be filled after the rest of the cast – Anna Wheaton, Marie Carroll, Edna May Oliver and the others – had been signed up: and one morning Comstock asked Guy and Plum to look in at his office. They found him telephoning as usual.

'Can you fellows . . . I haven't time to talk to you now, honey, we're casting. And don't ask if there's anything for you, because there isn't . . . keep a secret?' he said.

They thought they could.

'Well, I don't promise, but I think I'm going to steal the two top *Follies* beauties away from Flo Ziegfeld.'

'You don't mean – ?'

'That's right. Marion Davies and Justine Johnstone.'

'You're kidding, Ray. Why would they leave Flo? Look at the publicity he gives them.'

'They want to be actresses.'

'Ah!'

'And I caught them at just the right moment. They're sore about the dressing-room sketch.'

'What's the dressing-room sketch?' asked Plum.

'I know all about that,' said Guy. 'It's a thing Gene Buck wrote for the *Follies*, but it has never been used. It never will be, either. It's much too valuable to Flo for him to waste it on the public. You see, every year Flo has this same trouble with some of the girls getting ambitious. They tell him they won't sign on unless they're given lines to speak. So up pops the dressing-room sketch. The girls get their parts, and everybody's happy.'

'And then he says it's so bad it must come out?'

Guy was amazed.

'*Flo?* You think Flo would do anything as crude as that? Of course not. He tells them the sketch is great stuff and they're going to knock the customers endways. He says he never realized before how wonderful they were and thanks them for making him give them the opportunity of showing what they could do. But, come opening night at Atlantic City, he's all broken up to find that the costumes, owing to somebody's inexcusable carelessness, have been left behind. He yells and storms at the wardrobe mistress, but there's nothing to be done about it, of course, till tomorrow night. And before tomorrow night they've found out that the show is an hour too long and he's all broken up but the dressing-room sketch will have to go. Meanwhile, the girls have signed up for another year.'

The following afternoon when Guy and Plum arrived at the Princess, there were two 'town cars' parked at the kerb, a pair of uniformed chauffeurs standing beside them. The Delage bore no identifying insignia, but on the door of the Pierce-Arrow were two Js intertwined back to back like the double Ls emblazoned on the royal coach of the *Roi Soleil*.

Everything seemed to indicate that here were the Girls.

As the two authors entered Ray's office, it was evident to them that they had guessed right. The air was vibrant with silvery laughter, and the characteristic smell of a theatrical manager's office, which is a blend of dust, whisky, and old, dead scripts, had given place to something more pleasing, possibly Coty's 'l'Origan' or 'Quelques Fleurs'. The place was practically a boudoir.

The girls were quite breathtakingly lovely. Marion was eighteen, Justine a year and a half older. Both wore mink coats that even a masculine eye could see were the best that the mink family had to offer. Both wore a spray of orchids as if orchids were an everyday affair – which for them they were. Diamonds sparkled at their wrists and glistened more discreetly through the sheer black silk stocking that covered Marion's slender ankle.

Bob Milton, a mature and serious man, sat on the sofa beside

Marion, gazing at her as Bernard Berenson would gaze on a Botticelli Venus.

'Don't waste your time with them,' he said, as Guy and Plum were 'presented'. 'They're only writers. I'm the man that's going to make you into an actress.'

'Yes, b-but they'll have to write the w-words I'm to say.' Marion had an ever-so-faint and ever-so-attractive stammer.

Justine Johnstone was, if anything, even more likely than her friend to provoke the long, low whistle. Daughter of a Norwegian sea captain, she had that touch of aloofness and that faintly haughty carriage that seem to characterize the beauties claiming Viking ancestry.

'The girls are ready to sign up with us,' said Ray, 'provided they get parts.'

Guy assured them that they would have parts.

'And names,' said Justine. 'Not just "first girl" and "second girl".'

'Of course you have names. Yours is Polly Andrews.'

'Is that a play on polyandrous?'

'Good heavens, no.'

'It sounds like it.'

'What does polyandrous mean?' Bob Milton inquired. He was a Russian whose real name was Davidoff and a surprisingly short time before he had known no English words at all.

'It means the same thing about a woman that polygamous does about a man.'

'You're too well-educated,' said Marion. 'I just say snuggle-hound – that's what I hear Ray is. I hear he's the worst old snuggle-hound on Broadway.'

'I'm not a patch on Guy. A flick of the finger, a broken heart – that's Guy Bolton.'

'Really?'

'He once kissed a girl on Broadway, and she shot clear up to the top of the Woolworth Building.'

'You don't say?'

'I'm telling you. Just closed her eyes with a little moan and floated up and up and up.'

'And he looks so good. Are you married, Guy?'

'Not yet.'

'But you are?' said Marion to Plum.

'Oh, yes,' Guy told her. 'Plum is very happily married and he's constantly telling me I should be too.'

'You get married,' said Marion, 'and first thing you know you have a baby. Then in a few months – there's another baby. Mind you, I like babies, I like them a lot, but I'm glad I haven't one now.'

Then, as if it were an afterthought, she leaned over and rapped the top of Ray's desk. The laugh that rewarded her carried her to the door.

'Write me some funny stuff, boys,' she said. 'I want to be a comic.'

She went out.

'Marion will say anything to get a laugh,' Justine commented in her low, Ethel Barrymore voice, 'but really she's a perfectly good girl and lives at home with her mother.'

She gave a little gurgling laugh as if she too had said something funny, then raised her hand in the straight forearm salute associated with royalty. Her hand fluttered a farewell. 'Good-bye, boys.'

She followed Marion out. Through the open door they could see the actors craning their necks after her. There was a buzz of comment. Plum, who had been the little gentleman to spring up and open the door, closed it behind her.

'I feel as if I had stepped back into Good King Charles's golden reign,' he remarked. 'Saucy Nell must have been very like Saucy Marion.'

'Yes, Charles would have made them both duchesses,' agreed Guy.

'They'll get us a lot of publicity,' said Ray. 'But, great Godfrey, how the rest of the women in the show are going to hate them!'

2

The rehearsal period passed swiftly and uneventfully. It seemed no time before a day arrived when the company were gathering on a platform in the Grand Central, with the usual collection of dogs, fiancés, and anxious mothers that appear whenever a theatrical troupe is setting off 'on the road'.

The manager in charge was a young man named Jefferson Perry. He was new at the game, but anxious to learn all he could about it before embarking on some private ventures of a highbrow nature beside which *Oh, Boy!* seemed trivial indeed.

His wife, of no special moment – or so the boys supposed – was a rather severe-looking young woman with glasses, who wore a small brooch on which the letters 'D.A.R.' appeared in red-white-and-blue enamel.

Schenectady was the first stop, and there the authors were plunged into the depths of despair by a dress rehearsal at which all the things that can go wrong at dress rehearsals did.

The shoes, for instance. The gentleman from I. Miller sitting stolidly out front was a constant object of attack.

'These are my own shoes, Mr Comstock. The shoes from Miller don't fit.'

'You need them larger?'

'Larger on the inside – yes.'

The prop department had its share of blame.

'I'm supposed to have a letter to read but no one's given it to me.'

Then, most nerve-racking of all – the stage wait. 'What's the matter? What's supposed to be happening?' 'Miss Wheaton says she can't make the change. There'll have to be more dialogue.'

The two Ziegfeld lovelies appeared on the stage for a brief scene that lit the depressing gloom with a moment or two of comic relief. Marion, it seems, had suffered an attack of stage fright and, in an effort to dispel it, had downed a glass or two of champagne. This had the unfortunate effect of increasing her charming little stammer to a point at which she was unable to deliver her lines.

To cope with this situation the girls had arranged between them that Justine should speak not only her own lines but Marion's as well. The remarkable monologue ran as follows:

'Oh, so you're here? Yes, I'm here – what about it? You won't leave George Budd alone. That's my business. You don't stand a chance with him. Why not? He's in love with that little Carter girl. He isn't. Yes, darling he is. I don't care. I'll tell you something else, darling. They're married. They're *not*. Yes, they are – secretly married.'

Some effort at verisimilitude was made by Justine changing her voice on each alternate line, speaking first in a piping treble then in her own rich contralto. On the treble lines Marion kept moving her lips as if she were actually speaking. But mouthing and sound were a very poor fit.

The scattering of dressmakers, scene-painters, music-arrangers, house-managers, not to mention the gentleman from I. Miller, burst into shouts of laughter.

'Keep it in, Guy,' said Comstock grimly. 'At least you'll be sure of one laugh.'

The climax came with the sudden appearance of a reporter and a press photographer shepherded by the show's press agent. There was a whispered exchange with Ray Comstock who shook hands with the newcomers and then called Milton over.

'Stop the rehearsal,' he said. 'We're going to get a spread in the papers.'

The actors gathered together in little groups as the newsmen made their way on to the stage.

'Who do you want first?' asked the stage manager.

'We only want Miss Davies and Miss Johnstone.'

'You mean you're not going to take any pictures of the rest of the company?'

'No, that's our orders – just Miss Davies and Miss Johnstone.'

The company had come out front and sat watching the girls as they moved from pose to pose. The expressions on the faces of the female members of the cast were much the same as those of the bonnet rouge leading the mob in Delacroix's famous painting of the storming of the Tuileries. One heard the mutterings of the crowd coming from the seats where the chorus had grouped themselves.

'They're just a bunch of amateurs.' Guy and Plum, sitting together, numb and despairing, heard it without knowing who said it.

Then someone added, 'Like a college show.'

Finally the picture-taking was finished.

'Let's get on with the rehearsal,' Comstock called from the back of the theatre.

'Sorry, Mr Comstock, Miss Wheaton and Miss Carroll have gone. They said they'd have no voices tomorrow if they sat around in this cold theatre any longer.'

Comstock rose. 'Send 'em all home,' he said. 'No use going on. You'll just have to trust to luck tomorrow – and God knows you'll need plenty.'

He turned to Jerry Kern, ignoring the pair seated behind him, and delivered the *coup de grâce*.

'This is the lousiest, awfullest show I ever saw,' he said. 'I thought *Go To It* was bad, but it was a sweetheart compared to this turkey. It hasn't a hope.'

3

The two who had planned and written the atrocity made no reply. They slipped out of a side exit to avoid meeting anyone either on the stage or in the lobby. No conference was called. The thing was beyond conferences. The scribbled notes of errors detected earlier in the evening seemed too trivial to mention. To have wasted time on them would have been like cleaning spots off the deck of a vessel about to founder.

There was a bitter wind blowing, and when a bitter wind blows in Schenectady it is a matter of civic pride with the citizens that no other upstate city can claim a bitterer. Guy and Plum turned up the collars of substantial overcoats that felt as if they were fashioned of gossamer.

The empty streets were dark as were their thoughts. It was very late. The Schenectadians were abed, dreaming no doubt of the treat that awaited them tomorrow evening at the Gaiety Theatre.

They rounded a corner and were met by a blast that seemed to say, 'You thought it was cold on Main Street, did you? Now we'll show you what Canal Street can do.' They bowed their heads and pushed forward like Robert Peary and his Eskimo companion on 8th April, '99.

A figure suddenly appeared beside them. It was the red-

headed boy who played the waiter at the country club in Act
Two, a part of less than a dozen lines.

'How was I?' he asked, barring their path.

'You were fine, Eddie.' It was hard to speak without losing
your breath. 'You were wonderful.'

'I'd like to have a little chat about my part,' said Eddie. 'I
guess some of the things you wrote have more meaning than
I'm putting into them.'

'Not a bit, old man.'

'If I could go over them.'

'But for God's sake, Eddie – not here.'

'That last exit of mine. I'd like a laugh, if you could give me
one.'

'We haven't a laugh in us, Eddie.'

'I thought of something myself. I'd like to tell it to you, if
you won't get sore.'

'We won't get sore, but we may get pneumonia. I feel like
the corpse on ice in *Go To It*.'

'Yes, it's a bit chilly tonight, isn't it?' said Eddie, apparently
having just noticed it. 'But this won't take a minute. Of course,
it's a pretty fresh of me to be trying to put a line in a wonderful
show like *Oh, Boy!*'

'You think *Oh, Boy!* is wonderful?'

'I sure do.'

'Then,' said Guy, 'we're at your service until Hell freezes
over. And that, I should think, is liable to happen almost any
minute.'

'Well, you know the situation,' said Eddie, getting down to
it. 'Miss Wheaton has just got a flash of Sheriff Simms through
the window. He's been looking for her ever since she escaped
from that raid in the speakeasy – '

'Yes, yes, we know the plot.'

'Well, she runs into the Ladies' Room just as I'm going off
on the other side, and I thought maybe I could call to her,
"When you come out, would you mind bringing me my
umbrella?" Would that be okay?'

'Absolutely okay,' said Guy. 'And if you'd like to rewrite the
rest of the show you're more than welcome.'

4

The next night was a riot. Everything went like clockwork. The hand-props were all there, I. Miller's shoes were all there. When it came to the quick change, Anna Wheaton was there. Most important of all, the laughs were there, and none topped that put in by Eddie, the red-headed waiter.

Ray Comstock beamed.

'I knew it was all right last night,' he said. 'You could feel success in the air.'

They moved on to Syracuse, Rochester, Buffalo and Albany, the weather getting colder and colder and the audiences warmer and warmer, and the company, after the manner of theatrical touring companies, becoming what someone has cleverly described as 'one big happy family'. No team, no clique, no sworn band of blood-brothers has such a tendency to gang up as a company of travelling actors. They move like Xenophon's Ten Thousand through an alien country, speaking a different language. They think of nothing but the show. Newspapers lose their interest. Burning questions may be exercising the rest of the populace, but to actors on the road the only burning question is, 'How's the show going to go tonight?'

But even a big happy family can have its rifts within the lute. The trouble with the *Oh, Boy!* one was, as might have been, predicted, the Girls. Not that they weren't nice to everybody, not that they were not good troupers. But they were too pretty.

And then there were the hotel suites, which rankled a little with important members of the company who had to rough it in humble bedrooms. These had started quite modestly, but as the tour progressed they became larger, and the flowers with which they were bedecked appeared in more lavish profusion. Somebody – possibly her mother – was intent on seeing to it that while on the road Marion got all the comforts of home, and this mother – or it may have been an aunt – was plainly a woman of spacious ideas. In the Hollenden Hotel in Cleveland what Marion drew was a reception room, a large sitting-room, a small sitting-room, a dining-room, two bedrooms, two baths, a clothes pressing room, maid's room and maid's bath.

Invited to share it, Justine looked dubious. 'Where do I put my maid?' she queried.

'That's all right,' said Marion cheerily. 'We'll tell them to tack on another room and bath.'

5

It was in this cosy little chummery that the famous party was given, but before the party came the arrival of Ethel Wodehouse and before the arrival of Ethel Wodehouse came the contretemps.

Mrs Jefferson Perry, the wife of the company manager, was, here in Cleveland, treading her native heath. Her mother, still extant, was of the *crème de la crème* of Cleveland society. And in those days there was no nonsense about 'café society'. As Ward McAlister could tell you, you were either born to it or you weren't.

Mrs Jefferson Perry, Mrs Jefferson Perry's mother, Mrs Pell and the Kerns were having supper following the Cleveland opening of *Oh, Boy!* the reception of which had been all that could be desired. At another table in the Hollenden dining-room the Girls were the guests of Plum and Guy. Their meal was the first to finish and the quartette filed out, passing the Kern-Perry-Pell table. A pause was indicated.

'Went well, didn't it?' said Guy, and turned to Mrs Perry who with downcast eye was busying herself with a Nesselrode pudding.

'You don't know Miss Davies and Miss Johnstone, do you, Mrs Perry?'

'No, and I don't care to,' said Mrs Perry.

This devastating rejoinder broke up the little gathering.

The one big happy family was no longer one and no longer happy. The story quickly went the rounds and produced varying reactions. Most of the company sided with the Girls but there were exceptions. At least two of the members of the company laughed when they heard the story and said 'Good'. This was duly reported to the Girls by one of those little birds that goes around poking his bill into other people's business. Also

Eva Kern continued to be seen about with Mrs Jefferson Perry. It made her a marked woman.

It had reached the point where certain members of the company were not speaking to each other, and at which unpleasant words were muttered half audibly as some member of the opposing camp passed by, when the party was augmented by the arrival of Ethel. She loved the show, but was appalled by the 'atmosphere'.

'It's the best way to get a failure,' she said. 'You can't have a company bickering and quarrelling. People can't work together unless there is harmony.'

'Nonsense,' said Plum. 'Look at Gilbert and Sullivan, they were like a dose of Paris green to each other but they worked together all right.'

'There may be exceptions, but that doesn't alter the fact that in most cases dissension destroys the team spirit.'

'What can we do about it?'

'You must give a party, you and Guy – Jerry too if you like. A real bang-up "get-together". And when they're all there and have had plenty to drink you must make a little speech about the importance of harmony.'

'My instinct is against it, but I know from experience that once you make up your mind to give a party, no man or elemental power may stay your course.'

'I'm only doing it for you and Guy. You neither of you seem to think it important to have everyone pulling together, but I feel sure that it is.'

'What do you think, Guy?'

'I think if Ethel wants us to give a party we'll give a party.'

'It needn't be anything elaborate. Lots of beer and a few bottles of whisky.'

'And sandwiches?'

'Yes, and a few other odds and ends. "Picnic style" I'd call it. Songs round the piano. By the time it's over they'll all be one big happy family.'

6

Two evenings later the party took place. Ethel assured Plum and Guy that they need not involve themselves in the preparations. She would take care of everything. Ray Comstock, she said, had promised to find a room of suitable size. Everyone was coming, chorus as well as principals.

The two hosts were the first to arrive. Ethel had said that they would find her there, but she wasn't visible.

'Anybody here?' called Plum.

'Only us tables and chairs.'

'And a hell of a lot of expensive-looking flowers.'

They peered into adjoining rooms. In the dining-room was a U-shaped table with American Beauty roses strewn about artistically between the places. Standing at one end of the room was a marvellous buffet of cold dishes that included a big salmon encased in ice. There was a platter of Chicken Jeannette and another of some small birds that looked like quail in aspic.

Guy pointed to it. 'Picnic style,' he said. 'For the love of Pete, what has Ethel been up to? The show will have to run six months for us to break even.'

'Gosh, yes, look at this – there are music stands. She's engaged an orchestra.'

'And what about these champagne buckets? There are bottles and bottles.'

'What kind of champagne is it?'

'I'm afraid to look.'

'Suffering Pete – Bollinger 1911.'

Max Hirschfeld, the company's conductor, arrived with three or four of his musicians. He said that Ray Comstock had told him there would be dancing. The musicians started in to play the music from the show. Some of the girls and boys came trooping in and took the floor. Then came the magnetic Anna Wheaton and her opposite number, Hal Forde. Marie Carroll and Tom Powers followed, then the Kerns accompanied by the Perrys and the inevitable Mrs Pell.

'Say, what *is* all this?' exclaimed Jerry. 'Putting on the dog a bit, aren't you?'

'What about yourself? What about those pearls Eva is wearing?' countered Plum.

'Aren't they lovely?' said Eva. 'Jerry said he'd get them for me when he was sure the show would be a big hit.'

'Expensive, of course,' said Jerry. '$7500, no less.'

As he spoke they became aware of a sudden hush in the room. All eyes had turned to the door. It was the Girls. They paused just inside the door waiting for the lovely ermine wraps to knock 'em dead. They looked ravishing in sheath-like dinner dresses that showed off the flowing lines of their young figures. They both wore sprays of orchids and pearl necklaces. The other women, looking them over with microscopic carelessness, knew that they might as well pack up and go home. They'd had it.

The two hosts went forward and greeted them. 'Let's dance,' said the Girls simultaneously.

As Guy danced with Justine, she asked him what it was Jerry was saying when they arrived. 'Something about a pearl necklace.'

The music stopped and Plum suggested they come in to supper. Four waiters had appeared. The champagne had begun to flow.

'Don't look now,' said Plum to his fellow-sufferer, 'but I think the stuff in those crocks the waiters are passing is caviar.'

It was caviar – the big grey kind that nowadays never gets farther than the tables of particular friends of the boys in the back-room at the Kremlin.

Then at last, pale and scared, Ethel appeared. She drew the hosts aside.

'I've been looking everywhere for Ray Comstock. I gave him my lists, but left the ordering to him. He's changed everything.'

'You didn't order caviar?'

'Good Heavens, no.'

'How about Bollinger '11?'

'I asked for whisky and beer as I said I would – everything Bohemian and informal.'

'And the performers on sackbut and psaltery?'

'No, I told Ray to make sure there was a piano for Jerry and whoever else might play.'

'Ray thinks it's a joke, I suppose. He's always making cracks about all the money we have rolling in.'

Save for the bad moment when the Girls appeared, Mrs Jefferson Perry was having a good time.

'I adore caviar,' she said. 'I've never had enough, but I'm really making the most of my opportunity tonight. And this champagne is the last word.'

'I love the peeled hot-house peaches in the glasses,' chimed in her mother.

Ethel closed her eyes and drew a long breath. 'Hot-house peaches!' she murmured.

The Girls seated across the table from Jerry, Eva and the Perry contingent, were engaged in a conversation about jewellery.

'Lillian Lorraine has a new pearl necklace,' said Miss Johnstone casually.

'What, another one?'

'Oh, this isn't like her real one. It's just something to wear when she's slumming. It only cost $7500.'

'I wouldn't be seen dead in a thing like that,' said Miss Davies disdainfully. 'My motto is don't have it if you can't have it good.'

'You're so right, darling,' agreed Miss Johnstone. 'Of course, for $7500 all you get is one of those cultured Japanese jobs. The Japs tease the oyster into making the pearl by pushing a bit of grit into his shell. He makes a pearl, but his heart isn't in the work.'

'Serves the Japs right,' said Miss Davies. 'Why should an oyster be annoyed like that just to make second-class pearls for cheap necklaces? Left alone he might some day make a really good pearl – something an oyster could be proud of.'

It was at this point that Eva said that she had a headache and thought she'd go to bed. Mrs Jefferson Perry downed a final glass of Bollinger and said if Eva was going she would go too.

'Oh, don't go yet,' protested Marion. 'I ordered Nesselrode pudding especially for you – I know how fond you are of it.'

'*You* ordered it?' cried Mrs Perry. 'I was told this party was being given by Mr Wodehouse and Mr Bolton.'

'Not *this* party, dear,' said Marion. '*This* party is mine. I believe their party is in one of the banqueting rooms on the second floor.'

'But we were told to come here.'

'Yes, Ray thought you might all enjoy coming to my party first.' She turned her charming smile full on Mrs Perry. 'Perhaps he knew how fond you are of caviar.'

'Are *we* invited to your party?' asked Marion, turning to the authors.

'Of course,' said Plum, fastening his gaze on Ethel. 'Ours is for everybody – a get-together. The entire big happy family.'

'That's lovely,' said Marion, 'but anyone who wants to stay here can. How are you doing, girls?' she asked, addressing the female principals at their table. 'Are they giving you plenty of champagne?'

It was the day of the gold-mesh bag. Each of the girls was carrying one. Marion opened hers.

'Oh, dear,' she said, turning to Justine. 'Have you a loose $100 on you, darling? I want to leave something for the waiter.'

The definition of a smash-hit in the theatre is one that has varied a good deal from age to age. In Shakespeare's time anything that ran two nights was good, and if you did three you went out and bought a new fur coat. In the nineties authors became offensively conceited if they broke the hundred mark. Today a musical comedy which runs less than five years is presumed to have had some structural weakness in it. It ought to have been fixed up out of town, people say, even if it meant calling in a couple of play-doctors.

It is difficult, therefore, to estimate the degree of success which *Oh, Boy!* achieved. One can only say that it was sufficient to make one chuck one's chest out quite considerably when it happened. It did not run five years, but it did do 475 performances in New York, and during its Broadway run there were four companies out on the road, one playing Chicago, another Boston, a third the one-week cities and a fourth the one-night stands. It cost $29,262.56 to produce, this including a seven-week tour during which two authors, a composer, a book director, a dance director and a manager had to be supported in luxury, and it made a profit of $181,641.54.

For those days it was a socko, and it left Bolton and Wodehouse – the latter now better known as the Sweet-Singing Thrush of 39th Street – sitting on top of the world and loving it. It seemed as though Fate had decided that there was nothing she could deny to these favourite sons of hers. They were in. As they sauntered past Cain's Storehouse of a morning, taking snuff from their jewelled snuff-boxes and sneering at the lower orders whom they jostled off the pavement, there was never a thought in their minds that the time was coming when that gaunt building would play an impressive part in their lives and that before many more suns had set its proprietor, when asked by friends how business was, would be saying, 'Quiet at the moment, boys, a little quiet at the moment, but it'll pick up. Bolton and Wodehouse have a couple of shows coming on.' Like most young authors who get a run of luck, the unhappy saps had taken on much more work than they could do even fairly well. They had so many irons in the fire that they put the fire out.

Writing musical comedies is like eating salted almonds – you can always manage one more. Every time the two partners met, they vowed that they would go on the musical comedy wagon, but nothing ever came of their good resolutions. Somehow they found themselves in Charlie Dillingham's office, and there was the box of cigars on the desk and Mr Ziegfeld in a chair by the window and Mr Dillingham saying, 'Wouldn't it be fun to get up some theatricals?' and Mr Ziegfeld saying, 'Yes, wouldn't it?', and then a voice through the smoke cooed, 'Sign here, boys,' and the boys woke up and found that they were booked to do a colossal revue for the Century Theatre.

And after that . . . Cain's hospital storehouse.

Cain's Storehouse, like so many monuments of the past, no longer exists. One is not quite sure what happens now to the scenery of shows that have failed to attract. You probably have to cart it out into the wilds somewhere and set fire to it with matches. But in the days of which we are writing Cain's was a great institution, a sort of Sargasso Sea into which the wrecks of dramatic Hesperuses drifted automatically. Or you might call it a morgue. To this morgue it was inevitable that sooner or later Bolton and Wodehouse would be contributing a corpse or two. In actual fact, they contributed three, one after the other.

There was once a manager who, examining his books, made the discovery that his box-office man had been cheating him for years. He sent for the culprit.

'How much do I pay you a week?' he asked.

'$60, sir.'

'It's raised to $75.'

'Oh, thank you, sir!'

'Or, rather, $100.'

'Oh, thank you, sir!'

'No, wait. That's not enough. $150. And when I say $150, I mean, of course, $200.'

'Oh, *thank* you, sir!'

'Just one thing more,' said the manager, beaming at him like a Cheeryble Brother, 'You're fired. You see,' he explained to a friend when telling him of the incident later, 'I wanted to fire the son of a what-not from a really *good* job.'

It is in a precisely similar way that Fate likes to work, waiting with the brass knucks and the sock full of sand until its victims are at the peak of one of those boom periods when life appears to be roses, roses all the way. As Shakespeare, who often hits off a thing rather neatly, once said:

> This is the state of man. Today he puts forth
> The tender leaves of hopes, tomorrow blossoms,
> And bears his blushing honours thick upon him.
> The third day comes a frost, a killing frost;
> And when he thinks, good easy men, full surely
> His greatness is a-ripening, nips his root.

It was just like that with Guy and Plum. They couldn't have put it better themselves.

The first V-shaped depressions to darken their lives after the unbroken fine weather in which they had been basking came along, ironically, in the season when they had set a mark for all other authors to shoot at by having five shows running simultaneously on Broadway . . . or, in Guy's case, six, for Belasco had taken sufficient time off from his picture hanging to produce the Bolton-Middleton comedy, *Polly With A Past*, starring Ina Claire, and it had settled down to a long and prosperous run.

These were the five: *Oh, Boy!*, *Leave it to Jane*, *The Rose of China*, *The Riviera Girl*, *The Second Century Show*.

Oh, Boy!, as we say, was a smash-hit, and so to a lesser extent was *Leave it to Jane*, a rather free adaptation of George Ade's *College Widow*.

But the others. . . .

1 The Rose of China

The writing of this blot on the New York theatrical scene was
due entirely to too much rich food, too much potent liquor and
the heady effect of Oriental music on top of these. The con-
sumers of the food and the liquor were the pair so shortly to
become the toast of Cain's Storehouse, and the music was that
of Armand Vecsey, rendered by himself in the Oval Room of
the Ritz-Carlton Hotel, where he was the *chef d'orchestre.*

In the song 'Yip-i-addy' we are told that,

> Young Herman von Bellow
> A musical fellow,
> Performed on the 'cello each night
> At a restaurant where
> All the brave and the fair
> Would look in for a chat and a bite.
> He played tunes that you know
> From Wagner and Gounod
> To give the gay building a tone,
> But the place started swaying
> When he began playing
> A sweet little thing of his own.

It was precisely the same with Armand Vecsey, except that his
instrument was the violin. He played superbly, and when he
dished out the Chinese suite he had composed, the brave and
the fair curled up like carbon paper and the Messrs Bolton and
Wodehouse, puffing their cigars and taking another beaker of
old brandy, told each other emotionally that this was the stuff.
Not realizing that practically anything sounds good after a well-
lubricated dinner, they agreed that a musical play written
around these marvellous melodies could not fail to bring home
the gravy. A week later they were writing *The Rose of
China.*

It just shows how overwork can dull the senses that neither
of the gifted youths realized what was bound to happen if they
started getting mixed up with things of that sort. The advice
that should be given to all aspiring young authors is: Have
nothing to do with anything with a title like *The Rose of China*
or *The Willow Pattern Plate* or *The Siren of Shanghai* or *Me Velly*

Solly . . . in fact, avoid Chinese plays altogether. Much misery may thus be averted.

What happens when you write a Chinese play is that before you know where you are your heroine has gone cute on you, adding just that touch of glucose to the part which renders it unsuitable for human consumption. She twitters through the evening saying, 'Me Plum Blossom. Me good girl. Me love Chlistian god velly much,' and things of that sort, like the heroine of Sammy Shipman's *East is West*, by which, one supposes now that the agony has abated and it is possible to think clearly, the Bolton-Wodehouse opus must have been – if that is the right word – inspired.

It is the view of competent critics that – with the possible exception of *Abie's Irish Rose* and *Grandma's Diary* – *East is West* is the ghastliest mess ever put on the American stage, but this is an opinion held only by those who did not see *The Rose of China*. It was of *The Rose of China* that Ring Lardner, one of the scattered few who caught it during its New York run, said, 'Cain's horses are *snorting* for this one,' and how right he was. It was the sort of piece where the eyes of the audience keep wandering to that cheering notice at the top of the programme: 'This theatre can be emptied in three minutes. Look around, choose the nearest exit to your seat and walk (do not run) to that exit.'

Without referring to the script, a thing they are naturally reluctant to do, the authors cannot say after this length of time whether or not the heroine of *The Rose of China* turned out in the end to be the daughter of an American missionary, kidnapped by Chinese bandits in her infancy, but it would seem virtually certain that she did. All heroines of Chinese plays turn out in the end to be the daughters of American missionaries, kidnapped by bandits in their infancy. This is known as Shipman's Law. There is no reason to suppose that in this instance there would have been any deviation from the straight party line.

2 *The Riviera Girl*

By all the ruling of the form book this one should have been all right, for it was a Klaw and Erlanger production, put in with

Joseph Urban scenery at the New Amsterdam, and the score was by Kalman, the composer of *Sari* and *Miss Springtime*, with additional numbers by Jerome Kern.

The Kalman score was not only the best that gifted Hungarian ever wrote but about the best anybody ever wrote. After thirty-odd years it is still played constantly on the radio, and in the early fifties it was revived, with another libretto, in Paris, and pulled in the cash customers in their thousands. Which seems to place the responsibility for its deplorable failure on Broadway squarely on the shoulders of the boys who wrote the book. They feel that where they went wrong was in being too ingenious in devising a plot to replace the original Viennese libretto, which, like all Viennese librettos, was simply terrible.

It was one of those plots where somebody poses as somebody else and it turns out that he really was somebody else, they just think he is pretending to be somebody else. (It would be nice to make it a little clearer, but that is the best we can do.) And the odd thing is that – till the critics got at it with their hatchets – both authors thought highly of it. 'Boy,' Guy would say to Plum, his eyes sparkling, 'you could take that plot down to the bank and borrow money on it,' and Plum, his eyes sparkling, too, would agree that you certainly could.

And then the rude awakening.

3 *The Second Century Show*

This was the one mentioned earlier, into which the authors were lured by the combined persuasiveness of C. B. Dillingham and Florenz Ziegfeld, the former of whom alone was capable – for there never was a more genial man than Charlie Dillingham – of luring an author into anything. The two had gone into partnership in the previous year to produce a mammoth revue at the Century Theatre called *The Century Show*, and they now wanted another, equally mammoth, to follow it. The Century, long since pulled down, stood at the bottom of Central Park West and was the last word in theatres, its girders made of gold and $1000 bills used instead of carpets. It was built by a syndicate of millionaires. At least, they were millionaires when they began building it.

The thing that turned the scale and decided the Bolton-

Wodehouse duo to sign on the dotted line was the fact that the latter a few years earlier had collaborated on a revue for the Empire Theatre in London and had found it the most delightful experience. As he told Bolton, all the author of a revue had to do was put his name on the thing. The dialogue was written by the artists, worthy fellows who asked nothing better than to write their own stuff, while publishers vied with one another to contribute songs. Doing *The Second Century Show*, he said, would be a nice rest.

The awakening – another rude one – came with the discovery that the New York method of assembling a revue differed from that in vogue in London. The authors found that they were expected to do the work themselves. It was an unpleasant shock, but they rallied from it and sat down to think what sort of a masterpiece they should give the customers.

On one thing they were resolved – there should be a plot, a real, coherent, consecutive story. Not like that show last year. They were frightfully contemptuous and superior about that last year's show. They called it a mere vaudeville entertainment and other harsh things. They could do a little better than that, they rather felt.

The first jarring note was struck when they learned that the cast of principals as selected – and given contracts – to date consisted of three classical dancers, three acrobatic dancers, a Spanish dancer, forty-eight buck-and-wing dancers, two trained cows and Harry Kelly and his dog Lizzie. (Does anybody remember Harry Kelly and Lizzie? 'She's a hunting dog. Sometimes she hunts here, sometimes she hunts there.' Harry would say, 'Roll over,' and Lizzie would take not the slightest notice, and Harry would say, 'Good dog,' and the act would proceed.)

This did not seem what you might call a balanced cast for a plotty show, but the management urged them to go ahead and fear nothing. They said they would see to it that performers were provided, and they certainly were. Scarcely a day went by without the addition to the cast of some new juggler or trapeze artist, and the gallant little plot swallowed them all like a frog swallowing flies, till at last, in a heroic attempt to absorb a performing seal, it burst and died, regretted by all.

You could find fragments of it splashed about all over the final version of *The Second Century Show*, gruesome fragments like the remains of the man who died of spontaneous combustion in Bleak House. Guy was at the sick-bed to the last, hoping for the best, for he loved that plot. He would pick it up and nurse it back to consciousness after some frightful blow had stunned it, but just as it was beginning to recover, along would come somebody and cram a couple of cross-talk comedians down its throat, and all the weary work was to do again.

Plum was more occupied with the lyrics. Occasionally a sharp scream from the tortured plot would make him wince, but it was the lyrics that etched those lines on his face and were responsible for the dark circles under his eyes.

A revue lyric of that period was a monstrous freak with one verse and twelve refrains, each introducing a separate girl in some distinctive costume. The lyric was written round the dresses. On arriving at the theatre in the morning, the sensitive poet was handed a pile of costume designs. One would represent a butterfly, another the Woolworth Building, a third a fish, a fourth a bird, a fifth a fruit salad and the others the Spirit of American Womanhood, Education Enlightening The Backward South, Venus Rising From The Sea, and so on, and Mr Ziegfeld says will you please have it ready for tomorrow's rehearsal, as the girls are threatening to walk out because they have nothing to do. ('Walking out' was the technical term when a show-girl stepped into her Rolls-Royce, said, 'Home James,' to the chauffeur and drove off, never to be seen again.)

When the bard had finished twelve refrains, cunningly introducing the butterfly, the Woolworth Building, the Growing Unrest In The Balkans and Venus Rising From The Sea, the management decided that they didn't want to use those costumes after all, and handed him another batch. Critics have often commented on the sombre gloom which permeates all Wodehouse novels like the smell of muddy shoes in a locker-room and have wished that, fine as they are, there was not quite so much of the Russian spirit of pessimism and hopelessness in them, but now that it has been revealed that he wrote the lyrics for *The Second Century Show*, they will understand and sympathize.

It was an axiom in the theatre of those days that if you had a clientele you could not fail to bring home the bacon. The Empire had its clientele. So had the Princess and one or two other houses. But the real clientele boys, head and shoulders above all the rest, were C. B. Dillingham and Florenz Ziegfeld. With the two of them joining forces, it seemed obvious that *The Second Century Show* must be a success. But it was not. In the immortal words of whoever it was, the clientele didn't come to that one.

Have you ever been distressed and mortified at the unexpected refusal of your dog to accept the proffered morsel? You are enjoying a quiet meal, when the hound intimates by every means at his disposal that he wishes to come in on the ground floor. You offer him a bit of the delicacy you are consuming, and he sniffs at it and then turns away with an expression on his face that suggests that you have wounded him in his finest feelings, leaving you piqued, chagrined and frustrated. Just so does an author feel when the public, who have been pawing and whining at him for some particular brand of entertainment, turn away on being offered it and leave it untouched.

If there was one thing it was certain that the New York public wanted at this time, it was large, lavish revue crammed with lovely girls, and this was what they had been given. Nothing could have been larger and more lavish than *The Second Century Show*, and there were lovely girls in every nook and cranny of it. And yet it was withdrawn after thirty performances. Which was perhaps just as well, come to think of it, for it was discovered later that it was so large and lavish that if it had played to absolute capacity with two rows of standees every night, the weekly loss would have been between $3000 and $4000.

There was only one thing about *The Second Century Show* that is of historic interest. The pianist who played the piano at rehearsals was a young fellow named George Gershwin.

SEVEN

I

For two ardent young men who have made it their mission in life to raise the lighter musical drama to new heights there are few things more unpleasant than a resounding flop. Let them have three such flops in rapid succession, and they begin to feel like a couple of lepers who have been expelled from their club for cheating at cards. After *The Rose of China*, *The Riviera Girl* and *The Second Century Show* the guilty pair were afraid to walk past the Lambs Club lest they run into some reproachful ham who had appeared briefly in one or other of these outstanding turkeys. A jocular boulevardier induced in them a strong distaste for all jocular boulevardiers by saying to the jocular boulevardiers with whom he was drinking synthetic Scotch that he felt nervous about leaving town for the weekend these days because he might be missing a Bolton-Wodehouse show.

It was the tragedy of *The Rose of China* that they found hardest to bear. The other two had been commissions, and nobody could have been expected to turn down a commission for a big musical from Klaw and Erlanger and what had seemed like an even bigger musical from pre-eminent managers like Dillingham and Ziegfeld. But they had gone into *The Rose of China* entirely on their own initiative, just because a fiddler had hypnotized them with his violin at a moment when their better judgment had been clouded by a good dinner at the Ritz-Carlton.

They were not eating at the Ritz-Carlton now but at the Columbus Circle Childs'. There were three reasons for this – the first the prices on the right-hand side at the former of the two hostelries, the second the understandable shrinking from being pointed out as the pariahs of Broadway, and the third, most potent of all, a desire never again to lay eyes on or lend ears to the Ritz-Carlton's *chef d'orchestre*.

At this very moment, they felt, as the waitress slammed down their buckwheat cakes and coffee, Armand Vecsey was probably tying himself in knots as he rendered some excerpt from *The Rose of China* designed to show the luncheon patrons that its failure had not been the fault of the composer.

They were just squaring their elbows and getting at the wholesome foodstuffs when Plum gave a start and sat rigid, the buckwheat cake frozen on his fork. The expression on his face was that of someone passing a sewer excavation.

'What's that noise I hear?' he asked in a low, toneless voice. 'I don't mean the waitress throwing used dishes down the chute, I mean that music. It's Chinese music!'

'Nonsense. You're hearing things.'

'Don't tell me. That's Chinese music. Listen.'

'Do you know, I believe you're right.'

They hailed a waitress, who explained that the music was indeed Chinese music and was filtering through the ceiling from the Far East restaurant immediately above.

'We shall not be coming to this Childs' again,' said Plum coldly.

'Decidedly not. I'm darned if it isn't *The Rose of China* they're playing. They must have got hold of one of the records. Even here we can't escape it. And do you realize,' said Guy, 'that if a certain man had not happened to walk down a certain street in a certain Hungarian town on a certain evening *The Rose of China* would never have happened?'

'What do you mean?'

'It was owing to this son of a Hungarian that Armand Vecsey got his musical education. I had it from Armand himself. It seems that he began life as a poor boy in a farming district near Budapest called the Puszta. He wanted to be a violinist, but his family wouldn't hear of it, so one day he ran off with his fiddle, and what little money he had managed to save, to a place with the impossible name of Papa. It's the Heidelberg of Hungary, I gather, and there is a famous Conservatory of Music there.'

'How do you spell Papa?'

'P-a-p-a.'

'The students, no doubt, refer to it as their Alma Pater.'

'Please! Not now. Well, in next to no time, of course, Armand ran out of money, and his landlady said that if he didn't pay his back rent, she would kick him out and keep his violin.'

'So he packed it in his trunk and tried to sneak away?'

'Exactly. And he got it as far as the front door when this man came along. Seeing that Armand was in difficulties, he stopped and asked if he could give him a hand. Armand explained the situation, and they started down the front steps, carrying the trunk. At this moment the landlady appeared.'

'Embarrassing. I suppose Armand was nonplussed.'

'He was. But the man wasn't. He told the landlady that he was a friend of Armand's, and Armand had inflamed him with his stories of what a delightful dump this of the landlady's was, so here he was with his trunk and he would like, if possible, a room with a southern exposure.'

'Ingenious.'

'Yes, he was one of those quick-thinking Hungarians. Well, the landlady not unnaturally blew her top. "I don't want any friends of this little so-and-so in my house," she said, speaking of course in Hungarian. "You take that trunk and get out of here!" Which they did. Are you laughing heartily?'

'Very.'

'Well, save it up, because there's a lot more coming. When they were out of sight of the house, they put down the trunk and sat on it. Armand thanked the man, and told him all about his ambition to become a violinist, but how on earth he was ever going to become a violinist he didn't know, he added, because he hadn't the cash to study at the Conservatory, and if you're a musician and don't study at conservatories, you haven't a hope.'

'Like that line in *Leave it to Jane*. "If you don't get an eddiccation, you can't be a lawyer." '

'Exactly. Well, when he heard this, the man pricked up his ears. "Now, that's a funny thing," he said. "I've been sent to the Conservatory to study, and I want no piece of it. What I like is pottering around and having a good time. I've not been near the place yet. How would you react to the idea of going there and studying in my place?"

'Armand felt that this must be some beautiful dream.

' "You're offering me a musical education? Your education?"

' "Why not? I don't want it. I hate music. But my grandmother told me to come here, and her word is law. She has supplied me with ample funds to see me through the Conservatory, so it seems to me our path lies clear before us. We split the money, you taking one quarter, me threequarters, and you go and study till you're blue in the face, leaving me to continue pottering around and, as I say, having a good time." '

'Gosh! This thing's beginning to shape. Armand, who of course takes the other fellow's name, is a great success at the Conservatory and writes a diploma-number that enchants one and all, and the grandmother comes hot-footing to applaud the young genius – '

'And the chap who knows nothing about music has to play for the old lady, so he sits at the player-piano and – '

' – half-way through he gets absent-minded and gets up – '

' – and the piano goes on playing . . . There's a show there.'

'If we were going to write any more shows.'

'But we aren't.'

'No. Still, it's a good story.'

'Very good.'

'The only thing wrong with it,' said Guy broodingly, 'is that, to make it dramatic, after a start like that Armand should have finished up as a world famous composer instead of sawing a fiddle in a New York hash-house. In which event he wouldn't have intrigued us with a lot of pseudo-Chinese music and we wouldn't have written a prize bust called *The Rose of China*.'

2

Despondency continued to grip the two. After three failures in a row it seemed impossible that they would ever again find a manager with confidence enough in their motheaten talent to entrust them with a commission. And it was just when Guy was saying that, come right down to it, there was no life like the architect's, and Plum had begun to mutter that if he had to do it all over again he would certainly think twice before he gave up a steady job at £3 a week, that Ray Comstock brought the sunshine back into their lives by asking them to look in and discuss a new piece for the Princess. They were in his presence twenty minutes after the receipt of the telephone message, not even stopping to wonder how Ray could have staved off the honeys long enough to be able to give them a call.

In the familiar surroundings of the Princess their flagging spirits revived. True, the actors on either side of the waiting-room eyed them distrustfully as they appeared at the wicket and one of their number rose, pocketed his *Variety* and left, glancing at them in a meaning way as he passed through the door.

'There's a fellow doesn't want to be in anything of ours,' said Guy, as they went into the inner office and found Ray with the receiver propped on his shoulder as usual. The conversation he was conducting had apparently reached its end, for he said, 'Good-bye, sugar,' and hung up.

'*Sugar?*' said Plum, startled. It seemed very unorthodox.

'He's giving the South a play,' said Guy.

Ray smiled his Sphinx-like smile.

'Where have you boys been keeping yourselves?' he asked genially. 'Time you stopped loafing and got down to work.'

They exchanged glances. Was this tact, or had he not noticed certain things that had been happening around the corner on Broadway?

Presumably he had not, for his faith in them appeared to be unimpaired.

'Another *Oh, Boy!* is what we want,' he said. 'Oh, hello, honey.'

'How do you like *Oh, Lady, Lady* for a title?' asked Guy. It was a phrase which Bert Williams, the negro comedian, was using at the moment.

'H'm. . . . Go jump in the lake, honey. . . . Yes, good. Well, if you boys want contracts, you can have them now, and an advance of $1000 apiece. I'm adding a half per cent to your royalty. Every time you give me a hit, the next time. . . . I said Go jump in the lake, honey . . . will be a half per cent more.'

The two partners were so moved by the thought that some-body still considered them capable of writing hits that they nearly broke down. As they left the office, they agreed that there was no manager like Ray Comstock and no theatre like the Princess.

'I shall be practically next door to it, which will be convenient,' said Plum. 'Ethel's taken an apartment for the winter in the Beaux Arts.'

This new abode was a handsome studio-apartment recently vacated by the well-known artist, Leon Gordon. It was here that Guy and Plum met one morning to work on *Oh, Lady, Lady*. Ethel had gone out, leaving them to get on with it.

But they had struck a snag. A story was shaping itself, but they could not decide where the action was to be laid. Also, what to do with the second love-interest was bothering them. 'Bill', the hero, and 'Molly', the heroine, would take care of the main plot, but running parallel with it there had to be a second love-interest, and it had to be funny. And to make the process of composition tougher, they had run out of tobacco, without which it was impossible to think properly. Guy said he would go out and buy some.

'I wish you would,' said Plum. 'I ought not to leave here. There's a lady decorator coming to collect that settee there.'

'A bastard piece,' said Guy, surveying it. 'Early American top with Victorian legs.'

He went out, and in the lobby encountered Audrey Munson, New York's leading artists' model, whose acquaintance he had made in a friend's studio. It is Audrey Munson whom the passer-by sees when he walks down Fifth Avenue and arrives at 59th Street, for she is the lady on top of the fountain in the Plaza, who seems to be awaiting, from the other side of 59th Street, the imminent arrival of General Sherman, rather inconveniently chaperoned by an angel. She may also be seen in the Modern Room of the Metropolitan as Phryne dropping her cloak at the trial, as Hagar driven into the wilderness, and as an unnamed female strolling in the nude along a presumably unfrequented beach.

'What are you doing?' asked Guy after the customary greetings and civilities had been exchanged.

'Oh, I'm making the rounds of the artists' studios, seeing if I can't drum up a little trade,' said Audrey. 'In my line you've got to make the most of what you've got while you've still got it.'

Guy went on his way, and Audrey looked in on a few likely prospects. None of them wanted a model at the moment, but one of them suggested she try Leon Gordon. To the Leon Gordon studio she went, and in response to her ring Plum opened the door.

'Oh, come in,' he said cordially. He waved a hand toward the settee. 'There's the old sofa.'

Miss Munson interpreted this as an invitation to be seated.

'I'm Audrey Munson,' she said. 'Have you any work for me?'

Plum had not paid much attention to the name of the lady decorator when Ethel had mentioned it, but it seemed to him that it had been something like Munson. (Actually, it was McFarland.)

'Oh, rather, quite a bit of work,' he chirruped brightly, and, remembering his instructions, added, 'and more to come later, if your figure is all right.'

Miss Munson bridled slightly.

'My figure is generally supposed to be all right.'

Plum knitted his brow, trying to remember just what Ethel had told him about that settee. The back and the arms were okay, if he recalled, but. . . . Ah, yes.

'It's the legs that are the problem.'

'You need have no anxiety about those.'

'That's good. And how much will it be altogether?'

'You want the altogether.'

'Oh, while I remember, the seat. It should be covered with a piece of chintz. To hide the legs, if they show too much sign of wear and tear.'

Miss Munson smiled indulgently.

'I guess I'm being kidded,' she said. 'You fooled me at first with that deadpan stuff.' She rose and glanced about the room. 'Do you have a screen?'

'I don't believe so. Should we, do you think?'

'It doesn't matter. I can manage. You want to work now, right away?'

'Yes, I've got to get to work.'

'Fine,' said Audrey. She walked over to the bedroom door. 'Anyone in there?'

'No, I'm all alone.'

'Good. I'll only be a minute.'

Plum told Guy later that it did occur to him as a trifle odd that a lady decorator should have accompanied the foregoing remarks by starting to unfasten the buttons of her dress. However, he knew that lady decorators had their own way of doing things. Assuming that she had gone into the bedroom to inspect something Ethel had asked her to inspect in there, he dismissed her from his thoughts and turned back to the lyric he had been working on for *Oh, Lady*, a trio for Bill, the hero, Hale, his friend, and Cyril Twombley, the aristocratic private detective subsequently played so perfectly by Reginald Mason. It was entitled – appropriately in view of what was so soon to happen – 'It's a Hard World for a Man'.

He had just written the last line when the door of the bedroom opened and Audrey Munson emerged in an advanced state of nudity. And as he stood gaping, with the feeling that this was pretty eccentric even for a lady decorator, there was a ring at the bell and there entered another strange young woman.

'I've come for – ' she began, then stopped, having caught a glimpse of what should have been covered with a piece of chintz disappearing upstage left. 'Perhaps it would be more convenient if I were to look in some other time,' she added frigidly, and Plum observed that behind her there was standing a man in overalls, obviously one of those sons of toil whose function it is to heave furniture about. Quick on the uptake, like all the Wodehouses, he saw that this new arrival must be the authentic female decorator. Who the other had been, he could not say. Probably just one of the neighbours making a social call.

'Oh, good morning,' he said, and was about to add that that was the settee over there and, as he had been saying only a moment ago to the lady who has just left us, the legs didn't match with the upper part, when his visitor withdrew, taking the man in overalls with her. The latter, he noticed, seemed reluctant to leave, as if he were feeling that by doing so he might be missing something of more than passing interest. His eyes, as they rested on the bedroom door, were protruding some inches from the parent sockets.

It was a few minutes later that Guy returned with the tobacco. Plum welcomed him warmly. He was glad to have at his disposal the advice of this seasoned man of the world.

'Listen, old boy,' he said. 'I have a problem, and one that seems to me to call for sophisticated handling. There's a girl in there.'

'A girl?'

'Yes, it's a girl, all right.' It was a point on which no room had been left for doubt. 'She came in while you were out and after a few civil remarks had been exchanged took all her clothes off.'

'Took her *clothes* off?'

'Yes. It struck me at the time as peculiar. And the problem, as I envisage it, is: Taking into consideration the fact that Ethel will be back at any moment, what do we do for the best?'

Even as he spoke, the inspiration of Puvis de Chavannes and Homer St Gaudens came out, fully clad, and Guy was able to effect the introductions. Plum apologized gracefully to Miss Munson for having proved so distrait a host, and Audrey, as good a sport as ever sat on a model throne, apologized for having made it necessary for him to apologize to her. They sketched out for Guy's benefit the story of the recent misunderstandings, and it was just after Miss Munson had left that Guy leaped from his chair as Archimedes leaped from his bath when he made that historic observation of his – 'Eureka!'

'That's it,' he said 'There's our scene.'

'What scene?'

'The comedy scene we want for the first meeting of Bill's friend Hale and our soubrette – "May Barber", or whatever we were going to call her. Bill must be an artist, and he leaves Hale with instructions about the settee, and in comes May, who's a model. The thing will write itself, and it gives us our setting – Greenwich Village. I can't remember a Greenwich Village set in a musical comedy, so it'll be brand new. There ought to be a Greenwich Village lyric.'

'There will be,' said Plum, and next day he was able to hand it over to Jerry, complete.

Way down in Greenwich Village
There's something, 'twould appear,
Demoralizing in the atmosphere.
Quite ordinary people,
Who come to live down here,
Get changed to perfect nuts within a year.
They learn to eat spaghetti
(That's hard enough, as *you* know)
They leave off frocks
And wear Greek smocks
And study Guido Bruno.
For there's something in the air
Down here in Greenwich Village
That makes a fellow feel he doesn't care:
And as soon as he is in it, he
Gets hold of an affinity
Who's long on modern Art but short on hair.
Though he may have been a model,
Ever since he learned to toddle,
To his relatives and neighbours everywhere,
When he hits our Latin Quarter
He does things he shouldn't oughter:
It's a sort of,
Sort of kind of,
It's a sort of kind of something in the air.

3

Oh, Lady, Lady opened out of town in Wilmington, Delaware, three days before Christmas, and the authors thought highly of it.

The integration of book and music was better than in *Oh, Boy!*, the story – for a musical play – exceptionally strong, so much so that Plum was able later to use it for a full length novel, *The Small Bachelor*, and the score one long succession of those Kern melodies of his early youthful days that were so gay and carefree compared with his maturer style. After *Show Boat* he turned to more serious things, and the light duets and trios of the Princess era were no more for him.

The Wednesday matinée fell on Christmas Eve, and the number of Wilmingtonians who preferred to finish their shopping was in considerable excess of those who visited the Dupont Theatre. Guy and Plum sat surrounded by a vast acreage of empty seats. What audience there was was in the first two rows, and the authors hardly knew they were there.

For the paying customers did little to draw attention to themselves. In theatre parlance they 'sat on their hands' and were pretty defiant towards any attempt to make them laugh. The best that could be said of them is that they were not the barking seal type. They were quiet.

So quiet that half-way through the first act Bolton, forgetting their existence, rose and addressed Harry Brown, who was playing his opening scene with Carroll McComas.

'That's wrong, Harry,' he said. 'You'll kill the laughs if you keep pointing to the settee. Carroll would be bound to know what you were talking about.'

His voice trailed off in silence as he became aware of thirty-six blank faces which had turned and were regarding him with astonishment from rows one and two. There was a long moment of silence. Plum came to the rescue.

'Ladies and gentlemen,' he said 'we must apologize. We're down here trying to get this show right for New York, and Mr Bolton has just spotted something that is wrong. Would you mind if we fixed it?'

Some civil person said, 'Not at all. Go ahead,' and Guy, encouraged, found his voice.

'There are so few of you,' he said, 'and you were keeping so quiet that I had quite forgotten you were there.'

This got a better laugh than any of the lines in the show, and Guy said, 'We're all a little dizzy these days, and I thought we were having a rehearsal. If you don't mind, we'll have one now.'

It was one of the most successful rehearsals in the history of the stage. The audience listened with rapt attention as the authors made their corrections. Many of them contributed suggestions. When the performance ended, the cast came down to the footlights and signed the programmes that were handed up to them.

'If only we could have you people with us for our first night in New York!' said Vivienne Segal.

'They certainly liked it,' said Plum, as he and Guy crossed the corridor that separates the theatre from the hotel. 'There was a delightful woman with a face like a weasel who called it a gem.'

'If they call this a gem,' said Guy, 'can you imagine what they'd say about *The Little Thing*?'

'You know what,' said Plum. 'I almost hope *The Little Thing* is never produced. Then you'll always have something to look forward to.'

The shaping-up tour of *Oh, Lady, Lady* was a long one, taking the play through eight one-week stands.

What happens in such cases is that you cosy-up and become one big happy family. The chorus of twelve girls, chosen less for their abilities – although of course they must be able to dance and sing – than their good looks, were about average. That is, all except one.

She was the youngest of the troup with enchanting big blue eyes, a lovely, transparent skin inherited from an English mother, beautiful everything, figure, face, smile, speaking voice, a smile that bestows kindness on everyone, everyone but especially Plum, with whom she fell in love.

Guy called it Plum's 'one wild oat', but Plum insisted there was nothing sexual about it. Fleur – that was her name – Fleur Marsden had fallen in love with his books.

She has several copies of them and she'd marked things she didn't quite understand. She longed to have him help her, she was terribly badly educated. Her mother had married an explorer and she'd been moved about to all sorts of strange places and had actually never been to school at all. And Plum longed to help her.

It was fun and they laughed and chaffed and treated Plum's 'one wild oat' as a proper subject for banter. Fleur hadn't understood what it meant. Guy told her.

It was late when the train rolled into the Grand Central. Guy dropped Plum at his abode on the roof of an office building, 22nd Street and Madison Avenue. Ethel greeted him coolly.

'The show's a big hit,' he told her.

'Good,' Ethel said, 'perhaps it will pay for the expense of the tour.'

'What do you mean? The tour is paid for by the management even to the box of cigars for Guy and me.'

'I'm speaking about the diamond watch-bracelet you gave your girlfriend, the receipted bill for which arrived here yesterday morning.'

'It was her birthday, her nineteenth, and no one sent her anything, not even a card.'

'And you didn't know it's a racket. Six birthdays a year though she's not likely to meet up with another costing close on a thousand dollars.'

'Even if you think of it as an affair, which it wasn't. . . .' Ethel broke in. 'Don't give me that! I'm not a fool.'

'No, you're an angry wife and if you won't believe what I say you'll just have to go on believing what you think. And now I suppose we might talk about the play. It's the best job any one of us three has done. Guy's story is both charming and terribly funny.'

'I hate the play and I hope it turns out a stinker. . . .' She turned away.

'You're the woman I work for. You are my inspiration. . . .'

He was following her as he spoke. She cut off his speech with a sharp bang of the door.

4

Oh, Lady, Lady turned out to be what Comstock had asked for – another *Oh, Boy!* All the New York critics – there were about twenty of them in those days – were enthusiastic and complimentary. One even burst into song:

This is the trio of musical fame,
  Bolton and Wodehouse and Kern:
Better than anyone else you can name,
  Bolton and Wodehouse and Kern.
Nobody knows what on earth they've been bitten by:
All I can say is I mean to get lit an' buy
Orchestra seats for the next one that's written by
  Bolton and Wodehouse and Kern.

And Dorothy Parker, never easy to please, wrote:

Well, Bolton and Wodehouse and Kern have done it again. Every time these three gather together, the Princess Theatre is sold out for months in advance. You can get a seat for *Oh Lady, Lady* somewhere around the middle of August for just about the price of one on the Stock Exchange. Only moving-picture artists and food-profiteers will be able to attend for the first six months. After that, owners of munition-plants may be able to get a couple of standing-rooms.

If you ask me, I will look you fearlessly in the eye and tell you in low, throbbing tones that it has it over any other musical comedy in town. I was completely sold on it. But then Bolton and Wodehouse and Kern are my favourite indoor sport, anyway. I like the way they go about musical comedy. I like the way the action slides casually into the songs. I like the deft rhyming of the song that is always sung in the last act by two comedians and a comedienne. And Oh, how I do like Jerome Kern's music! And all these things are even more so in *Oh, Lady, Lady* than they were in *Oh, Boy!*

All of which was as rare as refreshing fruit to two battered wrecks who had just groped their way out of the ruins of *The Riviera Girl*, *The Rose of China*, and *The Second Century Show*. Life began to animate the rigid limbs again, and Cain's Storehouse became once more merely a number in the telephone-book.

Oh, Lady had a very long run at the Princess, and was actually played simultaneously at the Casino by a second company. It also had the distinction of being put on at Sing-Sing with an all-convict cast.

One of the most popular numbers in it was the duet between Spike Hudkins, the ex-burglar, and Fainting Fanny, the shop-lifter, which ran as follows:

SPIKE

Since first I was a burglar, I have saved in every way
Against the time when some nice girl should name the happy day.
When I retired from active work and ceased at nights to roam,
I meant to have enough nice things to furnish up the home.

> And I achieved, as you will find,
> The object that I had in mind.

> Our home will be so bright and cheery
> That you will bless your burglar boy:

I got some nifty silver, dearie,
When I cracked that crib in Troy:
And I got stuff enough in Yonkers
To fill a fairly good-sized chest,
And at a house in Mineola
I got away with their victrola,
So we'll have music in the evenings
When we are in our little nest.

FANNY

I've made a nice collection, too, to add, my love, to yours
Since I began professionally visiting the stores.
I've been a prudent little girl, and I have saved, like you:
I never started squandering as girls are apt to do:
          Each time I stole a brush and comb,
          I said 'There's something for the home'.

          Our home will be so bright and cheery
          With all the stuff I swiped from Stern's
          And all the knick-knacks from McCreery
          And from Bloomingdale's and Hearn's.
          And I've got stacks from Saks and Macy's
          Of all the things that you'll like best,
          And when at night we're roasting peanuts
          Upon the stove I pinched from Greenhut's,
          Although it's humble, you won't grumble,
          You'll love our cosy little nest.

This number was, as they say, 'well received' up Ossining way, where it must have brought nostalgic memories to many a first nighter. Playwrights who nowadays console themselves for a flop on Broadway with the thought that, 'They liked us in New Haven,' know nothing of the thrill of being able to say, 'They liked us in Sing-Sing.'

One odd thing in connection with the piece was that the song 'My Bill', subsequently so popular when sung by Helen Morgan in *Show Boat*, was written for *Oh, Lady, Lady* tried on the road and cut out before the New York opening.

EIGHT

Experience brings wisdom. The two alumni of Cain's Storehouse had learned their lesson. The vital thing for brainworkers, they saw now, is to husband their energies and never attempt to do too much. That way disaster lies.

'We must have been crazy,' said Guy as they walked down Fifth Avenue one morning about a week after *Oh, Lady* had opened. 'We just said, Yes, yes, yes, to everything anybody offered us, forgetting that if the machine is not to break down it must have constant intervals for rest and repose. The reservoir needs to fill itself. But never again. At least six months must elapse before we consider writing another show. It will be embarrassing, of course. Managers will come pleading with us to accept contracts, but we shall be firm . . . resolute . . . and – what's the word?'

'Adamant?'

'Yes, adamant. We shall say, "Sorry, boys, but nothing doing. We are husbanding our energies and filling the reservoir. We hate to disappoint you, dear old chaps, but in a word – " '

'No!'

'No!'

It was at this point that Colonel Henry W. Savage suddenly appeared on the steps of a brownstone church which they were approaching.

'Just the boys I was looking for,' he said, beaming. 'Would you like to write a show for me starring W. C. Fields?'

'Yes!' said Plum.

'You betcher!' said Guy.

'Then what I would suggest is that you come for a few days'

run in my boat, the *Dorinda*. A yacht is a perfect place for conferences.'

'A yachting trip? We'd love it.'

'Good. The *Dorinda* has been lucky for me as a workshop. It was aboard her that poor Browne and I laid out *Everywoman*.'

The reference to 'poor' Browne coupled with the ominous phrase 'laid out' cast a momentary chill, but the Colonel's pleasure at the prospect of having them as guests on his luxury yacht was so evident that the unfortunate allusion was soon forgotten. The following Friday – Friday the thirteenth, they realized later – was fixed for the start of the cruise.

'And now I must be getting back to my trustees' meeting,' said the Colonel. 'The church has had a handsome offer for its property, but they want me to see if I can't get a bit more. They seem to think I'm a pretty good bargainer.'

There was silence for some moments as the two authors continued on their way down the avenue.

'Yes, I know,' said Guy, speaking a little defensively. 'But one can't husband energies and fill reservoirs when one's offered W. C. Fields. And, anyway, you said "Yes" first.'

'And I'd say it again,' said Plum. 'W. C. Fields! The greatest comedian there is. And W. C. Fields plus a yachting cruise. . . .'

'Have you ever been on a yachting cruise?'

'No, but I know what it's like. I've seen it in the movies. Deep cushioned chairs on the after-deck, stewards in white coats handing round cocktails and canapés. . . . You realize what has happened, of course? Remorse has been gnawing old Hank because he did us down over that Billy Van thing. Quite possibly he heard an organ playing a hymn his mother used to play on the harmonium in his childhood, and it softened him. "I must atone," he said to himself, "I must atone," so regardless of expense he gives us this yachting trip. It does him credit, I say.'

'Great credit,' agreed Guy.

Friday was a spring-like day and the yachts at the Columbia anchorage made an attractive picture. They found the Colonel in the club house attired in an ancient serge suit and a yachting cap which the passage of time had changed from blue to green.

He greeted them warmly, but seemed surprised by the spruce-
ness of their appearance.

'You lads look rather dressed up,' he said, 'but I think I've
some dungarees aboard that will fit you.'

'Dungarees?'

'You'll need dungarees,' said the Colonel, and he never spoke
a truer word.

The *Dorinda* was a large boat – seventy-three feet six on the
waterline, eighteen feet two beam, four master-cabins and two
baths – but its crew consisted merely of an engineer called
Peasemarch, a name Plum registered for future use, a cook
called Palmer, quickly christened Palmer the Poisoner by the
guests, and a captain, Henry W. Savage. The thing that struck
Guy and Plum immediately was that what it needed was a
couple of deck-hands to do the dirty work, and this, events
were to prove, it got.

'I thought of asking Jerry along,' said the Colonel as he
showed them to their cabins, 'but he's such a little chap.'

This puzzled the two pleasure-seekers. Why Jerry's delicate
physique should rule him out as a reveller aboard the *Dorinda*
they were unable to understand.

'We thought we might have Bill Fields with us,' said Guy.

'Bill Fields?' The Colonel spoke the name a little blankly, as
if it were new to him. 'Ah, yes,' he said. 'Bill Fields. No, no, too
fat and lazy.'

The guests had rather expected that the course would lie
north to Spuyten Duyvil and through that waterway to the
Harlem and Long Island Sound. The northern shore of the
Island with its charming harbours and the great houses of
Morgan, Mackey, Otto Kahn and Mrs Belmont would make
an ideal cruising ground, and then they could slip through the
Shinnecock Canal to the romantic south shore lagoons or
perhaps cross the Sound to Newport and Narragansett, then
in the Indian Summer of their glory.

But the Colonel had other plans. Erect at the wheel, he
steered down the bay passed Guttenberg and Weehawken and,
hugging a shore lined with factories, foundries and coal yards,
through the oily waters of Bayonne to the narrow inlet that
separates Staten Island from the mainland.

'Afraid lunch will be a bit late,' he said. 'I want to hit the Raritan canal on the incoming tide. Tide's quite a help until you get to the locks.'

Locks! That magic word. Visions of Boulter's Lock on Jerome K. Jerome's Thames with its punts and skiffs, its girls with parasols and its young men in club blazers rose before the eyes.

When the locks on the Raritan and Delaware rose before the eyes, they proved to be somewhat different. The traffic consisted mostly of barges laden with gravel or coal. One that was preceding the *Dorinda* had a cargo of fish destined, the Colonel explained, for a glue factory on the Delaware River. Only the riper and more elderly fish are used for manufacturing glue, and those aboard the *Shirley B* were well stricken in years and almost excessively ripe.

As they approached the first lock they brought the matter up.

'Think we might slip past *Shirley*?' asked Plum.

'The barge ahead?'

'That's the one. It reminds me of Cleopatra's. "Purple the sails and so perfumed that the winds were love-sick with them".'

'We find *Shirley* a little on the niffy side,' said Guy.

The Colonel was unsympathetic.

'Come, come, you lads are a bit finicky, aren't you? You aren't here to sniff dead fish. You've work to do. There's a lot of handling needed in the locks.'

There was. Quite a lot. There were three boats swung outboard on davits, a launch, a dory for fishing and a dinghy, and these had to be swung inboard before the *Dorinda* was able to enter the lock.

'First get the boats stowed and then when we're in the lock go ashore and secure the hawsers. You'll have to remove a few sections of the rail first,' said the Colonel, and his guests at last realized what all that stuff about dungarees and Jerry Kern's lack of robustness had meant. The scales fell from their eyes. For all practical purposes, they saw, they might have been aboard the Savage grandfather's slave-ship.

'Morning, Cap'n,' said the Colonel genially to the mate of the *Shirley B*. 'Carrying fish, eh?'

'Ah.'

'I've got two dudes aboard who don't like the way you smell.'

'Sissies,' said the old salt briefly.

After an eternity of removing sections of rail, stowing boats and securing hawsers and trying not to inhale, they were past and the *Dorinda* drew away down the long straight waterway. Guy cautiously lowered the handkerchief from his nose.

'Good-bye, *Shirley*! Thank heaven we've seen the last of the lady.'

'Lock ahoy!' called the Colonel.

The work began again. The boats were hauled inboard, the lock gates opened, the amateur deck-hands seized the hawsers as Peasemarch threw them and made the *Dorinda* fast. They stood waiting expectantly for the lock gates to close and the water to be poured in. Nothing happened.

'What's the matter, Colonel?'

'Lock master's waiting for the barge. He doesn't like to work the lock for one vessel.'

Presently the *Shirley B* bore slowly down on them, preceded by its noisome effluvium. There are – or were – eleven locks on the New Jersey canal system, and in every one of them *Shirley* snuggled in cosily beside the *Dorinda*.

'Got any fresh fish, Cap'n?' inquired the Colonel on their third encounter.

'My God, he wouldn't!' muttered Plum, aghast.

They were spared. The barge captain shook his head.

'Never eat it.'

'You should. Healthiest food in the world.'

'I guess maybe I'll try a piece sometime,' said the barge captain.

They tied up for the night at the side of the canal. When they sat down to dinner they noticed that the table was laid for four. The extra place, it appeared, was for Palmer.

'I always have him in for dinner,' said the Colonel.

'Like Cesare Borgia,' said Plum. 'He used to have the cook dine with him and always made him eat a bit of each course before he sailed into it himself. So if it was poisoned, all that happened was that he was a cook short.'

'Ha, ha!' laughed the Colonel merrily. Then, as Palmer

entered bearing a dish of boiled potatoes and another of turnips, the smile faded from his lips. 'What, *two* vegetables?' he said frowning like someone austere contemplating one of those orgies that preceded the fall of Babylon. 'Oh, well,' he said resignedly. 'I suppose this *is* something of an occasion.'

Palmer was a weedy young man with a pale intellectual face and large horn-rimmed spectacles. He deposited the turnips and potatoes and went back for the *plat de jour*, a dish of brined herring. When this had been distributed, the two authors got down to business.

'We've roughed out a tentative idea for the Bill Fields play,' said Guy.

'Oh?' said the Colonel.

'Let's hear it,' said Palmer, closing his eyes and putting the tips of his fingers together.

'Well, Bill's a man who's lost his memory through over-working – '

'What at?' said Palmer.

'It doesn't matter what at. The point is, he's lost his memory. He ties bits of string round his fingers to remind him to do things, and then can't remember what they're to remind him to do.

'So his wife takes him to a psychiatrist.'

'I don't like it,' said Palmer.

'Nor did the man, because the psychiatrist fell in love with his wife and she with him. They start an affair.'

'I don't like it,' said Palmer.

'Well, of course, this makes the man unhappy, though for the life of him he can't remember what he's unhappy about. He ties a bit of string round his finger to remind him, but next day it holds no message for him. However, he knows he's unhappy, so he decides to end it all. He tells his wife he proposes to commit suicide. He goes into the kitchen, and she hears him dragging out a table. She hears him climb on to the table, and then there is a long silence. She is just wondering what is going on, when the man suddenly appears with the rope around his neck. He points at it and says, "Now what on earth was that to remind me to do?"'

Palmer shook his head.

'I don't like it,' he said. 'It seems to me to contain nothing that would make an appeal to the more advanced appreciators.'

'What do you mean, the more advanced appreciators?'

'The *avant garde*,' said Palmer. 'In writing a play the scale of values should be at once objective and rational, hence absolute and authentic. One aims to achieve in these days of mere impressionism a newness – if I may use the term – which is continually intended and essentially correct. One's explorations should be eruptive, vital and intense. How do you like the herring, Colonel?'

The Colonel said the herring was fine, which was a black lie. Palmer seemed gratified.

'It has nuances,' he agreed.

Guy tried again.

'Well, if that idea doesn't attract you, we have another.'

'Eruptive, I hope?' said Palmer.

'In this one Bill Fields is a pawnbroker, the last of a long line. His family have been pawnbrokers for centuries, and one of them was the fellow who loaned the money on Queen Isabella's pearls when she pawned them to finance Columbus. She signed a document to say that the pawnbroker was to get 10 per cent on whatever Columbus discovered. Well, he discovered America, and this old Spanish grant turns up, so there is Bill Fields in the position of having an iron-clad claim to 10 per cent of America. Then some crooks get hold of him – '

'Crooks!' said Palmer. 'Why must there always be crooks in these things? Thematic archaism. And just as I was beginning to think that you were groping for something esoteric and foreign to the debauched conception the public of today has of the theatre. I've made a steamed pudding,' he said, rising. 'I'll go and get it.'

He disappeared in the direction of the galley.

'That's an odd cook you've got, Colonel,' said Guy.

'Yes, not any great shakes at his job, I'm afraid, but what are you to do nowadays? You have to take what you can get. And it doesn't really matter to me. I was shipwrecked once and lived for three weeks on dog biscuits. Ever since then I find everything wonderful.'

Palmer returned with the pudding, a large glutinous lump

that tasted not unlike a pair of old boiled slippers. The authors declined it and shortly afterwards went out on deck. The air was still vibrant with the scent of dead fish.

The next morning they were roused at daybreak. The moorings had to be dealt with and after that there were more locks ahead. They came out on deck to find rain falling in a manner which Palmer would no doubt have described as eruptive, vital and intense. They negotiated the last of the locks and the *Dorinda* sailed on down the Delaware, slipping into the Chesapeake and Delaware Canal and thence through the Elk River into Chesapeake Bay. As Guy and Plum sat huddled under a tattered and inadequate awning, Palmer popped out of the galley and bore down on them.

'Good morning,' he said. 'Lovely weather. Have you ever studied the dominant impulse of the unconscious as exemplified in the plays of Pirandello?'

The two stared at him.

'You seem to know a great deal about plays,' said Guy.

'Well, naturally. I'm a playwright.'

'I thought you were a cook – well, when I say a cook. . . .'

'Oh, no, I'm a playwright really. The Colonel's got a play of mine which he's going to do as soon as he finds the right star. It's called *Ophelia* – Hamlet from the woman's angle. Meanwhile, he's given me this job. He doesn't pay me anything, of course. But I must be getting back to my galley. I'm doing you a bouillabaisse for lunch. An experiment, but I think it will have significant form.'

'Hold on a moment,' said Guy. 'How long has the Colonel had this *Ophelia* of yours?'

Palmer considered. 'Let's see. This is my fifth trip to Florida on the *Dorinda*. . . .'

'Florida? You mean we're on our way to Florida?'

'Of course. Didn't the Colonel tell you?'

'He didn't say a word about it. He just suggested a cruise.'

'We haven't brought any clothes for Florida,' said Plum.

'Oh, *you're* not going to Florida,' said Palmer, reassuring him. 'He'll put you ashore somewhere round here. That's what he has always done before.'

'What do you mean, "before"?'

'With the other authors he's brought along to work the *Dorinda* through the locks. As we've passed the last of the locks, I should imagine he will be landing you shortly. Excuse me, I must be looking after that bouillabaisse. If all goes well, it should be an entertaining little *morceau*. I think you will be amused by its *naïveté*.'

The two authors made their way to where the Colonel, clad in glistening oilskins, stood at the wheel.

'You didn't tell us you were going to Florida, Colonel,' said Guy.

'Didn't I?' said the Colonel mildly. 'Stupid of me.'

'If you had warned us before we started – '

'Of course, yes, I ought to have done. It slipped my mind. I'm sorry. I'll land you boys after lunch. You can get a train from Annapolis. It will give you a chance to look around the Naval Academy.'

'You realize,' said Guy, 'that we haven't discussed the play yet?'

The Colonel looked at him a little vaguely. Then his face lit up.

'The play? Ah, yes, the play. I'm sorry about that. I didn't want to cloud your enjoyment of the trip by telling you before. That's off. I'm not doing it. Fields wants too much money.'

It was as they sat in the draughty station at Annapolis, waiting for their train to arrive, that Guy observed that Plum was scribbling on the back of an envelope.

'What's that?' he asked. 'A lyric?'

'No, just an idea I've had for a mystery thriller. It's a little out of my usual line – but I think it will be good. A corpse has been discovered with its head bashed in by a blunt instrument, and the police lieutenant has come with his sergeant to the scene of the crime.

' "A foul and brutal murder," he says. "Cost what it may, we must spare no effort to bring the perpetrator of this hideous outrage to justice." (You know how these police lieutenants talk.) "Has the identity of the deceased been ascertained?"

' "It has," says the sergeant. "The stiff is a theatrical manager – Colonel Henry W. Savage."

' "Oh, well," says the lieutenant, "in that case, let's not bother."

'And they go off to lunch. It will run a bit short, I suppose, but it should have a wide appeal.'

'Very wide,' said Guy. 'You've got a winner.'

NINE

I

Another result of the substantial clicking of *Oh, Lady, Lady* was that Abraham Lincoln Erlanger, who during the bleak *Riviera Girl* days had shown a tendency to be as aloof to the authors of that musical gumboil as in his incarnation as Napoleon he would have been to a couple of Marshals who had lost an important battle, abandoned his resolve to have them shot at sunrise and invited them to do a piece for the New Amsterdam with Ivan Caryll, the composer of a long list of shows at George Edwardes's London Gaiety Theatre and of that historic success of 1911, *The Pink Lady*, the 'Beautiful Lady' waltz from which is still sung even now in many bath-tubs both in England and America, mostly off key.

Caryll – he was a Belgian, and his real name was Felix Tilken – was widely known as 'Fabulous Felix'. He had made a great deal of money in the theatre and, whatever else you might say about him, you could not say that he did not do himself well. He lived *en prince*, as much *en prince* as if his first name had been Flo and his second Ziegfeld, having apartments in both London and Paris, as well as a villa containing five bathrooms, overlooking the Deauville racecourse. A man, as he sometimes said, or if he didn't, he should have done, needs plenty of elbow room and, if he has five children, as 'Fabulous Felix' had, how can he possibly do with fewer than five baths, one for each child to sing 'Beautiful Lady' in?

When visiting New York, he did not actually charter a private liner, but he took most of Deck C on whichever was the best boat crossing, and on arrival settled down with his five children, his wife Maud and a cohort of nurses, tutors, governesses, valets and ladies' maids in a vast suite at the Hotel Knickerbocker. Then, instead of calling on the managers like the rest of the *canaille*, he would send word to them that he was, so to speak, in residence, ready to receive them and consider offers. And they came trotting round like rabbits.

It has never been decided whether or not 'Fabulous Felix' did it with mirrors, but he had a hypnotic effect on all the big musical comedy impresarios of Broadway. Harry Kelly's dog Lizzie could have picked up some useful hints on technique from the way these normally hard-boiled characters rolled over with their paws in the air in this man's presence. Some authorities claim that it was his beard that did the trick, and it may be that they were right. It was one of those long, black, square-cut, bushy numbers, as worn by Ozymandias, King of Kings, and other prominent Assyrians, concealing the whole face with the exception of the eyes and lending to its proprietor's appearance a suggestion of some dangerous creature of the wild peering out through a jungle. It is not surprising that sensitive managers, accustomed from childhood to composers who shaved daily and pink-cheeked authors smelling of bay rum, should have been as wax in his hands.

What happened on these occasions was that 'Felix' would say he had found a wonderful play in Paris which would make an ideal musical and, being an impulsive sort of fellow who had taken a sudden fancy to the manager whom he had selected to be the goat, was prepared to let him have this and to write the score for the customary composer's royalty of 3 per cent. No need for you to read the thing, my dear boy – it was, he assured his dear boy, superb, and he had the contracts here, all ready to sign.

'You couldn't give me some idea of what it's about?' the manager would say timidly.

'It's about a man who's in love with a girl.'

'I see. Yes, that sounds fine.'

'And there's another man. He's in love with a girl, too. It's tremendous. There's just one point. The French author's royalties. These French authors come high. I doubt if I could beat them down below 7 per cent.'

And just as the manager was about to say 'ouch!' or 'Zowie!'

or whatever managers say when they are asked to part with 7 per of the gross to a bunch of French authors, he would catch sight of that beard, quivering a little as though what was inside it was crouching for the spring, and his nerve would fail him. Quaking, he signed on the dotted line.

And what 'Felix' in the rush and bustle of the conversation had completely forgotten to mention was that, as he had bought the French authors out for a few thousand francs before leaving Paris and was sole owner of the property, the entire 7 per cent would be added to his personal take-home pay. No wonder he could afford to launch out a bit in the matter of bathrooms. He must have been astounded sometimes at his moderation in confining himself to five.

This time he had deviated from his normal routine. What he had sold to Erlanger was not a French play but a mere idea of his own which had occurred to him on the voyage over. It concerned the Parisian ladies who during the first world war had adopted army 'godsons' to whom they wrote letters and sent cigarettes and books and food. It seemed to 'Felix' that out of this pleasant custom there might grow a romance.

The thing presented possibilities. Guy and Plum felt that they could do something with it, making the lady a star of the Paris stage and the 'godson' a struggling playwright who had written a play and wanted to get acquainted with her in order to persuade her to act in it. With this end in view, he exchanges identity books with the star's actual 'godson', an army cook, and presents himself at her home in the country. Add a comic husband, whom the star has caught cheating and is determined to punish in kind: a rich uncle who, finding the star and the playwright in each other's arms, assumes the latter to be the husband; and bring the playwright's fiancée on the scene, she being a co-worker with the star in an army canteen; and you have something which, if not literature, is certainly a French farce. And it was a French farce on which 'Felix' insisted, for his *Pink Lady* had been founded on one and he believed in sticking to a formula.

So gradually *The Girl Behind the Gun* – it became *Kissing Time* when produced in London – took shape.

2

Rehearsals began in the middle of September and, one morning a week later, Plum, arriving at Guy's apartment, nearly collided with a strikingly handsome brunette in a very exotic costume who was coming out. She beamed upon him in friendly fashion.

'Are you Mr Wodehouse?'

Plum said he was.

'How do you do? I'm Marguerite Namara.'

'Of course, yes. I recognized you at once.'

Marguerite Namara was a well-known opera singer. She had appeared recently in a Schubert operetta, *Alone at Last*.

'I'm so glad to meet you,' she said. 'Guy has told me so much about you.' She looked at her wrist-watch. 'Oh, dear, is that really the time? I must rush. We shall be seeing one another again at dinner tonight.'

She hurried off, and Plum went in and found Guy settling down to work.

'Oh, there you are,' said Guy. 'Did you see Marguerite?'

'We met in the doorway. She says we're dining tonight.'

'Yes.'

'Will she be joining us in those Czechoslovak reach-me-downs?'

'That dress isn't Czechoslovak. It's Greek. She's wearing what is called a peplum.'

'Will she expect me to wear a peplum?'

'A peplum is a feminine garment. If you wore anything, it would be a *sakos* or possibly the *esorroko* or *palto*.'

'Does she always dress like that?'

'Generally.'

'Slightly cuckoo is she, by any chance?'

Guy stiffened.

'You are speaking of the woman I love.'

'I thought you loved them all.'

'Not as I love Marguerite. You're the one who has kept telling me I ought to find myself a wife. Well, now I've done it.'

'You aren't married?'

'We're going to be.'

'A thousand congratulations. This means that your lightest wish is law to her. Ask her not to wear that Greek costume tonight.'

'Why not?'

'I don't like it, as Palmer would say. It's too eruptive, vital and intense.'

'Very well. I think it's charming myself, but perhaps it is more suited for the privacy of the home.'

Marguerite, the soul of amiability, cheerfully consented to substitute for the Greek costume something simple and inconspicuous. When Guy called for her that night, she was wearing a bright scarlet dress trimmed with astrakan and a matching *shlyapa*, or, as we would say, hat. Around her neck was a collar decorated with silver bells similar in design to those seen in paintings of *troikas* pursued through the Siberian woods by wolves. Short red Russian boots completed the costume, each having a large bell hanging where one would have expected a tassel. The *tout ensemble*, though perfect for Old Home Week at Nijni-Novgorod, was not so good, Guy felt, for the Ritz-Carlton, where he had been intending to dine. Didn't she think, he said, that the Ritz-Carlton was a bit stodgy, and wouldn't a Bohemian place be more fun?

'Oh, yes, let's go to Mouquin's. We'll see all the people from the Met.'

Guy could think of no reasonable excuse for avoiding an encounter with the Metropolitan Opera personnel. At any rate it was better than braving the stares of the aristocratic feeders at the Ritz-Carlton's Oval Room. He telephoned Plum to meet them there with a flask and to order some 'set-ups' if he got there first.

He did get there first and was seated sipping something that had been sold to him as bourbon, when he was startled by what sounded like a *troika* with a bevy of wolves after it. The jingling appeared to be coming from his immediate rear, and turning, he found himself confronted by what might have been The Spirit of the Volga in one of the twelve refrains of a number for the girls in *The Second Century Show*.

His imitation, a very close one, of the late Sir Henry Irving in his most famous role ('Eah! daun't you hear . . . the sund of bell-ll-s?') was interrupted by the converging on the table of a *maître d'hôtel*, an assistant head-waiter, two ordinary waiters and a bus-boy, for Marguerite was an established and popular patron at Mouquin's. Wine was brought – in a teapot – and the soup had just been served when several new arrivals came through the swing doors that faced Sixth Avenue.

'*Scotti!*' screamed Marguerite in that carrying voice of hers which had so often given the back rows of the Paris Opéra Comique their money's worth. 'Scotti, my *angel!*'

Guy and Plum, the latter a little unsteady on his feet, for he was feeling as if he had just been hit by something solid between the eyes, rose as the great Scarpia of the Met came over, and stood politely while an animated conversation took place in Italian. Finally, after Scotti had delivered a long speech, accompanied by passionate gestures, they were at liberty to resume the soup at which they had been looking longingly for the last ten minutes.

'What was all that excitement?' asked Guy.

'No excitement,' said Marguerite. 'Antonio was just saying he doesn't like the steam-heat in New York. I love Antonio.'

'Charming chap,' agreed Plum, 'but he made it a little difficult to concentrate on soup. I often say that it is fatal to let soup – '

'*Pavel!*' shrieked Marguerite. 'Pavel, my *dear!*'

The new arrival was Pavel Solokolov of the Ballet Russe. He had known Marguerite in Moscow when she had appeared at the Malenskia Theatre with Isadora Duncan and her troupe of dancers. Guy and Plum once more rose politely, but contributed little to the conversation. It was in Russian, and their Russian was a bit rusty. They were inclined to be peevish as they resumed their soup, and Guy was just saying that the next one that came along he was going to fix three of these straws together and get his standing up, when Marguerite interrupted him.

'*Feodor!* Feodor, my *pet!*'

This time it was something spectacular, the great Chaliapin in person, looking, as he always did, like a benevolent all-in wrestler. Both Guy and Plum had often admired him, but never more so than now, for his first act was to thrust them back into their seats with a ham-like hand and insist jovially that they get on with the serious business of the evening.

'Zoop is zoop,' he said, speaking in English with an accent in which a spoon would have stood upright, and they felt he could not have phrased it more neatly.

'These are two playwrights that I am dining with,' said Marguerite, performing a belated introduction.

'We do musical comedies,' said Guy, pegging away at his soup.

'A low form of art, of course,' said Plum, pegging away at his.

Chaliapin would have none of this self-deprecation.

'*Not* a low form of art,' he insisted vehemently. 'When I am a student at the gymnasium, I too write a musical comedy. In it there is a scene which I will give to you, Mr Bolton, as a present. It is a bum scene and very phoney.'

It seemed to Plum that the great man was too modest.

'Oh, I'm sure it isn't,' he said politely.

Marguerite interpreted.

'Bomb scene. Very funny.'

'Yes, so phoney you will laugh off your heads,' said Chaliapin. 'You are to imagine that I am a cruel Governor and you two are revolutionists who have come to blow me up with a bum. But I catch you, and my men they tie you to a bench and I put the bum beneath the bench. It is a time-bum and it goes tick-tock, tick-tock. I laugh. It tickles me like a horsehair undervest. Because it is a fine torture for you to hear that tick-tock, tick-tock, tick-tock.'

'Like someone reading the minutes at a meeting,' said Guy brightly. 'What happens then?'

'I tell you. The bum is going tick-tock, tick-tock, when a noise outside distracts my attention, and I turn my back for a moment. You have one hand free, and you take the bum and slip it into the pocket of my *palto*, my big overcoat. There are more noises outside and I go out to ask, "What the hell?", and the bum she goes with me.'

He illustrated this bit of action by turning away and squeezing past a party of two elderly ladies and a deaf old gentleman who were taking their places at the next table.

'But wait,' bellowed Chaliapin from a distance of several

yards, his organ-tones ringing through the restaurant. 'You have not seen the last of me. I come back now to gloot over you.'

He began to creep back, his face wearing a hideous and menacing scowl. The two ladies at the next table stirred uneasily.

'Remember I have the bum in my pocket.' He patted his pocket. 'I am coming back to laugh, to gloot over you. The bum is ticking – any minute now she is going off – and I am glooting. Pigs! Children of pigs! In a little moment you will be sausage meat. You will be buttered all over the walls. It makes me laugh to think of it. Ha, ha, ha, ha.'

It was a good laugh, and it sent the two elderly ladies scurrying to the door, leaving their deaf escort to his fate. People were standing up, trying to see what the commotion was about. There was a sense of relief, mingled perhaps with a certain disappointment, when Chaliapin, reaching the table, sat down and helped himself to wine from the teapot, his face wreathed in smiles.

'Phoney?' he said.

'Very phoney,' agreed Guy faintly.

Chaliapin looked about him, inspecting the table closely. He seemed puzzled.

'Where is the other gentleman? There were two gentlemen, two musical-comedy writers, drinking zoop. Now there is one gentleman.'

'Mr Wodehouse had to leave hurriedly,' Guy explained. 'A sudden seizure. He gets them sometimes. I understand he hears buzzing sounds – '

'Like a bum going tick-tock, tick-tock, tick-tock?'

'Exactly. Accompanied by an occasional cow-bell.'

As Guy was going to bed, the telephone rang.

'Sorry about running away like that,' said Plum.

'I don't blame you. Heaven deliver us from opera stars with comedy scenes.'

'How did it end?'

'The bum scene? I couldn't tell you.'

'You mean that ruddy basso left without giving you the finish?'

'He never mentioned it. He went on to speak of other things. Why, are you interested?'

'Interested! I shall dream about it for weeks. You and me tied to a bench and Chaliapin coming back and forth, glooting over us, and the bum going tick-tock, tick-tock.'

'I'll get Marguerite to call him up and ask him to tell us who blew up whom in the end. Oh, by the way. Marguerite. Charming, don't you think?'

'Very charming. And I'll tell you something else I think – something you probably know already. I think you're going to have a wonderfully exciting married life.

3

The Girl Behind the Gun opened in New York in November, settling down at once to a long run, and the authors were able to concentrate on the next show for the Princess, on which they had been working for some time in their intervals of leisure.

It seemed to both Guy and Plum that these Princess shows were running too much to type and that the formula was becoming evident. They begged Ray to strike out in a new direction with *The Little Thing*, but he insisted that the pattern be followed just once more. Even if this one were not so success-ful as its predecessors, there was, he argued, plenty of slack to take up.

This one – they called it *Oh, My Dear* – was certainly not another *Oh, Boy!* or *Oh, Lady*, but it did quite well when, a few weeks after *The Girl Behind the Gun* had opened at the New Amsterdam, it made its bow on 39th Street. It was a lively musical farce, the scene of which was a sanatorium in the country, where a young man who thought he had inadvertently committed a murder found it convenient to hide out. It was the first comedy to bring the psychiatrist to the stage and also the only Princess show to have a non-Kern score. Jerry was busy elsewhere, and Lou Hirsch, composer of 'The Love Nest', a song still heard after all these years, wrote the music but without – unfortunately – contributing another 'Love Nest'. It was one of those pieces which are quite all right – business excellent – nothing to complain of – but not sensational. It was the 'Ruddigore' of the series.

4

A couple of weeks after the *Oh, My Dear* opening the two authors met for lunch.

'I suppose you're spending your Christmas with Marguerite?' said Plum.

'No,' said Guy. 'On Christmas Day Marguerite will be appearing in the Bull Ring in Mexico City with Titta Ruffo.'

'Become a lady bullfighter, has she?'

'She's singing *Carmen*, ass.'

'I trust she won't wear that red dress.'

'There are no bulls in the Bull Ring while they are singing.'

'A pity. It would make the thing so much more exciting. So she's in Mexico City, eh? Your fiancée does get about, doesn't she? How's the romance going?'

'It's in a state of suspended animation.'

His partner asked him to elucidate. Had there been a lover's quarrel? No, nothing like that, only Marguerite had doubts as to whether their divergent tastes, their disparate careers could be welded into a workable marriage.

'It'll probably end in her going her way and you going hers.'

'It'll probably end where it is right now,' replied Guy pessimistically.

Plum looked at him.

'The thing you need is a holiday,' he said. 'You pack your traps and come off to Palm Beach with Ethel and me.'

'Don't you have to be a Rockefeller or something?'

'Not at all. Theatrical managers and other lower type Fauna Americana are migrating there in flocks.'

'You call consorting with managers a holiday?'

'There is other companionship. It is a spot favoured by members of the *Follies* ensemble to rest up after the ardours of a New York run.'

'I don't want *Follies* girls either.'

'That remark alone proves you are far from being yourself.'

At the moment they were comparatively idle. Plum had just published *A Damsel in Distress* and in his spare moments was at work on *The Indiscretions of Archie*. Guy was collaborating on two comedies, *The Five Million* with Frank Mandel and *Adam and Eva* with George Middleton. Still these things were not being written to order. There was no deadline to meet. Though Guy was still inclined to demur, Plum remained firm. They bought straw hats and pongee slacks. They bought bathing-suits. They bought tickets to Palm Beach.

TEN

I

Anyone in those days arriving for the first time in America's number one winter playground would have had to be very blasé not to experience a thrill. There was magic in the place. Nowadays the visitor is deposited at a shabby station in the least glamorous section of Palm Beach's frowsy namesake on the wrong side of the tracks, but when Guy and Plum opened their eyes at eight o'clock that December morning they found their train crossing a blue lagoon fringed with royal palms and a little later were deposited in a shining, white-painted terminus festooned with scarlet bougainvillaea. Coloured bell-boys and porters, all in spotless uniforms, stood lined up, awaiting them. On the pathway that ran along the shore of Lake Worth the hansom cab of Palm Beach, the open basket-chair with the driver mounted behind, sped by, carrying a couple attired in, of all things, evening dress.

'Must have been some party,' commented Guy.

'Probably spent the night at Bradley's,' said a fellow-traveller who was sorting out his luggage beside him. He pointed to a large frame building on the opposite side of the palm-lined avenue, and they looked with interest at the most famous gambling casino in America. One of the unobtrusive corps of guards, armed with a sawn-off shotgun, was strolling round between the big flowering bushes that dotted the lawn.

Back in New York it had been snowing, but here the sun shone brightly. Little puffy white clouds like dabs of whipped cream moved lazily across a sky of the deepest blue. The two mounted the steps that led from the station through a covered way into the longest hotel in the world, the 1400 feet Royal

Poinciana, with one employee for each foot. Shops lined the way, New York's top couturiers, Charvet of Paris, Beale and Inman of London, bag shops, flower shops, jewellery shops. Plum waved a hand at one of the last named.

'Remind me to tell you a story about Arch Selwyn.'

'Who's Arch Selwyn?' asked Ethel.

'New York manager.'

'Then don't tell me about him,' said Ethel. 'I'm trying to forget that there is such a place as New York. Why can't we stay for ever in this Paradise?'

Their rooms overlooked the golf-course. To one side were a couple of spurs running from the railway. On these, packed closely together, stood the private cars which had brought the wealthy down from Manhattan. One of them, which had been attached to the back of their train, was being shunted into place. The owner strolled out on to the spacious lounging platform. There seemed something familiar about his appearance.

'Good Lord! It's Flo!'

'Gosh, so it is. What does it cost to travel in one of those?'

'I can tell you,' said Plum. 'I asked. Not because I was toying with the idea of booking one for the homeward journey. I wanted to use it in a story. The tariff is ninety fares.'

'You mean ninety times what we paid?'

'That's right. Flo must be feeling rich.'

'Flo Ziegfeld always feels rich. The trouble is, it's just a feeling. The most extravagant man of our time. The arch-squanderer. . . . That reminds me. What was that about Arch Selwyn?'

'Oh, that? It was something Ray told me. It seems that last year Arch made his first trip to Palm Beach, and the night of his arrival found him at Bradley's plunging with the best of them. Birdie tried her best to stop him – '

' "Birdie"?' queried Ethel.

'His wife – but when she saw him scooping in the counters – '

'Oh, he won?'

'A packet. Couldn't go wrong. He was so loaded with the stuff when he left that he had to lean on her all the way home. She said "My hero!" or words to that effect, and next day steered him into one of those shops downstairs. He bought her a gorgeous diamond clip costing about $2000.'

'Nice man.'

'Oh, yes, Arch is fine.'

'Well, the next night he went back to Bradley's, and you can guess what happened. First he lost the price of the clip and after that the price of his shirt and mesh-knit underwear. The next night it was the same, and the next and the next, and all the time Birdie was chirruping around showing her clip and saying what a thing it was to have a generous husband. And when Arch dropped hints about marriage being a partnership in which the loyal little comrade should share the downs as well as the ups, she didn't seem to get it.

'Finally Arch pleaded with her to put the clip away somewhere. He said he couldn't bear to look at it.

'Then one evening it disappeared. It wasn't insured, and Birdie kept the loss to herself. It was only when they were back in New York that Arch happened to ask her why she never wore that diamond clip he had bought her in Palm Beach. She explained what had happened.

'When Arch at last gathered that the clip had been stolen, he nearly had a fit. "Why in heaven's name didn't you notify the hotel detective, the police?"

' "How could I? It would have got into the papers. It would have looked terrible – ARCH SELWYN STEALS WIFE'S JEWELS."

'Arch tottered. "You thought *that* of me? You really supposed that I would stoop – My God!"

'Arch was properly indignant, but he admitted to Ray privately that the thing that made him really so sore was to think of all those weary hours he had spent hunting everywhere for the clip after Birdie was asleep, and all the while some dirty crook had beaten him to it.'

2

They swam and lay in the sun. They played a round of golf on that odd little course where the hazards were palm trees and the greens – in those days – were of sand.

That night they went to Bradley's and Sam Harris, of Cohan

and Harris, who came in with Charlie Dillingham, took them into the office and introduced them to the Colonel and his brother.

'Two writin' fellers, Colonel,' said Charlie. 'They want membership cards.'

'Can they afford to lose?'

'Up to a point, and I guess you know what that is.'

The Colonel told his brother to make out the cards.

'I don't like to win money from people who can't afford it,' he said. 'I think that's pretty well known . . . too well known, perhaps. At any rate, I got caught nicely the other day. Man came in and started to play big. In less than an hour he'd dropped $17,000. I went myself and watched him at the end. Seemed to me he looked kind of upset, and it worried me. Then the next day his wife came in and asked to see me. She was terribly wrought up. Said her husband must have been crazy. What he'd lost, she said, was the money they had been saving up for years to buy a home in Florida. A real tear-jerker it was. Well, I did what I've done quite a few times when this sort of thing has happened: I gave her back half the money and told her to tell her old man that if he ever tried to come sneaking into my place again, I'd make it my business to kick him out personally. That woman was certainly grateful. Tears coursed down her cheeks. She grabbed my hand and kissed it. She said she wished there were more men like me in the world.'

'I'll bet she did,' said Sam Harris. 'I've known a lot of gamblers in my time, from Dick Canfield down, but you're the only one that would hand back $8500 just because a dame cried at you.'

'You haven't heard the pay-off,' said the Colonel, and his brother, sitting at the desk, started to laugh. 'Spite of my warning, darned if the husband didn't come in again that very same night, and sat down calm as a codfish on ice, and began to high-roll all over the board. I was hopping mad. I sent one of my table-men to fetch him to the office, and when he came in I started to lay him out. "Didn't your wife tell you I said you weren't to come here?" I yelled at him. He looked sort of surprised. "My wife, Colonel?" he said. "I haven't got a wife!" I said, "You mean you haven't got a wife who came in here this morning and told me you'd lost the money you had been saving for years to buy a home?'' "Certainly not," said the fellow. "Why would I buy a home?" he said. "I'm lousy with homes. Homes are what I've got nothing else but. I own the biggest hotel chain on the West Coast." '

'Women aren't gentlemen,' said Charlie Dillingham.

'But Ed hasn't told you the real snapper,' said the Colonel's brother. 'The fellow he'd been so big-hearted about had a run of fool's luck that night. He nicked us for close on $80,000.'

They went into the gambling rooms, which were filled with men in dress-clothes and women laden down with jewels. Europe had not yet regained its pre-war popularity, and everyone was coming to Palm Beach. The recently established tax on income, crushing though it was – 4 per cent, if we remember rightly – had not removed any of the gilt from the gilded set. The two writers, who had but recently acquired the feeling of solvency, shrank back into the ranks of the under-privileged as they saw the walnut-sized diamonds and the piles of green $20 chips strewn across the roulette tables.

There were a few faces that they recognized . . . Otto Kahn with his neat white moustache . . . General Pershing accompanied by his friend Coleman Dupont . . . Willie K. Vanderbilt, Junior . . . Mrs O. H. P. Belmont . . . the impish-faced Margaret Lawrence with her husband, Orson Munn. Most of these they knew from having seen their photographs in papers and magazines, but there was a leavening of characters from their own bailiwick . . . Arch Selwyn, Condé Nast, Addison Mizner.

'Take a look round,' said Plum, 'and tell me – who, if you didn't know who any of them were, would you say was head man, most assured, most at home?'

Guy could answer that without a moment's hesitation.

'Ziegfeld.'

'That's right. He's got an air. You feel that $100 bills mean no more to him than paper matches to a cigar store.'

'And half the time he hasn't enough to buy a knitted waistcoat for a smallish gnat.'

Ziegfeld was standing by a table with a handful of the costly green chips, dropping them carelessly on the numbers and turning to talk to the woman next him without watching the wheel. He won, but went on talking, leaving the chips where they lay. He won again. It was quite a win, but only when his companion squealed excitedly and pointed to the piled-up counters did he motion languidly to the croupier to push them toward him.

'The lady seems more thrilled at his win than he is,' said Guy.

'So I notice. "Blasé" about sums it up.'

'Know who she is? I just heard someone say. Mrs Edward B. McLean of Washington.'

'Do you mean to say that that blue thing she's wearing round her neck is the Hope diamond?'

'That's it. The stone Tavernier stole from the idol Rama-Sita. Fifteen violent deaths laid to its account.'

'Is that really the score?'

'So far. You wouldn't catch me playing roulette with that thing alongside me.'

But the Hope diamond seemed to have lost its malignant power tonight. Ziegfeld continued to win. Then, apparently bored, he pushed his counters over to the table-man and received a slip of paper in exchange. Two famous beauties from the *Follies* came up to him, Helen Lee Worthing and Olive Thomas. He fished some loose chips from his pocket and handed them to the girls. He caught sight of Guy and Plum and came over to them. He asked them how long they had been in Palm Beach. They told him they had arrived that morning by the same train as himself.

'Why didn't you come in my car?' he said. 'It's a lot more comfortable than those stuffy drawing-rooms.'

They did not mention that they had travelled down in humble 'lowers'.

'You didn't bring Jerry with you?'

'No.'

'He's coming. I reserved a room for him at the Breakers. He and I have been talking about a show for Marilyn Miller.'

This was news. Presumably Jerry had not mentioned this because there was another librettist involved.

'You ought to have a huge success with her,' said Guy. 'She's got the same sort of quality Maud Adams had. A wistful charm that goes right to the heart.'

'Have you settled on a story?' asked Plum.

'Practically settled. It's a musical version of *Be Calm, Camilla*, that Clare Kummer comedy. Clare will do the book and lyrics.'

'Isn't that the play in which the heroine breaks her ankle in the first act?' inquired Plum innocently.

'That's it.'

'I shouldn't have thought it would be an ideal vehicle for a dancer.'

Ziegfeld stared at him for a moment, then he laughed.

'Jerry and I ought to have our heads examined.'

'However, that's the only objection.' Plum's smile was benevolent. 'It's a very charming play otherwise.'

Ziegfeld eyed them thoughtfully.

'Have you fellows got a story?'

'Guy has. Scheherazade had nothing on that boy. He's full of stories.'

'We must get together when Jerry arrives and have a talk,' said Ziegfeld. He turned away, but came back as if struck by an afterthought. 'You boys like yachting?'

With the hint of an *arrière pensée* the boys said they did.

'I've chartered the *Wench*, Len Replogle's boat. We might take a cruise through the Indian River and possibly run up the Loxahackie in one of the launches. You'll see alligators and orchids growing wild.'

'That should be quite a saving for you, gathering a few wild orchids,' said Plum. Ziegfeld was famous as an orchid-giver.

'Are there any locks?' asked Guy.

'Locks? No. Why?'

'I was just thinking of something. How many do you carry as crew?'

'Fourteen, including the Captain.'

Guy drew a deep breath.

'We'd love to come, wouldn't we, Plum?' he said.

An immediate conference seemed to be called for. Watching millionaires winning and losing fortunes had its thrills, but it was not so thrilling as the contemplation of a show for Ziegfeld with Marilyn Miller as star. They left Bradley's and climbed into one of the chairs lined up at the entrance. They told the coloured owner to take them where he pleased. A full moon was shining. The air was soft and balmy. Though wearing dinner-jackets without overcoats they had no sense of chill even when they turned down the broad cedar-lined way that led to the ocean.

No motor vehicles were allowed on the island in those days. Bicycles and the bicycle-chairs were the only means of transit on pathways that wound through the semi-tropical clusters of palm, cedar and banyan.

They agreed that a show for Ziegfeld would be the biggest thing that had happened to them. Quite aside from New York, his name on the road was dynamite. The *Ziegfeld Follies* were the top drawing-card of America. And a show for Ziegfeld *with* Marilyn Miller . . . You couldn't beat that for a combination.

Inevitably Guy suggested *The Little Thing*. Plum was dubious. It seemed to him that the setting and costumes would strike Flo as giving insufficient opportunity for glamour.

The first scene of *The Little Thing* was the backyard of an actors' boarding-house, the heroine a little drudge who loathed washing dishes and longed to be a ballet dancer like the great Esmeralda, one of the boarders. Esmeralda, now an old woman with nothing left of her days of glory but an imperious temper, was certainly not a Ziegfeld type, nor was Mr Tolly, the old actor who had loved Esmeralda when she was the toast of Broadway and who had surreptitiously fastened a gold star to the door of her hall-bedroom. 'Not much there for Flo,' said Plum.

'But can't you just see Marilyn in that scene with the writer who'd do the article on the old-timers?'

'Which scene do you mean?'

'He says, "What's your last name, Sally?" "Rhinelander." "Oh, a society lady?" "No, that was just the telephone district. I was found in a telephone booth wrapped in an old shawl. I go and put flowers in it every Mother's Day." '

'Yes, yes.' Guy, once started on the subject of *The Little Thing*, was not easy to stop. 'Yes, I remember.'

' "The last time I saw Mother," ' Guy went on, ' "one of her hinges was broken and she had a sign on her 'Out of Order'. It's kinda sad, don't you think?" '

'What I remember most clearly about *The Little Thing*,' said Plum, 'is the lyrics. You secured a very gifted man to write those, some name beginning with W.'

'You are thinking of "Joan of Arc"?'

'No. Good, but not W at his best. "Church Round the Corner" was more up to the W mark. "Church Round the Corner" – did I ever tell you Ethel and I were married there?'

'No. Were you?' Guy sighed enviously.

'We had $126 between us in the world, and we were standing there waiting for the parson to appear and beginning to wonder if he had stood us up, when he came bounding in with a six-inch grin across his face.

' "Hello, folks!" he yodelled. "I've just made $10,000 on the Stock Exchange." I was as sick as mud. $10,000! There ought to be a law.'

They lapsed into silence as their chair turtled along beside a sea spread out like a dark-blue counterpane lace-edged with white where it touched the shore. Presently Plum spoke.

'By and large, not a bad world,' he said.

3

Jerry Kern arrived, and after a talk with Ziegfeld said, 'Well, boys, it looks as if you'd done Clare Kummer out of a job.'

Guy disagreed.

'All we did was point out that a play where the heroine spends the entire evening on crutches with a plaster cast on her leg might not be just right for Marilyn Miller. But Clare Kummer is so clever that I'm sure she will be able to think up something that will give a dancer more scope.'

'Come off it. You two hi-jackers are after the thing for yourselves.'

'Naturally we would like the job. But only if Clare Kummer turns it down.'

'She has turned it down. She's at work on a play called *A Successful Calamity*. She might have managed an adaptation, but isn't equal to inventing a new story, starting from scratch.'

'Well, tell Flo we are in residence, ready to receive him and consider offers.'

'Eh?'

'I was thinking of "Fabulous Felix",' said Guy.

But Ziegfeld, having raised their hopes, did nothing to sustain them. They ran into him every day, but on the subject of shows for Marilyn Miller he preserved a proud silence. His conversation was of golf, of gossip, of gambling. He talked quite a lot, but he did not talk turkey. One morning, meeting them pottering round the Country Club course, he told them that the yachting trip was set to start next Sunday morning.

'Do you boys like terrapin?' he asked in that curious, melancholy way of his.

Jerry Kern said he was crazy about terrapin. Plum and Guy, neither of whom had ever tasted it, said they were, too. (As he later admitted, Jerry had never tasted it, either.)

'Well, don't eat too much breakfast,' said Flo. 'We'll have terrapin for lunch that beats any you've ever eaten. The ship's cook has a special way of preparing it.'

The *Wench* was something very different from the *Dorinda* of evil memory, a real dream-boat with a cocktail shaker for every port-hole. Confident this time of finding a steward in a white coat deferentially serving refreshment, the visitors found three stewards in three white coats, each more deferential than the last. Everything capable of glistening glistened. Everything fashioned to glow glowed. The deckchairs were lower, deeper and more luxuriously cushioned than those of any other vessel to be seen about the yacht-club pier. Each single item was the best money could buy, from the giant Havana Perfectos to the three long-limbed young ladies stretched at their ease under an awning of the famous Ziegfeld rose pink. Their costumes were to the last degree what Palmer would have called *avant garde*. In a day when girls were arrested if they appeared on a bathing beach without stockings, the three nymphs justified Will Rogers's famous crack, 'I never expected to see the day when girls would get sunburned in the places they do.'

The other men of the party were Messmore Kendall, a theatrical manager, Paul Block, the newspaper owner, and Walter Chrysler. Just before they were ready to sail, Arthur Somers Roche, the novelist, came aboard with his bride, Ethel Pettit, who had played the heroine of *Miss Springtime* in the

Chicago company and later, when Sari Petrass, the Hungarian prima donna, retired from the New York company, had taken her place. In this gathering of millionaires and *Follies* girls it was pleasant to meet one of the gang.

The *Wench* turned through the inlet and headed up the coast past the tall red column of Jupiter Light standing at the end of the island which had been the home of Joseph Jefferson. Messmore Kendall had known one of the Jefferson sons – four of them, all actors – and this younger Jefferson had told him that, when his father had moved there, Jupiter Island had had only one other inhabitant, a hermit who had not exchanged a word with another human being for thirty years. The story ran that he had had his tongue cut out by a tribe of Seminoles, he having told a lie about one of them. (Seminoles are touchy.) He was held up as an awful warning to the younger Jeffersons.

The legend lost considerably in impressiveness when it was discovered that not only could he talk, but that once started it was impossible to stop him. Conversation, the accumulation of thirty years of silence, poured from him in an unending stream. He attached himself to the Jeffersons, and nothing they could do would rid them of him. Finally they accepted the inevitable and he became old Joe's constant companion on his fishing, hunting and painting expeditions. One day Joe asked him if it was true that he had remained silent for thirty years.

'Yeppy, that's right.'

'Why?'

'Weren't nobody worth talking to.'

Old Joe said he considered that one of the highest compliments ever paid him.

Jerry sat down at the little yacht piano that had been moved out of the saloon for the occasion, and began to play.

'What's that?' asked Olive Thomas.

'It's a delicious melody,' said Ethel Pettit. 'Are there any words?'

'You bet there are words and I'd love to hear you sing them. The song was written for *Oh, Lady* but we took it out.'

Jerry asked Plum to scribble down the lyric for Ethel and, while he did so, he told them something more of the song's origin. The melody was one of several that Jerry had assembled to play Charles Frohman back in 1906 or thereabouts. He wanted to get in on the writing of those extra numbers which were interpolated into the scores of the Austrian composers. These at that time were always supplied by some member of the 'English school' – Lionel Monckton, Paul Rubens, Howard Talbot and the rest, Frohman having that odd passion of his for anything English.

Frohman refused to see Jerry, sending word that he bought all his material in England, and anybody but Jerry would have accepted the situation meekly and given up the struggle. But the fellow who said, 'You can't keep a good man down,' must have been thinking of Jerome D. Kern. He scraped together his few pennies and went to London. There he succeeded in selling a number called 'Won't You Come and Flirt with Me?' to George Edwardes, who put it into one of his productions. It had girls in swings that swung out over the audience displaying black-stockinged legs and frilly petticoats, and was the hit of the show.

On the second night, when Jerry was standing at the back of the circle glooting, as Chaliapin would have said, over his success, Charles Frohman came up. He told Jerry that he had been pointed out to him as the composer of the number. He was enthusiastic.

'When it comes to this sort of thing,' he said, 'you Englishmen are in a class by yourselves. We haven't anyone who can do it on the other side.'

He asked Jerry if he would consider coming to America. Jerry thought he might be able to fit in a trip – he had often wanted to see America – and they sailed back on the same ship. As the boat went up the bay, C. F. pointed out the various objects of interest to the bit of imported English talent at his side.

'The highest building of all is the Manhattan Life. The one with the gold dome is the World Building. This is the Hudson River, navigable by quite large vessels for 100 miles.'

'Coo!' said Jerry. 'Really? 100 miles? Lord-love-a-duck! Makes a chap think a bit, that sort of thing, what?'

At this point a lady, a poor sailor, who had remained in her state-room during the voyage, espied Jerry and came up to him.

'Why, Jerry Kern!' she cried, 'How did you like London?

Weren't you homesick? After all, there's no place like dear old Newark, is there?'

'What did Frohman say?' asked Paul Block.

'He behaved like the sport he always was,' said Jerry. 'He laughed and laughed, and finally I was sufficiently reassured to join in. We became great friends, and the next time C.F. went abroad, he asked me to come with him. There were a couple of new musicals in London and he wanted my opinion on them. Well, naturally I jumped at the invitation, and the night before we were to sail a bunch of my friends gave me a farewell party, at which I did a thing I don't often do. I got pie-eyed. I was just sober enough to ask whoever it was that brought me home to set the alarm-clock for seven, and when seven came there was a little croak from the clock, but it was enough to wake me up, and I staggered out of bed and started getting dressed. The boat was sailing at ten, and I wanted to have plenty of time.

'I made myself a cup of coffee and got my clothes on. It was a miserable day, and all the time it kept getting darker, until I thought there must be a terrible storm coming up. By the time I got into a taxi, the sky was almost black. I said to the driver, "What on earth's happening? Is there going to be a thunderstorm?" He said he didn't think so. "Then what's making the sky so dark?" I said. "Why wouldn't the sky be dark?" he said. "It's close on eight-thirty."

'And suddenly I got it. It was eight-thirty at *night*. I'd slept right through the day. The alarm-clock hadn't wakened me, and that croaking sound which I had finally managed to hear had been the little bit of alarm left for the next time the hour it's set at comes round.'

'So of course you had missed the boat?' said Chrysler.

'Yes. And do you know what boat it was? The *Lusitania*, sailing 2nd May 1915.'

<h1 style="text-align:center">4</h1>

Plum handed the lyric he had been writing out to Ethel Pettit, but before she had a chance to sing it one of the stewards announced luncheon. They all filed through the big lounge into the dining-saloon. The meal started with grapefruit au Kirsch, caviar having already been served with the cocktails. Then came the terrapin.

'Wait till you taste this,' said Ziegfeld.

But after the first mouthfuls and the appreciative 'Ohs' and 'Ahs' he shook his head.

'There's something wrong,' he said. 'This isn't it. It's not bad, but nothing like what I promised you.' He turned to the steward. 'Did Shimo cook this?'

He was told that Shimo had not cooked it, having been fired by the Captain for impertinence. Ziegfeld nodded moodily, but said nothing.

While they were still at lunch, the *Wench* put into Port Pierce. A steward went ashore with a sheaf of Ziegfeld telegrams. This was routine. Few hours of the day passed without Ziegfeld sending a telegram to someone.

It was on the return journey, when the sky had begun to glow with one of those magical Florida sunsets, that Ethel Pettit sang the song that had been dropped from the score of *Oh, Lady, Lady*:

> I used to dream that I would discover
>> The perfect lover
>>> Some day:
> I knew I'd recognize him if ever
>> He came round my way:
> He'd have hair of gold
>> And a noble head
> Like the heroes bold
>> In the books I'd read.
>
> Then along came Bill,
>> Who's not like that at all:
> You'd pass him on the street and never notice him.
>> His form and face,
>> His manly grace,
>> Are not the sort that you
>> Would find in a statue:
> I can't explain . . .
> It's surely not his brain
>> That makes me thrill:
> I love him because . . . oh, I don't know,
>> Because he's just my Bill.

'I've got to have that song,' said Ziegfeld. 'What do you boys want for it?'

'It's not for sale,' said Jerry. 'It's a valuable adjunct to a show.'

'I'll have Fanny Brice sing it and give it a big set-up – plenty of *schmalz*.'

'It's no good for a revue, Flo. It needs a situation back of it. It needs a guy named Bill and the girl who loves him.'

He turned to Plum. 'Am I right or am I right?'

'Of course you're right. I wrote it for Molly to sing about Bill in *Oh, Lady*. The whole point is that the audience has seen Bill and has been wondering what a girl like her can find to love in a chap like that. . . . And she tells them. It's no good except for a book show.'

'Well, I'm going to do a book show – plenty of them before I'm through,' said Flo. 'I'm starting next season with one for Marilyn Miller.'

'Okay, we'll put it aside till we see who you offer us to sing it.'

'Ruth Etting suit you?'

'Yes, Ruth Etting would suit us fine. So would Ethel Pettit.'

'Sorry, I've retired,' said Ethel. 'Though I admit,' she added, 'if anything would tempt me back, it would be a song like that.'

'Nora Bayes, Elizabeth Brice, Fanny . . . there's plenty who could sing it,' said Jerry, 'but let's get the show first.'

'We'll get a show.'

'If that song is in it and Ollie Thomas, I'll back it,' said Chrysler.

'You'll have a little competition, Walter,' said Paul Block. 'I'm already elected to back Flo's show for Marilyn, and I may say I don't mind having Ollie in it either.'

That's how simple it was to get backing in those days when big musicals cost $50,000 to put on and not $300,000 . . . a well-staged party with a few pretty girls . . . Irving or Jerry, Lou Hirsch or Rudy Friml at the piano . . . and one lady guest carefully chosen for her voice.

When the *Wench* came into the yacht harbour, there was a Jap standing on the clubhouse pier. Ziegfeld went over to the Captain.

'I'm told you fired Shimo because he was fresh,' he said. 'You were quite right, but I wired him that he's hired again. He won't be the ship's cook. He'll live in a hotel and come aboard only when we're having terrapin. That's all he's for – just terrapin.'

Chrysler laughed.

'You and Paul and I,' he said, turning to Messmore Kendall, 'have quite a bit of money between us, but it takes a Ziegfeld to do a thing like that.'

5

The two partners had one more encounter with the Glorifier before they left. It was on the golf course that had been laid out between the Breakers and the Royal Poinciana. There were only nine holes, and though it was quite late in the afternoon Plum thought he would be able to make it before dark. Guy, who had blistered his hands in a country-club match the day before, was walking round with him. On the first tee they found Ziegfeld, who was likewise accompanied by a non-player, Freddie Zimmerman. It seemed only fitting that the two active members of the quartette should team up.

'What'll we play for?' asked Flo. '$5?'

'All right,' said Plum, getting ready to drive. 'And if it gets too dark to finish, we'll give the $10 to Freddie to hold for tomorrow.'

'I meant $5 a hole.'

Plum was actually swinging as Flo said it. He foozled his drive. Flo, however, following his almost invariable custom, foozled his, and Plum won the first two holes. As he addressed his ball on the third tee, Ziegfeld called out 'Double or quits', which caused his opponent to slice, and the ball, striking a palm tree, returned almost to the starting point. In these circumstances a protest regarding the wager would hardly have been sporting, so Plum agreed and Ziegfeld sent a topped shot a matter of eighty yards down the fairway. Once more Plum won the hole, and once more Ziegfeld said 'Double or quits'.

By the time they holed out at the seventh, Plum again winning, two things had begun to gather – darkness and a gallery. Guy and Freddie, working it out with pencils and bits of paper, announced that the contest for the short eighth would be for $640.

The eighth was a mashie-niblick shot on to a narrow green surrounded by bunkers.

'You shoot first,' said Plum. 'It may change your luck,' and Ziegfeld proceeded to make a shot Francis Ouimet might have been proud of. The ball rose in a beautiful arc against the still faintly glowing western sky. It dropped a yard from the hole, and there was a round of applause that was probably as gratifying to the master-manager's ear as any earned for him by his artists.

It was unnerving for Plum to have to follow such an effort, and he topped his shot badly. The ball took off on a flat trajectory, whizzed across the green, hit one of the private cars in the siding behind it, came whistling back, ricochetted off a caddy, soared into the air, fell ten inches from the cup and trickled in.

Plum was relieved. It had been a near thing.

'Thought for a moment I'd missed it,' he said.

'Double or quits,' said Ziegfeld.

'Or suppose we make it an even thousand?'

'Okay. Mind if I shoot first again?'

'Go ahead.'

The shades of night were falling fast now. There was just enough visibility for the spectators to be aware that this time Ziegfeld meant business. They could see him only vaguely, a dim form in the darkness, but even that glimpse was sufficient to tell them that there stood a man who intended that his stance should be right, his grip right, his body still, his head unmoved, and his eye on the ball; a man who proposed to come back slow, bring the arms well through, roll the wrists, let the club-head lead and pivot on the ball of the left foot, being careful not to duck the right knee. A man, in short, whose driver would travel from point A to point B along dotted line C, winding up at point D, as recommended in all the golf books.

And so it proved. It was a superb drive. It was unhurried. It had rhythm. The arms were straight, the wrists cocked at the top of the swing, the elbows close to the body, the weight shifting at precisely the right moment from leg to leg, the wrists uncocking to give the final snap, the whole winding up with a perfect follow-through. A ball hit by a man doing all that sort of thing has to go places. Ziegfeld's did. It shot from the tee as if Walter Hagen were behind it, and was immediately swallowed up by the night.

'Watch it!' yelled Flo, apparently crediting those present with the "patent double million magnifyin' gas microscopes of hextra power" which Sam Weller claimed not to possess in place of eyes, and the caddies ran ahead, the gallery following. The hunt was up. Ziegfeld, his caddy, Freddy Zimmerman, Guy, Plum and perhaps twenty pleasure-loving followers of sport were searching hither and thither about the fairway, striking matches and lining up in arm-linked squads. They combed the ground in every direction, but the ball was nowhere to be found.

Plum, meanwhile, having given up the search, had holed out, using his mashie-niblick, not trying for distance but being content with smooth, wristy shots that travelled from eighteen inches to two feet. Ziegfeld, joining him on the ninth green, pulled out a roll of bills and extracted one. It was a beautiful thing with a yellow back on which was a portrait of President Garfield and a printed promise that it could be redeemed at the US Treasury for $1000. The two authors gazed at it respectfully. It was the first thing of the sort they had ever seen.

They walked back to the Poinciana.

'What I like about show business is that you meet such interesting people,' said Plum, taking out the $1000 bill and fondling it. 'Flo Ziegfeld, to name but one.'

'Yes, and "Felix", Ray, Arch Selwyn, Charlie Dillingham, Hank Savage and the rest of them. I suppose that's why the theatre draws one like a maggot, as Joe Urban would say.'

They came to the hotel. Inquiring at the desk for mail, they were handed a cablegram. It was from 'Fabulous Felix', urging them to come to London. *The Girl Behind The Gun*, its title changed to *Kissing Time*, was to go into rehearsal in a week or two with a cast of stars – George Grossmith, Leslie Henson, Phyllis Dare, Yvonne Arnaud, Tom Walls, Stanley Holloway . . . a breath-taking roster of talent.

'*Kissing Time*!' said Guy. 'My God, what a title! We'd better get over there quick and change it.'

'It may not be so bad for London. "Kissing Time" was the hit song of *Chu Chin Chow*.'

They cabled 'Felix' that they would come, but a few days later Guy had developed doubts.

'Suppose Flo suddenly comes through with the Miller show?'

'One of us could always jump on a boat and come back.'

'One of us, yes. I suppose one would also be able to look after things in London.'

Guy had personal reasons for not wanting to go to England at this time. He had hopes that he might be able to convince his prima donna that if Jack Sprat and his wife could make a go of it with such contrary tastes, why couldn't they? She was still in Mexico and there was no hint of an early return. Unless things were taken in hand their romance seemed destined to dwindle to extinction in a dismal and occasional exchange of picture-postcards.

'All right,' said Plum. 'You stay here. You can keep in touch with Flo, and I can do anything that needs to be done in London.'

A week later he and Ethel sailed for Southampton on the *Majestic*.

6

Guy went to see them off, joining the crowd at the end of the pier and waving as the queen of the White Star fleet turned from the pack of bustling tugs and moved slowly down stream. A couple unrecognizable at the distance were waving. They looked like Plum and Ethel. Guy waved back, then turned away disconsolately. When he returned to his 57th Street apartment he was conscious of a lost feeling. For the first time since he and Plum had met and formed their partnership, he faced the ups and downs of their strange theatre world alone, and he could not help feeling that it was the end of a phase – a period. Something told him that there would be no more Princess shows. Jerry had drifted away and was writing with other librettists, while Plum, he knew, was in process of capturing a public with

his books and short stories that would give him a more secure
position, a more solid standing than the theatre ever could.

It depressed Guy to think that this separation might mean
the end of a writing partnership which had been so pleasant and
so successful. He knew that Plum had been feeling the need of
refreshing his view of the English scene. England was the
background of his stories, and he had said while they were
waiting for the boat to sail that he might settle there for a while.
How long was 'a while'?

However, there was work to do, as always, and Guy got down
to it and finished *The Five Million* and *Adam and Eva* and went
on to tinker a comedy George Middleton had written called
The Cave Girl. He and George also wrote a rather strange play
about Oberammergau Passion Players, *The Light of the World*.
He was steering away from musical comedy. He started work
on a serious play all his own with a wartime background, *The
Dark Angel*.

Letters passed back and forth between him and Plum.
Kissing Time – the London management had insisted on keeping
the title – had opened at the Winter Garden and was the success
it was bound to be with that galaxy of stars. It ran for nineteen
months.

Several times during that period Guy was on the point of
boarding a liner and joining Plum, who had settled down in
Kensington, but something always happened to stop him.
Marguerite was singing with the Chicago Opera, and he
journeyed there and back between rehearsals and bouts of
intensive writing at Atlantic City.

She still held off on their marriage, arguing that, for his own
sake, he should find himself a wife who would fit into the pattern
of his life without having any conflicting pattern of her own. It
was on this note that they parted when, the Chicago Opera
season ended, Marguerite started off on a tour with the St
Louis Symphony Orchestra while Guy returned to New York
for the *Adam and Eva* rehearsals.

Then, with the seeming inconsequence associated with
feminine decisions, came a letter saying that she had changed
her mind. She told Guy she was ready to get married as fast as
he could get himself out to San Francisco where her tour was

ending. They would be free then to buy a car and spend an enchanting honeymoon roving the Pacific coast. Only pausing on his way to the Grand Central to pay a quick visit to Tiffany's, Guy boarded the Twentieth Century.

The four-and-a-half day journey seemed endless but the Overland Ltd, to which he had changed in Chicago, finally ambled through vast fields of artichokes into the delightful City of Hills. It was early and San Francisco was wrapped in its pearly morning mist. To Guy's surprise Marguerite was waiting on the platform.

'Come on,' she said. 'We've got time to go over to the Cliff House for breakfast.'

' "Got time"? What do you mean? Where are we going?'

'You're going back to New York on the noon train.'

'What are you talking about?'

'You've had a wire from Jerry Kern and heaven knows how many from Ziegfeld. They want you at once for the Marilyn Miller show.'

'Are you coming back with me?'

'I can't, darling. I've got two more concerts.'

'Well then, I shall chuck it.'

'Oh, no, you won't. I'm not going to have you looking at me some morning when I've a cold in the head and saying, "It was for that I turned down the biggest opportunity of my life." '

They took a taxi and breakfasted at a table looking down on the seal rocks. Guy saw in the seals a symbol of separation.

'Those aren't loving couples,' he explained in answer to her question. 'Those are all females. The males never bother with California. They are up in the Misty Islands where the fishing is better.'

'And don't these wives of theirs suffer from the same qualms as I do? Wondering whether the old boy isn't playing house with some little Misty Island chorus-seal.'

'Not a chance. The bull seals are sick to death of women once the mating season is over.' Marguerite laughed.

'There's an idea there,' she said.

She looked at the diamond wrist-watch that had occasioned the stop at Tiffany's. It was time to go back to the station.

A little later Guy was staring out of the train window wondering who it was that ate all those artichokes.

7

The Marilyn Miller show was to be called *Sally*. Ziegfeld had originally planned three shows, one for Marilyn, one for Leon Errol and the third for Walter Catlett, but after *Sally* was completed he decided to have Errol co-star with Marilyn. This necessitated a complete reconstruction, and not more than a week after it was finished he sent for Guy and asked him to 'put in' a part for Catlett which would be equal to Errol's but must take nothing away from it, as Errol had already seen the script. Just one of those simple little rewrite jobs that are so common in the world of musical comedy. Guy, as he toiled away, found himself thinking enviously of Plum, who about now was probably writing a serial for the *Saturday Evening Post* which would be accepted, paid for on the nail and printed without the change of a comma. These novelists, he felt, had it soft. It was some slight consolation to him, as he courted brain-fever in the effort to make the Catlett part screamingly funny but not so funny as to provoke growls of anger from his fellow-star, to reflect that it would hardly be possible not to reap a small fortune from a Miller-Errol-Catlett show with Kern's music, Ziegfeld's girls and Joe Urban's scenery to help it along. Ziegfeld authors might wind up sticking straws in their hair and cutting out paper dolls, but they could afford expensive nursing-homes in which to do it.

Plum having written that it was impossible for him to leave England at the moment, he was working alone. He shipped a script over to his partner in London, and a certain amount of long-distance collaboration took place. Plum wrote two or three lyrics, at the same time urging Guy to use 'Bill' and extract 'Church Round the Corner' from *The Little Thing*. He did use the latter, and the final scene was built around it, but Marilyn's voice was not suited to the singing of 'Bill', which needed – and finally got – a Helen Morgan. Two more lyrics were taken from a musical adaptation of *Brewster's Millions* which Jerry and Guy had started but abandoned. These –

'Whip-poor-will' and 'Look for the Silver Lining' – were by Buddy de Silva. Two other lyricists, Clifford Grey and Anne Caldwell, also had lyrics included. It was all pretty haphazard and very different from the Princess days.

The script called for a funny woman to play opposite Catlett. Guy suggested Ada Lewis. Flo wouldn't hear of it.

'Make her young and cute,' he said. 'I hate women comics.'

He gave the role to little Mary Hay, and again overruled the author in the matter of the casting of the elderly society matron who was mixed up with Sally's fortunes. Guy presented the names of several of the leading theatrical *grandes dames*, but Flo refused to consider them. He engaged Dolores, the lovely six-feet-one amazon who had been the central figure of the Ben Ali Hagan tableaux in the *Follies*.

'I don't want old people in my shows,' he said. 'What you look at is just as important as what you listen to.'

One argument, however, Guy did win. Ziegfeld wanted a 'star' entrance for Marilyn, and Guy had introduced her as one of the six orphan girls who came on early in Act One in a line, all dressed alike in cotton frocks and laced-up ankle-boots, to be inspected by the restaurant owner, who had applied to the orphanage for a dishwasher.

Ziegfeld hated the idea. So did Jerry Kern. But, of all people in the world, Guy found an ally in Marilyn, who might have been expected to be the first to recoil in horror at the suggestion that she should make an entrance like that.

'It's fine,' she said. 'Just right for my eccentric dance.'

'We'll try it together in Baltimore,' said Flo grudgingly. 'But be prepared to rewrite it for New York.'

It did not have to be rewritten. It was an immediate success. A delighted gasp went up all over the theatre when the last of the row of orphans was yanked out of the line by the restaurant owner and revealed herself as Marilyn. Charlie Case, the vaudeville comedian, used to tell a story in his act which culminated in the line 'He tore off his whiskers, and it was Jim!' Marilyn's entrance had much the same effect, not only in Baltimore but two weeks later when she made it at the New Amsterdam.

But Flo had been right about Dolores. Not only was she

lovely to look at, she was the perfect foil for Errol, the Balkan
Grand Duke who had been thrown out of his country by a
revolution and was making a living as a waiter. When the pair
emerged together from 'The Little Church round the Corner'
they were greeted with a storm of applause. The finale was the
number that Plum had written for *The Little Thing*.

> There's a church around the corner that's waiting for us:
>   It's just above Madison Square.
> I'll borrow a dollar and buy a clean collar,
>   And then I'll be meeting you there.
> There'll be crowds in the pews and excitement and fuss,
>   For I mean to be married in style,
> And the girls will go dizzy and whisper 'Who is he?'
>   When I start to step up the aisle.
>
> Dear little, dear little Church Round the Corner,
>   Where so many lives have begun,
> Where folks without money see nothing that's funny
>   In two living cheaper than one.
> Our hearts to each other we've trusted:
>   We're busted, but what do we care?
>   For a moderate price
>   You can start dodging rice
>   At the Church Round the Corner,
>   It's just round the corner,
>   The corner of Madison Square.

Few who were there on that opening night will ever forget the
reception that was accorded the little star when she came down
the steps of the church in the lovely lace bridal-robe that
Ziegfeld had dressed her in. Many things contributed to the
magic of that night – Jerry's wonderful score, the *Follies*
beauties in their lovely costumes; the Urban scenery and still
more the Urban lighting; the two comedians, each turning in
the best performance of his career. But it was Marilyn that
really mattered, Marilyn who gave to the play a curious
enchantment that no reproduction in other lands or other
mediums ever captured.

8

'Church Round the Corner' had a significance that carried beyond its role in *Sally*. It served as admonishment and happy omen for a real life wedding. Marguerite and Guy got married, with Jerry as best man in lieu of Plum.

'How are the mighty fallen!' said Jerry when he and Eva were sipping champagne with the newly married pair. ' "Marriage means giving up your comfort and your ideal of woman, in trying to be some woman's ideal of man." Line by Guy Bolton. "Marriage isn't a process for prolonging the life of love but for mummifying its corpse", a further comment on the institution from the same source. "Marriage is the net in which the jade snares the jaded." "Marriage — " '

'Listen,' said Guy. 'Just because I write of a cynical woman-hater is no reason I should subscribe to his views. My opinion of woman as the priceless pearl of creation is well known.'

'Let us trust,' said Marguerite, 'that I'm the last bead on the string.'

'I wish to propose a toast,' said Guy. 'Here's to the author of "Church Round the Corner".'

'You'll be seeing the old boy soon.'

'Let's hope,' said Guy. 'We're sailing for England next week.'

Actually it was five weeks later that they sailed for England on the *Olympic*, a delay occasioned by discussions with Max Marcin concerning a comedy melodrama which he and Guy were writing together. Among their fellow passengers were Charlie Chaplin and Eddie Knoblock, the author of *Kismet*.

At the ship's concert Marguerite sang and Chaplin did a pantomimic act in which he portrayed an out-of-work actor applying for a job. As the manager, played by Knoblock, described each aspect of the character, Chaplin became successively humble, aggressive, charming, ultra-aristocratic. Told he was too short for the role, he seemingly grew several inches taller. Questioned as to his romantic qualifications, he hurled himself into the manager's lap. Finally he is asked to run through a scene in which he is supposed to come home and find his wife in the arms of his best friend. In a frenzy of jealous rage he is called on to kill his betrayer. The manager shakes his head and says he fears Charlie can never be sufficiently convincing in the scene, whereupon the actor, determined to win the coveted role, seizes the manager by the throat. When he at last relaxes his grip and turns away to get his hat and stick, the manager is a corpse on the floor. Charlie, turning back with an ingratiating smile to receive his applause, was Chaplin at his best. His surprise on seeing the empty chair, his consternation on discovering the body that has slipped down under the desk were done as only Chaplin could do it. And then his famous shuffling exit, looking back over his shoulder and raising his hat to the corpse. It made a perfect finish.

9

The first thing Guy did on reaching London and depositing their bags at the Berkeley was to go in search of Plum. He was living in bachelor quarters in a tall, old-fashioned building in Queen Street. His flat was on the fourth floor. There was no lift and Guy, travel-tired, toiled up the long staircase to arrive somewhat breathless as he entered the already opened door. Plum had just finished a letter and he called out a cheery 'Hurray, you're here. Just a tick while I get this letter off.' So saying he walked to the half-open window and tossed it out.

'What on earth,' exclaimed Guy. 'Has the joy at seeing me brought on some sort of mental lapse?'

'You're referring to that letter? I throw all my letters out of the window. I can't be bothered to toil up and down stairs every time I post a letter. These are honest people, you know, each one is his brother's keeper, whoever picks it up will quicken his pace as he hurries it to the nearest letter-box.'

'Well, I wish you'd write me a letter while I'm here, I'd like to show it round in America. Quite a score for good old England.'

Guy turned from the window to Plum's battered old typewriter.

'The same old girl,' he said, 'I duly salute her. But what is that large affair with a great big roll of paper hitched up behind her?'

'That,' responded Plum, 'is the great Wodehouse invention.'

'You type directly on to that roll of paper?'

Plum explained. 'Nothing is more destructive,' he said, 'when the steam's up and ideas are tripping over each other to suddenly arrive at the bottom of the page. You have to take the page out, lay it on the pile, find another sheet, put it in, then find yourself uncertain what the last word was, find it, realize you've misspelt it. . . . But, with this Wodehouse invention you just type merrily on, words flowing like a purling stream.'

Guy took over, 'Witticism after witticism, yes, yes, brilliant, brilliant! What a man!'

'But,' resumed Plum, 'every silver lining has its cloud. Last Thursday I was having a wonderful day, I had typed a good seventy feet and I felt I could easily pass the hundred mark when a smouldering odour seemed to have come into the room. I leapt to my feet in the middle of a big laugh, the seventy-foot page had made its way across the floor, passing a pile of books, an old-fashioned spittoon, and had curled up round the little electric heater that I use to take the chill off the room. I rushed over and started stamping on some of the best comedy lines I had ever written.'

'What a tragedy!' Guy exclaimed sympathetically. 'Nothing you put in its place ever seems any good.'

It was two days later that Guy heard a timid knocking on his door. He opened it and a man said, 'Your name "Bolton"?' Guy said it was.

'I've got a letter for you, sir.'

Guy put his hand toward his trouser's pocket.

'Thank you, sir, but I'm not looking for any tip, I was coming this way.' He felt differently about a beer and Guy poured him one. While he was drinking it Guy went to the telephone and called Plum.

'I've got your letter,' he said.

Plum said, 'Are you sure it's mine?'

'Yes, of course I'm sure.'

'I only threw it out of the window twenty minutes ago.'

Guy said, 'The GPO had better look to their laurels.'

'And keep an eye on their laburnums,' Plum added, 'That sure beats everything if you want it to go fast.'

ELEVEN

I

Guy was having a business honeymoon. He had hoped to be able to buy a car and tour the British Isles at his leisure, but a playwright's programme is always subject to changes without notice. Work fell on him out of the skies. Gilbert Miller was putting on *Polly With a Past* at the St James's, and he suddenly decided to advance the opening date and called on Guy to attend rehearsals.

Miller had assembled a brilliant cast for *Polly* – Edna Best, a newly arrived star who had made a great success in a play called *Brown Sugar*, Edith Evans, Claude Rains, Aubrey Smith, Henry Kendall, Helen Haye, Donald Calthrop and a young man named Noel Coward. Altogether quite an array of talent and one that would be on the expensive side today.

It led off the season on 2nd March. The following night Maugham's *The Circle* opened at that most delectable of theatres, the Haymarket. Then on the 14th came *A Bill of Divorcement*, followed by Cyril Maude's revival of *Grumpy* on the 26th, and *Bulldog Drummond* on the 29th. And the players – Gerald du Maurier, Marie Tempest, Meggie Albanesi, Allan Aynesworth, Lottie Venne. Marguerite and Guy had chosen a good month for their theatre-going.

'The London theatre is wonderful,' said Guy. He had dropped in to pay a morning call on Plum.

'Surely not as vital as New York?'

'I'm worried about New York – not the plays but the way the men up top are running things. Take this ticket-speculating. The managers could stop it in a minute if they wanted to, but half of them are getting rake-offs. They're driving people away from the theatre. That boy and his best girl that we used to talk about can't afford to come any more. We're getting the out-of-town buyers – tickets bought for them at inflated prices by the firms they do business with – and the new rich who sprang up during the war. And the kind of audience you get largely determines the kind of plays you get.'

'The musicals are better in New York.'

'Yes, but the costs are sky-rocketing. They tell me you have to have close on $50,000 in the kitty to put on a big musical today.'

'I wonder what our old friend Hank Savage would say to that.'

'Even an *Oh, Boy!* would cost between $30,000 and $35,000. In London things are reasonable. And the theatres look so much better here with everyone dressing and most of the men in white ties. It seems as if the audiences are out to enjoy themselves. They don't have that grim I-wonder-if-I'm-going-to-get-my-money's-worth attitude that paralyses you in New York.'

'Not the people in the stalls, perhaps, but how about the gallery boys?'

'Yes, they're tough, of course. I would hate to be booed.'

'There are worse things than booing. Did I ever tell you about the very first play I ever had produced?'

'I don't think so. In London?'

'At the Vaudeville. It was supposed to be funny, but you would never have thought it from the way the audience reacted. Not a laugh from start to finish, as I remember it. When the final curtain fell, there was a dead silence all over the house. Then a voice in the gallery said, "Well, good night, all," and they went home to bed. I would much have preferred the loudest booing. What a ghastly thing a real solid flop in the theatre is.'

'All the same, I'd sooner have one in London than on Broadway. And I still maintain that London audiences are better than New York audiences and London plays – most of them – better than New York plays.'

'Well, if you're so keen on them, you'd better come and lunch with me at the Dramatists' Club and meet some of the fellows who write them.'

'What's the Dramatists' Club?'

'It's . . . how shall I put it? . . . it's the Dramatists' Club.'

'I see. The Dramatists' Club.'

'That's right.'

The Dramatists' Club had no clubhouse. Its members met once a month in the private dining-room of a hotel in Northumberland Avenue, where they lunched and exchanged views. Its president at this time was Sir Arthur Pinero.

Today there was a distinguished gathering. Barrie was in the seat next to Pinero and on his other side the club's secretary, Ian Hay and, beside Ian, Edward Knoblock.

The man next to Knoblock was a rather colourless looking little fellow with blondish, greying hair.

'Who's that?' whispered Guy.

'Jacobs.'

'Not W.W.?'

'There's only one Jacobs.'

'There certainly is,' said Guy reverently. He knew practically all Jacobs by heart. Sam, Ginger, Bob Pretty and the rest of them were his familiar friends. If there had been a deliberate attempt to thrill him, they could not have done better. Louis Parker came in, and with him Clemence Dane, and shortly afterwards Cyril McNeile, who wrote under the name of Sapper. His *Bulldog Drummond*, with Gerald du Maurier starring, had just opened and was a tremendous success. Of those who had big hits running in London, only Willie Maugham was missing.

As they were sitting over coffee and cigars, Barrie rose, looking, even when standing, not much taller than his sitting neighbours.

'I know speeches are not in order,' he said with his faint Scottish burr, 'but I haven't been to one of these meetings for some time and I've got to tell you of the wee little thrill I always get when I come here. It's some years now since we founded this club, Arthur here and poor Haddon Chambers, whom we've just lost, and Harry Esmond and Kipling and Hornung and one or two more. We were all pretty young then and we talked a lot about the things we'd written and the things we were going to write. There was one fellow talked more than all the rest of us put together. A tall, Irish chap with a red beard . . . I've often wondered what became of him.'

Guy asked the man seated next to him, if it was true, as Barrie had seemed to imply, that Shaw never came to these lunches and, if so, why.

'There was a lot of unpleasantness during the war,' his neighbour told him. 'He wrote stuff praising the Germans and it infuriated a good many people, Kipling particularly. The atmosphere got so strained that Shaw finally resigned. Pinero announced it at the next meeting. "Mr Shaw has handed in his resignation," he said, then paused for a moment. "Mr Shaw's resignation," he added, "is as nothing compared to ours." '

2

Sally was to be presented at the Winter Garden in the autumn at the end of the long run of *Kissing Time*. The management was again that of Grossmith and Laurillard and discussions regarding book adjustments, casting and other matters called for daily meetings with George Grossmith, who thus took his place in the Bolton-Wodehouse gallery of theatrical managers.

'Tell me about Grossmith,' said Guy one morning.

'What do you want to know about him?'

'He's a strange bird compared with our New York gang.'

'George isn't only a manager, he's one of London's top musical comedy actors.'

'Yes, I know. He's a brilliant light comedian, but he can't have been so hot in the Donald Brian part in *Kissing Time*.'

'Hotter than he was as Prince Karl in an Austrian operetta I once caught him in. The trouble with George is that if there's a prince in the show you can't keep him away from it with an injunction. Show him a white uniform with gold frogs across the chest and a lot of medals, and he starts making mewing noises.'

'A snob, perchance?'

'A priceless snob, but the looking-up kind, not the looking-down. The looking-up snob longs to know a duke, the looking-down variety can't afford to know a dustman. George reads himself to sleep with Burke's *Peerage*, but he'll go pub-crawling with the stage-door man.'

'I like him.'

'Everybody likes him. Women especially.'

'Oh, he's a ladies' man?'

'Second to none. I heard a funny story about George the other day. I don't know if it's true or not, but it sounds just like him. He had gone to see the Grand National and, strolling through the paddock, met his friend Lord Lathom, who introduced him to a very pretty woman, Lady something – I can't quite remember – Mudge – that's not quite it.'

'Peeress?'

'No, wife of a baronet – but that would be enough to endear her to George. They got along together like ham and eggs and, when she said that racing bored her and that she couldn't bear seeing the horses fall at the jumps, he gallantly insisted on remaining with her in the paddock during the running of the race. The friendship ripened on the journey back to London and when they parted she invited George to come and spend the next weekend at the old home. She said her husband would be delighted. A touch of gout had kept him away from Aintree but she was sure George would brighten him up.

'George accepted but when he met the gentleman he had misgivings. If the Bart was delighted his manner didn't show it. He had heard about the meeting in the paddock and he started right in asking George why the devil he had gone halfway across England to see a race and then chosen to turn his back on it and talk to a woman instead. This had evidently aroused his worst suspicions.

'The dinner was a ghastly affair with the host whipping the carving-knife back and forth across the steel until his wife complained that he was setting her teeth on edge. George tried to talk about the house, which was ancient to the point of mouldering. Hosts are usually to be drawn out on the subject of the family manse. "Fascinating old place," he said.

' "A lot of people have died in it," said Bart darkly.

' "Probably from the damp," said his wife. "It's the dampest place I was ever in."

'This disturbed George. He has a horror of damp. However,

he beamed as cheerfully as he could manage. He was glad when the time came for bed.

'But he wasn't glad long. It suddenly came back to him what his hostess had said about the place being damp. The room they had put him in smelled musty, and he was sure the sheets must be wringing.'

'I thought it was an established custom before getting into any bed in England to make a test for dampness by putting a hand-mirror between the sheets?'

'It is. And don't think old hypochondriac George didn't think of it, but unfortunately the only mirror in the room was a thing six feet by eight, fastened to the wall with brass nails. Then he remembered something. He was pretty sure he had seen a mirror in a carved frame standing on the piano in the drawing-room. And what could be simpler than to toddle downstairs and fetch it? With the Grossmiths, to think is to act. He set off in his white silk pyjamas with the gold frogs across the chest, got the mirror and started back again. As he reached the landing, a door was suddenly thrown open and there was the Bart, looking like Othello.

' "What the devil are you doing, prowling about the house at this time of night in your pyjamas?" he inquired, clenching and unclenching his fists, his eyes burning with a green flame.

' "I came to get this," said George, exhibiting the mirror.

'Only it wasn't a mirror, it was a photograph of Lady Mudge.'

'Good Lord! What happened then?'

'I don't know,' said Plum. 'That's where the story ends.'

3

The chief problem in casting *Sally* was, of course, to find a Sally. Leslie Henson and Grossmith could handle the Errol and Catlett parts, but there were no Marilyn Millers in England – only one in America. It was decided to engage Dorothy Dickson.

Dorothy was an old friend of Guy's and Plum's. Ray Comstock had discovered her dancing with her husband, Carl Hyson, at the College Inn in Chicago, and had signed them up as a speciality dance team for *Oh, Boy!* Their success had been sensational. Dorothy used to make up with a round spot of rouge on each cheek like a painted doll, and accentuated this effect by wearing a little Dutch cap. She was prettier than any of her rivals in the field of ballroom dancing and, good though Carl Hyson was, this was the only team – except the Astaires – in which the female partner was the equal of the male. Vernon Castle, Maurice, De Marco and the others made it their business to show off the girl they were dancing with, but, had they wanted to, they could just as easily have shown her up. Not even the best of them could have done that to Dorothy.

She was ambitious to become something more than a ball-room dancer and took vocal and acting lessons, but the first two parts she played were in failures – *Girl o' Mine* and *Rock-a-bye-Baby*. She then went to London, rejoining Carl, and appeared in the Cochran revue, *London, Paris and New York*. It was not an impressive record, and both Ziegfeld and Kern were vehemently against entrusting her with such a vitally important role as Sally, Ziegfeld eclipsing himself in the matter of violent cables. Guy, however, remained firm and insisted on her playing the part.

He wanted to get the matter settled so that he could get over to Paris. He had had a letter from Marguerite in which she told of an offer from the Opéra Comique of an engagement that would assign her the top lyric soprano roles, Louise, Manon, Mimi and Butterfly. He knew such an opportunity was her dearest ambition.

'Are you going to say "Yes"?' Plum asked him.

'There's nothing else I can do. I can't help remembering what she said to me when I wanted to chuck *Sally* and stay in California. "I don't want you to be looking at me in years to come and saying – for that I gave up my biggest oppor-tunity." '

'I was afraid it was going to be like that, two ambitious people.'

'Oh, well, I can pop back and forth – London, Paris and New York – not a bad life.'

'You've got to go to New York for that farce-melodrama, haven't you?'

'*The Nightcap?* Yes. I've only a week or two to spend with Marguerite.'

Guy raised the question of when they might hope to get together on another show. Plum suggested that they should reunite the old triumvirate, Bolton, Wodehouse and Kern. Guy said it couldn't be a 'Princess' show. Jerry had set his face against writing again for the tiny playhouse.

'If we can't have Jerry, who else is there?'

'Irving.'

'Fine, but he wouldn't want me. He writes his own lyrics.'

'Do you remember that boy who was rehearsal pianist at the Century?'

'You mean the lad who could make a piano sound like a whole jazz orchestra?'

'That's the one. He said he'd like to play us some of his music.'

'Every rehearsal pianist wants to play you his music.'

'I know, but I was with some people not long ago and they talked about this chap and someone said he was a genius.'

'You're sure it was the same fellow?'

'Yes, I'd clean forgotten his name but when they said it I remembered it. I've written it down so I won't forget it again and when I get back I think I'll look him up.'

'What was the name?'

'George Gershwin.'

'That's right, I recall him now. Pink cheeks, nice smile, a terrifically strong beard that even the closest shave couldn't conceal.'

'If I decide he'll do, will you come over?'

'Yes, but try to get Jerry. After all there's only one Kern.'

'True. Still, who knows? Maybe there's only one George Gershwin.'

4

Guy went to Paris. The opera engagement offered to Marguerite was for the autumn. He saw how eager she was to do it and told her to accept. It was for a year with an option for a second one.

'You'll just have to commute,' she said.

'I know how you hate to leave the stage for more than a minute but you'll have to when the baby arrives.'

'Not necessarily. Tonelli told me he was born in a dressing-room at the Scala during a performance of *Traviata*.'

'Don't tell me the lady was playing Violetta?'

'I wouldn't be surprised, dear. Crinolines you know. It's *the* opera for expectant prima donnas.'

They went to Italy – Rome, Florence and Venice – returning to Paris where Marguerite was due for rehearsals. *The Nightcap* rehearsals were starting in New York. Guy phoned Plum to say good-bye, Plum again urging him to try and re-establish the Princess team. He sailed from Cherbourg on the *Olympic*, the ship that he and Marguerite called their honeymoon boat.

Meanwhile Plum had retreated to the charming village of Rogate in the Petersfield district and was embarked on that intensive programme of novel writing which turned out, in rapid succession, *The Girl on the Boat*, *The Adventures of Sally*, *The Inimitable Jeeves*, *Leave it to Psmith*, *The Heart of a Goof*, and *The Small Bachelor*, the last named *Oh, Lady, Lady* in new guise.

Just to keep his hand in he wrote the lyrics for *The Golden Moth*, for which Fred Thompson supplied the book.

The Nightcap opened early and then Guy, who happened to be in Atlantic City, saw the first performance of a show called *Tangerine* which was written by the head of the New York Theatre Guild, Lawrence Langner. Langner had received some help from Philip Bartholomæ but it wasn't sufficient. The show fell flat on its face. Carl Carleton, the husband of Edith Day, was the manager. He asked Guy if he thought the piece could be saved. Guy thought it could, and he was right. His revised version ran for more than 300 performances.

Guy barely waited for the opening night, then sailed for Europe. *Sally* was already in rehearsal in London so there was no time to travel via Paris. He wired Marguerite asking her to meet him in London but when he got there he found a letter saying that she was singing *Traviata*. The role sounded significant. She begged him to come over. He phoned and told her he must stick with rehearsals for at least a week or so.

Plum was back in London, living in a house in Onslow Square, next door to the one that had been the home of William

Makepiece Thackeray. When Guy went to see him, the door was opened by a butler. Plum explained that this wasn't swank.

'It's business,' he said. 'This chap is an author's model.'

'A what?'

'Come, come, you've heard of artists' models. Audrey Munson was one, if you remember. Well, he's an author's model. I'm writing some stories about a butler. At least, he's not a butler, he's a valet, but the two species are almost identical. I study this bird and make copious notes. Do you like the name Jeeves?'

'Is that what he's called?'

'No, that's the name of the man in my stories. This one is Robinson. You couldn't sell a butler called Robinson to the public. Not box-office. For a long time I was stumped for a name, then I remembered a cricketer, in the years before the war, called Jeeves. Played for Gloucestershire, I think. Calling a character after a county cricketer is lucky. Sherlock and Holmes were both county cricketers. I believe Doyle had decided on Sherrinford Holmes, when he suddenly thought of Mordecai Sherlock, who used to keep wicket for Yorkshire. Jeeves seemed to me just right for the sort of bloke I wanted.'

'What sort of a bloke is this Jeeves of yours?'

'He's omniscient. And, what is more, as Abe Erlanger would say, he knows everything. Robinson's like that. You can't broach a subject he isn't up on. Think of one.'

'Spats.'

'Too easy.'

'Spiders.'

'Right.' Plum pressed the bell. 'Do you know anything about spiders?'

'If you wish to live and thrive, let the spider run alive.'

'Damned silly saying. You wouldn't thrive very long with a family of tarantulas running around. Oh, Robinson.'

'Sir?'

'Mr Bolton is writing a play with an entomologist in it and he wants some inside stuff about spiders.'

'From what aspect, sir?'

'Their domestic life and all that sort of thing.'

'The domestic life of the spider is something that does not bear a close scrutiny, sir.'

'Things not too good in the home?'

'No, sir. The spider's is a matriarchal society. The husband, if we may call him such, has but one function . . . if I may put it that way.'

'Carry on. Mr Bolton understands. I've told him all about the bees and flowers.'

'When this function is fulfilled, the lady has him for dinner.'

'Nothing formal, I suppose? Just a black tie?'

'I speak in a literal sense, sir.'

'You mean she eats him?'

'Precisely, sir. As Shakespeare so well put it, "Oh, curse of marriage, that we can call these delicate creatures ours, but not their appetites." '

'Would you say "delicate" was the—'

'*Mot juste*, sir? Possibly not, sir. One confesses that one is inclined to look askance at the female spider and to view her activities with concern. She deceives the male with a tenderness which, in the light of what is to follow, one cannot but regard as in dubious taste. She flirts and plays, inviting him to swing with her on a long thread, holding him gently in her arms.'

'And all the time she is planning—'

'Precisely, sir.'

'Good God! Women! . . . I hope you're listening, Guy.'

'Would there be anything further, sir?'

'No, that will be all. Thank you, Robinson.'

'Thank *you*, sir.'

The door closed.

'There you are,' said Plum. 'And it would have been just the same if I had asked him about anything else.'

'Useful chap to have around. But a bit on the sombre side, isn't he? Doesn't he ever smile?'

'Faintly, at times.'

'I can't imagine him laughing.'

Plum seemed shocked.

'I should say not. Butlers don't laugh. They aren't allowed

to by the rules of their Guild. Though – yes – I did once see one convulsed with mirth. It is one of my most painful memories.'

'You didn't like him laughing?'

'I didn't like what led up to the laughter. It happened when I was very young and very shy and very hard up. So hard up that I relied for my clothing mostly on the leavings of other members of the family. Thus – if you're interested – I had a frockcoat and a topper discarded by my brother Armine, an overcoat discarded by my Uncle George and a suit of dress-clothes once the property of my Uncle Hugh. It was in this suit of dress-clothes that I went to dine one night at the house where this butler held office. Some people who had known my father in Hong Kong. Rich blokes. All very posh. I was the only one at the dinner table who was of the *canaille*.'

'Still, you were properly dressed.'

'It depends on what you mean by "properly". And I wasn't dressed so much as swathed. This uncle of mine, this Hugh, was a man who weighed close on seventeen stone, and he liked his clothes roomy, the trousers in particular. And they kept climbing up over my shirt-front. Well, that was all right so long as I had my hands free, because I could shove them down again. But came a moment when I was helping myself to some dish, and they shot clear up over my white tie. And it was at that moment that this butler gave way to his baser nature. There was a sound like a paper bag exploding and he rushed from the room. He squared himself with his Guild later, I believe, by saying that he had had a fit.'

'You should have had the things altered by a tailor.'

'Talk sense,' said Plum. 'It would have cost about a quid.'

5

Sally opened at the Winter Garden, and was an instantaneous success. The only mishap was that Dorothy's toe-slipper came off just as the ballet started. Twice she tried to slip it back on and the audience applauded. Up to that point she had turned in a charming performance. In the dressing-room scene that followed she was delightful.

The next morning, after a breakfast of excellent notices, supplemented by a little light refreshment, Guy took off for Paris. Marguerite had reluctantly left the stage, her last performance having taken place ten days previous.

'Even then you were taking chances on being a second Madame Tonelli.'

They dined in the seclusion of Marguerite's studio-apartment in the Val du Grâce. The phone rang. It was from London. Plum reported *Sally* a complete sell-out. The show had gone like a breeze, the only mishap was that Dot's toe-slipper had come off.

'But, good Lord,' said Guy. 'Is this going to happen every night?'

'Every night, old boy, and at matinées. But don't worry. That pathetic slipping slipper has become one of the high spots of the show.'

'She can stop the show with any other kind of dancing.'

'She'll stop it in the ballet spot, too, before she's through. Don't worry.'

'It's your birthday this week, isn't it?'

'Yes, this coming Sunday, why?'

'Nothing. I just had an idea.'

His idea was right, the baby was born on Sunday. He couldn't call it Pelham so they compromised on Pamela, Pamela Marguerite.

A week or two later Guy had a cable from Sam Harris. It asked him to get together with the Duncan Sisters. He commissioned Guy to write a show for them. Irving Berlin would supply the score. Guy wired back saying he would like to work with Plum – Sam cabled to go ahead, only Irving would do his own lyrics.

Guy was delighted. The young lady who had arrived on Plum's birthday seemed to have been a happy omen. He called Plum and told him the news.

'The Duncan Sisters? You can't miss with them. I saw them the other night. They're terrific.'

'I'm glad you're so enthusiastic. What about you coming in with me?'

'Good Lord! Do you want me?'

'I sure do.'

'Then I'm with you. We can write the show here and then sail.'

'But what about Jeeves?'

'Jeeves can wait,' said Plum.

TWELVE

I

The Duncan Sisters, in case the present generation needs reminding of it, were two small girls who created the impression of being about twelve years old. Their names were Rosetta and Vivian, though their friends, and their friends were legion, called them Heim and Jake. Their forte was the delivery of numbers like 'The Bull-Frog Patrol' in close harmony, and they were – there is no other word – terrific. The revue they were starring in at the Royalty was called *Pins and Needles*, and was about London's biggest success, crowded at every performance.

Guy invited them to have supper with him at the Embassy Club. Plum warned him not to, saying that a formal business meeting in the afternoon with pencils and notebooks was the right approach, but Guy would make it the Embassy, a place he adored. Plum said he would not be present. Guy could have the talented artists all to himself.

Guy went to see their new show and after a due interval to permit them to change and remove their stage make-up presented himself at their dressing-room. He found them ready to leave, but they had not changed their revue costumes, nor had they removed their stage make-up. All they had done was stick huge bows in their hair, one pink, one blue. In the final scene of the revue they had worn short dresses and socks. They were still wearing short dresses and socks. They looked like something left over from a defunct kindergarten, and Guy was conscious of a sinking feeling. The Embassy Club in those days, when the great Luigi presided over it, was the smartest, most exclusive supper place in London, posh to the eyebrows.

Dukes and duchesses jostled countesses and earls, and it was a very exceptional evening when you could throw a brick in it without beaning some member of the royal family. It seemed to Guy that in such surroundings the Sisters Duncan and their socks were likely to make something of a sensation.

Propped up against the wall of the dressing-room was a huge floral horseshoe. It was taller than the Duncan Sisters. It was taller than a Duncan Sister mounted on another Duncan Sister's shoulders, and he gazed at it with a wild surmise.

'What's all this?' he asked, and Heim explained that it was a present from their manager, Mr de Courville, tonight being the 200th performance of the show.

They were now ready to be escorted to the taxi which Guy had asked the stage-doorman to have in readiness. Heim spoke to this worthy as they came out, and he ducked back into the theatre, emerging a few moments later accompanied by the stage manager and the assistant stage manager. They were cautiously negotiating the horseshoe through the stage door.

'We're not taking that with us?' faltered Guy.

'Of course we're taking it with us. We're not leaving all those lovely flowers here to die.'

'But what will we do with it at the Embassy?'

'We'll have it at our table. It'll look cute.'

'And another thing,' said Jake. 'It's lucky. It's a lucky horseshoe. Seems like a good omen to have it there when we sit down to talk about the new show.'

Guy tottered on his base. If there was one thing from which his sensitive nature recoiled, it was looking conspicuous, and it was plain that he was scheduled to look even more conspicuous than when giving Marguerite a bite to eat in those Greek reach-me-downs of hers which had so intimidated Plum, the Athenian stole and the serpent armlets. Broodingly he helped Heim into the cab while the driver and the stage manager secured the horseshoe on the truck stand. He was able to have a brief word with the driver before they started off.

'Ten bob extra,' was what he said, and the driver nodded intelligently.

When the cab drew up at its destination, the girls gave a simultaneous cry of dismay.

'It's gone – the horsehoe!'

'My God!' cried Guy, shocked to the core.

The driver was apologetic.

'Sorry, gov'ner, it slipped off and another cab ran over it. Didn't think it was worth while stoppin' to pick it up.'

Guy gave the faithful fellow a pound note, and they went into the club.

'It's a bad omen for the new show,' said Jake Duncan as they took their seats.

'Yes,' agreed her sister. 'It's put me clean off it. When you've got a good luck horseshoe and it falls off the taxi, that means something.'

'Yessir,' echoed Jake. 'That sure means something. Maybe we'd best get busy on that Topsy and Eva thing.'

Guy was aware of a sinister foreboding. What, he wondered, was the Topsy and Eva thing? He did not like the sound of it.

2

Sitting Pretty was the title of the show. They wrote it in Plum's study in Onslow Square. It's central figures were two sisters in an orphan asylum, one of whom was adopted by a wealthy old man whose passion was eugenics. He had already adopted a boy, and it was his aim to marry these two, not knowing that Horace, the boy, was in partnership with an amiable burglar named Uncle Joe, who insinuated him into rich houses to prepare the way for him by leaving doors and windows open.

Irving Berlin had written that he had no objection to Plum contributing a lyric or two if he felt so inclined, and a comedy song being needed for Uncle Joe, Plum attended to it with a number called 'Tulip Time in Sing-Sing'.

> In Broadway haunt of pleasure
> Where they dine and tread the measure
> A young burglar was becoming slowly fried.
> When the waiter saw this mobster
> Sitting sobbing in his lobster,
> He stole up and asked him softly why he cried.
> And the egg said with a quiver
> 'There's a college up the river

Which I yearn for. That's the reason of my gloom.
For the little birds each Spring sing
Aren't you coming back to Sing-Sing
Now it's April and the tulips are a-bloom?
When it's Tulip Time in Sing-Sing,
Oh, it's there that I would be:
There are gentle hearts in Sing-Sing
Watching and waiting for me:
Take me back, take me back,
Give me lots of rocks to crack
With my pals of the class of '99:
For I'd rather have neuralgia
Than be tortured by nostalgia
For that dear old-fashioned prison of mine.

Early in the autumn Guy returned with Plum and Ethel to New York.

'Look,' said Sam Harris, when they reported at his office, 'I'm afraid there's been a hold-up. Irving hasn't been able to work on the score because this *Music Box Revue* has been taking up all his time. I'm going to do *Sitting Pretty* all right, but it will have to be next season. The delay doesn't mean much to you boys, but it does to the Duncan girls, and they've asked me if I will consent to their filling in by doing a thing of their own on the Coast. I don't have to say yes, because I've got them under contract and I can put them in the *Music Box* till we're ready for them, but I don't see any harm in letting them do this thing of theirs if they want to, do you?'

Guy and Plum thought it would be a good idea. If the girls appeared in the *Music Box Revue*, it would take a lot of the freshness out of *Sitting Pretty*.

'What is this thing out on the Coast?' asked Guy.

'Oh, it's some idea of their own that they say they've had for quite a while. They've written the numbers themselves. It's a sort of half-amateur affair. *Topsy and Eva* they're calling it. It's a sort of comic *Uncle Tom's Cabin*.'

Guy's head gave a side jerk as if he had suddenly received a left jab to the jaw. *Topsy and Eva!* He recalled the night at the Embassy with a dim foreboding.

'What's the matter?' asked Plum, noting his friend's silence.

'I was just thinking. *Uncle Tom's Cabin* – it's never missed yet.'

3

Some premonition of disaster seemed to be disturbing Irving Berlin when they dined with him two days after seeing Sam.

The dinner took place at Irving's apartment on West 46th Street. This was a novel duplex penthouse that had taken his fancy. He had had to buy the building in order to get it, but that sort of thing was a trifle to Irving. Like 'Fabulous Felix', he believed in doing himself well.

There was a broad corridor that descended in a series of steps, each step an eight-feet-square platform, to the big living-room that faced the street. Moulded glass panels by Lalique lighted this handsome passage. These were fringed with big potted plants, and standing in front of two of them were tall wooden stands on which stood a pair of brilliant-hued toucans. They added the final touch of magnificence, and it occurred to the authors that 'Felix' must be kicking himself for never having thought of toucans. Only 'Felix' would have had five.

As they came down from the dining-room, their host put out his hand to one of the birds, which immediately proceeded to strike like an offended rattlesnake, its terrifying bill missing the hand by the fraction of an inch.

'I'd be a bit more distant with those fowls, if I were you,' said Plum. 'They're liable to take your finger off.'

'Yes,' laughed Irving, quite unperturbed. 'And it might be the one I play the piano with.'

His piano playing was, of course, as exceptional as everything else about him. He could . . . but why are we using the past tense about Irving? If anyone is perpetually present-tense, it is the one-man Hit Parade. . . . He can play only in the key of F sharp. But of course, if you're a composer, you can't have everything in one key, so Irving's pianos have a transposing keyboard, equipped with a lever that can be set here and there at any key desired, while Irving goes blithely along hitting his black notes. Blithely and magically hit after hit.

After dinner Irving played a couple of tunes he had designed for the Duncan show, then swung round on the piano stool.

'This *Sitting Pretty* book,' he said. 'I've read it, and I think it's darned good. But—'

'But?'

'Well, as I figure it out, it's no use without the Duncans. The high spots come when the sisters, the rich one and the poor one, meet and do numbers together. With the Duncans these'll be smashes. We know what those babies can do with a number when they work together. But without the Duncans. . . .'

'You think we may not get them?'

'I'm wondering. My grapevine tells me this *Topsy and Eva* of theirs is pretty big. It may surprise us all.'

As they went down in the little push-button elevator, Guy was looking grave.

'I suppose you got that?' he said. 'Irving doesn't mean to write that score till he's sure we've got the Duncans. One show more or less means nothing to that bird. He can always make another million or so whenever he feels like it. Lucky devil!'

'Yes, he must have been born in a bed of horseshoes.'

'Don't speak of horseshoes, I'm superstitious about them.'

'I thought they were lucky.'

'Not to me,' said Guy.

A day or two later came a letter from George Grossmith saying that the end of the *Sally* run was in sight and that a new show would be needed at the Winter Garden. He proposed that this would be home-made and, indeed, indicated that he was nominating himself as part-author. Jerry was to write the score.

'You'd better go and do it with George,' said Guy gloomily. 'It looks like a long wait on *Sitting Pretty*.'

'Why don't you come too?'

'How can I? I've got *Polly Preferred* going into rehearsal and there's more than a chance that Gilbert will do *The Dark Angel* with Bart Marshall.'

So Plum sailed back and set to work with George Grossmith on a show called *The Cabaret Girl*, in which Dorothy Dickson was to co-star with Leslie Henson as the author-actor-manager, while Guy went to Paris and the Val du Grâce studio, where his infant daughter regarded the stranger with doubtful eyes.

4

While Jerry was working with Plum on *The Cabaret Girl*, he had read the *Sitting Pretty* book and had offered himself as composer if Irving Berlin was dropping out.

Irving was dropping out. *Topsy and Eva* was now in the twenty-seventh week of its Chicago run with no end in sight. Thus when Guy received a letter from Plum saying here was the old firm back together at last, he shot a wire to Ray Comstock and everything was fixed up. He crossed to England and settled down to fit the numbers Plum and Jerry were writing into the *Sitting Pretty* book.

Then one morning the letters that came up with his breakfast tray included one from Marguerite written in her most slap-dash style. It seemed that a crisis had arisen, not in Marguerite's affairs but in those of a friend. Marguerite collected crises. She would gladly involve herself in one that was the property of people she hardly knew. Like a boy scout, she believed in doing her daily act of kindness.

A woman of prodigal generosity, she had one pet economy. She hated to waste writing-paper. In consequence it was her custom not merely to write on both sides of a piece of thin writing-paper but to turn the page sideways and write slap across the writing already there. A great deal of no doubt interesting gossip was thus lost to her friends.

In this letter she had really outdone herself. There was some talk of Robert Milton's wife who was in Paris, and there was some stuff about a child. Whether it was the Miltons' child or the child or a woman travelling with Mrs Milton was not clear. Guy, remembering somewhat vaguely that the Miltons had a child, inclined to the view that this was it. Anyhow the child was a problem – 'I don't mean a problem child,' Marguerite wrote in brackets. His name was Ben or possibly Hen – that was Marguerite's handwriting. And his mother was paying a flying visit to Geneva or Genoa where a hick (possibly sick) relative demanded her presence. Meanwhile Ben or Hen – now it looked more like Len – was coming over to spend a week with Guy in England. That part was painfully clear. His mother would collect him at the end of that time on her way back to America. In the meanwhile the little fellow would be entertained by visits to the Tower of London, Madame Tussaud's and the Black Museum at Scotland Yard.

Guy took the letter round to Plum. Bob Milton had staged the Princess musicals for both of them, and it seemed to Guy that they should share this burden that had been thrust upon him, standing shoulder to shoulder like the Boys of the Old Brigade. A partnership, as he pointed out to Plum after Robinson-Jeeves had conducted him to the latter's study, is a partnership.

'How old is this little excrescence?'

'Nine.'

'I know that American children are extremely precocious, but a child of nine who has his heart set on visiting the Black Museum at Scotland Yard should be given a wide berth. I'll bet that he has six toes on each foot and that his hairline starts one inch above his eyebrows.'

'Marguerite says he is extremely well-behaved. She goes into details though unfortunately a good deal of it is impossible to read. I did manage to make out that he does not flip butter-pats at the ceiling, a pastime all too prevalent in juvenile American circles.'

'That may be, but let me point out to you that people who regard their nine-year-old offspring as a treasure would hardly be shipping it from Paris to London unguarded. The fact that Mrs Milton is willing to do so is the tip-off.'

'Well anyway,' said Guy, 'the point is I can't put the child up in that mousehole I'm living in at the Mayfair. Here you have lots of space. You also have a butler who might well be a college professor did he not prefer the freer life and higher pay of domestic service. You can turn Ben over to Robinson without a qualm.'

'When is the little louse arriving?'

'Tonight on the Golden Arrow. I'm to meet him at Victoria.'

The notes of the conversation as given in the Wodehouse diary break off at this point. They are followed by a one-line entry: 'Went with G. to meet Ben. Biggest mistake of my life.'

The cryptic statement is not enlarged on. On the other hand the Bolton entry is extremely detailed, if somewhat incoherent. It was evidently written under the influence of strong emotion.

The basic trouble seems to have lain in the fact that trunks are frequently sent from France to England in bond, thus saving a hold-up in the Dover Customs shed. The owner of the trunk can, and usually does, proceed to the spot where these trunks are assembled immediately upon alighting in Victoria Station. Should such a person be travelling with a child, it is not unnatural – though perhaps unwise – to tell the little half-wit to take a seat on the platform and look at a picture-book of which he, she or it is sick to death after the seven-hour journey from Paris.

'Be a good little honey-cub and sit down there with the bags and the Mommer-bear will be back right away.'

Why should a poor, unsuspecting American mother imagine that, in orderly England, two kidnappers were on their way ready to pounce on her innocent offspring at this first moment of arrival? Plum and Guy were just a fraction late or they would have seen the Mommer-bear and not have found an unaccompanied child goggling vacantly amidst an assortment of hand-luggage.

'Sure that's the one?'

'Of course. See his stars and stripes buttons? Also he looks like Bob Milton, the same sort of puddingy face and red hair.'

'How'y'r, Ben?' said Guy holding out a hand to the young-ster.

'I'm okay. How's yourself?'

The complaint, widely circulated, that American children are badly brought up is not necessarily true. This specimen had clearly been taught to be bright and friendly with strangers.

'Come along,' said Guy, taking the little fellow's arm. 'I bet I know someone who's ready for some ice-cream.' The chauffeur, who accompanied them, gathered up Ben's surprisingly voluminous hand luggage and they all moved off to the car.

'I hear you want to see Madame Tussaud's?' said Plum chattily.

'Yes, and the Tower of London.'

After that the two writers may well be pardoned for believing they were in possession of the rightful Ben. It did not occur to them that all small boys are told when they visit London that they will be taken to Madame Tussaud's and the Tower.

During the journey to Onslow Square the child remained sunk in a gloomy silence. When the car drew up in front of the house he looked at it disparagingly.

'Rabbit hutch,' he said.

The remark wounded Plum who was rather proud of his little home. He had no notion that his guest was supposing this to be one of London's luxury hotels.

'This is your room,' he said, leading the way upstairs. 'The bathroom is the third door down the passage.'

'No bathroom?' rejoined Ben with a haughty stare. 'In America, hotels that don't have baths with every room is dumps.'

'Dinner will be in ten minutes.'

'Watcher mean dinner will be in ten minutes? Mom an' me eat dinner when we like.'

Plum went downstairs and joined Guy in the study.

'Correct me in a tendency to dislike this child,' he said. 'I don't mind a little healthy criticism but this blister treats my home as if it were a Bowery flop-joint.'

'He's certainly not what I expected from Marguerite's description.'

'I don't know why a man like Milton insists on propagating his species unless reasonably assured he can do a bit better than this.'

'Wait,' said Guy. He seemed agitated. 'Do you know what has just occurred to me? I'm pretty sure Bob has only one son.'

'One like this is plenty.'

'And that son, whose name as I recall it is Paul, not Ben, is editor of the *Dance Magazine* and, if I am not mistaken, has been married for some years.'

At this point the door was swung open by the Mystery Child.

'Where's my Mom?' he demanded.

'Your mother is on her way to Geneva – or Genoa.'

'You're a liar.'

'See here,' said Guy, 'if you go on like this, there'll be no Tower of London for you.'

'Phooey.'

'And you must be polite to Uncle Plum. He's being very kind to keep you here for a week.'

'A week my foot. We're going back home. My Grannie wants me. Me Pop wants me. My Auntie wants me. I guess most everybody wants me.'

'You guess wrong,' said Plum.

Ben surveyed them malevolently.

'You think 'cause they all want me they'll pay you money to get me back. My Mom'll fix you. She'll get the police after you. They'll get you under the lights. They'll beat you up with rubber hoses – that's what they'll do.' He turned abruptly and left the room.

'What on earth is the child talking about?'

There was a knock followed by the entrance of Robinson.

'Pardon me, sir, but what are your instructions regarding dinner? Master Breckenridge has informed me that under no circumstances will he eat boiled cod.'

' "Master Breckenridge"?'

'I gather from his observations that that is the young gentleman's name, sir.'

'If it is, I shall make it my business to present Mr Bolton's wife with a typewriter.'

Guy leapt to his feet.

'This isn't any question of spelling, of Milton or Wilson. We've got hold of the wrong child!'

'What? Do you think Mr Bolton is right, Robinson?'

'It seems a tenable theory, sir. It explains certain oddities in Master Breckenridge's behaviour.'

'Then for heaven's sake let's race this maverick back to the Lost Property Office.'

The car was summoned, the bags brought down and Master Breckenridge hustled into his coat.

'Where are we going?' he demanded.

'We're taking you back to your mother.'

On the chance that Mrs Breckenridge might have left Victoria in despair, they asked the youngster if he knew where his mother was planning to stay. He shook his head.

'With your approval, sir,' said Robinson, 'I will establish

telephonic communication with all the leading hotels. The Breckenridges are, I believe, wealthy, and I fancy the lady will have booked rooms at the most expensive.'

As they were getting into the car Junior Breckenridge eyed them unpleasantly.

'Are you gorillas taking me for a ride?'

'Don't be crazy.'

'Then let me have your guns.'

He started to frisk them, rubbing his hands over their pockets. Plum pushed him into the car.

As they arrived at the station Junior nipped out of the car and rushed to where he saw a policeman standing.

'I bin kidnapped,' he said. 'I guess it's in the papers. I guess there's a reward – a mighty big reward. You take me to my Mom and you'll get it.'

The policeman turned to Plum and Guy.

'What's all this?' he asked. 'There's been some talk around here about a missing child. Are you the men who made off with him?'

'Sure. These are the ones,' said Junior. 'They know my Mom is rich. One of 'em said so. Get 'em under the lights!'

Speaking at once the two writers tried to explain. Guy pulled out Marguerite's letter and held it out waveringly to the policeman.

'I think you'd better come with me over to the station.'

'Must we? Can't you just take the little fellow and the bags? My man will drive you.'

The policeman was unrelenting. He insisted on taking them to the Westminster Police Station. There they found that a police call had been sent out asking for a report on two men seen leaving Victoria Station with a child and some purloined bags. They had, so the blotter read, joined an accomplice at the wheel of a battered car.

The Wodehouse Sunbeam was far from battered. Whoever had supplied the information was, doubtless, a devotee of crime literature. The sergeant in charge took their names. He had clearly never heard of either of them. Something in Guy's accent made him look up.

'You're an American, aren't you?'

'Yes.'

'Did you know these people in the States?'

'No.'

He eyed Guy keenly. 'Sure you didn't follow them over?'

Plum came to the rescue.

'Mr Bolton is a writer,' he said.

'He has no regular occupation?'

Plum, who might well have been expected to furnish a cutting reply merely faltered 'no'. It was not the stern-faced sergeant that made him go so suddenly jittery, it was Junior. The child had become fascinated by a notice on the station bulletin board headed 'Wanted for Murder', and depicting two thugs who had figured in a Thames warehouse crime. He was now switching his gaze back and forth from the printed portraits to the faces of the two writers. Plum's nerves, already so many tattered dish-rags, could stand no added strain.

'Well,' said the sergeant in a tone that suggested capitulation. 'It's unfortunate you men got hold of the wrong child. It was a piece of carelessness that caused this little lad's mother a lot of anxiety and distress. I have no doubt your excuse is that the other boy resembled this one. But still—'

'What other boy?' interrupted Junior.

'There was another little boy on the train with you that these gentlemen came to meet.'

This sounded better. They were now described as gentlemen.

'That's a lie,' said Junior. 'There was no kid on that train but me. I went through it and through it looking for someone to play with.'

The 'gentlemen' period was short-lived. They were now 'men' again and men in a most uncomfortable position. Junior Breckenridge was driven off to Claridge's with a policeman guarding him. Plum and Guy were still held answering questions regarding the non-existent Ben, their uncertainty as to his precise name, age or appearance imparting a quality of fishiness to their story.

It was on this intensely delicate situation that Robinson entered. He was looking his most dignified and ambassadorial. The sergeant was visibly impressed.

'Who are you?'

'My name is Eugene Robinson, sir. I am Mr Wodehouse's major-domo.'

'His what?'

'Butler,' said Plum.

'Your butler?' It was clear what was passing in the sergeant's mind. An employer of butlers, especially such a butler as this, must, like Cæsar's wife, be above suspicion.

'What about the child these gentlemen were supposed to meet?'

'That is precisely the point that I have come here to elucidate, sir. In the course of my inquiries regarding Mrs Breckenridge, I telephoned the Mayfair Hotel where Mr Bolton resides and was informed that there was a Continental telegram there addressed to him. I took the liberty of having it opened and the contents read to me. It was from Mrs Bolton and conveyed the information that the child Mr Bolton was desired to meet would not, after all, be visiting the Metropolis, the young gentleman's mother having changed her plans. Might I ask, sir,' he added, addressing Plum, 'if you plan to return home shortly? When I left, the cook was expressing anxiety about the soufflé.'

On the way back to Onslow Square Robinson produced the telegram.

'I stopped at the Mayfair and collected this, sir,' he said. 'However, I feared that if I showed it to the sergeant, it might occasion further confusion.'

The telegram read: LITTLE NAN NOT COMING. HER MOTHER CANCELLING GERMANY VISIT. MRS NELSON THANKS YOU AND SENDS REGARDS.'

There was another wire, a cable. It was from Aarons and Freedley, a newly established management, asking Guy if he was prepared to write a show for the Astaires with a score by George Gershwin.

THIRTEEN

I

It was a day or two after this shattering experience that Plum and Guy saw Gertrude Lawrence in a revue called *Rats* at the Vaudeville.

Plum had seen her before in *A to Z* and in the *Midnight Frolic* at the Hotel Metropole, an entertainment that was a close imitation of the one which Flo Ziegfeld had done on the New Amsterdam roof, but in *Rats* she had far greater scope than in either of those vehicles. Her performance affected Guy and Plum rather as his first perusal of Chapman's *Homer* affected the poet Keats. It seemed to them – a view that was to be shared later by the New York public – that she had everything. She could play sophisticated comedy, low comedy, sing every possible type of song, and she looked enchanting. When Guy got back to Mayfair, he wrote her an enthusiastic note in which he said that if she would come to New York he would guarantee to star her in a revue, a musical comedy or a straight comedy, whichever she preferred.

Getting the Ziegfeld spirit, she replied with a six-page telegram which could have been condensed into the words 'Right oh'. She was committed to play in a Charlot revue in New York, but after that she would be at his disposal. (The result of this exchange of civilities was *Oh, Kay*, the musical comedy which Guy and Plum wrote for her with music by George Gershwin and lyrics by his brother Ira when she was finally free to leave André Charlot's management.)

However the immediate problem was the casting of *Sitting Pretty*. Letters passed back and forth with Ray and Jerry who was now back in New York. Frank McIntyre was engaged for the part of Uncle Joe, the sentimental burglar. The sole problem was the two girls who were to take the place of the Duncans. Queenie Smith was decided on for one, but who could play the other?

'I've just had a wire from Ray,' said Guy, bursting in on Plum at work in his study. If we cable "yes" Ray will book Gertrude Bryan.'

'Gertrude Bryan? You don't mean that Gertrude Bryan will come back to the stage?'

'I'm just telling you. All he's waiting for is "yes".'

'He'll get the loudest "yes" he's ever heard. Some cocktails, Robinson, and put your best effort into them. This is an occasion.'

'Oh yes, indeed, sir. In that brief visit I paid to New York with my late employer I had the privilege of seeing the young lady you refer to in *Little Boy Blue*. You have my warmest congratulations, sir.'

There are no doubt by this time a whole generation of voting age who will fail to see the significance of all this enthusiasm. Let them learn now that to have seen Gertrude Bryan in *Little Boy Blue* is to have wandered in a garden of enchantment. Her eyes were like the bluebirds in the spring, and her hair like finches' feathers a-wing. Gertrude Bryan, even more than Marilyn Miller, might well have worn the mantle of Maud Adams, had she not married at the very outset of her career and retired.

'I'll tell you what I think,' said Plum. 'I vote we board the first liner that's sailing and bend to the task of fitting this re-born star with the material that best suits her.'

'Yes, you're right, we mustn't waste a moment.'

'Your tone sounds a bit regretful.'

'Well, Marguerite and I had planned a little trip in the *roulotte*.'

'In the what?'

'Didn't I tell you about it? I suppose you'd call it a caravan, but the front part is a smart little car built by the Minerva people. You pull a lever and the *roulotte* is released and away you dash to do the family shopping.'

'Where did you acquire this monstrosity?'

'It was made for the King of the Belgians but he passed it up and I bought it for Marguerite. It sleeps four and has a bath, a kitchenette and a bar.'

'What, no ball-room?'

'However, I'll forget the *roulotte* until we've got *Sitting Pretty* on. Now where's *The Times*? Let's see what is the first boat going.'

'Don't bother. Robinson carries these matters in his head.'

Even as he spoke, Robinson had entered with the tray containing glasses and shaker.

'If I may be permitted to put two and two together, sir,' said Robinson, 'I fancy your remark indicates an immediate departure for New York.'

'Exactly.'

'The *Mauretania* on Wednesday, sir, the *Majestic* on Saturday.'

'We'll take the *Mauretania*,' said Plum. 'Ask Mrs Wodehouse if she's prepared to sail on such short notice, then book our passage.'

2

But, as Robinson might well have said, *surgit semper aliquid amari*. It is sad to have to record that the last effort of the Princess triumvirate, who had worked together so much and so happily, was their least successful, was in fact a flat failure. Jerry turned out a first-class score, the cast was excellent, the staging and mounting all that could be desired, but Irving, the lad who never made a mistake, had put his finger on it when he had insisted that the Duncans were, as Robinson would have said, of the essence. Charming Gertrude Bryan and clever Queenie Smith, brilliant individually, were not a team. When they met, when they performed together, the electric spark was missing, and the play was so written that these were the vital spots.

Poor *Sitting Pretty*, which had seemed to have so much to offer but which nobody wanted!

'We're like two flower-girls,' said Plum, waxing sentimental. 'Stretching out our small, grubby hands with a pathetic nosegay which the passers-by – blister their insides – curtly ignore as they hurry past.'

'For heaven's sake don't talk about flowers,' said Guy. 'It reminds me of a certain floral horseshoe.'

Who knows? Perhaps it is because of that horseshoe – the Horseshoe of Fate it might be called – that *Sitting Pretty* is a name remembered only as that of a film in which Clifton Webb was baby-sitter to an infant Junior Breckenridge.

3

There was no time for the licking of wounds. Guy had signed contracts with Aarons and Freedley for two shows, one for the Astaires and one to follow Plum's *Beauty Prize* at the Winter Garden. Since the Astaires were in London, playing in *Stop Flirting*, and Aarons and Gershwin also there busily occupied with the preliminaries of the two shows, an immediate return was indicated. As to Plum there was *Jeeves*.

The new Winter Garden show, which Aarons and Freedley were presenting jointly with Grossmith and Laurillard, had been sketched out by Guy on the voyage to America and a scenario sent back, of which the combined management had approved. It was now at the casting-stage and, on arriving in London (he had travelled via Paris), Guy went to report at the Winter Garden, whose bar is the tiny Drury Lane Tavern frequented by Nell Gwyn in her orange-selling days. Plum's *Beauty Prize* was coming to the end of a successful run, and George Grossmith was holding a chorus audition for *Primrose*, which was the name of the new show. He sat with George Gershwin and Alex Aarons, surrounded by pressmen, yesmen, vocal experts and beauty experts, testing applicants as to voice, diction and appearance.

George, though one of the boys in private life, was, in his managerial aspect, rather pompous – nay, even stuffy. He had issued a ukase to the effect that all members of the chorus of *The Beauty Prize* should appear and bring a bit of music with them. He had recently lost a girl to Charlie Cochran because her talent had passed unnoticed in the choruses of *Sally* and *The Cabaret Girl*, and he wasn't having that happen again.

As Guy entered the theatre, coming in through the Nell Gwyn tavern, George was having difficulty in persuading one of the showgirls to demonstrate her vocal powers. It seemed that here was a young lady who, while willing to accept £3 a week for decorating the stage of the Winter Garden for a season or two, very definitely had other fish to fry. She was, as a fryer of fish, to make quite a name for herself. Several names in fact, two of them those of peeresses of the realm.

'Must I sing, Mr Grossmith?'

'Yes, Sylvia, you must. All of you have to sing if you want jobs as showgirls in *Primrose*. The Gershwin score demands it.'

'Oh, very well,' she replied petulantly, and, going down to 'the floats', she handed over a piece of music to the pianist in the pit. The piano struck a chord.

> God save our gracious King,
> Long live our noble King,
> God save the King.

George, a strict observer of ritual, rose and stood at attention. His minions rose and stood at attention. Guy, on his way to announce his arrival, stood at attention.

As the anthem came to the normal stopping point, George started to sit down, but there is more, much more of the fine old choral than is generally known. James Carey is credited with a three-stanza version; in another version John Bull, composer, singer and organist at Antwerp cathedral, has expressed the same sentiment in his own way; while James Oswald, a Scot, who was chamber-music composer to George the Third, also got into the act. A printing is extant giving them all. Sylvia Hawkes sang them all. The pianist stopped playing but that didn't stop Sylvia. They wanted her to sing, did they? Well, sing she would. Of course no one dared to call a halt. The national anthem is sacrosanct – especially if you're an actor-manager clinging to the hope of a belated knighthood.

Sylvia Hawkes said afterwards that she expected to be fired then and there. Perhaps she would have been had she not been so deliciously pretty. There are, it is true, more pretty girls to the square foot in the USA than in the British Isles. But, when they're really trying, the parent race can turn out an article of highly exportable value. Witness Ziegfeld's Dolores, also his Kathleen Martin and his June McKay, witness the Jersey Lily, witness Connie Carpenter, Deborah Kerr and, as we say, Sylvia Hawkes.

Sylvia Hawkes was not only pretty, she had a pretty sense of humour. George Gershwin was swept off his feet by her, so was Lord Ashley, heir of the Earl of Shaftesbury, so was Douglas Fairbanks, Sr, so was Lord Stanley of Alderley and so, finally, was the very sure-footed Mr Clark Gable. All of these, except George Gershwin, laid their fortunes and/or coronets at Sylvia's feet. George might well have done the same had he possessed at the time either fortune or coronet. Nobody ever cut a wider swathe than Sylvia Hawkes. But then, if you have those looks, combined with those brains, not to mention that charm, you don't have to invent a new mouse-trap to have the world beat a path to your door.

Primrose did somewhat less well than the most decorative member of its cast. It managed to hang on for 255 performances, which was a shade better than its predecessor, *The Beauty Prize*, and definitely better than it deserved.

It had one engaging ditty in which Leslie Henson and Claude Hulbert were overcome with pity when recalling the fate of some of the heroines of history. One quatrain ran:

> Oh, isn't it terrible what they did to Mary-Queen-of-Scots?
> When playing at St Andrew's she would *not* replace div-ots,
> So, after quite a bothering day,
> They locked her up in Fotheringay,
> Oh, isn't it terrible what they did to Mary-Queen-of-Scots?

Though not by Wodehouse, it was written in the Wodehouse style with triple rhymes. It somehow made Guy feel more at home.

FOURTEEN

I

That 1924 season in London when the first two of the Gershwin
series of shows were written was one of extraordinary gaiety.
Was it because the Astaires were there to hobnob with – the
Astaires, George Gershwin and his piano, George Grossmith
who knew everyone in London?

Adele had the faculty of making any party from two to
fifty-two into a success. Such words as enchanting, delicious,
captivating did not seem like tired adjectives from a Hollywood
pressbook when applied to her. How nice if she could have gone
on and on with brother Fred. How nice if George Gershwin
could have gone on and on writing for them. His music suited
them to perfection.

One weekend Guy encountered Adele at Knole. Knole is
one of the top great houses of England. For those who don't
know it, or who have not read the books of Victoria Sackville-
West, in which its atmosphere is wonderfully evoked, a thumb-
nail sketch might be in order.

Belonging to Elizabeth's reign, Knole is all of one style as so
few great houses are, and so is generally conceded to be the
finest example of domestic Tudor architecture in England. It
is built on a chronological plan containing 365 rooms, fifty-two
staircases, twelve courtyards, and twenty bathrooms – including one that is haunted. It is packed with art treasures, Van-
dycks, Reynolds, Gainsboroughs and Romneys elbowing each
other for the spot on the wall with the best light. All in all,
quite a lot of house.

At the time Adele and Guy were weekending there, the
family were living in reduced circumstances. They were

huddled into a corner of the cosy edifice, where their simple wants were tended by a staff of only twenty-two servants. The gardens, which had been laid out on a scale commensurate with that of the house, had fifteen gardeners hustling round to do the work which had once commanded the services of thirty.

What were Broadway characters doing in such surroundings? Well, Adele had already had several offers to supply her with some such setting of her own, but Guy—?

Guy was there because Lady Sackville had also been, but a few years before, a Broadway character. She had appeared in Guy's first play *The Rule of Three* and then again in *Polly-with-a-Past* . . . Anne Meredith, a charming and talented actress.

A wonderful dinner, some extraordinary bridge, a little dancing – there was a fresh supply of American phonograph records, and Adele Astaire to dance with, if you could buck the line.

Then came the hour when whisky-and-sodas were at the nightcap stage and the company drifted into corners, breaking up into little groups of fours, threes and twos. Lord Sackville made announcement of what the doings would be on the morrow, church or golf, and an expedition, by invitation of the Astors, to visit nearby Hever, home of the Boleyns, where poor Anne had first met Henry. These suggestions were all on a take-it-or-leave-it basis. You could breakfast when you pleased from the row of hot-plates in the dining-room. You could lunch or not as you pleased, so long as you told the butler. The only 'must' was the cocktail-hour, dinner and a white tie. That was weekending in England as still surviving in 1924. Not much left of that sort of thing today, my masters, save only at Blandings Castle.

Guy was paddling round his bedroom in his pyjamas, inspecting the Rowlandsons on its panelled walls, when there was a knock at the door. He opened it to find Adele attired in a heady negligé.

'Come right in,' he said heartily. 'This is what I call good old-fashioned hospitality. I didn't know Anne made such charming provision for her guests.'

'It's a cute idea,' said Adele, 'but I'm holding out for a

wedding ring and I understand the one your girlfriends used to rent their apartments with is gone.'

'Then to what do I owe the pleasure?'

'I want you to change rooms with me. I've got the haunted bathroom.'

'Haunted bathroom? Must be rather a modern ghost?'

'Yes, and the poor thing is very upset or nervous or something.'

'How do you know?'

'Well, every now and then you'll hear the johnny flush.'

'And there's nobody there?'

'No, but the eerie part of it is that this particular convenience is the difficult kind. You know how it is with English privies – there are the overheads, the buttons, the levers, the foot release and ye olde worlde pull-up. Then with the overheads with dangling handle, of which this specimen is one, for some smart, quick pull, with others a long, steady, slow one. This one's a devil – the coax-me-variety.'

'But yet the ghost?'

'Oh, the ghost has no trouble at all, just a gruesome rattle of the chain followed by an immediate "whoosh". Somehow it gives you a creepy feeling when a ghost seems to be more at home in your room than you are. I know I won't sleep a wink.'

'We'll change, of course. I'm rather keen on ghosts. A bit of an amateur psychic researcher.'

The shiftover was effected. The phenomenon continued at intervals and was certainly disturbing. Eventually Guy wriggled down under the covers so that hearing was sufficiently impeded for him to get to sleep. He was still in a state of concealment when a soft-footed lady's maid entered, drew the curtains, and then laid him out a pair of demi-tasse shorts, a lace brassière, a pair of stockings and a fetching sports-costume.

He wakened during this operation but, being by inclination a slow getter-up, he decided to remain doggo. As he had supposed would happen, the maid withdrew without disturbing him. He dozed again and this time was awakened by what he presumed to be the ghost taking a bath. He cocked an eye in the direction of the bathroom and was startled to see a feminine form, partly concealed by a towel, flit across the open doorway.

He had evidently made some slight noise, for the nymph came to the bathroom door rubbing herself with the towel. She was not only very pleasant to look at but she was a lady whose name was one of the most honoured in Debrett.

'I thought you wouldn't mind my coming in here, dahling,' she said. 'George was barricaded in ours and you know what men are in a bathroom. They fall asleep in the tub, I believe.'

Guy made some inarticulate noise from under the covers, pitched in as high a key as he could manage. The lovely peeress donned her robe and started out. As she passed the bed, she gave Guy a hearty smack.

'Get up, you lazy girl,' she said. 'We're playing golf, remember?'

She went out into the hall and Guy heard a sharp cry. A moment later Adele appeared.

'For heaven's sake what's happened?' she said. 'I just ran into Alex and when she saw me she almost fainted dead away.'

Guy put on a scarf and dressing-gown and went down to breakfast. Although the custom for ladies was a bedroom tray there was no rule in the matter. Adele elected to go with him. They found one of Britain's forty marquises lifting the covers of a line of silver hot-plates, weighing his choice.

'Did you come into my room this morning and take a bath?' inquired Guy.

'Me? No, but—'

'Funny,' said Guy, 'I'd have sworn it was you. Of course I wasn't properly awake.'

The marquis replaced the lid on the kedgeree.

'Excuse me a minute. I must pop up and have a word with the better half. She was in a bit of a dither about something.'

He disappeared.

'Quite the gentleman, what?' laughed Adele. 'I suppose it's the influence of all those belted earls looking down on you from the walls.'

2

'So you've been hobnobbing with the upper-crusters, have you?' said Plum, meeting Guy on his return from Knole. 'I remember the last time I dined with Johnny Galsworthy—'

'When was that?'

'Two days ago. It was the first time, too. Ethel met Mrs Galsworthy at a garden party – the house we've taken for the summer is near his – and she invited us to dinner. A very charming woman, we thought her.'

'Did he know your books?'

'He'd just bought one.'

'How do you know he had "just" bought it?'

'Because there was a mark in it. It seems it's been his habit when he stops reading to make a pencil note in the margin, so he'll know where he was.'

'Which book was it?'

'*Right Ho, Jeeves.* The mark was on the side of page ten.'

'Did he say anything matey like, "I laughed my pants off at that chapter in which Gussie Fink-Nottle presents the prizes?" '

'I somehow gathered the impression that he found it more tactful not to broach the subject.'

'Just you and Ethel?'

'Good Lord, no. There were twelve or possibly fourteen guests. As we took our seats at the dinner-table Galsworthy immediately began to discuss the deteriorating effect of educational uniformity on the incidence and development of genius.'

'You don't mean that you had to talk about that?'

'Apparently it's a time-honoured custom. The woman next to me told me that Galsworthy abominates desultory conversation.'

'But what happened when the subject became exhausted?'

'It never did. If the conversation lagged, Galsworthy would rap on the table with the end of his knife and present a new aspect of the problem. "To what extent is genius influenced by the educational standards of parents; with special reference to the cases of Thomas Chatterton and Shakespeare?" '

'What a dinner!'

'I was punch drunk by the time we got to the sweet.'

3

Lady be Good was the new Bolton-Gershwin show for the Astaires, and as soon as the script was ready Guy sailed for

New York to help with the staging. Aarons and Freedley's
idea was to make *Lady be Good* the start of a new series of musical
comedies like those at the old Princess only on a larger scale,
and Guy, while he approved of the scheme, felt a certain
melancholy at the thought that he would not be working with
Plum. George Gershwin always stipulated that his brother Ira
should do his lyrics, and Plum did not blame him, for he had a
great admiration for Ira's work. Ira Gershwin was the man who
wrote the immortal couplet:

> Let's sing to every citizen and for'ner
> 'Prosperity is just around the corner'.

The substitution of George for Jerry did not bother Guy. The
young man who had played the piano at the rehearsals of *The
Second Century Show* was beginning to look uncommonly like a
genius. But it would seem all wrong, working without Plum.
There would undoubtedly be a lot of success, but there wouldn't
be the same fun. It was with a pang that Guy envisaged the
end of the partnership which had begun on that Christmas
Eve after the first performance of *Very Good Eddie*.

The opening of his *Grounds for Divorce* at the St James's did
nothing to cheer him up. Madge Titheradge, Owen Nares,
and Lawrence Grossmith were the featured players, and very
good they were . . . till on the second night Lawrence collapsed
and was taken to hospital, and almost simultaneously Madge
Titheradge developed laryngitis and became practically inaudible for three weeks. It surprised Guy that Owen Nares
did not fall a victim to some wasting sickness, for once bad luck
hits a show, it seldom knows where to stop.

'You're on the right side of the fence,' he said to Plum.
'Novels don't give you the headaches plays do.'

Lady be Good was a success. The first scene of Act One
showed the Astaires – playing brother and sister – thrown out
with their few goods and chattels on the sidewalk. Adele,
behaving as she unquestionably would have done in real life,
arranged the furniture neatly about a lamp-post, hung up a
'God Bless Our Home' motto and with the help of a passing
workman – destined to become the hero – attached the perco-

lator and fixed the hydrant so that water would be constantly available.

After which, of course, it began to rain, and she and Fred did a number called 'Hang On To Me', dancing together under a big umbrella.

Given perfect artists like Fred and Adele, it was just the sort of charming little scene to start a musical comedy off with a bang and, this being so, Alex Aarons, being a manager, could see no virtue in it. Only Guy's proviso that this would have to be done over his dead body had saved it from being thrown into the discard after the dress rehearsal.

He was behind on the opening night when Alex Aarons suddenly appeared, pale and agitated and reproachful.

'I told you!' he cried. 'I told you how it would be if we kept that scene in. They're howling and booing!'

'Not so much howling and booing,' said Guy, 'as cheering their heads off. You don't often hear cheering like that in a theatre. The scene has knocked them cock-eyed. But of course you're the boss and what you say goes, so we'll cut it out tomorrow night.'

'Over my dead body,' said Alex.

Lady be Good was a smash-hit and was equally successful when eventually it arrived in London. There, after a long run, it closed the famous old Empire. The Astaires appeared in one more Gershwin show, *Funny Face*, after which Adele closed her career with a triumphant performance in *The Band Wagon*, by George S. Kaufman, Howard Dietz and Arthur Schwartz. She then married the Duke of Devonshire's second son and retired to Lismore Castle in Ireland, leaving a gap that can never be filled. Fred struggled on without her for a while, but finally threw his hand in and disappeared. There is a rumour that he turned up in Hollywood.

4

It was two years before Guy was able to leave America. He had done several shows there, among them the second of the Aarons and Freedley series – *Tiptoes*, written with Fred Thompson – and he came away with a couple of contracts in his pocket. Philip Goodman, an advertising man turned manager, wanted him to do a big musical for Clark and McCullough with score and lyrics by a new team named Kalmar and Ruby. This subsequently became the very successful *The Ramblers*. (In passing, it was to Philip Goodman that Jerry Kern, arriving in his office to discuss a new piece and meeting the manager for the first time, introduced himself with the historic words 'Good morning, Mr Goodman. I'm Kern. I hear you're a son of a bitch, and you probably aren't – and you've heard I'm a son of a bitch, and I most certainly am.'

The other contract was with Aarons and Freedley for a musical for Gertrude Lawrence, who had written to Guy saying that she was now available. Guy had debated whether to take her to Aarons and Freedley or to Ziegfeld, and it was George Gershwin's connection with Alex and Vinton that tipped the scale in their favour (and eventually put several hundred thousand dollars in their bank accounts). The most attractive aspect of the thing to Guy was that the book was to be written in collaboration with Plum. The old firm was in being again.

Marguerite had returned to Paris and the Opéra Comique. She met Guy at Le Havre with the *roulotte* and Peggy, and they had their long-postponed trip through the château country. After ten days of perfect weather they rumbled back from Châlons to Paris in a torrential downpour, and then Guy had to go to London to start work with Plum on the Gertie Lawrence show.

'Why don't you come with me?' he said to Marguerite when they were back in the studio.

'How can I? They've given me *Thaïs*, the one role I've always wanted to sing. Besides,' said Marguerite, 'you're going to be terribly busy with those two shows to write. You won't want to be bothered with Peggy and me.'

Guy agreed that there was certainly no worse company than an author in the throes of composition.

'*L'absence est à l'amour ce qu'est au feu le vent. Il éteint le petit, il allume le grand.*'

'Since I recognize the word *vent*,' said Guy, 'I conclude that that is something about absence being like the wind. Or does *vent* mean stomach?'

'The wind puts out small flames but fans strong ones.'

'It's humiliating, this language thing,' said Guy. 'There's that daughter of ours – no ball of fire, as you must admit – and I'll bet she grabbed it right off the bat. At three years old!'

'It's your own fault. Why don't you learn French?'

'I've tried, but I don't seem to get anywhere. I decided to start by learning how to count, because, having had some experience with the French I thought that – next to being able to say, *"Où est le Messieurs?"* – that would come in most useful. And I got along fine till I stubbed my toe on "seventy". Apparently *"septante"* wouldn't do.'

'It's *soixante-dix*.'

'Exactly. "Sixty-ten". A fine way to say "seventy". And when you get to "eighty", it isn't "seventy-ten", it's "four-twenty". And they call the French logical!'

'As a matter of fact, the Belgians do say *"septante"*. The Italians say *"Sessanta," "settanta", "ottanta"*. And in Spanish it's *"sesenta", "ochenta".*'

'It must be great to be educated. How about this young woman goggling at me over there on the sofa? I suppose she's got the whole thing down cold?'

'Oh, yes, she's wonderful at languages. You understood what Daddy and Mummy were talking about, didn't you, darling?'

Peggy nodded.

'Well, say those figures for Daddy.'

'*Sechzig, siebzig, achtzig.*'

'Before she says it in Russian,' said Guy bitterly, 'I'll call up and get that reservation on the Golden Arrow.'

'Flèche d'Or,' said Peggy.

She danced away and her richly bedecked mother took her place.

'I want words with you, Mister,' she said.

'Alas, they must be brief.'

'As per usual.'

'Alas again. I have a ship to catch.'

'With sailings widely spaced this time of year.'

'The occasional marriage. I have a feeling we should be introduced before getting into bed together.'

'You said to me, you'll have to commute.'

'I well remember. I'm not blaming you in the least but what about calling it a day? You're a success in one continent, I'm a success in another.'

There was a pause.

'Before they make a joke of it,' she added.

'Call it a day, you said,' Guy repeated it thoughtfully. 'It's been a nice day.'

'A wonderful day!' she repeated and held out her arms to him. They went into an embrace.

'You mustn't miss your boat.'

Peggy reappeared as she spoke.

'I just came to kiss you good-bye, Daddy,' she said.

5

In London Guy found Plum finishing an adaptation of Molnar's *Spiel Im Schloss* – later produced in New York and London as *The Play's the Thing*, and in order to be able to give uninterrupted attention to *Oh, Kay*, the Gertie Lawrence show, they took the train at Paddington and settled in at the Impney Hotel outside what is, next to A. E. Housman's Clun, the quietest place under the sun – Droitwich in Worcestershire, where the brine-baths are.

In the long English twilights that last until ten at night – the faint western glow may continue even later – they paced the terrace of the Impney – it's hard to say the name without giving the impression that you have a hare-lip – and worked out their plot, pausing occasionally to listen to the nightingales which collect in these parts in gangs. It was probably at Droitwich that the conversation – recorded by *Punch* – between the romantic man and his deaf friend took place. 'Have you ever,' sighed the romantic man as they strolled through the lanes one summer night, 'heard anything so perfectly wonderful as these nightingales?' 'Eh?' said the deaf man. 'I said, "Aren't the nightingales simply marvellous"?' 'Huh?' 'The nightingales. They're superb, don't you think? The nightingales. The *nightingales*.' The deaf man shook his head regretfully. 'I'm sorry,' he said. 'I can't hear a word you're saying. These nightingales are kicking up such an infernal noise.'

Worcestershire is next door to Shropshire, and they drove there one day in the hope of finding Blandings Castle and catching a glimpse of Lord Emsworth's pig. In this they were unsuccessful, but they found the minute hamlet of Stableford, seven miles outside the town of Bridgnorth, where Plum had lived as a young man.

'Pretty remote sort of spot,' said Guy, studying the old home through the window of the car.

'Yes, quite remote,' Plum agreed. 'I loved it. I've never found a better place for work. At the age of twenty I once wrote fourteen short stories there in ten days. They were never printed, which was a break for the reading public, but I wrote 'em.'

'Had you any neighbours in this grim solitude?'

'One family about a mile away. We quarrelled with them two days after we arrived and never spoke to them again. It was milk that caused the rift. At least, they said it was milk when they sold it to us, and we said it was skim-milk. Harsh words and dirty looks passed to and fro, and the thing culminated in us cutting them or them cutting us, we never quite made out which. That always happens in rural England. It's pure routine. Directly you have moved in and got your trunks unpacked, you have a hell of a row with the nearest neighbours about milk. Make a note of that.'

'I will.'

'Father sorts out his things, has a wash and brush-up, and looks in on Mother. "All set?" he asks. "All set," says Mother. "Fine," says Father. "Then let's go and beat the stuffing out of those swindling crooks down the road who've been selling us that so-called milk." And off they go, Father with his Roget's *Thesaurus* under his arm in case he runs short of adjectives.'

'It sounds a jolly life.'

'Oh, it was. Though my mother didn't like it much. She found it a little on the lonely side. My father had seen this house advertised in one of the papers, and he and she went down to take a look at it. As they were driving away, my mother said, "Well, thank goodness I shall never see that awful place again." "Eh?" said my father. "I was saying that it was a relief to me to think I should never see that frightful house again." "Oh, the house?" said my father. "You are speaking of the house. I was meaning to tell you about that. I've signed a twenty-year lease on it." Victorian husbands were like that. Men of steel.'

'I'd like to see you springing that sort of surprise on Ethel.' Plum shivered.

'Don't say such things, even in fun. But, as I was saying, I loved the place. Miles of smiling countryside, and not a Henry W. Savage to be seen as far as the eye could reach. The only thing I didn't like in my formative, or Stableford, period was the social stuff. Owners of big estates round about would keep inviting me for the weekend.'

'*You?*'

'I don't wonder you're surprised. Even today I'm about as pronounced an oaf as ever went around with his lower jaw drooping and a glassy look in his eyes, but you have literally no conception what I was like in my early twenties. Do you remember what Brichoux said about the chambermaid in the third act of *The Girl Behind The Gun*?'

' "She was a nice girl, but she had no conversation." '

'That was me. I was completely inarticulate. Picture to yourself a Trappist monk with large feet and a tendency to upset tables with priceless china on them, and you will have the young Wodehouse. The solution of the mystery of my mixing with the County is that my brother Armine was very popular. He played the piano like a Gershwin and could converse pleasantly on any subject you cared to bring up, and I suppose what happened was that one of these territorial magnates would run into Mother at a garden party or somewhere and say "I do wish you would persuade your son to come to us for the weekend." "Why, of course," Mother would reply. "My sons will be there with their hair in a braid." The magnate would start like a man seeing a serpent in his path.

' "Did you say *sons*?"

' "Yes, I have two – Armine and Pelham."

' "Oh? . . . Well, of course, we were rather thinking of Armine, but if Pelham can come as well, we shall be charmed . . . that is to say . . . oh, yes, charmed."

'And he would totter off and tell his wife that the curse had come upon them and she had better put the best china away till I had blown over.'

6

Gertie Lawrence was back in England after playing in the second edition of *The Charlot Revue* on Broadway. Guy and Plum felt that it would be advisable to see her and discuss her part in *Oh, Kay*. They telephoned her and arranged a meeting at her flat and drove back to London through those delicious Cotswold villages, Moreton-in-the-Marsh, Stow-on-the-Wold, Lower Slaughter, Weston-sub-Edge and possibly those hamlets of which Plum had written in his Mulliner stories, Chickenham-infra-Mud, Lower Smattering-on-the-Wissel and Higgleford-cum-Wortlebury-beneath-the-Hill! There was time to do some straying. They were not seeing Gertie till teatime.

On the piano in her sitting-room there was a photograph of a child dancing. It caught the eye immediately as they came in.

'Is that you?' inquired Plum.

'Yes, dearies, that's me at the time of my début in the Brixton Pantomime.'

'You took to the stage early?'

'For a good year before that photo was taken I'd been learning the ABC of my trade from dear old Italia Conti.'

'What a lot of distinguished pupils she had!'

'I'll tell you a little tale about one of them. It was the annual show that was put on for friends and relatives every June. I was just under ten – my birthday's 4th July – so you can imagine my surprise when, at the first rehearsal, Madame Conti's assistant handed me a part. Most of the children were "pixies" or "villagers" but I was to be a character. I was going to see my name on the programme: "*Jane* . . . Gertrude Lawrence." The theatre has given me a lot of thrills but never one quite as big as that moment when I held my first part in my hand.

' "Jane" it said on the cover. Jane was one of a party of children who steal out into the garden on Midsummer Night and find the flowers have changed into Little People and are giving a ball, a crafty lead into "The Dance of the Flowers", chief feature of this juvenile turkey. I delayed before turning the slightly battered blue cover, savouring the great moment. I opened it. There was a single line: "Oh, look, children! Pansy has turned into a Pierrot and he's dancing with Columbine!"

'I was standing there weighing the problem of how best to characterize Jane when I heard Mme Conti's voice say: "That's your cue, Gertie." Good God! I had missed my first cue. Properly flustered, I went charging on to the stage and said, "Jane pants."

' "Jane pants? You don't *say* that, dear. That's the stage direction. You've been running and you're excited."

' "Of course. I was upset at being late on cue, I just read it without thinking."

' "Well, you *must* think. Never do anything on the stage without thinking. Now make the entrance again and say the line."

' "Oh, look, children! Pansy has changed into a Pierrot and he's dancing with Concubine."

'The brats sniggered. Mme Conti explained patiently that the name was "Columbine", adding that if I said "Concubine" on the afternoon of the performance some of the parents might not think this was a very nice school to send their child to.

' "Whenever you're flustered, take a long, deep breath and pause. Always remember a slight pause never hurts." I paused. I took a long, deep breath. As I did so I heard a childish treble voice repeat my line, reading it beautifully, with wonder and excitement and just that little catch in the breath that was indicated by "Jane pants." "Don't you think, Mme Conti," the voice went on, and it had now changed to a budding baritone, "don't you think it would be *safer* if *I* said the line?"

'I was stunned, speechless, unable to find words in which to protest.

' "Yes, dear," I heard Mme Conti say. "I think perhaps it would be, I'm sure Gertie won't mind. Give Noel the part, will you, dear?" '

'It wasn't—?' exclaimed Guy.

'Yes, it was, duckie. Noel Coward, the little ham. If I had had a blunt instrument in my hand at the time the English speaking stage would have lost one of its most brilliant talents.'

'He calmly walked off with your first part?'

'Darned unprofessional, I call it,' laughed Plum.

'Yes, but wait, boys. For years I've had a dream. In it I'm playing opposite him and, on opening night, just as we're coming to his favourite line, his most amusing bon mot, I say it myself and then give him the cue. Then, when he's left flat on his bumpty, I whisper, "Come on, Jane, old girl. Let's hear you pant."

'And let me tell you something – it's coming, Gertie's Revenge!' She waved a hand at her desk where stood a photograph of this distinguished author-actor-composer, lovingly inscribed. 'He's writing a play in which I'm to be with him. He calls it *Private Lives* and it's to be ready by the time I'm finished with your show.'

'Well, much as I look forward to that opening night, I trust it's a long way off,' said Plum.

'So do I,' said Gertie. 'And now you boys help yourselves to drinks and tell me about this *Oh, Kay*.'

7

Oh, Kay was a musical comedy about bootleggers. It was 1926 and the noble experiment had been in operation for seven years. People had learned to cope with it at least to the extent of having their liquor analysed or, in an emergency, of pouring some into a saucer in a darkened room, setting fire to it, and, if it burned with a reddish flame, changing their bootlegger.

It was the 'Hooch Age', and the spirit that made bath-tub gin (the human spirit, not the stuff you bought at the druggist with a doctor's prescription) was the same devil-may-care quality that accounted for flagpole-sitters, marathon dancing and the bull market.

It is hard to imagine two worlds more different than the one the authors said good-bye to as they left the Impney and that into which they plunged upon disembarking from the *Aquitania*.

It was not only missing the wine card from which they could select, even in that unfashionable retreat, a Chambertin or a Pouilly, as well as the bottle of crusted 'Taylor '96' that would supply the accompaniment to their after-dinner savoury. The whole tempo of life was different. People walked faster, laughed louder and became nervously excited – lost their tempers more readily.

The pace had, seemingly, quickened since the *Sitting Pretty* period of two years ago, the last time the two writers had been in New York together. When they dropped in at the Ritz barber shop on the afternoon of their arrival, the barbers of their adjacent chairs both got immediately on to the subject of stocks as if that were the one thing that anybody would want to talk about. The market had taken another upward spurt, it seemed, and each of the lads manipulating the razors had come appreciably nearer to East Street that everyone seemed bent on moving into.

'Have-a you gotta the Alice Charmers?' inquired Plum's barber.

' "Alice Charmers"? Never met the lady.'

The barber laughed.

'Lady! It sure acta like a lady. De mosta sweet stock on de board.'

'You watcha your foot with thatta Alice,' said the other barber. ' "Like a lady," you say. Sure, a lady you no canna trust.'

The coloured boy shining Guy's shoes looked up.

'I got a friend uptown made $400 last week. Beds it was. He bought beds an' sold 'em again. $400 he made.'

'$400!' said the barber disparagingly. 'Whatsa $400?'

'It ain't hay,' said the coloured boy. 'He's gwine back in again an' he's buying a couple for me.'

'Coupla beds?'

'No, couple of shares.'

'Oh, it's Simmons's beds?'

'That's right. Mr Simmons's beds.'

'There's a new bed company started,' said the manicurist, who was sitting at her small table reading the paper. 'It'll put Simmons clean out of business.'

'Howsa dat, Elsie?' inquired one of the barbers.

'One of my customers was telling me about it. He's in on the ground floor. They got wonderful improvements – buttons you

press. One closes the window, another turns on the bath water.
They're in the head of the bed. Then there's a radio that you
listen to while you go to sleep. It's under your pillow. No one
can hear it but you. And if there's someone in bed with you,
they can listen to a different programme under their pillow.'

The barber removed the towel from Plum's face and pushed
the chair into an erect position.

'What you tink, boss? You tink datta bed business is good
thing for to putta de money?'

Plum didn't know.

'I'd like to get the name of the company,' said Guy. 'I've a
theme song for them to play on those radios of theirs.'

He started to chant:

> Bed, bed, beautiful bed,
> Pull it all over your head
> Wrap up your heels in it
> Have all your meals in it
> Make a hotel of your bed.

'What's that?' inquired Plum.

'A relic of my pre-Wodehouse days.'

> Though your wife may desert you
> Don't let that fact hurt you
> So long as she leaves you the bed.

'There's a lot more, four verses and four refrains if you'd care
to hear them?'

'Some other time,' said Plum, stepping out of the chair.

'I might have made a lyric writer,' said Guy, 'if I'd stuck to
it.'

Plum wasn't listening. The barber was reciting a list of good
stock-buys based on information gleaned from customers. He
wasn't listening to that either.

'This country's gone nuts,' he said, as they made their way
down the stair.

'Shall we have dinner in the Oak Room or the Oval Room?'

'I never like the Oak Room at night. It's depressing.'

'On the other hand in the Oval Room you will have to listen
to Vecsey playing *The Rose of China* – and that is even more
depressing.'

They were greeted at the door of the Oak Room by the younger of the Ritz's two 'Theodores'.

'What about a drink, Theodore?'

'Certainly, Mr Bolton. Two old customers, of course.'

When the drinks arrived with a long lemon twist disguising them as 'horse-necks', Guy asked Theodore if the essential ingredient was of unquestioned reliability. Theodore reassured him.

'But I heard that two Detroit millionaires woke up dead after drinking some bootleg hooch in this hotel.'

Theodore explained that if the story were true (it was) the thing had nothing to do with the hotel.

The gentlemen in question, if they ever existed (he was admitting nothing), had sent a bell-boy to a bootlegger they knew of and he had given them a bottle of whisky made from alcohol that the government had poisoned.

'You don't mean to tell us that the government are running a poisoning department?'

'Oh, yes, Mr Wodehouse. You've got to be very careful today. They're putting formaldehyde in it.'

'Embalming fluid?'

'Yes, sir, and wood alcohol. The enforcement people think it's the best way to stop drinking.'

'It stopped those two Detroit boys, all right.'

'One would think that even Andy Volstead might consider death a somewhat severe punishment for infraction of his famous Act.'

Theodore shook his head. Under the Baumes Law a woman had, only last week, been sent to prison for life for selling a pint of gin. Rum-runners were frequently shot down by government officers when crossing the Canadian border. The figure of 197 persons killed by prohibition agents had just been published.

They asked Theodore for the names of some reliable speakeasies. He recommended The Hyena Club, The Ha! Ha!, The Jail Club and The Day Breakers.

'We're interested in the subject because we're writing a play in which bootlegging is the main theme,' explained Plum.

It was a few minutes later that Bob Benchley strolled in.

'Well, as I live and attempt to breathe,' said Bob. 'If it isn't

"Book and Lyrics". How are you, lads, and when does it open?'

They invited him to join them for dinner, and he said he would try to peck a bit, though not having much appetite. He was feeling a little down at the moment, he explained, as he had not yet shaken off the hangover caused by attending a party on the previous night.

'Was it a pleasant party?'

'I can't remember, but I think so. Bob Barbour was our host. Do you know Bob?'

'Yes, quite well.' Robert Barbour, the brother of the New Jersey Senator, was an old friend.

'Did you ever hear the story about him and his private stock?'

'No.'

'Thank God. Now it can be told. He kept it in an old family manse which was next door to the old family plant at Paterson, New Jersey, where I fancy, from the fact that they have so much of it, they print money, and came a day when he decided to move in to his apartment in New York.'

'He was taking a risk, wasn't he?'

'A grave risk. The one thing that wakes the fiend that sleeps in the authorities is someone conveying potables across a state line. In some of the more tolerable communities you are given the benefit of a trial, but the general view is that this is a bit sissy.'

'We live in stirring times.'

'We do, indeed. Well, Bob, knowing this, decided not to risk any minion's hide but to carry through the operation himself. So he loaded the stuff into his station-wagon, covered it over with some rugs and started to wend his way to Gomorrah-on-Hudson. And hardly had he wended a couple of parasangs when he heard that most unpleasant of all noises, the whine of a following motor-cycle.'

'Golly!'

'You may well say "Golly!" It was late. The road was empty. There could be no doubt that it was he who was the object of the attention of the hellhound of the law. He tried turning a corner quickly and doubling back on his tracks, but nothing could shake off the pursuer. Just clear of the town the state trooper rolled up beside him and signalled to him to stop.

'Mr Barbour?'

'Y-y-y-yes.'

'Look, Mr Barbour,' said the state trooper. 'You're a drinking man, aren't you? Could I interest you in some of our stock? We've got the best line of wet goods in Bergen County'.

Guy was impressed.

'Is that a true story?'

'You bet it's true. I could tell you a dozen more of a similar nature, if you like your stories by the dozen. I'll tell you what you two ought to do, if, as I understand it, you are writing about rum-running on Long Island. You should get this R. Barbour of whom I have been speaking to take you on that floating café of his that he calls a yacht to view the liquor fleet off Montauk. Scores of launches and fishing boats darting back and forth like nesting swallows. It's a heartening sight for those of a convivial kidney. I use the word playfully. Most of us old-timers have only half a kidney left after a seven-years' bout with prohibition.'

Guy and Plum thought of the Impney and George, the head waiter, leaning over with the wine-card.

'Since it is so warm this evening, sir, perhaps a glass of Château Yquem instead of the port? We still have a little of the '92. A very engaging wine, sir.'

'Everything ends in "—est" over here,' said Guy. 'When this country makes a bloomer, it's a beaut.'

8

Oh, Kay was a great success and so was Gertie Lawrence after which the play went to England, where Gertie, in sole command, pinched the good lines out of other people's parts and put them in her own.

Plum too went to Europe, choosing the French Riviera as his domicile, while Guy went to Hollywood where he wrote *The Love Parade* for Maurice Chevalier, making the transition from writing for the stage to writing for films with astonishing ease, but only because he had the helpful tutelage of that great Austrian director, Ernst Lubitsch. He went on to write *The*

Love Doctor and collaborated on *The Yellow Ticket* for Elissa Landi and Laurence Olivier.

All this covered quite a lengthy period in which Guy and 'the little thing' bought them a charming house in Beverly Hills and settled down with a dog, a cat and a parrot that had an astonishing range of the English language at its lowest.

And then came a day in which Ethel Wodehouse appeared with the news that she had just signed a contract for Plum with Metro-Goldwyn-Meyer to give them his services for the length of a year.

After the longest lapse there was to be in their joint lives, the two were once more together.

'What is to happen to the wonderful stream of books about Jeeves and Bertie, Blandings, Uncle Henry and the rest?' Guy asked her.

'He can keep on with those as well,' Ethel replied. 'You know how easy writing is for him.'

'I know how easy it looks,' Guy responded.

They were in a beautiful Cadillac that Ethel had just bought, on their way to meet Plum in Pasadena. The train was the famed Santa Fe wonder, The Chief. Guy was thrilled as the familiar figure came down the steps.

The two old friends embraced. Guy noticed that Plum's hand was trembling slightly.

'Let's get going,' he said. 'These two bags are all I've got on me.' He added, 'And I want to have a look at the grand new car.'

Guy reflected that he still knew Plum better than anyone else did. There was someone on that train that he didn't want to meet.

In the car Guy said, 'You still need me to tie your bow ties for you,' and they both laughed. Plum knew that Guy knew there had been some happening that had shaken him.

Arrived at the Beverly Hills Hotel, there were cordial greetings, hearty handshakes, someone took a couple of snapshots of the two writers and then Guy whisked Plum away to what was to be his writing room until he and Ethel took possession of the big Spanish-roofed hacienda with the gorgeous swimming-pool that Ethel had taken for the coming year.

There was a momentary silence and then Plum said, 'Can you put your mind back to *Oh, Lady, Lady*?'

'To the greatest of our Princess Theatre's triumphs, when the doyen of New York critics wrote a tribute in verse and Dorothy Parker proclaimed. . . .'

Plum interrupted him. 'And you can put your mind back to the five weeks we spent touring various cities working to get the show in shape for New York?'

'When we were like one cosy little family the world forgot.'

'And where we shared a giant hotel suite with Marion Davies which her boyfriend was paying for,' said Plum.

'And where P. G. Wodehouse sowed his one wild oat,' said Guy.

'I've told you that wasn't true.'

'But you told Ethel it was.'

'I was tired of arguing and thought if I said yes it would end the thing and we could get to talking about something else.'

'I hope Ethel appreciates the wonderful compliments you pay her.'

'Look, let's get down to modern times, shall we? When the mighty Chief pulled out of Chicago, who do you think suddenly appeared?'

'Who?'

'That beautiful little lady from the past. Fleur by name, straight out of *Oh, Lady, Lady*!'

There was a stunned silence.

'It isn't true!'

'It's true all right.'

'You mean to tell me that adorable pussycat with the matchless English complexion and the lovely long legs, and the beautiful lips always held partly open, the luscious . . . [breaking off] what does the poor old girl look like today?'

'She hasn't changed the veriest fraction from the description you've just given of her. Oh, of course she's changed in some ways, as she says she's "learned to read" and she adores my books.'

'Did she know you were going to be on the train?'

'Yes, she'd read it in the papers, so she booked to go on the same, she had some business in Hollywood. She's to appear as the leader at some big function.'

'Was it a touch?'

'What do you mean?'

'I mean getting on the same train and. . . .'

'You mean money? She's loaded, married a Texan and, as she herself expressed it, she's up to her nose in cattle ranches.'

'Thank heaven I'm anchored to My Little Thing,' said Guy.

'Yes, four wives should be enough even for you.'

'Go on with your story.'

'We dined together. She'd brought along a rare wine. She said I'd find it better than the champagne that was also from her cellars.' He paused.

'And then?'

'The train was halted for what seemed a long stop, the porters were down on the platform. I was sitting up, reading, when a lady came to me and said "your lady friend wants you to come. It seems something has happened. It's urgent." '

'I went with her. The curtains that lined the way were all drawn but, as I heard my name spoken, a pair parted. . . . Fleur was lying with a transparent something affording a slight cover for her nudity. She said, "Get on. The porters are down on the platform. Get in quick." '

'And did you?'

Plum paused before answering.

'No,' he said, 'no, I didn't.'

'What did you do – or say, for that matter?'

'I don't quite know. I remember hearing myself repeating the words "my wife" – and, I also seem to remember being swept into an outburst on how ravishingly lovely Fleur was without her clothes, I also asked her what the magic perfume was – if it wasn't just her, herself, that was wafted to me, an intoxicating fragrance – and I then became suddenly aware that the train was moving, the porter was at my elbow and I turned and fled back to "Cactus Flower". The door was closed but I opened it. And there, to my bewilderment, instead of "Cactus Flower", was the giant locomotive.

' "Youse belong on de 'Scenic Route'," the porter was telling me the train split in half and wouldn't unite again until we were at Pasadena. "An' everybody's wonderin' what's kep you back here." '

'A great story,' Guy said, 'with a splendid climax, but the one thing we must do is keep it out of the papers.'

'More important still,' said Plum, 'is to keep Fleur from meeting Ethel. She's longing to. She thinks Ethel must be such a very wonderful woman.'

And just at that moment Ethel arrived and said, 'How did you enjoy your trip through the Grand Canyon?'

FIFTEEN

I

Oh, Kay opened in Philadelphia. On the third night of the engagement Guy and Plum were leaning on the barrier behind the last row of the stalls, happy in the fact that in the whole of the capacious Shubert Theatre there was not a seat for them to sit in.

The comedian – Victor Moore – had just gone off to a rousing hand. Gertie Lawrence and Oscar Shaw were in the midst of a romantic passage, and anyone looking at Guy would have realized that here at least was one man who found the scene utterly captivating. Plum, while perhaps equally enchanted, could mask his feelings more readily, nor had he the habit of repeating the lines in unison with the actors, a Bolton practice which he, not infrequently supported by members of the audience, had tried vainly to correct.

A more unfortunate moment for a dog to select for making his appearance on the stage could hardly have been thought of. Long windows stood half open on a moonlit beach; the door to the library was unclosed; there was also a stair. None of these appealed to the canine visitor. He preferred instead to come in through the fireplace, where a log fire was flickering realistically. He paid no attention to the actors but walked straight to the footlights and stared at the audience from under shaggy brows like a Scottish elder rebuking sin from the pulpit.

He then walked over to the proscenium arch, cocked his leg, then scuffled with his feet and made his exit – through the fireplace.

Guy was outraged.

'What are you laughing at?' he said. 'The love story has gone clean out of the window.'

'Out of the fireplace, you mean, don't you?'

The actors had stumbled through the buzzing and the ripples of laughter to the duet.

> I remember the bliss
> Of that wonderful kiss . . .
> Oh, how I'd adore it
> If you would encore it.

The dog made a second appearance, pausing this time while still in the fireplace, his paws resting on the log as he glanced archly from side to side of the room. He jumped the log and came in wagging his tail. He was a grey, rough-coated animal something like an oversize Cairn but, if such was his mother's stock, it seemed certain that her pride of race had been tried beyond the breaking point by a lop-eared hound.

> Oh, do, do, do what you done, done, done
>   before, baby

sang the lovers.

The storm of laughter drowned the orchestra and, when the wretched animal, as if in response to the repeated admonitions, made his way again to the proscenium arch, there was no continuing with the number.

The pair on the stage were not as badly shaken as was Victor Moore, waiting, on the side opposite the fireplace, to make his re-entrance. He knew the authors had been busy writing in some new stuff for Gertie and Oscar. He knew that Oscar was an accomplished light comedian and he was further aware that, given encouragement, Gertie revelled in 'hoke'.

But, dash it all, if the so-called 'straight' people were going to get laughs like this he would have to pull up his socks. Then, shattering him completely, came a terrific 'scene-call' from the audience far in excess of the hand he had received. He could hardly have been expected to guess that a dog had decided that a stage fireplace was an excellent substitute for a kennel.

'I should have left Bugs at his club,' said Betty Compton afterwards.

'His club?' queried Plum.

'Oh, yes there are dogs' clubs in all the big cities. The top one in New York is The Blue Ribbon but poor Buggsie could never get into *that*. You have to have been shown before you're eligible, so of course Buggsie hasn't a hope. Jimmy pulled some wires and got him into The Beefsteak. The food is wonderful but it's full of mutts.'

Plum, an old-time dog-lover, was interested. Betty explained that there were some single-breed clubs and in those pets of both sexes were catered for. Then should there be any 'romances', as Betty termed them, the result would not be too disastrous. There was one for poodles called Colonie Caniche, and another exclusively for police dogs known as The Sentinel. The clubs were, she explained, a great convenience, especially for hotel dwellers.

'A car calls for Buggsie in the morning and he comes home at cocktail-time.'

'What do the dogs do at these clubs?' asked Guy.

Betty gave him rather a blank look.

'What does anyone do at a club? They eat lunch and play games.'

'Of course.'

2

'They're getting pretty nutty in this adopted land of mine,' said Guy a few days later when they were sitting over the Great Neck breakfast-table. 'I'm just reading about the funeral yesterday of the Chicago gangster, Dion O'Bannion. The casket with handles of solid gold, cost $10,000 and on top of it lay a wreath inscribed "From Al", sent by the man who had had him murdered.'

'Yes, I've been reading about it, too. There were twenty-six truckloads of flowers. Also three widows in weeds so heavy that they couldn't be identified.'

'But life even over here isn't all murders,' said Guy. 'Turn to the sporting page. "The Dixmoor Country Club has installed loud-speakers round the courses so that Sunday morning golfers can listen to the church services and still get their game".'

'Some game, too, if they play the latest style of golf match which a writer here says is growing in popularity. You're allowed to cheat in any way you like, but if caught cheating you lose the hole.'

'The crossword puzzle craze is now at such a pitch, my paper informs me, that a Pittsburgh pastor is handing out crossword slips which, when solved, give the text of his sermon. They're all loony.'

'The particular type of looniness that has sprung up in Florida seems to have been given a sharp lesson.'

'The hurricane? Yes, pretty ghastly, isn't it?'

'It says that the streets of Miami are littered with yachts – not one of them Hank Savage's, unfortunately – and that a five-masted steel schooner is standing in the garden of one of the new hotels.'

'400 dead, 5000 homeless. Even Nature goes a bit screwball in America.'

'But show business is booming.'

'Yes, it's never been better.'

'How's your *Ramblers* doing?'

'All the Lyric Theatre will hold.'

Plum's adaptation of *The Play's the Thing* opened at the Henry Miller on 3rd November and *Oh, Kay* at the Imperial five days later. They were both instantaneous successes. The old firm was doing all right.

Immediately after the first night of *Oh, Kay* Guy rushed over to London, where a show he had written, with a score by Rodgers and Hart, was already in rehearsal and due to open at the London Gaiety on 1st December. It was for Cicely Courtneidge, Jack Hulbert and Phyllis Dare and was called *Lido Lady*.

Plum was at Rogate in Sussex writing a novel called *The Small Bachelor*, an amplified version of *Oh Lady, Lady*. Guy journeyed down there and found the Wodehouse family settled in at Rogate Lodge in that delightful region of hill and woodland. Plum was in his study. The windows looked over a long slope of garden to a valley at the far end of which lay Winchester, but Guy had no eyes for scenery, his attention was occupied with the long coil of paper on the floor, curling its way past chairs and tables and finally doubling over when it reached the wall.

'At the end of the day's work, I suppose you snip the thing up into pages with the scissors?' asked Guy.

'Exactly. Did you notice the walls?'

Yes, Guy had noticed the walls. Always observant, he had seen that they were covered with typewritten sheets.

'I pin them up, and when they first go up, they're all at the same level. Then I walk round, scanning them, and when I find one where the story seems to drop, I put that sheet on a lower level. The gaps are where there are holes in the story that need filling.'

'And when the sheet's hanging crooked?'

'That means that a twist is required at that spot.'

'Rather a good idea,' said Guy.

'What do you mean, "rather a good idea"?' said Plum. 'It's genius.'

Gertie Lawrence was arriving from America the next week to start preparations for the London presentation of *Oh, Kay*, and they went up to London to welcome her and discuss with her the possibility of making changes in the book. It had occurred to them that a musical comedy about bootleggers might not appeal to a British audience, and in their gloomier moments they had even felt that it might be necessary to construct a completely new story and fit the Gershwin numbers into it.

They were at Waterloo when the boat train rolled in, but found that they had not reckoned for Gertie's popularity. A dense crowd of friends and admirers were on the platform. André Charlot was there, so were Jack Buchanan, Ivor Novello and, so it seemed, half the population of London.

Clearly there was no hope of getting her attention now, and, when Ivor invited them to a party in her honour that night at his flat, they accepted gratefully, hoping that they might get a minute or two with her alone in the course of the evening.

It was very much wishful thinking. In the Novello flat above the Strand Theatre Gertie was always the centre of a group except when she stepped out to sing a song or give her impersonation of her cockney dresser, Clarrie, famous in the profession. Clarrie had an old grandmother who, too, had been a dresser, and the dialogue between them, as rendered by Gertie, ran thus:

'Grannie,' I says, 'I want your advice about sailors, Grannie.'

'Sailors?' she says. 'Listen, my girl. Cheer for the Navy every chance you get, but don't go round with it. A bunch of scamps, all of them, that's what sailors are.'

'How about actors?' I says.

'Must it be one or the other?' she says.

'As things are at present,' I says.

'Well, it's a 'ell of a choice,' says Grannie, 'but speakin' as a woman as was born in a wardrobe hamper, I'd say take the sailor.'

Having finished her act, Gertie became the centre of a crowd again, and to her intense indignation Clara Novello Davies, Ivor's mother, found herself deserted and standing alone with none to pay her reverence, a thing to which she was by no means accustomed. She was a woman whose powerful voice, dominating manner and majestically flowing robes made her seem like a blend of the Cumaean Sybil and the Statue of Liberty, and she was wont to hold court, not to be left in solitude.

'Well!' she said, giving the word the full force of that voice of hers.

A hush fell on the assembly. Clara Novello Davies strode to the door and, flinging it open, turned.

'I have been grossly insulted,' she boomed, 'and I am leaving my son's home for ever. I shall never again cross this threshold.' And she strode through the door, slamming it behind her.

Most unfortunately, it was the door of the coats and hats cupboard, and she emerged a moment later in floods of tears. Ivor rushed to console her, and the incident ended with the whole company singing 'For She's a Jolly Novello.'

On 15th December rehearsals of *Rio Rita* were to begin in New York, so Guy's visit to London was necessarily a brief one.

Rio Rita opened the new Ziegfeld Theatre on 2nd February. It had a most effective score by Tierney and McCarthy, the team which had written *Kid Boots* for Ziegfeld as well as the record-breaking *Irene*.

Ziegfeld drew Guy aside after the opening and told him that he had signed Marilyn Miller and Jack Donahue for the following season. Would Guy write a show for them and, if so, did he want a partner? He said he did and of course named Plum.

The two set to work immediately and turned out a scenario. The play, tentatively entitled *The Gibson Girl*, was in complete scenario form inside of ten days. They read it to both the stars and both approved. Ziegfeld was in Palm Beach so they decided to go down there and close the deal.

SIXTEEN

I

It was in 1918 that they had paid their previous visit to the Florida resort – now it was 1927. The real-estate boom had come in the interval and, having reached its climax in the previous year, was in a state of recession. It had not yet, however, by any means collapsed.

Plum bought a paper when their train stopped at Fort Pierce and regaled his companion with a joint proclamation by the mayors of the East coast littoral announcing 'The Fiesta of the American Tropics' – 'Our Season of Mardi Gras when Love, Merrymaking and Wholesome Sport shall prevail throughout Our Domains.' They promised unitedly, 'Parades in which a Glorious Pageantry of Sublime Beauty shall depict in Floral Loveliness the Blessing Bestowed upon us by Friendly Sun, Gracious Rain and Soothing Tropic Winds.'

'I wonder,' said Guy, 'how the 1600 people injured in the great September hurricane feel about those "Soothing Tropic Winds."'

Ziegfeld was staying with Leonard Replogle, the financier, and wasn't in when they phoned. They spent the day swimming and playing a round of golf on the new Everglades course. They returned to the hotel expecting to find a message from the manager but there was none. They dressed, dined and went to Bradley's. There the Colonel told them that Ziegfeld was upstairs in the Chemin-de-Fer room. He said he was afraid Flo had had a bad night.

'Lucky that *Rio Rita* of his is such a hit,' he said. 'He's had nothing but bad luck down here.'

A man with a shock of pale straw-coloured hair standing nearby turned to them.

'You're talking about Flo?' he said. 'Did you ever see anybody like him? He was flat-broke before this new show of his went on, with a grocery bill up at Hastings that a greyhound couldn't jump over. But a week after the Ziegfeld opened he came down here in a private car.'

'There never was such extravagance,' agreed Bradley.

'I knew him out in Chicago when we were both knee-high to a grasshopper,' said the light-haired man. 'The first thing I remember about him was he'd buy an all-day sucker at six o'clock at night.' Everybody laughed.

'Suckers he had even then, had he?' commented a man who had been standing near them listening to the conversation.

As they turned to him he placed a finger on his chest.

'When I say "suckers" I'm pointing right at the biggest one. Believe me, gentlemen, that loafer still owes me for the costumes of the *Follies* of 1923. And then he had the nerve to ask for me to dress the Spanish Shawl number in *Rio Rita*. Real Spanish shawls he wants and, what you think? I am damn fool enough to get them for him.'

'Who was the chap who said he'd known Flo as a kid?' asked Guy as the Colonel escorted them to the stair.

'Jesse Livermore.'

'The Wolf of Wall Street!'

'Yes, I don't know why he wastes his time coming in here.'

'Shemmy' was an innovation since Guy and Plum had last visited Bradley's. When they were there in 1918 there had been only Roulette and 'Hazard', or 'Birdcage' as it is sometimes called. Now Bradley's 'Shemmy' game had the reputation of being the steepest in the world.

Ziegfeld was seated at the table. He greeted them gaily.

'Hello boys, what are you doing down here? Bad place, bad game.' He addressed the dealer. 'Card, please.'

'I never learned to play "Shemmy",' said Guy.

'Seems like I never did either,' said Ziegfeld, turning over a ten. 'You boys got some money on you?'

'Yes.' Guy, who was acting as the team's treasurer, pulled out his wallet.

'Give me $1000.'

'That's all we've got.'

'It's all I asked for.'

Guy handed him a small sheaf of crisp, new hundreds. Ziegfeld tossed them all on the table and pulled the 'shoe' toward him.

'That's pretty rich, isn't it?' protested one of the players.

'That's what the bank opens for, gentlemen, $1000.'

As the punters placed their bets, Flo conversed with the two writers standing beside him.

He turned his cards as he spoke. He had eight. The money was raked into the bank. They watched the play for a few minutes, then: 'We've brought down the lay-out of the Miller show,' Guy told him.

'Oh, good. I want it to be the biggest thing I've ever done. Incidentally Erlanger won't come in. He says $100,000 is too much to risk on any show.' He turned back to the table.

Ziegfeld continued to win steadily. The croupier announced that there was $24,000 in the bank. A voice said *'banco.'* Ziegfeld looked up and saw Jesse Livermore.

'Hello, Pinkie.' Livermore, a virtual albino, had that characteristic pink look about the eyes. 'Don't come round here with that hot streak of yours.'

Ziegfeld dealt the cards with the same careless flip.

' "Shooting for the stick", eh? That's always been your style.'

He turned over a natural.

'The Magoo, Pinkie. Looks like you aren't wearing your horseshoes tonight.'

Jesse Livermore laughed and threw in a wad of bills.

'Seems as if you boys have brought me luck,' said Ziegfeld.

'You're not going to leave that money in the bank, are you?'

'Why not? I'm doing all right.'

'You've run the bank for fourteen coups,' said Plum. 'You don't think it's going on for ever, do you?'

'I'll run it one more.'

'Well, I won't watch.'

'You stay right where you are. Maybe it's you that's the mascot.'

He won again.

'All right, boys, the bank passes. I'm going to go on gambling with this money,' he told the table. 'I'm going to use it to produce a show by these two gentlemen. What's it called, boys?'

'*The Gibson Girl.*'

'Yes, not bad. Come on, let's go down and have a drink.'

But Ziegfeld seemed lukewarm. He listened, nodded and said nothing. A day or two later Guy learned the reason. Flo produced a rough outline for a show which had been sent to him by Bill McGuire. It was 'timely', having to do with the recent visit to the US of Queen Marie of Romania and her daughter. The Princess was in love with a West Point cadet who, somewhat improbably, had flown the Atlantic with a cadet pal (Donahue). Still more improbably they had landed in Romania.

Neither Bill nor Ziegfeld was strong on geography, nor were they acquainted with the regulations covering West Point cadets. Guy had, in his architectural youth, spent two years at the Point, and he thought this might give him some advantage in dealing with the cuckoo about to lay its egg (a prophetic phrase he fancied) in the cosy nest that Plum and he were building.

But McGuire had done one thing which, for Ziegfeld, had a subtle appeal. He had telegraphed his story. As has been pointed out before, Ziggy was the telegraph-kid. He handled the forty-two yellow sheets, with Bill's name on the last one, with loving care.

So it was that *Rosalie* came into being. Flo told Guy he wanted him to team with McGuire. 'I know Bill,' he said. 'This telegram is about all I'll ever get from him.'

'But what about Plum?'

'He can write the lyrics.'

'How can he? You're getting Gershwin. He'll only work with Ira.'

'I'm having Romberg as well. He knows Romania. He's been there. Plum knows Europe too. It's a good combination.'

'Two book writers, two lyric writers, two composers?'

'Why not?'

'It's all right if you can pay for it.'

'If I can't pay for it, you won't get paid.'

This simple axiom summed up the principle on which all Ziegfeld undertakings were based. He had one disciple who adhered to this philosophy as strictly as he did, his pet author, William Anthony McGuire. Bill had his own way of putting it: 'If I haven't got it, they can't get it,' was his phrase, and the fact that he so frequently didn't have it because, like Ziegfeld, he'd bought what he couldn't pay for, seemingly troubled him as little as it did the manager.

Once when a scene that Bill had written in *Whoopee* was dubbed 'old-fashioned', he refuted it hotly.

'Damn it all, Flo and I are ahead of the times. Look at the way we both live on next year's income.'

He was constantly just one jump ahead of the sheriff. Once indeed the sheriff was one jump ahead of him. Guy was expecting Bill to come and spend a week at a shore cottage he had taken at Westhampton. Together they were going to put the finishing touches to *Rosalie*. Half an hour before the train was due, three men, one of whom wore a large silver star, tramped up the wooden path and displayed to the Bolton factotum a body-warrant that called for Bill's arrest and incarceration.

Though clad in a wet bathing-suit, Guy flew to his car and drove to Speonk, where he told his collaborator what was awaiting him at Westhampton. Bill and his bag were then driven back to Patchogue so that he could catch a train for New York. All there was of the polishing process took place during the drive.

It was a few days after that that Bill disappeared. He was living at the Hotel Warwick, but when Guy and Plum, who were working together on a spot where a new number was needed, phoned him, they were told he was no longer there. They called Flo.

'That's where he was last night. I'll see what I can find out. You boys had better come on over to the Ziegfeld.'

'I don't know where the man's got to,' were the words he greeted them with when they entered the office. 'His things are still at the Warwick. They're holding them for the rent.'

'I hope the revised script of *Rosalie* isn't impounded.'

'Holy cats! If he's got the script, God help us! That fellow is a crackpot. You know what he did to me once? Sold me a sketch – I bought it outright for $1500. He put the money in his pocket but forgot to leave the sketch. The *Follies* was already in rehearsal so I combed the town for him. His wife didn't know where he was – but it wasn't often she did. Then *The Passing Show* opened and there was my sketch. The stinker had sold it to Lee Shubert two days before he did to me. And all he'd charged Lee was $1000!'

The phone rang. It was Bill. Ziegfeld told him to beat it over as fast as he could come and to bring the script.

'He's got it,' Ziegfeld told them as he hung up. 'The Warwick people wouldn't let him take a thing but he sneaked *Rosalie* out tucked under his waistband. Then what do you think he did? He moved into the Plaza. He says he likes it better there, he's got a nice view of the park.'

Bill arrived, cheerful as usual.

'So you're at the Plaza now?'

'Yes, only trouble is it's a bit grand. You have to have a shave before you'd venture into the barber shop.'

'What did you do for luggage?'

'Oh, I always keep a bag at the club with a couple of old telephone books in it. Then I go and buy what I need and have it paid for at the desk.'

The phone rang again. Ziegfeld answered it. 'That was the box-office,' he said. 'They say there's a sheriff waiting for you downstairs, Bill.'

'Jeez! That's what I get for coming here.'

'Look,' said Flo, 'I tell you what. I'll go down and say you've gone. Turn out the lights. I'll tell them there's nobody up here.'

It was about seven-thirty. They turned out the lights and sat in the dark discussing the show in whispers. A strange sort of story-conference, but then things were apt to be strange around Bill McGuire.

Then the door was opened and Ziegfeld switched on the lights. He held a folded paper in his hands.

'You son-of-a-bitch,' he said. 'He wasn't after you, he was after me.'

McGuire clicked his tongue disapprovingly.
'Why don't you pay your bills, Flo?' he said.

2

To compensate Plum for substituting McGuire as Guy's collaborator, Flo engaged him to write *The Three Musketeers*, a musical designed to serve as a twin starring vehicle for Dennis King and Vivienne Segal. The composer was Rudy Friml, whom Plum had worked with before on the lyrics of a dead and gone turkey of 1916 called *Kitty Darlin'*. On the book he, in turn, was teamed with McGuire.

About the same time he was commissioned by Gilbert Miller to adapt *Her Cardboard Lover* for Jeanne Eagles and Leslie Howard. He had, further, a comedy he had written for an English management called *Good Morning Bill*. All four of these, including *Rosalie*, were produced within the space of four months.

At the same time Guy was engaged with Fred Thompson on a new Astaire show, *Funny Face*, another Philip Goodman musical, *The Five O'Clock Girl, Rosalie* and *She's My Baby*, a Dillingham show written in collaboration with Kalmar and Ruby and with a score by Rodgers and Hart.

Guy, finding conflicting demands too much for him, bowed out of *Funny Face* after the play had passed its scenario stage. He suggested Bob Benchley to take his place. Bob took over.

Altogether Plum and Guy had, singly or together, nineteen opening nights in the three years 1926-7-8. Fourteen of these were new shows, five productions in one country of plays first presented in the other.

Looking through the diaries, every day seems to have been given to either writing or rehearsing. The protracted tours of the Princess days had given place to a more or less standard two weeks try-out. This was a period of intensive effort, of re-writing, of early and late rehearsals, of the continual watching of performances in an effort to gauge audience reactions.

Four shows a year meant two months of this, the hardest and most exacting work of all. The chief intervals of rest were those spent on ocean liner – though even there you would most likely have found the team, rug-wrapped in adjoining deck-chairs, busy with pad and pencil.

3

Although Plum was deeply preoccupied with his books – *The Small Bachelor*, *Meet Mr Mulliner* and *Money for Nothing* all published in the year, with *Summer Lightning* and *Carry on Jeeves* coming along in the next – he still found time to do a little dramatic work. With Ian Hay he wrote *A Damsel in Distress*, based on an earlier novel, and he accepted a commission from Gilbert Miller to adapt the German play, *By Candlelight*. The fact that Gertie Lawrence was to be the heroine of the last-named was too great a temptation to be resisted.

This particular chore took Plum to America in the early summer of '29. He and Guy had not met for exactly a year.

'You're looking a little drawn,' said Plum. 'I know it can't be overdrawn, ha, ha, so there must be some other reason. Are you worried about anything? Which reminds me of a story about Eva Kern. Do you remember a play called *Six-Cylinder Love*?'

'Vaguely. Ernie Truex starred in it. He was a little clerk—'

'That's right. Well, Eva came to Jerry one day and said "I'm terribly anxious about poor Ernie Truex. I've just seen him and he looked awful, as if he had got something dreadful on his mind. Honestly, I was afraid he might be going to commit suicide." So Jerry trotted off to investigate. It seemed to him, when he met him, that Ernie was looking reasonably cheerful, but he started making inquiries. "Are you all right, Ernie?" he asked. Ernie said he was fine. "No money troubles? Nothing wrong with your home life? Doctor hasn't told you you've got an incurable disease?" "No," said Ernie. "Plenty of money, home life terrific, and I haven't gone to a doctor for years." "Then what on earth was Eva talking about?" said Jerry. "She told me she had seen you and you were in a fright-ful state, contemplating suicide and all that sort of thing." "But I haven't met Eva for quite a while," said Ernie. "When did she see me?" "At the Thursday matinée." "Ah," said

Ernie, enlightened. "Well, at the Thursday matinée and the Saturday matinée and also six times a week nightly I lose my job, I have my life's savings stolen, my wife tells me she's going to leave me, and I am expecting every moment to be arrested. Maybe I did look a little worried when Eva saw me." After which digression, is anything the matter with you?'

'Just the rat-race. I don't quite know why I've been doing it.'

'I don't quite know why either of us have. Youth's been knocking at the door for some time now.'

'Yes . . . only what do you do when you stop working? Just sit there listening to the hardening of your arteries.'

'It's not as bad as all that. We're still quite young.'

'Yes, quite.'

'Quite.'

'I hate that word "quite".'

Plum regarded him speculatively.

'The only symptom of approaching age I detect in you is that you don't talk about *The Little Thing*, as much as you used to.'

'I'm still as keen about it as ever.'

'Are you? They why don't we put in on ourselves?'

'Become managers?'

'Don't say it in that awed voice. There's no trick to being a manager.'

'Are you sure there isn't? All my life – my theatrical life – I've mentally been saying "sir" to them. They may be "Ray" and "Flo" and "Charlie" to talk to, but in my innermost soul they are Mr Comstock, Mr Ziegfeld and Mr Dillingham, I find myself waiting for them to ask me to sit down.'

The conversation was taking place in the Ritz where they were both staying. Guy's Great Neck home was rented. In answer to a question he said that Marguerite had been in America but was now in Italy.

'Let's talk over this *Little Thing* thing at lunch.'

'Where shall we go?'

'The Algonquin?'

'The Round Table? I'm never comfortable there. I feel like one does when one's trying to think up a funny opening-night telegram to the comic, which you know will be pasted on his mirror for the run of the show.'

'You seem to be in a very diminished state. What's happened to you?'

'Oh, a bit of this and that – nothing.'

'I suspect woman trouble – that old complaint of yours.'

'Nonsense. I nailed my flag to the masthead years ago. "Women are wonderful." It's still there, a bit tattered and battle-scarred but flying just the same.'

They went downstairs to the Japanese Garden where, ironically enough after their decision not to go to the Algonquin Round Table, Theodore (the big one this time) put them next a table where Alec Woollcott was seated with Bob Benchley, Arthur Richman and Phil Barry. Plum received a warm welcome and he and Guy were told to move over.

'Don't tell me you two fellows are planning another assault on Broadway,' said Phil. 'You're a menace.'

'Speak to those men respectfully, young fellow,' said Bob. 'They've written more musical comedies than any other four men in the world. I wrote *one* – that chap Guy landed me with it – and oh, boy, was that something. I always keep saying "Oh, boy" whenever these two are around,' he added. 'I like to see those nostalgic smiles steal across their faces.'

'What *are* you up to, Plum?' said Woollcott, 'if it's rude to ask.'

'I'm here to see Gilbert Miller about an adaptation I'm doing for him.'

'Gilbert Miller?' echoed Woollcott and, rising, he held up his coffee cup in a toast. 'Gentlemen, I give you Gilbert Miller. I give him to you freely. All I ask in exchange is a 5¢ cigar-butt and a Coolidge campaign button.'

'Come, come now,' said Plum. 'After all he is our most literate manager.'

'True,' agreed Woollcott resuming his seat. 'To quote one of his lady stars, "The man has his faults but, after all, he does speak our language."'

Everyone laughed, but this time Guy rushed to Gilbert's defence.

'It's the old story,' he said. 'When it's someone you like and admire, their faults are of moment to you. You notice a blemish in your sweetheart that would pass unchallenged in another woman.'

'Gilbert may be your sweetheart,' said Woollcott. 'He isn't mine.'

'But you must admit—'

'Yes, yes, yes,' interrupted the critic testily. 'I admit everything. I admit his impeccable taste in stage décor, his shrewdness in casting, his enterprise, his courage. . . . His stories have both pith and point, and I pay tribute to his admirable restraint when, with far more justification than have others who do – he does not attempt to rewrite his authors' plays. It is on a matter, not of sense, but of sensibility that I arraign him. . . . Mr Arthur Richman has the floor.'

'Oh, no you don't!' laughed Arthur. 'I'm not telling that story!'

'Are you not the author of the famous line: "You have to know Gilbert really well in order to dislike him"?'

'That was just a crack – not to be taken seriously.'

'Very well, if you won't tell the story, I will.' He turned to the table:

'The talented gentleman on my right recently received a dinner invitation from the Millers, and, in response to its instructions, presented himself at the door of the Bache-Miller residence, 814 Fifth Avenue, attired in white tie and with dark red carnation in buttonhole.

'Ushered into one of the sumptuous reception rooms where Fragonards and Watteaus rub shoulders, and where bergères, encased in lovely Oudry Tapestries, implore you not to sit on them, our author was set to wondering why he had been invited. It was clearly one of the fancier Miller occasions and he realized that all save himself enjoyed high rating by either social or cash-register standards, if not by both.

'In an effort to make him feel more at ease, or possibly because he was tired, Gilbert came and leaned on his shoulder, a rather favourite habit of the most literate of our managers.

' "Come with me," he said suddenly and rather abruptly, and, turning, he led the way to the elevator. . . . Oh, yes there is an elevator, known, because of its being hung with Gobelins, as the *ascenseur*. There are also solid gold fittings on the plumbing fixtures. Kitty maintains they are economical – they never have to be cleaned.

'Little Arthur, following in the wake of big Gilbert, thought to himself hopefully, "Ha, a business chat . . . Ina Claire . . . that comedy of mine that would have been collecting dust on Gilbert's desk this past twelve month, were not Gilbert's desk so constantly dusted."

'But no, it was not that. Gilbert shot the *ascenseur* upwards and stopped it between floors. He turned to Arthur with that, as always, ominous phrase: "Arthur, we've known each other a long time, so I think I may speak freely."

' "Go ahead," said Arthur.

' "You have a terrible case of halitosis."

' "Oh, no," protested Arthur, as perspiration beaded his forehead. "It can't be true. I'm a very healthy man with an excellent digestion and—"

' "Blow at me," said Gilbert.

'Arthur blew.

' "Blow again."

'Arthur blew again.

' "No, it isn't you," said Gilbert, and shot the *ascenseur* down again. To describe Arthur as shattered would be an understatement. His collar had wilted, two damp spots showed on his shirt-front, he felt that if Gilbert came and leant on him again he would collapse.

'But Gilbert was leaning on other shoulders. Arthur was free to stand there alone and try to recover his shattered morale. He, naturally, realized the reason for the mistake. Gilbert had not supposed that anyone who had their name in the Social Register could possibly have halitosis – well, now he had learned his lesson. Arthur watched as the host ambled off once again to the *ascenseur* with a prominent young upper-cruster in tow.

'When he returned Arthur could not resist an inquiry.

' "Yes, he's the one," said Gilbert, "but I think I've got him pretty well fixed up with some of Kitty's mouth-wash." '

Woollcott paused.

'If I was a pitiful object,' said Arthur, 'you should have seen this other poor wretch. Whenever one of the women on either side of him spoke to him, he never turned his head by the fraction of an inch. He spoke straight . . . out . . . front.'

'An engaging story,' said Plum, 'but still, reverting from sensibility to sense, isn't it better to know if you've got halitosis? Personally I find it comforting to reflect that, if your best friends won't tell you, Gilbert Miller will.'

4

The idea of turning manager and putting on *The Little Thing* themselves burgeoned as a bud in May. Guy, seemingly dubious when Plum first suggested it, grew daily more enthusiastic. Even when investigation revealed that costs had pyramided so that they must budget for close to $100,000 he was not discouraged – what was $100,000? Plenty of smart lads were making that every other day down in Wall Street.

The script was hauled out and completely revised. Some of the scenes had the 'colour' of *Sally*. These were eliminated. Bits of the material that they had designed for *The Gibson Girl* were fitted in. They chose Vincent Youmans as composer. Plum and he set to work on the score.

They took offices in the Brill Building. They interviewed Marilyn, miraculously free. She read the script and liked it.

'Why was this never done before?' she asked. 'You say you wrote it some time ago.'

'I'd hate to tell you how long.'

'It's a shame Jack can't play the comedy part but he's going into something he's written with Fred Thompson.'

'*Sons of Guns*? Yes, we know about that. How do you like that new chap they're all talking about who's playing in a thing at the Shubert called *Ups-a-Daisy*?'

'Lester Hope?'

'He's changing his name to "Bob" – "Bob Hope".'

'I think he'd be just right.'

'We'll get him.' It was said with confidence. Not, 'We'll get him if Mr Freedley agrees.' No nonsense about the management not being willing to pay the salary – the thing Savage had pulled when they asked for Billy Van.

'You're right,' said Guy, 'there's no trick to being a manager.

It's like trying the handle of a door that you'd always imagined was locked and bolted, and finding it's been open all the time.'

'I suppose we ought to sell some securities and deposit that hundred grand in the bank?'

'Oh, we don't need it yet. My broker says the bull market's good for another six months. Seems a shame to pull the money out when every day you leave it there it keeps getting more.'

They hired a company manager, Jim O'Leary, an old-timer who knew the ropes and had costs at his fingertips. They had an excellent secretary, Lillian Hartman, who had worked for Guy years before. Everything seemed set. The only annoyance was what they always referred to as the *ascenseurs*. There never was a building whose elevators were so jammed. People seemed to pour in and out of the Brill Building in waves. Frequently three of four elevators would go by their floor as they were waiting to go to lunch. A little thing, but, when you want to go to lunch, you want to go to lunch.

'Let's move before we produce our next show,' said Plum.

Guy nodded. 'This is an anniversary,' he said, 'and I suggest that, for good and practical reasons, we go somewhere where they know us.'

'What's it an anniversary of?'

'Just thirteen years ago today we walked into Ray Comstock's office. *Go To It* had laid an egg the night before.'

'The *Oh, Boy!* contract.'

'That's right the *Oh, Boy!* contract. 8th October.'

'Good old 8th October!'

5

It was the following day that the roof started to fall in, but it wasn't until 24th October that the floor gave way and the two authors began to wonder how far down bottom was. Each hour the seismographs registered a further shock. Auburn Auto, in which they both had holdings, dropped sixty points in one day. After that bit of news came through, things got blurred and there seemed to be a general impression that Judgement Day had set in with unusual severity. Looking over one's shoulder one would not have been surprised to see a brace of those peculiar beasts with an unnecessary number of heads, as described in the Book of Revelations, flexing their muscles before starting in to do their stuff.

Plum and Guy closed the door of their Brill Building office with the knowledge that they would never have need to return. They pressed the 'down' button. The elevator that stopped at their floor was miraculously empty.

'That's funny,' said Guy.

'Not at all,' said Plum. 'Everybody is using the windows.'

Guy's reception of the witticism was not hearty.

'Where shall we go to lunch?' It was Plum who asked the question. 'Ever try the Automat? The food's darn good. I used to go there when I was writing *Polly Preferred*.'

'No,' said Plum firmly, 'I'm damned if we will. We'll take a leaf out of the Ziegfeld-Maguire book and go to the Ritz.'

'What smart fellows those two were: they *spent* their money.'

'Yes, I bet they're busy right now popping champagne corks and patting each other on the back.'

'Wise guys, eh?' I can hear them jeering. 'Now these smart Alecs will be coming round to us for some tips on sheriff dodging.'

They went to the Ritz and Theodore produced two smashing horses' necks that were not horses' necks. They didn't even mind when Vecsey struck up with *The Rose of China*.

'Funny, the failures don't matter any more. If we'd cleaned up with *The Rose of China*, today it would be alleesamee bottomside.'

'For heaven's sake don't start talking pidgin. That'll finish me.'

'How do you actually stand?'

'The books balance exactly – the red and the black. They did a thorough job on me.'

'They didn't get quite all of mine, thanks to Ethel.'

'Well, that's fine.'

'What about you taking a bit of it till the tide starts coming in again?'

'No, thanks a lot, but I'm all right. I've got enough for car fare.'

Guy took a letter from his pocket and extracted an oblong green slip from it.

'The three sweetest words in the language,' said Plum. ' "Enclosed find cheque." Remember which show that was from?'

'*Very Good Eddie.*'

'Right. Is it a big cheque?'

'Quite big. I'm sending it back.'

'You doing *what*?'

'Sending it back . . . to Marguerite. She heard about what's happened and sold all the bits and pieces I ever gave her. She even sold her beloved *roulotte*.'

'She's a wonderful wife.'

'Yes . . . but not mine.'

'What on earth do you mean?'

'The divorce was made final that day sixteen months ago . . . the day we lunched with Alec Woollcott and the others at the Ritz. It didn't work, you see. She needed someone who would be on hand to talk to and have a bit of fun with . . . what's the phrase . . . ? "Turn out the pocketful of daily doings." '

'I'm terribly sorry.'

'Oh, I'm all right now. I've found a girl.'

'I'm glad to hear that.'

'And I've got a job.'

'That's odd. *I've* got a job.'

'I'm off to Hollywood.'

'I'm off to Hollywood.'

'Well, that's wonderful. I thought this time really had broken up the old firm. I'm with MGM.'

'*I'm* with MGM. They're putting me on a picture for W. C. Fields.'

Guy drew a deep breath.

'Do you think,' he said, 'the clientele would object if I sang a few bars?'

'MGM are putting *me* on that Fields picture, too.'

Plum gaped.

'You're kidding me.'

'It's the truth.'

'You mean we'll be working together?'

'But this is terrific!'

'Pretty good, I agree.'

'I think this calls for another one, don't you?'

'I certainly do.'

'Do you realize,' said Plum, 'that we've been working together for thirteen years and not a dirty look from start to finish? Most collaborators hate each other's guts after the first couple of shows. It's extraordinary.'

'Amazing.'

'Twin souls about sums it up, in my opinion.'

'In mine, too.'

They drank to Hollywood, to MGM, to W. C. Fields and to the further prosperity of the partnership.

'And now,' said Plum, when this ritual was concluded, 'tell me about this girl of yours.'

'I'd rather wait till you see her.'

'When will that be?'

'She'll be meeting me at Pasadena.'

'What's her name?'

'No, I'm not even going to tell you that. I'll tell you her nickname though. And she had it before I met her.'

'Yes?'

'The Little Thing,' said Guy.

SEVENTEEN

I

The train to the coast – the famous Chief – was rolling along through the wide open spaces where men are men. It was the second day out from Chicago and Guy and Plum were finishing their lunch in the diner. Ethel was to come on later after they had settled in.

The exodus from the East, which had begun with the coming of sound to the motion pictures, was at its height. Already on the train the two had met a number of authors, composers, directors and other Broadway fauna with whom they had worked in the days before the big crash. Rudolf Friml was there and Vincent Youmans and Arthur Richman and a dozen more. It was like one of those great race movements of the middle ages.

'Well,' said Guy, 'California, here we come! How do you feel?'

'I feel,' said Plum, 'as I should think Alice must have felt when, after mixing with all those weird creatures in Wonderland, she knelt on the mantelpiece preparatory to climbing through the looking-glass.'

'I see what you mean – wondering what kind of freaks she was going to meet this time. Still, maybe it won't be so bad. Hollywood can't have many terrors for two men who have survived Erlanger, Savage, a little Plymouth, junior Brecken-ridge, the Sisters Duncan – not to mention "Fabulous Felix" and Palmer.'

'Palmer?'

'Hank Savage's private poisoner.'

'Good Lord, I haven't thought of him for years. I wonder what became of him.'

'I hope he perished of his own cooking. I've never forgiven that bird for the supercilious way he sneered at that really excellent plot of ours about the pawnbroker.'

'I remember dimly something about a pawnbroker—'

'Good heavens, man, it was a superb plot and we might do worse than spring it on W. C. Fields when we get to Hollywood. You can't have forgotten. About a fellow who was the last of a long line of pawnbrokers and his ancestor had loaned the money to Queen Isabella to finance Columbus. . . .'

'I remember! The contract turned up, and he found that he owned 10 per cent of America. It was a darned good idea.'

'It was a terrific idea, and that hash-slinging sea cook crabbed it with a lot of stuff about thematic archaism.'

At this moment a man in horn-rimmed spectacles paused at their table.

'Oh, there you are,' he said. 'I'll come and have a chat in a minute or two. Can't stop now. See you later.'

He passed on, and they looked after him, puzzled.

'Now who on earth was that?' said Guy. 'He seemed to know us.'

'Probably somebody who was in one of our shows. The train's stiff with actors.'

They dismissed the man from their thoughts and returned to the subject of Hollywood.

'Have you talked to anyone who's been there?' asked Guy.

'Only Bob Benchley, and you know the sort of information you would get from him. He said I mustn't believe the stories I had heard about ill-treatment of inmates at the studios, for there was very little actual brutality. Most of the big executives, he said, were kindly men, and he had often seen Louis B. Mayer stop outside some nodder's hutch and push a piece of lettuce through the bars.'

'What's a nodder?'

'Bob explained that. A sort of Yes-man, only lower in the social scale. When there is a story conference and the supervisor throws out some suggestion or idea, the Yes-men all say "Yes". After they have finished saying "Yes", the nodders nod.

Bob said there is also a sub-species known as nodders' assistants, but he didn't want to get too technical.'

'What else? Is it true that they're all lunatics out in Hollywood?'

'Bob says no. He says he knows fully half a dozen people there who are practically sane – except of course at the time of the full moon. . . . Good Lord!'

'What's the matter?'

'I've remembered who that chap was who spoke to us.'

'Who?'

'Palmer.'

'It can't have been.'

'It was. Palmer in person.'

Guy considered.

'I believe you're right. But we shall soon know. He's coming this way.'

It was Palmer – older and with a new and rather horrible briskness about him, but still Palmer. He reached their table and sat down, looking snappy and efficient.

'Well, well,' said Guy.

'Well, well,' said Plum. 'It's a long time since that yacht cruise. How's *Ophelia*?'

Palmer cocked a puzzled eyebrow.

'Ophelia?'

'Your play?'

'Oh, that?' Palmer's face cleared. 'I got tired of waiting for the Colonel to do something about it – he kept changing the subject to corned beef hash whenever I mentioned it – so I threw up my job as cook on the *Dorinda* and came out here. Do you know something?'

'What?'

Palmer's voice was grave.

'I don't want to wrong him, but I've sometimes thought that Colonel Savage may have been stringing me along all the time.'

'Colonel *Savage*?' cried Guy and Plum, horrified.

'I know the idea sounds bizarre, but it has occasionally crossed my mind that he encouraged me to think that he was going to produce my play simply in order to get a free cook on that boat of his. We shall never know, I suppose. Well, as I was

saying, after the seventh – or was it the eighth? – trip to
Florida I got tired of waiting and came out here. I had a hard
time of it for a year or two, but I won through in the end and
am now doing extremely well. I'm a cousin by marriage.'

'A . . . what was that?'

'I married the cousin of one of the top executives and from
that moment never looked back. Of course, cousins are fairly
small fry, but I happen to know that there's a lot of talk going
around the front office of giving me brevet rank as a brother-in-
law before very long.'

'A brother-in-law is good, is it?'

Palmer stared.

'My dear fellow! Practically as high up as a nephew.'

The two authors offered congratulations.

'Well, now we're all going to be in Hollywood together,' said
Guy, 'I hope we shall see something of one another.'

'We shall. I'm your supervisor.'

'Eh?'

'On this W. C. Fields picture. If you've finished your lunch,
I'll take you along to meet him. What's the time?'

'Two-thirty.'

'Ah, then he may be sober.'

They made their way along the train to the Fields drawing-
room, Guy and Plum a little dubious and inclined to shake
their heads. They were not at all sure how they were going to
like being supervised by a man who thought that in writing a
play – and presumably a talking-picture – the scale of values
should be at once objective and rational, hence absolute and
authentic. And their uneasiness was increased when their
overlord said graciously that he hoped they would come to
dinner at his Beverly Hills home on the following Saturday,
adding that for the sake of old times he would cook the meal
himself.

'I'm as good a cook as I ever was,' he said.

Just about, they imagined, and shivered a little.

2

In the semi-darkness of the drawing-room the first thing the authors heard was a hollow groan and the first thing they saw was a vast something bulging beneath the bed-clothes. It stirred as they entered and there rose from the pillow a face rendered impressive by what must have been one of the largest and most incandescent nasal jobs ever issued to a human being. It reminded Plum – who had read his Edward Lear – of the hero of one of that eminent Victorian's best known poems.

> And all who watch at the midnight hour
> From hall or terrace or lofty tower
> Cry, as they trace the meteor bright
> Moving along through the dreary night
>   'This is the hour when forth he goes,
>   The Dong With The Luminous Nose'.

They were to learn later that the comedian was very sensitive about what he considered the only flaw in an otherwise classic countenance and permitted no facetious allusions to it even from his closest friends.

He switched on the light and regarded the visitors with aversion.

'And to what, my merry buzzards, do I owe this intrusion at daybreak?' he asked coldly.

Palmer explained that Mr Bolton and Mr Wodehouse were the two authors to whom had been assigned the task of assembling – under his supervision – the next Fields picture, and the great man softened visibly. He was fond of authors – being, as he often said, an author himself.

'Sit down, my little chickadees,' he said, 'and pass the aspirin. Are you in possession of aspirin?'

Palmer – who no doubt had foreseen this query – produced a small tin box.

'Thank you, thank you. Don't slam the lid. What I need this morning is kindness and understanding, for I am a little nervous. I was up late last night, seeing the new year in. Yes, I am aware,' proceeded Fields, 'that the general consensus of

informed opinion in these degenerate days is that the year
begins on 1st January – but what reason have we for supposing
so? One only ... that the ancient Romans said it did. But what
ancient Romans? Probably a bunch of souses who were well
into their fifth bottle of Falernian wine. The Phoenicians held
that it began on 21st November. The medieval Christians threw
celluloid balls at one another on the night of 15th March. The
Greeks were broadminded. Some of them thought New Year's
Day came on 20th September, while others voted for 10th
June. This was good for the restaurateurs – who could count on
two big nights in the year – but confusing for the Income Tax
authorities, who couldn't decide when to send in their demands.'

'I never knew that before, Mr Fields,' said Palmer respectfully. There was that about the majestic comedian that made
even supervisors respectful.

'Stick around me and you'll learn a lot. Well, you can
readily appreciate the result of this confusion of thought, my
dream-princes. It makes it difficult for a conscientious man to
do the right thing. He starts out simply and straightforwardly
by booking a reserved table for the last night in December, and
feels that that is that. But mark the sequel. As March approaches,
doubts begin to assail him. "Those medieval Christians were
shrewd fellows," he says to himself. "Who knows whether they
may not have had the right idea?"

'The only way he can square his conscience is by going out
and investing heavily in squeakers and rattles and paper caps
on the night of 15th March. And scarcely has the doctor left
his bedside next morning, when he starts to brood on the fact
that the Phoenicians, who were nobody's fools, were convinced
that 21st November was New Year's Eve. Many a young man
in the springtime of life has developed cirrhosis of the liver
simply by overdoing his researches into New Year's Eve. Last
night I was pure Phoenician, and I would appreciate the loan
of that aspirin once more.'

He mused in silence for a moment.

'So you're coming out to Dottyville-on-the-Pacific, are you,
boys?' he said, changing the subject. 'Poor lads, poor lads!
Well, let me give you a word of advice. Don't try to escape.
They'll chase you across the ice with bloodhounds. And even

if the bloodhounds miss you, the pitiless Californian climate drives you back. The only thing to do is to stick it out. But you'll suffer, my unhappy tenderfeet, you'll suffer. Conditions were appalling enough B.S., but they're far worse now.'

'B.S.?'

'Before Sound – sometimes called the Stereoptician Age, rich in fossils. Pictures first learned to walk. Now they've learned to talk. But the thing they've always managed to do is smell. In this year A.S. confusion is rife. Not a soul at the studios but is clutching its head and walking around in circles, saying, "Where am I?" And can you blame them? Think how they must have felt at MGM when they found that Jack Gilbert could only talk soprano.

'Yes,' Fields went on, 'confusion is rife. I was out to Pathé in Culver City last month and found the place in an uproar. One of their most popular vice-presidents had just been carted off to the loony-bin, strong men sitting on his head while others rushed off to fetch strait waistcoats and ambulances. It came about thus. As you doubtless know, the Pathé trademark is a handsome white rooster. For years he's been popping up on the screen ahead of their pictures and newsreels, flapping his wings and a-gaping open his beak. And when Sound came in, of course the directors held a meeting and it was duly resolved that from now on he had got to crow right out loud.

'Well, they set to work and brought out all the fancy sound equipment into the front yard. The countryside had been scoured for the biggest, all-firedest rooster the sovereign state of California could provide. It was a beaut – pure white with a great red comb on him – and they had a swell background fixed up behind him and the sound machines all waiting to catch that mighty cock-a-doodle-do – and – what do you know? – not a yip could they get out of him. He'd strut about, he'd flap his wings, he'd scrabble with his feet, but he wouldn't crow.

'Well, sir, they tried everything. They even went back to the first principle of show business – they brought on the girls. But he wasn't interested, and they began to wonder if it wouldn't be best to send for a psychiatrist. Then one of their top idea men told them that the sure way to make a rooster crow was to get another rooster to crow. He remembered that the second vice-president was pretty good at barnyard imitations, though his crow wasn't his best number. His quack was better and his sow-with-a-litter-of-baby-pigs was his topper. But they thought his crow might get by, so they fetched him out of his office.

' "Crow," they said.

' "Crow?" said he.

' "That's right. Crow."

' "Oh, you mean *crow*?" said the vice-president, getting it. "Like a rooster?"

'And they all said that the more like a rooster he was the better they'd be pleased.

'Well, these vice-presidents don't spare themselves when duty calls. He crowed and crowed and crowed until he rasped his larynx, but not a sign of audience reaction. The rooster just looked at him and went on scrabbling his feet.

' "Now let's all be very calm and rational about this," said the director who had been assigned to shoot the scene. "I'll tell you what's wrong, Adolf. This bird's no fool. He sees you in those yellow slacks and that rainbow shirt and the crimson tie and he's on to it right away that you're no rooster. 'Something wrong here,' he says to himself, and your act don't get over."

' "So here's what you do, Adolf," said the president. "You go out in the street round behind the studio wall where the bird can't see you and start crowing out there. That ought to do it."

'So the vice-president went out on the street and began to crow, and at last the old rooster started to perk up and take notice. He jumped on the perch they had built for him and cleared his throat, and it looked like they were all set to go, when darned if Adolf didn't stop crowing.

' "What's the matter with the fellow?" said the director, and the president yells over the wall:

' "Crow, Adolf, crow!"

'But not a yip out of Adolf, and then someone goes outside to see what's wrong, and there's two cops pushing him into the wagon. They're talking to him kinda soft and soothing.

' "Take it easy," they're saying. "Yes, yes, *sure* we understand why you were crowing. You're a rooster, aren't you? So you come with us, pal, and we'll take you back to the hen-house." '

3

It was only after they had left the drawing-room that Guy remembered that they had not told the comedian their pawn-broker plot. They had not, of course, had much opportunity, and they consoled themselves with the thought that later on there would no doubt be a formal story conference where only business would be talked.

The long journey was coming to an end. They breakfasted next morning as the train was pulling out of San Bernadino. There was a strong scent of orange-blossoms in the air, turning Guy's mind to thoughts of marriage. He mentioned this to Plum, as they sat in the diner gazing out at the mountains, at snow-capped Old Baldy and the distant shimmering peak of Mt Wilson.

'When are you getting married?' Plum asked.

'As soon as possible, now that we are both out here.'

'You'll probably settle down in Hollywood and spend the rest of your life there.'

Guy shook his head.

'Not if they paid me!'

'Well, they would pay you. Bob Benchley says that's the one redeeming feature of the place – the little man in the cage who hands you out the $100 bills each Thursday.'

'I mean, not if they paid me untold gold. Hollywood may turn out all right for a visit, but—'

'You wouldn't live there if they gave you the place?'

'Exactly. Not even if they made me a brother-in-law, like Palmer. I'm going to get back into the theatre again.'

'Me, too.'

'Venton Freedley said he liked that story of ours about the fellow who's such a hit with women and the millionaire father who hires him to stop his daughter marrying a titled half-wit.'

'You mean *Anything Goes*?'

'Yes. You still like that title?'

'I think it's great.'

'Vinton says Cole Porter would write the score.'

'Cole does his own lyrics.'

'Yes.'

'That means I'm out. What pests these lyric-writing composers are! Taking the bread out of a man's mouth.'

'You would do the book with me.'

'Do you want me to?'

'Of course I do. You had an idea about a crook escaping on the boat from New York dressed as a clergyman.'

'Public Enemy Number Thirteen.'

'A superstitious crook. Never had any luck when he was Thirteen, so wants to murder one of the top dozen and get promoted to Twelve. We ought to start jotting down some of these ideas before we get all tangled up with Hollywood.'

'Write on the back of the menu.'

Cups and plates were pushed aside. They paid no further attention to the orange groves, the mountains, the advertisements of the secondhand-car dealers, the flaming twenty-four sheets of the picture-houses. They were working.

'I see the whole of the action taking place on a transatlantic liner.'

'Giving the hero six days to disentangle the girl.'

'There'll be another girl – a comic – who's mixed up with the hero. He was out with her on a supper-date when the heroine's father gave him the job, and she follows him aboard. You never saw *Girl Crazy*, did you?'

'No, I was in England.'

'There was a girl called Ethel Merman in it. It was her first job and she made a terrific hit, singing that "I've Got Rhythm" thing of Gershwin's. She puts a song over better than anybody and is great on comedy.'

'She sounds right for this part.'

'Exactly right. We're rolling!'

'Yes, we're rolling.'

But they were also rolling into Pasadena. They had to hurry back to their compartment for their things.

Held on the car platform while suit-cases, golf-bags and typewriters were handed down by the porters, they looked out at the strange new land that was to be their home. Tall eucalyptus . . . blue-flowered jacarandas, feathery pepper trees dotted with red. . . . And what looked like a thousand shiny new cars, one of which, they felt, must unquestionably belong to Palmer.

Guy saw all these things without really seeing them. His eyes were on a girl farther down the platform who was searching the faces of the passengers waiting to alight. She turned and saw him . . . smiled and waved.

'Journey's End,' felt Guy.

Palmer came bustling up.

'I wanted to see you two boys,' he said briskly. 'I've had an idea for the Bill Fields picture. Just an outline at present, but something for you to be mulling over. Bill's a pawnbroker, the last of a long line of pawnbrokers. His family have been pawnbrokers for centuries. They started originally in Spain and – get this – it was an ancestor of Bill's who loaned Queen Isabella the money to finance Columbus. She signed a regular contract—'

Guy drew a deep breath. His eyes had glazed a little. So had Plum's.

'—giving this ancestor 10 per cent of anything Columbus discovered,' continued Palmer. 'Well, what he discovered – see what I mean – was America. So – this is going to slay you – there's good old Bill with a legal claim to ten per cent of America. Take it from there. Isn't that great?' said Palmer, his horn-rimmed spectacles flashing. 'Isn't that terrific? Isn't that the most colossal idea for a comedian's picture anyone ever-heard?'

There was a long silence. The two authors struggled for words. Then they found them.

'Yes, Mr Palmer,' said Guy.

'Oh, *yes*, Mr Palmer,' said Plum.

And they knew they were really in Hollywood.

ACKNOWLEDGEMENTS

The authors wish to extend their sincere thanks to Messrs Chappell & Co. for permission granted them to reprint lyrics from a number of musical comedies. Those lyrics are copyright as follows:

From *Very Good Eddie*, copyright, 1916, by T. B. Harms Co.
From *Have a Heart*, copyright, 1916, by T. B. Harms Co.
From *Miss Springtime*, copyright, 1916, by T. B. Harms Co.
From *Oh, Boy!* copyright, 1917, by T. B. Harms Co.
From *The Riviera Girl*, copyright, 1917, by T. B. Harms Co.
From *Oh, Lady, Lady*, copyright, 1918, by T. B. Harms Co.
From *The Rose of China*, copyright, 1919, by T. B. Harms Co.
From *Sally*, copyright, 1920, by T. B. Harms Co.
From *Sitting Pretty*, copyright, 1924, by T. B. Harms Co.
From *Show Boat* (the song 'Bill'), copyright, 1927, by T. B. Harms Co.

PERFORMING FLEA

A Self-Portrait in Letters

With an introduction and additional notes by

W. Townend

Contents

Introduction

It was only a few months ago – though I had been receiving them for more than thirty years – that the thought occurred to me that an amusing and instructive book could be made of these letters of P. G. Wodehouse, eliminating the purely private passages which would be unintelligible to anyone but myself.

Amusing? . . . Well, they amused me. And instructive? Yes, I think so. It seems to me that they are full of sound advice on the art and craft of writing fiction, and to the aspiring author, who has to learn by the arduous and heart-breaking process of trial and error, advice from a writer of worldwide fame is more precious than rubies – or should be.

In my impecunious youth in San Francisco, an equally impecunious friend from Omaha, Nebraska, with whom I had toiled for a pittance on a ranch in Mendocino County, near Russian River, walked with me one day on Market Street – the world's finest thoroughfare – and revealed a scheme whereby we could both make what Plum's Ukridge would have called 'a vast fortune'.

He suggested that we should combine what small amount of cash we had and insert advertisements in the San Francisco newspapers, stating that we were prepared to criticize and revise short stories and novels at a fee of so much per thousand words, and for a further fee would advise the writers of these how best to earn a living from authorship. He said, with some accuracy, that most people in San Francisco either had written or were planning to write, so why should we not make a bit by instructing them how to do it?

I was horrified and firmly refused, much to his regret, but

without impairing our friendship. I said I knew nothing about writing fiction. He said he knew rather less than I did, but seemed puzzled that I should think that that mattered. Was I, he asked, going to throw away a chance of picking up some easy money?

I was.

Now Plum, I think, would have been qualified even then to take on such a project. Almost from the very beginning he knew his job. As Peter Quennell wrote of him a year or two ago:

Though not one non-literary reader in a thousand will lift his eyes from the page to consider Wodehouse as an artist, a fellow-hack cannot fail to admire the extraordinary skill with which, judged by professional literary standards, he goes about his business. Every sentence has a job to do and – in spite of the air of lunatic irresponsibility which hangs around a Wodehouse novel – does it neatly and efficiently. Bertie Wooster may live in a perpetual haze, but P. G. Wodehouse knows at any moment of the story exactly what he is aiming for.

In these letters – the earlier ones, at any rate – he certainly gave me some excellent tips on how to write, from which I hope I have profited.

It is nearly fifteen years since I last met Plum, but I have a feeling that I know him even better now than when we saw each other every week or month or so; for even when he lived in Le Touquet in France my wife and I were living in Dover and he would call in and see us each time he crossed the English Channel on his many visits to London. I think that the explanation for this is that with the passage of time his letters have grown in depth and understanding, and one can read in what he has written – written with no thought that they would ever be seen by other eyes than mine – an awareness of what life has come to mean, of man's responsibilities and duties in a world beset by fear, of the narrowness of mind that leads to war and the pettiness many men and more women show in their contacts with other people, and of a tendency to see both sides of a problem at issue.

I may be wrong, but this is my reading of much that Plum has written. I am, however, right in saying that no one I have ever met has in his disposition so great a zeal for friendship and is so faithful to his ideals.

Plum and I were at school together at Dulwich College, a school situated in delightful surroundings of field and woodland where one can imagine oneself – or could at the turn of the century – in the heart of the country. We were in the same house, slept in the same small dormitory, and shared the same small study, but outside the house our paths divided. Plum was in the classical sixth and a school prefect, he played for the school two years at cricket, but although tried for the football fifteen occasionally in 1897 and 1898 did not get his honour cap till the 1899 season, by which time I had left.

He was, in fact, someone of importance in the life of Dulwich, and was already at the age of seventeen an author, having among other things written a series of plays after the pattern of the Greek tragedies, outrageously funny, dealing with boys and masters. I would give a good deal to have those plays in my possession now.

Unlike Plum I was of no importance in the school: I had been kept by my father at a private school far too long: my education was unbalanced and, knowing a fair amount of Latin, but little Greek, a fair amount of French but no German, I was forced to specialize in mathematics which, fortunately for me, meant that I passed many hours each week by myself in the master's private library, surrounded by books, and with no supervision save my own conscience which was elastic.

I was at Dulwich for four terms only, but save for my four years on the Pacific Coast and my Army Service from 1915 to 1919, no period of my life has made so great an impression on me. I look back on those few short months as among the happiest I have ever known and I owe this happiness to Plum Wodehouse with whom I spent evening after evening, when we should have been preparing the next day's work, in reading and in conversation.

Should there be anyone in the year 1951 ignorant of but interested in the life of a great English public school in the last years of Queen Victoria's reign I suggest that a perusal of

Plum's school stories would be advantageous. Wrykyn, the school about which he wrote, is Dulwich, a Dulwich not situated in a London suburb but in the country. But whereas the boys of Wrykyn are practically all boarders Dulwich, like Bedford and St Paul's, though with four large boarding-houses, now increased to five, is in the main a day school; nevertheless elderly men who were at Dulwich between the years 1895 and 1901 will recognize and appreciate Plum's masterly delineation of the life we lived so long ago. *The Gold Bat*, *The White Feather*, *The Head of Kay's* and *Mike* are still, I believe, popular with the present generation of schoolboys.

Had I, in the course of years, earned even a pittance as a black-and-white artist – which was what I tried to be on leaving Dulwich – the letters that form this book would never have been written, but Chance – I can think of no better term, rejecting Incompetence as too humiliating, however true – turned me to the writing of fiction as a means of livelihood.

In the year 1906 I was living in one room in Arundel Street, a cul-de-sac off Coventry Street, where Lyons' Corner House now stands, my expenses being paid by Plum, a *quid pro quo*, as it were, for a service I had quite unwittingly done him. I had one day, when in a talkative mood, a normal condition, I fear, insisted on telling him the story of an eccentric acquaintance who had helped another man, equally eccentric, so I gathered, to manage a chicken farm in Devonshire. Neither my friend nor the man who was his partner had known the first thing about the raising and feeding of chickens and they might with no more chance of success have embarked on the rearing of seagulls. Every mistake that could be made by a chicken farmer was made by these two and in the end creditors, like vultures about a carcass, arrived in force and the partnership was dissolved in scenes of incredible tumult.

Plum was so amused by this story that he asked if he could use it in a book. He wrote the book, *Love Among the Chickens*, and it was a success, and on my share of the proceeds I came to live in Arundel Street.

Toward the end of that wonderful summer of 1906, discouraged by my failure as an artist, I felt that I needed a new source of material for my pictures, though actually what I needed was talent. Someone suggested that I should go for a voyage in a tramp steamer. Plum said that if I really wanted to go – 'and rather you than me' – he would pay my expenses.

I went for my voyage, to Sulina in Romania, and returned after three months with a broken nose and no hat, with no pictures, but with notebooks filled with stories I had heard on board my tramp, scraps of fo'c's'le and engine-room gossip, local colour, details of everyday routine, anecdotes and so on, which I had jotted down more or less idly with no thought in my mind that in years to come they might be of use to me.

Later when I had finally decided that I should never earn a living as an artist, I unearthed these notebooks, read through them, much as I have read through Plum Wodehouse's letters, and set to work to write a sea story, *The Tramp*, the first of the thirty-nine books which I have had published in the last thirty years.

W. TOWNEND

ONE

1920–1925

It is usually difficult to decide at what point to begin a book, fiction or otherwise, but the problem here is settled by the fact that the letters I received from Plum between 1899 and 1920 have, with very few exceptions, been either lost or destroyed.

From 1922 the letters follow at frequent intervals. If at times there are gaps in the sequence, this was because Plum and I lived near enough to each other to make letter-writing unnecessary.

I begin with one written twelve months after I was demobilized from the Army. Plum, who had gone to New York in 1909, was rejected for military service because of bad eyesight and had remained in America during the war, earning a precarious living as a freelance writer.

Feb. 28, 1920   *Great Neck,*
                                                       Long Island, NY

Dear Bill,

Your letter arrived this morning, and it's great to know that you are in the pink as it leaves me at present. I have seen a lot of your stuff in *Adventure,* and I wrote to you care of them, but I suppose it never reached you. Letters are always going wrong these days.

Gosh, what a time since we corresponded! When you last heard from me, I was living in Bellport, wasn't I? Or was it Central Park West? Anyway, I know that wherever I was I was having the dickens of a job, keeping the wolf the right side of the door. Nobody would buy my short stories. I couldn't sell a damn one anywhere. If it hadn't been for Frank Crowninshield, the editor of *Vanity Fair,* liking my stuff and taking all I could do, I should have been very much against it.

Vanity Fair is a swanky magazine 'devoted to Society and the Arts', and I used to write about half of it each month under a number of names – P. G. Wodehouse, Pelham Grenville, J. Plum, C. P. West, P. Brooke-Haven and so on. (Comic articles, not short stories. They don't use fiction.) The payment wasn't high, but high enough to keep me going. I also became the *VF* dramatic critic.

I was plugging along like this, when suddenly everything changed and the millennium set in. The *Saturday Evening Post* took my serial *Something Fresh*, an amazing bit of luck which stunned me, as it had never really occurred to me as possible that a long story by an unknown writer would have a chance there. Since then I have had three more in the *SEP* – *Uneasy Money*, *Piccadilly Jim* and *A Damsel in Distress*. (I deduce that you saw one of them, as your letter was forwarded from the *Post*.) They gave me a raise with each one – $3500, $5000, $7500, and for the *Damsel* $10,000 – so now I can afford an occasional meat meal, not only for self but for wife and resident kitten and bulldog – all of whom can do with a cut off the joint.

But my big source of income these last years has been from the theatre. Do you remember a song of mine called 'Mr Chamberlain' that Seymour Hicks sang in *The Beauty of Bath* in 1906? The music was by Jerome Kern, and I happened to run into Jerry over here – it was at the Princess Theatre the first night of a very successful small musical comedy which he had written with Guy Bolton – and he introduced me to Guy, who suggested that we three should team up, Guy doing the book and me the lyrics. I was delighted, of course, because I love writing lyrics. We wrote a fairly successful show called *Have a Heart* and then had a terrific smash with a thing called *Oh Boy!* after which all the managers were after us with commissions. One season Guy and I actually had five shows running simultaneously on Broadway, and about a dozen companies out on the road.

Guy and I clicked from the start like Damon and Pythias. We love working together. Never a harsh word or a dirty look. He is one of the nicest chaps I ever met and the supreme worker of all time. I help him as much as I can with the 'book' end of the things, but he really does the whole job and I just do the lyrics, which are easy when one has Jerry to work with.

In spite of all this theatre work, I have managed to write a number of short stories for the *SEP* – about a bloke called Bertie Wooster and his valet, and I am now doing a serial for *Collier's* and another for – if you'll believe it – the *Woman's Home Companion*. Heaven knows what a women's magazine wants with my sort of stuff, but they are giving me 15,000 of the best for it.

The short stories to which Plum refers were those later published by Herbert Jenkins under the title *The Inimitable Jeeves*. The *Collier's* serial was 'Jill the Reckless' the *Woman's Home Companion's*, 'The Girl on the Boat'.

Here are the answers to your questions:

(1) I now write stories at terrific speed. I've started a habit of rushing them through and then working over them very carefully, instead of trying to get the first draft exactly right, and have just finished the rough draft of an 8000 word story in two days. It nearly slew me. As a rule, I find a week long enough for a short story, if I have the plot well thought out.

(2) On a novel I generally do eight pages a day, i.e. about 2500 words.

(3) Recently I have had a great time with my work. We have been snowed up here after a record blizzard, and nobody has been able to get at me for ages. As a rule I like to start work in the mornings, knock off for a breather, and then do a bit more before dinner. I never work after dinner. Yet in the old days that was my best time. Odd.

(4) Plots. They've been coming along fine of late.

(5) I think a good agent the best investment in the world. The point is that an agent can fight for your stuff as you can't possibly fight yourself. I would never have the nerve to refuse a fairly good offer in the hope of getting more elsewhere, but an agent will.

Funny you should have had that trouble about a story getting longer and longer in spite of yourself. I'm suffering that way now. This new novel of mine is already 15,000 words longer than anything I have done, and the worst is yet to come.

I must get hold of Alec Waugh's book *The Loom of Youth*, that you speak so highly of. I've heard a lot about it. He must be pretty good to be able to do anything big at seventeen. I was practically an imbecile at that age.

We sail on the *Adriatic* on April 24th, as follows: Ethel, carrying the black kitten, followed by myself with parrot in cage and Loretta, our maid, with any other animals we may acquire in the meantime. We shall have to leave Sammy, the bulldog, behind, worse luck, owing to the quarantine laws. It's a nuisance and we shall miss him sorely, but fortunately it won't break his heart being parted from us, as he is the most amiable soul in the world and can be happy with anyone. This is the dog I was given by one of the girls in the revue Guy and I wrote for the Century Theatre (Gosh, what a flop that one was!), and he cost us a fortune when we first had him, because he was always liking the looks of passers-by outside our garden gate and trotting out and following them. The first time he disappeared, we gave the man who brought him back ten dollars, and this got around among the local children, and stirred up their business instincts. They would come to our gate and call, 'Sammy, Sammy, Sammy,' and out old Sam would waddle, and then they would bring him back with a cheery 'We found your dog wandering around down the road, mister,' and cash in. I may add that the bottom has dropped out of the market and today any child who collects 25¢ thinks he has done well.

That I then received no letter of any importance from Plum until June 1922 is explained by the fact that we were living within easy reach of each other in London and so met frequently.

June 27th, 1922   *4 Onslow Square, SW7*

I've just wired to you to say that I think the story is great. The only criticism I would make is that, as a reader, I wished that Overeck (what ghastly names you give these poor blighters! – when you read your stamp story you will be pained to see that I have changed your characters to Smith, Evans, Jones and so on) had got it in the neck a bit more directly. Still, it's all right as it stands.

Listen, Bill, any funny plots you can send me will be heartily welcomed. I've got to start another series in the *Strand*, February number, and haven't any ideas except that I think I'll write some stories with Ukridge as the chief character. At the date of the series he is still unmarried and I can make him always in love with some girl or other, like Bingo Little, if necessary. The keynote is that he and his pals are all very hard-up, and a plot which has as a punch Ukridge just missing touching someone for two bob would be quite in order.

I am afraid your eyes won't be gladdened yet awhile by the sight of *Leave it to Psmith*. I have suddenly decided to introduce another character, and this has created the most extraordinary confusion in the earlier chapters, so that my MS is all anyhow.

I have now contracted to finish a novel, six short stories and a musical show with Guy Bolton, by the end of October. I have no ideas and don't expect to get any. By the way, am off to Dinard on July 15th. Probably only for a fortnight, or three weeks, as rehearsals of *The Cabaret Girl*, the thing I've written with George Grossmith, for the Winter Garden – music by Jerry Kern – begin in August.

The puppy was run over by a motor bike the other day and emerged perfectly unhurt but a bit emotional. We had to chase him half across London before he simmered down. He just started running and kept on running till he felt better.

77 North Drive,
Great Neck,
December 16th, 1922   *Long Island, NY*

Life has been one damned bit of work after another ever since I landed here. First, Guy Bolton and I settled down and wrote a musical comedy – tentatively called *Pat*, a rotten title – in two weeks for Flo Ziegfeld. It has been lying in a drawer ever since, Ziegfeld having been busy over another play, and doesn't look like getting put on this year. This, I should mention, is the play Ziegfeld was cabling about with such boyish excitement – the one I came over to do. You never heard anything like the fuss he made when I announced I couldn't make the Wednesday boat but would sail on the Saturday. He gave me to understand that my loitering would ruin everything.

I then sat down to finish *Leave it to Psmith*, for the *Saturday Evening Post*. I wrote 40,000 words in three weeks.

Since then I have been working with Guy on a musical

comedy, *Sitting Pretty*, for the Duncan Sisters, music by Irving Berlin. This is complicated by the fact that Guy's new comedy has just started rehearsals, and he is up to his neck in it. So the work is proceeding by jerks.

The *Saturday Evening Post* has done me proud. Although they never commission anything, they liked the first 60,000 words of *Leave it to Psmith* so much that they announced it in the papers before I sent in the remainder. I mailed them the last part on a Wednesday and got a cheque for $20,000 on the following Tuesday.

The story will start late in January, I think. Do you get the *Post* now? If not, let me know, and I'll have it sent to you. I want you to cast a fatherly eye over the first two instalments in particular. There is a tremendous amount of plot to be got across in these and I want you to see if I could improve the construction. There is no possible way of avoiding telling part of the story twice over, which is a nuisance, but I think it's pretty good though I'm doubtful about the final chapter.

December 22nd, 1922   *Great Neck,*
                                                        Long Island

More or less down with lumbago. It started by my putting my hip out while playing golf and this set up an irritation. I went to an osteopath yesterday who practically tore me limb from limb. I must say I feel better after the treatment, though not at all sure that all of me is still there. I wonder what an osteopath does if a patient suddenly comes apart in his hands. ('Quick, Watson, the seccotine!')

We are having the devil of a time over this Duncan Sisters show. All attempts to get hold of Irving Berlin about the music have failed. We went into New York last Monday to keep an appointment with him and found that he had had to rush off to the dentist. He then made a date with me over the phone to lunch with him on Thursday and work all the afternoon. I went in and called at his flat and he was out and had left no message. Heaven knows when the thing will ever be finished!

December 29th, 1922   *Great Neck*

Well, well, well. So everything's all right. Yesterday morning when I got down to breakfast, there was a letter from Hoffman, saying that he was buying your novel, *The Tramp*, for *Adventure*. I cabled you yesterday (cursing you violently for having such a long address). What I said was . . . 'Tramp Sold', but I expect the cable people will think that that didn't make sense and will edit it. You probably got it as 'Trump Solid' or 'Stamp Gold', but anyhow, I hope you read the hidden meaning.

You don't know how bucked I am over this. I have been worrying myself like the dickens about this yarn. I felt that if they turned it down after you had sweated eleven weeks over it, you might turn your face to the wall and give up. But I think this proves that you are OK.

I don't want to come the heavy expert, but I'll tell you what has been wrong with some of your stuff in the past – you have been too easily satisfied with the *bones* of a story. Every time you have had a good story to tell, you have done a corker. If you look back, you'll see that the only ones of yours which have failed are those which have had a weak plot.

Another thing. Your stuff is really too good for the ordinary magazine, so that when you don't have a plot which is all right for the flatheads anyway, editors are apt to turn you down.

All this sounds rather incoherent – but, well, look here: your story, *The Horse Thief*, was sure-fire for any magazine because the actual plot was so exactly right for any type of reader that it didn't matter that it was well written instead of cheaply. But *The Price of the Picture* was no good for popular magazines unless thoroughly cheapened.

And now I know what I am driving at is: When you get a plot, examine it carefully and say to yourself, 'Is this a popular magazine plot?' If it isn't, simply don't attempt to make it a popular magazine story. Just put all you know into it and write it the very best you can and confine its field to the really decent magazines like *Blackwood's*, the *Cornhill*, etc.

I think that now you have had such an instant response from the *Cornhill* you should follow up that line as hard as you can. It may not be so immediately profitable as the more popular magazines, but you make up for that in reputation.

I have got to start the *Cosmopolitan* series at once, and the editor likes the character of Ukridge, so if you have any more plots, ship them over.

May 28th, 1923   *Southampton,*
                                                       Long Island

I have at last got the *Strand* with *A Couple of Down-And-Outs* in it. I think the illustrations are good and the story reads fine. It has given me an illuminating idea about your work – to wit, that you make all your characters so real that you can't afford a grey ending. You simply must make a point of having them all right in the end, or the reader feels miserable. And you have got to make the happy ending definite, too, as in this story.

Another thing is: what you want to put your stuff over is *action*. In *A Couple of Down-And-Outs* the story jumps from one vivid scene to another. The more I write, the more I am convinced that the only way to write a popular story is to split it up into scenes, and have as little stuff between the scenes as possible. See what I mean? Well, look here. I wrote a story the other day – *The Return of Battling Billson* – and the only thing that was arrived at in the first 1500 words was that I met Battling Billson down in the East End and gave him Ukridge's address, which he had lost. But by having me go into a pub and get a drink and have lost my money and be chucked out by the barman and picked up by Billson, who happened to be passing, and then having Billson go in and clean up the pub and manhandle the barman I got some darned good stud which, I think, absolutely concealed the fact that nothing haff really happened except my giving him the address.

Do you see what I mean? I think that for a magazine story you *must* start off with a good scene. Of course, you probably know this already, but here it is again with my blessing.

I'm going up to New York tomorrow for a few days, as George Grossmith is arriving to work on the next Winter Garden show with me.

I was awfully glad to get your letter containing the welcome statement that you thought on reading it again that Ukridge's Dog College was all right. I had to rush that story in the most horrible way. I think I told you that the *Cosmopolitan* wanted it for the April number, and I had about five days to deliver it and got it all wrong, and had to write about 20,000 words before I got it set. And then, when I reached Palm Beach, I found that the artist had illustrated a scene which was not in the final version, and I had to add a new one by telephone!

I have done two more stories in the last three weeks, and am now well ahead again, having completed eight. I'm so glad you like the series. Now that I've got well into it, I think it better than any of the others. It was difficult at first having the 'I' chap a straight character instead of a sort of Bertie Wooster, but now I find it rather a relief, as it seems to make the thing more real.

I have had a stream of letters cursing the end of *Leave it to Psmith*, and I shall have to rewrite it. But what a sweat it is altering a story that has gone cold!

Easthampton,
Long Island

July 23rd, 1923

Have you ever been knocked over by a car? If not, don't. There's no percentage in it. I was strolling along yesterday evening to meet Ethel who had gone down to the station in our Buick, and half-way to the village she sighted me and pulled in to the sidewalk. The roads here are cement, with a sort of No Man's Land of dirt between side-walk and road. I had just got on to this when I saw a Ford coming down behind our car. Naturally, I thought it would pull up when it realized that Ethel had stopped, but it must have been going too fast, for I suddenly observed with interest that it wasn't stopping but was swinging in straight for me on the wrong side of the road. I gave one gazelle-like spring sideways and the damned thing's right front wheel caught my left leg squarely and I thought the world had ended. I took the most awful toss and came down on the side of my face and skinned my nose, my left leg and my right arm. This morning all sorts of unsuspected muscles and bones are aching, and I can hardly move my right arm. But, my gosh! doesn't it just show that we are here today and gone tomorrow! If I had been a trifle less fit and active, I should have got the entire car in the wishbone. Oh, well, it's all in a lifetime!

Last night I went to bed early and read your story, *Peter the Greek*. For the first half I thought it was the best thing you had ever done, full of action and suspense. But, honestly, as you seem to think yourself from your letter, it does drop a bit after that. Mogger (my Heaven! what names you give your characters!) whom you have established as a sinister menace, is weakened by that scene where Teame hits him. It is an error, I think, ever to have your villain manhandled by a minor character. Just imagine Moriarty socked by Dr Watson. A villain ought to be a sort of scarcely human invulnerable figure. The reader ought to be in a constant state of panic, saying to himself, 'How the devil *is* this superman to be foiled?' The only person capable of hurting him should be the hero.

Bill, I've spoken of this before and I want to emphasize it again – you *must not* take any risk of humanizing your villains in a story of action. And by humanizing I mean treating them subjectively instead of objectively.

Taking Moriarty as the pattern villain, don't you see how much stronger he is by being an inscrutable figure and how much he would have been weakened if Conan Doyle had switched off to a chapter showing his thoughts? A villain ought to be a sort of malevolent force, not an intelligible person at all.

I wish the deuce we could meet and talk these things over. It is so hard to discuss a story by correspondence. The time to wrangle over the construction of a story is when it is being shaped, not after it has set.

I wish, too, that you were in London and not Switzerland. I am sailing next Saturday for the rehearsals of *The Beauty Prize* at the Winter Garden, and I shall be in London for three weeks or so. I suppose your wanderings can't possibly take you home for August?

Herbert Jenkins's death was a great shock to me. I was awfully fond of him, but I always had an idea that he could not last very long. He simply worked himself to death. He was very fragile with a terrific driving mind and no physique at all, one of those fellows who look transparent and are always tired. One used to wonder how long he could possibly carry on. He shirked his meals and exercise and concentrated entirely on work. You can't do it.

11 *King Street,*
St James's,
August 24th, 1923   *London*

I am at the above address and should like to see a specimen of your typing, with all the latest gossip from Switzerland, but mark you, laddie, I sail for New York on September 5th, so make it snappy!

I have the honour to report that the old bean is in a state of absolute stagnation. I wrote the best golf-story I have ever done on board the boat coming over – *The Coming of Gowf* – but since I landed I have not had the ghost of an idea for a plot of any kind – so much so – or so little so – that I shall be obliged to drop the Ukridge Series – at any rate for the moment – at the end of the ninth story. I wanted the last two stories to be about how he got married, and it looked as if it would be pretty easy, but I'm darned if I can think of anything for him to do. It may come later. I've done a lot of work this last year – twelve short stories and half a novel, besides my share of *The Beauty Prize,* including all the lyrics – and it may simply be that I need a rest.

The kitten has had a fit, but is all right again now. I allude to the animal at the Wodehouse home at Easthampton, whom you have never met. A cheery soul, with a fascinating habit of amusing the master at breakfast by chasing a ball of paper all over the room, and then suddenly dashing up the curtain from floor to ceiling at one bound. Sammy, the bulldog, has had an attack of eczema, but is doing well. No other news from home.

c/o Guaranty Trust Company,
44th St & 5th Avenue,
November 4th, 1923   *New York City*

I have been meaning to write to you for some time about *The Talking Doll.* It gripped me all through but if you are going to start anything in a story like the idea of the doll and Chutton, it is brutal to the reader to explain it away in the end. It is like the ghost turning out to be smugglers.

Just one more thing. I think you have made a mistake in starting interesting stuff and then dropping it. The principle I always go on in writing a long story is to think of the characters in terms of actors in a play. I say to myself, when I invent a good character for an early scene, 'If this were a musical comedy we should have to get somebody like Leslie Henson to play this part, and if he found that all he had was a short scene in act one, he would walk out. How, therefore, can I twist the story so as to give him more to do and keep him alive till the fall of the curtain?'

This generally works well and improves the story. A good instance of this was Baxter in *Leave it to Psmith*. It became plain to me as I constructed the story that Baxter was such an important character that he simply had to have a good scene somewhere in what would correspond to the latter part of act two, so I bunged in that flower-pot sequence.

I wish we could discuss these stories, as we used to, before you finish them. It is so much easier to see where a scenario goes off the rails. Why don't you send me your next scenario for me to make suggestions? I always get my own scenarios passed by two or three people before I start writing. If one has finished a long story, one goes cold on it and alterations are a torture. I had this experience with *Leave it to Psmith*. You and a number of other people told me the end was wrong, as I had already suspected myself, but I couldn't muster up energy and ideas enough to alter it. I finally did it, and it has held up the publication of the book and caused much agony of spirit at the Herbert Jenkins office. Still, it is all right now, I think.

I am half-way through mapping out a new novel, which looks like being a pippin. I am going on a new system this time, making the scenario very full, putting in atmosphere and dialogue etc., so that when I come actually to write it the work will be easy. So far I have scenarioed it out to about the 40,000 word mark; and it has taken me 13,000 words to do it! I have now reached a point where deep thought is required. I am not sure I haven't got too much plot, and may have to jettison the best idea in the story. I suppose the secret of writing is to go through your stuff till you come on something you think is particularly good, and then cut it out.

The new novel Plum speaks about here was published under the title of *Bill the Conqueror*.

                                                c/o Guy Bolton,
                                                17 Beverly Road,
January 26, 1924   *Great Neck, LINY*

Listen, Bill. Is this a crazy idea? I suddenly thought the other day, there are always rats on board ship, so why shouldn't one rat, starting by being a bit bigger than the others, gradually grow and grow, feeding on his little playmates, till he became the size of an Airedale terrier? Then there begin to be mysterious happenings on board the ship. Men are found dead with their faces chewed off, etc. And so on.

Is this any good to you? It certainly isn't to me. I give it you with my blessing.

An interesting letter – to me, at any rate. Plum's suggested giant rat story unexpectedly came to fruition ten years later when I wrote a story on the same theme, though dealing with an island in the South Pacific and not with a ship. This story was published in *Harper's Magazine* – and was, I suppose, one of the few good short stories I ever wrote, but the extraordinary part about the whole affair is that I had no idea Plum had given me the plot until, reading over his letter of January 26th 1924, I suddenly realized that the theme of the story had come from him, and was not my own invention. I have a good enough memory, but this was one of the things I had forgotten in twenty-seven years!

                                                Hôtel Campbell,
                                                Avenue Friedmann,
May 8th, 1924   *Paris*

Our plans for the summer are still very undecided, but it looks as if we are going to take a house in London in the autumn.

Are you working well these days? I haven't had an idea for a story for three months or more. I finished *The Adventures of Sally* at the beginning of April and since then my mind has been a blank. I had to write it under difficulties, as I was working with Guy and Jerry Kern on a musical comedy, the first we three have done together since the Princess Theatre days. It's called *Sitting Pretty*, and was doing all right when I left New York, but I have my doubts about it.

It's a good instance of the sort of trouble you run into when working in the theatre. Do you remember me telling you that Guy and I were doing a show for the Duncan Sisters with Irving Berlin? This is it. What happened was that we didn't plan to produce till October or later and the Duncans asked Sam Harris, our manager, if they could fill in during the summer with a little thing called *Topsy and Eva* – a sort of comic *Uncle Tom's Cabin* which they had written themselves. They just wanted to do it on the coast, they said. Sam said that would be all right, so they went ahead, expecting to play a couple of months or so, and darned if *Topsy and Eva* didn't turn out one of those colossal hits which run for ever. It's now in about its fiftieth week in Chicago with New York still to come, so we lost the Duncans and owing to losing them lost Irving Berlin, who liked *Sitting Pretty* but thought it wouldn't go without them. So we got hold of Jerry and carried on with him. He has done a fine score, but it still remains to be seen whether or not the show – written as a vehicle for a sister act – will succeed with its present cast. We have Gertrude Bryan and Queenie Smith for the two Duncan parts, and they are both very good, but in my opinion they aren't a team and this may dish us. A pity if it happens, as it's really a good show.

Sitting Pretty came off after a short run, the only one of the six Bolton-Wodehouse-Kern musical comedies that did not play a whole season in New York. Irving Berlin had been right.

Grand Hotel,
Harrogate,
Yorks

September 23rd, 1924

Awfully sorry I haven't written for so long. I've been very busy. I've done a couple of short stories since I got here and also practically completed the scenario of a new novel.

Ethel left yesterday to see about getting our new house ready. We have taken 23 Gilbert Street, Grosvenor Square, from October 1st. Isn't there any chance of your being in town at any rate through November? I have a feeling that Dulwich are going to have a good team this year.

Harrogate is a terrific place for work. I wrote an elaborate scenario of the first third of my novel yesterday. I've got a new system now, as it worked so well with *Bill the Conqueror*: that is to write a 30,000 word scenario before starting the novel. (Perhaps I've told you already.) By this means you avoid those ghastly moments when you suddenly come on a hole in the plot and are tied up for three days while you invent a situation. I found that the knowledge that I had a clear path ahead of me helped my grip on the thing. Also, writing a scenario of this length gives you ideas for dialogue scenes and you can jam them down in skeleton and there they are, ready for use later.

Do you like the title: *Sam The Sudden*?

You remember how we condemned Harry Leon Wilson's *Oh, Doctor!* on the strength of the first instalment in the *Post*? I have just been reading it in book form, and it's excellent. I think a story has to be pretty good to stand up against publication in the *Post*, with that small print and those solid pages. But I must say I'm not keen on his new one. Are you reading it? How that man does work that Addison Simms joke to death!

I think it must have been within the next twelve months that the *Saturday Evening Post* discarded the small type, that was so hard on their writers and adopted larger print altogether, which was a great improvement in every way.

October 1st, 1924   *Harrogate*

The short story I've just finished, entitled *Honeysuckle Cottage*, is the funniest idea I've ever had. A young writer of thrillers gets left five thousand quid and a house by his aunt, who was Leila May Pinkney, the famous writer of sentimental stories. He finds that her vibrations have set up a sort of miasma of sentimentalism in the place, so that all who come within its radius get soppy and maudlin. He then finds to his horror that he is – but it will be simpler to send you the story, so I am doing so. I polished it up a good bit in typing it out.

Key to the Addison Simms mystery. I don't know if it is still going, but there used to be an advertisement of a memory training course in all the American magazines. It showed the man who had not taken the course embarrassed and floundering when he met the old acquaintance whose name he had forgotten. Whereas the man who had taken the course just stretched out his hand with a beaming smile and said, 'Why, certainly, I remember you, Mr Addison Simms. We met at the Rotary Club dinner at Seattle on October 3rd, 1910. How are you, how are your wife and your three children? And how did you come out on that granary deal?'

In his letter of October 2nd, 1924, written once more from Harrogate, Plum discusses at great length the reasons why, in his opinion, my long story, *His Father's Son*, had been rejected when other of my stories which I considered not so good had been accepted and published. Plum wrote:

It seems to me that if you are to go on writing for popular magazines you will deliberately have to make your stuff cheaper. At present you are working from character to plot, and what they want, I'm convinced, is the story that contains only obvious characters who exist simply for the sake of the plot. Take a story like that one I thought was your very best, *In the Stokehold*. It was all subtlety. What they would have liked would have been the same idea with all the motives obvious. You've been trying to write for magazines that aren't good enough, and you are consequently caught in two minds. You can't bring yourself to start with a cheap, tawdry plot, and yet you torture the story to suit an editor by excluding everything he objects to.

Here is an exact parallel. Remember *The Luck Stone*, which with your assistance I wrote for *Chums*. School story full of kidnappings, attempted murders, etc. They were delighted with it. Then I tried them with a real school story and they threw a fit. 'What, no blood?' they cried, and shot the thing back at me.

I was thrilled and amused when on re-reading Plum's letters, I discovered by chance among them a note I had had from him, dated May 6th, 1906.

Dear Bill,

Here's a go. I've been commissioned by *Chums* to do a 70,000 word serial by July. They want it not so public-schooly as my usual stuff and with a rather a lurid plot. For Heaven's sake rally round and lend a hand. I've written off today

earnestly recommending you for the illustrations on the strength
of those you did for *The White Feather*.

In any case, give me an idea or two.

PS Your reward will be my blessing and at least a fiver.

Though a fiver was a fiver in those days, Plum sent me £10 for the
small amount of help I was able to give him. It should be of interest
to any student of the books of P. G. Wodehouse to obtain the
numbers of *Chums* for the latter part of 1906, if any still survive, and
read *The Luck Stone*, by – if I remember rightly – 'Basil Windham'.

A letter Plum wrote on October 28th from 23 Gilbert Street,
Mayfair, contains some valuable advice.

When you're doing a long story you have got to be most
infernally careful of the values of your characters. I believe I
told you once before that I classed all my characters as if they
were living salaried actors, and I'm convinced that this is a
rough but very good way of looking at them.

The one thing actors – important actors, I mean – won't
stand is being brought on to play a scene which is of no value
to them in order that they may feed some less important
character, and I believe this isn't vanity but is based on an
instinctive knowledge of stagecraft. They kick because they
know the balance isn't right.

I wish we could meet. How is the cottage working out? One
thing about living in the country is that, even if the windows
leak, you can get some work done. I find it's the hardest job
to get at the stuff here. We have damned dinners and lunches
which just eat up the time. I find that having a lunch hanging
over me kills my morning's work, and dinner isn't much better.
I'm at the stage now, if I drop my characters, they go cold.

I enclose a sheet of questions, which you will save my life by
answering. They come in Chapter Three of *Sam the Sudden*, the
chapter I ought to be working on now.

Chapter Three starts as follows:

Sam Shotter stood outside the galley of the tramp steamer
Araminta in pleasant conversation with Clarence – ('Soup')
Todhunter, the vessel's popular and energetic cook.

Now then:

(A) How was Sam dressed? (All his luggage had come over

on the *Mauretania* and he had sea-clothes on. This is very important, as in next chapter it is essential that Sam shall look like a dead-beat and be taken for a burglar.)

(B) What did Sam see, hear and smell, as he stood outside the galley?

(C) Sam is the stepson of a millionaire and has a penchant for travelling on tramps. He must have had at least one voyage on the *Araminta* before, because it is essential that he knows the skipper well. Therefore, in what capacity did he sail? Would it be ship's etiquette for him to chum up with the skipper as well as the cook?

(D) On the voyage the only thing Sam has had to look at has been a photograph of a girl cut out of the *Tatler*. Could he have a cabin to himself? And do you call it a cabin or a state-room?

(E) The *Araminta* is sailing from America to England. How long would the voyage take? Also, where would she start from, and where dock? Could she dock at Port of London, and be going on to Cardiff?

(F) I particularly want Sam to be in London when Chapter starts, so that he has an easy trip to the West End, which is the setting of the next chapter. Please give me some atmosphere for Port of London, or wherever it is, i.e. something for Sam to see from the deck of the ship.

(G) Can you possibly write me a description of Soup Todhunter from your knowledge of ship's cooks? It is immaterial what he looks like, of course, but it will help.

(H) I am probably taking Sam to the skipper's cabin, so what is the skipper doing when the boat has just docked? I mean, probably the boat is discharging cargo or has been during the day. I want Sam to get off the ship in nice time to take the skipper up to the West End for a bit of dinner.

Well, that's all I can think of at the moment. I'm keeping a carbon copy of these questions, so you'll only need to jot down notes under each heading.

I do hope you're not busy on anything just now, as I don't want to interrupt you. Also bear in mind that I can carry on quite well for at least three weeks without the information. I have got the story so mapped out that I can skip the sea stuff and go on working on the shore scenes till you are ready.

I answered all these questions with great care, but, alas, as you will see if you turn to *Sam the Sudden*, Sam Shotter never did stand outside the galley of the tramp steamer *Araminta* in pleasant conversation with Clarence ('Soup') Todhunter. In the final version the meeting took place off stage and is merely referred to in the words, 'He had dined well, having as his guest his old friend Hash Todhunter,' – not 'Soup', an honourable name bestowed later on Mr Slattery, the burglar in *Hot Water*. All I actually accomplished was putting Plum right about Sam's costume and Hash's looks. But that formidable list of questions shows the thoroughness with which he approached a job of work.

January 11th, 1925   *23 Gilbert Street,*
                                                            Grosvenor Square

I think that their criticism of this story means that your stuff is too real.

You have your heroes struggling against Life and Fate, and what they want are stories about men struggling with octopuses and pirates. You make the reader uneasy. He doesn't enjoy himself. He feels, 'Well, maybe this poor devil will struggle through all right, but what a wretched thought it is that the world is full of poor devils on the brink of being chucked out of jobs and put on the beach.' You make them think about life and popular magazine readers don't want to.

Another thought is that your method involves the elimination of comedy. Your hero, being real, can't approach his difficulties gaily and meet them in a dashing way. I do hope this is clear. What I mean is this: A man trapped in a ruined mill by pock-marked Mexicans and one-eyed Chinamen can be lively and facetious. A man in the position of most of your heroes can't be anything but dead serious. This tends to make a story heavy; it lifts it, in fact, into a class of literature in which your intended public simply doesn't belong.

April 28th, 1925   *23 Gilbert Street,*
                                                            Grosvenor Square

What an age since I wrote to you last. I have been in a sort of trance since I finished *Sam the Sudden*.

It was a frightful rush – so much so that I hadn't time to have it typed but had to send my original script (the only one in existence) over to America from Monte Carlo, and was in a considerable twitter till I heard that it had arrived safely, I having no confidence whatever in the postal arrangements of foreign countries. I sold it to the *Post* for $25,000, and they will eventually send proofs over here, which the Newnes people are anxiously waiting for. At present the Newnes editor has the first 30,000 words and no more. I do hate having to rush a thing like this.

I am having my usual struggle to get new ideas. So far I have got out what may be the framework of a novel, but the incidents don't seem to come.

I'm having lunch with Conan Doyle today. He has written a spiritualistic novel which starts in the July *Strand*.

Conan Doyle, a few words on the subject of. Don't you find as you age in the wood, as we are both doing, that the tragedy of life is that your early heroes lose their glamour? As a lad in the twenties you worship old whoever-it-is, the successful author, and by the time you're forty you find yourself blushing hotly at the thought that you could ever have admired the bilge he writes.

Now, with Doyle I don't have this feeling. I still revere his work as much as ever. I used to think it swell, and I still think it swell. Do you remember when we used to stand outside the bookstall at Dulwich station on the first of the month, waiting for Stanhope to open it so that we could get the new *Strand* with the latest instalment of *Rodney Stone* . . . and the agony of finding that something had happened to postpone the fight between Champion Harrison and Crab Wilson for another month? I would do it today if *Rodney Stone* was running now.

And apart from his work, I admire Doyle so much as a man. I should call him definitely a great man, and I don't imagine I'm the only one who thinks so. I love that solid, precise way he has of talking, like Sherlock Holmes. He was telling me once that when he was in America, he saw an advertisement in a paper: CONAN DOYLE'S SCHOOL OF WRITING. LET THE CONAN DOYLE SCHOOL OF WRITING TEACH YOU HOW TO SELL – or something to that effect. In other words, some blighter was using his name to swindle the public. Well, what most people in his place would have said would have been, 'Hullo! This looks fishy.' The way he put it when telling me the story was, 'I said to myself, "Ha! There is villainy afoot." '

May 27th, 1925

I'm very bucked about the *Post* giving you $600 for *Bolshevik*. I remember Lorimer telling me that he had paid $200 for a story by Bozeman Bulger (What's become of him, by the way? Do you remember, he used to write a lot for the *Post*) – and that very soon they would raise him to 250. He seemed to think that lavish. They only gave me $400 for my first story or two, so evidently they must have been hard hit by *Bolshevik*. I don't wonder. I always said it was a whale of a story.

Hotel Marguery,

New York

November 2nd, 1925

What a time since I wrote to you last. I don't know why it is, but when I'm staying with people, I can never write letters. I didn't write one while I was on Jim Stillman's yacht. However, now we have settled temporarily in New York.

Listen, laddie. I am putting together a serial plot and my only trouble is that, wishing to use that shanghaiing stuff about which I once consulted you, I find it necessary that my hero should know a lot of tramp skippers. Otherwise, the fact that he is shanghaied on the one boat of which he happens to know the skipper becomes too much of a coincidence.

Well, then. What I want him to be is the godson – original touch, this. You thought I was going to say nephew – of Jones Mickelbury (I bet you wish you'd thought of that name), the eminent shipowner. He starts in the firm, and his job involves going down to the docks at all sorts of unearthly morning hours to interview skippers of incoming boats belonging to the firm.

Now, is there such a job?

It must be something that would irk a lazy man, because the effect on him when he chucks it is to make him stay in bed all day, which annoys the heroine and leads to a good situation.

I've just got out a good Ukridge plot. U pawns his aunt's

diamond brooch to buy a half-share in a dog that is to win the
Waterloo Cup, and the dog dies. OK.

Extract from an undated letter written from New York.

Hotel Marguery,
270 Park Avenue

Did I tell you that a man came up to me the other day and
said, 'Mr Wodehouse, I want to thank you for the happy hours
you have given me with your book *Forty Years in China*!'

TWO

1926–1931

Hunstanton Hall,
Norfolk

June 26, 1926

The above address does not mean that I have bought a country
estate. It is a joint belonging to a friend of mine, and I am
putting in a week or two here. It's one of those enormous
houses, about two-thirds of which are derelict. There is a
whole wing which has not been lived in for half a century. You
know the sort of thing – it's happening all over the country
now – thousands of acres, park, gardens, moat, etc., and priceless heirlooms, but precious little ready money. The income
from farms and so on just about balances expenses.

I spend most of my time on the moat, which is really a
sizable lake. I'm writing this in the punt with my typewriter on
a bed-table wobbling on one of the seats. There is a duck close
by which utters occasional quacks that sound like a man with
an unpleasant voice saying nasty things in an undertone.
Beside me is a brick wall with the date 1623 on it. The only
catch is that the water is full of weeds, so I can't swim in it as
I would like to.

I've just had a cable from Guy Bolton asking me to sail on
July 8th and do a new show with him for Gertrude Lawrence.
I am trying to put it off till the 24th. Ethel isn't keen on going
to America just now, so I am torn between a dislike of leaving
her and a desire not to let a good thing get by me. Because
there's no question that it *is* a good thing. Gertie is terrifically
popular over there and a show for her can't miss, especially
as George Gershwin is doing the music. George being the
composer means that Ira Gershwin will write the lyrics, so

that I shall simply help Guy with the book as much as I can.

The show to which Plum refers was called *Oh, Kay*, and was produced in New York in November, 1926, and in London in September, 1927. It had 256 performances in New York and 214 in London.

> *17 Norfolk Street,*
> *Park Lane*

April 1, 1927

We have got a new Peke, Susan, three months old.

I was awfully glad to hear about your Gaumont deal. It ought to help the sale of the book a lot. I went round to the Jenkins headquarters the day I got back from Droitwich and had a long talk with Askew about your work, Grimsdick being away. He was very enthusiastic and said they thoroughly believed in you and thought your stuff fine, and intended to stick to it and build it up.

He realizes what I have always felt, that your sort of work has to be built up. Mine was just the same. I didn't sell over 2000 till I went to Jenkins with *Piccadilly Jim*. I don't think you can expect a big sale with an early book unless it happens to be one of those freak winners. The thing to do is to bung in book after book with one publisher. I'm sure that's the wheeze, as then each book helps the next.

Do stick to Jenkins. The more I see of them, the more I think they are the best publishers of the lot. Askew has been right through the bookselling business, starting as an apprentice and this gives him an enormous advantage. Sometimes when I see those column ads of other publishers in the Sunday papers, I get rather wistful, but I always come back to feeling that the Jenkins people do much more for you than any of them. I mean to say, while these other blokes are buying column ads, Askew is going round and taking some bookseller whom he used to play marbles with out for a drink and landing him with a hundred copies of your book.

> *Impney Hotel,*
> *Droitwich*

May 5th, 1927

Isn't that writing blurbs stuff the devil! You ought to let me write yours and you write mine. I simply can't put down on paper the sort of thing they want. What they would like from you is something on the lines of, 'When you meet Mr Townend, you are struck at once by a look in his eyes – it is the look of a man who has communed with his soul in the teeth of nor'-easters. One winter not many years ago, on a tramp steamer in the North Atlantic – etc.' It's hopeless trying to do that sort of thing yourself.

I am just finishing an adaptation (for America) of a serious play from the German. I was talking to Gilbert Miller, and Al Woods was there and I said to G.M., 'I wish you'd give me Molnár's next play to adapt!' He said, 'You couldn't do it. It's not in your line. It's a serious play!' I said, 'Boy, I can write anything!' And Al Woods, said 'I have a serious German play,' and I said, 'Gimme!' purely with the intention of scoring off Gilbert by showing him how I could do the heavy dramatic stuff, too. So I hope I don't flop. I'll bet I do! Of course, I can't really write serious stuff, and why I ever let myself in for the damned thing, I can't imagine. I must have been cuckoo.

Later Plum adapted Molnár's *The Play's the Thing*, which was a great success in New York, not only when put on in 1928, but also when revived after the Second World War in 1948. It was, strangely enough, considering Plum's reputation in this country and his vast following, a failure in London.

July 27th, 1927   *Hunstanton Hall*

I've just read your story in the *Strand*. It's fine. I love Captain Crupper, and you have the most extraordinary knack of making your minor characters live.

Listen, laddie. Have you read a thing of mine called *Pig-Hoo-o-o-ey*? I have a sort of idea you once wrote a story constructed on those lines, i.e. some perfectly trivial thing which is important to a man and the story is apparently how he gets it. But in the process of getting it he gets entangled in somebody else's love story and all sorts of things happen but he pays no attention to them, being wholly concentrated on his small thing. If you never did a yarn on these lines, try one with Captain Crupper. It's a good formula.

Anyway, bung-oh! I'm sweating blood over *Money for Nothing*, and have just finished 53,000 words of it. Meanwhile,

I have to anglicize *Oh, Kay*, by August 9th, attend rehearsals, adapt a French play, write a new musical comedy and do the rest of *Money for Nothing*, as far as I can see, by about September 1st. It'll all help to pass the time.

November 28th, 1927

14 East 60th Street,
New York

I would have written before this, but ever since I landed I have been in a terrible rush. I came over here with George Grossmith, to do *The Three Musketeers* for Flo Ziegfeld, and we finished a rough version on the boat. But like all work that is done quickly, it needed a terrible lot of fixing, which was left to me, as George went home. I was working gaily on it when a fuse blew out in Ziegfeld's Marilyn Miller show – book by Guy Bolton and Bill McGuire – owing to the lyrist and composer turning up on the day of the start of rehearsals and announcing that they had finished one number, and hoped to have another done shortly, though they couldn't guarantee this. Ziegfeld fired them and called in two new composers, Sigmund Romberg and George Gershwin, and asked me to do the lyrics with Ira. I wrote nine in a week and ever since then have been sweating away at the rest. Meanwhile Gilbert Miller wanted a show in a hurry for Irene Bordoni, so I started on that, too – fixing the *Musketeers* with my left hand the while. By writing the entire second act in one day I have managed to deliver the Bordoni show on time, and I have now finished the lyrics of the Flo show and the revised version of the *Musketeers*, and all is well – or will be until Flo wants all the lyrics rewritten, as he is sure to do. We open the Bolton-McGuire-Ira Gershwin-Wodehouse-George Gershwin-Romberg show in Boston next week. It's called *Rosalie*, and I don't like it much, though it's bound to be a success with Marilyn and Jack Donahue in it.

Just at present I feel as if I would never get another idea for a story. I suppose I shall eventually, but this theatrical work certainly saps one's energies. As I write this, it is six o'clock, so the play I wrote for Ernest Truex, *Good Morning, Bill*, must be finishing in London. I hope it has got over, as I know Gilbert Miller is waiting to see how it is received in London, before putting it on here.

New York is noisier than ever. I found my only way of getting any work done on the Flo lyrics was to take a room at the Great Neck Golf Club and work there. So I am the only man on record who commutes the wrong way. I catch the twelve o'clock train from New York every day and return after dinner. Flo thinks I play golf all day out there and is rather plaintive about it, but I soothe him by producing a series of lyrics.

Good Morning, Bill was a success. It ran for 146 performances at the Duke of York's Theatre and was revived seven years later at Daly's with Peter Haddon as the hero.

Rosalie – the Bolton-McGuire-Ira Gershwin-Wodehouse-George Gershwin-Romberg piece – turned out a credit to its platoon of authors and composers, doing 335 performances in New York at the New Amsterdam Theatre. It was never produced in London. Plum was later to undergo some headaches out in Hollywood, trying to turn it into a motion picture for Marion Davies.

17 Norfolk Street,
March 10th, 1928   *Park Lane, London*

Can you get anything to read these days? I was in the *Times* Library yesterday and came out empty-handed. There wasn't a thing I wanted. To fill in the time before Edgar Wallace writes another one, I am re-reading Dunsany. I never get tired of his stories. I can always let them cool off for a month or two and then come back to them. He is the only writer I know who opens up an entirely new world to me. What a mass of perfectly wonderful stuff he has done. (All this is probably wasted on you, as I don't suppose you have read him, unless you were attracted to his stories by the fact that they used to be illustrated by S. H. Sime. He has exactly the same eerie imagination as Sime. In fact, he told me once that quite a lot of his stuff was written from Sime's pictures. They would hand him a Sime drawing of a wintry scene with a sinister-looking bird flying over it and he would brood on it for a while and come up with *The Bird of the Difficult Eye*.)

His secret sorrow is that he wants to write plays and can't get them put on. I spent the afternoon with him once at his house down in Kent, and he read me three of his plays one after the other. All awfully good, but much too fantastic. One of them was about an unemployed ex-officer after the War who couldn't get a job, so he hired himself out as a watch-dog. He lived in a kennel, and the big scene was where he chased a cat up a tree and sat under it shouting abuse. I laughed heartily myself, but I could just picture the fishy, glazed eye of a manager listening to it.

Dunsany told me a story about the Troubles in Ireland, which amused me considerably. Lord Whoever-It-was had a big house near Cork somewhere, and one day a gang of Sinn Feiners rolled up and battered down the front door with axes. Inside they found a very English butler, a sort of Beach of Blandings Castle. He looked at them austerely and said coldly, 'His lordship is not at home.' They paid no attention to him and went in and wrecked the place from basement to attic, finally setting fire to it. On leaving, they found the butler still in the hall. Flames were darting all over the place and ceilings coming down with a bang, but Fotheringay – or whatever his name was – was quite unperturbed. 'Who shall I say called, sir?' he asked.

I've got Michael Arlen coming to dinner. Nice chap.

I had a profitable weekend at Droitwich, getting the missing links in *Summer Lighting*, which I had by me for eighteen months, and also a sort of lay-out for a novel, which, if I don't change the title, will be called *Big Money*. The short story jam also shows signs of breaking. The fact was I came back from America dead tired and then stayed in London for six weeks. What I needed was a few days among the trees. I feel fine now.

Edgar Wallace, I hear, now has a Rolls Royce and also a separate car for each of the five members of his family. Also a day butler and a night butler, so that there is never a time when you can go into his house and not find buttling going on. That's the way to live!

17 Norfolk Street,
Park Lane

April 30th, 1928

So sorry not to have written before, but I have been much tied up with a very difficult story. *Company for Gertrude*, I'm calling it. I wish to goodness you were here to help me with it. It's one of those maddening yarns where you get the beginning and the end all right, and only want a bit in the middle. The idea is that Lord Emsworth has been landed with a niece at the castle, said niece having got engaged to a man her family disapproves of, a pal of Freddie Threepwood's. Freddie has seen a film where the same thing happened and the man, disguised with false whiskers, went and curried favour with the family, and then when they were all crazy about him, tore off the whiskers and asked for their blessing. So he sends the young man to stay at Blandings, telling Lord E. he is a friend of his named Popjoy. He tells the young man to strain every nerve to ingratiate himself with Lord E.

Now, you see what happens. The fellow spends his whole time hanging round Lord E., helping him up out of chairs, asking him questions about the gardens, etc., etc., and it simply maddens Lord E., who feels he has never loathed a young man more.

See the idea? Well, what is bothering me is the getting of the cumulative details which lead up to Lord E. loathing the young man. Can you think of any? What *would* a young man in that position do, thinking he was making a big hit with the old man when really he was driving him off his head? It all leads up to my big scene, where Lord E., having at last, as he thinks, eluded the young man, goes and bathes in the lake and is so delighted at having got away from him for a couple of minutes, that he starts to sing and kick his feet from sheer joy. Which causes the young man, who is lurking in the bushes, to think he is drowning and dive in and save him, starting, of course, by beating him over the head to keep him from struggling.

I've done the first 2500 words, up to the moment of the young man's arrival at the castle, and I think it's good. I now have to think of some more details to fill in with before the rescue scene.

Rogate Lodge,
July 26, 1928   *Sussex*

We have been getting quite social lately. Guests in every nook and cranny. John Galsworthy came to lunch yesterday – he has a house near here – and we also had Leslie Howard, who is going to play opposite Tallulah Bankhead in that show I adapted, *Her Cardboard Lover*. Did you know that Leslie was at

Dulwich a year or two after our time? Leslie Howard is a stage name, so it's no good searching the school records. Probably Slacker knows all about him. He – L.H. – is an awfully nice fellow and a very good writer on the side. He wrote some excellent short things, very funny, which he showed me one day in New York, and I was able to get Frank Crowninshield, the editor of *Vanity Fair*, to use them.

Don't you think the tragedy of an author's life is the passion printers have for exclamation marks? They love to shove them in every second sentence. I've just been re-reading *Piccadilly Jim*, of which I did not correct the proofs, being in New York, and the book is bristling with them. Specimen sentence: 'But wait a minute! I don't get this!' It gives an impression of febrile excitement which spoils the whole run of the dialogue.

Ian Hay has been here, too, dramatizing *A Damsel in Distress*. Tom Miller and Basil Foster are putting it on. It opens in London on August 14th. We have formed a syndicate – the management, Ian and I each putting up £500. We needed another £500 to make up the necessary £2000, and A. A. Milne gallantly stepped forward and said he would like to come in. I don't think we shall lose our money, as Ian has done an awfully good job.

September 28th, 1928   *Rogate Lodge*

The two shows are doing marvellously. Both were well over the £2000 last week. *Her Cardboard Lover* hasn't dropped below £2200 yet, but I have an uneasy feeling all the time that it is one of those plays that may go all to nothing at short notice, though Tallulah is terrific, as is Leslie Howard. *Damsel In Distress* looks solid and ought to run a year. It has gone up steadily every week.

I have spent the summer writing and rewriting the first 30,000 words of *Summer Lighting*, and must have done – all told – about 100,000 words. It is one of those stories which one starts without getting the plot properly fixed and keeps going off the rails. I think all is well now, but I am shelving it to do some short stories.

How about C. E. Montague? Do you ever see his stuff? I've just found a good thing by him called *Judith*. Apart from that I, seem to have read nothing lately. Oh, yes, H. G. Wells's *Mr Blettsworthy*. Only fair, I thought.

(Nature note. A local cow starts mooing before dawn and goes steadily on and on. I now get, in consequence, about five hours sleep a night.)

Listen, Bill, something really must be done about Kip's '*Mrs Bathurst*'. I read it years ago and didn't understand a word of it. I thought to myself, 'Ah, youthful ignorance!' A week ago I re-read it. Result, precisely the same. What did the villain do to Mrs Bathurst? What did he tell the Captain in his cabin that made the Captain look very grave and send him up country where he was struck by lightning? Why was the other chap who was struck by lightning, too, introduced? And, above all, how was Kip allowed to get away with six solid pages of padding at the start of the story?

Have you any short story plots you want to dispose of? I need a Lord Emsworth plot and also an Ukridge. I am planning a vast campaign. I want to write six short stories simultaneously. I have three plots to begin with and I want three more. Don't you feel, when writing a story, that if only it were some other story you could write it on your head? I do. I'm sure it's the best way to have two or three going at the same time, so that when you get sick of the characters of one you can switch to another.

I laughed when I read Plum's 'I am planning a vast campaign', for in these words the creator of Ukridge is so clearly revealed. Again and again this is precisely what Ukridge planned to do, to be invariably in Plum's stories robbed of the fruits of his ingenuity.

The stories of Rudyard Kipling no longer seem to be popular and I wonder how many young men or women under thirty have read *Mrs Bathurst* a great short story in spite of its leisurely start. But even now, fifty years after that story was written, I should dearly like to know the solution to the mystery.

Can anyone explain what happened between Vickery and Mrs Bathurst or why Vickery, having seen her walking toward the camera in a motion picture of the arrival of a train at an English railway station, shown at a circus in Durban – or was it Capetown? – should have expressed such consternation? It was true, I know, that he had thought of her as still living in New Zealand, but why, even supposing that they had had a love affair, should her arrival in

England when he was in South Africa have so disturbed him? Why, too, should he have made that cryptic remark to Pyecroft that his lawful wife had died in childbirth? I often think I should like to insert a notice in *The Times* personal column asking if some clever person would clear up the mystery of *Mrs Bathurst* before it is too late.

The Impney Hotel,
Droitwich

October 18, 1928

I've just got a copy of *The Ship in the Swamp*. I think it's marvellous. My introduction is all wrong, of course, much too flippant. A book like that ought to have had something worthy of it. It's the best collection of short stories that has been published since *Where the Pavement Ends*. How infinitely better your stuff reads in book form than in magazine small print.

You've got to hand it to Grimsdick. This time he really has made a book. That jacket is terrific. And I feel now he was right in insisting on *The Ship in the Swamp* as the title. It's one of the few titles I've seen that grips the imagination. With that jacket, with the yellow flowers growing over the ship; you wonder what the deuce it is all about and you feel you must find out.

The only way to get a book public is to keep plugging away without any long intervals. They don't know you're writing till you've published about half a dozen. I produced five books which fell absolutely flat, and then got going with *Piccadilly Jim*. And when I say five I mean seven. I suppose if *Piccadilly Jim* had been published first it would have fallen as flat as the others, but all the time I must have been creating a public bit by bit and I feel it's going to be the same for you.

I enclose some letters in answer to some I wrote. Arnold Bennett's is a bit obscure. I also wrote to the *Daily Express*, etc. Are there any other reviewers you think would help? Why not send signed copies to all the editors who have used your stories – e.g. *Strand, Nash's, Storyteller*, etc.? You never know how much that sort of thing helps.

I'm going to write to Conan Doyle and Rudyard Kipling about it. After all, they can only snub me.

Dulwich have got a red-hot team this year. Nine old colours

from last year's side, which lost only to Bedford. Unfortunately, I hear Sherborne and Haileybury have got special teams, too. Still, I'm hoping we beat Bedford next Saturday. You must come up and see at least one game. Why not St Paul's at West Kensington on Saturday week?

Here is yet another instance of what trouble Plum went to in order to help a friend. His efforts regarding *The Ship in the Swamp* bore fruit as I had a succession of excellent notices for the book.

Owen Seaman wrote:

'My dear Wodehouse,

The Ship in the Swamp is being sent out to be reviewed by our maritime expert. I look forward to seeing you soon at the Beefsteak, especially as I want a personal talk with you.'

Arnold Bennett wrote:

'Dear Wodehouse,

Thank you for your letter of the 12th, about Mr Townend. If I come across the book, and if I think it is better than yours, I will say so. But I very much doubt whether this will happen. As a contributor to the *Evening Standard*, I am the most callous fellow that God ever created.'

Which, though obscure, as Plum said, shows a sturdy and commendable independence, at least, and a belief that God created Arnold Bennett.

December 1st, 1928   *17 Norfolk Street*

I had a letter from New York on November 10th, saying that *Collier's* must have my serial by January 1st! Only 30,000 words written then and those all wrong. I have rewritten them and another 20,000, sweating like blazes! They now say that January 15th will be all right, so I think I'll deliver on time. But, my gosh, what a rush!

And now, omitting pages of advice and guidance on dead-and-gone stories, let us turn to a topic that has for more than a quarter of a century been dear to Plum Wodehouse's heart: Pekes.

There is a tendency for people, young people especially, to despise Pekes as pampered lap-dogs, but though small in size no breed of dog is more courageous or attractive than the Pekinese. The Wodehouses' Peke, Susan, had lately had puppies and Ethel Wodehouse had asked my wife if she would like one. The answer was that she would, of course. In a long letter, dated December 15th, 1928, Plum wrote:

In *re* Bimmy. The great point is that a Peke needs a frightful lot of petting. Is Rene game to leave off doing whatever she is doing in order to pick Bimmy up and pet her?

Plum need have had no anxiety. Bimmy became the centre around which our household life revolved, as it were, and no more lovable or more sporting little dog ever breathed. She was quite without fear and used to paralyse us by dashing excitedly at the big farm bull when she met him being exercised on the road by the cowman. The bull, a normally sullen beast, was never hostile as he might have been toward a larger dog, merely a little confused and perplexed.

Bimmy, a miniature red brindle, was friendly toward all other animals, cows, horses, pigs – though pigs puzzled her – and cats. Only once did we see her angry and that was when an Alsatian who lived nearby rushed out of his garden gate as Bimmy went racing by and hustled her roughly. Bimmy, without checking her pace, turned, snarling, and snapped at him fiercely, resenting his interference, and the Alsatian halted and gazed after her in consternation, astounded that so small an animal should dare quarrel with him.

April 13th, 1929

If you haven't been paid in advance for your stuff, you must be rolling now. I see nothing but your stories wherever I look.

Now about America. Harold Ober, Reynolds's partner, is in London now, and I should very much like you to meet him. Couldn't you come up one day next week and stay the night? I shall have a show on at the Golder's Green theatre (it comes to the Globe Monday week), and you and Rene could see that. We could give Ober a lunch and have a valuable talk about your work.

I was down at Southsea a week ago, opening this new show by Ian Hay and me, called *Baa, Baa, Black Sheep*, and I don't wonder you used to hate living there in the old days. What a particularly melancholy place it is with that beastly common between you and the sea. I like Portsmouth, but I can't stand Southsea. The show went marvellously there. Terrific enthusiasm, and we took £1150 in the week, which, of course, is very good for a try-out. I only hope London will like it as well.

April 27th, 1929   *Hunstanton Hall*

I would have written before, but I have had a hell of a week. On Sunday I had to condense *Good Morning, Bill* into a sketch for Heather Thatcher. (She opens at the Coliseum on Whit Monday.) From Monday to Thursday night I was writing a Jeeves story in response to an urgent demand from America that I get it off by Saturday's boat, which meant mailing it from here not later than noon on Friday. (And why they wanted it so soon I can't think. It is for the October number of the *Cosmopolitan.*) On Friday and yesterday I was so exhausted I couldn't write. (Incidentally, you surely aren't aiming at writing a story a week? The strain would be too awful. Three a month is just possible, but even so, don't you think you would lose in merit what you gained in production? I find that if I work really quick on a story, I become incapable of judging it, and have to lay it aside for a week to let it get cool.)

It's wonderful being back at Hunstanton again, though things aren't so frightfully bright at the moment, as host has had a row with butler, who has given notice. The butler is a cheery soul who used to be the life and soul of the party, joining in the conversation at meals and laughing appreciatively if one made a joke, but now he hovers like a spectre, very strong and silent. I'm hoping peace will be declared soon.

I think I like Hunstanton as well in winter as in summer, though, of course, I don't get the moat in the winter months. I laid the scene of *Money for Nothing* at Hunstanton Hall.

What bloodstained books you seem to read! I haven't seen any of them. Down here I am limited to what there is in the house – principally Elizabethan dramatists – and what I can get from the twopence-a-go library in the town. How are you on the Elizabethan dramatists? My opinion, now that I have read them all, is that they are a shade better than Restoration dramatists, but as you rightly remark, that is not saying much.

These seaside libraries are a bit apt to have nothing later than *By Order of the Czar*, but the Hunstanton one is quite good. I have been able to get a number of tuppennyworths of E. V. Lucas and W. B. Maxwell, which I had read before, of course, but found I could read again. Do you know Lucas's novels – *London Lavender*, etc? He takes a character and sends him wandering around and meeting all sorts of odd people, or else he tells the thing in letters. I've read them all about a dozen times each, but I can always go back to them.

The first time I met Lucas was soon after I had begun writing 'By the Way' on the *Globe*. He had been doing a column a year or two before with C. L. Graves. The thing I can't understand about him is that in those days – 1903 or thereabouts – he was morbidly shy, so shy that it was really agony for him to meet people. He told me once that he would often bury his face in his hands just to avoid seeing his fellow men for a minute or so. Yet now he seems to be a regular mixer. Odd.

And talking of Maxwell. He came to dinner one night at Norfolk Street when I wasn't there, and Ethel, greeting him in the library, told him that he was one of my favourite authors (which was quite true), and that I was never happier than when among his books, so to speak. And then to her horror she saw his eye swivelling round the shelves and realized that there wasn't a single Maxwell book there. The solution, of course, was that all his were in my study upstairs, where I keep the books I like best. But I suppose for the rest of his life he will regard me as a fraud and a humbug. No means of letting him know the truth, of course.

I don't think any of those books you mention really amount to much. It seems to me that at least two-thirds of the stuff published nowadays is by one-book people. You know, *A Stirring Revelation of a Young Girl's Soul*, by Jane Emmeline Banks, who never writes another damn book in her life. The test is, can you write three?

August 17, 1929   *Hunstanton Hall*

I did curse when I got your letter saying that Rene had been staying at her sister's for a week and that you had been all alone – just the very week I was up in London by myself. You could have come and stayed with me, and we could have sat up all night talking. All that week – which was given up per day to duty lunches and rehearsals – I used to get back to the house at nine-thirty and sit reading till one a.m. It never occurred to me to try to get in touch with you, as I knew you were working, and my days were full up. Blast it! However –

The day before yesterday I was rung up and told that Flo Ziegfeld wanted to speak to me from New York. After a lot of waiting, I was told that the phone call had been cancelled. He cabled instead. He wants me to go out immediately to help with a musical comedy. I had been wavering about going out for the production of *Candlelight* and this has decided me. His last cable said that he was arranging my passage through an agency who would communicate with me. It might mean next Wednesday, though I hope not. I don't expect to be over more than six weeks this time, and hope to return early in October.

Susan's devotion is beginning to affect my liver. I can't get a bit of exercise. She won't let me out of her sight, and she won't come for long walks. If I try to take her, she just sits down and looks pathetic. What she likes is to lie in the middle of the lawn and have me walk round and round her. She won't let me go on the moat, and if I bicycle to the town I have to take her along, tucked into my sweater. I hope she won't miss me too much when I leave. I don't think she will, as she will be with Ethel and will have Winks.

I lunched with Askew and Grimsdick the other day and they both almost wept at the idea of your not doing another long novel. Askew looks on you as the greatest sea story writer going and Grimsdick said he knew your stuff would sell, if you kept up the supply.

I'll try to see the *Saturday Evening Post* people when I'm in New York and ask them about your stuff. I might get a line on what they want. Broadly, of course, they like action as opposed to subtlety. The longer I write, the more I realize the necessity for telling a story as far as possible in *scenes*, especially at the start.

October 2nd, 1929   *14 East 60th Street,*
                                                         New York

I am having the usual Ziegfeld experience. I have been here six weeks and nothing has happened yet. I don't expect to be back in England before Christmas.

The show I'm doing is a musical version of a – lousy in my opinion but very successful – play called *East is West*, done in 1918, all about a Chinese girl who goes around saying, 'Me love Chlistian god velly much,' and that sort of thing, and turns out in the end to be the daughter of an American missionary, kidnapped by Chinese in her infancy. I think it's frightful, but I suppose Flo is fascinated by the thought of how he will be able to spread himself over the costumes, and anyway I haven't anything to do with the writing of the book. Bill McGuire is doing that, at least he's supposed to be, but as far as I can make out he hasn't started yet. You would love Bill McGuire. He is exactly like Ukridge. Remind me to tell you when I get back, the story of him and the gangsters and the diamond ring. Much too long to relate here, but a laugh in every line.

The music is by Vincent Youmans, if he ever gets around to doing any, and I am collaborating on the lyrics with a very pleasant lad named Billy Rose, who broke into the Hall of Fame with a song entitled, 'Does the Chewing-Gum Lose its Flavour on the Bedpost Overnight?' As far as I can make out, Billy and I are the only members of the gang who are doing a stroke of work. I go around to his hotel every morning and we hammer out a lyric together and turn it into Youmans, after which nothing more is heard of it.

So what with this and what with that it seemed to me a good idea to take a few days off and go to Hollywood. I wanted to see what the place was like before committing myself to it for an extended period. I was there three days, but having in an absent-minded moment forgotten to tell Flo and Gilbert Miller that this was only a flying visit, I created something of an upheaval in the bosoms of both. Flo wanted to have me around as he expected Bill McGuire and Youmans to come out of their respective trances at any moment, and rehearsals of my adaptation of *Candlelight* for Gertie Lawrence were nearing their end and the out-of-town opening coming along, so Gilbert wanted me around, too. It was a nasty jar, therefore, when they were told that I had gone to Hollywood, presumably for good.

It hit Flo hardest, because he loves sending 1000 word telegrams telling people what he thinks of them, and he had no address where he could reach me. From what Billie Burke (Mrs Flo) told me later, I gather that he nearly had apoplexy. However, all was forgotten and forgiven when I returned on the ninth day. I went to Baltimore, where *Candlelight* was playing, and got a rather chilly reception from Gertie, but was eventually taken back into the fold.

Candlelight has since opened in New York and looks like a hit. We did $18,060 the first week. Gertie is wonderful, as always. This is the first time she has done a straight show without music, but she is just as good as she was in *Oh, Kay*. I don't believe there's anybody on the stage who can do comedy better.

I liked what little I saw of Hollywood and expect to return there in the summer. I have had three offers of a year's work, but I held out for only five months.

The only person I knew really well out there was Marion Davies, who was in the show *Oh, Boy*, which Guy Bolton, Jerry Kern and I did for the Princess Theatre. She took me out to her house in Santa Monica and worked me into a big lunch at the Metro-Goldwyn which they were giving for Winston Churchill. All very pleasant. Churchill made a speech at the lunch, and when he had finished Louis B. Mayer said, 'That was a very good speech. I think we would all like to hear it again,' and it was played back from an apparatus concealed in the flowers on the table. Churchill seemed rather taken aback.

I wanted to go to Chula Vista, but of course hadn't time. I must do it when I come here again.

I have reluctantly come to the conclusion that I must have one of those meaningless faces which make no impression whatever on the beholder. This was – I think – the seventh time I had been introduced to Churchill, and I could see that I came upon him as a complete surprise once more. Not a trace of that, 'Why, of course I remember you, Mr Addison Simms of Seattle,' stuff.

Chula Vista which Plum speaks of was in my day – 1910 to 1913 – a small ranch town south of San Diego some eight miles from the Mexican line. I lived there for some time and earned a precarious living at sundry jobs while writing stories in the evenings after the day's work was done. Chula Vista was a lovely little place, situated between the Pacific Ocean and the Coast Range of mountains in a setting of orange and lemon orchards, and palms and pepper and eucalyptus trees. Quite recently, Raymond Chandler in one of his letters told me that if I saw the place I would not like it, so greatly changed was it from the little town I had known.

The Billy Rose whom Plum mentions as his collaborator in the lyrics of the Chinese musical play shortly afterwards became a millionaire. During the great fair, he ran what was called the Acquacade, a swimming-and-diving-belle entertainment out near La Guardia airfield. His expenses per week were $30,000, and he never failed to take in $100,000, one bumper week topping $260,000. This went on all through the summer, and it was at a time when the American income tax was a mere 19 per cent.

November 11th, 1929   *17 Norfolk Street*

I'm longing to get down and see you all, but I'm in the middle of a story, which I must finish before I can make any move. I've gone and let myself in for one of those stories which lead up to a big comic scene and now I'm faced with writing the scene and it looks as if it was going to be difficult to make funny. It's a village Rugger match, where everybody tries to slay everybody else, described by Bertie Wooster who, of course, knows nothing about Rugger. It's damned hard to describe a game you know backward through the eyes of somebody who doesn't know it. However, I suppose, it will come. These things always do. But it isn't easy.

I went down to Dulwich and saw the Mill Hill game. It was very one-sided and dull. We have a great side this year and I'm hoping we beat Haileybury on Saturday. It's rather funny how we regard the Bedford match. Nobody seems a bit pleased at having beaten them by twenty-five points. They take it for granted that Bedford must have a very bad team, and not that we have a good one. They appear to think there's something rather indecent about beating Bedford by twenty-five points.

Aren't Peke puppies the most fascinating things on earth? What are you going to do with them?

I want to talk to you about that story you sent me. It doesn't seem to be quite right, and I think I have spotted the flaw.

The remainder of the letter is taken up by another of Plum's masterly analyses of where a story had gone wrong and some suggestions as to how it could be improved.

December 9th, 1929

What a sweat a novel is till you are sure of your characters. And what a vital thing it is to have plenty of things for a major character to *do*. That is the test. If they aren't in situations, characters can't be major characters, not even if you have the rest of the troupe talk their heads off about them.

I have just had a cable from Hollywood. They want me to do a picture for Evelyn Laye. This may mean a long trip out there pretty soon, but I don't expect to stay very long. I shall know more on December 21st when Sam Goldwyn arrives in England.

January 8th, 1930   17 Norfolk Street

My novel, *Big Money*, is coming out terrifically, and I am very nearly half-way through. The aunt has been eliminated altogether, and so has the hero's father – after four distinct and concrete versions were scrapped.

My main trouble is that my heroine refuses to come alive, and what makes it worse is that the second girl is a pippin. I'm afraid the reader will skip all the stuff dealing with the hero and heroine and concentrate on the scenes between the second man and the second girl.

It looks as if Hollywood was off. I had some sessions with Goldwyn, but he wouldn't meet my price. The poor chump seemed to think he was doing me a favour offering about half what I get for a serial for doing a job which would be the most ghastly sweat. He said, when he sailed today, that he would think things over and let me know, but I'm hoping I have made the price too stiff for him. I don't want to go to Hollywood just now a bit. Later on, in the Spring, I should like it. But I feel now I want to be left alone with my novel.

I'm glad Christmas is over. I came in for the New Year festivities at Hunstanton, and had to wear a white waistcoat every night.

Four months later Plum set out for Hollywood. Ethel Wodehouse, who had gone to New York at the end of 1929, arranged a contract for him with Metro-Goldwyn-Mayer – six months at $2500 a week with an option for another six months.

Metro-Goldwyn-Mayer Studios,
June 26th, 1930   *Culver City, California*

I have been meaning to write to you for ages, but I have been in a tremendous whirl of work ever since I arrived in Hollywood. For some obscure reason, after being absolutely dead for months, my brain suddenly started going like a dynamo. I got a new plot for a short story every day for a week. Then I started writing, and in well under a month have done three short stories, an act of a play, and all the dialogue for a picture.

There is something about this place that breeds work. We have a delightful house – Norma Shearer's – with a small but lovely garden and a big swimming pool, the whole enclosed in patio form. The three wings of the house occupy three sides, a high wall, looking on to a deserted road, the other. So that one feels quite isolated. I have arranged with the studio to work at home, so often I spend three or four days on end without going out of the garden: I get up, swim, breakfast, work till two, swim again, have a lunch-tea, work till seven, swim for the third time, then dinner and the day is over. It is wonderful. I have never had such a frenzy of composition.

One of the stories I have written is your cat plot. The story of Webster, do you remember – the artist and the dignified cat? I have added a lot to the plot. It now ends differently. Hero has a row with his girl, flies to whiskey bottle, sees cat staring gravely and rebukingly at him, drops bottle, cat laps up whiskey, gets tight, springs through window and cleans up an alley cat which has been saying rude things to him for weeks. Hero realizes cat is one of the boys after all, and all is well. It has worked out as one of the best things I have ever done.

How is everything your end? I hope you have been selling stuff lately. Write and tell me all about everything.

I haven't made my pilgrimage to Chula Vista yet. Nor has Ethel arrived. I shall wait till she comes.

California is all right. It's a wonderful relief not having to worry about the weather. Incidentally, it is only in the past few days that it has been really hot and sunny. We had three weeks of dull English weather. Still, it never rained.

I don't see much of the movie world. My studio is five miles from where I live, and I only go there occasionally. If I ever dine out or go to parties, it is with other exiles – New York writers, etc. Most of my New York theatre friends are here.

Odd place this. Miles and miles of one-story bungalows, mostly Spanish, each with a little lawn in front and a pocket-handkerchief garden at the back, all jammed together in rows. Beverly Hills, where I am, is the rather aristocratic sector. Very pretty. Our house has a garden the size of the garden of any small house at Dulwich, and we pay £200 a month for it.

Metro-Goldwyn Studio,
August 18th, 1930   *Culver City*

Awfully glad to hear from you. That's fine about the story the *Saturday Evening Post* bought.

There is a writer here called John Farrow. Have you ever heard of him? He was saying something to someone the other day about how much he liked your work, especially *Tiger Bay*. He is a man who served before the mast. I met him not long ago and he said how well you know the sea and wanted to know if you had ever been a sailor.

Ethel arrived a month ago, with Winks under her arm. Winks has settled down finely and seems to be very happy. We are devoted to her, and she seems to have taken on a lot of Susan's characteristics. She barks furiously at our Japanese gardener.

I expect to be out here till next Spring. I might dash back to England for a week or two before that, but I am not counting on it, as I expect they will want me to stick on without going away.

As regards ideas I have had another barren spell. Isn't it the devil, how you get these brilliant periods when nothing seems easier than to plot out stories, and then comes the blank? Oddly enough, Hollywood hasn't inspired me in the least. I feel as if everything that could be written about it has already been done.

As a matter of fact, I don't think there is much to be written about this place. What it was like in the early days, I don't know, but nowadays the studio life is all perfectly normal, not a bit crazy. I haven't seen any swooning directors or temperamental stars. They seem just to do their job, and to be quite ordinary people, especially the directors, who are quiet, unemotional men who just work and don't throw any fits. Same with the stars. I don't believe I shall get a single story out of my stay here.

This letter was written about ten months before Plum was to shake the film industry to its foundations and, quite unintentionally, bring about what amounted to a major revolution. His forebodings about not getting a single story out of his stay in Hollywood were quite unjustified. Before he left for home he wrote the funniest skits on film stars and the making of films ever written. The yesmen of his stories became portents of the financial storm that was to break with such devastating fury. They can be found among the stories in the book entitled *Blandings Castle*.

October 28th, 1930   *Metro-Goldwyn Studios*

I was delighted to get your long letter. What a shame you had to alter the title of the new book. I agree I can't see why, in these days when there are so many books coming out, it matters if two titles clash. I see a man has just published a book called *Seventeen*. Well, you'd have thought Booth Tarkington had established the sole right to that title, but I'll bet nobody notices anything funny.

Well, laddie, it begins to look as if it would be some time before I return to England. The Metro people have taken up my option, and I am with them for another six months and Ethel has just taken a new house for a year. Which means that I shall probably stay that long.

If you came over here and settled down, I think I would spend at least six months in every year here. I like the place. I think Californian scenery is the most loathsome on earth – a cross between Coney Island and the Riviera – but by sticking in one's garden all the time and shutting one's eyes when one goes out, it is possible to get by.

As life goes on, though, don't you find that all you need is a wife, a few real friends, a regular supply of books, and a Peke? (Make that two Pekes and add a swimming-pool.)

MGM bought that musical comedy *Rosalie* – the thing Guy Bolton, Bill McGuire, George Gershwin, Sigmund Romberg, Ira Gershwin, and I did for Ziegfeld for Marilyn Miller – for Marion Davies. Everyone in the studio had a go at it, and then they told me to try. After I had messed about with it with no success, Irving Thalberg, the big boss (and a most charming fellow incidentally, about the nicest chap I've run into out here – he is Norma Shearer's husband) worked out a story on his own and summoned me to Santa Barbara, where he was spending a few days, to hear it. I drove down there with a stenographer from the studio, and he dictated a complete scenario. When he had finished, he leaned back and mopped his brow, and asked me if I wanted to have it read over to me. I was about to say Yes (just to make the party go), when I suddenly caught the stenographer's eye and was startled to see a look of agonized entreaty in it. I couldn't imagine what was wrong, but I gathered that for some reason she wanted me to say No, so I said No. When we were driving home, she told me that she had had a latish night the night before and had fallen sleep at the outset of the proceedings and slept peacefully throughout, not having heard or taken down a word.

Fortunately, I could remember the high spots of the thing, well enough to start working on it. Unfortunately for some inscrutable reason Thalberg wants me to write it not in picture form but as a novelette, after which I suppose it will be turned into a picture. The prospect of this appals me, and I am hoping that the whole thing will eventually blow over, as things do out here.

What did Sheila Kaye-Smith object to in *Angel Pavement*? I thought it a splendid book. Curious method of writing Priestley has, though. Have you noticed it? A lot of characters with practically no connection with each other are attended to in turn, e.g. Smeeth and Dersingham. You get fifty pages of Smeeth at home, then fifty pages of Dersingham at home. Then a hunk of some other character. I always feel that I have got to link up, and that I couldn't show Dersingham at home without bringing Smeeth on, too, to play a scene with him.

I am still bathing vigorously three times a day, though in the early morning the water is pretty chilly. They tell me that with care you can bathe all through the winter.

Winks is barking like blazes in the garden. I think it must be the Japanese gardener, whom she hasn't accepted even after seeing him every day for six months.

Last night Maureen O'Sullivan brought her new Peke round here, and Winks was very austere. Do you remember the day you and Rene and Bimmy arrived in Norfolk Street? I had been looking forward sentimentally to the reunion of the two sisters and as I came downstairs I heard the most frightful snarling and yapping, and there was Winks trying to eat Bimmy. Odd, too, how the row stopped directly we took them out on to the steps. Apparently a Peke only resents Peke visitors in the actual house.

Leave it to Psmith seems to have got over all right in London. Thanks for the notices. Of course no one else ever thought of sending me any. (Aren't people funny about that? They write and tell you there was something awfully nice about you in *the Phoenix (Arizona) Intelligencer*, and take it for granted that you must have seen it yourself.)

Psmith did £2400 at Golder's Green and £2017 the first week at the Shaftesbury, during which week, of course, a lot of free seats had to be given away. *Damsel in Distress* only did £1600 its first week in London.

I am at last reading *The Good Companions*. I love it. That's the sort of book I would like to write.

February 25th, 1931

Only time for a scribble. The studio has just given me a job which will take up all my time for weeks, though I'll bet when I've finished it, it will be pigeon-holed and never heard of again.

I'm afraid just now is a bad time for stories unless commissioned. All the Mags, except the *SEP*, are living on their accumulated stuff. This can't last much longer, and business conditions seem to be improving already.

I have been away for a week at Hearst's ranch. He owns 440,000 acres, more than the whole of Long Island! We took Winks, who was a great hit.

The ranch is about half-way between Hollywood and San Francisco. It is on the top of a high hill, and just inside the entrance gates is a great pile of stones, which, if you ever put them together, would form an old abbey which Hearst bought in France and shipped over and didn't know what to do with so left lying by the wayside. The next thing you see, having driven past this, is a yak or a buffalo or something in the middle of the road. Hearst collects animals and has a zoo on the premises, and the ones considered reasonably harmless are allowed to roam at large. You're apt to meet a bear or two before you get to the house.

The house is enormous, and there are always at least fifty guests staying there. All the furniture is period, and you probably sleep on a bed originally occupied by Napoleon or somebody. Ethel and I shared the Venetian suite with Sidney Blackmer, who had blown in from one of the studios.

The train that takes guests away leaves after midnight, and the one that brings new guests arrives early in the morning, so you have dinner with one lot of people and come down to breakfast next morning and find an entirely fresh crowd.

Meals are in an enormous room, and are served at a long table, with Hearst sitting in the middle on one side and Marion Davies in the middle on the other. The longer you are there, the further you get from the middle. I sat on Marion's right the first night, then found myself being edged further and further away till I got to the extreme end, when I thought it time to leave. Another day, and I should have been feeding on the floor.

March 14th, 1931   *MGM Studio*

I wish you were here for this weather. It is as warm as summer, and I am bathing regularly. The pool is a nice 62 degrees.

I am doing a picture version of *By Candlelight* now for John Gilbert. This looks as if it really might come to something. Everything else I have done so far has been scrapped. But I doubt if they intend to give me another contract. The enclosed paragraph from *Variety* can only refer to me, and it looks darned sinister. My only hope is that I have made myself so pleasant to all the studio heads that by now I may count as a cousin by marriage or something.

I must stop now, as we have to go out to dinner. Corinne Griffith.

Winks is in great form, and has got quite reconciled to having Johnnie, Maureen O'Sullivan's Peke, as a guest. We are putting Johnnie up while Maureen is in Ireland. Sex female in spite of the name, and age about a year. Very rowdy towards Winks, who disapproves rather. Johnnie is the only ugly Peke I have ever seen. She was run over by a car some months ago and has lost an eye. She looks like one of your tougher sailors.

This was the paragraph from *Variety* to which Plum refers:

'Following *Variety*'s report of the ludicrous writer talent situation, eastern executives interrogated the studios as to instances such as concerned one English playwright and author who has been collecting $2500 a week at one of the major studios for eleven months, without contributing anything really worth while to the screen.'

I personally, having seen many bad Hollywood films and very few good ones, am convinced that Plum's non-success was due to the fact that the people responsible for making films were unable to recognize a good idea when it was given them. Unless a story conformed to their low standards, it was no use to them.

May 19th, 1931   *Metro-Goldwyn Studio*

Everything is very wobbly and depressed over here these days. We seem to be getting a sort of second instalment of the 1929 crash. The movies are in a bad state, and MGM showed no desire to engage me again when my contract lapsed last week. Meanwhile I am plugging along with *Hot Water* and have done 60,000 words, but it looks like being one of those long ones and I doubt if I shall finish it before mid-August.

Two Hollywood stories, one previous to that interview of mine, the other more recent. The first is supposed to illustrate the Hollywood idea of poverty. A supervisor was giving a writer instructions about the picture he wanted him to work on. He said the outline was that a father has a ne'er-do-well son and gets fed up with his escapades and thinks the only thing to make a man of the young fellow is to force him to battle with the world for himself. So he cuts him off with $500 a week. The other story is quite a recent one, and has to do with the current depression. A man standing in the crowd outside a movie theatre here after a big opening hears the carriage starter calling for 'Mr Warner's automobile', 'Mr Lasky's automobile', 'Mr Louis B. Mayer's automobile', and so on, and he shakes his head. 'At an opening a year from now,' he says, 'there won't be any of this stuff about automobiles. You'll hear them call for Mr Warner's bicycle, Mr Lasky's kiddie car and Mr Louis B. Mayer's roller-skates.'

I'm afraid that interview of mine has had a lot to do with the depression in the picture world. Yet I was only saying what everybody has been saying for years. Apparently what caused the explosion was my giving figures and mentioning a definite studio in print. But, damn it all, it never ought to have been in print. It was just a casual remark I happened to drop off the record (though, like an ass, I didn't say that it was off the record). It just shows that with these American reporters you must weigh every word before you speak.

Another story, not a Hollywood one. Wilton Lackaye, the actor, was playing in San Francisco and invited the editor of one of the San Francisco papers to dinner one night. The editor said he was sorry but he couldn't come, because he had a conference. 'A conference?' said Lackaye. 'What's that for?' The editor explained. 'We get together every day for an hour or so and decide what is to be in the next day's paper – matters of policy, emphasis on news and all that sort of thing.' 'Good heavens!' said Lackaye, amazed. 'Do you mean to tell me that you get out that paper *deliberately*?'

We have been having a heat wave for the last week. I never noticed the heat last year, but this has been terrific. At that, though, it isn't as bad as it was sometimes in the East. I remember when Guy Bolton and I were at Great Neck writing *Oh, Kay*, for Gertie Lawrence in the summer of 1926, I used to have to change my shirt three times in a morning.

Heather Thatcher has turned up to spend a couple of months with us. We gave a big party for her yesterday, which I found rather loathsome, as it seemed to pollute our nice garden. There was a mob milling round in it from four in the afternoon till eleven at night. About twenty people in the pool at one time. The only beauty of having a party in your own home is that you can sneak away. I went upstairs to my room at five and only appeared for dinner, returning to my room at eight sharp. (The perfect host.) I re-read *Cakes and Ale*. What a masterly book it is. Have you read it? Incidentally, if they were going to pick on anyone for being irreverent towards the old Victorian master, why not Hugh Walpole for his *Hans Frost*? Did you read that one?

I can't remember if you said you liked or disliked Dorothy Parker's *Lament for the Living*. I have just got it out of the library, and it's good.

We are toying with a scheme for going round the world in December on the *Empress of Britain*. Sometimes we feel we should like it, and then we ask ourselves if we really want to see the ruddy world. I'm darned if I know. I have never seen any spectacular spot yet that didn't disappoint me. Notably, the Grand Canyon, and also Niagara Falls.

Personally, I've always liked wandering around in the background. I mean, I get much more kick out of a place like Droitwich, which has no real merits, than out of something like the Taj Mahal.

Maureen O'Sullivan's Peke is still with us. She – the Peke, not Maureen – snores like twenty dogs and sleeps under my bed. I'm getting used to it. She is the ugliest and greediest hound I ever met, but full of charm.

The first intimation we had at home that anything had gone wrong was reading in *The Times* a brief report of the interview that was to rock Hollywood.

Although his contract had lapsed the Metro-Goldwyn-Mayer people rang Plum up one day to ask if he would give an interview to a woman reporter for the *Los Angeles Times*. Plum said he would be delighted.

The woman reporter duly arrived and was received by Plum politely and cheerfully. She asked Plum how he liked Hollywood. Plum said amiably that he liked Hollywood and its inhabitants immensely; he said how much he had enjoyed his stay and added, to fill in time and make conversation before the interview proper began, that his one regret was he had been paid such an enormous sum of money without having done anything to earn it.

And what was that.

The interview then got under way and was conducted by both parties on normal question and answer lines. The woman reporter withdrew, having got her scoop.

Early the next morning before Plum was out of bed the telephone rang. Someone wanted to speak to Mr P. G. Wodehouse. Plum answered: rather sleepily, I take it. A voice at the other end of the line said it was Reuter's Los Angeles correspondent speaking, and would Mr Wodehouse kindly say if the interview with him in that day's *Los Angeles Times* was authentic. Plum, rather startled at having been aroused at that hour to be asked so trite a question, said that it was. Reuter's correspondent then asked if he might have Mr Wodehouse's permission to cable it across to London and Plum, even more startled, said that he might!

A brief interval elapsed and then the telephone bell rang again. This time an agitated voice demanded if Mr Wodehouse had seen the interview in the *Los Angeles Times*, because if he had –

Plum dashed downstairs and grabbed the *Times* and almost the first thing he saw under scare headlines was the interview that was destined to revolutionize the motion picture industry and put it on a sound basis and cut out the dead wood, the woman reporter having printed every word he had said about his regret at having been paid such an enormous sum of money without having done a thing to earn it!

Before nightfall Plum was the most talked of man in the United States of America and the bankers went into action.

Some years later I read what the well-known American writer, Rupert Hughes, had to say about this strange episode in the *Saturday Evening Post*:

'Many authors have been badly treated in Hollywood, but Hollywood has paid high for this idiocy. One of the gentlest and one of the most valuable for Hollywood – P. G. Wodehouse – quietly regretted that he had been paid a hundred thousand dollars for doing next to nothing. This remark was taken up, and it stirred the bankers deeply, as it should have done. But Mr Wodehouse has written no ferocious assaults on those who slighted him.'

Sept. 14, 1931   *Beverly Hills*

This business of writing to you has taken on a graver aspect, the postal authorities here having raised the ante to 5¢ per letter.

I can bear it bravely as far as you are concerned, but I do grudge having to spend 5¢ on a letter to some female in East Grinstead who wants to know if I pronounce my name Wood-house or Wode-house.

My art is not going too well at the moment. I have six more stories to do for the *American* magazine, and ye Ed has put me right out of my stride by asking me to make them about American characters in an American setting, like knowing that if I try to do American stuff, the result is awful. Apparently he doesn't care for Mulliner stories, though I'll swear things like 'Fate' and 'The Fiery Wooing of Mordred' aren't bad, always provided you like my sort of stuff. What puzzles me about it all is that when he commissioned the series he must have known the sort of thing I wrote. It can't have come on him as a stunning shock to find that I was laying my scene in England. What did he expect from me? Thoughtful studies of life in the Arkansas foothills?

I suppose I ought to have taken a strong line and refused haughtily to change my act, but I'm all for strewing a little happiness as I go by, so I told him I would have a pop at some Hollywood stories.

Talking of taking a strong line, a negro out west somewhere had been cheated at a street-fair gambling concern and was pretty sore about it. He said to the man running the thing, 'I shall get even with you.' 'How?' said the gambler. 'You are coming here next year?' asked the negro. The gambler said he was. 'Well,' said the negro, 'when I see a white man coming up to gamble with you, I shall stand nearby and say, "Oo! Oo!"'

We dined last night with Douglas Fairbanks and Mary Pickford. She is a most intelligent woman, quite unlike the usual movie star. I talked to her all the evening. (Probably bored her stiff.)

Have you read A. A. Milne's serial, *Two People* in the *Daily Mail*? It's colossal. The sort of book I shall buy and re-read every six months or so. What a genius he is at drawing character. Did you ever see his *The Dover Road*? My favourite play.

Hollywood story. Couple of boxers at the American Legion stadium put on a very mild show, and a spectator, meeting one of them after the fight, reproached him for giving such an inadequate exhibition. The boxer admitted that he had not mixed it up very vigorously, but had a satisfactory explanation. 'Couldn't take no chances of getting mussed up,' he said, 'not with a part in Mae West's new picture coming along.'

A New York actress has just got back to Broadway after a year in Hollywood. She says that she has been so long among the false fronts and papier-mâché mansions on the set that nowadays she finds herself sneaking a look at her husband to see if he goes all the way round or is just a profile.

Non-Hollywood story. Inez Haynes Irwin, wife of Will Irwin, applied for a passport the other day and, assisted by Will Irwin and Wallace Irwin, started to fill up the 'description' form. One of the questions was 'Mouth?' Well, that was all right. She wrote 'Brilliant crimson Cupid's bow with delicious shadowy corners,' but the next question, 'Face?' puzzled her. 'What do I say to that?' she aked. 'Write "Yes",' said Wallace Irwin.

THREE

1932–1938

The above is now our address. We move in on Thursday. We
have taken it for a year. It is a sort of Provençal country-house,
with 100 acres of hillside and large grounds and a huge swimming-pool. It ought to be lovely in summer. Just at the moment
it is a bit bleak.

I have written one goodish story since I got here, and two
others which aren't right. I think I can fix them, but a comic
story which goes off the rails is worse than any other kind. One
gets the feeling that one's stuff isn't funny, which is deadly.

Do you ever read Claude Houghton? Writes darned well.

I bought Aldous Huxley's *Brave World* thing, but simply
can't read it. What a bore these stories of the future are. The
whole point of Huxley is that he can write better about modern
life than anybody else, so of course he goes and writes about the
future, blast him. Michael Arlen is down here, writing a novel
the scene of which is laid in the future. It's a ruddy epidemic.

I have had rotten luck with books lately. All my favourite
authors have let me down, and I've had to fall back on the
French. I've read everything by Colette I could get hold of,
including her autobiography, *Mes Apprentissages*. In *re* Colette
a thing I've never been able to understand is how her husband,
Willy, got away with it. Did you ever hear of Willy? He must
have been quite a chap. He was a hack journalist of sorts, and
shortly after they were married he spotted Colette could write,

so he locked her in a room, and made her turn out the four *Claudine* books, which he published under his own name – 'par Willy' – and made a fortune out of. He would give her an occasional bit of the proceeds and expect her to be grateful for it, and he used to tell interviewers that his wife had been of considerable assistance to him in these works of his, helping him quite a bit.

Right. One can faintly understand that aspect of his literary production, because she was very young and scared stiff of him, so I suppose she didn't dare to object. But why did all the other fellows whose work he published as his own put up with it?

What he used to do was to get a central idea for a novel, and write a page or two, then he would send it to a friend with a letter saying that he had got as far as this but what was needed now was the friend's magic touch. Would he, the friend, mind dashing off a few thousand words in his own inimitable style, just to get the thing going?

When the script came back with the added stuff, he had it typed and sent it to another friend. 'To the rescue, old man! You will see that enclosed is beginning to shape, but it needs you to add the touches. Could you take the time to etc.' The script – plus the added stuff – would then go to a third friend, then a fourth and possibly a fifth, until eventually it was finished and another novel 'par Willy' was in the book-shops.

How did he *do* it? It must have been hypnotism or something.

We have settled down here very comfortably. Weather bad so far, but they say from now on we get six months of unbroken sunshine. It's a good place for work. I have written sixty-four pages of *Thank You, Jeeves*, in seventeen days, and would have done more but I went off the rails and had to rewrite three times. That is the curse of my type of story. Unless I get the construction absolutely smooth, it bores the reader. In this story, for instance, I had Bertie meet the heroine in London, scene, then again in the country, another scene. I found I had to boil all this down to one meeting, as it was talky. By the way, it's not all jam writing a story in the first person. The reader can know nothing except what Bertie tells him, and Bertie can know only a limited amount himself.

I have just got Denis Mackail's *David's Day*. Very good. You ought to read it.

Grimsdick wants me to do a preface for the Bindle Omnibus book. Damned difficult. Easy enough if I could do a kidding preface like I did for *The Ship in the Swamp* – I could describe a Jenkins day, with H. J. doing everybody's work including the office boy's. But, dash it, the man killed himself by overwork, so bim goes that.

If there is any reader who does not yet know how a writer's mind works and would like to know, let him ponder on how in the course of writing this letter Plum's Bertie Wooster story developed. To me the most interesting and remarkable feature of Plum's methods of writing a story is that, however many false starts he may have made and however difficult it may have been for him to find the right way of presenting his theme, the finished result always reads as though the story had simply poured out without check.

April 23, 1932   *Domaine de la Fréyère*

The stuff you sent me about the house with monkeys and mice in it is just what I needed for *Thank You, Jeeves*. It fits in perfectly. (This sounds like Willy, doesn't it?) Bertie's pal Chuffy lives at Chuffnell Hall, Chuffy's aunt and her small son at the Dower House in the park. The son breeds white mice. They smell, and the aunt thinks it's drains, so they shift to the Hall and only a caretaker is in the Dower House. So when Bertie breaks in to get a night's lodging, with his face covered with black boot polish. . . . Golly, what rot it sounds when one writes it down! Come, come, Wodehouse, is *this* the best you can do in the way of carrying on the great tradition of English Literature? Still, I'll bet the plot of *Hamlet* seemed just as lousy when Shakespeare was trying to tell it to Ben Jonson in the Mermaid Tavern. ('Well, Ben, see what I mean, the central character is this guy, see, who's in love with this girl, see, but her old man doesn't think he's on the level, see, so he tells her – wait a minute, I better start at the beginning. Well, so this guy's in college, see, and he's come home because his mother's gone and married his uncle, see, and he sees a ghost, see. So this ghost turns out to be the guy's father. . . .')

I haven't read *Magnolia Street*, so I don't know how good it is, but as a rule I think most novels would be better, if shorter.

I think we shall open Norfolk Street in March next, when we get it back.

August 13th, 1932   *Domaine de la Fréyère*

How's everything going with you? I liked your 'Before and After' story in *Collier's*.

Would this idea be any good to you? Downtrodden young peer, much snootered by aunts, etc., has become engaged to two girls at once, and feels that the only way out is to vanish. He runs away to sea and has adventures. It might work out into something.

I am hoping that this rise in the American stock market means the beginning of better times out there. There is no doubt that the magazines in New York are having a bad time. Fancy the *Saturday Evening Post* people having to pass their dividend! Two years ago they were paying eight dollars a share. I sold *Thank You, Jeeves* to the *Cosmopolitan* for $50,000 – my record – and they are paying me so much a month and not the whole amount down in a lump. I've never heard of that happening before. Hearst can't be as hard up as all that.

August 24, 1932   *Domaine de la Fréyère*

Odd your not getting *Louder and Funnier*. I sent it off quite a month ago. This confirms my view that only about one letter in five sent out from this bally place ever arrives anywhere, and parcels simply haven't a hope. The postman probably drops anything at all heavy down a ravine. And I don't blame him. The poor devil has to walk miles up and down hill in the blazing sun. I'll write to the Fabers to send you a copy. The best thing about *Louder and Funnier* is the jacket by Rex Whistler.

H. G. Wells lives not far from here, and I have been seeing him occasionally. He lunched here yesterday. I knew him slightly in London, at the time when he had some complicated row on with a man who had worked for him on his *Outline of History*. He asked a bunch of authors to dinner to hear his side of the thing. Why he included me, I don't know. Arnold Bennett was there and we walked home together. He was pleasant but patronizing.

I like Wells. An odd bird, though. The first time I met him, we had barely finished the initial pip-pippings when he said, apropos of nothing, 'My Father was a professional cricketer.' If there's a good answer to that, you tell me. I thought of saying, 'Mine had a white moustache,' but finally settled for, 'Oh, ah,' and we went on to speak of other things.

Don't you find that the chief difficulty in writing novels is getting the love interest set? Boy meets girl. Right. But what happens then? I'm gradually assembling a plot where a rising young artist is sent for to Blandings to paint a portrait. He says to himself, 'Ah, some prominent Duchess, no doubt,' and of course it turns out that Lord Emsworth wants a portrait of his pig, to celebrate her winning the silver medal at the Shropshire Agricultural Show in the Fat Pigs class. Artist, deeply offended, speaks disparagingly of pigs and Lord E. kicks him out. On his way out, he – the artist – sees a wonderful girl, falls in love at first sight and realizes that he has now made it impossible for himself ever to enter the Blandings premises again. So he is obliged to hang round the place, seeking furtive meetings.

Now then. Who is the girl? Why is she at Blandings? I can't get on till I find out what her position is.

Which reminds me of a story I read somewhere – by S. J. Perelman? I can't remember – about a movie magnate who had a wonderful idea for a picture, and he sends to New York for an author, telling him, when he arrives, that every writer on the payroll has been stumped for three months by one detail in the story. Get that one small detail, and the thing will be set.

'We fade in on a street in London,' he says, 'and there's a guy in rags dragging himself along through the fog, a Lon Chaney type guy. He's all twisted and crippled up. He comes to a colossal house in Berkeley Square and lets himself in with a latchkey, and he's in a gorgeous hall full of Chinese rugs and Ming vases, and the minute he's inside he straightens up, takes off his harness and unties his leg, and by golly, he's as normal as you and me, not a cripple at all. Then we truck with him through a door, and he's like in a hospital corridor, and he pulls on rubber gloves and an operating gown and he goes into a room where there's ten, fifteen beautiful dames chained to the wall with practically nothing on. We follow him to a bench that's full of test tubes and scientific stuff, and he grabs a hypodermic needle and he goes around laughing like a hyena and jabbing it into these beautiful dames. And that's where you got to figure out this one thing: *What kind of a business is this guy in?*'

December 1st, 1932

*Dorchester Hotel,
London*

When I see you I want to talk over an idea for a secret collaboration on a series of sensational stories. I think it would be fun having a shot at these. I don't suppose we shall be able to do anything till I settle in London again, but it now looks as if we should open Norfolk Street in March or earlier.

I never in my life experienced such suspense as during that second half of the Sherborne match, culminating in Bill Griffith scoring that superb try. Isn't it strange that one can still be absorbed by Dulwich footer? I never saw such splendid defensive work as we put up. It was easily the best school match I have seen.

Don't you find, as you get on in life, that the actual things you really want cost about £200 a year? I have examined my soul, and I find that my needs are a library subscription and tobacco money, plus an extra bit for holidays.

When I see you, I want to take away a pile of your stories. I feel there must be so many of them that just need a bit of fixing. We might use some of them for the collaboration. Shall we revive Basil Windham?

January 4th, 1933

Domaine de la Fréyère

I hope to have my novel finished before I return to England. If I put off my return till March, that is to say. At present, we plan to come back at the end of January and open Norfolk Street.

I shall be glad to be settled in England again. This country is fine, but we are too far from everything. And if one lives in Cannes, there is the constant temptation of the Casino. London is the best spot, all round.

How have you been doing? Any luck? I'm afraid it is still a bad time for the magazines.

Second Test Match. How about it? What a bunch of rabbits! Isn't it odd how cricketers during the county season seem such marvels yet no good in Australia.

Have you ever read Warwick Deeping? I hadn't till the other day when Ethel took *New Wine and Old* out of the library. He is good. His stuff reminds me a little of yours.

The catch about that sort of stuff, of course, is that it is quiet and does not make a punching appeal, so that it is necessary to build book on book and get a public gradually.

I have had a devil of a time with my new one. It is a sequel to *Summer Lightning*, to be called *Heavy Weather*, and the first chapters were terribly hard to write, because I had to be careful not to assume that people had read *S. L.* and at the same time not to put in yards of explanation which would have bored those who had. In order to get 100 pages of OK stuff, I must have written nearly 100,000 words.

This place is congested with Ethel's adopted cats, all having kittens.

Domaine de la Fréyère,
February 9th, 1933   *Auribeau, A.M.*

Sorry I haven't answered yours of January 23rd before. I have been sweating at *Heavy Weather*, and must be getting a bit stale, as I simply hadn't any energy left to write a line after the day's work. It's a curious thing about this novel, and probably means that it's going to be good, but I must have written at least 200,000 words so far. For a long time I couldn't get the thing straight. I kept getting dissatisfied with the first 30,000 words and starting again. Today I reached page 254 and have a very detailed scenario of the rest, and all up to page 254 now looks all right. It really reads as if I had written it straight off without a pause.

My plans are a little uncertain. I am waiting to hear from Ethel, who left on Sunday to open Norfolk Street, leaving me with Winky! I think the idea is that she is going to find out about quarantine and then write me. I expect a letter to-morrow.

If she says come along, I shall start at once. I am thoroughly sick of this place. These last four days have been rather trying.

I am alone in the house with the caretaker and his wife, who cooks for me. I take my meals on trays.

I could go and stay at a hotel in Cannes, of course, but Winky would be such a burden at a hotel. My God, she's bad enough here! She won't let me out of her sight. I feel rotten if I don't get an exercise walk in the afternoon, but every time I try to start on one Winky sits on the terrace and just looks at me. You can hear her saying, 'Going to leave me, eh? Well, of all the dirty tricks!' So I say, 'Well, come along, too.' And she says, 'What, sweat down that mountain and have to sweat up again? Not for me.' So it ends in my strolling about the garden.

November 5th, 1933   *17 Norfolk Street*

Thanks for card about telephone number. This will ease the situation a lot. I shall now be able to let you know of my visits on the day instead of having to give notice a week ahead.

Since returning from Hunstanton, I have been having rather a lull. I sold *Right-ho, Jeeves* to the *Saturday Evening Post*, and they are starting it on December 2nd, which will be a nasty knock for the *Cosmopolitan* who, after postponing publication for two years, God knows why, are starting *Thank You, Jeeves* on December 10th. I got the same price as for *Heavy Weather* – $40,000.

                                                              The Dorchester,
March 10, 1934   *Park Lane*

I've just had the foulest week of my career.

Which reminds me of the story of the engine-driver. This engine-driver overslept himself one morning, had to shave in a hurry, cut himself, went down to breakfast, found the coffee was cold and the toast burned, raced off to his train, tripped over a loose stone and barked his shin, and, finally, got aboard and started off. The train had just rounded a corner when he suddenly saw another train on the same line coming at him at fifty miles an hour. He heaved a weary sigh. 'Do *you* have days,' he said to the stoker, 'when *everything* seems to go wrong?'

But about this week. It included two visits to the dentist, a cold in the head, the opening of Crockford's Club (one of those ghastly functions where you're invited for ten o'clock and don't have any dinner because you think supper will be served the moment you arrive and then don't get any supper), an American interviewer who caught me just as the cold was at its worst, and a snack luncheon to celebrate the publication of a young author's new book. And, finally, the shifting of our fifteen trunks, twenty suit-cases and two Pekes from Seamore Court here.

I must say that luncheon was the limit. It seemed to take one into a new and dreadful world. Can you imagine giving a lunch to celebrate the publication of a book? With other authors, mostly fairies, twittering all over the place, screaming, 'Oh Lionel!' and photographs of you holding the book, etc. Gosh! Dumas was the boy. When he had finished a novel he kept on sitting and started another. No snack luncheons for him.

Thrilling about your voyage. Can't we manage to combine our trips? My idea is to go to Cannes again, but I am game to do anything. Why wouldn't a week or two at Marseilles do you just as well as the trip to Port Said? You ought to see the South of France, it would be very valuable to your work, and you have the gift of being able to collect material on a very short stay.

The Riviera isn't much good to me, but I should have thought you could have got a lot out of it. You have Marseilles, which is right up your street, and all the tough quarters of Nice, etc. Anyway, if we could arrange to meet at Marseilles and then think what to do next, it would be fine.

Hôtel Prince de Galles,
June 11th, 1934   *Paris*

I've been meaning to write for ages, but I've been tied up with *The Luck of the Bodkins*. I find that the longer I go on writing, the harder it becomes to get a story right without going over and over it. I have just reached page 180 and I suppose I must have done quite 400 pages! Still, it is in good shape now.

Paris is fine. I don't go out much, as I am working all the time. I have been here for exactly five weeks, except for one day at Le Touquet. I may be going to Le Touquet again for a few days soon, to talk with Guy Bolton about our play for

Vinton Freedley *Anything Goes*. But this address will always find me.

I had an offer from Paramount the other day to go to Hollywood, and had to refuse. But rather gratifying after the way Hollywood took a solemn vow three years ago never to mention my name again. Quite the olive branch!

Do you know, Bill, what was one of the most interesting periods in history? The year 1822 in France, when the ex-officers of the Old Guard were plotting to bring Napoleon's son to the throne. I am reading a book called *Les Demi-Soldes* (The Half-pay Officers) by Desparbes (which sounds like the sort of name you give the characters in your stories). It's thrilling.

Royal Picardy,
August 2nd, 1934   *Le Touquet-Paris-Plage*

Thanks for yours. I'm glad the novel is coming out well. What a sweat all that sea stuff must be.

The big item of news is that we have bought a house here. Isn't it odd? The only reason I came to Le Touquet was because I was writing this musical comedy with Guy Bolton, and he doesn't like Paris, so I said, all right, we'll meet half-way, I'll come to Le Touquet.

At first I didn't like the place, and then suddenly it began to get me, and it struck both Ethel and me that, as regards situation, it was the one ideal spot in the world. I can get over to England by boat in a few hours and by plane in one hour. It is only two and a half hours from Paris and within motoring distance of Cherbourg.

We shan't be moving in, I suppose, till next Spring, as the house wants fixing up.

I'm having a devil of a time with *Anything Goes*. I can't get hold of Guy or the composer, Cole Porter. What has become of Cole, Heaven knows. Last heard of at Heidelberg.

Golf Hotel,
September 13th, 1934   *Le Touquet*

The Ship in the Fanlight arrived this morning. I am looking forward to reading it tonight in bed. Don't you think they have given you a good jacket this time? It really seems as if they have turned over a new leaf in that respect.

Idea for a story for you: Mate of ship murders Captain to get his job, sets fire to ship to destroy all traces, becomes hero and lives happily ever afterwards – except for the moment when the Captain's ghost comes and breathes down the back of his neck, just as he is addressing his old school on *How to Succeed*.

I have been musing over what you say at the end of your letter about the passage of Time. I feel just the same. My particular trouble is that what I feel I should really like is to vegetate in one place all my life, and I spend my whole time whizzing about.

Of course, the trouble is that one is never quite happy unless one is working – and by working I don't so much mean the actual writing as the feeling that one could write if one wanted to. It is the in-between times that kill one.

I am now faced with a difficult job – a 16,000 word story for the *New York Herald-Tribune*, to run in four parts. But I can't seem to get the right idea. A short story of 7000 words is simple, and a novelette of 30,000, too, but this in-between length is trying. I haven't room to build up an elaborate plot, and yet the story must not be thin and must have at least a passable curtain for each instalment. Oh, well, I suppose it will come.

Hutchinsons have just sent me the *Century of Humour*. Have they sent you a copy? Your *Interlude in a Quiet Life* looks very good.

Low Wood,
Le Touquet

October 5th, 1934

I have been meaning to write to you for weeks, but I have been working on the 16,000 word story for the *New York Tribune* magazine. I finished it this morning, after much sweat.

Thanks for the ideas for stories. That one about sitting down on the chair that wasn't there is fine, but, laddie, did you ever read a *Saturday Evening Post* story by Nunnally Johnson called *There Ought To Be A Law*? It was about a wife who would keep moving the furniture, and the big scene was very similar.

There the husband chucks himself into bed in the dark, to find the bed is over in another corner of the room.

I'm much bitten with the idea of writing some stories under another name. I've been brooding on one you sent me, *The Old House*. I believe that if one got a slightly different angle on it, it would go? Do you remember the story? Young American wife shown over English country house by shabby old man, who turns out to be the owner. Arthur Morrison once did a very good one where a caller was shown over house by bloke who had just murdered the owner, whose body was lying in next room. Couldn't we do something on those lines?

I am very fit. The air here is wonderful, and I have got to go and fetch our papers every day from Paris Plage. That means a four mile walk, so what with taking the dogs for runs and generally messing about, I suppose I do a steady fifty miles a week. I notice the difference in my condition very much. In London, my four-mile walk used to leave me not exactly tired but feeling I had had all I wanted but here, I hardly feel it.

Low Wood,
December 4th, 1934   *Le Touquet*

Lady Dudley (Gertie Millar) lives a few doors off us and when she went to England asked me to exercise her spotted carriage dog occasionally. Well, of course, after I had taken it with me for two days on my walk to get the papers, it proceeded to regard this walk as a fixed ceremony. The day I had to go to Lille, I hear it refused all food and would not be comforted.

I finished *The Luck of the Bodkins* on November 20th, and ever since have been in a sort of coma. Do you get like that after a big bout of work?

As a matter of fact, my present collapse is the result of a strain that has gone on now for almost six months. While in the middle of *The Luck of the Bodkins*, and just beginning to see my way through it, I had to break off and start plotting out that musical comedy, *Anything Goes*, for New York with Howard Lindsay, the director. We toiled all through that blazing weather in Paris, and then we came down here and started all over again with Guy Bolton. In the end we got out a plot, and I wrote a rough version, and sent it off to Guy to rewrite.

Well, I eventually started on *The Luck of the Bodkins* again. Then I got the commission for the novelette for the *New York Herald-Tribune*, to be done in a hurry. So I started sweating at that and, just as I was in the middle of it, a cable came from America from Vinton Freedley, the manager, saying that the stuff which Guy and I had sent over wouldn't do, and that he was calling in two other people to rewrite it. So there I was, presumably out of that.

I got the novelette finished and sent it over, but was naturally in a panic about it after the débâcle of the musical comedy which, incidentally, had been preceded by the complete failure of the Bolton-Wodehouse comedy in London, because, though it was a commission, I wouldn't have felt able to stand on my rights and demand the money unless the stuff was acceptable. And for weeks I heard nothing.

Meanwhile, *The Luck of the Bodkins* was coming out with great difficulty. Have you had the experience of getting out what looks like a perfect scenario and then finding that it won't write and has to be completely changed?

And then suddenly – or, rather, not suddenly, but in a sort of series of bits of good news – everything came right. My arrangement about *Anything Goes* was that I was to get 2 per cent of the gross, if I was able to go to New York and attend rehearsals, but if I couldn't I was to give up half of the 1 per cent to Howard Lindsay. So I was looking on it all the time as 1½ per cent job (1½ per cent being the ordinary musical comedy royalty).

You can imagine my relief when I found that the rewriting was not going to affect my royalty very much. Russel Crouse, the rewriter, had consented to do the work for half of 1 per cent, so I am only down a quarter of 1 per cent on the normal royalty. Then we heard that the show was a huge success in Boston, and now it has been produced in New York and is the biggest hit for years and years and Cochran has bought it for London.

Meanwhile I had had a cable from the *New York Herald-Tribune*, which said, HAPPY ABOUT LORD HAVERSHOT (that was the name of the hero of the novelette), from which I inferred that it was all right – though don't you hate these ambiguous cables? I mean, the editor might quite easily really have written NOT HAPPY and the French postal officials cut out the word 'not' as not seeming to them important.

Finally, however, a letter arrived with the cheque, just about the time I heard the news of the success of the show.

By that time, I was struggling with the last chapters of *The Luck of the Bodkins*. Usually when I get to the last fifty pages of a story, it begins to write itself. But this time everything went wrong and I had to grope my way through it all at the rate of two pages a day. I began to get superstitious about it and felt that if I could ever get it finished my luck would be in. On November 29th I was within four pages of the end and suddenly all the lights in the house went out and stayed out.

Still, I finished it next day, and it is pretty good, I think. Frightfully long – 362 pages of typescript – it must be over the 100,000 words.

All this, added to the fact that Ethel has gone to London, and it has been raining from the moment she left, has left me pretty limp. I suppose I shall be all right in a day or so.

One of your old letters mentioned that you had been reading J. D. Beresford and that you admired his work a lot. I think he's darned good, too. Did you read a weird little story of his in the *Daily Express* about a dog?

Have you been following public school footer form this year? I have never known it so in and out.

> Bedford 30, Dulwich nil
> Dulwich nil, Haileybury 3
> Haileybury 9, Bedford 5
> Tonbridge 3, Haileybury 5
> Dulwich 11, Tonbridge nil.

Dulwich beat Mill Hill, Mill Hill beat Brighton, Brighton beat Dulwich.

The *Herald-Tribune* novelette Plum subsequently expanded into a full-length novel, *Laughing Gas*.

No letter ever illustrated more completely the trials and torments of even an eminent writer than this. Plum was, at the time his letter was written – December 1934 – pre-eminent in his profession, yet even he, as his letter showed, had his rebuffs, his moments of doubt and his difficulties. It must have been a consolation to him to read soon after this Hilaire Belloc's introduction to the book, *Week-End Wodehouse*. Mr Belloc wrote:

'Some two or three years ago I was asked in the United States to broadcast a few words on my own trade of writing – what I thought of it and why I disliked it.

'I understand that this broadcast was heard by a very large number – some millions, it seems. Now in the course of this broadcast I gave as the best writer of English now alive, Mr P. G. Wodehouse.

'It was not only a very sincere, but a reasonable and well-thought-out pronouncement. Yet I got a vast number of communications asking me what I exactly meant. Not that those who had heard me doubted Mr Wodehouse's genius. They had given proof of their perception of that genius by according him the very wide circulation which he enjoys on that side of the Atlantic, as I am glad to say he does elsewhere. No; their puzzlement was why I should call the author who was supreme in that particular line of country the 'best' writer of our time: the best living writer of *English*: why I should have called him, as I did call him, 'the head of my profession'.''

I shall quote no more of this profoundly erudite essay on Plum Wodehouse's art, so often decried by those without real understanding as being merely 'verbal' wit, but suggest the book in which Mr Belloc's essay appears should at once be either bought or borrowed from the nearest library because in *Week-End Wodehouse* there will be found what a critic in the *Observer* described as, 'A ravishing anthology from Mr Wodehouse's novels, some of his lighter papers, and choice morsels of comment and description.'

January 23rd, 1935   *Low Wood*

When I got to page 100 of *Voyage Without End*, I rushed to my typewriter and wrote a letter to Arthur Waugh, the head of Chapman & Hall, raving about the book. As I don't know him, this will probably cause him to reject the thing immediately. Still, I meant well.

Bill, it's an absolute masterpiece. It's the only book I've read for years that did really take me out of myself into another atmosphere, so that I got the sense of coming back to another world when I finished reading. I just live with those people.

What Ivor Nicholson's reader can be suffering from, I don't know, because it defeats me how anyone can say those characters aren't real. There isn't one of them that you can't visualize with perfect clearness as you read.

One of the best tips for writing a play is, 'Never let them sit down' – i.e. keep the characters buzzing about without a pause, and that's just what you have done here. There isn't a moment till you come to the end of Part One where you can stop reading. You always feel there is something round the corner.

Let's see what Chapman & Hall do. If they fail, I will write to Sir Tresham Lever, who is Thornton Butterworth, or E. V. Lucas.

I am contemplating writing to Ivor Nicholson, cursing his reader – who, I imagine, is a novelist of sorts. By the way, how does a publisher ever accept a novel on a reader's report? If you told the story of any book in the form of a reader's report, it would sound awful.

Reader's report of *Henry Fourth, Part One*, by W. Shakespeare: 'This is a story of life in London. The plot is improbable and does not carry conviction, as it deals with a Prince of Wales who apparently visits public houses. There is a fat man named Falstaff.'

I'll tell you one thing. From now on, in your novels, let yourself go, regardless of what the reader is going to think. For magazines one more or less has to study the public, but not for the novel public. I believe there are two ways of writing novels. One is mine, making the thing a sort of musical comedy without music, and ignoring real life altogether; the other is going right deep down into life and not caring a damn. The ones that fail are the ones where the writer loses his nerve and says, 'My God! I can't write this, I must tone it down.'

If you will let me have a copy of *Greenside Island*, I'll send it to young Lorimer on the *Saturday Evening Post*, telling him that it was submitted before, but that you have rewritten it. I gather that he has taken Costain's place, and Costain was the man who read it before. Costain is now Eastern editor of Fox Films – a good job, I suppose, so long as you stay in it, but I wouldn't trust myself to a movie company. You dine with the President on Monday, and he slaps you on the back and tells you you are the salt of the earth, and on Tuesday morning you get a letter from him saying you are fired. Still, I suppose Costain has a long contract.

Here's an idea you might be able to use: I see a man at Ascot with a rich-looking but unpleasant wife. I pity him, and you, who know him, tell me he is one of the happiest men you know. You tell me his story.

The point of this is that he is in love with a *house*. He is of hardish-up family, went to school in some awful suburb where he lived – not Dulwich, as Dulwich is too pleasant. He had some distant cousins who owned a lovely country house, a place like Hunstanton Hall. Out of pity they used to have him to stay for two weeks every summer, and those two weeks were his real life. He worshipped the house. I mean, really worshipped. It was the core of his whole inner life.

Then there came the war. The distant cousins lost all their sons, and in addition became broke. (Note: He stopped going to stay at the house when he was seventeen, when he went into an office, so it has remained a remote Paradise all this time.)

Some profiteers bought the house, and a chain of circumstances – he might be in the profiteer's office – brought him into contact with profiteer's daughter, a spoiled, awful girl.

You will have to give hero some quality of attraction. He might be very handsome. Because the daughter wants him and insists on having him. And he marries her, though thoroughly disliking her, because it will mean that he will get back to the house.

So there he is when I meet him. He is snubbed by the parents, and the girl nags him, because her brief infatuation is over and she realizes that she is landed with a nobody as a husband. He has a rotten time as far as his outward life goes, but he is perfectly happy. He has the house and can potter about and dream.

I think you could make something of that. It has something of the quality of your *The Rose House*.

I wrote Plum's story about the man in love with a house and it failed badly, which in a way did not surprise me as I felt when I had finished it that it was a thoroughly poor effort. But I know now what was wrong with it; it was not a short story plot at all, but the theme for a novel.

February 4th, 1935   *Low Wood*

Hell's foundations quivering briskly just now. The *Saturday Evening Post* have rejected *The Luck of the Bodkins* – my first rejection in America in twenty-one years. I have re-read the book as critically as if it were someone else's – all right someone's else, if you prefer it – and see now what's wrong. Gosh, isn't it awful the mistakes one can make and not see till too late? It's 25,000 words too long.

Do you know, I believe over-longness is the worst fault in writing. I had such a good farcical plot in this one that I got all hopped up and felt that it wasn't possible to give 'em too much of this superb stuff, so every scene I wrote was elaborated till it lost its grip. To give you some idea, I now reach on page 45 a situation which in the original I got on to page 100! That's 15,000 words out for a start. I expect to cut 30,000.

Just got the *Anything Goes* script from America. There are two lines of mine left in it, and so far I am receiving £50 a week apiece for them. That's about £3 10s. a word, which is pretty good payment, though less, of course, than my stuff is worth.

Letter from Arthur Waugh   *11 Henrietta Street,*
Chapman & Hall Ltd   *Covent Garden, WC2*

Dear Mr Wodehouse,
I was delighted to get your kind letter about Mr Townend's MS, and, as it happened, it could not have arrived at a more opportune moment. For only a couple of hours before it came, I had started on the MS and was struck at once by the conviction that these deckhands, seagoing men, and their womenkind were the real thing, drawn from life – not the stock figures from the novelist's cardboard tray. I must admit that I thought their world a bit sordid to please the general public; but when they get to sea the atmosphere may change. I was much helped by your letter, and encouraged at the start of my task of reading

the MS – no very light one, for it looks like 130,000 words at least. Thank you very much for writing to me about it.

Yes; it is true that we have never met in the body, but in the spirit we have travelled a good many miles together. There was a time, in Alec's schooldays, when we used to read your books together with enormous enjoyment; and, though we are never long enough together nowadays – to read more than a telegram – we still have preserved a sort of freemason's code of Psmithisms, which continually crops up in our letters. Indeed, I can truly say, in emulation of Wolfe, that I would far rather have created Psmith than have stormed Quebec.

Again thanking you for your very pleasant letter and hoping that I may like *Voyage Without End* as much as you do.

Sincerely yours
Arthur Waugh

Hôtel Lincoln,
Rue Bayard,
March 6th, 1935   *Paris*

I have been at above address since February 24th. I return to Low Wood on Saturday.

Your letter, forwarded on from Le Touquet, reached me last night. I am frightfully bucked that Chapman & Hall have taken *Voyage Without End*.

I must say I feel a bit uneasy about that huge cut they want to make, and particularly at your saying that they had cut 30,000 words already themselves. I think you should be in sole control of any cutting that has to be done.

Can you hang on for a few days, till I can get back to Le Touquet and read the story again? The only living soul at Low Wood at present is a Jugo-Slavian butler, and any attempt to get him to mail you the script would result in your receiving either (*a*) the MS of *The Luck of the Bodkins* or (*b*) a handsomely bound copy of the *Encyclopaedia Britannica*.

This cutting business is frightfully tricky, as I know from my own experience. I got 25,000 words out of *The Luck of the Bodkins* without any trouble at all, but not by paring down scenes. I reconstructed the first half of the story entirely, taking advantage of a really sound criticism from Reeves Shaw to eliminate one situation entirely. Isn't it odd how one can spoil a story by being too leisurely in telling it?

I thought your briar pipe thing in the *Strand* the best short story you had written for ages. Surely in Captain Shuffley you have got the character you were looking for, who would run through a series! He seems to me as good as Bob Pretty. I see him as a chap who might have adventure after adventure, doing the most chivalrous things but always making a bit out of them. You know what I mean – saves girl from low-down café in Buenos Aires and you find at the end that his main motive in starting the big rescue scene was that he hadn't any money to pay his bill, and wanted a way of creating a diversion.

Have you ever noticed how if you are expecting an important telegram some absolutely unimportant one arrives? I remember in 1922 when *The Beauty Prize* was produced at the Winter Garden, I sailed the day it opened, expecting a wireless about how it had gone. On the first day out along came a wireless and I tore it open and it was from Leslie Henson, wishing me *Bon Voyage*.

The same thing has happened now. I am on tenterhooks about the fate of some stuff I sent over to New York. I got a letter from my agent saying that the editor of the *Red Book* liked the stories, but that a snag had arisen in the shape of the president of the company, which also owns *McCall's*, because in 1922 I contracted to do six short stories for *McCall's* and never delivered them! The president has been brooding on it ever since, and agent says it rather looks as if he may have to shade our price a bit as compensation.

Well, as anything I get out of America nowadays with this income-tax dispute going on is like a bone sneaked from a dog, I cabled CLOSE DEAL AT ANY PRICE YOU CAN GET AND CABLE AT ONCE. Sure enough, a telegram arrived that night. It was from Gertie Millar at Le Touquet, thanking me for having exercised her Dalmatian dog in her absence.

March 10th, 1935   *Low Wood*

What asses Pekes are! We took Winky to Paris, leaving Boo
behind. Ten days later I bring her back. But was there a joyful
reunion? No, sir. Each poor fish had completely forgotten the
other, and each, seeing a stranger in her home, prepared to
fight to the death. They had six fights in the first ten minutes
and one the next morning, but have now settled down.

One of the fights was the funniest thing you ever saw. I had
put my typewriter case down in a corner and Winky was
behind it. Boo came up in front and they both reared up on their
hind legs and stood with their noses touching, snarling and
growling, but unable to get at each other. This went on for
about five minutes.

March 28th, 1935   *Low Wood*

Thank God, the sun has broken through the clouds and the
United States Marines have arrived just as the savages were
storming the stockade. A cable from my New York agent came,
saying that he had sold *The Luck of the Bodkins* and three short
stories to the *Red Book*. $25,000 for Bodkins as against the
$40,000 *The Post* would have paid, but what of it? 'Oo-la-la!'
as we say over here.

That hound Boo as near as a toucher got killed last night.
We were walking on left side of road. Two girls on bikes came
along on right side. Boo dashed across and gave chase, spilling
one girl. I stopped to pick her up, and Boo legged it after the
other one, spilling her also. I was twenty yards behind when I
saw a car coming and at that moment Boo swerved to the left.
I gave a yell and the car stopped with the wheel right over her.
Another revolution would have killed her. She then trotted
to Ethel and lay on her back, which is her idea of passing off a
delicate situation.

No date   *Low Wood*

I have just had a review of *Blandings Castle* in some provincial
paper, criticizing in an adverse spirit a scene which is not in
the book at all, but in Eric Linklater's *Ripeness Is All*.

Just had a testing job – reading the page proofs of the

Mulliner Omnibus book. 864 pages! It humbled me a good deal, as the stuff didn't seem good. Still, I suppose nothing would, if you read 864 pages of it straight off.

I can't get an idea for a novel. Maddening, as except for that I am fixed so solidly for the coming year – for there will be four companies of *Anything Goes* playing, not counting the London one, and I have an original play for Ralph Lynn – *The Inside Stand* – and an adaptation coming on in London, and I am well ahead with short stories. But all is useless unless I get started on a novel.

Oh, this will interest you. Askew was saying why doesn't Townend stick to sea stories, and said that one single bookseller in Glasgow sold a thousand copies of the half-crown edition of *The Tramp*. Of course, this is a hell of a time to tell you this, when you are in the middle of a non-sea novel, but as a guide for the future apparently what they want from you is the sea stuff.

PS – I thought your old address was pretty bad, but the new one beats it. I look on it as a good morning's work addressing an envelope to you now.

September 12th, 1935   *Low Wood*

In *re* short story series. My own experience is that you can't – unless you are extraordinarily inventive – write a series bang off. I started writing in 1902, and every day I said to myself, 'I must get a character for a series.' In 1916 I wrote the first *Jeeves* story. About a year later I wrote another. But it wasn't till I had done about six at long intervals that I realized I had got a series-character.

You remember that story you gave me, about the woman telling lies about the girl's relations, so that she could marry the humble suitor? It comes out in the Christmas *Strand*, called *Uncle Fred Flits By*. Now, in Uncle Fred I'm sure I have got a character, but at the moment I simply can't think of another plot for him. I'm just waiting and hoping one will come.

It's different if you have got a man with a definite job – Sherlock Holmes or Raffles. Then you can think of things for him to do. But I wouldn't sit down and do a series of *Adventures of Psmith*, because there is no definite line that he would take.

I expect to be over again very soon. Jack Waller's new musical comedy opens tonight, and I suppose that almost immediately after that he will start rehearsals of my Ralph Lynn show. In which case I shall stay over till the opening.

November 15th, 1935
Telegram

MOTORING PORTSMOUTH STOPPING TEA COODEN HOTEL FIVE. PLUM.

I met Plum for tea. Rain was pouring down and a high wind was blowing. He had motored from Le Touquet to Boulogne, had crossed to Folkestone, where he had hired a car to take him all the way to Portsmouth to attend the first performance of his new play. How he endured so dreadful a journey in pitch-black darkness I cannot imagine. He told me when I said goodbye to him, that he proposed to use the time involved in thinking out a new story; which was a convincing proof of Plum's power of concentration.

December 2nd, 1935   *Hilbre, Le Touquet*

Isn't it perfectly rotten – my old typewriter on which I have been working since 1911, has gone phut. I had it patched up in Boulogne, but now the shift key won't work, so I have had to discard it. I am writing this on a machine which has been knocking around for a year or so, while Ethel buys me a new one in London. I think she is getting a Royal. I believe that's what you use, isn't it?

Do you know if there is any way of having my old machine entirely rebuilt? Expense no object. My trouble is that this is a Monarch, and there is no Monarch firm now. Perhaps if I buy a Royal, the Royal people would fix it up.

Don't you find that after you've used a typewriter for a long time, you can't get used to the touch of any other?

I have been alone here with the dogs for exactly two weeks tomorrow. It's extraordinary how well one gets along – once one has fallen into a routine. I find the great thing is having something good to read after dinner. The rest of the day takes care of itself.

Talking of reading and the publisher's reader who said your stuff was 'nasty', the other evening, routing among the shelves of this house we're living in till Low Wood is ready, I came upon Faulkner's *Sanctuary*. Have you ever read it? It's one of the few books that have really given me the horrors and made me feel sick as well. Those Southerners! What a set! – as Matthew Arnold would say.

I'm glad you liked 'Uncle Fred'. But unless you give me another story as good as that one, I can't think of anything for him to do. He is really a sort of elderly Psmith, and I can see in a vague way that he ought to go about helping people – and at the same time getting Pongo into trouble – but it's details that are so hard to think of. I wish I had a more inventive mind.

Here's a rummy thing, Bill. For six months I have been hammering away at a plot, trying to make it come out, with no success. Last night I suddenly said, 'Could this be an Ukridge story?' Ten minutes later I had the plot complete. It's the treatment that matters, isn't it?

The Ralph Lynn play, alas! is not doing any too well. Whether this is due to its being no good or whether it is simply the pre-Christmas slump, I don't know. One good thing is that we can keep running at a low figure. But I rather think it has missed fire.

I've been bitten to pieces by mosquitoes – of all things in December! They must have turned in for the winter in the rooms here and woken up to find a square meal in their midst.

January 20th, 1936   *Low Wood*

Just off to Carlton Hotel, St Moritz, where I expect to stay for a few weeks. I don't know how I shall like it. I've always avoided Switzerland up to now.

Doesn't Kipling's death give you a sort of stunned feeling? He seems to leave such a gap. I didn't feel the same about Doyle or Bennett or Galsworthy. I suppose it is because he is so associated with one's boyhcod. It has made me feel older all of a sudden.

I am writing this on my new Royal. I have got quite used to it now, but I still can't feel as easy as I did on the old Monarch – which, I hope, some expert will be able to repair. I don't like these metal things which stick up and hold the paper down, so that you can't get a clear view of what you're writing.

Winks and Boo do nothing nowadays but fight. I think it is because they are not getting enough exercise. Have you ever studied the psychology of the Dirty Look in Pekes? Winks and Boo will be sleeping quite happily in their baskets at different ends of the room, and then suddenly one of them will lift her head and stare. The other then stares. This goes on for about ten seconds, and then they rush at one another snarling, and start a terrific battle. My theory is that dogs say things which the human ear can't hear, and during this period they are exchanging inaudible cracks. By the way, we're taking both Pekes to St Moritz.

Do you ever read Claude Houghton's stuff? (C. H. Oldfield, Dulwich, circ. 1908). His last book *Christina* is good. He sends me his books as they come out, but we've never met.

Low Wood is in a hideous mess now, but will emerge as a very nice house when it is finished. I hate being in our present place, which is just a shack and as cold as ice.

What Plum had said in his letter about the death of Rudyard Kipling found an echo in my heart. Ever since our schooldays Kipling had stood for something stable and permanent in our lives.

Plum and he corresponded quite often, having met at the Beefsteak Club of which both were members. Plum told me once, more or less in jest, that if he were to predecease me he would leave me Kipling's letters but added that I should find that Kipling invariably spelt his name *Woodhouse*. This puzzled me until I reflected that he was remembering the name he had used in two of his stories, or in one story, at least.

April 2nd, 1936   *Hilbre, Le Touquet*

I'm sorry you are going through a mistrustful phase in your book, but I am pretty certain it is only because you have been working so hard at it. I have had just the same experience with the one I am doing now – *Laughing Gas* – a novel-length version of a short serial which came out in *Pearson's* last year – did you see it? – about the man whose soul goes into the body of the child film star. A few days ago it all seemed absolutely idiotic, but it looks quite all right again now.

Listen. Extract from a book by Arnold Bennett called *How to Become an Author*.

'He should take care to produce books at regular short intervals. He may continue this process for years without any really striking result in fame or money, and he may pessimistically imagine that his prolonged labours are fruitless. And then newspapers will begin to refer to him as a known author, as an author the mention of whose name is sufficient to recall his productions, and he will discover that all the while the building of his reputation has been going on like a coral reef.

'Even mediocre talent, when combined with fixity of purpose and regular industry, will, infallibly, result in a gratifying success.

'But it must never be forgotten that while the reputation is being formed, the excellent and amiable public needs continuous diplomatic treatment. It must not be permitted to ignore his existence. At least once a year, and oftener if possible, a good solid well-made book should be flung into the libraries.'

He also advises against frittering away energy on a lot of small things – e.g. short stories.

That seems to me to sum up your position, except that you certainly can't call yours a 'mediocre talent'. Really good stuff like yours is bound to succeed if you keep turning it out. I think this plan of yours of doing a lot of novels is the right one. What you've got to remember is that, in a sense, you really started with *Voyage Without End*, because the other books were buried.

Arnold Bennett's own case was just the same. His early books didn't sell. But gradually one began to see his name about.

May 13th, 1936   *Hilbre,*
                                                         Le Touquet

I finished *Comox* last night, and I see exactly what you mean. It is a hybrid. It starts off as a leisurely, Arnold Bennett sort of novel and then turns into a story of action, and the effect of this is to make the last part seem all out of key. It seems to me that you will have to abandon the leisurely note and go for the action.

In writing a novel, I always imagine I am writing for a cast of actors. Some actors are natural minor actors and some are natural major ones. It is a matter of personality. Same in a book. Psmith, for instance, is a major character. If I am going to have Psmith in a story, he must be in the big situations.

Right ho, then. In this book, Sennen stands out as a major character. You have taken so much pains to make him live that you can't exclude him from the main thread of the story. What is the main thread of the story? Andrew's married life. Therefore, Sennen must affect that. But he doesn't. Comox does. And Comox is essentially a minor character. (And if you say he isn't, I come right back at you – quick as a flash – by saying that in that case you can't drop him casually into the story on page 200. He must run right through.)

I believe the solution of this book is to give Comox's stuff to Sennen.

Is there any particular point in having the action in the nineties? I imagine that this is a left-over from your original idea of the story being a manuscript found in the cabin of a dead, elderly man, isn't it? As I read, I couldn't see any reason why it all shouldn't be happening in the present.

It's awfully hard to put all I want to in a letter.

The main thing is, PULL THE STORY TOGETHER. At present it lacks grip. The stuff is all there, but the construction is wrong.

The thing that made *Voyage Without End* so marvellous was the way it zipped along. You can get just the same effect into this one, and I really think you've got a stronger theme.

ONE BIG CHARACTER IS WORTH TWO SMALL ONES. Don't diffuse the interest. Generally, the trouble is that you can't switch Character B's stuff so that it fits Character A, but here Comox can blend into Sennen without a hitch.

The absolute cast-iron good rule, I'm sure, in writing a story, is to introduce *all* your characters as early as possible – especially if they are going to play important parts later.

It will probably be agony to rewrite this book, as you must be sick of it, but I know you have got something just as big as *Voyage Without End*, if you only sweat at it. If you send it out in its present form, it won't be a failure, but it won't be nearly so successful. Even if it means later publication, do have a go at it.

I think the success of every novel depends largely on one or two high spots. The thing to do is to say to yourself, 'Which are my big scenes?' and then get every drop of juice out of them. You are a bit apt to give the same value to a minor scene as to a major. I believe that when one has really got a bit of action going, it can extend as long as you like.

Golf Hotel,
July 23rd, 1936   *Le Touquet*

I've just returned from a hurried visit to England, but simply couldn't get a moment to get in touch with you. I had a phone call from Ethel saying that Guy Bolton had been rushed into hospital at Worthing with acute appendicitis and nearly died, and I had to spend my time travelling up and down. He seems to be all right now, thank goodness, but it was a near thing.

Listen. How far are you from Folkestone? Couldn't you catch the morning boat, lunch here and spend the afternoon, and go back on the evening boat – unless you could stop the night? It's nothing of a trip. You pop into a taxi at Boulogne and say Hôtel du Golf, Le Touquet, and you're here in forty minutes. You wouldn't have to leave till six, which would give us the whole afternoon.

Enclosed will give you a laugh. Me and Mussolini!

In due course, within the week, we went to Le Touquet for the day by way of Folkestone and Boulogne where we were met and put into a taxi. Plum was waiting for us at the Golf Hotel, and took us to Low Wood to meet the Pekes, Winks, Bimmy's sister, and Boo, whom Rene had taken care of for some weeks at the end of 1931. There was, to be sure, a moment of apprehension when we entered Low Wood, which was in the hands of the builders and occupied only by Madge, the cook, and her husband, an Englishman, an ex-soldier of the 1914–18 War. Would the Pekes regard us as interlopers in their home; enemies to be driven off the premises, or would they show themselves friendly? Although neither dog could have remembered us, they accepted us at sight, which was a compliment, Boo, in particular, being apt to take an illogical dislike to strangers and bark furiously until soothed and assured that no actual harm could come to her or her home.

We had lunch with Plum at the Picardy, walked in the sun among sand dunes and pine trees, talked, saw what sights Le

Touquet had to offer, had tea and then departed to catch the evening boat back to Folkestone and a train to Walmer.

Readers may regard all this talk of Pekes and public school football and cricket as being 'small beer'. This may be so, but a celebrity's life is not confined solely to the major achievements with which his name is associated, the books he has written, the pictures he has painted, the battles he has taken part in, the money he has made, the public offices he has held and the honours he has received; to gain a full understanding of the man and his calibre it is necessary to know something about his hobbies and tastes and interests. It is, I find, almost impossible to think of Plum without a Peke as a companion.

A letter from the president of the International Mark Twain Society gives the explanation of 'Me and Mussolini'.

June 26th, 1936   *Webster Groves, Missouri*

Dear Mr Wodehouse:

In recognition of your outstanding and lasting contribution to the happiness of the world, it gives us much pleasure to offer you the Mark Twain Medal. The list enclosed will show you to whom the Medal has been given in the past.

With all good wishes,
Yours sincerely,
Cyril Clemens

The list included Mussolini.

In October Plum went to Hollywood for the second time.

             1315 Angelo Drive,
              Beverly Hills,
November 7th, 1936   *California*

I am sending this to Watt, because I am not sure if you are still at the flat.

Well, here we are, settled in a house miles away up at the top of a mountain, surrounded by canyons in which I am told rattlesnakes abound, and employing a protection agency to guard the place at nights! We looked at a lot of houses in the valley part of Beverly Hills, where we were before, but couldn't find one we liked, so took this, which is a lovely place with a nice pool, but, as I say, remote. Still, that's an advantage in a way, as we don't get everybody dropping in on us.

Did you ever hear anything from Doubleday? I wrote to him, urging him to publish your books in America, but have heard nothing, except that Watt told me D. had had a 'very nice' letter from me. What I wanted to know, of course, was if he was going to publish your books.

Winky has taken on a new lease of life through association with the puppy. (Did I tell you Ethel bought a female puppy just before we sailed?) She ignored her for six weeks, and then suddenly became devoted to her. She races about the garden, chased by the puppy.

The puppy is a comedian. In New York, we had put on Winky's lead and let it trail on the carpet, and we went out, but no Winky followed, though we called to her. When we went back, we found Winks trying hard to get out, but the puppy had seized the lead and was tugging at it.

Everything is very pleasant and placid here, and I am having a good time. But it doesn't seem as interesting as it was last time. I miss Thalberg very much, though I like Sam Katz, for whom I am working. I am collaborating on a musical picture with a man I last saw twenty years ago, when I was sympathizing with him for being chucked out of the cast of one of the Bolton-Wodehouse-Kern musical comedies. He is a wild Irishman named McGowan, who seems to be fighting the heads of the studio all the time. I get on very well with him myself.

Before starting for California, I went to Philadelphia to see Lorimer at the *Saturday Evening Post*. He was very friendly. Rather funny, when he bought *The Crime Wave at Blandings* after I had had nothing in the *SEP* for a couple of years owing to my American income-tax trouble, he paid me $2000 and wrote me a letter asking if that was all right. I wrote back, 'Dear Mr Lorimer. I am so intensely spiritual that money means nothing to me, but I must confess that that $2000 was a bit of a sock on the jaw, as I had always thought that a short story was supposed to fetch a tenth of the price of a serial, so I had been looking forward to $4000.' This apparently touched his heart, for the first thing he said to me when I came into his room was that he would give me $4000.

He seemed a little taken aback when I walked in, as he had not seen me since the days when I had thick black hair on my now bald head. Did I ever tell you about that? He bought *Something Fresh* as a serial, and when I wrote *Uneasy Money*, he asked me to spend the weekend at his house, bringing the script with me. On the Sunday he curled up on a sofa and started to read the script, with me sitting there, pretending to be absorbed in a bound volume of the *Post* but really, of course, listening in anguish in the hope of hearing him laugh. Which presently he began to do, and after about half an hour he said, 'I like this one better than the other.' I never heard such beautiful words in my life. At the end of the first hour he said he would buy it and give me $5000. For *Something Fresh* he had given me $3500. He said he would have given me $5000 for *Something Fresh*, but he had had a row with my agent and wanted to score off him. Tough luck on a writer to be caught in the middle of a feud like that, don't you think?

I've always thought that his buying *Something Fresh* showed what a wonderful editor he was. Here was a story by an absolutely unknown man, and a story, what is more, about life in England, a country he didn't like, but it amused him, so he decided without any hesitation that the public of the *Saturday Evening Post* were jolly well going to be amused by it, too, and he didn't give a damn if they weren't.

I think the reason the English magazines die off like flies is that the editors are wondering timidly all the time what their readers are going to like, and won't take a chance on anything that isn't on exactly the same lines as everything else they have ever published. Lorimer has always had an unswerving faith in his own judgment. His attitude is, 'I like this story, and to hell with what anyone else thinks.' That's how he has made the *Post* such a success.

He is retiring in January, to be succeeded by Wesley Stout.

I still swim every morning, but the water is beginning to get a bit chilly.

Haven't seen many celebrities yet. We don't see much of anybody except our beloved Maureen O'Sullivan and her husband, John Farrow. He is the man who likes your sea stories so much. I met Clark Gable the other day. Also Fred Astaire.

I think Fred is going to do a picture of my *A Damsel In Distress*, with music by George Gershwin. I shall know more about this later.

The puppy Plum mentions in this letter, which was soon to be known as Wonder, became in due course the most travelled, the most celebrated and the longest-lived of all the Wodehouse Pekes, and the only one we never met.

December 28th, 1936   *1315 Angelo Drive*

Thanks for your long letters with all the news about the school footer. Isn't it extraordinary how we never seem to get the breaks against Haileybury? I remember one very wet day when we scored four tries and they also scored four and converted one from the touch-line, a thing that wouldn't have happened again in a hundred times.

I call it a very good performance beating St Paul's. If they could take fifteen points off Bedford, they must be a good side.

(Incidentally, isn't it amazing that you and I, old buffers of fifty-five with Civilization shortly about to crash, can worry about school football? It is really almost the only thing I do worry about.)

By the way, a word about stories. Don't regard the rejected ones as hopeless. I wrote an Ukridge story last year which I tried to feel was all right, but inside me knew was not. It was sent to the *Red Book*, which chucked it. I have rewritten it, making it a Bingo Little story, and it is now fine. (I haven't actually sent it out yet, but I shall be amazed if the *Saturday Evening Post* don't take it.) See what I mean? The thing was wrong, because I told it in one way. Telling it in another made it all right.

I haven't finished my novel yet. I have had rather a big job to do at the studio, and this particularly story – *Summer Moonshine* – is so tricky that I can't just dash off a chapter at odd times. In my spare time I have been rewriting a couple of short stories. The one I mentioned above is one of them, and the other I have sold to the *Post*.

I have a story coming out in *SEP* week ending January 30th, which they think is the best I have ever done. It was sent to the *Red Book*, and they offered $2000 for it, having given me $3000 for my others, I refused this, and on landing in America rang up the editor and asked him to return my story – having called on Lorimer the previous day and, as I believe I told you, got him to agree that he would pay $4000 for any stories of mine which he accepted. The editor of the *Red Book* raised the offer to $2500; but I believed in the story so much that I turned it down, and am glad that I did, because the *Post* jumped at it. Title – *All's Well with Bingo*.

I heartily concur, as Watt would say, with your remarks about *Reggie and the Greasy Bird*. In that shape, rotten. It just shows how much depends on the telling of a story – which is what I mean about your rejected stuff. Half of it may be quite all right, except for one little thing that has put an editor off without his knowing why he was put off. That was what was wrong with the Ukridge story (see above). I had to have a scene where the hero gets in bad with the man who is about to give him a job, and I had a bad scene – and, what was worse, a very long one. Even when I had changed it to a Bingo Little story, I could see it was not quite right, and finally I spotted that what was wrong was this one scene.

I had Ukridge meeting the man at Charing Cross station – while they are talking, along comes one of U.'s creditors and U. breaks off in the middle of a sentence and legs it with the creditor after him, thus making the prospective employer feel that he is a bit too eccentric to employ.

Why that wasn't right, I'm still darned if I know. It sounds a good enough scene, and I may quite possibly use it somewhere eventually. But it was all wrong for this story. I have now substituted a quite short and simple scene at the employer's club.

We have now reached the rainy season here. Funny how one never minds rain in England, but in California it seems to upset everything.

March 7th, 1937   *1315 Angelo Drive*

I meant to send you a lot of clippings about the frosts here, but forgot. Anyway, the gist is that we have had a foul winter and the valley below this house has been wrapped in a dense London fog for weeks, because of the smudge pots which they have been burning to try to save the lemon crops.

Did smudge pots enter into your lemon-life at all when you were out in California? Or was it always warm here then in winter? Lemons have been practically wiped out this year.

I am leading a very quiet life here. Unless I have to go and see my producer, I stay around the house all day except for an hour's walk, and we go up to our rooms at eight-thirty and read and listen to the radio. I enjoy it, though I must say I would like to be nearer home. This place seems very far away sometimes.

Winks is very well. Also the puppy, who now has a new name – Wonder. My days starts when I hear the puppy bark in Ethel's room. I open the door, and the puppy comes leaping out. Winky then pokes her head out of my bed, in which she has been sleeping, and I take them downstairs and let them out. I bring them in when I come down to breakfast, and they then have to be let out again in order to bark at the gardener, whose arrival is always a terrific surprise and shock to them, though he has turned up at the same time every morning for four months.

Woman out here has just got a divorce. Stated that her husband had not worked for months and was a pretty low-down character altogether. 'He was always going to dances,' she said, 'and when he wanted to go to one the other night, he took the only pair of silk stockings I had and cut the tops off so that he could wear them as socks.'

1315 Angelo Drive,
Beverly Hills

March 24th, 1937

I finished *Summer Moonshine* yesterday. Young Lorimer, of the *Saturday Evening Post*, called on me about two weeks ago and took away 80,000 words of it, leaving me about another 10,000 to do. I must say the *SEP* are extraordinary. Lorimer left on a Friday, read the thing in the train, arrived Philadelphia Monday night, presumably went to the office Tuesday morning and gave the MS to somebody else, who must have read it Tuesday and given it to Stout, the chief editor, on Wednesday morning and Stout must have read it on Wednesday night, because on Thursday morning I got a telegram saying it had been accepted.

I don't see how they manage to be so quick. They get 75,000 MSS a year, all of which are read.

Price – $40,000.

Against this triumph I have to set the fact that Metro-Goldwyn-Mayer are not taking up my option, which expires in another two weeks. I have had another flop with them. I started gaily in working on a picture with Bill McGuire, and I gradually found myself being edged out. Eventually, they came out into the open and said they had wanted McGuire to write the thing by himself, all along. There seems to be a curse over MGM, so far as I am concerned.

Since then, I have had a number of offers from other studios for one picture apiece. It seems pretty certain that in about two weeks I shall be working on my *Damsel in Distress*, which RKO bought for Fred Astaire. Selznick wants me to do a thing called *The Earl of Chicago* and Walter Wanger asked me to go round, as he had something right in my line. It turned out to be Clarence Budington Kelland's *Stand-In*. I turned it down. I got myself in bad enough last time by criticizing Hollywood, and I didn't want to do a picture which would have been an indictment of the studios.

Raining in buckets today, and snow on the foothills yesterday! The latest gag here is about the New York man who came to Southern California for the winter – and found it!

May 6th, 1937   *1315 Angelo Drive*

Listen. What has become of the old-fashioned California climate? We had a couple of warm days last week, and then went right back to winter weather again. Today is absolutely freezing. And it's been the same ever since I got here.

I wish we had taken this house for six months instead of a year. There seems to be a probability that I shall do a four weeks' job on the *Damsel in Distress*, but except for that nothing is stirring. I was told that I was going to do *The Earl of Chicago*, but I see that Ben Hecht is doing it. The fact is, I'm not worth the money my agent insists on asking for me. After all, my record here is eighteen months, with only small bits of pictures to show for it. I'm no good to these people. Lay off old Pop Wodehouse, is the advice I would give to any studio that wants to get on in the world. There is no surer road to success.

May 7th, 1937

I have been seeing a lot of G. O. Allen, the England cricket captain, who came home from Australia via Hollywood. He told me the inside story of the bodyline crisis. He is a bit sick about the last English team, as everybody failed enthusiastically on every occasion, and the fast bowlers had to do all the work.

Our butler got home last night tight as a drum and is still sleeping it off. Over here, the help take every Thursday off, and he employed his holiday in getting thoroughly pickled.

I can't fathom the mentality of Pekes. Yesterday Roland Young came to tea and sat on the sofa with Winks snuggling up to him on one side and Wonder on the other. The moment he got up and started to leave, both Pekes sprang down and attacked his ankles with savage snarls. You would have thought they had never seen him before, and had spotted him breaking in through a window.

Interesting that about your visit to the specialist. It's nice to know that your heart is all right. Isn't it difficult to get accustomed to the idea that one is now at the age when most people settle down and don't do a thing? I am now exactly the age my father was when I left Dulwich, and I remember him as tottering to his armchair and settling in it for the day. That's one thing about being a writer – it does keep you young. Do you find you can't walk as far as you used to! I do out here, but I remember last year in Le Touquet I used to do my seven miles without feeling it. I think it's mainly the California climate.

Big strike now in the picture industry, which may close all the studios. That'll teach them not to take up my option.

June 24th, 1937   *1315 Angelo Drive*

Life here at present is a bit like being on your *Lancing Island*. We can't go on the mountains because of the rattlesnakes, the butler killed two Black Widow spiders in the garden (deadlier than snakes), and last night and this morning the following episodes occurred. We were taking the dogs for a stroll after dinner, and Wonder didn't follow. We went back and found her playing with a tarantula on the drive! And this morning, when I came out from my swim, I heard her gruffling at something on the steps of the pool, and there was another tarantula, bigger than the first one!

I am sweating away at a picture. The Fred Astaire one, *A Damsel in Distress*, with musical score by George Gershwin. When they bought it, they gave it to one of the RKO writers to adapt, and he turned out a script all about crooks – no resemblance to the novel. Then it struck them that it might be a good thing to stick to the story, so they chucked away the other script and called me in. I think it is going to make a good picture. But what uncongenial work picture-writing is. Somebody's got to do it, I suppose, but this is the last time they'll get me.

June 25th, 1937

Your letter of June 15th has just arrived.

We have got a big party on tomorrow night – seventy people coming – and there is no room for them all in the house, so we shall have to feed in the garden, and the fear that is haunting us is that it will be too cold. Up here in the mountains we get an odd sort of white mist which comes up from the sea. They don't get it in the valley. The days now are scorching, but it always cools off a lot at night. Still, last night was lovely.

I'm glad you liked the Peke story. I have a good one coming out next week. But I haven't had a short-story idea for ages. They don't seem to come nowadays.

I shall be glad to get away from California. It is too far away.

As far as I can make out, the American magazines are doing all right now, but prices have gone down a lot. The *Post* seems away ahead of the rest, and Lorimer's resignation doesn't seem to have hurt it at all.

September 4th, 1937   *1315 Angelo Drive*

I finished my work on *Damsel in Distress* three weeks ago, and with only one day's interval started on a picture with Eddie Goulding – Englishman whom I used to know in London before the war – now a director here. I am not finding it very pleasant, because he has his own ideas about the thing and rewrites all my stuff, thus inducing a what's-the-use feeling and making it hard not to shove down just anything. Also, I don't like the story.

The money is fine – $10,000 for six weeks and $2000 a week after that – but this blasted Administration has just knocked the bottom out of everything by altering the tax laws, so that instead of paying a flat 10 per cent as a non-resident alien I now have to pay ordinary citizen rates, which take away about a third of what one earns.

The taxes are fantastic here and very tough on Hollywood stars because they make so much over a short period and then go into the discard. Nelson Eddy, my neighbour, made $600,000 last year and when all his taxes and expenses were paid found that he had $50,000 left. Well, not bad, even so, one might say. But then the point is that in 1939 his income may be about tuppence! Stars shoot up and die away here before you can breathe.

I'm not enjoying life much just now. I don't like doing pictures. *A Damsel in Distress* was fun, because I was working with the best director here – George Stevens – and on my own story, but as a rule pictures are a bore. And just now I'm pining to get at a new novel, which I have all mapped out. I sneak in a page or two every now and then, but I want to concentrate on it.

October 11th, 1937   *1315 Angelo Drive*

Just a line to say that we are not staying here for the Spring, after all, but are sailing on October 28th, and I shall be back at Le Touquet on November 4th.

                                                       Low Wood,
November 9th, 1937   *Le Touquet*

Just had a misfortune with the old typewriter. Arrived here with a very faint ribbon and took out a spare, and found, after I had taken off the old ribbon that the new one was a Remington, and wouldn't fit. So I have been three days with the machine out of action.

I am coming over on Tuesday 16th. I am not quite certain where I shall go.

Frightful lot to talk about. Remind me to tell you about my visit to the *Saturday Evening Post*. One of the editors is Erd Brandt, who used to be your agent. He spoke very highly of you, and said you were now living in Brazil. I said yes, you were, and were looked on locally as quite one of the nuts, so you can now start writing a lot of Brazil stories for them. They want to see your stuff. They all remembered it and liked it.

November 22nd, 1937   *Low Wood*

Two things combined to make me scratch my visit. I shrank from a journey probably in rotten weather, and secondly I got a letter from Reynolds, enclosing one from the *Saturday Evening Post* about my serial, which made it necessary for me to pitch in on the thing.

It looks as if the *Post* are taking it for granted that they are going to buy the story – I sent them the first 50,000 words – but they felt that the early part needed cutting. 'Too many stage waits,' was what Brandt said. And when I looked at it, I saw they were right.

Here is the lay-out, as I had it:

1 Bertie goes to see his Aunt Dahlia.
2 She tells him to go and buy flowers for Aunt Agatha, who is ill.
3 Bertie goes back to his flat and she rings up and says she forgot to say that she has another job for him – which will necessitate a visit to an antique shop.
4 Bertie goes to flower shop and gets into trouble.
5 Bertie goes back to his flat and sobs on Jeeve's shoulder.
6 Bertie goes to antique shop and gets into more trouble.

Now, can you imagine that I had written that part quite a dozen times and only now spotted that it ought to go thus:

1 Bertie goes to Aunt Dahlia. She tells him to go to antique shop.
2 Bertie goes to antique shop, plays the scene which origi-

nally took place in flower shop, then plays the antique shop scene.

It cuts out fifteen pages without losing anything of value. And what I am driving at is that isn't it ghastly to think that after earning one's living as a writer for thirty-seven years one can make a blunder like that. Why on earth I kept taking Bertie back to the flat, where nothing whatever happened, I can't think.

This necessitated five days of intense work, and I now feel that I might as well get on with the thing and postpone my visit to England till December 16th.

Did you ever read an old book called *Helen's Babies*, about a young bachelor getting saddled with some kids? The *Ladies' Home Journal* editor has got a fixation that a splendid modern version could be done, and he has offered me $45,000 if I will do it. And here's the tragedy. I can't think of a single idea towards it. When *Helen's Babies* was published, all you had to do was to get the central idea and then have a monotonous stream of incidents where the kids caused trouble. Nobody seemed to mind in those days that you were being repetitious. But surely that sort of thing wouldn't go now. In any case, I can't work it. I'll never do a story, however much I'm offered, unless I like it and feel I can make it good.

The *LHJ* editor is Bruce Gould, who used to write those wonderful stories in the *Post* about a literary agent. Do you remember them? They were superb.

Even now, whenever I read one of Plum's books, I find it difficult to realize that he ever had the slightest difficulty in the construction or writing. In a way it was a comfort to me to learn that even he had written a book that limped at the start, because I had always thought that, if there was one thing he excelled in more than another, it was in the way he began his stories. As a reader, I felt that my attention and interest were captured from the very first sentences. Consider, for instance, the beginning of *The Luck of the Bodkins*:

'Into the face of the young man who sat on the terrace of the Hôtel Magnifique at Cannes there had crept a look of furtive shame, the shifty, hangdog look which announces that an Englishman is about to talk French. One of the things which Gertrude Butterick had impressed upon Monty Bodkin when he left for this holiday on the Riviera was that he must be sure to practise his French, and Gertrude's word was law. So now, though he knew that it was going to make his nose tickle, he said, "*Er, garçon.*"

"*M'sieur?*"

"*Er, garçon, esker-vous avez un spot de l'encre et une pièce de papier – notepapier, vous savez – et une enveloppe et une plume?*"

"*Bien, m'sieur.*"

The strain was too great. Monty relapsed into his native tongue.

"I want to write a letter," he said. And having, like all lovers, a tendency to share his romance with the world, he would probably have added, 'to the sweetest girl on earth,' had not the waiter already bounded off like a retriever, to return a few moments later with the fixings.

"*V'là*, sir! Zere you are, sir," said the waiter. He was engaged to a girl in Paris who had told him that when on the Riviera he must be sure to practise his English. "Eenk – pin, – pipper – enveloppe – and a liddle bit of bloddin' pipper." '

This brings the reader to the end of page 1. He will now turn to page 2 and read on.

The book with which Plum was having such trouble was *The Code of the Woosters*, and it is in this book, in Chapter VIII, that you will find the funniest of the Jeeves and Bertie scenes where the girl, Stiffy, enters her bedroom to find them treed on the top of the chest of drawers and the cupboard because of the menace of her Aberdeen terrier, Bartholomew.

January 4th, 1938   Low Wood

I am finding finishing *The Code of the Woosters* a ghastly sweat. I don't seem to have the drive and command of words I used to. Towards the end of *Thank You, Jeeves*, at La Fréyère, I wrote twenty-six pages one day! Now I find myself quarrying out the stuff. I imagine the trouble is that I have twice been stopped writing the book for long periods, and this has made me tired of it. Still, the story seems good enough when I get it down.

May 15th, 1938   Low Wood

It must be about two months since I wrote you. I have been sweating like blazes getting a new novel started. It's about 'Uncle Fred' – I'm calling it *Uncle Fred in the Springtime* – at

Blandings Castle. After writing 150 pages, I now have 40 which are right. Every time I write a book, I swear I'll never write another with a complicated plot. In this one – in the first 40 pages – I have either brought on to play a scene or mentioned heavily each of my principal characters – ten including Lord Emsworth's pig. So the going ought to be easier now.

Fancy Paddy Millar turning up at Low Wood!

I wish you had been with him.

How did *Sailor's Women* do?

(Staccato, disjointed style due to fact that this is the fifteenth letter I've written since tea-time.)

Today is Winky's tenth birthday! Great celebrations. Madge made a sponge cake with 'Happy Birthday' on it in white sugar.

I am hoping to come over on Friday week.

I find the most difficult thing in writing is to describe a character. Appearance, I mean.

Have you sold Reeves Shaw anything lately?

Don't you wish Watt's address was shorter?

Shall we ever get Bradman out in the Tests?

Love to Rene.

June 30th, 1938   *Low Wood*

Ethel is going over on Tuesday to look after Norfolk Street, so I shall probably come on Thursday.

Isn't writing in the summer a sweat! I find that my output slows down to about half, and if I can average three pages a day I think I am doing well. I started *Uncle Fred in the Springtime* on May the first and have only got up to near half-way – i.e. about a month behind my schedule. Still, I think the stuff is good. I find it so hard to write in the afternoons. If I go for an exercise walk, I'm too tired to write, and if I don't get any exercise, my brain won't work!

I liked the Gilkes book. I thought Leake had made a good job of it. Though you rather get the impression of Gilkes as a man who was always trying to damp people, to keep them from getting above themselves. ('So you made a century against Tonbridge, did you, my boy? Well, always remember that you will soon be dead, and in any case, the bowling was probably rotten!')

The 'Gilkes book' was a sort of history of Dulwich College, featuring A. H. Gilkes, the famous headmaster of our time.

July 19th, 1938   *Low Wood*

I can see what's wrong with that story. You have got a star character – Shuffley – and you don't give him enough to do. He just sits in the background up to page 22, and even then he doesn't really do anything *ingenious*. He just produces £50 and hands it over to Brogan. The story is all about the other characters. In fact, you might just as well not have Shuffley in the story at all, except as a mechanism for Brogan getting the money.

The conception of the story is good. What it needs is for Shuffley to do something very funny and ingenious in order to get the money for Brogan – he simply can't say, 'I've got £50, here you are.' I can't think of anything on the spur of the moment, but the sort of thing you need is something like they had in a play called *Turn to the Right*, where the comic crook learns from the old woman who has been kind to him that the local banker (The Menace) is going to sell her up, unless she pays $500 back rent. The banker comes in, the crook picks his pocket of a wad of money, and then when the banker starts demanding his cash comes forward and says, 'Here you are, paid in full – give me a receipt.'

See what I mean? It shows the principal actor *doing* something. You get the thing absolutely right in *Captain Shuffley's Briar Pipe*, which the *Strand* bought and Illingworth illustrated. In this one, Shuffley somehow ought to fool the two villains and get the money from them. I'm just thinking aloud now, but if he went to Beigel and said, 'Give me £25 and I can fool Kirtle out of buying the land, because I know there is going to be a hotel built there,' and, then went to Kirtle and told him a similar tale, he could give both sums to Brogan to make up the required £50.

Of course, this wouldn't work, I suppose. It might, if Kirtle and Beigel – you would call the poor devils names like that – were working secretly from each other. Suppose each had got a private tip that the hotel was to be built and Shuffley demands £25 from each as his price for not telling the other. That looks promising. Shuffley would say he wasn't interested in the thing except as the means of raising a few quid for himself – I mean, he would make it clear that he was not in the market against them.

To work this, I think you would have to conceal it from the reader that he was fooling them *both*. You would have to show him telling Kirtle that he knew what he was up to and that £25 would keep him quiet, and then in the end you would reveal that he had played the same game on Beigel. In fact, the more people you had working against one another, the easier it would be; because you could make Shuffley's silence money smaller. How would it be to have him get £5 from three chaps – or even two, and then run it up to the required sum by gambling?

I think this would work. Its great merit is that it makes Shuffley seem crooked till right at the end when you reveal that his motives were good. That is to say, it gives him character. I think what Rene found wrong, when she said the story was dull, was just what I am criticizing – i.e. that you engage Charles Laughton to play a star part and all the time the audience is saying, 'Hey, but isn't Laughton going to do *anything*?'

The reason why I have reproduced Plum's letter at such length is that I wished to show his methods of constructing a story or, at least, of turning a thoroughly bad story into quite a good one. Anyone who has ever written fiction or tried to write will understand how difficult a task it is to put right a story by someone else. Here, as so often in the past, Plum saw at a glance where I had gone wrong, and what was far more profitable made it possible for me to reconstruct my story on the right lines.

November 13th, 1938   *Low Wood*

I'm sorry your novel has stuck, but, boy, you don't know what trouble is! Two weeks ago I got a cable from Reynolds saying:

'*Saturday Evening Post* will buy *Uncle Fred in Springtime*, provided you make certain changes. They like story, but think at present it is difficult to follow week by week. They suggest you might want to eliminate a character or two and clarify relationships.'

You can imagine what it's like, taking two characters out of my sort of story, where a character is put in only because he is needed for at least two big scenes later on in the book! However, I cabled that I would do it, and for these last two weeks I have been hard at work.

I found that I could simplify the story enormously by dropping the whole of one motive and the two characters it involved, but this meant rewriting practically the whole book. Whenever I came to a spot where I had been hoping to be able just to rip a dozen pages out of the original version and pin them together, I found they were studded with allusions to the vanished characters.

Your troubles must have been pretty bad, but they were part of the first writing, when one expects to encounter a snag or two. But from the tone of Reynolds' cable, I gathered that mine practically got over as it stood, and then some ass in the office said, 'Of course, it wouldn't be a bad thing if there were fewer characters,' and the boss editor yawned and said, 'No, that's right. Tell him to cut out a couple of them.'

I am very interested in what you say about *Jill the Reckless*. It's what I always feel about my work – viz. that I go off the rails unless I stay all the time in a sort of artificial world of my own creation. A real character in one of my books sticks out like a sore thumb. You're absolutely right about Freddie Rooke. Just a stage dude – as Bertie Wooster was when I started writing him. If you look at the early Jeeves stories, you'll find Bertie quite a different character now.

The old gentleman blowing the other up with dynamite was in *Money for Nothing*. The burglar on the window-ledge is in *Hot Water*.

November 29th, 1938   *Low Wood*

Dear Bill,

Winkie is dead. I can hardly bear to write about it. The usual thing – tick fever. Same as Boo.

I went up to Paris to join Ethel on Monday, taking her with me, and I thought she was more than usually fit. She ran about on the platform at Boulogne Station and seemed splendid. On Tuesday morning Ethel took her and Wonder for a walk and told me that Winkie had refused to run and seemed out of sorts. On Wednesday morning we took her to the vet. and left her there. In the afternoon we went to see him, and he said it was tick fever. We saw her in her cage and she was obviously dying, and that night the vet. rang up and said it was all over. We had the body taken down here and she is buried beside Boo in the garden.

FOUR

1939–1946

On Wednesday, June 21st, 1939, at the Encaenia at Oxford University, Plum – on this occasion Mr Pelham Grenville Wodehouse – received the degree of D.Litt.

In its report of the proceedings in the Sheldonian *The Times* in its issue of June 22nd said:

Last, but in the opinion of the University far from least, came Mr. P. G. Wodehouse, whom the Public Orator presented as *festivum caput – Petroniumne dicam an Terentium nostrum?* The *Public Orator* fittingly marked almost his last public appearance, and delighted his audience by a passage of Horatian hexameters, an exemplum of his own *urbana felicitas*, in which he not only paid tribute to the kindly temper and finished style of Mr. Wodehouse's work, but also achieved the difficult task of presenting or suggesting in Latin the familiar figures of Bertie Wooster and Jeeves and Mr. Mulliner and Lord Emsworth and the Empress of Blandings and Psmith and even the Honourable Augustus Fink-Nottle and the love-life of the newts.'

In the same number of *The Times* there appeared the following verses:

D.Litt, 1939

Dear Mr. Wodehouse, who'll applaud your
D.Litt.? Jeeves, Mr. Mulliner, Bertie, Psmith,
Aunt Dahlia, Gussie Fink-Nottle, Tuppy, both
the Freddies.
   Threepwood and Widgeon,
Sam the Sudden, Ronnie, Empress and Lord Emsworth,
Stinker Pinker, Biscuit, Monty, Lotus Blossom,
Beach, Beefy Bingham, gay old Gally Threepwood,
   Albert E. Peasemarsh.

Who'll look austerely? Lady Constance Keeble,
Baxter, Sir Roderick, all the tribe of Parsloe,
Roderick Blackshorts (Eulalie in Secret).
  Tilbury, Pilbeam.
Ruler unquestioned of the Land of Laughter,
Scholar, creator, lord of apt quotation,
Master of words, of things yet unattempted,
  Thanks, Dr. Wodehouse.'

                                          K.A.E.*

Of Plum, a leader-writer in the June 22nd issue of *The Times* said:

'. . . but there is no question that in making Mr. P. G. Wodehouse
a doctor of letters the University has done the right and popular
thing. Everyone knows at least some of his many works and has felt
all the better for the gaiety of his wit and the freshness of his style.
Style goes a long way in Oxford; indeed the purity of Mr. Wodehouse's style was singled out for particular praise in the Public
Orator's happy Horatian summing up of Mr. Wodehouse's qualities
and achievements.'

Toward the latter end of July Plum was in England once more
and my wife and I met him in London; and he took us about with
him and was very kind and hospitable. On the Saturday of his short
visit he and I went down to Dulwich together to see the school play
St Paul's and we sat in the pavilion and met people we had known
years before and would have been happy but for the fact this was
the dullest cricket match, the slowest and most uneventful, either
of us had ever seen.

I said good-bye to Plum at about four o'clock, having arranged
to get back to town early, and I left him seated in the pavilion,
looking rather bored and rather disconsolate.

That was the last time I saw him.

Six weeks later war was declared. Plum was in Le Touquet. I was
in Dover.

And now I feel compelled to discuss at some length the impact of
war on one who had never in his life had a really unkind thought
concerning any other human being. As the reader will by now have
discovered, Plum Wodehouse is a man of simple tastes, a hard
worker at his chosen occupation, a writer of good English, of far
better English than his detractors who sprang up like mushrooms

* These initials concealed the identity of the late Mrs K. A. Esdaile, the
wife of Dr Arundell Esdaile, CBE.

the morning after his first broadcast from Berlin were willing to admit, a writer, too, who chose to depict the absurdities of his fellow countrymen while appreciating their worth. It was, of course, Plum's misfortune that he was capable of finding things to like in the most unlikeable of people, and, though loathing the Nazi way of life and their lust for conquest, and their uniforms and posturings, was unwilling to associate the individual German with the excesses and crimes of his Government.

Here is a personal note: one evening when I was working on the ground floor of the little house in Hildenborough where we lived after the military had requisitioned our house in Dover and before we returned to the coast, I heard my wife call to me from her bedroom, where she was listening to the radio. I went upstairs and she told me Plum was broadcasting. I listened anxiously and heard a far-away voice, easily recognizable as Plum's telling of his journey from Loos prison into Germany in a cattle truck without food or water. The broadcast ended with the remark that, so far as I remember, happier days were in store for soon he and his fellow prisoners were to be at Tost. The wavelength was, I believe, 525 medium.

I think it worth while here to put down some of the things said about Plum Wodehouse in the newspapers during and after the war, and in books, and in private letters.

Not everyone who wrote to Plum, sympathizing with him and wishing him well, was known to him. John F. Lemming, the author of a very successful book, *Always Tomorrow*, and a prisoner of war for two and a half years in Italy, wrote:

'I would like to tell you that, having read your broadcasts, I cannot see how anyone could possibly see anything in them the slightest degree pro-German or anti-British. But I will not give you my own opinion. I will tell you that of the late Air-Marshal Boyd, R.A.F. I was his personal assistant and we were prisoners together in Italy. He read your broadcasts and gave them to me, saying: "Why the Germans ever let him say all this I cannot think. They have either got more sense of humour than I credited them with or it was just slipped past the censor. There is some stuff about being packed in cattle trucks and a thing about Loos jail that you would think would send a Hun crazy. Wodehouse has probably been shot by now." '

In his book *Critical Essays*, George Orwell had this to say in his monograph, 'In Defence of P. G. Wodehouse':

'If my opinion of Wodehouse's mentality is accepted, the idea that in 1941 he consciously aided the Nazi propaganda machine becomes untenable and even ridiculous.

'The other thing one must remember is that Wodehouse happened to be taken prisoner at just the moment when the war reached its desperate phase. We forget these things now. There was hardly any fighting, the Chamberlain government was unpopular, eminent publicists were hinting that we should make a compromise peace as quickly as possible, trade union and Labour Party branches all over the country were passing anti-war resolutions. Afterwards, of course, things changed. The Army was with difficulty extricated from Dunkirk, France collapsed, Britain was alone, the bombs rained on London, Goebbels announced that Britain was to be "reduced to degradation and poverty". By the middle of 1941 the British people knew what they were up against and feelings against the enemy were far fiercer than before. But Wodehouse had spent the intervening year in internment, and his captors seemed to have treated him reasonably well. He had missed the turning point, of the war, and in 1941 he was still reacting in terms of 1939.'

George Orwell continued:

'In the desperate circumstances of the time, it was excusable to be angry at what Wodehouse did, but to go on denouncing him three or four years later – and more, to let an impression remain that he acted with conscious treachery – is not excusable. Few things in this war have been more morally disgusting than the present hunt after traitors and Quislings. At best it is largely the punishment of the guilty by the guilty. In France, all kinds of petty rats – police officials, penny-a-lining journalists, women who have slept with German soldiers – are hounded down, while almost without exception the big rats escape. In England the fiercest tirades against Quislings are uttered by Conservatives who were practising appeasements in 1938 and Communists who were advocating it in 1940. I have striven to show how Wodehouse – just because success and expatriation had allowed him to remain mentally in the Edwardian age – became the *corpus vile* in a propaganda experiment, and I suggest that it is now time to regard the incident as closed.'

In his book *Life With Topsy* Denis Mackail said:

'Again the door of a lift was the scene of another parting. It closed. We descended. And the next time I heard those mild and familiar tones was in August 1941, when Diana suddenly roused me from sleep and rushed me to the radio. She had been twiddling knobs, and Plum's voice – doubly removed, for it was a record that was being played over – was addressing us from Germany, where he had recently emerged from forty-nine weeks of internment. I was much moved, but I can't say that I was indignant. He was being funny; I thought he was being remarkably courageous; he seemed to be making a quiet and almost causal plea against intolerance. But this didn't stop a Minister of Information from overriding the authorities of the B.B.C., and putting up a journalist to blackguard him in another broadcast, to sneer at his Christian names, and to describe him as a "playboy". Plum! The most industrious author that I had ever known. But the war couldn't go on without hatred, and Plum hated no one. That was his crime.'

Sax Rohmer was one who defended Plum. He wrote:

'Mr. W. A. Darlington's reference to a claim for £50,000 made by the United States Revenue upon P. G. Wodehouse is calculated to mislead. I would like to point out that a similar claim (in my own case for a less staggering sum) was made upon all English novelists and playwrights, or all of those with whom I am acquainted, who derived any considerable revenue from the U.S.A.

These claims were based upon some obscure paragraph in the Statute book hitherto overlooked even by the lawyers. Never-the-less, assessment was made retrospective. Rafael Sabatini heroically took the matter to Court and fought a losing action which dragged on for more than a year.

In fairness to a man whose good name is at stake on other counts, I think the implication that Wodehouse's misfortune was due to conscious tax-dodging should be disclaimed.'

Ethel Mannin wrote:

'Since some fellow-authors have seen fit to censure P. G. Wode-house in a "We-wouldn't-do-that-sort-of-thing" manner, may I suggest that judgment be withheld, since we are none of us in a position to know the facts?

It is always difficult to gauge another person's motives; how can any of us say with certainty what we would do in given circum-stances? None of the people so busily censuring Mr. Wodehouse has had his experiences. I was always under the impression that part of the Christian ethic was "Judge not that ye be not judged." '

Not all the letters the *Daily Telegraph* published were from dis-tinguished writers. The one that I thought by far the best was by someone who signed himself 'disinterested'.

'In view of the letters you have received about Mr. P. G. Wodehouse, it may be of interest to know the facts surrounding his release from prison camp which have just come into my possession.

Mr. Wodehouse was captured last year because he refused to believe that the Germans were approaching his residence where he was working on a book. He wished to finish the last four chapters before leaving France. At that time he was over 58. The Germans are not interning enemy aliens over 60, and Mr. Wodehouse will be 60 within a few months.

The camp in which he was imprisoned is one of the best in Germany. A former asylum for the insane, its accommodation is comfortable, and its Commanding Officer, a British prisoner during the last war, moderate and lenient. Although he was offered a room to himself, Mr. Wodehouse refused to accept preferential treatment, and shared a room with sixty others. He was, however, given space in which to write. This was a large room in which a tap-dancer, a saxophonist and a pianist were also "working".

The Columbia Broadcasting Company and several other American agencies had been in touch with Mr. Wodehouse for some time with a view to securing his stories. His broadcasts for Columbia were arranged before he left the prison camp, and set for whatever time he might be released in the normal course of events. This came within a short time of his 60th birthday.

Released prisoners are free to live where they choose, within certain central districts. Mr. Wodehouse's considerable royalties from his books published in Germany undoubtedly decided him to select his greater comfort of the Adlon in preference to more modest accommodation elsewhere in the centre of Berlin.

I have no right or desire to comment or pass judgment on Mr. Wodehouse's action, but I would add the remarks made by one who knew him in Berlin. They agree with Mr. A. A. Milne that he is politically naïve, and with Miss Dorothy Sayers that he is unconscious of the propaganda value to the Germans of his action. It sprang, they say, from his desire to keep his name before his American reading public. But they do add, most emphatically, that he did not buy his release from prison camp by agreeing to broadcast.'

I wrote to Plum regularly while he was in enemy hands: a good many of my letters reached him, some were returned. The last letter I received from him from Le Touquet was dated April 6th, 1940. When I next heard from him, he wrote from Berlin on May 11th, 1942.

At last I am able to write to you. This is being taken to Lisbon by a German I used to know in Hollywood, who is accompanying the US Embassy crowd. He will mail it there, and I hope it will eventually arrive.

I'm so glad you liked *Money in the Bank*. The only novel, I should imagine, that has ever been written in an internment camp. I did it at the rate of about a page a day in a room with over fifty men playing cards and ping-pong and talking and singing. The first twelve chapters were written in a whirl of ping-pong balls. I suppose on an average morning I would get from fifteen to twenty on the side of the head just as I was searching for the *mot juste*.

As I was starting Chapter Thirteen the Library was opened and I was made President. The President of a Camp Library must not be confused with the Librarian. The Librarian does the rough work like handing out books and entering them in a ledger. The President presides. He stimulates and encourages. I, for instance, used to look in once a day and say 'Everything okay?' and go away again. It was amazing how it helped. Giving the Wodehouse Touch, I used to call it.

Being President of the Library, I became entitled to a padded cell all to myself, and I wrote the rest of the book in a peaceful seclusion disturbed only by the sound of musical gentlemen practising trombones, violoncellos, etc., next door, in the interests of the Entertainment Committee and somebody else lecturing on Chaucer or Beowulf (under the auspices of the Committee for Education). All that I know of Beowulf today I owe to these lectures.

After I had finished *Money in the Bank*, I started a Blandings Castle novel called *Full Moon* and had done about a third of it when I was released. Ethel then joined me in the country, bringing with her the Jeeves novel called *Joy in the Morning*, which I had written at Le Touquet during the occupation.

Those letters in the *Daily Telegraph* about my having found internment so terrible that I bought my release by making a bargain with the German Government were all wrong. I was released because I was on the verge of sixty. When I was in Loos Prison the first week, a dozen of our crowd were released because they were sixty, including my cellmate William

Cartmell, the Étaples piano tuner. Of course, he may have made a bargain with the German Government, offering if set free, to tune its piano half-price, but I don't think so. It all looked pretty genuine to me.

As for finding internment terrible, I didn't at all after the first few months. Loos Prison, Liège Barracks and the Citadel of Huy were on the tough side, but Tost was fine. One thing that helped us enormously there was the presence of the internees from Holland. A good many of them were language teachers, lecturers and musicians, so we were able to have concerts, shows and so on and brush up on our Beowulf. We also played cricket all through the summer. The prime difficulty in the way of playing cricket was that we had no ball, but the sailors from the *Orama* got round that. They got hold of a nut and wound string round it, and the result was as good a ball as you could want.

The most terrible thing that happened to me as an internee was my shower bath in Loos Prison. Once a week, if you are in the coop at Loos, you all troop up to the top floor and take a tepid shower under the supervision of a warder. You remove your clothes and queue up, and when you reach the head of the line a dab of soft soap is slapped into your hand and you go under the water. And where I went wrong was in making the mistake of supposing that I had lots of time.

I am one of those cautious shower bathers who put a toe in first and then, if all seems well, another toe, and, in a word, sort of work up to the thing: and it became apparent almost immediately that what the warder wanted to see was something in the nature of an imitation of forked lightning striking a mountain torrent.

The result was that just as I had soft-soaped myself all over, and was hovering on the brink, my feet, as Sir John Suckling beautifully puts it, like little mice stealing in and out, he informed me that my time was up, and told me to put my clothes on and go back to my cell. I don't know if you have ever put your clothes on over a foundation of soft soap, and then gone back to a prison cell, and tried to wash it off at the cold tap without a sponge, but it is one of those experiences that test you. You come out of it a finer, deeper, graver man, not perhaps so fond of French prison warders as you used to be, but with a wonderful feeling of having had your soul tried in the furnace and the realization that life is stern and earnest and that we are not put into this world for pleasure alone.

Did you see a book called – I forget what, but something by one of the American correspondents in Berlin?

If so, I hope you didn't believe the bilge he wrote about me – e.g. that some sinister German had come to the camp to see me and arrange about my being released and speaking on the radio. Nobody ever came near the camp.

The best proof that I did not 'make a bargain' with the German Government is supplied by the Stout-Wodehouse correspondence. Just after the last of the broadcasts I got a cable from Wesley Stout of the *Saturday Evening Post* about *Money in the Bank*. He said he liked it and wanted to buy it, but could do so only on my assurance that I would stop talking on the German radio. I cabled back that I had already stopped, that I had never intended to do more than these five descriptions of camp life, and that he could be perfectly easy in his mind, as I would not speak again on any subject whatsoever.

Now, this cable of mine was written in the presence of an official in the Wilhelmstrasse and sent off by him, and if there had ever been any idea that I had been released because of an agreement on my part to broadcast German propaganda, or, for that matter, to broadcast at all – I hardly think the German authorities would have made no protest when I announced that I intended to go back on the bargain.

Of course I ought to have had the sense to see that it was a loony thing to do to use the German radio for even the most harmless stuff, but I didn't. I suppose prison life saps the intellect.

I remember you saying once how much you liked the men in your regiment in the last war. It was the same with me when I was an internee. I had friends at Tost in every imaginable walk of life, from Calais dock touts upward, and they were one and all the salt of the earth. A patrol of Boy Scouts couldn't have been kinder than they were to me. I was snowed under with obligations. I remember once when I broke the crystal of my watch and seemed likely to have to abandon the thing as a total loss, which would have been a devastating tragedy, one of the fellows gave up the whole afternoon to making a case for it, out of an old tube of tooth paste, while another gave me a bit of string, roughly equivalent in value in camp to a diamond necklace, which I could use as a chain; and a third donated a button, which he could ill spare, to string the string on.

Whenever my bed broke down, somebody always rallied round with wedges. (You drive the wedges in at the end of the planks. Then they don't suddenly shift in the night and let you down with a bump.) When I strained a tendon in my leg, along came Sergeant-Major Fletcher night after night, when he might have been playing darts, to give me massage.

I was so touched by this that I broke into verse on the subject. As follows:

> I used to wobble in my walk
>   Like one who has a jag or bend on;
> It caused, of course, a lot of talk,
>   But really I had strained a tendon.
> And just as I was feeling I
>   Would need a crutch or else a stretcher.
> A kindly friend said: 'Why not try
>   A course of rubs from J. J. Fletcher?'
> He gave me massage day by day
>   Till I grew lissome, lithe and supple,
> And no one now is heard to say,
>   'Avoid that man. He's had a couple.'
> And so with gratitude profound
>   I shout 'Three cheers for good old Fletcher.
> He is the man to have around
>   When legs get out of joint, you betcher.
> Fletcher,
> I'm glad I metcher.'

Silly, of course, but that's how it goes.

Let's see. What else? Oh, yes, beards. A lot of us grew beards. Not me. What I felt was that there is surely enough sadness in life without going out of one's way to increase it by sprouting a spade-shaped beard. I found it a melancholy experience to be compelled to watch the loved features of some familiar friend becoming day by day less recognizable behind the undergrowth. A few fungus-fanciers looked about as repulsive as it is possible to look, and one felt a gentle pity for the corporal whose duty it was to wake them in the morning. What a way to start one's day!

O'Brien, one of the sailors, had a long Assyrian beard, falling like a cataract down his chest, and it gave me quite a start when at the beginning of the summer he suddenly shaved, revealing himself as a spruce young fellow in the early twenties. I had been looking on him all the time as about twenty years my senior, and only my natural breeding had kept me from addressing him as 'Grandpop'.

I shall have to stop now, as the deadline for writing is approaching. Love to Rene. Yours ever, Plum.

PS I was very interested to hear about Gilkes taking over Dulwich. I wonder how things will be there after the war. I'm afraid the public schools will have a pretty thin time.

Hôtel Lincoln,
December 30th, 1944   *Rue Bayard, Paris*

I am not actually at the above address, being at the moment in a hospital (though not ill), but letters sent there will be forwarded.

I am longing to hear how you have been getting on with your novels. I suppose the short story market in England has pretty well vanished, but Denis Mackail in a card which I received yesterday says that all books are selling like hot cakes, so I hope that you are flourishing.

I always think it such a pity that experiences happen to the wrong people. I don't suppose, for instance, I shall ever make anything of life in Paris during the liberation, whereas if you had been here then you would have got a wealth of material. The afternoon of the big parade down the Champs-Élysées, Ethel and I and Wonder went to the park near the Marigny Theatre and Ethel managed to wriggle into the front rank of the crowd, leaving me with Wonder. I was just starting to give Wonder a run on the grass near one of the restaurants which are in the gardens when I saw a policeman coming, so edged away, and at that moment a brisk burst of firing came from the restaurant, which would have outed me had I been on the grass. Then guns began to go off all over the place, and I was in a panic because I thought Ethel was still in the crowd. I rushed about, looking for her, and was swept into the Marigny with the crowd. A dead girl was brought in on a stretcher and laid down beside me. It was all rather ghastly. Eventually, the firing stopped and I was able to get back to the Hôtel Bristol, where we were staying then, and found Ethel there. She had gone back before the firing began, but had run into another battle outside and inside the hotel.

My arrest by the French came as a complete surprise. I have it from what is usually called a 'well-informed source' that an English woman was dining with the Prefect of Police, and said to him, 'Why don't you arrest P. G. Wodehouse?' He thought it a splendid idea and sent out the order over the coffee and liqueurs, with the result that I woke up at one o'clock in the morning of 22nd November to find an Inspecteur at my bedside. (Much the same thing, if you remember, happened to the late Abou Ben Adhem.) He took Ethel and me to the Palais de Justice, where we spent sixteen hours without food in a draughty corridor, sleeping on wooden chairs.

Aren't women wonderful? Ethel took the whole thing in her stride without a word of complaint. She was simply magnificent, and the love and admiration which she has inspired in me for the last thirty years hit a new high.

I don't know what was going on behind the scenes, but the news of our arrest apparently caused quite a stir in British official circles. They flew a Home Office representative over, who plunged into a series of talks with the Palais de Justice boys – heated ones, I should imagine, for the whole atmosphere suddenly changed like a flash. We were given beds, and Malcolm Muggeridge – what a pal that man has been! – arrived loaded with bread, corned beef, champagne and cigars, and we had a banquet.

Next day they released Ethel, and I spent four days in the Inspecteur's room, getting very matey with them all and resuming work on my novel. (Turn up your copy of *Uncle*

Dynamite and read Chapter Nine, the one that begins, 'It is a characteristic of England's splendid police force. . . .' The whole of that chapter was written in the Inspecteur's room at the Palais de Justice, with the lads crowding round to see how the stuff was going.)

On the evening of the fourth day I was brought to this hospital where I have been ever since.

I have a room to myself, quite good food and plenty of tobacco, and Ethel is allowed to come and see me, as are all my friends. So I might be considerably worse off.

I generally wake up at four a.m., lie in bed till six, then get up and boil water on a boiler lent me by one of the doctors and have breakfast. The concierge arrives with the *Paris Daily Mail* at nine, and after my room has been cleaned, that is by half-past nine, I start writing. Lunch at half-past twelve. At four I get a walk in the garden. In the evening I walk up and down the landing, and then go to bed, never later than eight. Light out at nine-thirty. I get on wonderfully with the Inspecteurs, and am improving my French. When I get visitors, they usually come at three. It isn't a bad sort of life, if you have a novel to write.

Did you happen to see a thing by George Orwell called 'In Defence of P. G. Wodehouse'? He says that my indiscretion (the broadcasts) gave a good propaganda opening to the left-wingers in England because 'it was a chance to expose a wealthy parasite'. Had it ever occurred to you that that is how authors are regarded in England? You, me, Shakespeare, all of us, just parasites. (Have you read any good parasites lately?) It's very different in France. Seeing me hammering out my wholesome fiction, the Inspecteurs treat me with reverence. For two pins (*épingles*) they would call me '*maître*'.

When I finish this one, I shall have five novels which have not been published in England, also ten short stories. I wonder if they ever will be published. If England won't have them, I shall have to content myself with appearing in Spain (and Sweden). There is a publisher in Barcelona who is bringing out *eight* of my books a year. He very decently sent me F350,000 a year ago, which came in very handy.

I'm afraid this letter is all about me. But I thought you would like to hear details about my life. It's good news to hear that Dulwich is going strong. I wonder if the public schools will survive the war.

By the way, I saw in the *Paris Daily Mail* that Hugh Bartlett and Billy Griffith were in the Arnhem show and got through safely, but since then someone has told me that Bartlett was blown up in a car. I hope it is not true. Have you heard anything? It's awful to think of all those fellows one used to know being in danger all the time.

Hôtel Lincoln,
February 5th, 1945   *Paris*

Malcolm Muggeridge is leaving for England this week and will post this. He will be in London about ten days, I think, so if you have time to write me a letter you could send it to me care of him. I will add his London address as a postscript, as I shall not know till I see him this afternoon. I am longing to get a letter from you, telling me all the news.

I was in the hospital when I wrote to you last. (I hope you got the letter all right.) I spent eight weeks there, and then Malcolm drove Ethel and Wonder and me down to Barbizon, about thirty miles from Paris, in the most awful blizzard. We lunched at a marvellous restaurant in the forest in front of a great log fire and thought things were going to be wonderful. But when we got to the hotel at Barbizon, we found it was a strictly summer hotel, no carpets, no heating and no running water owing to the frost freezing the pipes. However, we settled down and had a very good time for three weeks, though with icicles forming on us, and then the hotel was requisitioned by SHAEF, so we are back in Paris. I think eventually we shall go to Ethel's friends the De Rocquignys at their house near Hesdin; but in the meantime Paris is very pleasant, though living conditions are getting tougher every day and I don't like the look of the Seine, which may burst its banks at any moment. Still, Paris is always Paris, and we are quite happy.

(I was just writing this, when an air raid warning sounded. I thought all that sort of thing was over in Paris. Still, there it is. I will let you know how the matter develops.)

Where was I? Oh yes, Paris. It's all right. Quite a city. La

Ville Lumière, I have sometimes called it, though it is far from being that these days.

I was thrilled by what you told me about Dulwich winning all its school matches last cricket season, including Harrow and Malvern. It's odd, but I don't find that world cataclysms and my own personal troubles make any difference to my feelings about Dulwich.

The air raid is still apparently in progress, as there has been no 'All Clear', but nothing seems to be happening. We got a scare one night at Barbizon when terrific explosions suddenly shook the hotel. I believe it was some allied plane which had had to jettison its bombs in the neighbourhood.

Do tell me, when you write, about your work since the war started. You mention books you are writing but don't tell me how you're selling these days. I am longing to know the figures. You must have built up a large public by now. Is the *Strand* still going? Have you read ('All clear' just gone) Hesketh Pearson's life of Conan Doyle? Very interesting. It's curious to think what small prices he got for stories which are world famous. I can't remember off-hand, but I think he got £125 for the complete American rights of *The White Company*.

I have been plugging away at *Uncle Dynamite*. I managed to get 100 pages done while in the clinic, in spite of constant interruptions. I would start writing at nine in the morning and get a paragraph done when the nurse would come in and sluice water all over the floor. Then the concierge arrived with the morning paper, then the nurse with bread for lunch, then another nurse with wine, then a doctor and finally a couple of Inspecteurs. All the Inspecteurs were very interested in my writing. It was the same thing in camp, where I used to sit on my typewriter case with the machine balanced on a suitcase and work away with two German soldiers standing behind me with rifles, breathing down the back of my neck. They seemed fascinated by this glimpse into the life literary.

February 24th, 1945   *Hôtel Lincoln*
There seems to have been some hitch about Malcom's visit to England, as he is still here. We are meeting him at dinner tomorrow night, so I will give him this letter then. If he is not

going over himself, he will probably know of someone who is going.

Meanwhile, your two letters of January 19th and January 30th have arrived, within two days of each other. (So it looks as if letters now take about a month to come, which isn't so bad.) You can imagine how delighted I was to get them.

That story you told me in your letter about someone saying that while I was in camp the German officers talked to me in German amused me. I wonder why people invent these things. All the German I know is, '*Es ist schonus wetter*,' and I mispronounce that. As a matter of fact, they didn't even talk to me in English. It's extraordinary how things get twisted. When I was making my statement in Paris after the liberation to the Home Office representative, he started by questioning me keenly as to whether I had written for a German paper (in English) called *The Camp*, which was circulated among British prisoners. It seemed that somebody had denounced me as having done so, and all that had happened really was that in one number there was a parody of my Jeeves stuff under the title of 'Bertie At The War' or something like that, signed 'P. G. Roadhouse' or some such name.

When I was in camp, I had the most tremendous liking and admiration for the War Graves Commission men. With one of them, Bert Haskins, I formed a friendship which will last all our lives. He was pure gold, and we kept up a correspondence all the time after I left Tost until, a few weeks before the liberation, his letters suddenly ceased and I assumed that he had been repatriated. I hope so. Bert was the chap who, when we were spending that eight hours in the cattle trucks before leaving Loos, suddenly appeared at my side with half a loaf of bread, butter, radishes, a bottle of wine and a slab of potted meat. He didn't know me, but out of sheer goodness of heart he came and gave me the stuff. He was a splendid chap, and I was always so sorry that he was not in my dormitory. It's like being in a house at school. In camp you don't see much of people who aren't in your dormitory. Did I tell you that Lord Uffenham in *Money in the Bank* was drawn from a man in my dormitory? It isn't often that one has the luck to be in daily contact with the model for one's principal character.

I have become very interested in Shakespeare, and am reading books about him, having joined the American Library here. A thing I can never understand is why all the critics seem to assume that his plays are a reflection of his personal moods and dictated by the circumstances of his private life. You know the sort of thing I mean. They say *Timon of Athens* is a pretty gloomy piece of work, which means that Shakespeare must have been having a rotten time when he wrote it. I can't see it. Do you find that your private life affects your work? I don't.

Well, so long. I've probably left out a dozen things I wanted to say, but I will put them in my next.

Hôtel Lincoln,
April 5th, 1945   *Rue Bayard, Paris*

Will you address all future letters to the Hôtel Lincoln, as the girl at the Consulate is getting a bit sniffy about having to ring me up and tell me there is a letter waiting for me there. (Why she can't just re-address it, I don't know, but she seems to think that would be impossible.) Letters to the Lincoln will always reach me.

I was very interested in your long letter about your books. I wish I could get hold of them, and I suppose that will be possible fairly soon now. The last I read was *Sink and be Damned*, which I thought awfully good. What an infernal nuisance the paper shortage is. It must be maddening to sell out before publication and then not be able to follow it up because there is no paper for another edition. I sympathize with your trouble with the printers and their queries. The American cousins of these birds read the proofs of the *Saturday Evening Post* and I used to spend hours writing sarcastic replies in the margin. I remember in *Quick Service* they queried the grammar of some remark made by a barmaid in a moment of extreme agitation; and I wrote a long essay in the margin pointing out that when an English barmaid is agitated she very often speaks ungrammatically. Futile, of course.

I finished *Uncle Dynamite* last Sunday. What with one thing and another, it has taken me exactly a year to write, but I think the results are good. It was one of those difficult stories where you get everything into a tangle and then straighten it all out in the last chapter, and all the way through I was saying to myself, 'Well, it's all right so far, but that last chapter is going to let the whole thing down.' But, thank goodness, the last chapter came out all right. I now have the following books shuffling their feet nervously in the ante-room, wondering if they will ever get into print: *Money in the Bank*, *Joy in the Morning* (a Jeeves story), *Full Moon* (Blandings Castle Story), *Spring Fever* and this new one, *Uncle Dynamite*. Also ten short stories.

But it's a funny thing about writing. If you are a writer by nature, I don't believe you write for money or fame or even for publication, but simply for the pleasure of turning out the stuff. I really don't care much if these books are published or not. The great thing is that I've got them down on paper, and can read and re-read them and polish them and change an adjective for a better one and cut out dead lines.

A. A. Milne says much the same thing in *Two People*. He says that books ought not to be published. They ought to be written, and then one copy ought to be beautifully printed for the author to read.

This letter will reach you quickly, as Irene Ward, the MP, is taking it over to England with her tomorrow. I am going to the Consulate today and shall hope to find a letter from you there. All your others have arrived safely, and I have them all pinned together and re-read them continually.

78 Avenue Paul Doumer,
April 22nd, 1945   *Paris*

The above is now my official address. By an absolute miracle we have been able to get a furnished flat and move in to-morrow. Ethel made friends with the French wife of an Englishman at the Lincoln, who had found a flat and was moving in immediately, and then her plans were all changed by her having to go to the country, so she said we could have the place. I went to see it yesterday and it is just what we want. It is almost impossible to get a flat in Paris now, even people at the Embassy can't do it, so you can imagine how thankful we are. Ethel had managed to keep her room on at the Lincoln, but we never knew when she might not have to move, and there was absolutely nowhere I could go except to this Danish friend of mine, and I felt that he must be getting fed up after five weeks of me. So now we are all right.

Somebody, presumably Slacker, sent me the Dulwich Year Book for 1943 and 1944, which I was delighted to have, though it was saddening to see the Roll of Honour. Most of the names I did not know, but quite a few were of chaps I knew slightly as members of the cricket and football teams. I see Doulton's son and D. G. Donald's have both been killed, and also R. H. Spencer, who played half, and a fellow named Darby who was in the cricket team of 1935 and wrote to thank me for a notice I gave him in my report of the Tonbridge match.

By the way, was 1944 a very wet summer in England? I ask because that was the year we won all our seven school cricket matches and the lad at the head of the batting averages had an average of 25. We seem to have outed the opposition each time for about 83 and then to have made 84 for 8 ourselves. The top score seems to have been 60. Very odd.

Also by the way, I see that in the footer statements the game with Tonbridge is described as 'Abandoned', when we were leading by a goal and a try to nil. How in the name of goodness does a school footer match get abandoned? It can't have been the weather, as one plays through everything. Unless a dense fog suddenly came down.

You never told me if H. T. Bartlett was all right. He got through Arnhem with Billy Griffith, and then I heard a rumour that he had been blown up by a mine. I do hope it wasn't true. I had a message through an RAF man in September from A. C. Shirreff, so he was all right then, but you never know from one day to another, worse luck.

PS I have been reading Mark Twain's letters. Very interesting. He thought an enormous lot of W. D. Howells's books. Have you read any of them? I have taken *The Rise of Silas Lapham* out of the American Library here, and it certainly is good. It was written in 1884, but reads quite like a modern book.

May 22nd, 1945   *78 Avenue Paul Doumer*

I looked in at the Consulate a day or two ago and found two letters from you, and today your long one of May 2nd was forwarded on from the Lincoln, so I think it is about time I wrote.

I'm like you, I can't remember what I told you in previous letters.

I'm so glad you have got your novel finished. At least, you have done the first draft, and that is always the tough part. Personally, I love rewriting and polishing. Directly I have got something down on paper, however, rough it is, I feel the thing is in the bag.

I wish I could get hold of some of Raymond Chandler's stuff. It sounds from what you say just the kind of thing I like. An occasional new book creeps through to Paris, but it is very difficult to get hold of anything except pre-war books. I have just got the new Peter Cheyney, and it makes one realize there has been a war on to look at it. It is about an inch thick and printed on a sort of brown paper and the price is nine and six. Before the war no publisher would have put out a shilling edition like that. I think the paper shortage is worse than the food shortage. Here in Paris the papers don't come out on Monday, which must be maddening for them if something big happens on the previous day. One week the non-appearance day was shifted to Wednesday for some reason, with the result that the papers were not able to report the death of Hitler.

At the present moment I am in a state of suspense, wondering if Billy Griffith is playing for England in the Test at Lord's. The Paris *Daily Mail* gave the list of the team and said, 'Either Griffith or Evans will keep wicket.' The report of the first day's play merely gave the score, and today's paper does the same, plus a description of the Australian innings. I am going down town this afternoon in the hope of finding an English paper. I am hoping that Billy got in all right.

I am having trouble again with the American income tax people. They have now dug back to 1923 and claim that I made no return that year or in 1924. I have absolutely no means of proving that I did, but I must have done. I was in America both years and left for England, and you can't get on a boat at New York, unless you show that you have paid your income tax. I suppose what will happen is that after I have spent thousands of dollars on lawyer's fees they will drop the thing.

But it's an awful nuisance, and I wouldn't have thought that legally they were entitled to go back twenty-two years. But they just make up the rules as they go along. It reminds me of George Ade's story of the man who was in prison and a friend went to see him and asked what he had done. The man told him and the friend said, 'But they can't put you in prison for that,' and the man said, 'I know they can't, but they have.'

I have been meaning to send you a story a man told me some months ago. He was an ex-merchant-navy man, and during the war was in charge of various tough sea assignments. I only put down a hurried note; so I may have got the thing all wrong, but this was what I think he said. He was told off to take a vessel to somewhere off the east coast of England to recover forty tons of nickel which had been sunk in a torpedoed steamer. Right. Well, the sunken ship was in such a position that you had to approach it through E-boat alley. Does that convey anything to you? It didn't to me, though I imagine it must mean some sort of channel where there was a big risk of being attacked by enemy E-boats. The sunk ship was four miles beyond E-boat alley. My next note consists of the words 'Three mines', so I suppose they encountered three mines on their way. Now it gets a bit clearer. When the divers went down, they found on board the sunken ship a lot of unexploded bombs, and also a number of cylinders of poison gas for India. The point is that this made the enterprise very perilous, and you could work it up and invent a lot of stuff. Anyway, the blow-out is that after they had been risking their lives for quite a number of days they were informed by the Admiralty that it was sorry they had been troubled but the Admiralty had just discovered that previous to the sinking of the ship the nickel had been transhipped, and so they needn't bother.

It seems to me that there is a short story for you on the lines of my Hollywood one *The Castaways*, where the entire personnel of the cast sweat their guts out, writing a picture based on a popular novel and then the studio discovers that it doesn't own the rights to the novel. How about it? Do you think you can do anything with it?

78 Avenue Paul Doumer
June 30th, 1945   *Paris (16)*

Your letter of June 12th reached me about a quarter of an hour ago, when I came in from my afternoon walk. I am sending this by air mail, as they tell me that takes letters to England in a couple of days or so. So note carefully when it arrives. Thanks for sending me the books. I hope I get them all right.

Before I forget. In one of your letters you asked me if I ever had read anything by Trollope. At that time I hadn't, but the other day, reading in Edward Marsh's *A Number of People* that Barrie had been fascinated by a book of his called *Is He Popenjoy?* I took it out of the American Library. I found it almost intolerably slow at first, and then suddenly it gripped me, and now I am devouring it. It is rather like listening to somebody very long-winded telling you a story about real people. The characters live in the most extraordinary way and you feel that the whole thing is true. Of course I read Trollope's *Autobiography* and found it very interesting. But I still don't understand his methods of work. Did he sit down each morning and write exactly 1500 words, without knowing when he sat down how the story was going to develop, or had he a careful scenario on paper? I can't believe that an intricate story like *Popenjoy* could have been written without minute planning. Of course, if he did plan the whole thing out first, there is nothing so very bizarre in the idea of writing so many hundred words of it each day. After all, it is more or less what one does oneself. One sits down to work each morning, no matter whether one feels bright or lethargic, and before one gets up a certain amount of stuff, generally about 1500 words, has emerged. But to sit down before a blank sheet of paper without an idea of how the story is to proceed and just start writing, seems to me impossible.

I'm sorry the short story didn't get over with the *Saturday Evening Post*. How extraordinary that they should be so against war stories. It is a complete change of policy since the last number I read, which was only about a year ago. At that time the synopsis of a *SEP* serial would be something like this. 'Major Dwight van Renasseller, a young American officer in the FGI, has fallen in love with a mysterious veiled woman who turns out to be Irma Kraus, assistant Gauleiter of the Gestapo, who is in New York disguised as a Flight Lieutenant of the RAF, in order to secure the plans of the PBO. One night at a meeting of the ITD he meets "Spud" Murphy, in reality a colonel in the THB, who is posing as Himmler in the hope of getting a free lunch at a German restaurant on Eighty-fourth Street. They decide to merge the YFS with the PXQ, thus fascilitating the operations of WGC. Go on from there.'

At present, however, I take but a faint interest in the American market, as the US Government is claiming this large sum of money from me for income tax and would infallibly pouch anything I made over there. My case comes up in September, and I suppose will end, as before, in my paying about a tenth of what they claim. As the year now in dispute is 1921 and all my records have been lost and also, one imagines, all those of the Government, I don't see how any conclusion can be arrived at except a compromise.

I wrote a novel called *Spring Fever* in 1943, and the other day, not being able to get a plot for a novel, decided to make a play of it. It is coming out very well, but as always the agony of telling a story purely in dialogue and having to compress it and keep the action in one spot, is frightful. I have written the first scene of Act I half a dozen times, and it isn't right yet. The curse of a play is that you can't give people thoughts. It all has to be done in the dialogue.

78 Avenue Paul Doumer,
August 1st, 1945   *Paris*

Well, the books arrived safely and we have been revelling in them.

I'll tell you what's the whole trouble with you, Bill, and that is that you have never done anything except write the stuff and are competing with all these birds who hang around authors' lunches and go about lecturing and presenting prizes at girls' schools. I don't think it matters in the long run, but there's no doubt that all these other fellows who shove themselves forward and suck up to the critics do get a lot of publicity, and it helps them for a while. I always think Hugh Walpole's reputation was two-thirds publicity. He was always endorsing books and speaking at lunches and so on.

I can't remember if I ever told you about meeting Hugh when I was at Oxford getting my D.Litt. I was staying with the Vice-Chancellor at Magdelen and he blew in and spent the day. It was just after Hilaire Belloc had said that I was the best living English writer. It was just a gag, of course, but it worried Hugh terribly. He said to me, 'Did you see what Belloc said about you?' I said I had. 'I wonder why he said that.' 'I wonder,' I said. Long silence. 'I can't imagine why he said that,' said Hugh. I said I couldn't, either. Another long silence. 'It seems such an extraordinary thing to say!' 'Most extraordinary.' Long silence again. 'Ah, well,' said Hugh, having apparently found the solution, 'the old man's getting very old.'

We went for a long walk in the afternoon, and he told me that when somebody wrote a stinker about some book of his, he cried for hours. Can you imagine getting all worked up about a bad notice? I always feel about the critics that there are bound to be quite a number of them who don't like one's stuff and one just has to accept it. They don't get a sob out of me.

I never cared much for Walpole. There was a time when I seemed about to be registered as number fourteen or something on his list of friends – did you know that he used to list all his friends in order? – but nothing came of it. He wanted me to come to Majorca with him, but I backed out and this probably shoved me down to number thirty or off the list altogether.

I see in the *Express* that poor Damon Runyon has had an operation which has left him unable to speak. It sounds pretty serious. Do you like his stuff? I have just been reading a book of his stories and I thought they were great.

September 13th, 1945   *78 Avenue Paul Doumer*

Thanks for your letter of September 2nd, for sending Watt the clippings, and for *Sabina's Brother*, which arrived yesterday. I am looking forward to revelling in it directly I have cleared off a mass of correspondence which has been hung up.

Your California book sounds as if it would be very good. I

remember those movie stories you mention. They were by Charles E. Van Loan, a very nice fellow who lost his right arm and taught himself to play golf with his left so well that he used to go round in the seventies with one arm. The stories were published in book form by George Doran (now Doubleday Doran & Co.). I have them in the archives, but can't possibly get at them, and as to what they were called. . . . Isn't it extraordinary? I was on the point of saying I hadn't a notion when the title suddenly flashed into my mind. *Buck Parvin and the Movies*. I believe you could get a copy from Doubleday & Co., Rockefeller Center, New York City, though, of course, they may be out of print. Even if you don't need the book for your work, it would be fascinating to read now. Isn't it amazing to think that in 1910 movies were as primitive as that. As I remember Van Loan's book, you just got a camera and a few pals and went out into the desert and shot some pictures, and that was all.

I'm so sorry Rene is so tired. It must be very hard for her without a maid. We still have one whom Ethel fires on Mondays and Thursdays. On Tuesdays and Fridays she gives her own notice. On Saturdays and Sundays she goes home. So our big day is Wednesday. This is the time to catch us.

I don't know why it is, but I am enjoying life amazingly these days. Thunderclouds fill the sky in every direction, including a demand for $120,000 from the US income tax people (case starts on Monday unless they settle in advance); but I continue to be happy.

I don't know what we shall do this winter, but I imagine that we shall probably take on the flat for another three months and dig in. We have laid in a supply of wood big enough to last us through the winter and things seem much better as regards electricity, so that we shall have electric stoves. Last winter was awful. The electricity wasn't turned on till five in the afternoon. The year before it was worse, for as I remember the juice wasn't switched on till about nine. I shall never forget a dinner given us by a friend in a mysterious restaurant, somewhere near here, which was located in a flat. We dined in pitch darkness and there were three black poodles in the room, so that every time anyone moved, they stepped on them, and dinner was punctuated with agonized yelps.

I see in the Paris *Daily Mail* this morning that E. Phillips Oppenheim has managed to get back to his home in Guernsey by getting a lift on a yacht. He is seventy-nine, but must still be pretty fit, if he can dash about like that.

I have always been devoted to Oppy. I saw a lot of him when I was living at La Fréyère. I remember him coming to lunch one day not long after he had had a slight sunstroke, and he was taking no chances of getting another one. There was one of those Riviera trees on the terrace, a dense mass of leaves through which no ray of light could penetrate, and he sat under it with a sun helmet on his head holding a large umbrella over himself. Did you know that he used to dictate all his stuff? I found him in gloomy mood one day. He had had the perfect secretary, who used to squeal with excitement as the story got going on the international spies and mysterious veiled women, which bucked him up enormously, and she had left to get married and in her place had come one of those tall, statuesque, frozen-faced secs who took his dictation in an aloof, revolted sort of way as if the stuff soiled the paper of her notebook. He said it discouraged him.

How *can* anybody dictate? Could you? I should be feeling shy and apologetic all the time. The nearest I ever got to it was when Ethel bought me one of those machines Edgar Wallace used to use, where you talk on to a wax cylinder and then turn back to the beginning to hear how it sounds. I started *Thank You, Jeeves*, on it, and when I played it back, I was appalled how unfunny the stuff sounded. I hadn't known it till then but apparently I have a voice like a very pompous clergyman intoning. Either that or the instrument was pulling my leg. Anyway, I sold the damned thing next day.

36 Boulevard Suchet,
November 8th, 1945 *Paris (16)*

Note the above address. We move out of this flat in a day or two and go to this other one, a very ornate joint belonging to Lady Deterding, two doors off the Duke of Windsor. I think we shall be very comfortable. We have a store of wood, and there are fireplaces; and also a number of electric heaters.

About the only drawback to the place is that it is rather a long way from the shops, and, of course, everything has to be fetched – by me. By the way, the relief of having got rid of bread tickets is tremendous. I have always been O.C. Bread, going out in the morning before breakfast for it and being responsible for seeing that the tickets lasted out, and it was always a very near thing and a great anxiety. One month I had to borrow half a loaf from the concierge on the last day.

I was intending to write to you last night, but I wouldn't have had time to write a long letter, so I put it off till this morning, and at breakfast your letter of November 4th arrived. I'm so glad you managed to fix up the novel so that it did not clash with H. M. Tomlinson's, but what a lot of bother you have had about it and all unnecessary really. I don't think there was ever a chance that Tomlinson would have made a fuss. With the great number of novels published nowadays writers are bound to clash in the way of ideas. Still, it's best, of course, to avoid any possible trouble, as you have done.

I'll tell you what makes life hell for writers, and that is that you meet someone who tells you a story as having happened to himself or a friend, and you work it up and publish it, only to find that the gentleman read the thing in a magazine somewhere. But listen. What *is* plagiarism? Did you ever see a play by Freddie Lonsdale called *The Last of Mrs Cheyney*? It was about a society woman who was one of a band of crooks, and this is revealed to the audience at the end of Act I. An exactly similar situation was in an American play called *Cheating Cheaters*. And the big scene of Act II was where the hero gets Mrs Cheyney into his room at night and holds her up for something by saying he is going to keep her there till they are found in the morning, which is exactly the same as Pinero's *Gay Lord Quex*. And yet nobody has ever breathed a word against Freddie for plagiarizing. Quite rightly. The treatment is everything.

I had to break off at this point to take Wonder for her walk. I find it almost impossible to get anything done in the mornings, as I have to suit my time to hers. What I would like would be to hoik her out of bed at eight-thirty, exercise her and be able to settle down to work at ten. But if I try to do this she curses so much that I desist. It is generally about eleven-fifteen when I am just getting going, that there is a thud on my door, and in she bounds. There is a spaniel who lives at No. 72 and sits inside the front door, which is of thick glass, and every day Wonder toddles up to this door and she and the spaniel start a terrific fight through the glass, which lasts until I haul her away. The other day the spaniel nipped away and suddenly appeared at the open ground-floor window, whereupon a scene of perfect camaraderie ensued, both dogs immediately becoming bosom friends. But next day the fight started again.

Back to the subject of plagiarism. The best plagiarism story I know was the one Guy Bolton told me about Owen Davis, the American playwright. He had a show on in New York, a melodrama, and a tailor claimed that it was stolen from a play which he – the tailor – had dashed off in the intervals of tailoring. Davis got together with him, and asked him just what he based the accusation on. The tailor said his play was about a man accused of murder and all the time he was innocent, and so was Davis's. Davis then took him round to some of the other plays running on Broadway at the moment – *The Crimson Alibi, At 9.45, The Sign on the Door*, etc. – and pointed out that two of them were about men accused of murder and by golly in the end they turn out not to have done it after all. But you can't down an author with evidence of that sort. 'They've *all* stolen my play!' was his only comment.

Frank Sullivan wrote a very funny article at the time when a Miss Georges Lewis sued Eugene O'Neill, charging him with stealing *Strange Interlude* from a play of hers called *The Temple of Pallas Athene*. Asked for the examples of similarity between her play and his, she cited these:

> I have been sadly disillusioned. (*Lewis*)
> You have been sadly disillusioned? (*O'Neill*)

> Old fox. (*Lewis*)
> Old fox. (*O'Neill*)

> My goodness. (*Lewis*)
> My goodness. (*O'Neill*)

'I shall sue O'Neill, too!' Frank wrote. 'And I may even sue Georges as well, because, strangely enough, in my play *The Forgotten Galosh*, there occurs not only the line, "*He* has been sadly disillusioned," but also the line, "My goodness." This, to my mind, makes it look very very bad for Georges and Eugene. Even if great minds do jump, three of us would never have thought of that pearl. It looks fishy to me.'

He ends: 'I have plenty more evidence, which I propose to produce at the proper time unless the playwrights mentioned above see fit to settle out of court. I'll take ten dollars.

Well, five.

Not a cent under three. I'd be losing money.

Well, don't go, hold on a minute, I'll take a dollar.

A half-dollar I'll take.

Could you spare a nickel for a cup of coffee?'

Which is about how most of these plagiarism suits end.

December 7th, 1945   *36 Boulevard Suchet*

The new flat is a great success. It is like living in the country with all the advantages of town. I go out into the Bois every morning before breakfast in a sweater and golf knickers and do my exercises, and I wear golf clothes all day. The great merit of this part of Paris – up in Auteuil – is that nobody stares at you no matter what you do or wear. We have hot water here all the time, which is wonderful, and we can keep one room warm with wood fires, so we are well off. So far we have been able to get food, though at a terrific cost. Butter is £1 5s. a pound.

We have a female Pole who comes each morning at nine (or is supposed to) and leaves after getting us lunch, but there is so much to do that Ethel generally does all the cleaning of the flat. We have a very simple meal at night. I wonder when things will get easier. The effect it has on me is to mess up my work pretty completely. Whenever I try to settle down, there is always something to do like going to the cellar for wood or going out and buying vegetables.

I had a letter from Denis Mackail the other day, drawing a very gloomy picture of the short story situation in England. He says there is now practically no market, and if you do write

a short story it mustn't be over 2000 words. Bobbie Denby,
writing from America, says that over there you mustn't exceed
5000. This dishes me completely, as I can't keep under
7000.

January 11th, 1946   *36 Boulevard Suchet*

It shows the advantage of putting things off. I meant to write
this letter yesterday, but postponed it because I hadn't time
to write a really long one, and this morning yours of January
6th arrived, so I can answer that as well as yours of December
11th.

You've got me stumped on those things in the California
book. Who the dickens were the motion picture stars of 1911?
Mary Pickford, of course, but not Douglas Fairbanks, because
in 1911 he was an actor on the stage and incidentally playing
the part of Jimmy in my *Gentleman of Leisure*, at the Playhouse
in New York. It must have been at least two years after that
before he went into pictures. Ha! Something Bunny and Flora
Finch. Was Barbara La Marr going in 1911? Wallace Reid?
Fatty Arbuckle? It's darned hard to remember. But surely any
motion picture magazine would tell you. Theda Bara. Sidney
Drew.

Life continues very pleasant here. I am getting fonder and
fonder of Paris. It was a blow when they started rationing
bread again, but in actual practice it doesn't affect us much.
We now have a cook who buys the stuff and there always seems
enough. There is some sort of row on just now between the
wholesale and retail butchers, which has resulted in no meat
for the populace for about two weeks. But something always
seems to turn up. There is a mysterious Arab gentleman who
calls from time to time with offerings. He has just come and
fixed us up with a rabbit. Also a Dane (a stranger to me) has
sent me an enormous parcel from Copenhagen, the only
trouble being that all the contents are labelled in Danish, so
we don't know what they are. There are three large tins which
I hold contain bacon, but Ethel, who is in pessimistic mood
today, says that they are floor polish. But surely even the most
erratic Dane wouldn't send hungry Britons stuff for polishing
floors. The only way I can think of solving the mystery is to

ring up our Danish friend at Neuilly and spell the labels over the phone to him, and ask him to translate.

March 7th, 1946   *36 Boulevard Suchet*

I wrote to you yesterday and today got yours of March 4th.

It must be a great relief to you getting the new book off. I hope they won't make you cut it, but 200,000 words does seem a lot for these shortage-of-paper days. They'll probably print it all in smaller type than *MacRann*, in which case I shall have to use a magnifying glass.

Odd about the shortage of reviews of *MacRann*. Denis Mackail tells me he has seen none at all of *Huddleston House*. I can't understand the reviewing situation in England. Ethel brought me home an *Observer* and a *Sunday Times* yesterday and the books they reviewed seemed the sort that nobody could possibly want to read. (With the exception of *George Brown's School Days*, by Bruce Marshall, which looks as if it might be interesting, though apparently the same old anti-public-school stuff. I often wonder if you and I were unusually fortunate in our schooldays. To me the years between 1896 and 1900 seem like Heaven. Was the average man really unhappy at school? Or was Dulwich in our time an exceptionally good school?)

Back to the subject of reviews. I believe the only thing that matters to an author is word-of-mouth advertising. My experience has been that the ordinary member of the public, like myself when I am not a writer but a reader, is always on the look-out for authors that he can read but is very wary about taking on new ones. Quite by accident, generally, he dips into a book by someone who has been writing for years, likes it and says to himself, 'Here's a chap to keep an eye on. I'll read the rest of his stuff.' When a sufficient number of people have done that, the author has a public. I think this is what is happening to you. All the time single readers all over the country have been coming across stray books of yours in seaside libraries and so on, and have put you on their list. As an instance of this, the other day, browsing in the American library, I picked up a book by Naomi Jacob, saw that it was about music-hall performers, was interested in music-hall performers, decided that after all I wasn't taking such a big chance, as I could change it next day, took it home, liked it and now am resolved to read all her others. Have you ever read any of her stuff, by the way? This book *Straws in Amber* was good.

April 29th, 1946   *36 Boulevard Suchet*

A rush of correspondence prevented me answering your April 3rd letter, and this morning yours of April 26th arrived with the good news about *South of Forty-Five* and the bad news about *Fool's Gold*.

First, congratulations on the 12,000 sale. Terrific! This must have done a lot to offset the other knock.

Of course I shall be delighted to read *Fool's Gold*. I may be able to suggest cuts. Reading the two readers' reports, I got the impression that the length was all that was wrong with it. I mean to say, dash it, 215,000 words! At a time when they've probably only got about half a dozen bits of paper in the office.

Did you read Kipling's autobiography? In that he maintains that the principal thing in writing is to cut. Somerset Maugham says the same. Kipling says it's like raking slag out of a fire to make the fire burn brighter. I know just what he means. You can skip as you read, but if the superfluous stuff is there, it affects you just the same. The trouble is to know what to cut. I generally find with my own stuff that it's unnecessary lines in the dialogue that are wrong, but then my books are principally dialogue. I should say at a guess that in *Fool's Gold*, in the effort to put down all you knew, you had rambled a bit.

I can't make out what's happening in the book world these days. Someone sent me a copy of the *New York Sunday Times* the other day, and I see that Daphne du Maurier's new book has sold over a million already. I suppose it's all these book clubs they have in America. If you have the luck to be selected by one of the big ones, that means a 600,000 sale right away.

Here's another odd thing. Almost without exception these enormous sellers are historical novels. It's curious, the passion for historical stuff in America. When I first went there in 1904, all the big sellers were historical novels, and now they are at it again. I suppose they are entitled to read what they like, but it does seem strange that, when we are living in about as interesting a period as the world has known, what people want is all that stuff about plain John Blunt following his dear lord to the wars and bigger and better hussies at the court of Charles the Second.

Probably it won't be till around 2500 AD that the boys will start writing about the glamorous days of 1946.

We have had so many parcels from America that the food situation is much better now. My trouble is that the shortage of bread in the prison camp has left me with a yearning for the stuff, and the present rations are pretty small. We just get through the month. Luckily there is a shop around the corner where you can get biscottes, so we manage. But what I want to know is what has become of the potato? I had always supposed that in times of food shortage you just lived on potatoes, but they are like jewellery in Paris.

I've just read Raymond Chandler's *Farewell, My Lovely*. It's good. But a thing I've never been able to understand is how detectives in fiction drink so much and yet remain in the hardest physical condition. And how do Peter Cheyney's detectives manage to get all that whisky in London in war-time? They must be millionaires, as I believe the stuff is about £4 a bottle. Do you ever read Rex Stout's Nero Wolfe stories? A good many of them came out in the *Saturday Evening Post*. They're good. He has rather ingeniously made his tough detective drink milk.

George Orwell. I wish I could get hold of that book of his, as it's just the sort of thing I like reading nowadays. He is a friend of my friend Malcolm Muggeridge and about a year ago or more came over to Paris and gave us a very good lunch at a place down by Les Halles (the Markets to you). I liked him very much indeed.

May 22nd, 1946   *36 Boulevard Suchet*

I started *Fool's Gold* last night and have just reached page 136, and my opinion so far is that it is the most fascinating thing I have ever read. The idea of cutting a line of it revolts me. And at the same time I am saying to myself, 'Am I all wrong about this book? I mean, is my mind so constituted that I am the only person who would enjoy it?' – this of course, being due to the two publisher's readers' criticisms. (This, I gather from your letter is exactly the impression it makes on you. You say, 'I do not believe anyone would be interested in the book save myself.')

I think the reception of the book depends entirely on what the reader is led to expect. I mean, if he thinks he is going to get a quick-moving, dramatic story of the old West, then I suppose he would be disappointed. But I can't imagine anyone in the right mental attitude not liking it.

Anyway, I love the thing! Which reminds me of the story of the actress's sister who telegraphed her on the opening night of her new show, 'Whatever happens, always remember that Mother and I love you.'

Money in the Bank appears on Monday, when I expect you will get your copy. Jenkins assure me that 25,000 copies at least will be sold, which will be nice.

June 3rd, 1946   *36 Boulevard Suchet*

My pleasure in reading your kind words about *Money in the Bank* was slightly marred by the sudden arrival of a spectacled Frenchman with a bill for thirteen mille for electricity, this including nine mille penalty for over-indulgence during the winter. Ethel nearly fainted and I, though a strong man, was shaken. I always knew we were for it, as we went in freely for hot water and heaters during those cold months, but I had supposed that they would just shake a playful finger at us and fine us about a quid. Still, it's better than being cold.

August 27th, 1946   *36 Boulevard Suchet*

Thanks for your letters. I would have written to you a long time ago, but have been tensely occupied with a rush job which started on August 8th and finished last night, viz. the dramatization of *Leave it to Psmith* for America.

The effect of this has been to give me eye trouble and it was, a great comfort to read what you said in your letter of July 29th about paying no attention to those floating specks. If they don't matter, that's fine. But now when I move my right eye a sort of black thing swings across it. If it is only a blood vessel, right ho, but, like you, I was brought up on *The Light that Failed* and suspect any funny business along those lines.

Incidentally, why do all these critics – George Orwell, for instance – assume that *The Light that Failed* was a flop and is recognized as such by the reading world? It certainly didn't flop in the sense of not making money, as it probably sold several hundred thousand in the ordinary edition and was also serialized and successfully dramatized. And if they mean that it's a failure because it doesn't grip you, they are simply talking through their hats.

It's odd, this hostility to Kipling. How the intelligentsia do seem to loathe the poor blighter, and how we of the *canaille* revel in his stuff. One thing I do think is pretty unjust – when they tick him off for not having spotted the future of the India Movement and all that sort of thing. I mean, considering that he left India for ever at the age of about twenty-two.

I wish these critics wouldn't distort facts in order to make a point. George Orwell calls my stuff Edwardian (which God knows it is. No argument about that, George) and says the reason for it being Edwardian is that I did not set foot in England for sixteen years and so lost touch with conditions there. Sixteen years, mark you, during most of which I was living in London and was known as Beau Wodehouse of Norfolk Street. He is also apt to take some book which I wrote in 1907 and draw all sorts of portentous conclusions from it. Dash it, in 1907 I was practically in swaddling clothes, and it was extremely creditable to me that I was able to write at all. Still, a thoroughly nice chap, and we correspond regularly. In his latest he says he has taken a house twenty-six miles from anywhere, up in the north of Scotland.

We are now making arrangements for going to America. I don't want to fly, and if one goes by boat it will mean sharing a cabin with about thirty other men on a 10,000 ton Liberty Ship. Though I am not sure if on the Liberty ships the number of passengers isn't limited. Are they really cargo boats? What I would like would be to get a passage on one of your tramp steamers, but how is this managed? Anyway, I expect I shall leave somehow towards the middle of September. We have to give up this flat on October 15th, and Ethel wants me out of the way during the move. I am hoping that she will clean everything up and join me in New York in about a month.

The news about my books is good. Jenkins writes that they have about 4000 left of the 30,000 they printed of *Money in the Bank* and are preparing a new edition, and Doubleday in New York sold 15,000 in advance of *Joy in the Morning*, which came out in America on August 22nd, and are very pleased about it and expect to sell a lot more.

Since I wrote last, we have had a short holiday at Le Touquet where I ran into several men from my camp. I went several times to see Low Wood. It isn't in such bad shape as I had feared. The walls, ceilings, staircases and mantelpieces are still there. It would apparently cost about £2000 to put it right, and Ethel has given a man an option till next Monday to buy at £4000. Our trouble is that, until they relax this rule about not being able to touch our English money, we simply can't raise £2000, and £4000 paid over in cash would be the salvation of us. At present we are living on driblets from America, just enough to keep us going.

I met Madge at Le Touquet, looking just the same. She has taken over Mrs Miffen, the Peke, the one we had in 1940. I met Mrs Miffen – now called Poppy, of all ghastly names – and of course she didn't know me from Adam. She is one of those square, ugly Pekes, but very nice.

You say you tend to get tired nowadays. Me, too. After all, we're both heading for seventy. Silver threads amongst the gold, laddie! (Extract from book I was reading the other day: 'Latterly his mind had been going to seed rather. He was getting on toward seventy, you see.')

August 30th, 1946   *36 Boulevard Suchet*

I sent you a copy of *Joy in the Morning* yesterday. I hope you will like it. I don't think it's bad, considering that it was written during the German occupation of Le Touquet, with Germans soldiers prowling about under my window, plus necessity of having to walk to Paris Plage every morning to report to the Kommandant.

When you say you liked Priestley's book, do you mean *Bright Day*? I read that and liked it, and I also liked *Daylight on Saturday*. I haven't seen any others by him. I am now reading Evelyn Waugh's *Put Out More Flags*, and am absolutely stunned by his brilliance. As a comic satiric writer he stands alone. That interview between Basil Seal and the Guards Colonel is simply marvellous. And what a masterpiece *Decline and Fall* was.

September 11th, 1946   *36 Boulevard Suchet*

I ought to be working, I suppose, but I feel I must write to you, as it may relieve the gloom which has come upon me strongly this morning, due principally to the problem of where we go from here.

I envy you having a place of your own where you can dig in. The only thing to do these days is to follow Voltaire's advice and cultivate your garden. If only Low Wood were habitable.

We have to move from here in October, and then what? I feel I ought to go to America and make some money, but against this is the fact that I would be separated from Ethel, added to the fact that I should have to doss in with three or four other men on the boat. As you say, when you get to sixty-five, you want sleeping accommodation to yourself. Here's an odd thing, though. When I was in camp, I slept in a dormitory with sixty-six other men and loved it. I don't think I would mind mucking in with twenty or thirty men on board a liner. The trouble would be, though, where would I get a place to write in? Incidentally, when I first went to America in 1904, I travelled second-class with three other men in the cabin, so the wheel has come full circle, as you might say.

I shall sail for America directly I can get a passage on something. When that will be, with all these shipping strikes raging, I don't know, but soon, I hope. I hear these Liberty ships are quite comfortable. Talking of which, I met a woman the other day and mentioned that I was thinking of sailing on a Liberty ship, and she said, 'Oh, did you hear that one broke in half not long ago outside Dieppe?'

November 1st, 1946   *Pavillon Henri Quatre, St Germain-en-Laye*

After booking my passage on the *America*, supposed to be sailing on October 26th but, owing to strikes, not likely to leave before the middle of November, I thought it over and decided to postpone my visit to the USA. I suddenly realized how impossible it would be to leave Ethel for probably months, and there was really no immediate need for me to be in New York. I don't suppose I shall sail now until the Spring. I want to get the novel I'm doing, *The Mating Season*, finished before I leave.

This is a heavenly place. Nine miles out of Paris, but right in the country. This hotel is on the edge of a terrace a mile and a half long which looks all over Paris, and to the left of the terrace there is a forest. Trains to Paris every quarter of an hour do the journey in twenty-five minutes, so that I am really just as near to the American Library as I was at Boulevard Suchet. This is the house where Louis the Fourteenth was born, if that interests you.

I am following the doings of the Dulwich team this season with interest. So far they have won their first four school matches, running up a total of 91 points to 17. I wonder if it is going to turn out one of the big sides, like 1909?

How is the novel going? And what do Rich and Cowan think of the revised version of *Fool's Gold*? And again, Bill, I have to say that Kipling was right about cutting. I think one has to be ruthless with one's books. I find I have a tendency to write a funny line and then add another, elaborating it when there is no necessity for the second bit. I keep coming on such bits in the thing I'm doing now. I go through the story every day and hack them out.

Do you find you write more slowly than you used to? I don't know if it is because *The Mating Season* is a Jeeves story, and in a Jeeves story every line has to have some entertainment value, but I consider it a good day's work if I get three pages done. I remember I used to do eight a day regularly. This present thing is growing like a coral reef. I am only up to page 130 after months of work. Still, the consolation is that the stuff seems good, and there is no hurry, as I am so much ahead of the game. But I wish now and then that I could strike one of those spots where the thing really flows.

The manageress here has a Peke called Ming, which I take for walks. Have you ever considered how odd it is that female Pekes don't like male Pekes? Just as chorus girls don't like chorus boys. If Wonder sees another dog miles away on the horizon, she races up to fraternize, but she takes no notice of Ming whatsoever, though he is a most attractive dog. On their walks together they never exchange a word.

Things seem pretty gloomy in England. Here they are distinctly better. For one thing, we find we can get ham, which makes an enormous difference to the budget. It means that, instead of getting soaked in the restaurant downstairs, we can dine for practically nothing in our room. Paris in the summer was full of fruit and vegetables. Meat was off the ration. In fact, I think France is picking up, though, of course, everything is terribly expensive.

Do you ever read John O'Hara? I have got his last book, *Pipe Night*. What curious stuff the modern American short story is. The reader has to do all the work. The writer just shoves down something that seems to have no meaning whatever, and it is up to you to puzzle out what is between the lines.

It must be quite a job, though, writing anything for the American magazines these days. Here is a cautionary manifesto which one of them has sent out to its contributors. The editor says he won't consider any of the following:

> Stories about gangsters, politics, regional problems. Stories with historical settings. Military stories, World War Two. Stories with a college background. Sex stories. Stories with smart-alec dialogue. Stories in which characters drink. Stories with a newspaper background. Dialect stories. Stories about writers or editors or advertising men. Radio stories. Stories about religion. Stories concerning insanity. Crime stories. Mistaken identity stories. Stories of the First World War. Stories about adolescent characters.

Apart from that, you're as free as the birds in the tree tops and can write anything you like.

What about that England team in Australia? I don't like the look of it. I don't think we shall ever get them out in a Test match. They were crazy not to take Billy Griffith along.

Pavillon Henri Quatre,
November 20th, 1946   *St Germain-en-Laye*

Isn't it odd, when one ought to be worrying about the state of the world and one's troubles generally, that the only thing I can think of nowadays is that Dulwich looks like winning all its school matches and surpassing the 1909 record (because now they play nine schools, and in 1909 it was only five). There are no papers published here on Sundays, so I had to wait till yesterday to go to Paris and get hold of a *Sunday Times* and learn the result of the Bedford match. It must have been a close thing. But I repeat, isn't it odd that after all these years one can still be as keen as ever on school football?

What you said about laughing immoderately over the prize-giving scene in *Right Ho, Jeeves* made me wince a bit, as I am headed for a similar scene in *The Mating Season*, and I'm haunted with an awful feeling that it is going to fall flat. The set-up is that Bertie has got to recite A. A. Milne's 'Christopher Robin' poems at a village concert, and I shall have to try to make the village concert a big scene. And at the moment I can't see how I am going to make it funny. Still, I suppose it will be all right when I get to it. It generally happens that after I have got momentum on in a story the various hurdles come easily. I haven't got down to thinking of the scene yet. Meanwhile, the story is coming out very well, though, as I told you in my last letter, slowly.

December 24th, 1946   *St Germaine-en-Laye*

It was a great relief to get your letter of December 8th and to hear that Rene was better. I was very worried after getting your first letter. I do hope that now she will be all right and that she won't find the conditions of life too much of a strain. Life is really terrible for women these days. (Wonder has just insisted on jumping on my lap, so I am finding it hard to type!)

It's curious how life nowadays has got down to simplicities. All that matters is three meals a day and light and warmth. Here we are all right for food, in fact extremely well off, but every Monday and Friday there is no electric light till six in the evening, which means that the heating subsides to nothing.

These last few days have been frightful, as I suppose they have been in England. The only person who seems to like the cold spell is the manageress's Peke. I take it out for a three-mile walk every day, and it races about like a greyhound, revelling in the cold.

I return the Rich & Cowan letter. Publishers do think up the darnedest objections to an author's book. As you say, how could David Copperfield possibly have remembered word for word the conversations he had with Mr Micawber, at the age of ten or thereabouts. They might just as well argue that in real life, when a man says, 'I am Hawkshaw, the detective!' or, 'So, Maria, it was really you, after all,' a curtain doesn't fall and cut off the reply. If you are going to bar all conventions in novels and plays; why should a novel or a play ever end?

I, too, have had my troubles. In *Joy in the Morning*, Bertie speaks of himself as eating a steak and Boko is described as having fried eggs for breakfast, and Grimsdick of Jenkins is very agitated about this, because he says the English public is so touchy about food that stuff like this will probably cause an uproar. I have changed the fried egg to a sardine and cut out the steak, so I hope the situation is saved. But I was reading Agatha Christie's *The Hollow*, just now, presumably a 1946 story, and the people in it simply gorge roast duck and soufflés and caramel cream and so on, besides having a butler, several parlour-maids, a kitchen-maid and a cook. I must say it encouraged me to read *The Hollow* and to see that Agatha was ignoring present conditions in England.

Do you ever write a book knowing that it will stand or fall by some chapter near the end? I'm up against that in *The Mating Season*. It's fine as far as I've got – about two-thirds of the way – but unless I can make the village concert chapter as funny as the prize-giving one in *Right Ho, Jeeves*, the thing will flop. At least, it won't exactly flop, because I pick up immediately after the concert with a lot of good stuff, but it needs a solid punch at that spot to make it perfect.

FIVE

1947–1952

February 14th, 1947   *St Germain*

I agree with you absolutely about cut-backs. I hate the type of
novel which starts off in childhood, so that you don't get to
the interesting stuff till about page 234. There is something,
too, about the cut-back in itself which is valuable. It gives the
reader a sort of double-angle. I mean, as he has become
absorbed with the story of old Jones as a grown-up and then
suddenly he gets a glimpse of him as a kid, and the fact that
he has been absorbed with him as a grown-up makes the kid
stuff twice as vivid as it would have been if simply dished up
as kid stuff at the start of the book. Rottenly put, but you know
what I mean. Denis Mackail works the thing in his new book,
Our Hero, but there he does it in alternate chapters. He gives
you a scene with his hero as of today, then the next chapter is
back in the fellow's childhood. It's very effective.

And now let us speak of parcels. As far as I can gather, the
entire postal service of the world has gone cock-eyed, though
I may be wronging the rest of the world and the fault may lie
entirely in France. If you sent me the second script last Saturday
why haven't I had it yet, today being Friday? And if Nelson
Doubleday sent me a parcel on November 27th, why did it
reach me on February 10th? And why hasn't another parcel
sent from England got here at all? My bet is that your first
script will eventually arrive. I hope you registered the second
one, as I believe they really do take a certain amount of trouble
over registered parcels.

Ethel came back from Paris yesterday bringing a book called

Night and the City by Gerald Kersh. Do you know his work? I have seen his name about in literary papers, but the only thing of his I had read was a short serial in *Collier's*. This book is terrific. Sordid to a degree, with only one moderately decent character in it, but tremendously gripping. An odd thing is that the book was published originally in 1938 by Michael Joseph and is now issued by Heinemann. I should imagine that what happened was this. M. Joseph sold about 2000 copies, and then called it a day and the plates or whatever they call them returned to the author. Then there were six years of war, ending with a general coarsening – or at any rate a toughening – of the public taste, and what was too sordid for them in 1938 is now just their dish. (For I gather that Kersh is the big noise of the moment.)

Ethel and I have our passage booked on the *America*, sailing April 18th.

Since I last wrote, things have been moving on the Low Wood front. Ethel has now decided to rebuild, so that we can live there. (We expect the French Government to chip in with something pretty good in the way of footing the bills, but we have to pay out first and then they pay us back.)

The catch is that the French Government is cagey. It says, 'Oh, so you lost all your baths, did you? Well, okay, here are some to replace them,' but whereas your baths were expensive jobs in pink and mauve and so on, the Government take the line that a bath is a bath and give you the cheapest available. Same with chairs. You lose your posh chair for which you paid a fortune, and they give you a kitchen chair, and when you kick, they say, 'Well, it's a chair, isn't it?' (Or, more probably, '*C'est une chaise, hein?*') So we shall have to dig down and pay the difference if we want the good stuff. Still, it'll be worth it, to have a home.

Wonder has just been discovered chewing tobacco on the floor.

April 1st, 1947   *St Germain*

I found your letter on my desk when I came in just now after taking Wonder for her walk, and am answering it two minutes after finishing reading it, which is quick service.

I shall be writing to you again before I leave, but meanwhile an address which will always find me in America is care of my lawyers (Perkins, Malone and Washburn) at 36 West 44th Street, New York City, 18. Of course, the moment I'm settled, I will let you know my address, but Washburn's last letter said that he was having some difficulty in finding a hotel.

The latest news, which will make you laugh, is this: Inquiries have revealed that throughout the war the American War Department was using my broadcasts in its Intelligence School at Camp Ritchie as models of anti-Nazi propaganda for the instruction of the lads they were teaching how to do it. Washburn in his last letter said that on March 24th he wrote to the War Department for further particulars, so I shall know more when he next writes. But it's funny, isn't it?

I'm so glad the new book is going well, but what bad news about the paper shortage crisis! It does seem a shame that when the public is snapping up books as they are the publishers can't produce them. Did I tell you that I broke off *The Mating Season* in order to rewrite that play which George Abbott turned down in 1945? I sweated blood over the play, and Marcel Bernard, the French Davis Cup player, took it over with him to New York. I have now got a letter from Abbott saying it is greatly improved, but I can't write plays without Guy.

Meanwhile, I have just had a letter from a New York manager saying he is putting on a piece by Molnár and Molnár thinks I am the only person capable of doing a decent adaptation of his stuff, and can I possibly get over in time to attend rehearsals and fix the thing up? They have just gone into rehearsal, so, of course, I shall arrive as they are finishing, but I have written saying that I shall be delighted to come on the road and do anything I can. So perhaps when I land in New York I shall have to go straight to Boston or somewhere. My adaptation in 1926 of Molnár's *The Play's the Thing* was a great success, and apparently he has never forgotten it. I met him once at the Casino in Cannes and he stopped the play at the table for about five minutes while he delivered a long speech in praise of me – in French, unfortunately, so I couldn't understand it, not being the linguist then that I am today.

About not being able to realize that other people have grown

older. Yes. I saw in the paper this morning something about
Ivor Novello: 'a lean Welshman of 54'. It seems incredible that
he can be that age. I thought he was about thirty. It's worse
with actresses. You do a play and think, 'the ingénue will be
a great part for Jane Jones,' and you suddenly realize that Jane
is now in the late fifties. I remember some years ago a grey-
haired matron accosting me in a restaurant, and she turned
out to be a girl who had been in the chorus of one of the shows
which I did with Guy Bolton and Jerry Kern at the Princess
Theatre.

I say, are you sure those specks that dance in front of one's
eyes are all right? Mine are pretty bad now, and I view them
with concern.

April 12th, 1947

My address in New York will probably be Savoy Plaza Hotel,
Fifth Avenue. At any rate to start with. The Savoy Plaza has
the enormous advantage that it is just opposite the Park, so
that airing Wonder (which is after all the most important
thing in life) will be simple.

Thank goodness my American income tax trouble has been
settled after dead silence on the part of the Tax Court since
October 1945! What happened was that the tax people suddenly got the idea that I had not paid taxes for 1921–1924, if you
can imagine it. They impounded all my money over there. The
Court now decides that I did pay tax in the years mentioned
(as of course I did, only naturally all records have been destroyed years ago). The net result of all the various cases is
that they will stick to about $20,000 and I shall get a refund
of about $19,000, and the extraordinary thing is that instead
of mourning over the lost $20,000 I am feeling frightfully rich,
as if I had just been left $19,000 by an uncle in Australia. I
find nowadays that any cash these Governments allow one to
keep seems like money for jam. Anyway, my whole financial
position in America has changed overnight, and instead of
landing without a penny and having to make a quick touch
from Doubleday or someone, I have become self-supporting.
Great relief.

What a business it is, making this trip to America. Poor

Ethel stayed up till six o'clock this morning, packing. The unfortunate thing is that she is buying some new clothes, not having had any for six years, and so has had to go to Paris every day. We have to get the heavy trunks off on Tuesday, and after that the situation ought to become simpler. I have just found that the train journey to Cherbourg takes six hours. Thank goodness we have a good stateroom. It would have been awful to have got on the boat all tired out and had to pig it. The great question now is can we by tipping right and left smuggle Wonder into our stateroom! I can't see her turning in for the night in a cage on a lower deck!

I wonder if you would like T. H. White's stuff. I love it. He started off with a beauty, *The Sword in the Stone*, and has just got one out called *Mistress Masham's Repose*, which I liked very much. They are sort of fairy stories, full of charm and lots of humour.

I find the only way to get anything to read nowadays is to go to a public library and browse round the shelves and get the sort of books nobody has ever heard of.

I have now completed *The Mating Season* all but the final chapter, which should be only three or four pages, but I can't seem to get the right kick-off for it. Do you have the same trouble with your stuff? I find the opening words of each chapter more difficult than anything. I shall probably have to wait and write it on board ship.

Hotel Weylin,
East 54th Street,
New York

May 15, 1947

Well, as you will have deduced from the above address, here I am in New York and still feeling a bit dizzy.

We had one of those rough voyages that the sailors in your books are always having on the western ocean, which seems unjust at this time of year. But the worst part was before it started. We arrived at Cherbourg and got on the tender and then we had a five hours' wait before the *America* turned up, it having been delayed by fog in the Channel. I've never felt so hungry in my life, not even at the Citadel of Huy. We just sat there, hour after hour, starving. We finally got aboard at ten o'clock at night and had a belated dinner, which was worth waiting for. Poor Wonder was carried off to a cage on the boat-deck, but next day we managed to sneak her down to our state-room, where she was as good as gold for the rest of the trip.

It's just ten years since I was last in New York. Scott Mere-dith, my agent, has sold a couple of my short stories, so I am hoping gradually to get back into the swim of things, though there are very few markets now for my type of work. Everything in the magazines has to be American nowadays and – as far as I can tell from a cursory glance – pretty bloody awful.

Did I ever tell you about Scott? An amazing chap. Only about twenty-five years old, but already one of the leading literary agents in New York. He started off as a writer at the age of fourteen, and by the time he was twenty had sold over 400 things to the *Saturday Evening Post* and other magazines. He then was in the army, and on coming out got a job with a moribund lit. agency which he and his brother subsequently bought with the bit of money they had been able to save. From then on he went steadily ahead, first with a tiny business and now with one that employs a whole squad of assistants. I don't know anyone I admire more. When I think how utterly incompetent I was at his age . . .! I suppose the sort of life he has had develops one quickly. He told me that he was in a school in Brooklyn when he was a boy, the personnel of which consisted almost entirely of negroes, and he had a fight with someone every day for four years. That kind of thing must toughen a chap!

It's quite a business arriving in New York now. In the old days the only newspaper man one saw was the ship reporter of the *NY Times*, who sauntered up as one was seeing one's stuff through the customs and asked if one had had a pleasant voyage, but now a whole gang of reporters flock aboard at Quarantine and a steward comes to you and tells you that the gentlemen of the press are in the saloon and request your presence. It's like being summoned before a Senate Committee.

I always get on well with reporters, and I found them very pleasant, especially the man from *PM*, one of the evening papers. We became inseparable and last Monday he gave a big dinner for Ethel and me at his house down in Greenwich Village.

My second morning I held a formal 'press conference' at the Doubleday offices, with a candid camera man taking surreptitious photographs all the time. These were the literary columnists. I am going to a cocktail-party at the house of one of them next week.

Next day I was interviewed on the radio, reaching 350 stations, and the day after that on television. All this sounds as if I were a hell of a celebrity, but the explanation is that Doubleday's publicity hound arranges it all in the hope that it will lead to the sale of a copy or two of *Joy in the Morning*. I don't suppose it helps a bit, really. I don't imagine the great public sits listening spellbound while I answer questions from the interlocutor, and says, 'My God! So that's Wodehouse! How intelligent he looks! What a noble brow! I must certainly buy that last book of his!' Much more probably they reach out and twiddle the knob and get another station.

Guy Bolton tells me that *Sally* is going to be revived with lyrics by me extracted from other Bolton-Wodehouse-Kern shows, and another management is doing *The Play's the Thing* with Louis Calhern in the Holbrook Blinn part, but apart from that I don't think there is much chance of theatrical work. The whole situation has altered completely since I was here last. There don't seem to be any regular managers now, the sort who used to put on their three or four shows every season. Today what happens is that some complete novice decides that he would like to have a pop, and he gets hold of a play and then passes the hat round in the hope of raising enough money to produce it. When it fails, he goes back into the suit and cloak trade.

How anybody ever does raise the money beats me, for today you need a minimum of $50,000 for a straight play with only one set and for a big musical anything from $250,000 up. Of course, if you get a colossal smash like *Oklahoma*, it doesn't take very long to get your money back at $6 or $7 per ticket, but with even a fairly successful show the position seems to me hopeless. A man who had put up some money for a musical that's running now showed me the week's balance sheet the other day. The gross box office receipts were $36,442.90 and the profit on the week was $3697.83. In other words they will have to go on doing nearly $37,000 a week for about seventy weeks before they can begin making anything. They start off by coughing up $10,000 for the rent of the theatre, then the company's salaries are another $10,000, the 'crew' takes $1700, the extra musicians $2200 and the authors and composer another $2200. You have to do $50,000 a week, like *Oklahoma*, if you're going to get anywhere.

The story of *Oklahoma* is quite a romance. Oscar Hammerstein, who adapted it from Lynn Riggs's *Green Grow the Lilacs*, had had no great success since he wrote *Show Boat* twelve years ago. The thing looked like a flop out of town and the Theatre Guild, which produced it, needed another $20,000 and couldn't raise it. They were about reconciled to calling it a day and closing, when someone thought of S. H. Behrman, the playwright. He had had some hits in the past with the Theatre Guild, so they went to him and pleaded with him for the sake of Auld Lang Syne to come to the rescue. Moved by their anguish, he wrote a cheque for $20,000 and got in return 10 per cent of the show. Then they opened in New York and were a sensation and have played to capacity ever since. Difficult to say how much Behrman will make out of it, but somewhere around half a million dollars, I suppose, which isn't bad on a $20,000 investment.

But the really romantic figure to me is Lynn Riggs. His original play was one of those sixty or seventy performances things, and he must have written it off as a complete loss. And then out of a blue sky it becomes a gold mine, for he can't be getting less than 1 per cent of the gross, more probably 2.

Talking of raising money in the theatre, there's a manager here who got a rich man to back a show by reading him Eugene O'Neill's *Hairy Ape*. The millionaire thought it sounded pretty good, and gladly coughed up. The manager then used the money to finance a bedroom farce he had written. The backer, seeing it on the first night, complained, 'But this isn't the show I originally heard.' 'Oh, well,' said the manager, 'you know how these things always get changed around a bit at rehearsals.'

New York is simply incredible. About five times larger than

when I last saw it. I said in my radio talk that every time I came back to New York it was like meeting an old sweetheart and finding she had put on a lot of weight. The prosperity stuns one after being in France so long. There is nothing in the way of food and drink you can't get here. And that brings me to a most important point. I want to start sending you food parcels, but before I do I should like to know what you and Rene are most in need of. I could put in a standing order with the British Food Parcels people, but the trouble with the British Food Parcels people is that they don't use their intelligence. When I was in France, I asked for tobacco, and they sent me a pound of it and a box of fifty cigars. Right. The happy ending, you would say. But mark the sequel. The following week another pound of tobacco and another box of fifty cigars arrived, and so on week after week, with the result that among my effects in storage in Paris are ten one-pound tins of tobacco and a ton of cigars. So I don't want to go wrong with your parcels. Just write and tell me what you particularly need.

(I'm glad the flannel bags arrived all right. Do you really mean to say they weren't long enough? They came up round my neck.)

2 East 86th Street,
New York

January 15, 1949

I have sent you – at enormous expense, $4, no less – a book that has headed the American best-seller list for months, *The Naked and the Dead*. I can't give you a better idea of how things have changed over here than by submitting that novel to your notice. It's good, mind you – in fact, I found it absorbing – but isn't it incredible that you can print in a book nowadays stuff which when we were young was found only on the walls of public lavatories. One thing which struck me about it – you'll get this letter weeks before you get the book, so all this won't make sense to you – is how little formal discipline there seems to be in the American Army. A lieutenant talking to a general never seems to call him 'sir', and so on. But whatever you think about the book, I'm sure it will interest you.

I have just received from the US Treasury a cheque for $4500. What it is and why they sent it, I simply can't imagine.

My lawyer says it's something to do with repaid interest on my 1941 tax. But the thing doesn't make sense. The Government put a lien on my money and won't let Doubleday pay me what they owe me till the last of the cases is settled, and at the same time they send me these doubloons. The more I have to do with Governments, the less I understand them. The result of my case before the Supreme Court isn't out yet, but I can't see why there should have been a case at all. The point at issue was, Does the money I got for *Saturday Evening Post* serials count as income? Any normal person would say, 'Yes, of course it does, what else do you think it was?' But the Government is solemnly deliberating the point and it's quite possible that they will refund me all the money I have paid in taxes on those serials. . . .

Practically all Governments ought to be in Colney Hatch.

March 30, 1949

The more I try to cope with the modern American magazine, the more I realize that if you are English it is terribly difficult to pretend in a story that you are American. I find that, if I try to, I get self-conscious. I realize now what stupendous luck I had, being able to get away with English stories in the old days. There are a few English writers whom the magazines will accept, like Gerald Kersh and Evelyn Waugh, but as a general rule they seem to insist on American stuff.

But what asses editors are! I met one at a cocktail-party the other day, and he asked me if I had any short stories that would suit him. I said I had a couple lying around and I sent them to him next day. He accepted them with enthusiasm, and it then turned out that Scott Meredith had offered them to him a month or two previously and he had refused them. They were the same stories – not a word changed – so how do you explain it? My considered opinion, after a careful study of today's American magazines, is that 90 per cent of the editors are cuckoo. I think that when one of them applies for a job on a magazine, they ask him, 'Any insanity in your family?' and if he says, 'You bet there is. My father thought he was Napoleon and nothing would convince my mother that she was not a teapot,' they engage him at a large salary.

The odd thing nowadays is that – except for Clarence

Budington Kelland – there seem to be no regular professional writers in the American magazine world. You never see a name you know. All the stories seem to be the work of amateurs who do one story and then are never heard of again.

I see that English nurses are protesting against the movie, *The Snake Pit*, because it represents nurses as hard and un-sympathetic. The curse of today is the Pressure Group, especi-ally in America. You can't take a step without getting picketed by someone. One odd aspect of it is that you can no longer put a negro on the stage unless you make him very dignified. Owing to the activities of the negro pressure group, comic negro characters are absolutely taboo. The result is that all the negro actors are out of work, because the playwrights won't write parts for them.

2 East 86th Street,
May 2nd, 1949   *New York*

Did I tell you that we were housing Guy Bolton's Peke, Squeaky, while Guy is in England? She is an enormous success, and Wonder gets on splendidly with her. She is an angel and loves everybody. She is pure white, and her way of expressing affection and joy is to scream like a lost soul, or partly like a lost soul and partly like a scalded cat. When the Boltons were in Hollywood, the neighbours on each side reported them to the authorities, saying that they had a small dog which they were torturing. They said its cries were heartrending. So a policeman came round to investigate, and Squeaky fortunately took a fancy to him and started screaming at the top of her voice, so all was well.

1000 Park Avenue,
June 20th, 1949   *New York*

Note new address. We now have what the licentious New York clubman has in the movies, a duplex Park Avenue penthouse. There is a room downstairs where I work, and upstairs a long gallery with French windows opening out on to our terrace, which is about the size of a small suburban garden. At the end of the terrace is a fence with a door in it, through which you get on the public roof of the building, invaluable for airing Wonder and Squeaky. We have fitted the terrace up with a big hedge, trees, geraniums, etc., and it looks wonderful. We have all our meals there, and at night I sit out there and read. We are very lucky in that there are no high buildings within two blocks, so we get a fine view of the park and perfect quiet. We are on the thirteenth floor, and at night we don't hear a sound. I never want to go away from the place, even in the summer.

We are only two blocks away from the best part of Central Park, where the reservoir is. I had never been up in the Eighties before – we are on 84th Street – and it is extraordinary how different it is from the rest of New York. It's almost like being in the country.

Squeaky refuses to leave me for an instant. She is under my desk now and has just shoved her head up, which means that I shall have to pick her up and try to write with her on my lap. She really is the most amiable dog in the world.

Great excitement yesterday. Ethel had left a melon to ripen on the terrace, and Wonder, apparently suspecting its intentions, started a fierce fight with it. She kept rushing at it, barking furiously, and then losing her nerve and jumping back ten feet. The melon preserved an unmoved calm throughout.

Story in the paper this morning. Wealthy-looking woman in mink coat gets on a Fifth Avenue bus, and looks about her amusedly. 'Goodness!' she says to the conductor as she gives him her fare. 'It does seem strange to be riding in a bus instead of in my car. I haven't ridden in a bus in two years.' 'You don't know how we missed you,' the conductor assured her.

1000 Park Avenue,
New York

December 13th, 1949

Sad bit of news in the *Herald-Tribune* this morning:

FAMED BRITISH MAGAZINE
GOES OUT OF BUSINESS

is the headline, and it goes on to say that the final number of the *Strand* will be published in March. As practically everything I have written since July, 1905, appeared in the *Strand*, I drop a silent tear, but I can't say I'm much surprised, for anything sicker-looking than the little midget it had shrunk to I never saw. Inevitably, I suppose, because of paper shortage. And in my opinion never anything worth reading in it, either, the last year or two.

How on earth does a young writer of light fiction get going these days? Where can he sell his stories? When you and I were breaking in, we might get turned down by the *Strand* and *Pearson's*, but there was always the hope of landing with *Nash's*, the *Story-teller*, the *London*, the *Royal*, the *Red*, the *Yellow*, *Cassell's*, the *New*, the *Novel*, the *Grand*, the *Pall Mall* and the *Windsor*, not to mention *Blackwood*, *Cornhill*, *Chambers's* and probably about a dozen more I've forgotten. I was looking at the book of acceptances and payments which I kept for the first five years of my literary career, and I note that in July, 1901, I sold a story to something called the *Universal and Ludgate Magazine* and got a guinea for it. Where nowadays can the eager beginner pick up £1 1s. one like that?

People wag their heads and tell you that what killed the English magazine was the competition of movies, motors, radio and so on, but, dash it, laddie, these things are not unknown in America, and American magazines still go merrily along with circulations of 3 and 4 million. My view is that the English magazine died of 'names' and what is known over here as 'slanting'.

The slanter, in case you don't know, is a bird who studies what editors want. He reads the magazines carefully, and slings in a story as like the stories they are publishing as he can manage without actual plagiarism. And the editors, if they are fatheads – and they nearly always were in the days I'm thinking of, say 'Fine!' and accept the things, with the result that after a while the public begin to find it a bit monotonous and stop buying.

Names, though, were almost as deadly as poison. The *Strand* was better than most of them, but practically every English magazine would buy any sort of bilge, provided it was by somebody with a big name as a novelist. The reason the *Saturday Evening Post* was always so darned good was that Lorimer never fell into this trap. Have you read *George Horace Lorimer and the 'Saturday Evening Post'* by a man named John Tebbel? Probably not, as I don't think it has been published in England. But here's what Tebbel says on page 241:

> No writer was bigger than the *Post*. If one chose to leave, there were always others to succeed him. Nor could he give any less than his best for the *Post*. Lorimer would not hesitate to turn down the work of the highest-paid writers if he thought it fell below standard. He read every contribution as though it were the first piece the writer had submitted.

That's absolutely true. Mary Roberts Rinehart in her *My Story* says, 'I once saw him turn down some stories by Rudyard Kipling, with the brief comment, "Not good enough." ' And Ben Ames Williams sold 162 stories to the *Post* between 1917 and 1936, but several of his things were rejected during that time. The Boss was an autocrat, all right, but my God, what an editor to work for. He kept you up on your toes. I had twenty-one serials in the *Post*, but I never felt safe till I got the cable saying each had got over with Lorimer.

1000 Park Avenue,
December 16th, 1949   *New York*

I returned this morning from Niagara Falls, where I crossed to the Canadian side, spent a couple of nights and came back into the USA on the quota, thus stabilizing my position and avoiding having to keep getting renewals of my visitor's visa. (I got three altogether, each for six months.)

What a business it is doing this sort of thing nowadays. I had to make three trips to Ellis Island, and I had to be there at nine in the morning, which meant that I woke myself up at four a.m. and stayed awake so as not to be late. The boats to Ellis Island run every hour. If you miss the return boat, you have to wait for another hour, and I always did miss it by a couple of minutes. And nowhere to go except the corridor and nothing to do except pace up and down it. If I never see Ellis Island again, it will be all right with me.

I also had to have X-rays done of my chest, I suppose to prove that there was nothing deleterious inside it. I took the X-rays home and stored them in a cupboard, and on arrival at the American Consul's at Niagara Falls found that I ought to have brought them with me and couldn't get my visa without them. It seemed for a moment what we French call an *impasse*, but fortunately the Consul was a splendid fellow and let me wire to the Ellis Island doctor, asking him to wire back that I was OK. When the doc's wire arrived, saying that my chest was the talk of New York and had five stars in Baedeker, I was given my visa. Next day the Consul drove me in his car to Buffalo, which saved me some tedious railway travelling, and I am now back home on the quota, so unless I plot to upset the American Government by violence – which I doubt if I shall do; you know how busy one is – I can't be taken by the seat of the trousers and slung out.

But, gosh, what a lot of red tape, as the man said when they tried him for murdering his wife. I remember the time when I would be strolling along Piccadilly on a Tuesday morning and suddenly say to myself, 'I think I'll go to America,' and at noon on the Wednesday I would be on the boat en route for New York. No passports, no visas, nothing. Just like that.

I always find a great charm in Canada, and sometimes toy with the idea of settling there. The last time I was there was when I came back from Hollywood, in 1931, and spent a very pleasant day with Stephen Leacock. I liked him enormously, and felt sad to think that in all probability two such kindred spirits would never set eyes on each other again. (We didn't.)

1000 Park Avenue,
New York

May 2nd, 1950

Two interesting lunches this week. The first was with Michael Arlen, whom I had run into one day when I was having a bite at the Colony with Evelyn Waugh. Talking of Arlen, I always remember the time when we were out on the road with one of the Princess shows and one of those small-town know-it-alls fastened on to Guy and me in Utica, I think it was, and started gassing about how he was just like that with all the celebrities in the literary world. I asked him if he knew Michael Arlen, and he said, 'Michael Arlen? Do *I* know Michael Arlen? I should say I do. Wild Irishman. Nice fellow, but like so many of these Irish, too belligerently patriotic.'

The reason I bring M.A. up is that, if you'll believe me, he hasn't written a line in the last fifteen (I think he said) years. He says business men retire, so why shouldn't an author retire? How he fills in his time, I don't know. Can you imagine yourself not writing for fifteen years?

The other lunch I had was with Molnár, if you could call it having lunch with Molnár. When I arrived at one o'clock at the little Italian restaurant on 58th Street, he was there all right, but he had done his stoking-up at eleven, so I tucked in by myself with him looking on and encouraging me with word and gesture. For the last few years he has lived at the Plaza Hotel on 59th Street, and he never moves off the block where the Plaza is. He goes to bed at nine, gets up at five, has a cup of coffee and writes till eleven, when he toddles round to this Italian restaurant – never going off the pavement which runs to Sixth Avenue and down to 58th – has his lunch and then toddles back and is in for the night. Central Park is just across from the Plaza, but he never sets foot inside it. As I say, he doesn't move off the pavement – ever. An old friend of his from Buda-Pesth had trouble with his wife the other day, and as it was in all the papers and he knew Molnár must have heard about it, he was hurt that Molnár didn't come to see him and console him, and wrote him a stiff letter, reproaching him. 'My dear fellow,' Molnár wrote back, 'I am a very nervous man. I fear this New York traffic. You cannot expect me to risk driving through it in a cab every time your wife deceives you.'

Well, there's one thing to be said for being in the New York theatre world – you meet such interesting people.

I am always terribly sorry for Molnár. What he wants is the *café* life of Buda-Pesth – it no longer exists, of course – and I can see he is miserable in New York. He is homesick all the time, and nothing to be done about it. Also, these modern managers look on him as a back number and won't do his plays. I have adapted two of them – *Arthur* and *A Game of Hearts* – and I don't think there is an earthly chance of them being put on. *Arthur* has a different (and elaborate) set for each of the three acts, and the cost of producing it would be prohibitive.

Long silence on my part due to the fact that I have only just got back from my travels. I can't remember if I told you that I had written a play. (Not the one I sent to George Abbott, another one.) Anyway, I had, and a management decided to try it out on what they call the 'straw hat circuit' here – i.e. the summer resorts. A good many of these summer resorts have theatres now, and it is a good way of trying out a new play. You go from spot to spot, playing a week at each.

We went first to Skowhegan, Maine, rehearsed eleven days and opened at the wonderful theatre they have there. But before proceeding I must tell you a story a Maine man I met at Skowhegan, Maine, told me about a Maine farmer. The farmer's wife, it seems, was subject to fits, and the farmer used to get very fed up because people were always calling him in from his work when they came on, and by the time he reached the house she would be all right again. So time went on, and one day he was busy ploughing, when someone shouted to him, 'Go to the house quick, Joe, your wife is in a bad way.' And this time, when he got to the house, he found her lying dead on the kitchen floor. 'Well,' he said, 'that's more like it.'

Right. Where were we? Skowhegan, Maine. We did our eight performances, and on the Saturday the management informed us that our next port of call would be Watkins Glen, New York. We would drive there in a couple of station wagons. No one seemed to know anything about Watkins Glen. 'Somewhere near here?' we asked. 'Oh, pretty near,' said the management. About 650 miles, they thought. Or it might be 700.

So on the Sunday morning we started off. We got up at five-thirty, stopped in Skowhegan for a bite of breakfast, and then off through New Hampshire, Vermont and Massachusetts. It was a great moment when we crossed the Massachusetts border into New York state, because there we could get a drink, a thing barred elsewhere on Sundays. (By the way, in Maine you may drink sitting down, but you mustn't drink standing up. If you are having a snifter and start to your feet to welcome an old friend who has entered the bar, you must be careful that you aren't holding your glass as you do so, because if you are, you're breaking the law and rendering yourself liable to a big fine.)

So picture us, *mon vieux*, tooling on and on through the long summer day on a journey about the equivalent in England of starting at Land's End and finishing up somewhere near the Hebrides. I enjoy my little bit of motoring as a rule, but it's a pretty gruesome experience to realize, after you have gone 300 miles, that you have scarcely scratched the surface, so to speak, and there are still another 400 to go. Even assuming, mind you, that there was such a place as Watkins Glen. We only had the management's word for it, and they might quite easily have made a mistake.

Years ago, when I had a penthouse apartment on the twenty-second floor of an office building on East 41st Street, I became temporary host to an alley cat which I had found on the front doorstep resting up after what must have been the battle of the century. I took him in, and for a few days he was a docile and appreciative guest, seeming to have settled down snugly to bourgeois respectability and to be contented with regular meals and a spacious roof for purposes of exercise. There, you would have said, was a cat that had dug in for the duration.

But all the while, it appeared, the old wild life had been calling to him, and one morning he nipped out of the door and headed for the open spaces. And not having the intelligence to ring for the lift, he started to walk downstairs.

I stood above and watched him with a heavy heart, for I knew that he was asking for it and that remorse must inevitably creep in. And so it proved. For the first few floors he was jauntiness itself. He walked with an air, carrying his tail like a banner. And then suddenly – it must have been on floor twelve – I could see the thought strike him like a bullet that this was going on for ever and that he had got to Hell and was being heavily penalized for not having been a better cat. He sat down and stared bleakly into an eternity of going on and on and arriving nowhere. If ever a cat regretted that he had not stayed put, this cat was that cat.

After 300 miles in that station wagon, I could understand just how he had felt.

Well, sir, it turned out that there really was a place called

Watkins Glen, and we reached it at four in the morning. We stayed there a week, playing in the High School Auditorium with an enormous basketball arena behind the stage. This rendered the show completely inaudible. We then went on to Bradford, a journey of 150 miles, where we got a theatre but ran into Old Home Week, with the entire population dancing in the streets and refusing to come anywhere near our little entertainment, with the result that we played to about $11 on eight performances. The management then announced that on the Sunday we would be leaving for Chicago. 'Isn't that rather far?' we asked. 'Far?' they said. 'What do you mean, far? It's only about 1000 miles.'

At this point I put the old foot down firmly. I said I wished them well and would follow their future career with considerable interest, but I was going back to New York. Which I did. The unfortunate company went off in an aeroplane, and I never saw them again, for from Chicago they went to Easthampton, Long Island – 1200 miles – and when I motored to Easthampton the Friday before Labour Day, I found there wasn't a bed to be had in the place, so twenty minutes after arrival I motored back again.

I was told later that I hadn't missed much. Our star had laryngitis and was inaudible, and the principal comic character started drinking, became violent, wrecked the house where he was staying and was taken to prison. The police let him out each night to play his part and on Saturday for the matinée, and then took him back to the jug again.

The net result is that unless I can find another management to put on the show – say one that was dropped on its head as a baby and is not too bright – it may be considered dead. I see now that the trouble with it was the same that James Thurber found in a play of his when he analysed it.

'It had only one fault,' he said, 'it was kind of lousy.'

1000 Park Avenue,
New York

October 30th, 1950

The night before last I was interviewed on the radio by none other than Mrs Franklin D. Roosevelt. A charming woman, and I would have liked to have lolled back in my chair afterwards and had a long and interesting conversation about life in the White House. Unfortunately she threw me out on my ear the moment the thing was over – we did it on a record for release in a couple of weeks – because John Steinbeck had come in to do his interview. I think my performance was adequate. We kidded back and forth with quite a bit of *élan* and *espièglerie*, and I wound up by telling that story about the woman who sat next to me at dinner and said how much her family admired my work, my invariable procedure when interviewed on the radio.

Why does one always say the wrong thing? Just to put him at his ease and to show him that my heart was in the right place, I said to John Steinbeck, 'And how is your play going, Mr Steinbeck?' he having had one produced a day or two before. He gave me a long, wan, sad look and made no reply. I then remembered reading in the paper that it had come off after four performances.

How did you like Raymond Chandler's book? Denis Mackail sent me his new one, which I liked very much. The other day I got hold of a book called *Brimstone in the Garden*, by Elizabeth Cadell, which I liked so much that I bought everything she has written. They are gentle English character stuff with lots of comedy, rather like Margery Sharp. (Making four times in five lines that I've used the word 'like'. Thank goodness one doesn't have to polish a letter.)

It's hard to say whether what you say – there I go again – about the English being disliked in New York is exaggerated or not. I fancy someone like one of your sailors, mixing with the tougher elements of the community, would have unpleasant experiences which someone like the Marquis of Milford Haven, mixing with the rich, wouldn't. Living as I do in the Eighties, which is a sort of village where one knows everybody, I find everyone very friendly. You find a lot of anti-British sentiment in some of the papers. On the other hand, you get a book like *Assignment to Austerity*, by the London correspondent of the *New York Times*, and it raves about the English character and virtues. It's all very puzzling. But don't you think that everybody except you and me hates everybody else's guts nowadays? I don't imagine Americans dislike Englishmen any more than they dislike Americans.

By the way, I have just heard from Watt that the BBC want to do my *Damsel in Distress* on their Light Programme. Always up to now they have told him that nothing by P. G. Wodehouse would even be considered. Well, what I'm driving at is that I had always said to myself, 'One of these days the BBC will come asking for something of mine, and then won't I just draw myself up to my full height and write them a stinker saying that after what has occurred I am amazed – nay, astounded – at their crust – etc. etc. Of course what actually happened was that I wrote to Watt saying Okay, go ahead.

The story to which Plum refers was of a nice old lady who sat next to him at dinner one night and raved about his work. She said that her sons had great masses of his books piled on their tables, and never missed reading each new one as it came out. 'And when I tell them,' she concluded, 'that I have actually been sitting at dinner next to Edgar Wallace, I don't know what they will say.'

1000 Park Avenue,
March 8th, 1951   *New York*

Do you remember a year or so ago my telling you about a giddy attack I had? I got all right in a day and had no more trouble. But about three weeks ago I suddenly got another. This was on a Sunday. On the Monday I felt fine, went for a five-mile walk and went to the dentist and so on. Then on the Tuesday after lunch, still feeling all right, I started to walk down to change my library books, and I had got to 82nd Street and Park Avenue when, without any warning, I suddenly felt giddy again. (At least, it's not exactly giddiness. The scenery doesn't get blurred or jump about. It's just that I lose control of my legs.) Well, Park Avenue fortunately is full of doctors, and I groped my way to the nearest, about half a dozen yards. I had great luck, as I happened to hit on one of the best doctors in New York, quite a celebrated man who attends Gertrude Lawrence, Oscar Hammerstein and other nibs.

Since then I have been taking every known form of test, and the general view is that I have got a tumour on the brain. If this is correct, it is presumably the finish, as I don't suppose I can survive a brain operation at my time of life.

1000 Park Avenue,
March 14th, 1951   *New York*

After a great many consultations and more tests, including that ghastly job of taking fluid out of the spine, the docs have decided that I have not got a tumour on the brain. (And, I have been feeling recently, not much brain for it to be on.) Nobody seems actually to know what is the matter and there is a school of thought which says it's probably my eyes. I never know what oculists mean when they talk technical language, but mine says my eyes are 'off' fifteen points or degrees or something. This, I take it, is not so hot, and I'm wishing I had never read *The Light that Failed*. The score, then, to date is that I am deaf in the left ear, bald, subject to mysterious giddy fits and practically cock-eyed. I suppose the moral of the whole thing is that I have simply got to realize that I am a few months off being seventy. I had been going along as if I were in the forties, eating and drinking everything I wanted to and smoking far too much. I had always looked on myself as a sort of freak whom age could not touch, which was where I made my ruddy error, because I'm really a senile wreck with about one and a half feet in the grave.

(My doctor, by the way, summing up on the subject of the giddy fits and, confessing his inability to explain them, said, 'Well, if you have any more, you'd better just *have* them.' I said I would.)

We now come to the subject of basketball, a game unknown in England – hence the term 'Merrie England' – but played throughout America in schools and colleges between the football and baseball seasons. At each end of the arena is a basket, perched high up on the wall, and the object of the game is to throw the ball into these. It sounds silly, and it is silly. Well-obviously, then, the taller you are, the easier it is for you to basket the ball, and the various teams scour the country for human giraffes, who can just walk up and drop it in. And now the gamblers have turned their attention to the game and basketball scandals are popping up all over the place.

All of which is leading up to an article John Lardner has in one of the weekly papers this week. Apparently the head man of the Littlewood pools stated in an interview that England has been shocked by the news of these basketball 'fixes'.

'We don't fix amateur sports in England,' he said.

Lardner writes:

To summarize conditions to date, then, England is (1) honest, but, (2) shocked. But I would like to tell the story of a college basketball game that was not fixed, some years ago. It seems that there was a fellow who went out on the street and met a tall man. The fellow stuck $500 in the man's pocket, which he could just reach, and whispered hoarsely, through a megaphone, 'The spread tonight against Kansas City is eight points.'

'Oh, is it?' said the tall man politely. 'Well, so long,' and he went down to the railroad station, bought a ticket to Albany, settled in that city as part owner of a coal and ice business, and lived happily ever afterwards.

Basketball would be wholly honest if more people worked like that, because it is the wrong way to fix a game. For textbook purposes, the principle might be stated thus: You cannot assume that every tall man you see is a basketball player. Some of them are deadbeats, some are taxidermists, and some are wearing elevator shoes.

John Lardner is the son of Ring Lardner, one of the most formidable blokes I ever met. He was at least eight feet high, with a grim, poker face, like Buster Keaton's. When you spoke to him, he never uttered but just stood staring coldly over your head. I sometimes think he must have been the hero of the story I once heard Clarence Budington Kelland tell. Late one night this fellow rang the bell of a neighbour's house, and the neighbour, donning bathrobe and slippers, went downstairs and let him in, and it was apparent to him right away that the visitor had recently been hoisting a few.

'Hello,' said the householder. 'Nice evening.' No answer. 'What keeps you out so late?' No answer. 'Have a drink?' No answer. 'Have a cigar?' No answer.

The belated guest then sat down and stared at his host for two hours without saying a word, and the host finally went to sleep in an armchair. He awoke as dawn was breaking, to find his guest still sitting and staring at him. Finally the guest broke his long silence.

'Say, why the hell don't you go home and let a man go to bed?' he said.

The only thing that makes me doubtful about it being Ring Lardner is that final speech. I don't believe Ring ever said as many words as that at one time in his life.

John Lardner is quite different, very genial and pleasant. I had lunch with him the other day and was dying to ask him if his father had ever spoken to him, but hadn't the nerve.

1000 Park Avenue,
May 11th, 1952   *New York*

Life in New York continues jolly, but it would be much jollier if it wasn't for the ruddy Crime Wave. The liquor store a few blocks up from where we are was held up a few days ago, also a hotel which is even nearer, and last week Ethel was held up at a dressmaker's on Madison Avenue. She was in the middle of being fitted, when a man came in brandishing a large knife and asked for contributions. He got $18 off Ethel and disappeared into the void. Wonder, who had accompanied Ethel, slept peacefully throughout.

This seems to have been one of those routine business transactions, conducted – like conferences between statesmen – in a spirit of the utmost cordiality, but the binge at the hotel was very stirring. At half-past five in the morning a gang of six ankled in with the idea of cracking the hotel safe, unaware that there was a cop on the premises having a wash and brush-up in the basement. He emerged just as the intruders were telling the night clerk at the desk to put his hands up, and started shooting in all directions. The gang started shooting back, and things were getting brisk, when more policemen arrived and eventually three of the blokes were captured on the roof and the other three in the beauty parlour.

'There was about a million bucks in the place, the way we had it figured,' one of the bandits said, as they loaded him into the wagon. 'It's too bad,' he added, probably clicking his tongue a bit, 'that this young cop went and ruined everything.'

They are very strong over here for what is known as the parole system. Some enterprising person is caught burgling a bank and sentenced to seven years in the coop. After about six months he is released on parole and immediately goes off and burgles another bank. He then gets ten years and six months later is again released on parole, when he immediately. . . . But you get the idea. It must be a dog's life running a bank in these parts. Never a peaceful moment.

Listen Bill. If you want to make a pot of money, come over here and go into domestic service. You can't fail to clean up.

A man and his wife came here from England some years ago and got a job as butler and cook at $200 a month plus their board and lodging. They were able to salt away $150 each pay day. After they had been in this place for a while they accepted an offer from a wealthier family at $300. They had two rooms and bath and everything they wanted in the way of food and wines and were able to put away $250 a month.

About a year later their employer made the mistake of entertaining a Hollywood producer for the weekend, and the producer was so struck by the couple's virtuosity that he lured them away with an offer of $400, to include all expenses plus a car. They now banked $350 a month. And when a rival producer tried to snatch them, the original producer raised their salary to $500, at which figure it remains at moment of going to press. They now own an apartment house in Los Angeles.

We have had a series of blisters – both white and black – in our little home, each more incompetent than the last and each getting into our ribs for $60 a week – which tots up to something over £1000 a year – in spite of the fact that Ethel does all the real work with some slight assistance from me. 90 per cent of them have been fiends in human shape, our star exhibit being dear old Horace, a coloured gentleman of lethargic disposition who scarcely moved except to pinch our whisky when we were out. We had laid in a stock of Haig and Haig Five Star for guests and an inferior brand for ourselves, and after it had been melting away for a week or two, we confronted Horace. 'Horace,' we said, 'you've been stealing our Haig and Haig and, what's more, you've also been stealing our. . . .' He gave us a look of contempt and disgust. 'Me?' he said. 'I wouldn't touch that stuff. I only drink Haig and Haig Five Star.' Well, nice to think that we had something he liked.

I heard of some people here who engaged a maid who had just come over from Finland. She seemed a nice girl and willing, but it turned out that there were chinks in her armour. 'How is your cooking?' they asked. She said she couldn't cook. At home her mother had always done all the cooking. 'How about house work?' No, she couldn't do house work – back in Finland her aunt had attended to all that sort of thing – nor could she look after children, her eldest sister's speciality. 'Well, what *can* you do?' they asked. She thought for a moment. 'I can milk reindeer,' she said brightly.

So if you can milk reindeer, come along. Wealth and fame await you.

June 20th, 1952   *Remsenburg,*
                                     Long Island

The above is where we have just bought a house. When writing, address the letter 'Remsenburg, LI' because it's one of those primitive hamlets where you don't have a postman, but go and fetch your mail from the post office.

Guy Bolton has a house here, and Ethel and I have been staying with him and Virginia, as Guy and I were writing a play together. While we were working, Ethel explored the neighbourhood and came back one evening to say that she had bought this house. It's at the end of what is picturesquely known as Basket Neck Lane, and has five acres of ground which lead down, through a wood, to a very attractive creek. Unfortunately one can't bathe in the creek, as it is full of houses. Which sounds peculiar, but what happened was that when that hurricane hit Long Island a few years ago it uprooted all the houses on the shore and blew them into the bay, whence they drifted into our creek and sank. So if I dived in, I would probably bump my head on a kitchen or a master's bedroom. I do my bathing at Westhampton, about four miles away, where one gets the ocean.

The play looks good. We wrote it with London in mind, not

New York, and Klift and Rea are going to put it on next year some time. I am now turning it into a novel called *Ring for Jeeves*. Our original title was *Derby Day*, but someone has told us that that was used for a film. It's too English to have a chance here, I think. It's about a hard-up young peer who becomes a Silver Ring bookie.

Guy, who always likes to have something to occupy his time, is also writing two musicals and a straight play, and weird collaborators keep turning up here to confer with him. One of them used to be a taxi-driver. He was always thinking of funny gags and, when one day Eddie Cantor happened to take his cab, he sprang a dozen or so of his best ones on him, and Cantor was so impressed that he engaged him as one of his official gag writers. Since when this chap – Eddie Davis his name is – has never looked back. During the war he had an idea for a musical comedy, but was, of course, incapable of writing it by himself, so the management called Guy in and the thing ran two years. Eddie has the invaluable gift of being able to raise money. He belongs to some strange club in the heart of Broadway where he is always meeting men who are eager to put $100,000 into a show. So they have collected the $200,000 they need for this one, and it is now simply a matter of waiting till they can get a satisfactory cast.

I say 'simply', but, my gosh, there's nothing simple about casting a play for Broadway nowadays. Everybody you want is either in Hollywood or has a television contract he can't break. I can't remember if I told you about that play of mine, the one I made into my novel, *The Old Reliable*. I wrote about six versions of it, but couldn't get it right, and finally handed it over to Guy, who wrote almost a completely new play, which was wonderful. We have a manager, and he has the money, and Joe E. Brown wants to star in it, but everything has been held up because Brown has this television show of his. So we shall have to wait till the autumn of 1953. It makes one sigh for the old days when actors needed jobs.

Remsenburg,
LI

August 11th, 1952

We are down here till the cold weather starts, when we shall return to 1000 Park Avenue with Squeaky, two kittens and a foxhound.

I went up to New York for a few days while Ethel stayed here to see the furniture put in. I rang her up one night and asked how things were going, and she said everything looked pretty smooth. 'But,' she added in a melancholy voice, 'a foxhound has turned up.' It seems that she was just warming to her work when she looked round and there was this foxhound. It came into the garden and sat down, looking on. It was in an advanced state of starvation, and so covered with ticks that it took two hours to get them off. These beastly ticks get on the dogs and swell to the size of marbles. The poor animal had hardly any blood left in him, and had to be taken to the vet for transfusions.

When I came down, he was quite restored and full of beans. We can't imagine where he came from. He is a beautiful dog and an expert here tells us that he is one of the famous Colonel Whacker hounds from Kentucky. There are one or two packs on Long Island, and I suppose he must have strayed. He had evidently been wandering in the woods for days, getting nothing to eat and accumulating ticks.

The next thing that happened was that we went to a man's birthday party in Quogue and somebody had given him two guinea hens as a present. Ethel asked him what he was going to do with them, and he said, 'Eat 'em.' Ethel was horrified, and asked if she could have them. So we took them away and built a large run for them in the garden; and they settled down very happily.

A few nights later we heard something crying in the dark and went out and there was a tiny white kitten. This was added to the strength.

About a week after that I was walking to get the mail when I saw a car ahead of me suddenly swerve and it seemed to me that there was a small dark object in the middle of the road. I went up, and it was a black kitten. I picked it up and put it on my shoulder, and it sang to me all the way to the post office and back, shoving its nose against my face. It, too, has been added to the menagerie, so the score now is one foxhound, two guinea hens, Squeaky, and two kittens, and we are hourly expecting more cats and dogs to arrive. I think the word must have gone round the animal kingdom that if you want a home, just drop in at Basket Neck Lane, where the Wodehouses keep open house.

The bright side is that all our animals get along together like sailors on shore leave. Bill, the foxhound, has the most angelic disposition and lets the kittens run all over him, while Squeaky of course would never dream of hurting anything. A very united family, thank goodness.

As soon as I have got this novel out of the way, Guy and I are going to start writing our reminiscences of the New York theatre. It is now just forty years since we started working on Broadway, during which time we wrote twenty-three shows together and met every freak that ever squeaked and gibbered along the Great White Way, so it ought to make an interesting book. It may turn out something which we can publish only in America, but I don't think so, as there will be a lot of London stuff in it, so many of our shows having been produced in England.

The drawback to Remsenburg is the mosquitoes and the ticks. We have had a very hot summer and the mosquitoes have rolled up in droves. Fortunately, the tick season isn't a very long one – it ought to be over by next month – but while it lasts things are very strenuous. Everybody tells me that these ticks don't fasten on to human beings, but they seem to be saying 'Who made that rule?' because twice this week I have been horrified by finding them glued to my person, enlarged to bursting point.

1000 Park Avenue
New York

September 10th, 1952

Up in New York for a few days, then back to Remsenburg.

Have you a television set? I always swore I would never get one, but finally yielded, so now I am in a position to see all the films of 1930, each of which seems to have been shot through a blinding snowstorm. What a loathsome invention it is. You hear people say it's going to wipe out books, theatres, radio and motion pictures, but I wonder. I don't see how they can help running out of material eventually. The stuff they dish out is bad enough now, and will presumably get worse. (Not that you can go by what I predict. I was the man who told Alexander Graham Bell not to expect too much of that thing he had invented called the telephone or some such name, as it could never be more than an amusing toy.)

There's only one thing worth watching on television – even when I am appearing on it – and that's the fights. Those are superb. They have them every Friday, and you get a much better view than if you were in a ringside seat. The second Joe Louis–Jersey Joe Walcott fight cured me of attending these binges in person. Ethel and I bought a couple of seats for some enormous price, and found that they were about a mile and a quarter away from the ring. (This was an open-air bout at the Yankee Stadium.)

Talking of fights, is there a short story for you in this thing I read in the paper the other day? It was very long, but I'll try to condense it.

College Inn, Chicago, the year Jack Johnson beat Jeffries. (In case you've forgotten, Johnson was the negro who had won the heavyweight championship by knocking out Tommy Burns, and Jeffries was the White Hope, who was coming back to the ring to regain the supremacy for the Caucasian race, and all that sort of thing.) Well, anyway, there was a gang of newspaper men who lunched at the College Inn every day, among them a chap called Lou Housman who was going to Jeffries's training camp to report on his progress till the day of the fight. He said as he was leaving, 'Don't any of you bet a dollar till you hear from me. As soon as I decide how the thing's going to go, I'll wire Billy Aaronson.' Billy Aaronson was the head waiter at the College Inn.

Well, Housman went off to Nevada to the Jeffries camp, and a week later Aaronson suddenly dropped dead. A new man, Marcel, succeeded him. And one night Marcel came in with a telegram.

'I don't get this,' he said. 'I open all wires addressed to Aaronson, because they keep coming to him from people wanting reservations who don't know he's dead. But this one is different.'

He showed them the telegram. It ran:

AARONSON
COLLEGE INN
SHERMAN HOTEL,
CHICAGO.
BLACK. — LOU.

Well, of course, the newspaper men knew that it meant that
Housman was sure Johnson was going to win, and they had
complete faith in his judgement, so they went out and put their
shirts on Johnson. And they also made up a pool and betted it
for Aaronson's widow. The fight came off. Johnson knocked
Jeffries out. They all cleaned up big.

Days went by. They knew Housman must be back in
Chicago, but nobody saw him. He didn't come to the College
Inn. And then, about two weeks later, one of them bumped
into him and he confessed.

'I hadn't the nerve to face you fellows,' he said. 'I was so sure.
I thought I knew it all. I shouldn't have dragged you boys in
with me!'

'What do you mean?' his friend said. 'We were all set to bet
on Jeffries, when your wire switched us. We made a killing on
Johnson.'

'On Johnson? Didn't Aaronson explain?'

His friend told him of Aaronson's death, and said that the
wire had reached them and they had bet accordingly.

Housman nearly swooned.

'When I said good-bye to Billy that night,' he said, 'I gave
him a code. I didn't want the telegraph office there or here to
know my pick. So we arranged that "white" would mean
Johnson and "black" would mean Jeffries. I didn't think
Johnson had a chance.'

Can you do anything with that? Wouldn't O. Henry have
jumped at it!

1000 Park Avenue,
November 18th, 1952   *New York*

Life, always difficult, has been much complicated of late by the
eccentricities of Bill the foxhound. We brought him up from
Remsenburg, having nobody to leave him with down there, and

he decided right away that city life was not for him. Alighting from the car, he flatly refused to enter our apartment house, evidently suspecting a trap. With a terrific expenditure of energy I dragged him as far as the lift, and again he jibbed. I finally got him in, and he then refused to emerge. Assisted by the lift man, I got him out, and he then stoutly declined to go through our door, which he obviously assumed led to the Den of the Secret Nine. When the time came to take him for an airing, he refused to go out of the door, into the lift, out of the lift, across the lobby and out of the front door, and on returning from our stroll showed the same disinclination to go through the front door, across the lobby, into the lift, out of the lift and through our door.

This went on for about a week, when he suddenly decided that his fears had been ill-founded and that there were no plots against his person. The only trouble is that he now wants to be taken for a walk every quarter of an hour or so, and I see no prospect of ever doing any more work. I take him for a mile hike before breakfast, a three miler in the afternoon and perhaps another mile after dinner. It's doing wonders for my figure, of course, but it has made me practically a spent force as a writer.

Though I sometimes wonder if I really am a writer. When I look at the sixty-odd books in the shelf with my name on them, and reflect that 10 million of them have been sold, it amazes me that I can have done it. I don't know anything, and I seem incapable of learning . . . I feel I've been fooling the public for fifty years.

I mean, take that prison camp, for instance. I was cooped up for a year with 1300 men of all trades and professions and nothing to do all day but talk to them and find out about their jobs, and I didn't bring a thing away with me. You in a similar position would have collected material enough for twenty novels. There is this, of course, to be said in excuse for me, that it takes a steam drill to extract anything of any interest from anyone. I tried to get some inside stuff from a man who ran a hotel in Boulogne – just my dish, I thought – and all he could tell me was that sometimes a customer asked him to have a drink. You can't make a powerful 80,000 word novel out of that.

I met a woman the other day whom I used to know back in 1912 or thereabouts, and she said, 'Why don't you write about *real* things?' 'Such as?' I asked. 'Well, my life, for instance.' 'Tell me all about your life,' I said. And she thought for a while and came up with the hot news that when in Singapore during the war she had gone about with a tin helmet on her head. I explained to her that that would be terrific for – say – the first 20,000 words, but that after that one would be stuck.

Talking of war and prison camps, I am sending you the script of my Camp book. I ought to have let you have it years ago, but in some mysterious way all the copies disappeared. I have now found one *chez* my lawyer. It will never be published, but I hope it will amuse you. I wrote it at Tost after I had finished *Money in the Bank*, except of course for the diary stuff about my life at the Citadel of Huy, which was jotted down day by day during my stay there.

I naturally read the Camp book – Plum had given it the title of *Wodehouse in Wonderland* – with intense interest. If the book is never to be published, that, of course, is that. But I propose to give here some extracts from it, beginning with – what he calls 'the diary stuff' about life at the Citadel of Huy.

SIX

Huy Day by Day

August 3rd

First night at Huy. Arrived four-thirty. Glad to be out of our cattle trucks, but things don't look too good. They have put forty of us in a room large enough for about fifteen. No beds. Not even straw on the floor. I am writing this at eight-thirty, half an hour before lights out, and it looks as if we should have to sit up all night.

August 4th

Our first night was not so bad as I had thought it was going to be. At the last moment we were moved into a larger room, and somebody suddenly remembered that there was straw in the cellars, so we went and fetched it – 110 steps down and ditto up. There was only enough to form a very thin deposit on the floor, and it stank to heaven. Still, it was straw. No blankets. I slept in flannel trousers, shirt, sweater and my red cardigan, using my other trousers, my grey cardigan and my suitcase as a pillow.

Parade was at eight-thirty on the first morning. The morning was given up to cleaning. We cleaned passages and wash-rooms. It is gradually borne in on me that we are a ruddy peripatetic fatigue party. We cleaned up Liège barracks and they moved us on, and now we shall presumably clean up the Citadel of Huy and move on again. By the time we have finished, you will be able to eat your dinner off Belgium.

A nasty jolt for our sensibilities today. We hear that all the Germans have been able to get for us in the way of food tomorrow is fourteen kilos of macaroni.

August 6th

Rumour proved true. Our buckets contained a sort of sweet hot water with prunes floating in it. I have seldom tasted anything so loathsome, but it was really rather a *tour de force* on the part of our cook, for it is not easy to brew soup for 800 men on a foundation of twenty-eight pounds of macaroni. In adding prunes I think he overstressed the bizarre note, but I suppose he had to add something. A less conscientious man might have put in a couple of small Belgians.

August 7th

Big day. Just after breakfast the rumour spread through the camp that one of the Belgian boys had escaped, and unlike most of our rumours turned out to be true. He had got out through one of the window slits in the wall at the end of the passage, leaving rope behind him tied to the water pipe.

Atmosphere rather like Dotheboys Hall after escape of Smike. At eleven-thirty Kommandant is heard bellowing orders outside. We are all told to go to our rooms and stay there. Presently four soldiers with bayonets enter our dormitory. They take away our washing cords and even small bits of string which we were saving up for shoe laces. There is a moment when it seems as if our belts will go, too, but this final disaster does not happen. No doubt it would be embarrassing for all concerned to have 800 internees parading with their trousers hanging round their ankles. Prevent smartness and snap.

Old Scotch windjammer sailor comes and sits on our window-sill and discusses the affair in a broad Glasgow drawl. He also touches on conditions here, which he thinks might be worse. Says he was in prison in Glasgow for five days and this is luxury in comparison. 'Ye had a wooden pillow, and ye didn't need to turn it over, 'cos it was the same both sides.' He doesn't like the Belgian boy who escaped, says he was in his room at Liège and they couldn't get him to wash! 'A greasy young—' he says, which explains how he managed to slide through that slit in the wall.

Opinion is divided between appreciation of the lad's enterprise and the feeling that he showed a lack of public spirit in getting away and leaving us to receive the kick-back. God knows what the reaction will be. We had just got all set to ask the Kommandant if we couldn't have a little more bread, but when we heard his voice outside commenting on the big news, we felt that this was not the moment.

August 9th

Horrible shock today. The bread ration failed and we each got thirty biscuits instead, about the size of those which restaurants used to give you to go with your order of oysters. Felt like a tiger which has been offered a cheese straw. The great problem is how to split up one's ration, i.e. whether to gorge half your biscuits for breakfast, or hold off at breakfast, relying on the heat of the coffee to give you the illusion of having fed, and go a buster at supper.

August 13th

I have now been sleeping for ten nights without a blanket, and it gets bitterly cold at night at this height. Today I went to the Sergeant, accompanied by Enke, our linguist, and complained. The Sergeant was apologetic, but it seems there are no blankets. His attitude seemed to be that you can't have everything.

Parade this morning at seven-thirty. Further parades at nine, ten and eleven, and again in the afternoon. Sandy Youl says – apropos of this constant parading – that if he has enough money after the war, he is going to buy a German soldier and keep him in the garden and count him six times a day.

I have a theory about these parades. They have dug this blighted Kommandant out after years of obscurity and given him this fairly important job, and it has gone to his head. He loves the feeling of strutting up and down, giving out orders. He is a man of sixty-two and used to be an inspector of police. The German soldiers assure us – through Enke – that he is a pain in the neck to them. They call him the Thief-Catcher.

The German soldiers themselves are all right. Being cooped up with them in this small place, we see a lot of them and they are always friendly. They are all elderly reservists longing to get home to their wives and children, whose photographs they constantly show us, and they sympathize with us. One of them gave Arthur Grant and me his soup yesterday. Full of rice with bits of meat in it.

There is one particularly genial sergeant, whose only fault is that he has got entirely the wrong angle on these damned parades. He wants us to go through the motions smartly, with lots of snap. 'Come on, boys,' he seems to be saying. 'Get the carnival spirit. Switch on the charm. Give us the old personality.'

He actually suggested the other day that we should come on parade at the double. When we were convinced that we had really heard what we thought we had heard, we looked at one another with raised eyebrows and asked Enke to explain to this visionary that in order to attend parade we had to climb twenty-seven steep stone steps. It was unreasonable, we felt, to expect us to behave like mountain goats on a diet of biscuits about the size of aspirin tablets and one small mug of thin soup a day.

'Try to make him understand,' we urged Enke, 'that it is pretty dashed creditable of us getting on parade at all. Tell him he has sized us up all wrong. We are elderly internees, most of us with corns and swollen joints, not Alpine climbers. If we are supposed to be youths who bear 'mid snow and ice a banner with the strange device "Excelsior", there ought to be Saint Bernard dogs stationed here and there, dispensing free brandy. Ask him if he expects us to yodel.'

Enke put these points and the man saw reason. Only once has our iron front broken down. That was the day before yesterday, when a spruce young lieutenant, a stranger to us, took over and electrified us by suddenly shouting '*Achtung!*' in a voice like someone calling the cattle home across the Sands of Dee. It startled us so much that we sprang to attention like a Guards regiment.

But we were waiting for him in the evening. He shouted '*Achtung*' again, and didn't get a ripple.

August 16th

Met cook today and congratulated him on yesterday's soup. He was grateful for my kind words, for his professional pride had been wounded by grumblers who criticized the quantity.

422   WODEHOUSE ON WODEHOUSE·

He said he could have produced more soup by adding water, but that would have weakened it, and he refused to prostitute his art. I said he was quite right and that it was the same in my business. A short story is a short story. Try to pad it out into a novel, and you lose the flavour.

August 17th

A 'Camp incident' today. Extra parade is called, and Sergeant and three Privates go down the ranks with a spectacled internee, the man we call the Snake, who looks after the electric lights. They seem to be chasing something, and it gradually develops that the Snake has been 'insulted' by a boy who said that he would throw him into the river . . . whereby, as lawyers say, our client goes in fear of his life.

To us the idea of this as a threat seems a bit comic because (a) it would require a super hurler to perform the feat, as the party of the second part would have to be lofted over a high wall, after which there would be a carry of several hundred yards, and (b) because there is nothing the majority of us would welcome more than being thrown into the river. Give us a couple of days' rations and a little money for railway expenses and then throw us into the river, and leave the rest to us . . . that is our view.

We stand on parade for about three-quarters of an hour while the Snake seeks vainly for the villain of the piece. After a while, in order to narrow the search down, all those under the age of thirty are lined up apart. But does that mean that we who are in the middle and late fifties are allowed to dismiss? Not a bit of it! The Snake had distinctly stated that the Menace was a 'boy', which ought to let out at least the grandfathers. But no, we go on standing there while the Snake potters hither and thither with a questioning look on his face, like a witch-doctor from one of Rider Haggard's early African romances smelling out the evil-minded, but still with no result.

Things are getting difficult. We are told that if the criminal does not confess pretty soon, we shall all be confined to barracks.

Our intelligent minds instantly spot the flaw in this. The snag in the way of confining internees to barracks is that they are jolly well confined to barracks already. About the only way you could confine us to barracks any more would be to put us in the cellar. We saw the thing was going to be a wash-out and it was. About twenty minutes later, the Sergeant, who is presumably as sick of it as we are, offers to settle it out of court if we all promise not to do it again. We do, enthusiastically, and go off to rest our feet.

Two hours later there is another parade. A strange new big pot arrives, inspects us, goes through the dormitories and disappears. We never see him again. Probably just someone slumming.

August 18th

The coming of the biscuit has made us all more and more obsessed with the subject of food. There is a man here with whom I got friendly at Liège. A very earnest sort of bloke. He was always telling me what a wonderful spiritual experience this is and how altruistic it is bound to make us all. This morning he came to me frothing at the mouth because – so he says – other dormitories are getting more potatoes in their soup than his. I never saw a man so bitter.

The windjammer sailor tells me that all this is nothing compared with what he has been through in his time. He says his first voyage lasted 345 days, and that they had been living for weeks on one weevily biscuit and an inch of water a day, when they eventually fetched up at Pitcairn Island. He didn't actually say so, but I got the impression that he rather disapproved of the high living at Huy and was wondering what it was going to do to his figure.

Still no bread. We get nothing but biscuits now, thirty per man and only just visible to the naked eye. It seems to date from the day when we complained to the Kommandant that we were not getting enough bread. He took the statesmanlike course of giving us no bread at all. ('Bread?' says the windjammer sailor. 'Why, on my third voyage. . . .' And then we get some revolting anecdote about biscuits and weevils.)

August 24th

A genuine General arrived today to inspect the camp. Our spirits soared when the word went round that he was making inquiries about the food, but unfortunately the two men he asked if we were getting enough to eat were Enke and the Snake. Enke, the stoutest man in the place, said we were being starved, and the General glanced sceptically at his tummy, Enke endeavoured by waggling his waistcoat to show that there had been a lot of wastage and that the tummy was nothing to what it had been, but there was such a lot still left that the demonstration achieved nothing. The General then buttonholed the Snake, who let the side down by saying that he had plenty to eat, omitting – blast him! – to add that he was getting double rations for looking after the electric light.

August 25th

The General's visit was a wash-out. Biscuits again today. A man tells me that one of the coloured internees, who describes himself as having been in peace-time a 'dancer and bottle-washer in a circus', has been able to put by a reserve of 128 biscuits. This must be the fellow I have noticed dancing about in front of the guard-room. Apparently he amuses the German soldiers with his comedy act, and they give him bread, thus enabling him to save his biscuit ration.

All one's values change in a place like this. This revelation makes me look on the bottlewasher as a millionaire. It is like hearing someone talk of Henry Ford or the Aga Khan. As Emerson said, 'Give me health and 128 biscuits, and I will make the pomp of Emperors ridiculous.'

My friend tells me that this morning the bottlewasher's comedy fell flat with a new lot of German soldiers who have just arrived. It seems that in the recent fighting a Senegambian killed one of their crowd by biting him in the throat, and this has prejudiced them against gentlemen of colour. In fact, when they saw our coloured contingent, they recoiled and asked, 'Are they dangerous?'

This new lot of Germans are simply baffled as to who on earth we are. One of them took an internee to the dentist's this morning, and the dentist asked him if we were prisoners of war. He said he didn't think so. 'Civil prisoners?' 'No.' 'Then who are they?' The soldier said he didn't know. He seemed to look on us as just acts of God.

I'm bound to say the whole thing puzzles me a bit, too. Why Germany should think it worth its while to round up and corral a bunch of spavined old deadbeats like myself and the rest of us it is beyond me to imagine. Silly horseplay is the way I look at it.

The idea, I suppose, is that if left at large, we would go about selling the plans of forts. But one would have thought that a single glance at me would have been enough to tell them that if somebody handed me a fort on a plate with watercress round it, I wouldn't know what to do with it.

I wouldn't even know what price to charge.

August 27th

We were given forms to fill out today – questionnaires regarding age, health, etc. In the space allotted to health Max Enke wrote, 'Tolerably sound but with some weakness. Reduced girth, skeletal construction more apparent,' and had to write it over again.

A great experiment is being tried. Two men have clubbed together and taken their biscuit ration to the cookhouse to be baked. They hope to get a cake, but they are running an awful risk of wasting good biscuits.

August 28th

The cake turned out a sensational success and has revolutionized thought throughout the camp. Everybody's doing it now. One great talking point for cake is the fact that if you have false teeth you don't have to chew. Algy, soaring above mere cakes, has argued our little group into subscribing to a pudding. We all donated biscuits, and I had a tin of condensed milk and Arthur Grant a pot of jam and somebody else some sugar, so we threw it all into the venture. The result was wonderful. I have never tasted anything so good. But, as in all good things, there is a catch. . . . One's bit of pudding just slides down one's throat and is gone, and a man with good teeth, like myself, can make a biscuit last out half the morning with careful nibbling.

Terrible disaster at lunch today. I put my mug of soup on my suitcase and upset it. Practically all the soup went west, most of it seeping through into the interior of the suitcase. Amazing how soup can spread itself. Life seemed to become for a moment all soup. I was able to lick some of it off my shirts, but I should have fed sparingly if Algy had not given me a couple of bits of potato from his ration.

September 1st

The pudding problem is becoming acute. Today I gave up fifteen biscuits, and I am wondering if it is worth it. By careful chewing, I could have made fifteen biscuits last out all day.

September 2nd

Reluctantly decide to stand out of pudding quartette.

September 3rd

Jeff went to the town to oculist's this morning and came back with a chunk of bread, given to him by sympathizer in street. He very sportingly divided it up among dormitory. Split twenty ways, it ran to about a mouthful apiece. Very welcome.

About this going to town. Internees are let out with a guard to go to dentist, oculist, etc. At first they used to smuggle in food with great caution and secrecy, one man coming back with a jam tart wrapped round his chest. Then they got bold and went out with bags and sacks, egged on by the guards, who were all for it. Jeff tells me his guard was a married man with children and hadn't been home for two years. He spoke a little English, and they became very friendly. Offered a drink, he told Jeff not to spend his money on him, but to save it for food for himself.

This golden age lasted about a week, and then men got too reckless. An unexpected Colonel found them roaming about the shops, buying up everything in sight, and the order has now gone out that no one is to be allowed down town! We are hoping that this is only temporary, as most of these *verboten* orders are.

September 4th

Canteen started again today, after having been *verboten* for some unknown reason for quite a time. Jock got quite a lot of cheese, but we hear that the Dutch frontier has been closed, so this is probably the last cheese we shall get. (The windjammer sailor says we ought to have been with him on his fifth voyage. They made half a pound of gorgonzola last from Liverpool to San Francisco, and towards the end, it kept escaping into the top-gallants, and had to be brought back by search parties. The more I listen to this man's conversation, the gladder I am that I did not adopt the merchant marine as a profession in my youth. It never seems to have occurred to anyone to victual the ship properly at the start of the voyage. Apparently they just bought a cheese and a few biscuits and trusted to luck. And then the breeze failed two days out, and there they were.)

September 8th

We are suddenly told at two-thirty that we are to parade and be ready to leave. I had just washed my clothes and had to pack them all wet. We parade for two hours, and there is an issue of half a loaf of bread per man and half a sausage. We then march down the hill to the station. I am faced with the problem of how to tote my baggage. I have the suitcase I came away with, a briefcase full of papers (including copious notes for *Money in the Bank*) and the enormous suitcase which Bunny sent me, weighing a ton. Fortunately I manage to get hold of a stick and Joe McCandless, always a friend in need, shoves this through the handle of the suitcase and I take one end and he takes the other, and somehow we get it to the station. And so off into the unknown.

The next chapter, 'Journey's End', describes the arrival at Tost in Upper Silesia, where the internees from Huy were housed in the local lunatic asylum.

A man I was always very sorry for at Tost was Internee Bob Shepherd. His was quite a sad case. If we had got to Tost in 1926, instead of 1940, we should have been in Poland, for it was in that year that a plebiscite was held to decide whether this slice of territory should be German or Polish and the Poles drew the short straw.

To assist in keeping order during this plebiscite a contingent of English soldiers was sent over, and one day about a week after our arrival Internee Bob Shepherd, the camp trombonist, was seen wandering to and fro with a puzzled look on his face, like a dog confronted with some lamp-post of its puppyhood, muttering, 'I have been here before.' It turned out that he had been one of the English soldiers who, like us, were quartered at the local lunatic asylum. It was the barbed wire that had prevented Bob recognizing the old place at first. It confused him, he said.

What the emotions are of a man who comes to stay at Tost Lunatic Asylum twice I cannot say, for Bob was always reticent on the point. If you asked him, he just blew his trombone in a thoughtful sort of way. But I should imagine they are pretty poignant.

Tost is no beauty spot. It lies in the heart of the sugar-beet country, and if you are going in for growing sugar-beets on a large scale, you have to make up your mind to dispense with wild, romantic scenery. There is a flat dullness about the country-side which has led many a visitor to say, 'If this is Upper Silesia, what must Lower Silesia be like?' And the charm of any lunatic asylum never strikes you immediately. You have to let it grow on you.

I came in time to be very contented in this Upper Silesian loony bin, but I was always aware that what I liked was the pleasant society rather than the actual surroundings. These screwball repositories are built for utility, not comfort. There is a bleakness about their interiors which might exercise a depressing effect if you had not the conversation of dormitory 309 to divert your thoughts. The walls are bare and the floors are bare, and when you go in or out you climb or descend echoing stone stairs. And the bars on the windows lower your spirits till you stop noticing them.

All the windows at Tost were heavily barred, even those of the dining-room, though why the most unbalanced lunatic should want to get out of a dining-room by the window when the door was at his disposal I cannot say. The gratifying result of this was to cause me to take a step up in the animal kingdom. At Huy I had felt like a water beetle. At Tost my emotions were more those of one of the residents of a monkey house at the zoo. If I had had a perch to swing on and somebody outside pushing nuts through the bars, the illusion would have been perfect.

At first sight Tost looks as if it were near nothing, except possibly the North Pole, but actually it is but a stone's throw from Slupska, Koppienitz, Peiskretscham and Pnibw. It was not immediately that I discovered this, but when I did the lyrist in me awoke and I sat down at a table in the upper dining-room and wrote a song hit.

As follows:

A young man was sipping soda in a gilded cabaret,
When a song of home sweet home the orches*trah* did
    start to play:
And he thought he'd ought to tie a can to dreams of
    wealth and fame
And go right back to the simple shack from which he once
    had came.
        And as for his soda he did pay,
To the head waiter these words he then did say:
        'Good-bye, Broadway'.

There's a choo-choo leaving for dear old Pnibw
Where the black-eyed susans grow
        (I wanna go, I wanna go).
There's a girl who's waiting in dear old Pnibw
        (Oh, vo-de-o-de-o-de-o)
        Tender and dreamy,
        Yearning to see me.

There are girls in Koppienitz and girls in Peiskretscham
And possibly in Slupska too,
But the honey for my money is the one who's sitting
    knitting
Underneath the magnolias in dear old Pnibw.
America, I love you with your eyes of blue,
But I'm going back, back, back to the land where dreams
    come true.
P-n-i-b-w spells Pnibw,
And, as Ogden Nash would say, what the hell did you
    think it was going to do?

It is a little rough at present, as I have not had time to polish it, but the stuff is there. It has the mucus.

The journey to Tost took three days and three nights, and it was rendered more trying than it need have been by the fact that we were not given the slightest clue as to how long it was going to last. We just sat and sat and sat and the train rolled on and on and on.

It was rather like being on the ship of the dead in *Outward Bound*.

A little trying the whole thing was. The Citadel of Huy had had its defects, but at least when there we had known where we were. Now we did not know where we were or where we were going, if anywhere. It seemed to us quite possible that the engine-driver had been told just to keep on taking us about the countryside until Headquarters had cleaned up a heavy lot of outstanding business on its desk and was at leisure to get around to deciding where it wanted us dumped.

And even if the man had received definite instructions as to our destination, he might have forgotten them. The conviction to which we came on the second day was that he had lost his way and was too proud to make inquiries. Sometimes he would stop at a siding for an hour or two, and we knew that he was thinking things out.

'Now let me see,' we could hear him saying, an elbow on his knee and his chin supported by his hand, like Rodin's "Penseur". 'They told me at Huy to go straight on till I came to the church and then bear to the left. Or was it to the right? And was it the church or the duck-pond? Well, anyway, I'm pretty sure I'm going in the right *direction*, because I'm in Germany and if I'd been going the wrong way I should be in France. I suppose I *am* in Germany? There's a thing one wants to get straight about before going any further. Hey, mister, I'm looking for a place called Tost.'

The passer-by pauses and stands listening to the hiss of the steam in the boiler.

'I don't like the sound of that engine,' he says. 'Sort of wheezy noise it's making. I'd say your sprockets weren't running true with the differential gear.'

This offends the driver.

'Never mind about my engine,' he retorts, nettled. 'You leave my engine alone and it'll leave you alone. I want to go to Tost.'

'Where?'

'Tost.'

'All right. Don't be long.'

'Do you know the way there?'

'Where?'

'Tost.'

'How do you spell it?'

'T-o-s-t.'

'Oh, *Tost*? I thought you said Vienna.'

'You know Tost?'

'Never heard of it.'

'Well, anyway, is this Germany?'

'I'm afraid I couldn't tell you,' says the passer-by. 'I'm a stranger in these parts myself.'

He saunters on, and the engine-driver rises to his feet with a weary grunt.

'Well,' he reflects, 'I suppose the only thing is to keep going on. Must get somewhere, if you keep going on. Stands to reason. Ho hum, back to the old grind.'

And when we did get to Tost he passed it without a glance and took us on to Gleiwitz, where we remained at a siding for six hours before somebody happened along and told him to go back till he came to Farmer Schmidt's barn and then left as far as the old mill and after that he'd better ask somebody.

For several days after our arrival I had a private yard to myself; not through any special dispensation on the part of the authorities, but because I was the only man with the quick intelligence to realize that we were allowed there. It lay in the angle formed by the main building and was fenced in with wire, and its whole aspect was of a place that is *verboten*. You would see men staring wistfully into it, and you knew that they were saying, 'Boy! What a place to go and spit,' but they never got any further than peering in.

I was the first who took a chance on it. I felt a little breathless the first day when soldiers passed, but I heard no raucous cry of '*Raus*' and decided that all was well. And so for quite a time it was. For some reason the story went through the camp that I had been allotted this haven by the Lagerführer as a special tribute to my general worth, and though faces continued to peer in, nobody ventured to crash the gate. I basked there in the sunshine alone, and very pleasant it was. For the artist soul loves to muse, and it is much easier musing in solitude than when you are rubbing elbows with 1300 of your fellow men.

It could not last. Came a day when a venturous Dutchman faltered in and finding that nothing happened stayed in. He was followed by others. Presently the spitters began to arrive, and one morning, seeking my favourite corner, I found it occupied by my old friend Spotty, the camp's champion spitter, playing like a Versailles fountain. I knew then that the end had come.

Spotty, by the way, was the only man I have ever met who could express his every emotion by spitting. Where you or I would have rapped out an oath or thrown off an epigram, Spotty spat. It was constant association with him that inspired me to begin a poem which, if I ever get it finished, will be in all the anthologies. These were the opening lines:

> This is my case
> Against the human race:
> It
> Has a tendency to spit
> On mountain, vale and lea
> And frequently on me . . .

But here, I must confess, I wronged Spotty. He always avoided what Shakespeare would call the Spit Direct. The Spit Courteous, the Spit Modest, the Spit Churlish, the Spit Quarrelsome and the Spit with circumstance, yes, but never the Spit Direct. He would shoot all round you till you felt like a knife-thrower's assistant, but you were really quite safe. His control was perfect, and there was nothing you could teach him about allowing for windage. (Young spitters *must* remember to allow for windage. On several occasions at Tost members of the crew of the *Orama*, operating from their window on the fourth floor, very nearly missed me as I sat in the yard below through overlooking this.)

The windjammer sailor says that there has been no real spitting since the days of sail. Precision in the true sense of the word, what they would have called precision in the fo'c's'le of the *Bertha May*, in which he made his eighth voyage, vanished with the coming of steam. Naturally almost anybody can hit a sitting author, but let them try to pick off a passing albatross in a high gale, said the windjammer sailor. That is where Class tells.

Checking in at an Ilag where you may be going to stay for several years is a much more elaborate affair than taking up a temporary abode in a prison or a barracks. There is about it a certain ceremonial pomp which, if you have just come from a three-days' and three-nights' trip on a train, you find a little trying. By the time the formalities had been concluded, we were in rather weary mood and the general feeling was that after all this Tost had better be good.

When we actually arrived at Tost station, we felt more lenient towards that engine-driver and less inclined to blame him for having experienced a little difficulty in finding the place. It consists of some planks dumped down in the middle of the woods, and it was not surprising that the man at the controls should have failed to recognize it for what it was. Only when we observed that the platform was filled with steel-helmeted soldiers and the compartment doors began to be unlocked did we ourselves suspect that this was where we got off.

We could have betted what would happen next. Yes, there was a parade. Then the baggage which looked too heavy to be carried was sorted out from the lighter stuff and loaded on trucks. We then started to march to the village, distant about two miles, and eventually found ourselves parading again outside the White House.

Here there was a restful pause of about an hour and three-quarters, pleasantly occupied in shifting from one leg to the other and wondering when we were going to eat. It was so long since we had done so that we were afraid we might have forgotten the technique. Then, at long last, soldiers appeared carrying large wicker-work baskets, and from these, like benevolent Santa Clauses, the corporals produced porcelain

bowls, tin mugs, spoons, knives and forks, which they proceeded to distribute – to each man:

> A bowl
> A mug
> A spoon
> A knife
> and
> A fork.

They passed these out in a careless, off-hand way, as if there
was nothing unusual about it all, but gasps of amazement
escaped us and we looked at one another with rising eyebrows,
awed by such lavishness. This, we felt, was stepping high. At
Huy we had had no forks or spoons and the tin mug which we
used for coffee in the morning had to serve for soup at midday.
And at Liège we had been obliged to get along with what we
could dig out of the dustbin. It was rather like coming to stay
with a millionaire uncle after living for years on the wrong side
of the railroad tracks. One regretted not having brought one's
white *piqué* waistcoat and one's copy of *Manners and Rules of
Good Society*.

I mentioned this to Spotty, who was next to me in the ranks,
and he spat twice. I knew what he meant. He was saying, '*And*
one's gold toothpick.'

As we numbered 800, the distribution took a considerable
time, as did the subsequent march to the cookhouse, and the
filling of the porcelain bowls with soup. But we were so proud
of having porcelain bowls and it was so jolly seeing soup again
that our spirits rose, and we looked forward gaily to the prospect
of collecting our mattresses and turning in for the night.

It was, accordingly, something of a shock to discover that
there weren't going to be any mattresses. When we returned to
the White House, we found that we had got to sleep on the
floor. And if anybody wants a testing experience, let him travel
for three days and three nights on hard wooden seats in a
crowded compartment of a train and then turn in for the night
on a cold stone floor. In the little brochure which I am preparing, entitled 'Stone Floors I Have Slept On', this one at the
White House at Tost will be singled out for special mention. I

do not accuse the German Authorities of having deliberately iced it, but the illusion of being a pound of butter in a refrigerator was extraordinarily strong and grew during the night. A philosopher, I suppose, would have consoled himself with the thought that he was not going bad.

In the morning we were paraded and marched off in batches to the laundry above the cookhouse, where we found a number of enormous wooden tubs and were enabled to scour off the geological strata which had accumulated during our journey. To save time, three men used a tub simultaneously, and I remember thinking that a word of apology was owing to the two who were going to share mine. I felt that I ought really to have been sent to the cleaner's.

I need not have worried. I drew Spotty and the windjammer sailor, who were even more deeply encrusted than I was. But even we, it seemed, could not claim the European record. The windjammer sailor said we ought to have seen Joe Purkiss at the conclusion of the voyage of the *Saucy Sally* from Pernambuco to Hull. They had to dig him out with spades.

After that, all pink and rosy, we took our baggage to the lower dining-room, where it was closely examined, everything of a suspicious nature being pounced on and removed. I can still recall the agony with which I watched the notes for *Money in the Bank* being trousered by a stern official, who plainly thought that he had got hold of something hot in the way of espionage codes and could hardly wait to pop it into the incinerator.

In this connection, I would point out the curious fact that from the German viewpoint there is something fishy about Tennyson's poems but not about Shakespeare's plays. They impounded my Tennyson, returning it to me some weeks later after it had presumably been gone through for subversive matter, but Shakespeare got by without a hitch. It just shows – I don't know what, but something.

We were then given our numbers and the metal discs which we were told must never leave our necks. And I must admit that my sensitive spirit, which had been keeping its end up nicely until now, winced at this point, as if it had bitten into a bad oyster. I had the unpleasant feeling of having sunk in the social scale. In Loos Prison I had at least been Widhorse. Here I was merely Number 796.

After that we were sent off to find our dormitories. Upon the choice of these hung our future happiness or discomfort. The internee's social life centres in his dormitory, and it is essential, accordingly, that he gets into the right one. I cannot imagine a more delightful one than mine – Number 309, the Pride of the Ilag. Presided over by George Travers and his lieutenant Sam Mayo and containing such rare souls as Arthur Grant, Sandy Youl, George Pickard, Smyth, Czarny, Tom Sarginsson, Max Enke, Charlie Webb, Mackenzie, the Moores, father and son, and Joe McCandless, it was an earthly paradise. Its only flaw was that old Bert Haskins was not a member of it.

None of us snored: and if Arthur Grant sometimes started giving a golf lesson in his sleep and somebody else dreamed that he was watching a football match and suddenly sprang from between the blankets at two in the morning with yells of advice and encouragement, these were small things and did nothing to mar the general harmony.

This leads into a chapter entitled 'The Dormitory'.

What its slice of gorgonzola is to the cheesemite, his dormitory is to the internee. It is the only place where he can really nestle and invite his soul, the only spot where he can find something moderately soft to sit on. Elsewhere throughout the establishment there are nothing but benches of an indescribable hardness, very wearing on the fleshy parts, but in the dormitory he has his bed.

Dormitories at Tost were of all sizes, ranging from Number 302, the Belgian room, with its 110 occupants, to the luxury suite which the Camp Captain shared with the Camp Adjutant. Number 309 was a long room with two doors, three large tables with benches, a small table where George Travers worked, three electric lights and seven windows. It also contained three wooden chairs and a stool. Its floor was of wood, its walls distempered. There were no cupboards and no hooks. When you went to bed, you dropped your clothes on the floor or slept in them.

The window-sills were used as storage depots for tin cans, cardboard boxes, cold potatoes and other properties. When you wanted to open a window you dropped these on the floor. The space between the double windows served as a frigidaire. That was where you put your butter and what was left of your potted meat. There were two radiators, useful for heating potatoes in the winter.

The population of Dormitory 309 fluctuated between a high of sixty-eight and a low of fifty-seven. (But that was in the very early days, before there were any new arrivals.) During most of my time at Tost we stayed firm at sixty-six, and our constant endeavour was to prevent our numbers being added to. It was not that we were unsociable; we just wanted to be able to breathe. The room had originally been designed to accommodate thirty, which made sixty-six a nice cosy number by internee standards. Sixty-seven, we felt, would have been a squash.

Every time a fresh bunch of internees filtered into the camp we sat bristling and defiant prepared to resist to the utmost all attempts to ring them in on us.

I have the following entry in my diary for December 11th, 1940:

Today was one of our fractious days, when we become more like small boys than ever. Word was brought by the Corporal that a man from the sailors' room was to be moved to our dormitory. Apparently he had asked the authorities if he might join us, as he was getting on in years and disliked the boisterousness of the younger set in his room.

We appreciated the compliment implied in his desire to be with us, but regretted that we were compelled to reject this contribution owing to lack of space. We pointed out to the Corporal that we were wedged into a solid mass already and that the addition of a sailor would make life impossible.

The Corporal, speaking through Max Enke as interpreter, pleaded that it was a very small sailor. We stood firm. We all admired the Merchant Navy enormously, and only a couple of days before had made up a collection of clothes for the *Orama* boys, who had had to go overboard without stopping to pack, but we insisted that even a powder-monkey or a midshipmite would ruin our comfort irretrievably.

Unfortunately we had to say all this in English, which didn't register, and Enke, who has one of those ingenious minds and loves trying to solve problems, he being the Camp's chess champion, started to demonstrate to the Corporal that by squeezing the beds on our side of the room together space could be made for one more bed.

Charlie Webb thereupon flatly refused to move his bed an inch, saying that by international law he was entitled to the present amount of space between beds. Enke, swiftly changing his strategy of attack, said that Charlie's chair wasn't really Charlie's chair but a communal chair, and that Charlie had a nerve treating as a private chair what was in fact a chair provided for the use of the entire dormitory, and Charlie said he wasn't talking about the bloody chair but about the bloody space between the bloody beds.

I thought his point well taken. It so often happens in these arguments of ours that people wander from the main issue. I have known a discussion on the Life to Come, inspired by one of the Salvation Army Colonel's sermons, to change in the space of a quarter of a minute into an inquiry as to who put their potted meat on somebody else's butter.

Arthur Grant then urged Enke to listen to the voice of his better self, accusing him of being jealous of us single-bedders just because he, Enke, happened to be sleeping in a double-decker. These things, he pointed out, were simply the luck of the draw.

Charlie Webb said that the whole question of space between beds had been thoroughly thrashed out at the Hague Convention.

Enke, coming back strongly, accused Arthur of treating the radiator as a private radiator, when it was really a communal radiator. I said Arthur didn't treat the radiator as a private radiator, but Enke had his answer to this. He said, 'Well, you keep your suitcase between your bed and the wall, which makes your bed stand out six inches from the wall, and it ought to be up against the wall.' McCandless, coming to my rescue, said, 'Well, you upset my coffee last night.'

Charlie Webb said if we didn't believe him, go to the Hague. Just go to the Hague, mention his name and ask them.

Enke was starting what promised to be a longish speech about McCandless inviting friends from other dormitories to come and sit on his bed, when somebody told him to put a sock in it, and he said, 'I won't put a sock in it. Can't I talk?' To which Smyth, who has a simple dignity which we all respect, said, 'Oh, for God's sake go and boil your damned head. The trouble with you is that you're always talking. When you're not talking about chess, you're talking rot,' this closing the debate.

It was exactly like the sort of squabble one used to have in a junior dormitory at school, and when you consider that nobody taking part in it was under the age of fifty, I think it does us credit. Internment may have its drawbacks, but it certainly restores one's youth.

I don't know how we managed it, but we didn't get the sailor. It was one of our notable victories.

When sixty-six men lounge all day and sleep all night in a room designed for thirty, the problem of ventilation is bound to arise; and it was unfortunate for those of us who had always been accustomed to breathe at night that many of our companions had for years been married to French wives and had imbibed from them those strong views on the closed window which are so characteristic of French wives. A Frenchwoman of the sturdy lower middle class considers that to inhale air in which a spoon will not stand upright is to court pneumonia.

From the moment of our arrival a silent war – and not always so silent, at that – had broken out between the fresh air brigade and the fug lovers, causing the only jarring note that ever disturbed the pleasant harmony of Dormitory 309 for more than a passing moment. The forces ranged in opposition were numerically unequal, but we fresh airers, though heavily outnumbered, enjoyed an important strategical advantage. Five of the seven windows in the room were always kept hermetically sealed, but the other two were commanded by the beds of

Arthur Grant, myself, McCandless and Smyth, and we usually managed to sneak one open for a while.

This sometimes led to complications, as witness the entry in my diary for February 27th, 1941:

> Dormitory row this morning. Last night McCandless opened his window after Lights Out and got away with it till about midnight. Then Enke across the way became aware of coolness and feeling that he was entitled by international law to frowst at night lumbered over and shut it.
>
> In the morning Mac discovered that his cold coffee had been upset, either by Enke or by the breeze. The row arose from a desire on the part of all to fix the responsibility. Enke stoutly denied having upset the coffee, and Mac said he must have done it. High words and black looks.
>
> What makes the thing so dramatic and lifts it to the level of a crisis is that this is the fourth time Mac's coffee has been upset; once by me, once by George Travers, and twice by Enke. He puts the stuff on the window-sill in a cloth-covered jam-pot, which nobody would recognize for what it is. I know that on the occasion when I was the guilty party, I thought there must be hairbrushes or something inside, and nobody more surprised than myself when I found cold coffee gushing out.
>
> Charlie Webb made the best suggestion for the avoidance of further disasters of the sort. 'Why don't you drink your blasted coffee at the proper time?' he asked. 'Nobody but you would be able to swallow the muck cold, let alone hoard it up as a treat for the morning.' I must say I thought he was right. Mac is a man of strange pleasures.

Yet in spite of the difficulty of keeping the atmosphere from resembling that which makes the French provincial home so memorable to all who have had to experience it, I loved my dormitory dearly. It was not too good, perhaps, at six o'clock on a cold winter morning, when the steam and electric light had not been turned on and we were all getting up simultaneously and tramping over each other in the dark as we groped for our clothes, but from seven onward it was as jolly and cosy a place as you could wish for.

It is difficult to say when it was actually at its best – at nine
in the morning, when we brewed our cup of tea; between two
and four in the afternoon, when we took our siesta; between
seven and eight in the evening, with the harmonicas going; or
at nine at night, when the lights went out and one lay in bed
staring drowsily at the barred window and listening to the
raconteurs at the top end telling their stories.

I have never slept better in my life than on that plank bed,
and I am convinced that the secret of health and well-being is
to turn in at nine and get up at six.

To make a really luxurious plank bed you need four planks.
Owing to a shortage of wood, we got only three. We could
arrange these as we liked – a solid mass of planks in the middle,
if we pleased, or, if we preferred it, a plank here, a plank there
and a plank there. The great thing was to get the springy one
in the middle.

Getting the pillow just the right height was always a difficulty.
Some men used suitcases for bolsters, but I found that I obtained the best results with a sweater, a cardigan, a pair of
trousers, a Red Cross parcel and the Complete Works of
William Shakespeare. Shakespeare, who wrote not for an age
but for all time, produced exactly the right amount of stuff to
make him an ideal foundation on which to build.

Internees for the most part sleep in layers. There were only
seven single beds in Dormitory 309, and it may surprise people
that a dreamy artist like myself was able to secure one. The
explanation is that when the rush began I had the shrewdness
to stick close to Algy, whom I had recognized from the very
beginning of my internment as one of those men who always
manage to get things. He had been a Quartermaster-Sergeant
in the first world war, and once a Quartermaster-Sergeant,
always a Quartermaster-Sergeant.

'Algy,' I said to him, as I surveyed the milling mob, 'I place
my affairs unreservedly in your hands. Consider yourself my
accredited agent.'

And when all the tumult and the shouting had died, there
he was with a single bed for himself and a single bed for me in
the best spot in the room, right under the window.

I had become so used at Huy to burrowing into straw at

night like a rat in a barn that when I found myself with a bed, and not only a bed but a pillow (stuffed with straw), a mattress (the same) and a cotton sheet and two blankets, I received an impression of almost Oriental magnificence, which never quite left me during my stay at Tost. You might say that the place had me dazzled from the start.

When I came to mingle with the internees from Holland, I found that they judged their surroundings by different standards, and were inclined to be captious. It appeared that they had been brought to Tost from a camp near the Hague where the conditions, to hear them tell it, must have been rather like those prevailing in a Sultan's palace of the better class. To them Tost was a distinct come-down. To me, who had come up from the slums, it seemed staggering in its luxury.

'But we've got *beds*!' I used to say.

'Plank beds,' sneered the Dutchmen with a wistful look in their eyes as they recalled the swansdown on which they had slept in their last place. (If you didn't like swansdown, you could have rose petals.)

Well, after Huy, any Ilag that gave me a bed, plank or otherwise, was Claridge's to me, and I was prepared to write in the visitors' book to that effect.

And here is a chapter entitled 'Lagerführers, Landeschützen and What Not':

Two things about a regular internment camp impress themselves upon you very soon after your arrival there. The first is the ingenuity with which privacy has been guarded against, the second the smooth efficiency with which the place functions. There was at Tost none of the casual sloppiness which had been the keynote of Liège and Huy. Everything had been organized. Shortly after we clocked in a manifesto was issued from up top and passed round the dormitories.

It ran thus:

ILAG VIII (TOST)

Ilag Tost consists of –
1 (a) The outer camp with headquarters, Administration Offices, Barracks of the Landeschützen.

(b) Internee camp with barbed wire fence.

2 Kommandant of Camp and Deputy.

3 (a) All contact between the internees and headquarters goes through the Lagerführer.

(b) Internees have been detailed into four companies and those subdivided into platoons. German NCOs will act as Company Commanders. The platoons are commanded by suitable internees.

(c) Internee Officers:

Camp Captain	Floor Wardens
Deputy Camp Captains (2)	Room Wardens
Camp Adjutant	

The duty of the Camp Captain is to put into force the orders of the Kommandant and his Deputy and supervise their carrying out. He also reports to the Kommandant through his Deputy, all complaints, if he considers them justified.

(d) In each company a Room Warden is to be appointed by the Lagerführer on the recommendation of the Camp Captain. The Room Wardens have the same duties to their Companies as Camp Captains to the Camp as a whole.

Now I can see, of course, that in getting the stuff down on paper for our benefit the authorities meant well, and I could see it at the time. But the trouble about a document like this is that it suffers from the same defect as the Plan of House, showing Squire's room, Aunt Isobel's room, Lord Jasper's room, Cyril's room, Mabel's room, cupboard on landing and bloodstained section at foot of stairs (marked X) where body of masked dancer was found with dagger between third and fourth ribs, which writers of detective stories always insert at about page 20. It is intended to be helpful, but isn't.

You look at this manifesto, but you don't take it in. I still find my mind skidding off it as I read, just as it did when I read it for the first time over a mug of tea and a cheese sandwich in the dormitory.

'George,' I said to George Travers, 'what the hell is all this about?'

He confessed himself baffled. And when a thing baffles George Travers, it may be written off as beyond the scope of human ingenuity.

It will be best, therefore, if you don't give it another thought. Just forget you ever saw the thing and preserve an open mind while I tell you in a few simple words exactly:

How An Internment Camp Is Run

First Get Your Internees:

These are indispensable, for nothing looks sillier than a prison camp without prisoners. Internees of all sorts and sizes may be readily obtained at little cost and trouble. They come in every shade from midnight black to primrose yellow, or, like me, a pretty pink. Having stocked up with internees,

Buy Plenty Of Barbed Wire:

You can have lots of fun decorating the place with this. It will bring back old memories of the days when you used to hang up the mistletoe at Christmas.

Lice:

These may be provided, but probably the internees will bring their own.

You are now all set to begin, and you start off with a Lagerführer, some Captains, some Lieutenants, as many Sergeants and Corporals as you wish and a couple of hundred privates, and you put them in barracks outside the barbed wire.

To these, however, we need pay no attention, for they do not enter into the internee's life. It is nice to know they are there, in case of burglars, but apart from that they don't mean a thing to the internee. The only members of the crowd he ever sees are the Sentries, who are always getting relieved. I have been in the grounds of Ilag Tost at every hour of the day, and whenever I was there somebody was relieving the Sentries. German soldiers earn their money easily.

Practically, then, you need not let this Outer Camp worry you at all. Just dismiss it from your mind. All that interests you is:

The Inner Camp

comprising the buildings and all that portion of the grounds and messuages which is enclosed in the barbed wire.

The inner camp is a seething mass of internees presided over by the Lagerführer and four German Corporals, one to each floor. You also find Sergeants drifting about occasionally, and I have seen a Captain and a German dog, but the great thing is to avoid elaboration of detail, so forget everything except

The Lagerführer
and
The Corporals

and then we shall really get somewhere.

I cannot impress it too strongly upon the young internee that the great thing, when he is starting out in business, is to have a good Lagerführer. Get a bad one, and you're sunk. An outstanding example of the bad Lagerführer was the marble-eyed old dug-out who was in charge of us at Huy. It was not that he was actually hostile, oppressing us and grinding us under the iron heel. It was just that he was one of Nature's stinkers, and for the comfort of internees a complete absence of stinkers in the outer camp is essential.

At Tost we were lucky. Oberleutnant Buchelt, to whom the Kommandant had 'delegated the supervision of the inner camp', was nothing less than the answer to an internee's prayer. He might have been constructed from our own blueprints. There is no actual obligation binding a Lagerführer to do anything more than see that order is maintained and appear once a day on parade, but Buchelt was working all the time in our interests; not, it was rumoured, without a good deal of opposition on the part of the men higher up, who held the view that when you have given internees a nice lunatic asylum to live in you have done all that can be expected of you.

He had the White House thrown open, started the library and the *Tost Times*, encouraged education and entertainments, procured for us beer, boiling water and cook stoves, got us permission to go to the sports field in the village, held the parades indoors instead of out in the yard, allowed smoking in the corridors and got the ban against looking out of the corridor windows lifted.

This last concession may not sound much, but it made all the difference to our comfort. The corridor is the internee's club, and a clubman's whole enjoyment of a club depends on his being allowed to sit in the window goggling out like a fish in an aquarium. In the beginning it was *streng verboten* so much as to glance sideways when passing a corridor window, and scarcely a day passed without the Sentry on the path below reporting members who had been unable to resist the urge.

It was not that there was anything much to see when you did look out; just a village street with a deserted beer garden across the way; but that mattered little to us. We did not ask for the Grand Canyon or the Taj Mahal. What we wanted was to stand there and goggle. And this, thanks to Oberleutnant Buchelt, we were finally permitted to do. I am happy to say that the privilege was only once abused, when the Sentry reported that some internees on the second floor had been blowing kisses at him. But this was in the Spring, when that sort of thing is always liable to happen.

So much for the Lagerführer. As for the Corporals – Ginger, Rosebud, Pluto and Donald Duck – they gave us no cause for complaint. It was their job to see that we were counted before the Lagerführer came on parade and to pop up unexpectedly out of traps and catch us smoking in the corridor during prohibited hours, and they performed these duties with reasonable courtliness and suavity.

On the third floor we had Rosebud – of whom our only criticism was that he used to burst into the dormitory like the Charge of the Light Brigade at six a.m. and shout 'Auf!' at the top of his voice. And this was remedied later. Internee Mackenzie, who spoke German fluently, took him aside and told him that 'Auf!' was a little abrupt and hurt our feelings, besides making us think that a bomb had hit the building.

A few days later he had got him saying 'Git opp', but even this did not satisfy Mackenzie. He was a man who before becoming an internee had run a school for problem children in Warsaw, and he had infinite patience in training the budding mind. With gentle persistence he kept at it, and one morning we were all enchanted by a musical 'Git opp, gentlemen, if you please'. It was amazing what a difference it made.

Co-operating with the Lagerführer and the Corporals, we have, as the manifesto informed us,

The Camp Captain
The Camp Adjutant
The Deputy Camp Captains (2)
The Floor Wardens and the Room Wardens

Of these the Room Wardens rank lowest in the social scale –
a Deputy Camp Captain, for instance, would go into dinner
before a Room Warden – but they are able to console themselves
with the thought that it is they who do all the real work about
the place.

Let us turn the searchlight on the activities of their colleagues,
beginning with those almost inanimate objects, the Floor
Wardens.

The Floor Wardens may try to make us think that they earn
the double rations which go with their job by sweating themselves to the bone warding the floors, but we are too astute to
be fooled. One simple question is enough to unmask their
pretentions. If a Floor Warden's duties had involved even the
merest suggestion of work, would Jock Monaghan and Algy
have become Floor Wardens? We rather fancy we need say no
more.

None of these living corpses ever did a stroke of honest toil.
There were eight of them in a room at the end of our corridor,
and they used to lie on their beds all day eating their double
rations and dropping cigarette ashes on the floor which was
their sacred charge. A fat lot of warding they did. I don't suppose the floor knew they were there. Lilies of the field, that's
what they were, just lilies of the field. I said as much to Spotty
one day.

'Spotty,' I said, 'they're simply lilies of the field, nothing
more.'

And Spotty spat at a passing fly, and I knew that what he was
saying in his peculiar way was 'How right you are, my dear
fellow.'

(The story that I tried to become a Floor Warden and was
rejected has, I admit, a certain substance in fact. That is to say,
there were informal conversations on the subject, in the course
of which – with no thought of double rations in my mind but
purely out of public spirit, because I thought they ought to

have a good man – I indicated my willingness to take office. But the fact that I was not chosen has nothing to do with the heat of the above remarks which are dictated entirely by a civic conscience.)

So much for the Floor Wardens. Let us leave a distasteful subject. What of the Deputy Camp Captains (2)? Slightly more active than the human sloths to whom I have been alluding (with their double rations, forsooth), they bustle about, trying to look as if the whole welfare of the Ilag depended on them, but, coming right down to it, what do they *do*? They follow the Lagerführer up and down the ranks at morning parade, and that is all.

They don't even try to make a race of it. Many a time, standing at attention in the corridor and watching the Lagerführer round into the straight with Deputy Camp Captains Greenways and Tom Sarginsson lying a couple of lengths behind, I have felt that all that was required on the part of the last-named (my Selection for the Day), was a sudden spurt and a quick challenge and have muttered under my breath 'Come on, Tom'. But when the numbers went up on the board, it was always the same story.

 1 Lagerführer
 2 First Deputy Camp Captain
 3 Second Deputy Camp Captain
  Also Ran, Corporal

My private belief is that the thing was fixed.

The Camp Adjutant's existence was even more languorous. He just didn't do *anything*. Picture in your mind a Turkish odalisque on a warm day in Stamboul, and you will have the Camp Adjutant.

Nor was the Camp Captain's daily task of a nature to tax an able-bodied man. He acted as a connecting link between the internees and the Lagerführer, going to see the latter in his office once a week with hard-luck stories gleaned from the rabble – that is to say me and the rest of the boys.

If, for instance, the coffee had been cold two days in succession, we of the proletariat told the Camp Captain, who told the Lagerführer, who told the Kommandant, who presumably cursed the cook, and if the cook excused himself on the plea that the boiler had burst, made him sacrifice his chewing-gum to mend it.

It was also the Camp Captain's duty to come to us on parade after the Lagerführer's departure and say, 'Gentlemen, one moment, please,' and then scold us for our sins and threaten frightful penalties, like a short-tempered nurse with a family of children who are not too strong in the head. He would appeal and announce that if we looked out of the corridor windows we would be deprived for a month of the privilege of writing letters; that if we smoked in the corridor, we would be forbidden to smoke anywhere in the building; that if we shuffled our feet on parade we would be dragged out of bed and made to parade again. We would stare at him in an owlish way, gently shuffling our feet, and then light our pipes and go and look out of the corridor windows.

Occasionally he would get things mixed. One night he informed us that from tomorrow on we must move our heads as the Lagerführer passed on parade and follow him with our eyes. It was, he said, a special order that had gone out, and the penalty for not obeying it was – I forget what, but something lingering with boiling oil in it. It was only after a blushing Lagerführer had hurried coyly up and down the ranks next morning under the penetrating scrutiny of 200 men, each with his eyes bulging like a snail's and performing the motion picture gesture known as the slow double take, that the Camp Captain returned and explained that there had been a slight error. What he had meant to say was that we must *not* move our heads as the Lagerführer passed on parade and follow him with our eyes.

It straightened out the whole thing.

Well, that is what a Camp Captain's job is, and you can't say that is is very strenuous or makes any great demand on the intelligence. I possess few of the qualities which go to make an executive, but I have always felt that I could have been a Camp Captain without straining a sinew. But I wouldn't have become a Room Warden to please a dying grandmother.

Each dormitory, as soon as it has fixed up the distribution of beds and put its potted meat on the window-sill, elects a Room

Warden and points at him with pride . . . and also with that gentle pity which the kind-hearted always feel when they regard the fellow whom Fate has called upon to be the Patsy, the Squidge or, putting it another way, the man who has been left holding the baby. They know what he has let himself in for.

In Dormitory 309 the People's Choice was good old George Travers, in private life the proprietor of a *café* at Arras, as fine a man as ever worked like a beaver all day and said, 'Well, good night all,' a quarter of an hour after Lights Out.

You take George, now. Never idle for a moment. He improved each shining hour and perspired at every pore. He was a kind of combination of Postmaster General, nursemaid, laundry van and messenger boy. He had to sort out and distribute incoming mail, see that outgoing mail was properly addressed, supply us with letter cards, collect letter cards when written, give out clean towels, collect dirty towels, distribute clean sheets, collect dirty sheets, put up the parcels list on the board, fill up forms, represent the dormitory at the canteen and hound us out of the room before morning and evening parade and line us up and count us, remembering who were absent in hospital, getting parcels, on fatigue and so on.

And when he had done all this, the Floor Warden would saunter along, bulging with his double rations, and say, 'Everything Okay, George?' and that completed the Floor Warden's duties.

High up on the list of World's Workers I Have Met comes the name of George Travers. The canteen aspect of his job alone was enough to intimidate anyone but a man of chilled steel.

Fairly early in our sojourn at Tost it was discovered that if 1300 men go to a canteen in a body and try to get served simultaneously, confusion results, so it was decreed that all orders must be placed through the Room Wardens. You went to George Travers and said, 'George, I want six of beer, a pair of shoelaces, some salt, some saccharine, half a dozen pencils, as much paper as you can get and one of those little gadgets, I forget what they're called, but you know what I mean,' and he would say, 'Rightyho'.

And then fifty other men would come to him with their commissions, and he would say, 'Rightyho'. And before you knew where you were he was back in the room, having carried the stuff across the yard and up three flights of stairs, and nothing forgotten or left behind.

Only the fact that I am writing this bare-headed prevents me at this point raising my hat to George ('What a man') Travers.

And finally a chapter entitled 'The Eats':

Food!

That magic word, at whose sound the internee starts like a warhorse hearing the bugle.

It may seem rather gross of me to devote a whole chapter to the subject of food. Already there has been quite a good deal about it in this book, and I can hear spiritual-minded critics asking disgustedly, 'Did this man never think of anything but his stomach?'

The answer is, 'Never' – or, at least, 'Very seldom'.

Under certain conditions the mind is bound to dwell on food. Shackleton once told me that when he was in the Polar seas, he used to dream every night that he was running about a field chasing those three-cornered jam tarts which were such a feature of life at our mutual school. And if that was how Shackleton felt, I am not ashamed of having felt that way myself.

It is not as if I had been the only one to give food priority in my mind. We were 1300 internees with but a single thought. A bevy of tapeworms could not have been more preoccupied with the matter of nourishment than the inmates of Ilag VIII. Some of us played darts, and some of us sang hymns to the accompaniment of a piano which would have been the better for half an hour with William Cartmell. Some of us walked in the park of an afternoon, and some of us took off our boots and slept. Some of us crouched over the chessboard, and some of us studied Spanish. But whether we are hurling the dart or bellowing the hymn, saying 'check' or whatever it is that people say when they are learning Spanish, subconsciously we were all thinking of food.

At the sight of it, even if it was only barley soup, our hearts leaped up as if we had beheld a rainbow in the sky. We sprang at the black pudding like wolves at a Russian peasant. Even the

windjammer sailor, a man who, having passed his formative
years in the society of weevily biscuits, might have been
supposed to be above human weakness, never failed to show
visible emotion when the whistle blew for meals.

Before lunch we would speculate as to what we were going to
have for lunch. After lunch we would discuss what we had had
for lunch, generally in a derogatory spirit, for we were not easy
critics. You may take it as a fact that no matter how apparently
absorbed an internee may be in some passing task or recreation,
his thoughts are really on his last or his next meal. And when
he talks, he talks of little esle.

A man told me once that, sickening of the universal topic,
he followed Father Reeves, the Roman Catholic priest, and
myself round the park one morning, hoping to get a bit of
mental and spiritual uplift. What he actually drew was a
discussion of the respective merits of sauerkraut and those
peculiar slices of sausage which we used to call 'rubber heels'
and some rather strong remarks on my part on swedes, criticizing sharply the habit of these vegetables of swimming in a
curious black juice which looks like swamp water.

This, I should mention, was in the early days of our stay,
before parcels started coming in and we were at liberty to turn
our thoughts into broader fields. If he had caught me a few
weeks later, he might have heard something good about neo-
post-vorticist poetry or the influence of James Joyce on the
younger English novelists. But I'm not sure. Even when we
were living highest my conversation was always a little apt to
touch on the browsing and sluicing.

With me, during the lean times at Huy and through the first
few weeks at Tost, the obsession took the form of a wild regret
that when I had been in the midst of plenty, I had not made
better use of my opportunities. I used to sit and marvel at the
thought that I had walked the streets of New York and passed
lightly by candy-shop windows, full from end to end of assorted
chocolates; that in London I had often lunched at Simpson's in
the Strand and taken only one helping of the juicy joints the
high priests wheel around there; that in Paris I had frequently
been satisfied with a mere omelette. I felt like a prodigal who
had thrown away all his chances in life.

What I craved for principally was bread. It is a curious thing about bread. As Compton Mackenzie points out in one of his books, nobody ever eats bread for pleasure. There is nothing in bread as bread that offers the least attraction. It is really used as a kind of anaesthetic for all other food. But how I longed for it at Tost. There was never a moment when I would not have traded the finest tin of sardines or even a slab of chocolate for bread.

And when I say bread, I mean the stuff the authorities laughingly called bread, made of leather substitute and sawdust.

The only time when we were in possession of enough bread was on Saturday nights, when a double ration was issued. But then we were compelled to force ourselves to hold back from it, for it had to see us through Sunday and breakfast on Monday. It was splendid moral exercise to peep into one's suitcase and see all that bread lying there and to know that only one's will-power prevented one swooping on it, but what I felt, and others have told me they felt the same, was, 'To Hell with moral exercise!' What I wanted was bread. Sometimes I would gladly have been back in Loos prison where, though conditions were cramped and I had had to sleep on the floor with my head up against the family one-holer, I had been given a whole loaf to myself every morning.

But one was not hidebound. One did not insist on bread. Any sort of food would have been welcome. And what aggravated the agony of having to get along on the diet of a banting canary was that nearly every book one read went into such close particulars about food. It was not pleasant, when one had just supped on three small biscuits and a mug of sewage overflow, to come upon the passage in an Agatha Christie thriller where Monsieur Poirot and Scotland Yard are discussing the contents of the corpse and to read:

> As for what he ate at dinner, it was the same as everybody else had. Soup, grilled sole, pheasant and chipped potatoes, chocolate *soufflé*, soft roes on toast.

Give me one blow-out like that, I used to feel, and you wouldn't find me making a fuss if somebody added a dose of some little-known Asiatic poison as a chaser.

But corpses in detective stories always have all the luck. It seems to me sometimes that they live for pleasure alone. I have never known one that had fewer than five courses inside it, not counting the arsenic.

An internee's diet is carefully thought out by committees of experienced German medical men, so they tell me. I don't believe it. I see behind it the hand of some foul vegetarian society. Nobody else would be capable of so stressing the vegetable note. These men had apparently never heard of such things as chops and steaks and cuts off the joint. And here is the final damning proof – they looked on swedes as human food.

If any of my readers, by the way, is reading this aloud to the tots, I should like him to make it quite clear that when I say swedes I don't mean Swedes, I mean swedes. Between the Swede who comes from Sweden and the swede which tries to mask its malevolence by hiding in black juice there is a great gulf fixed. I yield to no man in my respect for Swedes, but swedes give me a pain in the neck, and elsewhere.

'In reading the books of explorers,' says Somerset Maugham in his *Gentleman in the Parlour*, 'I have been very much struck by the fact that they never tell you what they eat and drink unless they are driven to extremities and shoot a deer or a buffalo that replenishes their larder when they have drawn their belts to the last hole. But I am no explorer and my food and drink are sufficiently important matters to me to persuade me in these pages to dwell on them at some length.'

I am glad to have the moral support of a writer whom I admire so much as I do Mr Maugham. Following his firm policy, I will now give details of what we got to eat at Tost.

At supper two loaves of brunette bread were deposited on each of the tables and divided up among the nine men who sat there. And when I say divided, I mean divided. There was none of that casual business of saying, 'Help yourself, George and pass it along.' At my table Tom Sarginsson got out his slide rule and started measuring, and the rest of us watched him like hawks to see that his hand didn't slip. For our share had to last us till supper-time the next day.

If you divide two regulation German army loaves among

nine men, each reveller gets a chunk about so thick and about so long – well, say about as thick as what reviewers call 'this slim volume of verse' and about as long as a pipe with shortish stem. About the amount which in times of peace you would eat while waiting for the waiter to bring the smoked salmon.

With the bread came a small piece of margarine, a minute spoonful of grease, an almost invisible dab of *ersatz* jam or one of those silver paper bits of cheese which, like the tables in the cells at Loos prison, are designed for the use of Singer's Midgets. Also a mug of imitation coffee. And sometimes instead of the cheese or jam we had those slivers of sausage which I have referred to as 'rubber heels', purple in colour like an angry sunset and snapping back like elastic when you bent them.

Occasionally – very occasionally – there were great days when the internee in charge of the dining-room would call for silence at lunch and intone these words: 'Gentlemen, bring your bowls tonight.' This meant that in addition to the ordinary ration there would be soup for supper, a soft, clinging soup made from yellow peas, very grateful to the palate and, what was better, filling.

For breakfast next morning we had what we had been able to resist eating of our bread overnight and a mug of coffee.

The luncheon menu was more varied. There were always potatoes – three per man during the first two months and then suddenly a welcome increase to eight or nine – but different days brought different things to go with them. The great danger was always that the cook, a man of lethargic mentality, would lose his inspiration and fall back on swedes. If he did not, we would get a fish stew once a week, an odd sort of barley porridge once a week, and on other days cabbage, carrots, sauerkraut or black pudding.

From start to finish of my career as an internee I lost forty-two pounds in weight. I don't say it has not made me feel better and look better. It has. I feel terrific and I look like Fred Astaire. All I am saying is that that amount of me has perished from the earth. It is rather sad in a way – all those lovely dimpled curves vanished, probably for ever, but that's how it goes. If you have global wars, you can't have plump, well-fed authors.

The official diet in a camp being on the somewhat ascetic lines which I have indicated, it will be readily understood that the arrival of a parcel is a big event in an internee's life. If you have a parcel, you are in a position to laugh at barley porridge and sneer at swedes. The list goes up in the dormitory after lunch, and the lucky ones proceed in groups to the building where parcels are distributed and wait there till their numbers are called.

This may not be for a considerable time, and in cold weather the conditions of waiting are not too agreeable. In the parcels room itself there is a stove, but in the stone-flagged hall where you keep your vigil you get the Upper Silesian air untempered. For this reason kind donors should be careful what they put in an internee's parcel. I suppose there is no spiritual agony so keen as that caused by the discovery, after you have hung around for three-quarters of an hour and got frostbite in both feet, that your little bit of burlap contains not cake and chocolate but a jigsaw puzzle.

Close friends generally arranged to share their parcels. Which brings to my mind the story of the two Belgian buddies.

These two buddies agreed to share and share alike, and one day Buddy A. went to Buddy B. and told him regretfully that this time his wife had been able to send only a small piece of gingerbread, and here was his, Buddy B.'s, share with comps. At the same time exhibiting something that looked like a Huy biscuit.

Buddy B. thanked him and suggested that, as there was so little, Buddy A. should take it all. Buddy A. said he would not dream of it, and Buddy B., as he started to dig in, said that if there were more fellows in the world with big, generous hearts like Buddy A.'s, the world would be a better place.

So far so good. A pretty little incident, you would say, and one reflecting great credit on human nature.

Unfortunately a few days later Buddy A. got a letter from his wife, a Flemish girl, written in Flemish, which he could not read, and took it to Buddy B., who could read Flemish, for translation. The gist of the letter was that Mrs Buddy A. was in the pink and trusted that this found Buddy A. as it left her at present, and she hoped he had enjoyed the parcel she had sent him containing the two cakes, the two bags of biscuits, the three tins of sardines, the four pieces of gingerbread and the jar of home-made jam. No blood was spilled, for internees who spill blood get bunged into the cells for from two to five days, but I should be deceiving my public if I said that this beautiful friendship was ever quite the same again.

Sometimes unfortunate misunderstandings would occur. One afternoon Smyth found his name on the parcels list, and having only recently recovered from pneumonia, asked me to go down for his parcel. (You give the substitute your disc, and this enables him to collect.)

When I got back, Smyth gratefully presented me with a packet of sliced ham by way of agent's fee. I gave a bit to Arthur Grant and a bit to Czerny and a bit to Joe McCandless and another bit to Sandy Youl and then took a bit myself, and we were all munching happily when there was a stifled cry and we saw Smyth standing there aghast. Apparently he had meant me to take a slice for myself, and give the rest back.

Madness, of course, to go handing packets of sliced ham about in an Ilag if you ever expect to see the contents again. I told him so. It didn't go very well.

All this luxurious living, I should mention, took place in the later stages of my internment. Long months passed during which we were entirely dependent on the camp meals, such as I have described, and after a year of camp meals I am still only slowly re-learning the technique of dining.

Even now it sometimes seems to me that the only way of dining is to wait till somebody blows a whistle and then grab a bowl and cigar-box and queue up till one's turn comes, and I still cannot accustom myself to the peace-time method of securing potatoes. In Camp, when you want potatoes, you hold out the cigar-box and old George Marsh plunges both hands into the crate and comes up with the spuds and dumps them in. And if it is old George, he will catch my pleading eye and add a brace of small ones.

If it is old George, I repeat. There were servers, I regret to say, who lacked his splendid humanity, servers with hearts of flint. Yes, I am looking right at you, young Hoddinott.

Though, of course, even hard-hearted servers were better

than no servers at all. I had a great respect for the servers, who did a lot of hard work and got not much in return except an occasional 'Hoy! Where's my ninth potato?'

We took our food in three sittings. As soon as the carriers had delivered the stuff, staggering over from the cookhouse with enormous baskets, we formed up in a queue, each man with a porcelain bowl for the *plat de jour* and a plate or a tin or a cigar-box for the potatoes. The servers then started serving, and it was extremely interesting to watch and compare their various styles.

Too many nervous young servers, I noticed, trying for distance, were apt to overswing and to forget that what puts ginger into the shot is that last-second crisp snap of the wrists. The moment a really first-class server started his swing, you could recognize his mastery of the ladle. He had learned the fundamental lesson – slow back, don't press, and keep your eye on the bowl.

With the low handicap man what you got was a nice easy half-swing, the ladle never rising much above the shoulder; and then, as you braced yourself to take the shock, down came the fish stew, bursting right in the centre of the bowl. A server anywhere near amateur championship class, like George Marsh, could always hit the bowl three times out of four and only splash you in odd spots.

Postscript

Early in April, 1953, I sent Plum the script of this book, and received the following reply:

1000 Park Avenue,
April 18th, 1953   *New York*

Dear Bill,

The book arrived safely a couple of days ago, and I have just finished a first quick perusal.

It gives one an odd feeling reading letters one has written over a period of thirty years. Rather like drowning and having one's whole life pass before one. How few of the people I mention are still alive. Flo Ziegfeld, Al Woods, Marilyn Miller, George Gershwin, Jerry Kern, George Grossmith, Bill McGuire, Lorimer, Kipling, Molnár . . . dozens of them, all gone.

The impression these letters have left me with is the rather humbling one that I am a bad case of arrested mental development. Mentally, I seem not to have progressed a step since I was eighteen. With world convulsions happening every hour on the hour, I appear to be still the rather backward lad I was when we brewed our first cup of tea in our study together, my only concern the outcome of a Rugby football match.

Though I believe there are quite a number of people like me in that respect. I remember lunching with Lord Birkenhead once, and my opening remark, 'Well, Birkenhead, and how are politics these days?' left him listless. He merely muttered something about politics being all right, and crumbled bread. But when I said, 'Tell me, my dear fellow – I have often wanted to ask you – what came unstuck at Oxford in 1893, or whenever it was? Why was it that you didn't get your Rugger blue?' – his eyes lit up and he talked for twenty minutes without stopping, giving me no chance to tell him what I did to Haileybury in 1899.

You ask, Do I approve of your publishing this book, with all the stuff about my German troubles? Certainly. But mark this, laddie, I don't suppose that anything you say or anything I say will make the slightest damn bit of difference. You need dynamite to dislodge an idea that has got itself firmly rooted in the public mind.

When I was interned, a man on *Time*, sitting down to write something picturesque and amusing about me, produced the following:

> When the German army was sweeping toward Paris last Spring, 'Plum' (to his friends) was throwing a cocktail-party in the jolly old pine woods at Le Touquet. Suddenly a motor-cycle Gendarme tore up, shouted, 'the Germans will be here in an hour,' tore off. The guests, thoroughly familiar with this sort of drollery from Wodehouse novels, continued to toss down cocktails. The Germans arrived punctually, first having taken care to block all the roads. They arrested the Wodehouses and guests, later permitted Mrs Wodehouse and celebrants to depart southward.

You wouldn't think anyone would have believed such an idiotic story, but apparently everyone did. In 1941 someone wrote in the *Daily Express*:

> He lived in Le Touquet. He was drinking a cocktail when the Germans arrived, and he was led away quite happily into captivity.

And in 1945 someone else thus in the *Daily Mail*:

> He was, in fact, just sinking a cocktail when, in 1940, someone dashed in and cried that the Germans would be there in an hour or less. The party stayed put with a phlegm worthy of Drake's game of bowls.

So after four years the thing was still going as strong as ever, and presumably still is. It is embedded in the world's folklore, and nothing will ever get it out. I wonder where I am supposed to have collected these light-hearted guests whom I am described as entertaining. By the time the Germans were threatening Paris, the resident population of Le Touquet had shrunk so considerably that the most determined host would have found it impossible to assemble even the nucleus of a cocktail-party, and the few of us who had been unable to get away were not at all in the mood for revelry. We were pensive and preoccupied, starting at sudden noises and trying to overcome the illusion of having swallowed a heaping teaspoonful of butterflies.

Odd, too, that a motor-cycle Gendarme should have torn up and shouted, 'The Germans will be here in an hour,' when they had been there two months. They entered Le Touquet on May 22nd. I was interned on July 21st. At the time when the incident is supposed to have taken place we were all confined to our houses except when we went to Paris Plage to report at the Kommandatur to a German Kommandant who had a glass eye.

This matter of glass-eyed German Kommandants, by the way, is one that should be carefully gone into by the United Nations. One recognizes, of course, that in modern total warfare the innocent bystander can no longer consider himself immune from unpleasantness, but there are surely limits to what should be inflicted upon him.

I used to amble down to Paris Plage of a morning like Pippa passing, and I would go in at the door of the Kommandatur and meet that eye and wilt. It was like the boss's eye you read about in the advertisements, and everyone knows how hopeless it is to try to meet that without wilting unless you have subscribed to the correspondence course in character-building and self-confidence.

But writers on daily and weekly papers always will go all out for the picturesque. When they interview you, they invariably alter and embroider.

As a rule, this does not matter much. If on your arrival in New York you are asked, 'What do you think of our high buildings?' and you reply, 'I think your high buildings are wonderful,' and it comes out as, 'I think your high buildings are wonderful. I should like to see some of these income tax guys jump off the top of them,' no harm is done. The sentiment pleases the general public, and even the officials of the Internal Revenue Department probably smile indulgently, as men who know that they are going to have the last laugh. But when a war is in progress, it is kinder to the interviewee not to indulge the imagination.

When I arrived in Berlin, I told an interviewer that I had found it difficult to be belligerent in camp, a mild pleasantry by which I intended to convey the feeling of helplessness – of having to be just a number and a well-behaved number at that, which comes over you when you find yourself on the wrong side of the barbed wire. But it did not get over. It was too subtle. The interviewer sniffed at it, patted it with his paws, wrinkled his forehead over it. Then he thought he saw what I was driving at, and penned the following:

'I have never been able to work up a belligerent feeling,' said Mr Wodehouse. 'Just as I am about to feel belligerent about some country, I meet some nice fellow from it and lose my belligerency.' (Have you ever heard me talk like that?)

With the result that I was accused of expressing unpatriotic sentiments and being indifferent to the outcome of the war.

Even George Orwell, who was writing in my defence, said:

He was placed under house-arrest, and from his subsequent statement it appears that he was treated in a fairly friendly way, German officers in the neighbourhood frequently 'dropping in for a bath or a party'.

From Orwell's article you would think I had *invited* the blighters to come and scour their damned bodies in my bathroom. What actually happened was that at the end of the second week of occupation the house next door became full of German Labour Corps workers, and they seemed to have got me muddled up with Tennyson's Sir Walter Vivian, the gentleman who 'all a summer's day gave his broad lawns until the set of sun up to the people'. I suppose to a man fond of German Labour Corps workers and liking to hear them singing in his bath, the conditions would have been almost ideal, but they didn't suit me. I chafed, and a fat lot of good chafing did me. They came again next day and brought their friends.

Some of the charges made against me at the time of the broadcasts were, of course, quite true. W. D. Connor, for instance, in his article in the *Daily Mirror* and subsequent speech on the BBC, accused me, not mincing his words, of having the Christian names of Pelham Grenville, and he was perfectly right.

In the year 1881 I *was* christened Pelham Grenville – after a godfather, and not a thing to show for it except a small silver mug. I remember protesting at the time, vigorously, but it did no good. The clergyman stuck to his point. 'Be that as it may,' he said firmly, having waited for a lull, 'I name thee Pelham Grenville.' All I can do is to express my regrets to Mr Connor, coupled with the hope that his Christian names are Walpurgis Diarmid or something of that sort, and that some day he will have to admit this in public.

The complaint of E. C. Bentley is that I was given a D.Litt. by Oxford University under false pretences, being nothing but a wretched humorist – one who 'has never written a serious line in his life'. He doesn't like it and I don't blame him. Nobody would. And again I have no satisfactory answer to make. If it is any comfort to Bentley and the thousands of others who have grudged me the honour, I may say that never in a career greatly devoted to feeling like 30¢ have I felt more like 30¢ than when in a borrowed cap and gown (with scarlet facings) I stood in the Senate House, taking the treatment.

With Sean O'Casey's statement that I am 'English literature's performing flea' I scarcely know how to deal. Thinking it over, I believe he meant to be complimentary, for all the performing fleas I have met have impressed me with their sterling artistry and that indefinable something which makes the good trouper.

But Mr Colin Vincent of Cheltenham, who wrote in the *Daily Telegraph*, 'Pick up any book by Wodehouse and you will find it peopled by men who have never worked and are moneyed and bored,' I can answer.

Moneyed, forsooth! It is true that Mr Donaldson, president of Donaldson's Dog Biscuits, Inc. of Long Island City and father-in-law of the Hon. Freddie Threepwood, had a pittance, but as he explained to Lord Emsworth, it did not amount to more than $9 or $10 million at the outside. And as for the rest of my characters, I look back over the long line of them, and it seems to me that, whether their name is Bingo or Pongo or Ronnie or Archie or Stanley Featherstonehaugh Ukridge, they are all down to their last bean and peering about with gleaming eyes for someone into whose ribs they can get for a fiver. And those who in an iron age like this have succeeded in prising fivers out of a hard-hearted world cannot be said never to have worked. It is a task that calls for all that a man has or energy, courage and the will to win.

And as for being bored, if the experiences through which they have passed in my books induced ennui in Bertie Wooster or the Efficient Baxter or Lord Emsworth's pig, they must have been extraordinarily *blasé*.

Yours for fewer and better Vincents, Plum.

OVER SEVENTY

An Autobiography With Digressions

P. G. Wodehouse

Contents

Foreword

There is a rare treat in store for the reader[1] of this book. Except in the Foreword,[2] which will soon be over, it is entirely free from footnotes.

I am not, I think, an irascible man,[3] but after reading a number of recent biographies and histories I have begun to feel pretty sore about these footnotes and not in the mood to be put upon much longer.[4] It is high time,[5] in my opinion, that this nuisance was abated and biographers and essayists restrained from strewing these unsightly blemishes[6] through their pages as if they were ploughing the fields and scattering the good seed o'er the land.[7]

I see no need for the bally things.[8] I have just finished reading Carl Sandburg's *Abraham Lincoln, The War Years*, and Carl manages to fill four fat volumes without once resorting to this exasperating practice.[9] If he can do it, why can't everyone?[10]

Frank Sullivan, the American writer,[11] has already raised his voice[12] on this subject,[13] being particularly severe on the historian Gibbon for his habit of getting you all worked up,

[1] Or readers. Let's be optimistic.

[2] Sometimes called Preface. See *Romeo and Juliet*, Act Two, Scene One – 'A rose by any other name would smell as sweet'.

[3] Sunny Jim, many people call me.

[4] See *King Lear*, Act One, Scene Two – 'Some villain hath done me wrong'.

[5] Greenwich Mean or, in America, Eastern Standard.

[6] Footnotes.

[7] Hymns A. and M.

[8] Footnotes.

[9] Bunging in a footnote every second paragraph.

[10] Answer me that.

[11] One of the Saratoga, N.Y., Sullivans.

[12] A light baritone, a little uncertain in the upper register.

[13] Footnotes.

thinking now that you are going to hear full details of the vices of the later Roman emperors, and then switching you off to a Latin footnote which defies translation for the ordinary man who forgot all the Latin he ever knew back in 1920.[14]

I know just how Frank feels. It is the same with me. When I read a book I am like someone strolling across a level lawn, thinking how jolly it all is, and when I am suddenly confronted with a [1] or a [2] it is as though I had stepped on the teeth of a rake and had the handle spring up and hit me on the bridge of the nose. I stop dead and my eyes flicker and swivel. I tell myself that this time I will not be fooled into looking at the beastly thing,[15] but I always am, and it nearly always maddens me by beginning with the word 'see'. 'See the *Reader's Digest*, April 1950,' says one writer on page 7 of his latest work, and again on page 181, 'See the *Reader's Digest*, October 1940.'

How do you mean, 'See' it, my good fellow?[16] Are you under the impression that I am a regular subscriber to the *Reader's Digest* and save up all the back numbers? Let me tell you that if in the waiting-room of my dentist or some such place my eye falls on a copy of this widely circulated little periodical, I wince away from it like a salted snail, knowing that in it lurks some ghastly Most Unforgettable Character I Ever Met.

Slightly, but not much, better than the footnotes which jerk your eye to the bottom of the page are those which are lumped together somewhere in the back of the book. These allow of continuous reading, or at any rate are supposed to, but it is only a man of iron will who, coming on a [6] or a [7], can keep from dropping everything and bounding off after it like a basset hound after a basset.[17]

This involves turning back to ascertain which chapter you are on, turning forward and finding yourself in the Index,

---

[14] Or, in my case, earlier. The sort of thing Sullivan dislikes is when Gibbon says you simply wouldn't believe the things the Empress Theodora used to get up to, and tells you in the footnote that she was *in tres partes divisa* and much given to the *argumentum ad hominem et usque ad hoc.*

[15] The footnote.

[16] The man's an ass.

[17] What *is* a basset? I've often wondered.

turning back and fetching up on Sources, turning forward and getting entangled in Bibliography and only at long last hooking the Notes; and how seldom the result is worth the trouble. I was reading the other day that bit in Carrington's *Life of Rudyard Kipling* where Kipling and his uncle Fred Macdonald go to America and Kipling tries to sneak in incog. and Fred Macdonald gives him away to the reporters. When I saw a [7] appended to this I was all keyed up. Now, I felt, we're going to get something good. The footnote, I told myself, will reveal in detail what Kipling said to Fred Macdonald about his fatheadedness and I shall pick up some powerful epithets invaluable for use in conversations with taxi-drivers and traffic policemen.

Here is [7] *in toto*:

F. W. MACDONALD

If that is not asking for bread and being given a stone, it would be interesting to know what it is. The only thing you can say for a footnote like that is that it is not dragged in, as are most footnotes, just to show off the writer's erudition, as when the author of – say – *The Life of Sir Leonard Hutton* says:

It was in the pavilion at Leeds – not, as has sometimes been stated, at Manchester – that Sir Leonard first uttered those memorable words, 'I've been having a spot of trouble with my lumbago.'

and then with a [6] directs you to the foot of the page, where you find:

Unlike Giraldus Cambrensis, who in *Happy Days at Bognor Regis* mentions suffering from measles and chickenpox as a child but says that he never had lumbago. See also Caecilius Status, Dio Chrysostom and Abu Mohammed Kasim Ben Ali Hariri.

Which is intolerable.[18]

No footnotes, then, in this book of mine, and I think on the whole no Dedication.

Nobody seems to be doing these now, and it just shows how things have changed since the days when I was starting out to

[18] It is what Shakespeare would have called a fardel. See *Hamlet*, Act Three, Scene One – 'Who would fardels bear?'

give a shot in the arm to English Literature. At the turn of the century the Dedication was the thing on which we authors all spread ourselves. It was the *bonne bouche* and the *sine qua non*.

We went in for variety in those days. When you opened a novel, you never knew what you were going to get. It might be the curt, take-it-or-leave-it dedication:

To

J. Smith

and the somewhat warmer:

To

My friend Percy Brown

one of those cryptic things with a bit of poetry in italics:

To

F.B.O.

> *Stark winds*
> *And sunset over the moors*
> *Why?*
> *Whither?*
> *Whence?*
> *And the roll of distant drums*

or possibly the nasty dedication, intended to sting:

To

J. Alastair Frisby

Who

Told Me I Would Never Have A Book Published

And

Advised me

To

Get a job selling jellied eels

SUCKSTOYOU, FRISBY

It was all great fun and kept our pores open and our blood circulating, but it is not difficult to see why the custom died out. Inevitably a time came when there crept into authors' minds the question, 'What is there in this for me?' I know it was so in my own case. 'What is Wodehouse getting out of this?' I asked myself, and the answer, as far as I could see, was, 'Not a thing.'

When the eighteenth-century author inserted on page 1 something like

To

The Most Noble and Puissant Lord Knubble of Knopp
This book is dedicated
By
His very Humble Servant, the Author

My Lord,
It is with inexpressible admiration for your lordships transcendent gifts that the poor slob who now addresses your lordship presents to your lordship this trifling work, so unworthy of your lordships distinguished consideration,

he expected to do himself a bit of good. Lord Knubble was his patron and could be relied on, unless having one of his attacks of gout, to come through with at least a couple of guineas. But where does a modern author like myself get off? I pluck – let us say – P. B. Biffen from the ranks of the unsung millions and make him immortal, and what does Biffen do in return? He does nothing. He just stands there. I probably won't get so much as a lunch out of it.

So no Dedication and, as I say, none of those obscene little fly-specks scattered about all over the page.[19]

I must conclude by expressing my gratitude to Mr P. G. Wodehouse for giving me permission to include in these pages an extract from his book, *Louder and Funnier*. Pretty decent of him, I call it.[20]

Here ends the Foreword. Now we're off.

[19] Footnotes.
[20] The whitest man I know.

ONE

Introducing J. P. Winkler

I

Interesting letter the other day from J. P. Winkler.

You don't know J. P. Winkler? Nor, as a matter of fact, though he addresses me as friend, do I, but he seems to be a man of enterprise and a go-getter.

He says, writing from out Chicago way:

Friend Wodehouse,
For some time I have been presenting in newspapers and on radio a feature entitled *Over Seventy*, being expressions on living by those who have passed their seventieth year, and I should like to include you in this series.

Here are some of the questions I would like you to answer. What changes do you notice particularly in your daily life now? What changes in the American scene? Have you a regimen for health? Are you influenced by criticism of your books? Have you ever written poetry? Have you ever lectured? What do you think of television and the motion pictures?

I see you are living in the country now. Do you prefer it to the city? Give us the overall picture of your home life and describe your methods of work. And any information concerning your experiences in the theatre and any observations on life in general, as seen from the angle of over seventy, will be welcome.

You have been doing much these last fifty years, perhaps you can tell us something about it.

Naturally I was flattered, for we all know that it isn't everybody who gets included in a series. Nevertheless, that 'fifty years' piqued me a little. Long before fifty years ago I was leaving footprints on the sands of time, and good large footprints at that. In my early twenties it would not be too much to say that I was the talk of London. If you had not seen me riding my bicycle down the Strand to the offices of the *Globe* newspaper, where I was at that time employed, frequently using no hands and sometimes bending over to pick up a handkerchief with my teeth, it was pretty generally agreed that you had not seen anything. And the public's memory must be very short if the 22 not out I made for the printers of the *Globe* against the printers of the *Evening News* one Sunday in 1904 has been forgotten.

However, I get the idea, Winkler. You want to start the old gaffer mumbling away in the chimney corner over his clay pipe in the hope that something will emerge which you can present in newspapers and on radio. You would have me survey mankind from China to Peru, touching now on this subject, now on that, like a butterfly flitting from flower to flower, and every now and then coming up with some red-hot personal stuff by way of supplying the human interest.

Right ho. Let's get cracking and see what we can do about it.

2

I am relieved, old man, that you do not insist on the thing being exclusively autobiographical, for as an autobiographer I am rather badly handicapped.

On several occasions it has been suggested to me that I might take a pop at writing my reminiscences. 'Yours has been a long life,' people say. 'You look about a hundred and four. You should make a book of it and cash in.'

It's a thought, of course, but I don't see how I could do it. The three essentials for an autobiography are that its compiler shall have had an eccentric father, a miserable misunderstood childhood and a hell of a time at his public school, and I enjoyed none of these advantages. My father was as normal as rice pudding, my childhood went like a breeze from start to finish, with everybody I met understanding me perfectly, while as for my schooldays at Dulwich they were just six years of unbroken bliss. It would be laughable for me to attempt a formal autobiography. I have not got the material. Anything on the lines of

Wodehouse, The Story of a Wonder Man

starting with

> Chapter One: The Infant
> Chapter Two: Childhood Days
> Chapter Three: Sturm und Drang of Adolescence

is, I feel, out of the question.

Another thing about an autobiography is that, to attract the cash customers, it must be full of good stories about the famous, and I never can think of any. If it were just a matter of dropping names, I could do that with the best of them, but mere name-dropping is not enough. You have to have the sparkling anecdote as well, and any I could provide would be like the one Young Griffo, the boxer, told me in 1904 about his meeting with Joe Gans, the then lightweight champion. Having just been matched to fight Gans, he was naturally anxious to get a look at him before the formal proceedings began, and here is how he told the dramatic tale of their encounter.

'I was going over to Philadelphia to see a fight,' he said, 'and my manager asks me would I like to meet Joe Gans. He asks me I like to meet Joe Gans, see, and I said I would. So we arrive in Philadelphia and we start out for one of the big sporting places where the gang all held out, and my manager asks me again do I want to see Joe Gans, and I say I do. So we go to this big sporting place where the gang all held out, and there's a big crowd standing around one of the tables, and somebody asks me would I like to meet Joe Gans, he's over at that table. Would I like to meet Joe Gans, he says, he's over at that table, he says, and I say I would. So he takes me to the table and says "Here's Young Griffo, Joe," he says. "He wants to meet you," he says. And sure enough it was Joe all right. He gets up from the table and comes right at me.'

I was leaning forward by this time and clutching the arms of my chair. How cleverly, I thought, just as if he had been a professional author, this rather untutored man had led up to the big moment.

'Yes?' I gasped. 'And then?'

'Huh?'

'What happened then?'

'He shakes hands with me. "Hullo, Griff,' he says. And I say "Hullo, Joe".'

That was all. You might have thought more was coming, but no. He had met Gans, Gans had met him. It was the end of the story. My autobiography would be full of stuff like that.

'I had long wished to make the acquaintance of Mr (now Lord) Attlee, but it was not for some years that I was enabled to gratify this ambition. A friend took me to the House of Commons, and we were enjoying tea on the terrace when Mr Attlee came by.

'Oh, Clem,' said my friend, 'I want you to meet Mr Wodehouse.'

'How do you do?' said Mr Attlee.

'How do you do?' I replied.

You can't charge people sixteen bob or whatever it is for that sort of thing.

Still, I quite see, J.P., that I must give you something personal on which your radio public can chew, or we shall have them kicking holes in their sets. I could mention, for instance, that when I was four years old I used to play with an orange, but I doubt if that would interest them, and that at the age of six I read the whole of Pope's *Iliad*, which of course they wouldn't believe. Better, I think, to skip childhood and adolescence and go straight to the Autumn of 1900, when, a comely youth of some eighteen summers, I accepted employment in the Lombard Street office of the Hong Kong and Shanghai Bank. Reluctantly, I may mention. As the song says, I didn't want to do it, I didn't want to do it, but my hand was forced.

The trouble in the Wodehouse home at the beginning of the century was that money was a good deal tighter than could have been wished. The wolf was not actually whining at the door and there was always a little something in the kitty for the butcher and the grocer, but the finances would not run to anything in the nature of a splash. My father, after many years in Hong Kong, had retired on a pension, and the authorities paid it to him in rupees. A thoroughly dirty trick, in my opinion, for the rupee is the last thing in the world – or was then – with which anyone who valued his peace of mind would wish to be associated. It never stayed put for a second. It was always jumping up and down and throwing fits, and expenditure had to be regulated in the light of what mood it happened to be in at the moment. 'Watch that rupee!' was the cry in the Wodehouse family.

The result was that during my schooldays my future was always uncertain. The Boy, What Will He Become? was a question that received a different answer almost daily. My brother Armine had got a scholarship and gone to Oxford, and the idea was that, if I got a scholarship too, I would join him there. All through my last term at Dulwich I sprang from my bed at five sharp each morning, ate a couple of *petit beurre* biscuits and worked like a beaver at my Homer and Thucydides, but just as scholarship time was approaching, with me full to the brim with classic lore and just spoiling for a good whack at the examiners, the rupee started creating again, and it seemed to my father that two sons at the University would be a son more than the privy purse could handle. So Learning drew the loser's end, and Commerce got me.

You are probably thinking, Winkler, that this was a nice slice of luck for Commerce, but you are wrong. Possibly because I was a dedicated literary artist with a soul above huckstering or possibly – this was the view more widely held in the office – because I was just a plain dumb brick, I proved to be the most inefficient clerk whose trouser seat ever polished the surface of a high stool. I was all right as long as they kept me in the postal department, where I had nothing to do but stamp and post letters, a task for which my abilities well fitted me, but when they took me out of there and put me in Fixed Deposits the whisper went round Lombard Street, 'Wodehouse is at a loss. He cannot cope.'

If there was a moment in the course of my banking career when I had the foggiest notion of what it was all about, I am unable to recall it. From Fixed Deposits I drifted to Inward Bills – no use asking me what inward bills are. I never found out – and then to Outward Bills and to Cash, always with a weak, apologetic smile on my face and hoping that suavity of

manner would see me through when, as I knew must happen
'ere long, I fell short in the performance of my mystic duties.
My total inability to grasp what was going on made me something of a legend in the place. Years afterwards, when the
ineptness of a new clerk was under discussion in the manager's
inner sanctum and the disposition of those present at the conference was to condemn him as the worst bungler who had
ever entered the Hong Kong and Shanghai Bank's portals,
some white-haired veteran in charge of one of the departments
would shake his head and murmur, 'No, no, you're wrong.
Young Robinson is, I agree, an almost total loss and ought to
have been chloroformed at birth, but you should have seen
P. G. Wodehouse. Ah, they don't make them like that
nowadays. They've lost the pattern.'

Only two things connected with the banking industry did I
really get into my head. One was that from now on all I
would be able to afford in the way of lunch would be a roll and
butter and a cup of coffee, a discovery which, after the lavish
midday meals of school, shook me to my foundations. The
other was that, if I got to the office late three mornings
in a month, I would lose my Christmas bonus. One of
the great sights in the City in the years 1901–2 was me
rounding into the straight with my coat-tails flying and my
feet going pitter pitter pat and just making it across the
threshold while thousands cheered. It kept me in superb
condition, and gave me a rare appetite for the daily roll and
butter.

Owing to this slowness of uptake where commerce was concerned, I was never very happy in the bank, though probably
happier than the heads of the various departments through
which I made my stumbling way. What I would have liked
to do on leaving school was to dig in at home and concentrate
on my writing. My parents were living in Shropshire – lovely
scenery and Blandings Castle just round the corner – and
nothing would have suited me better than to withdraw to that
earthly Paradise and devote myself to turning out short stories,
which I used to do at that time at the rate of one a day. (In
the summer of 1901 I contracted mumps and went home to
have them in the bosom of my family. I was there three

weeks, swelling all the time, and wrote nineteen short stories, all of which, I regret to say, editors were compelled to decline owing to lack of space. The editors regretted it, too. They said so.)

Putting this project up to my parents, I found them cold towards it. The cross all young writers have to bear is that, while they know that they are going to be spectacularly successful some day, they find it impossible to convince their nearest and dearest that they will ever amount to a row of beans. Write in your spare time, if you really must write, parents say, and they pull that old one about literature being a good something but a bad crutch. I do not blame mine for feeling that a son in a bank making his £80 a year, just like finding it in the street, was a sounder commercial proposition than one living at home and spending a fortune on stamps. (The editor is always glad to consider contributions, but a stamped and addressed envelope should be enclosed in case of rejection.)

So for two years I continued to pass my days in Lombard Street and write at night in my bed-sitting-room, and a testing experience it was, for all I got out of it was a collection of rejection slips with which I could have papered the walls of a good-sized banqueting hall. The best you could say of these was that some of them were rather pretty. I am thinking chiefly of the ones *Tit-Bits* used to send out, with a picture of the Newnes' offices in an attractive shade of green. I like those. But what I always feel about rejection slips is that their glamour soon wears off. When you've seen one, I often say, you've seen them all.

The handicap under which most beginning writers struggle is that they don't know how to write. I was no exception to this rule. Worse bilge than mine may have been submitted to the editors of London in 1901 and 1902, but I should think it very unlikely. I was sorry for myself at the time, when the stamped and addressed envelopes came homing back to me, but my sympathy now is for the men who had to read my contributions. I can imagine nothing more depressing than being an editor and coming to the office on a rainy morning in February with a nail in one shoe and damp trouser legs and finding oneself confronted with an early Wodehouse – written, to make it more difficult, in longhand.

H. G. Wells in his autobiography says that he was much influenced at the outset of his career by a book by J. M. Barrie called *When A Man's Single*. So was I. It was all about authors and journalists and it urged young writers to write not what they liked but what editors liked, and it seemed to me that I had discovered the prime grand secret. The result was that I avoided the humorous story, which was where my inclinations lay, and went in exclusively for the mushy sentiment which, judging from the magazines, was the thing most likely to bring a sparkle into an editor's eyes. It never worked. My only successes were with two-line He and She jokes for the baser weeklies.

At The Servants' Ball

COUNTESS (waltzing with her butler): I'm afraid I must stop, Wilberforce. I'm so danced out.
BUTLER: Oh, no, m'lady, just pleasantly so.

I got 1s. for that, and I still think it ought to have been 1s. 6d.

The curious thing about those early days is that, in spite of the blizzard of rejection slips, I had the most complete confidence in myself. I knew I was good. It was only later that doubts on this point began to creep in and to burgeon as time went by. Today I am a mass of diffidence and I-wonder-if-this-is-going-to-be-all-right-ness, and I envy those tough authors, square-jawed and spitting out of the side of their mouths, who are perfectly sure, every time they start a new book, that it will be a masterpiece. My own attitude resembles that of Bill, my foxhound, when he brings a decaying bone into the dining-room at lunch-time.

'Will this one go?' he seems to be saying, as he eyes us anxiously. 'Will my public consider this bone the sort of bone they have been led to expect from me, or will there be a sense of disappointment and the verdict that William is slipping?'

As a matter of fact, each of Bill's bones is just as dynamic and compelling as the last one, and he has nothing to fear at the bar of critical opinion, but with each new book of mine I have, as I say, always that feeling that this time I have picked a lemon in the garden of literature. A good thing, really, I suppose. Keeps one up on one's toes and makes one write every sentence ten times. Or in many cases twenty times. My books may not be the sort of books the cognoscenti feel justified in blowing the 12s. 6d. on, but I do work at them. When in due course Charon ferries me across the Styx and everyone is telling everyone else what a rotten writer I was, I hope at least one voice will be heard piping up, 'But he did take trouble.'

3

I was getting, then, in the years 1901–2, so little audience response from the men in the editorial chairs that it began to seem that I might have done better to have taken up in my spare time some such hobby as fretwork or collecting bus tickets. But if only a writer keeps on writing, something generally breaks eventually. I had been working assiduously for eighteen months, glued to my chair and taking no part in London's night life except for a weekly dinner – half a crown and 6d. for the waiter – at the Trocadero grill-room, when somebody started a magazine for boys called the *Public School Magazine*, and on top of that came another called *The Captain*, and I had a market for the only sort of work I could do reasonably well – articles and short stories about school life. Wodehouse Preferred, until then down in the cellar with no takers, began to rise a bit. The *Public School Magazine* paid 10s. 6d. for an article and *The Captain* as much as £3 for a short story, and as I was now getting an occasional guinea from *Tit-Bits* and *Answers* I was becoming something of a capitalist. So much so that I began to have thoughts of resigning from the bank and using literature not as a whatever-it-is but as a crutch, especially as it would not be long now before I would be getting my orders.

The London office of the Hong Kong and Shanghai Bank was a sort of kindergarten where the personnel learned their jobs. At the end of two years, presumably by that time having learned them, they were sent out East to Bombay, Bangkok, Batavia and suchlike places. This was called getting one's orders, and the thought of getting mine scared the pants off me. As far as I could make out, when you were sent East you immediately became a branch manager or something of that sort, and the picture of myself managing a branch was one I preferred not to examine too closely. I couldn't have managed a whelk-stall.

And what of my Art? I knew in a vague sort of way that there were writers who had done well writing of life in foreign parts, but I could not see myself making a success of it. My line was good sound English stuff, the kind of thing the magazines liked – stories of rich girls who wanted to be loved for themselves alone, and escaped convicts breaking into lonely country houses on Christmas Eve, when the white snow lay all around, and articles for *Tit-Bits* and school stories for *The Captain*. Could I carry on with these, enclosing a stamped addressed envelope in case of rejection, if I were out in Singapore or Sourabaya?

I thought not and, as I say, toyed with the idea of resigning. And then one day the thing was taken out of my hands and the decision made for me.

Let me tell you the story of the new ledger.

4

One of the things that sour authors, as every author knows, is being asked by people to write something clever in the front pages of their books. It was, I believe, George Eliot who in a moment of despondency made this rather bitter entry in her diary:

Dear Diary, am I a wreck tonight! I feel I never want to see another great admirer of my work again. It's not writing novels that's hard. I can write novels till the cows come home. What slays you is this gosh-darned autographing. 'Oh, *please!* Not just your *name*. Won't you write something *clever*.' I wish the whole bunch of them were in gaol, and I'd laugh myself sick if the gaol burned down.

And Richard Powell, the whodunit author, was complaining of this in a recent issue of *The American Writer*. 'I begin sweating,' he said, 'as soon as someone approaches me with a copy of one of my books.'

I feel the same. When I write a book, the golden words come pouring out like syrup, but let a smiling woman steal up to me with my latest and ask me to dash off something clever on the front page, and it is as though some hidden hand had removed my brain and substituted for it an order of cauliflower. There may be authors capable of writing something clever on the spur of the moment, but I am not of their number. I like at least a month's notice, and even then I don't guarantee anything.

Sometimes the quickness of the hand will get me by, but not often. When I am not typing I use one of those pen-pencil things which call for no blotting paper. The ink, or whatever the substance is that comes out at the top, dries as you write, so I take the book and scribble, 'Best wishes, P. G. Wodehouse' and with equal haste slam the lid, hoping that the party of the second part will have the decency not to peer inside till I am well out of the way. It seldom happens. Nine times out of ten she snaps the thing open like a waiter opening an oyster, and then the disappointed look, the awkward pause and the pained, 'But I wanted something *clever*.'[1]

The only time I ever wrote anything really clever on the front page of a book was when I was in the cash department of the Hong Kong and Shanghai Bank and a new ledger came in and was placed in my charge. It had a white, gleaming front page and suddenly, as I sat gazing at it, there floated into my mind like drifting thistledown the idea of writing on it a richly comic description of the celebrations and rejoicings marking the Formal Opening of the New Ledger, and I immediately proceeded to do so.

It was the most terrific 'piece', as they call it now. Though

[1] I'm frightfully sorry, but I must have just one footnote here. I have recently taken to inscribing these books with the legend:

'You like my little stories do ya?

Oh, glory glory hallelujah.'

It sometimes goes well, sometimes not.

fifty-five years have passed since that day, it is still green in my memory. It had everything. There was a bit about my being presented to his Gracious Majesty the King (who, of course, attended the function) which would have had you gasping with mirth. ('From his tie he took a diamond tie-pin, and smiled at me, and then he put it back.') And that was just one passing incident in it. The whole thing was a knock-out. I can't give the details. You will have to take my word for it that it was one of the most screamingly funny things ever written. I sat back on my stool and felt like Dickens when he had finished *Pickwick*. I was all in a glow.

Then came the reaction. The head cashier was rather an austere man who on several occasions had expressed dissatisfaction with the young Wodehouse, and something seemed to whisper to me that, good as the thing was, it would not go any too well with him. Briefly, I got cold feet and started to turn stones and explore avenues in the hope of finding some way of making everything pleasant for all concerned. In the end I decided that the best thing to do was to cut the pages out with a sharp knife.

A few mornings later the stillness of the bank was shattered by a sudden yell of triumph, not unlike the cry of the Brazilian wild cat leaping on its prey. It was the head cashier discovering the absence of the page, and the reason he yelled triumphantly was that he was feuding with the stationers and for weeks had been trying to get the goods on them in some way. He was at the telephone in two strides, asking them if they called themselves stationers. I suppose they replied that they did, for he then touched off his bombshell, accusing them of having delivered an imperfect ledger, a ledger with the front page missing.

This brought the head stationer round in person calling heaven to witness that when the book left his hands it had been all that a ledger should be, if not more so.

'Somebody must have cut out the page,' he said.

'Absurd!' said the head cashier. 'Nobody but an imbecile would cut out the front page of a ledger.'

'Then,' said the stationer, coming right back at him, 'you must have an imbecile in your department. Have you?'

The head cashier started. This opened up a new line of thought.

'Why, yes,' he admitted, for he was a fair-minded man. 'There is P. G. Wodehouse.'

'Weak in the head, is he, this Wodehouse?'

'Very, so I have always thought.'

'Then send for him and question him narrowly,' said the stationer.

This was done. They got me under the lights and grilled me, and I had to come clean. It was immediately after this that I found myself at liberty to embark on the life literary.

TWO

Getting Started

I

From my earliest years I had always wanted to be a writer. I started turning out the stuff at the age of five. (What I was doing before that, I don't remember. Just loafing, I suppose.)

It was not that I had any particular message for humanity. I am still plugging away and not the ghost of one so far, so it begins to look as though, unless I suddenly hit mid-season form in my eighties, humanity will remain a message short. When I left the bank and turned pro, I just wanted to write, and was prepared to write anything that had a chance of getting into print. And as I surveyed the literary scene, everything looked pretty smooth to me, for the early years of the twentieth century in London – it was in 1902 that the Hong Kong and Shanghai Bank decided (and a very sensible decision, too) that the only way to keep solvent was to de-Wodehouse itself – were not too good for writers at the top of the tree, the big prices being still in the distant future, but they were fine for an industrious young hack who asked no more than to pick up the occasional half-guinea. The dregs, of whom I was one, sat extremely pretty *circa* 1902. There were so many morning papers and evening papers and weekly papers and monthly magazines that you were practically sure of landing your whimsical article on 'The Language of Flowers' or your parody of Omar Khayyám somewhere or other after say thirty-five shots.

I left the bank in September, and by the end of the year found that I had made £65 6s. 7d., so for a beginner I was doing pretty well. But what I needed, to top it off, I felt, was something in the way of a job with a regular salary, and I was fortunate enough to have one fall right into my lap.

There was an evening paper in those days called the *Globe*. It was 105 years old and was printed – so help me – on pink paper. (One of the other evening sheets was printed on green paper. Life was full then, very rich.) It had been a profitable source of income to me for some time because it ran on its front page what were called turnovers, 1000-word articles of almost unparalleled dullness which turned over on to the second page. You dug these out of reference books and got a guinea for them.

In addition to the turnovers the *Globe* carried on its front page a humorous column entitled 'By The Way', and one day I learned that the man who wrote it had been a master at Dulwich when I was there. Sir W. Beach Thomas, no other. These things form a bond. I asked him to work me in as his understudy when he wanted a day off, and he very decently did so, and when he was offered a better job elsewhere, I was taken on permanently. Three guineas a week was the stipend, and it was just what I needed. The work was over by noon, and I had all the rest of the day for freelancing.

What you would call the over-all picture, Winkler, now brightened considerably. There was quite a bit of prestige attached to doing 'By The Way' on the *Globe*. Some well-known writers had done it before Beach Thomas – E. V. Lucas was one of them – and being the man behind the column gave one a certain standing. A parody of Omar Khayyám submitted to a weekly paper – as it might be *Vanity Fair* or *The World* – by P. G. Wodehouse, 'By The Way', the *Globe*, 367 Strand, was much more sympathetically received than would have been a similar effort by P. G. Wodehouse, 21 Walpole Street, Chelsea.

My contributions appeared from time to time in *Punch*, and a couple of times I even got into the *Strand* magazine, which for a young writer in those days was roughly equivalent to being awarded the Order of the Garter. My savings began to mount up. And came a day when I realized that I was sufficiently well fixed to do what I had always dreamed of doing – pay a visit to America.

Why America? I have often wondered about that. Why, I mean, from my earliest years, almost back to the time when

I was playing with that orange, was it America that was always to me the land of romance? It is not as though I had been intoxicated by visions of cowboys and Red Indians. Even as a child I never became really cowboy-conscious, and to Red Indians I was definitely allergic, I wanted no piece of them.

And I had no affiliations with the country. My father had spent most of his life in Hong Kong. So had my Uncle Hugh. And two other uncles had been for years in Calcutta and Singapore. You would have expected it to be the Orient that would have called to me. 'Put me somewheres east of Suez,' you would have pictured me saying to myself. But it didn't work out that way. People would see me walking along with a glassy look in my eyes and my mouth hanging open as if I had adenoids and would whisper to one another, 'He's thinking of America.' And they were right.

The *Globe* gave its staff five weeks' holiday in the year. Eight days crossing the Atlantic and eight days crossing it back again was going to abbreviate my visit, but I should at least have nineteen days in New York, so I booked my passage and sailed.

This yearning I had to visit America, rather similar to that of a Tin Pan Alley song-writer longing to get back, back, back to his old Kentucky shack, was due principally, I think, to the fact that I was an enthusiastic boxer in those days and had a boyish reverence for America's pugilists – James J. Corbett, James J. Jeffries, Tom Sharkey, Kid McCoy and the rest of them. I particularly wanted to meet Corbett and shake the hand that had kay-oed John L. Sullivan. I had a letter of introduction to him, but he was in San Francisco when I landed, and I did not get to know him till a good many years later, when he was a charming old gentleman and one of Broadway's leading actors.

But I did meet Kid McCoy. I went out to the camp at White Plains where he was training for his championship fight with Philadelphia Jack O'Brien, and it was at the end of my afternoon there that I made what I can see now – in fact, I saw it almost immediately then – was a rash move. I asked him if I could put on the gloves and have a round with him.

thought it would be something to tell the boys back home, that I had sparred with Kid McCoy.

He assured me he would be delighted, and as we were preparing ourselves for the tourney he suddenly chuckled. He had been reminded, he said, of an entertaining incident in his professional career, when he was fighting a contender who had the misfortune to be stone deaf. It was not immediately that he became aware of the other's affliction, but when he did he acted promptly and shrewdly. As the third round entered its concluding stages he stepped back a pace and pointed to his adversary's corner, to indicate to him that the bell had rung, which of course was not the case but far from it.

'Oh, thank you so much,' said the adversary. 'Very civil of you.'

He dropped his hands and turned away, whereupon Kid McCoy immediately knocked him out.

It was as my host concluded his narrative, laughing heartily at the amusing recollection, that, in Robert Benchley's powerful phrase, I developed a yellow streak which was plainly visible through my clothing. The shape of things to come suddenly took on a most ominous aspect.

'Is this wise, Wodehouse?' I asked myself. 'Is it prudent to go getting yourself mixed up with a middleweight champion of the world whose sense of humour is so strongly marked and so what you might almost describe as warped? Is it not probable that a man with a mind like that will think it droll to knock your fat head off at the roots?'

Very probable indeed, I felt, and that yellow streak began to widen. I debated within myself the idea of calling the whole thing off and making a quick dash for the train. It was an attractive scheme, in which I could see no flaw except that the strategic rearward movement I was planning would put an awful dent in the pride of the Wodehouses. I had never gone much into the family history, but I assumed that my ancestors, like everybody else's, had done well at Crécy and Agincourt, and nobody likes to be a degenerate descendant. I was at a young man's crossroads.

At this moment, as I stood there this way and that dividing the swift mind, like Sir Bedivere, there was a clatter of horse's

hooves and a girl came riding up. This was the Kid's wife –
he had six of them in an interesting career which ended in a
life sentence for murder in Sing-Sing prison – and she caused
a welcome diversion. We all became very social, and the
McCoy-Wodehouse bout was adjourned *sine die*.

I remember that girl as the prettiest girl I ever saw in my
life. Or maybe she just looked good to me at the moment.

2

Right from the start of my sojourn in New York I don't think
I ever had any doubts as to this being the New York of which
I had heard so much. 'It looks like New York,' I said to
myself as I emerged from the Customs sheds. 'It smells like New
York. Yes, I should say it was New York all right.' In which
respect I differed completely from Sig. Guiseppe Bartholdi,
who, arriving on the plane there from Italy the other day,
insisted against all argument that he was in San Francisco.

What happened was that the signor was on his way to visit
his son in San Francisco and was not aware of the fact that to
get to that city from Italy you have to change at New York and
take a westbound plane. All he knew was that his son had
told him to come to Montgomery Street, where his – the son's –
house was, so when his plane grounded at Idlewild, he hopped
out and got into the airport bus, shouting the Italian equivalent
of 'California, here I come', and in due course the bus deposited
him at the terminus, where he hailed a cab and said ,'Montgomery Street, driver, and keep your foot on the accelerator.'

Now it so happens that there is a Montgomery Street in New
York, down on the lower east side, and the driver – Jose
Navarro of 20 Avenue D., not that it matters – took him there,
and pretty soon Sig. Bartholdi, like Othello, was perplexed
in the extreme. Nothing the eye could reach resembled the
photograph his son had sent him of the house for which he was
headed, so he decided to search on foot, and when he had not
returned at the end of an hour Mr Navarro drove to the
Clinton Street police station and told his story.

About seven p.m. Sig. Bartholdi arrived at the police station
escorted by Patrolman J. Aloysius Murphy, and that was where

things got complex and etched those deep lines which you can still see on the foreheads of the Clinton Street force. For, as I say, the signor stoutly refused to believe that he was not in San Francisco. Hadn't he seen Montgomery Street with his own eyes? The fact that some men of ill-will had spirited away his son's house had, he said, nothing to do with the case. Either a street is Montgomery Street or it is not Montgomery Street. There is no middle course.

After about forty minutes of this Mr Patrick Daly, the courteous and popular police lieutenant down Clinton Street way, drew Patrolman Murphy aside. There was a worried expression on his face, and his breathing was rather laboured.

'Look, Aloysius,' he said, 'are you absolutely sure this *is* New York?'

'It's how I always heard the story,' said Patrolman Murphy.

'You have no doubts?'

'Ah, now you're talking, Lieut. If you had asked me that question an hour ago – nay, forty minutes ago – I'd have said "None whatever", but right now I'm beginning to wonder.'

'Me, too. Tell me in your own words, Aloysius, what makes – or shall we say used to make – you think this is New York?'

Patrolman Murphy marshalled his thoughts.

'Well,' he said, 'I live in the Bronx. That's in New York.'

'There may be a Bronx in San Francisco.'

'And here's my badge. Lookut. See what it says on it. "New York City".'

The lieutenant shook his head.

'You can't go by badges. How do we know that some international gang did not steal your San Francisco badge and substitute this one?'

'Would an international gang do that?'

'You never can tell. They're always up to something,' said Lieutenant Daly with a weary sigh.

Well, it all ended happily, I am glad to say. Somebody rang up the signor's son and put the signor on the wire, and the son told him that New York really was New York and that he was to get on the westbound plane at once and come to San Francisco. And there he is now, plumb spang in Montgomery Street, and having a wonderful time. (On a recent picture postcard to a friend in Italy he asserts this in so many words, adding that he wishes he, the friend, were there.) It is a great weight off everybody's mind.

The whole episode has left the Clinton Street personnel a good deal shaken. They are inclined to start at sudden noises and to think that they are being followed about by little men with black beards, and I am not surprised, for they can never tell when something like this may not happen again. And, really, if I were the city of New York, I honestly don't see how I could prove it to a sceptical visitor from Italy. If I were London, yes. That would be simple. I would take the man by the ear and lead him into Trafalgar Square and show him those Landseer lions.

'Look,' I would say. 'Lions. Leeongze. Dash it, man, you know perfectly well that you would never find leeongze like those anywhere except in London.'

Upon which the fellow would say, '*Si, si. Grazie,*' and go away with his mind completely set at rest.

3

From 1904 to 1957 is fifty-three years, and I see that you ask in your questionnaire, Winkler, what changes I have noticed in the American scene during that half-century and a bit. Well, I should say that the principal one is the improvement in American manners.

In 1904 I found residents in the home of the brave and the land of the free, though probably delightful chaps if you got to know them, rather on the brusque side. They shoved you in the street and asked who you were shoving, and used, when spoken to, only one side of the mouth in replying. They were, in a word, pretty tough eggs.

One of my earliest recollections of that first visit of mine to New York is of watching a mob of travellers trying to enter a subway train and getting jammed in the doorway. Two subway officials were standing on the platform, and the first subway official said to the second subway official (speaking out of the starboard side of his mouth), 'Pile 'em in, George!'

Whereupon the two took a running dive at the mass of humanity and started to shove like second-row forwards. It was effective, but it could not happen today. George and his colleague would at least say, 'Pardon us, gentlemen,' before putting their heads down.

For in recent years America has become a nation of Chesterfields, its inhabitants as polite as pallbearers. It may be Emily Post's daily advice on deportment that has brought about this change for the better. Or perhaps it is because I have been over here, setting a good example.

You see it everywhere, this new courtesy.

A waitress in one of the cheaper restaurants on the west side was speaking highly of the polish of a regular customer of hers. 'Every time I serve him anything at the table,' she said, 'he stops eating and raises his hat.'

A man I know was driving in his car the other day and stalled his engine at a street intersection. The lights changed from yellow to green, from green to red, from red to yellow and from yellow to green, but his car remained rooted to the spot. A policeman sauntered up.

'What's the matter, son?' he asked sympathetically. 'Haven't we got any colours you like?'

It is difficult to see how he could have been nicer.

Boxers, too, not so long ago a somewhat uncouth section of the community who were seldom if ever mistaken for members of the Vere de Vere family, have taken on a polish which makes their society a pleasure. They have names like Cyril and Percy and Clarence and live up to them. I can remember the time when, if you asked Kid Biff (the Hoboken Assassin), what in his opinion were his chances in his impending contest with Boko Swat (the Bronx's answer to Civilization), he would reply, 'Dat bum? I'll moider him.' Today it would be, 'The question which you have propounded is by no means an easy one to answer. So many imponderables must be taken into consideration. It is, I mean to say, always difficul to predict before their entry into the arena the outcome of an encounter between two highly trained and skilful welterweights. I may say, however – I am, of course, open to correction – that I am confident of establishing my superiority on the twenty-fourth prox. My manager who, a good deal to my regret, is addicted to the argot, says I'll knock the blighter's block off.'

There was a boxer at the St Nicholas Rink a few weeks ago who came up against an opponent with an unpleasantly forceful left hook which he kept applying to the spot on the athlete's body where, when he was in mufti, his third waistcoat button would have been. His manager watched pallidly from outside the ropes, and when his tiger came back to his corner at the end of the round, was all concern and compassion.

'Joey,' he asked anxiously, 'how do you feel, Joey?'

'Fine, thank you,' said the boxer. 'And you?'

One can almost hear Emily Post cheering in the background.

Even the criminal classes have caught the spirit. From Passaic, New Jersey, comes the news that an unidentified assailant plunged a knife into the shoulder of a Mr James F. Dobson the other day, spun him round and then, seeing his face, clicked his tongue remorsefully.

'Oh, I beg your pardon,' he said. 'I got the wrong guy.'

Frank and manly. If you find yourself in the wrong, admit it and apologize.

Nobody could be more considerate than the modern American. In the Coronet motel outside the town of Danvers, Massachusetts, there is a notice posted asking clients to clean out their rooms before leaving. 'Certainly, certainly, certainly, by all means,' said a recent visitor, and he went off with two table lamps, an inkstand and pen, a mahogany nighttable, an ashtray, four sheets, two pillow-cases, two rubber foam pillows, two blankets, two bedspreads, two bath towels, two tumblers and a shower curtain. It was as near to cleaning out the room as he could get, and it must have been saddening to so conscientious a man to be compelled to leave the beds, the mattresses and a twenty-one-inch console television set.

Yes, Manners Makyth Man is the motto of the American of today, though, of course, even today you come across the occasional backslider, the fellow who is not in the movement. A 'slim, elderly man wearing a grey Homburg hat' attracted the notice of the Brooklyn police last week by his habit of going to the turnstile of the Atlantic Avenue subway station, pulling the bar towards him and slipping through the narrow opening, thus getting a free trip, a thing the subway people simply hate. And what I am leading up to is this. Appearing before Magistrate John R. Starley at the Flatbush Police Court, he continued to wear his Homburg hat. When a court official removed it, he put it on again, and kept putting it on all through the proceedings, though he must have been aware that this is not done. ('Unless you are a private detective, always *always* take your hat off indoors' . . . Emily Post.)

It is a pleasure to me to expose this gauche person in print. Michael Rafferty (67) of 812 Myrtle Avenue, Brooklyn. That'll learn you, Mike.

THREE

Bring on the Earls

I

Back in London, I found that I had done wisely in going to New York for even so brief a visit. The manner of editors towards me changed. Where before it had been, 'Throw this man out,' they now said, 'Come in, my dear fellow, come in and tell us all about America.' It is hard to believe in these days, when after breakfasting at the Berkeley you nip across the ocean and dine at the Stork Club, but in 1904 anyone in the London writing world who had been to America was regarded with awe and looked upon as an authority on that *terra incognita*. Well, when I tell you that a few weeks after my return *Tit-Bits* was paying me a guinea for an article on New York Crowds and *Sandow's Magazine* 30s. for my description of that happy day at Kid McCoy's training camp, I think I have made my point sufficiently clear.

After that trip to New York I was a man who counted. It was, 'Ask Wodehouse. Wodehouse will know,' when some intricate aspect of American politics had to be explained to the British public. My income rose like a rocketing pheasant. I made £505 1s. 7d. in 1906 and £527 17s. 1d. in 1907 and was living, I suppose, on about £203 4s. 9d. In fact, if on November 17th, 1907, I had not bought a secondhand Darracq car for £450 (and smashed it up in the first week) I should soon have been one of those economic royalists who get themselves so disliked. This unfortunate venture brought my capital back to about where it had started, and a long and dusty road had to be travelled before my finances were in a state sufficiently sound to justify another visit to America.

I was able to manage it in the spring of 1909.

2

At the time of this second trip to New York I was still on the *Globe* doing the 'By The Way' column, and had come over anticipating that after nineteen days I would have to tear myself away with many a longing lingering look behind and go back to the salt mines. But on the sixth day a strange thing happened. I had brought with me a couple of short stories, and I sold one of them to the *Cosmopolitan* and the other to *Collier's* for $200 and $300 respectively, both on the same morning. That was at that time roughly £40 and £60, and to one like myself whose highest price for similar bijoux had been ten guineas a throw, the discovery that American editors were prepared to pay on this stupendous scale was like suddenly finding a rich uncle from Australia. This, I said to myself, is the place for me.

I realized, of course, that New York was more expensive than London, but even so one could surely live there practically for ever on $500. Especially as there were always the good old *Cosmopolitan* and jolly old *Collier's* standing by with their cornucopias, all ready to start pouring. To seize pen and paper and post my resignation to the *Globe* was with me the work of an instant. Then, bubbling over with hope and ambition, I took a room at the Hotel Duke down in Greenwich Village and settled in with a secondhand typewriter, paper, pencils, envelopes and Bartlett's book of *Familiar Quotations*, that indispensable adjunct to literary success.

I wonder if Bartlett has been as good a friend to other authors as he has been to me. I don't know where I would have been all these years without him. It so happens that I am not very bright and find it hard to think up anything really clever off my own bat, but give me my Bartlett and I will slay you.

It has always been a puzzle to me how Bartlett did it, how he managed to compile a volume of 3 million quotations or whatever it is. One can see, of course, how he started. I picture him at a loose end one morning, going about shuffling his feet and whistling and kickings tones, and his mother looked out of the window and said, 'John, dear, I wish you wouldn't fidget like that. Why don't you find something to *do*?'

'Such as . . .?' said John Bartlett (born at Plymouth, Mass., in 1820).

'Dig in the garden.'

'Don't want to dig in the garden.'

'Or spin your top.'

'Don't *want* to spin my top.'

'Then why not compile a book of familiar quotations, a collection of passages, phrases and proverbs, traced to their sources in ancient and modern literature?'

John Bartlett's face lit up. He lost that sullen look.

'Mater,' he said, 'I believe you've got something there. I see what you mean. "To be or not to be" and all that guff. I'll start right away. Paper!' said John Bartlett. 'Lots of paper, and can anyone lend me a pencil?'

So far, so good. But after that what? One cannot believe that he had all literature at his fingers' ends and knew just what Aldus Manutius said in 1472 and Narcisse Achille, Comte de Salvandy, in 1797. I suppose he went about asking people.

'Know anything good?' he would say, button-holing an acquaintance.

'Shakespeare?'

'No, I've got Shakespeare.'

'How about Pliny the Younger?'

'Never heard of him, but shoot.'

'Pliny the Younger said, "Objects which are usually the motives of our travels by land and by sea are often overlooked if they lie under our eye." '

'He called that hot, did he?' says John Bartlett with an ugly sneer.

The acquaintance stiffens.

'If it was good enough for Pliny the Younger it ought to be good enough for a pop-eyed young pipsqueak born at Plymouth, Mass., in 1820.'

'All right, all right, no need to get steamed up about it. How are you on Pliny the Elder?'

'Pliny the Elder said "Everything is soothed by oil." '

'Everything is what by *what*?'

'Soothed by oil.'

'How about sardines?' says John Bartlett with a light laugh. 'Well, all right, I'll bung it down, but I don't think much of it.'

And so the book got written. In its original form it contained only 295 pages, but the latest edition runs to 1254, not counting 577 pages of index, and one rather unpleasant result of this continual bulging process is that Bartlett today has become frightfully mixed. It is like a conservative old club that has had to let down the barriers and let in a whole lot of rowdy young new members to lower the tone. There was a time when you couldn't get elected to Bartlett unless you were Richard Bethell, Lord Westbury (1800–73) or somebody like that, but now you never know who is going to pop out at you from its pages. Gabriel Romanovitch Dershavin (1743–1816) often says to Alexis Charles Henri Clerel de Tocqueville (1805–59) that it gives him a pain in the neck.

'Heaven knows I'm no snob,' he says, 'but really when it comes to being expected to mix with non-U outsiders like P. G. Wodehouse and the fellow who wrote *The Man Who Broke the Bank at Monte Carlo*, well, dash it!'

And Alexis Charles Henri says he knows exactly how Gabriel Romanovitch feels, and he has often felt the same way himself. They confess themselves at a loss to imagine what the world is coming to.

Nevertheless and be that as it may, Bartlett, with all thy faults we love thee still. How many an erudite little article of mine would not have been written without your never-failing sympathy, encouragement, and advice. So all together, boys.

'What's the matter with Bartlett?'

'He's all right!'

'Who's all right?'

'Bartlett! Bartlett! Bartlett! For he's a jolly good fellow, for he's a jolly good fellow, for he's a jolly good fe-hel-low. . . .'

And no heel-taps.

3

I was down having a nostalgic look at the Hotel Duke the other day, and was shocked to find that in the forty-seven years during which I had taken my eye off it it had blossomed out into no end of a high-class joint with a Champagne Room or a Diamond Horseshoe or something like that, where you can dance nightly to the strains of somebody's marimba band. In 1909 it was a seedy rookery inhabited by a group of young writers as impecunious as myself, who had no time or inclination for dancing. We paid weekly (meals included) about what you tip the waiter nowadays after a dinner for two, and it was lucky for me that the management did not charge more. If they had, I should have been in the red at the end of the first few months.

For it was not long before I made the unpleasant discovery that though I had a certain facility for dialogue and a nice light comedy touch – at least, I thought it was nice – my output was not everybody's dish. After that promising start both *Collier's* and the *Cosmopolitan* weakened and lost their grip. If it had not been for the pulps – God bless them – I should soon have been looking like a famine victim.

I have written elsewhere – in a book called *Heavy Weather*, if you don't mind me slipping in a quick advert – that the ideal towards which the City Fathers of all English country towns strive is to provide a public house for each individual inhabitant. It was much the same in New York in 1909 as regards the pulp magazines. There was practically one per person. They flooded the bookstalls, and it was entirely owing to them that I was able in those days to obtain the calories without which it is fruitless to try to keep the roses in the cheeks.

Not that I obtained such a frightful lot of calories, for there was nothing of the lavishness of *Collier's* and *Cosmopolitan* about the pulps. They believed in austerity for their contributors, and one was lucky to get $50 for a story. Still, $50 here and $50 there helps things along, and I was able to pay my weekly bill at the Duke and sometimes – very occasionally – to lunch at a good restaurant. And after a year or so a magazine called *Vanity Fair* was started and I was taken on as its dramatic critic.

I blush a little as I make that confession, for I know where dramatic critics rank in the social scale. Nobody loves them, and rightly, for they are creatures of the night. Has anybody ever seen a dramatic critic in the daytime? I doubt it. They come out after dark, and we know how we feel about things that come out after dark. Up to no good, we say to ourselves.

Representing a monthly magazine, I was excluded from the opening performance and got my seats on the second night. This of course was rather humiliating and made me feel I was not really a force, but I escaped the worries that beset the dramatic critic of a morning paper. The inkstained wretches who cover the new plays for the dailies have a tough assignment. Having to rush off to the office and get their notice in by midnight, every minute counts with them, and too often they find themselves on a first night barred from the exit door by a wall of humanity.

The great thing, according to John McLain of the *NY Journal-American*, is to beat the gun, and with this in mind he employs two methods. One is to keep his eye on the curtain, and the minute it starts to quiver at the top, showing that the evening's entertainment is about to conclude, to be off up the aisle like a jack-rabbit. The other is to anticipate the curtain line, but here too often the dramatist fools you. At a recent opening the heroine, taking the centre of the stage at about five minutes to eleven, passed a weary hand over her brow and whispered, 'And that . . . is all.' That seemed good enough to Mr McLain and he was out of the theatre in a whirl of dust, little knowing that after his departure the hero entered (l.) and said, 'All what?' and the play went on for another half-hour.

Having two weeks in which to write my critique, I missed all that.

So what with my $50 here and my $50 there and my salary from *Vanity Fair*, I was making out fairly well. All right so far, about summed it up.

But I was not satisfied. I wanted something much more on

the order of a success story, and I would be deceiving your newspaper and radio public, Winkler, if I were to say I did not chafe. I chafed very frequently.

You know how it is, J.P. You ask yourself what you are doing with this life of yours, and it is galling to have to answer, 'Well, if you must pin me down, not such a frightful lot.' It seemed to me that the time had arrived to analyse and evaluate my position with a view to taking steps through the proper channels. I was particularly anxious to put my finger on the reason why slick-paper magazines like the *Saturday Evening Post* did not appear to want their Wodehouse.

Quite suddenly I spotted what the trouble was. It came to me like a flash one day when I was lunching on a ham sandwich (with dill pickle) and a glass of milk.

My name was all wrong.

This matter of names is of vital importance to those who practise the Arts. There is nothing about which they have to be more careful. Consider the case of Frank Lovejoy, the movie star, who for a time was not getting anywhere in his profession and couldn't think why till one morning his agent explained it to him.

'We meet producer resistance,' the agent told him, 'on account of your name. The studio heads don't think Frank Lovejoy a suitable name for a movie star. You'll have to change it. What they want today is *strong* names, like Rock Hudson, Tab Hunter and so on. Try to think of something.'

'Stab Zanuch?'

'Not bad.'

'Or Max Million?'

'Better still. That's got it.'

But a week later Mr Lovejoy had a telephone call from his agent.

'Max Million speaking,' he said.

'It is, is it? Well, it better not be,' said the agent. 'The trend has changed. They don't want strong names any more, they want *sincere* names.'

'How do you mean, sincere names?'

'Well, like Abe Lincoln.'

'Abe Washington?'

'Abe Washington is fine.'

'Or Ike Franklin?'

'No, I think Abe Washington's better.'

For some days Abe Washington went about feeling that prosperity was just around the corner, and then the telephone rang once more.

'Sorry, kid,' said the agent, 'but the trend has changed again. They want *geographical* names, like John Ireland.'

So Frank Lovejoy became George Sweden, and all seemed well, with the sun smiling through and all that sort of thing, but his contentment was short-lived. The agent rang up to say that there had been another shift in the party line and the trend was now towards *familiar* names like Gary Stewart, Clark Cooper and Alan Gable. So Frank Lovejoy became Marlon Ladd and might be so to this day, had not he had another call from the agent.

'There's been a further shake-up,' the agent said. 'What they want now are *happy* names suggestive of love and joy.'

'How about Frank Lovejoy?'

'Swell,' said the agent.

But I was telling you about my name being wrong. All this while, you see, I had been labelling my stories.

BY

P. G. WODEHOUSE

and at this time when a writer for the American market who went about without three names was practically going around naked. Those were the days of Richard Harding Davis, of Margaret Culkin Banning, of James Warner Bellah, of Earl Derr Biggers, of Charles Francis Coe, Norman Reilly Raine, Mary Roberts Rinehart, Clarence Budington Kelland and Orison Swett – yes, really, I'm not kidding – Marden. And here was I, poor misguided simp, trying to get by with a couple of contemptible initials.

No wonder the slicks would not take my work. In anything like a decent magazine I would have stood out as conspicuously as a man in a sweater and cap at the Eton and Harrow match.

It frequently happens that when you get an inspiration, you

don't stop there but go right ahead and get another. My handicap when starting to write for American editors had always been that I knew so little of American life, and it now occurred to me that I had not yet tried them with anything about English life. I knew quite a lot about what went on in English country houses with their earls and butlers and younger sons. In my childhood in Worcestershire and later in my Shropshire days I had met earls and butlers and younger sons in some profusion, and it was quite possible, it now struck me, that the slick magazines would like to read about them.

I had a plot all ready and waiting, and two days later I was typing on a clean white page.

SOMETHING FRESH
BY
PELHAM GRENVILLE WODEHOUSE

and I had a feeling that I was going to hit the jackpot. It seemed incredible to me that all this time, like the base Indian who threw away a pearl richer than all his tribe, I should have been failing to cash in on such an income-producing combination as Pelham Grenville Wodehouse. It put me right up there with Harry Leon Wilson, David Graham Phillips, Arthur Somers Roche and Hugh McNair Kahler.

If you ask me to tell you frankly if I like the name Pelham Grenville Wodehouse, I must confess that I do not. I have my dark moods when it seems to me about as low as you can get. I was named after a godfather, and not a thing to show for it but a small silver mug which I lost in 1897. But I was born at a time when children came to the font not knowing what might not happen to them before they were dried off and taken home. My three brothers were christened respectively Philip Peveril, Ernest Armine and Lancelot Deane, so I was probably lucky not to get something wished on me like Hyacinth Augustus or Albert Prince Consort. And say what you will of Pelham Grenville, shudder though you may at it, it changed the luck. *Something Fresh* was bought as a serial by the *Saturday Evening Post* for what *Variety* would call a hotsy $3500. It was the first of the series which I may call the Blandings Castle saga, featuring Clarence, ninth Earl of Emsworth, his

pig Empress of Blandings, his son the Hon. Freddie Threepwood and his butler Beach, concerning whom I have since
written so much.

4

Too much, carpers have said. So have cavillers. They see
these chronicles multiplying like rabbits down the years
and the prospect appals them. Only the other day a critic,
with whose name I will not sully my typewriter, was giving
me the sleeve across the windpipe for this tendency of mine to
write so much about members of the British peerage. Specifi-
cally, he accused me of an undue fondness of earls.

Well, of course, now that I come to tot up the score, I do
realize that in the course of my literary career I have featured
quite a number of these fauna, but as I often say – well, perhaps
once a fortnight – why not? I see no objection to earls. A
most respectable class of men they seem to me. And one
admires their spirit. I mean, while some, of course, have come
up the easy way, many have had the dickens of a struggle,
starting at the bottom of the ladder as mere Hons., having to
go into dinner after the Vice-Chancellor of the Duchy of
Lancaster and all that sort of thing. Show me the Hon. who
by pluck and determination has raised himself step by step
from the depths till he has become entitled to keep a coronet
on the hat-peg in the downstairs cupboard, and I will show
you a man of whom any author might be proud to write.

Earls on the whole have made a very good showing in fiction.
With baronets setting them a bad example by being almost
uniformly steeped in crime, they have preserved a gratifyingly
high standard of behaviour. There is seldom anything wrong
with the earl in fiction, if you don't mind a touch of haughtiness
and a tendency to have heavy eyebrows and draw them together
in a formidable frown. And in real life I can think of almost
no earls whose hearts were not as pure and fair as those of
dwellers in the lowlier air of Seven Dials. I would trust the
average earl as implicitly as I trust bass singers, and I can't
say more than that. I should like to digress for a moment on
the subject of bass singers.

What splendid fellows they are, are they not? I would think twice before putting my confidence in the tenor who makes noises like gas escaping from a pipe, and baritones are not much better, but when a man brings it up from the soles of his feet, very loud and deep and manly, you know instinctively that his heart is in the right place. Anyone who has ever heard the curate at a village concert rendering 'Old Man River', particularly the 'He don't plant taters, he don't plant cotton' passage, with that odd effect of thunder rumbling in the distance, has little doubt that his spiritual needs are in safe hands.

Am I right in thinking that nowadays the supply of bass singers is giving out? At any rate, it is only rarely today that a bass singer gets a song to himself. As a general rule he is just a man with a side shirt-front who stands on one side and goes 'Zim-zim-zim' while the tenor is behaving like Shelley's skylark. It was not like this in the good old days. When I was a boy, no village concert was complete without the item:

6. Song: 'Asleep on the Deep' (Rev. Hubert Voules)

while if one went to a music-hall one was always confronted at about ten o'clock by a stout man in baggy evening dress with a diamond solitaire in his shirt-front, who walked on the stage in a resolute way and stood glaring at you with one hand in the armhole of his waistcoat.

You knew he was not a juggler or a conjurer, because he had no props and no female assistant in pink tights. And you knew he was not a dramatic twenty-minute sketch, because he would have had a gag along with him. And presently you had him tabbed. He was a – bass, naturally – patriotic singer, and he sang a song with some such refrain as:

> For England's England still.
> It is, and always will.
> Though foreign foes may brag,
> We love our dear old flag,
> And old Enger-land is Enger-land still.

But where is he now? And where is the curate with his 'Asleep on the Deep' (going right down into the cellar on that 'So beware, so beware' line)?

This gradual fading-out of the bass singer is due, I should imagine, to the occupational hazards inseparable from his line of work. When a bass singer finds that night after night he gets his chin caught in his collar or – on the deeper notes – makes his nose bleed, he becomes dispirited. 'Surely,' he says to himself, 'there must be other, less risky ways of entertaining one's public', and the next time you see him he has taken to card tricks or imitations of feathered songsters who are familiar to you all. Or, as I say, he just stands in the background going 'Zim-zim-zim' – this is fairly free from danger – and leaves the prizes of the profession to the sort of man who sings 'Trees' in a reedy falsetto.

I was very touched the other day when I read in one of the papers the following item:

Montgomery, Alabama. Orville P. Gray, twenty-seven-year-old bass singer serving a sentence at Kilby prison, has turned down a chance for parole. Gray told Parole Supervisor E. M. Parkman that he does not want to break up the prison quartette, of which he is a member.

Would you get a tenor making that supreme sacrifice? Or a baritone? Not in a million years. It takes a man who can reach down into the recesses of his socks and come up with

> He must know sumfin', he don't say nuffin',
> He just keeps rollin' along.

to do the square thing, with no thought of self, on such a majestic scale.

But to get back to earls (many of whom, I have no doubt, sing bass). They are, as I was saying, fine fellows all of them, not only in real life but on the printed page. English literature, lacking them, would have been a good deal poorer. Shakespeare would have been lost without them. Everyone who has written for the theatre knows how difficult it is to get people off the stage unless you can think of a good exit speech for them. Shakespeare had no such problem. With more earls at his disposal than he knew what to do with he was on velvet. One need only quote those well-known lines from his *Henry VII, Part Two*:

My lord of Sydenham, bear our royal word
To Brixton's earl, the Earl of Wormwood Scrubbs,
Our faithful liege, the Earl of Dulwich (East),
And those of Beckenham, Penge and Peckham Rye,
Together with the Earl of Hampton Wick
Bid them to haste like cats when struck with brick,
For they are needed in our battle line,
And stitch in time doth ever save full nine.

(Exeunt Omnes. Trumpets and hautboys.)

'Pie!' Shakespeare used to say to Burbage, and Burbage would agree that Shakespeare earned his money easily.

A thing about earls I have never understood, and never liked to ask anyone for fear of betraying my ignorance, is why one earl is the Earl of Whoosis and another earl just Earl Smith. I have an idea – I may be wrong – that the 'of' boys have a social edge on the others, like the aristocrats in Germany who are able to call themselves 'Von'. One can picture the Earl of Berkeley Square being introduced to Earl Piccadilly at a cocktail-party.

The host says, 'Oh, Percy, I want you to meet Earl Piccadilly,' and hurries off to attend to his other guests. There is a brief interval during which the two agree that this is the rottenest party they were ever at and that the duke, their host, is beginning to show his age terribly, then the Earl of Berkeley Square says: 'I didn't quite get the name. Earl of Piccadilly, did he say?'

'No, just Earl Piccadilly.'

The Earl of Berkeley Square starts. A coldness creeps into his manner. He looks like Nancy Mitford hearing the word 'serviette' mentioned in her presence.

'You mean *plain* Earl Piccadilly?'

'That's right.'

'No "of"?'

'No, no "of".'

There is a tense silence. You can see the Earl of Berkeley Square's lip curling. At a house like the duke's he had not expected to have to hobnob with the proletariat.

'Ah, well,' he says at length with a nasty little snigger, 'it

takes all sorts to make a world, does it not?' and Earl Piccadilly slinks off with his ears pinned back and drinks far too
many sherries in the hope of restoring his self-respect.

Practically all the earls who are thrown sobbing out of
cocktail-parties are non-ofs. They can't take it, poor devils.

NOTE. (Not a footnote, just a note.) A friend, to whom I
showed the manuscript of this book, does not see altogether
eye to eye with me in my eulogy of bass singers. You get, he
reminded me, some very dubious characters who sing bass.
Mephistopheles in *Faust*, for one. Would you, he said, trust
Mephistopheles with your wallet? And how about Demon
Kings in pantomime?

There is, I must admit, a certain amount of truth in this.
I don't suppose there is a man much lower in the social scale
than the typical Demon King. Not only does he never stop
plotting against the welfare of the principal boy and girl, but
he goes in for loud spangles and paints his face green, thus
making himself look like a dissipated lizard. Many good
judges claim that he is the worst thing that has happened to
England since the top hat. And yet he unquestionably sings
bass. One can only assume that he is a bass singer who went
wrong in early youth through mixing with bad companions.

FOUR

Good-bye to Butlers

The same critic who charged me with stressing the Earl
note too determinedly in my writings also said that I wrote
far too much about butlers.

How do you feel about that, Winkler? Do you think I do?
There may be something in it, of course.

The fact is, butlers have always fascinated me. As a child,
I lived on the fringe of the butler belt. As a young man, I
was a prominent pest at houses where butlers were maintained.
And later I employed butlers. So it might be said that I have
never gone off the butler standard. For fifty years I have
omitted no word or act to keep these supermen in the forefront
of public thought, and now – with all these social revolutions
and what not – they have ceased to be.

I once read an arresting story about a millionaire whose
life was darkened by a shortage of pigeons. He had the stuff
in sackfuls, but no pigeons. Or, rather, none of the particular
breed he wanted. In his boyhood these birds had been plenti-
ful, but now all his vast wealth could not procure a single
specimen, and this embittered him. 'Oh, bring back my
pigeon to me!' was his cry. I am feeling these days just as
he did. I can do without pigeons – Walter Pidgeon always
excepted, of course – but it does break me up to think that I
have been goggled at by my last butler.

It is possible that at this point, J.P., you will try to cheer me
up by mentioning a recent case in the London courts where a
young peer was charged with biting a lady friend in the leg
and much of the evidence was supplied by 'the butler'. I
read about that, too, and it did cheer me up for a moment.

But only for a moment. All too soon I was telling myself cynically that this 'butler' was probably merely another of these modern makeshifts. No doubt in many English homes there is still buttling of a sort going on, but it is done by ex-batmen, promoted odd-job boys and the like, callow youngsters not to be ranked as butlers by one who, like myself, was around and about in the London of 1903, and saw the real thing. Butlers? A pack of crude young amateurs without a double chin among them? Faugh, if you will permit me the expression.

A man I know has a butler, and I was congratulating him on this the last time we met. He listened to me, I thought, rather moodily.

'Yes,' he said when I had finished, 'Murgatroyd is all right, I suppose. Does his work well and all that sort of thing. But,' he added with a sigh, 'I wish I could break him of that habit of his of sliding down the banisters.'

The real crusted, vintage butler passed away with Edward the Seventh. One tried one's best to pretend that the Georgian Age had changed nothing, but it had. The post-First World War butler was a mere synthetic substitute for the ones we used to know. When we septuagenarians speak of butlers, we are thinking of what used to lurk behind the front doors of Mayfair at the turn of the century.

Those were the days of what – because they took place late in the afternoon – were known as morning calls. Somewhere around five o'clock one would put on the old frock-coat (with the white piping at the edge of the waistcoat), polish up the old top hat (a drop of stout helped the gloss), slide a glove over one's left hand (you carried the other one) and go out and pay morning calls. You mounted the steps of some stately home, you pulled the bell, and suddenly the door opened and there stood an august figure, weighing seventeen stone or so on the hoof, with mauve cheeks, three chins, supercilious lips and bulging gooseberry eyes that raked you with a forbidding stare as if you were something the carrion crow had deposited on the doorstep. 'Not at all what we have been accustomed to,' those eyes seemed to say.

That, at least, was the message I always read in them, owing no doubt to my extreme youth and the fact, of which I never ceased to be vividly aware, that my brother Armine's frock-coat and my cousin George's trousers did not begin to fit me. A certain anaemia of the exchequer caused me in those days to go about in the discarded clothes of relatives, and it was this that once enabled me to see that rarest of all sights, a laughing butler. (By the laws of their guild, butlers of the Edwardian epoch were sometimes permitted a quick, short smile, provided it was sardonic, but never a guffaw. I will come back to this later. Wait for the story of the laughing butler.)

My acquaintance with butlers and my awe of them started at a very early age. My parents were in Hong Kong most of the time when I was in the knickerbocker stage, and during my school holidays I was passed from aunt to aunt. A certain number of these aunts were the wives of clergymen, which meant official calls at the local great house, and when they paid these calls they took me along. Why, I have never been able to understand, for even at the age of ten I was a social bust, contributing little or nothing to the feast of reason and flow of soul beyond shuffling my feet and kicking the leg of the chair into which loving hands had dumped me. There always came a moment when my hostess, smiling one of those painful smiles, suggested that it would be nice for your little nephew to go and have tea in the servants' hall.

And she was right. I loved it. My mind today is fragrant with memories of kindly footmen and vivacious parlour-maids. In their society I forgot to be shy and kidded back and forth with the best of them. The life and the soul of the party, they probably described me as, if they ever wrote their reminiscences.

But these good times never lasted. Sooner or later in would come the butler, like the monstrous crow in *Through The Looking Glass*, and the quips would die on our lips. 'The young gentleman is wanted,' he would say morosely, and the young gentleman would shamble out, feeling like 30¢.

Butlers in those days, when they retired, married the cook and went and let lodgings to hard-up young men in Ebury Street and the King's Road, Chelsea, so, grown to man's estate, I found myself once more in contact with them. But we never at that time became intimate. Occasionally, in a dare-devil mood, encountering my landlord in the street, I would say, 'Good morning, Mr Briggs' or Biggs, or whatever it might be, but the coldness of his 'Good morning, sir' told me that he desired no advances from one so baggy at the trouser-knee as myself, and our relations continued distant. It was only in what my biographers will speak of as my second London period – *circa* 1930 – when I was in the chips and an employer of butlers, that I came to know them well and receive their confidences.

By that time I had reached the age when the hair whitens, the waistline expands and the terrors of youth leave us. The turning point came when I realized one morning that, while I was on the verge of fifty, my butler was a Johnny-come-lately of forty-six. It altered the whole situation. One likes to un-bend with the youngsters, and I unbent with this slip of a boy. From tentative discussions of the weather we progressed until I was telling him what hell it was to get stuck half-way through a novel, and he was telling me of former employers of his and how the thing that sours butlers is having to stand behind their employer's chair at dinner night after weary night and listen to the funny noise he makes when drinking soup. You serve the soup and stand back and clench your hands. 'Now comes the funny noise,' you say to yourself. Night after night after night. This explains what in my youth had always puzzled me, the universal gloom of butlers.

Only once – here comes that story I was speaking of – have I heard a butler laugh. On a certain night in the year 1903 I had been invited to dinner at a rather more stately home than usual and, owing to the friend who has appeared in some of my stories under the name of Ukridge having borrowed my dress clothes without telling me, I had to attend the function in a primitive suit of soup-and-fish bequeathed to me by my Uncle Hugh, a man who stood six feet four and weighed in the neighbourhood of fifteen stone.

Even as I dressed, the things seemed roomy. It was not, however, until the fish course that I realized how roomy they were, when, glancing down, I suddenly observed the trousers mounting like a rising tide over my shirt-front. I pushed them back, but I knew I was fighting a losing battle. I was up against the same trouble that bothered King Canute. Eventually when I was helping myself to potatoes and was off my guard, the tide swept up as far as my white tie, and it was then that Yates or Bates or Fotheringay or whatever his name was uttered a sound like a bursting paper bag and hurried from the room with his hand over his mouth, squaring himself with his guild later, I believe, by saying he had had some kind of fit. It was an unpleasant experience and one that clouded my life through most of the period 1903–4–5, but it is something to be able to tell my grandchildren that I once saw a butler laugh.

Among other things which contributed to make butlers gloomy was the fact that so many of their employers were sparkling raconteurs. Only a butler, my butler said, can realize what it means to a butler to be wedged against the sideboard, unable to escape, and to hear his employer working the conversation round to the point where he will be able to tell that good story of his which he, the butler, has heard so often before. It was when my butler mentioned this, with a kindly word of commendation to me for never having said anything even remotely clever or entertaining since he had entered my service, that I at last found myself understanding the inwardness of a rather peculiar episode of my early manhood.

A mutual friend had taken me to lunch at the house of W. S. (Savoy Operas) Gilbert, and midway through the meal the great man began to tell a story. It was one of those very long deceptively dull stories where you make the build-up as tedious as you can, knowing that the punch line is going to pay for everything, and pause before you reach the point so as to stun the audience with the unexpected snaperoo. In other words, a story which is pretty awful till the last line, when you have them rolling in the aisles.

Well, J.P., there was Sir William Schwenk Gilbert telling this long story, and there was I, tucked away inside my brother Armine's frock-coat and my cousin George's trousers, drinking it respectfully in. It did not seem to me a very funny story, but I knew it must be because this was W. S. Gilbert telling it, so when the pause before the punch line came, thinking that this was the end, I laughed.

I had rather an individual laugh in those days, something like the explosion of one of those gas mains that slay six. Infectious, I suppose you would call it, for the other guests, seeming a little puzzled, as if they had expected something better from the author of *The Mikado*, all laughed politely, and conversation became general. And it was at this juncture that I caught my host's eye.

I shall always remember the glare of pure hatred which I saw in it. If you have seen photographs of Gilbert, you will be aware that even when in repose his face was inclined to be formidable and his eye not the sort of eye you would willingly catch. And now his face was far from being in repose. His eyes, beneath their beetling brows, seared my very soul. In order to get away from them, I averted my gaze and found myself encountering that of the butler. His eyes were shining with a doglike devotion. For some reason which I was unable to understand, I appeared to have made his day. I know now what the reason was. I suppose he had heard that story build up like a glacier and rumble to its conclusion at least fifty times, probably more, and I had killed it.

And now, Gilbert has gone to his rest, and his butler has gone to his rest, and all the other butlers of those great days have gone to their rests. Time, like an ever-rolling stream, bears all its sons away, and even the Edwardian butler has not been immune. He has joined the Great Auk, Mah Jong and the snows of yesterday in limbo.

But I like to think that this separation of butler and butler-*aficionado* will not endure for ever. I tell myself that when Clarence, ninth Earl of Emsworth, finally hands in his dinner pail after his long and pleasant life, the first thing he will hear as he settles himself on his cloud will be the fruity voice of Beach, his faithful butler, saying, 'Nectar or ambrosia, m'lord?'

'Eh? Oh, hullo, Beach. I say, Beach, what's this dashed thing they handed me as I came in?'

'A harp, m'lord. Your lordship is supposed to play on it.'

'Eh? Play on it? Like Harpo Marx, you mean?'

'Precisely, m'lord.'

'Most extraordinary. Is everybody doing it?'

'Yes, m'lord.'

'My sister Constance? My brother Galahad? Sir Gregory Parsloe? Baxter? Everybody?'

'Yes, m'lord.'

'Well, it all sounds very odd to me. Still, if you say so. Give me your A, Beach.'

'Certainly, m'lord. Coming right up.'

FIVE

Critics and the Criticized

I

Those stray thoughts on earls and butlers which I have just
recorded were written as a dignified retort to a critic dissatisfied
with the pearls which I had cast before him, and I see, Winkler,
referring to your questionnaire, that you want to know if I am
influenced by criticisms of my work.

That, I suppose, depends on whether those who criticize my
work are good or bad critics. A typical instance of the bad
critic is the one who said, 'It is time that Mr Wodehouse
realized that Jeeves has become a bore.' When my press-
cutting bureau sends me something like that, an icy look
comes into my hard grey eyes and I mark my displeasure by
not pasting it into my scrapbook. Let us forget this type of
man and turn to the rare souls who can spot a good thing
when they see one, and shining like a beacon among these is
the woman who wrote to the daily paper the other day to say
that she considers Shakespeare 'grossly materialistic and much
overrated' and 'greatly prefers P. G. Wodehouse'.

Well, it is not for me to say whether she is right or not.
One cannot arbitrate in these matters of taste. Shakespeare's
stuff is different from mine, but that is not necessarily to say
that it is inferior. There are passages in Shakespeare to which
I would have been quite pleased to put my name. That
'Tomorrow and tomorrow and tomorrow' thing. Some spin
on the ball there. I doubt, too, if I have ever done anything
much better than Falstaff. The man may have been grossly
materialistic, but he could crack them through the covers all
right when he got his eye in. I would place him definitely in
the Wodehouse class.

One of the things people should remember when they compare Shakespeare with me and hand him the short straw is that he did not have my advantages. I have privacy for my work, he had none. When I write a novel I sit down and write it. I may have to break off from time to time to get up and let the foxhound out and let the foxhound in, and let the cat out and let the cat in, and let the senior Peke out and let the senior Peke in, and let the junior Peke out and let the junior Peke in, and let the cat out again, but nobody interrupts me, nobody comes breathing down the back of my neck and asks me how I am getting on. Shakespeare, on the other hand, never had a moment to himself.

Burbage, I imagine, was his worst handicap. Even today a dramatic author suffers from managers, but in Shakespeare's time anybody who got mixed up in the theatre was like somebody in a slave camp. The management never let him alone. In those days a good run for a play was one night. Anything over that was sensational. Shakespeare, accordingly, would dash off *Romeo and Juliet* for production on Monday, and on Tuesday morning at six o'clock round would come Burbage in a great state of excitement and wake him with a wet sponge.

'Asleep!' Burbage would say, seeming to address an invisible friend on whose sympathy he knew he could rely. 'Six o'clock in the morning and still wallowing in hoggish slumber! Is this a system? Don't I get no service and co-operation? Good heavens, Will, why aren't you working?'

Shakespeare sits up and rubs his eyes.

'Oh, hullo, Burb. That you? How are the notices?'

'Never mind the notices. Don't you realize we've gotta give 'em something tomorrow?'

'What about *Romeo and Juliet*?'

'Came off last night. How long do you expect these charades to run? If you haven't something to follow, we'll have to close the theatre. Got anything?'

'Not a thing.'

'Then what do you suggest?'

'Bring on the bears.'

'They don't want bears, they want a play, and stop groaning like that. Groaning won't get us anywhere.'

So Shakespeare would heave himself out of bed, and by lunch-time, with Burbage popping in and out with his eternal 'How ya gettin' on?' he would somehow manage to write *Othello*. And Burbage would skim through it and say, 'It'll need work,' but he supposed it would have to do.

An author cannot give of his best under these conditions, and this, I think accounts for a peculiarity in Shakespeare's output which has escaped the notice of the critics – to wit, the fact that while what he turns out sounds all right, it generally doesn't mean anything. There can be little doubt that when he was pushed for time – as when was he not? – William Shakespeare just shoved down anything and trusted to the charity of the audience to pull him through.

'What on earth does "abroach" mean, laddie?' Burbage would ask, halting the rehearsal of *Romeo and Juliet*.

'It's something girls wear,' Shakespeare would say. 'You know. Made of diamonds and fastened with a pin.'

'But you've got in the script, "Who set this ancient quarrel new abroach?" and it doesn't seem to make sense.'

'Oh, it's all in the acting,' Shakespeare would say. 'Just speak the line quick and nobody'll notice anything.'

And that would be that, till they were putting on *Pericles, Prince of Tyre*, and somebody had to say to somebody else, 'I'll fetch thee with a wanion.' Shakespeare would get round that by pretending that a wanion was the latest court slang for cab, but this gave him only a brief respite, for the next moment they would be asking him what a 'geck' was, or a 'loggat', or a 'cullion' or an 'egma' or a 'punto' and wanting to know what he meant by saying a character had become 'frampold' because he was 'rawly'.

It was a wearing life, and though Shakespeare would try to pass it off jocularly by telling the boys at the Mermaid that it was all in a lifetime and the first hundred years were the hardest and all that sort of thing, there can be little doubt that he felt the strain and that it affected the quality of his work.

So I think the woman who wrote to the paper ought to try to be kinder to Shakespeare. Still, awfully glad you like my stuff, old thing, and I hope you don't just get it out of the library. Even if you do, 'At-a-girl, and cheers.'

2

This episode had rather an unpleasant sequel. A letter was forwarded to me from the paper – addressed to the editor and signed 'Indignant' – which began:

Sir – I was completely confounded to read in this morning's ———— the statement by your correspondent 'Highland Lassie' that P. G. Wodehouse is a better writer than Shakespeare. As an authority on the latter I can definitely state he was the greatest genius of his time, to be compared only with Riley, Drake and Nelson.

These names convey very little to me. Drake, I suppose, is Alfred Drake, the actor who made such a hit in *Kismet* and was the original Curly in *Oklahoma*, but who is Nelson? Does he mean Harold Nicolson? And as for Riley, we know that his was a happy and prosperous career – we still speak of living the life of Riley – but I never heard of him as a writer. Can 'Indignant' have got mixed up and be referring to the popular hotel proprietor O'Reilly, of whom a poet once wrote:

> Are you the O'Reilly
> Who keeps the hotel?
> Are you the O'Reilly
> They speak of so well?
> If you're the O'Reilly
> They speak of so highly,
> Gawblimey, O'Reilly,
> You are looking well.

But I never heard of him writing anything, either. Evidently some mistake somewhere.

The letter continues:

I have followed the arts for some time now and can definitely state that even the works of Joshua Reynolds was not up to Shakespeare's standard.

He has stymied me again. I recall a reference to, I presume, Joshua Reynolds in a music-hall song by Miss Clarice Mayne, the refrain of which began:

> Joshua, Joshua,
> Sweeter than lemon squash you are

and gather from that that he must be an attractive sort of fellow with lots of oomph and sex appeal, whom I should enjoy meeting, but I can't place him. There is a baseball player named Reynolds who used to pitch for the New York Yankees, but his name is Allie, so it is probably not the same man. I shall be glad to hear more of this Joshua Reynolds, if some correspondent will fill in the blanks for me.

Up to this point in his letter 'Indignant', it will be seen, has confined himself to the decencies of debate and it has been a pleasure to read him. But now, I regret to say, he descends to personalities and what can only be called cracks. He says:

It is not my disposition to give predictions on this dispute, but let's see how Wodehouse compares with the great bard in 2356.

Now that, 'Indignant', is simply nasty. You are just trying to hurt my feelings. You know perfectly well that I have no means of proving that in the year 2356 my works will be on every shelf. I am convinced that they will, of course, if not in the stiff covers at 12s. 6d., surely in the Penguin edition at two bob. Dash it, I mean to say, I don't want to stick on dog and throw bouquets at myself, but if I were not pretty good, would Matthew Arnold have written that sonnet he wrote about me, which begins:

> Others abide our question. Thou art free.
> We ask and ask. Thou smilest and art still,
> Out-topping knowledge.

When a level-headed man of the Matthew Arnold type lets himself go like that, it means something.

I do not wish to labour this point, but I must draw Indignant's attention to a letter in *The Times* from Mr Verrier Elwyn, who lives at Patangarth, Mandla District, India. Mr Elwyn speaks of a cow which came into his bungalow one day and ate his copy of *Carry On, Jeeves*, 'selecting it from a shelf which contained, among other works, books by Galsworthy, Jane Austen and T. S. Eliot'. Surely a rather striking tribute.

And how about that very significant bit of news from one of our large public schools? The school librarian writes to the school magazine complaining that the young students will persist in pinching books from the school library, and, he says,

while these lovers of all that is best in literature have got away
with five John Buchans, seven Agatha Christies and twelve
Edgar Wallaces, they have swiped no fewer than thirty-six
P. G. Wodehouses. Figures like that tell a story. You should
think before you speak, 'Indignant'.

I suppose the fundamental distinction between Shakespeare
and myself is one of treatment. We get our effects differently.
Take the familiar farcical situation of the man who suddenly
discovers that something unpleasant is standing behind him.
Here is how Shakespeare handles it. (*The Winter's Tale*, Act
Three, Scene Three.)

> ... Farewell!

> The day frowns more and more: thou art like to have
> A lullaby too rough. I never saw
> The heavens so dim by day. A savage clamour!
> Well may I get aboard! This is the chase:
> I am gone for ever.
>
> *Exit, pursued by a bear.*

I should have adopted a somewhat different approach. Thus:

> I gave the man one of my looks.
> 'Touch of indigestion, Jeeves?'
> 'No, sir.'
> 'Then why is your tummy rumbling?'
> 'Pardon me, sir, the noise to which you allude does not emanate
> from my interior but from that of the animal that has just joined us.'
> 'Animal? What animal?'
> 'A bear, sir. If you will turn your head, you will observe that a
> bear is standing in your immediate rear inspecting you in a some-
> what menacing manner.'
> I pivoted the loaf. The honest fellow was perfectly correct. It was
> a bear. And not a small bear, either. One of the large economy size.
> Its eye was bleak, it gnashed a tooth or two, and I could see at a g.
> that it was going to be difficult for me to find a formula.
> 'Advise me, Jeeves,' I yipped. 'What do I do for the best?'
> 'I fancy it might be judicious if you were to exit, sir.'
> No sooner s. than d. I streaked for the horizon, closely followed
> across country by the dumb chum. And that, boys and girls, is how
> your grandfather clipped six seconds off Roger Bannister's mile.

Who can say which method is the superior?

3

It has never been definitely established what the attitude of
the criticized should be towards the critics. Many people
counsel those on the receiver's end to ignore hostile criticism,
but to my thinking this is pusillanimous and they will be missing
a lot of fun. This was certainly the view taken by the impresario of a recent revue in New York which got a uniformly bad
press. He has instructed his lawyers to file an immediate
damage suit against each of his critics 'to cover the costs of
their undisciplined and unwarranted remarks'. With special
attention, no doubt, to the one who said, 'The only good thing
about this show was that it was raining and the theatre didn't
leak.' This, one feels, would come under the head of that
'slanderous volley of humourless witticisms that defies the
most vivid imagination' to which the impresario alludes.

The case, when it comes to court, will no doubt be closely
watched by the New Orleans boxer, Freddie Biggs, of whom
reporting his latest fight, Mr Caswell Adams of the *NY Journal-
American* said that he flittered and fluttered as if he were
performing in a room full of wasps. 'The only thing bad so
far about the Louisiana Purchase in 1803,' added Mr Adams,
'was that we eventually got Freddie Biggs.'

I would not, perhaps, go so far as the impresario I have
quoted, but I do think that an author who gets an unfavourable
review should answer it promptly with a carefully composed
letter, which can be either (*a*) conciliatory or (*b*) belligerent.

Specimen (a) The Conciliatory

Dear Mr Worthington,
Not 'Sir'. 'Sir' is abrupt. And, of course, don't say 'Mr Worthington'
if the fellow's name is John Davenport or Cyril Connolly. Use your
intelligence, Junior. I am only sketching the thing out on broad
lines.

Dear Mr Worthington,
I was greatly impressed by your review in the *Booksy Weekly* of my
novel *Whither If Anywhere*, in which you say that my construction

is lamentable, my dialogue leaden and my characters stuffed with sawdust, and advise me to give up writing and start selling catsmeat.

Oddly enough, I am, during the day, a professional purveyor of catsmeat. I write in the evenings after I have disposed of the last skewerful. I should hate to give it up, and I feel sure that now I have read your most erudite and helpful criticisms I can correct the faults you mention and gradually improve my output until it meets with your approval. (And I need scarcely say that I would rather have the approval of Eustace Worthington than that of any other man in the world, for I have long been a sincere admirer of your brilliant work.)

I wonder if you would care to have lunch with me some time and go further into the matter of my book and its many defects. Shall we say Claridge's some day next week?

Yours faithfully,
G. G. Simmons

PS. What an excellent article that was of yours in the *Licensed Victuallers Gazette* some weeks ago on 'The Disintegration of Reality in the Interest of the Syncretic Principle'. I could hardly wait to see how it all came out.

PPS If you can make it for lunch, I will see if I can get Mrs Arthur Miller to come along. I know how much she would like to meet you.

This is good and nearly always makes friends and influences people, but I confess that I prefer the other kind, the belligerent. This is because the Wodehouses are notoriously hot-blooded. (It was a Wodehouse who in the year 1911 did seven days in Brixton Prison – rather than pay a fine – for failing to abate a smoky chimney.)

Specimen (b) The Belligerent

Sir,
Not 'Dear Sir'. Weak. And not 'You potbellied louse', which is strong but a little undignified. Myself, I have sometimes used 'Listen, you piefaced child of unmarried parents', but I prefer 'Sir'.

Sir,
So you think my novel *Storm Over Upper Tooting* would disgrace a child of three with water on the brain, do you? And who, may I ask,

are you to start throwing your weight about, you contemptible hack? If you were any good, you wouldn't be writing book reviews for a rag like the one you befoul with your half-witted ravings.

Your opinion, let me add, would carry greater authority with me, did I not know, having met people who (with difficulty) tolerate your society, that you still owe Moss Bros. for a pair of trousers they sold you in 1946 and that the lady who presides over the boarding-house which you infest is threatening, if you don't pay five weeks' back rent soon, to throw you out on the seat of them. May I be there to see it. That you will land on something hard and sharp and dislocate your pelvis is the sincere hope of

Yours faithfully,
Clyde Weatherbee

PS. *Where were you on the night of 15th June?*

Now that's good. That cleanses the bosom of the perilous stuff that weighs upon the heart. But don't send this sort of letter to the editor of the paper, because editors always allow the critic to shove in a reply in brackets at the end of it, thus giving him the last word.

4

The critics have always been particularly kind to me. As nice a bunch of square-shooters as I ever came across, is how I regard them. And one gets helpful bits of information from them every now and then. John Wain, reviewing a book of mine the other day in which one of the characters was an impecunious author living in dingy lodgings, said that this was quite out of date. Nowadays, he said, impecunious authors do not live in dingy lodgings. Where they do live, I have not ascertained – presumably in Park Lane – though as to how they pay the rent I remain vague. Still, thanks, John. A useful tip, if I ever do another impecunious author.

Of course, there are black sheep in every flock and, like all other writers, I occasionally find a brickbat mixed in with the bouquets. I was roughly handled not long ago by the man who does the book reviews on the *Daily Worker*. He called Jeeves a 'dim museum-piece' and 'a fusty reminder of what once amused the bourgeoisie.' Harsh words, these, and especially hard to bear from a paper of the large circulation and nationwide influence of the *Daily Worker*. But against this put the very complimentary remarks of the *Berlingske Tidende* of Denmark.

Its critics says (in part):

Skont Wodehouse laeses af verden over, betyder det dog ikke, at alle hat det i sig, at de er i Stand til at goutere ham. Jeg ved, at der er dannede Mennesker, som ikke vil spilde deres kostbare Tid paa hans Boger. Hvis man ikke er for Wodehouse, er man nodvendigvis imod ham, for der er kun Undskyldning for at laese ham, og det er, at man kan klukle over ham.

That is the sort of thing that warms an author's heart, but, come right down to it, I suppose the best and simplest way of getting a good notice for your book is to write it yourself. The great objection writers have always had to criticism done by outside critics is that they are too often fobbed off with a 'Quite readable' or even a '8½, 233 pp', which, they feel, do not do complete justice to their work. Getting the Do-It-Yourself spirit, the author of a novel recently published in America starts off with a Foreword in which he says:

This book is a major work of prose, powerful, moving, trenchant, full of colour, crackling with wit, wisdom and humour, not to mention a rare gift for narrative and characterization perhaps never before equalled. It is a performance which stands alone among the books of the world.

The book in question, by the way, is the story of the life of Mona Lisa and is to be published in nine volumes. The first consists of 1267 pages, and at the end of page 1276 Mona Lisa has not yet been born. But one feels that she is bound to be sooner or later, and when she is, watch for the interest to quicken.

SIX

Raw Eggs, Cuckoos and Patrons

I

And now, Winkler, we come to rather a moot point – to wit.
Where do we go from here?

I know you are waiting with ill-concealed impatience for me
to resume the saga of my literary career and asking yourself
why I don't get on with it, but I am hesitating and fingering
the chin, wondering if it would not be better for all concerned
if we let it go and changed the subject. Here is the position
as I see it, J.P. I have held you spellbound – or fairly spellbound – with the narrative of my early struggles, but with the
publication of *Something Fresh* in the *Saturday Evening Post* those
struggles ceased abruptly. Its editor, George Horace Lorimer,
liked my work, and except for an occasional commission from
some other magazine everything I wrote for the next twenty-
five years appeared in the *SEP*. All very jolly, of course,
and I would not have had it otherwise, but you do see, don't
you, that it does not make a good story. Suspense and drama
are both lacking.

It was at about this time, too, that I started to clean up in
the theatre. Just after the appearance of my second *Post*
serial, *Uneasy Money*, while I was writing my third serial,
Piccadilly Jim, I ran into Guy Bolton and Jerome Kern. I had
worked with Jerry for Seymour Hicks at the Aldwych Theatre
in 1906, and the three of us now wrote a series of musical
comedies, as Guy and I have related in *Bring on the Girls*, which
were produced at New York's Princess Theatre and were very
successful. At one time we had five shows running simultaneously on Broadway, with a dozen companies on the road.

So you see what I mean, J.P. All the zip has gone out of

the thing, and I think we should take my activities from now on as read. To my mind there is nothing so soporific as an author's account of his career after he has got over the tough part and can look his bank manager in the eye without a quiver. I have known novelists, writing the story of their lives, to give not only a complete list of their novels but the plots of several of them. No good to man or beast, that sort of thing. A writer who is tempted to write a book telling the world how good he is ought to remember the reply made by Mr Glyn Johns to an interviewer at Fort Erie, Ontario, last spring. . . . Ah, Fort Erie, Ontario, in the springtime, with the chestnut trees a-blossom . . . on the occasion of his winning the raw-egg-eating championship of Canada by getting outside twenty-four raw eggs in fourteen minutes.

A thing I never understand, when I read an item like that in the paper, is how these fellows do it. How, I mean, does a man so shape himself that he becomes able to eat twenty-four raw eggs in fourteen minutes?

One feels the same thing about performers at the circus. How did the man who dives through a hole in the roof into a small tank first get the impulse? One pictures him studying peacefully for the Church, without a thought in his mind of any other walk in life, when suddenly, as he sits poring over his theological books, a voice whispers in his ear.

'This is all very well,' says the voice, 'but what you were really intended to do was to dive through holes in the roof into tanks. Do not stifle your individuality. Remember the parable of the talents.'

And he throws away his books and goes out to see an agent. Some sort of spiritual revelation like this no doubt happened to Mr Johns.

From his remark to the interviewer, 'I owe it all to my mother,' I piece his story together like this. His, as I see it, was a happy home, one of those typical Canadian homes where a united family lives its life of love and laughter, but he found the most extraordinary difficulty in getting any raw eggs. No stint of boiled, and on Sundays generally a couple poached on toast, but never raw. And all the time he was conscious of this strange power within him.

'If only they would let me get at the raw eggs!' he would say to himself. 'There, I am convinced, is where my genius lies.'

And one day he found his mother had forgotten to shut the door of the larder – ('I owe it all to my mother') – and saw on a lower shelf a whole dozen smiling up at him, seeming to beckon to him. It was as he wolfed the last of the twelve that he knew he had found his life's work.

'Stick to it, boy,' said that inward voice. 'Lead a clean life and practise daily, and the time will come when you will be able to manage twenty-four.'

And from that moment he never looked back.

But I was going to tell you about the reply he made to the interviewer. Asked after the final egg how he had done it, he said, 'I ate twenty-one in twelve minutes, and then I ate another three, making twenty-four in all.'

'No, I mean how did you *start*?'

'With the first egg. Call it Egg A or (1). I ate that egg, then I ate another egg, then I ate another egg, then I ate another egg, then I ate another egg, then I ate another egg, then I ate another egg and, if you follow me, so on.'

Substitute 'wrote' for 'ate' and 'book' for 'egg', and an author with a bank balance has said everything about his career that needs to be said. I, to take the first instance that comes to hand, wrote *Something Fresh*, then *Uneasy Money*, then *Piccadilly Jim*, and after that I wrote another book, then I wrote another book, then I wrote another book, then I wrote another book, and continued to do so down the years.

They are all there on my shelves – seventy-five of them, one for each year of my life – and I would love to name them all, but for the reader it would be too tedious. It is not as if I had ever written one of those historic best-sellers which everybody wants to hear about. When Noel Coward gave us the inside story of *The Vortex* and *Cavalcade*, I drank in every word, as I suppose all the readers of *Present Indicative* did, but there has never been anything dramatic and sensational about any of my productions. I have always run a quiet, conservative business, just jogging along and endeavouring to give satisfaction by maintaining quality of output. *The Inimitable*

Jeeves, it is true, sold 2 million copies in America, but that was in the 25¢ paperback edition, which really does not count, and apart from that I have never stepped out of the status of a young fellow trying to get along. I would call myself a betwixt-and-between author – not on the one hand a total bust and yet not on the other a wham or a socko. Ask the first ten men you meet, 'Have you ever heard of P. G. Wodehouse?' and nine of them will answer 'No.' The tenth, being hard of hearing, will say, 'Down the passage, first door to the right.

For the benefit of the small minority who are interested in statistics I will state briefly that since 1902 I have produced ten books for boys, one book for children, forty-three novels, if you can call them novels, 315 short stories, 411 articles and a thing called *The Swoop*. I have also been author or part author of sixteen plays and twenty-two musical comedies. It has all helped to keep me busy and out of the public houses.

There was once a millionaire who, having devoted a long life to an unceasing struggle to amass his millions, looked up from his death-bed and said plaintively, 'And now, perhaps, someone will kindly tell me what's it's all been about.' I get that feeling sometimes, looking back. Couldn't I, I ask myself, have skipped one or two of those works of mine and gone off and played golf without doing English literature any irreparable harm? Take, for instance, that book *The Swoop*, which was one of the paper-covered shilling books so prevalent around 1909. I wrote the whole 25,000 words of it in five days, and the people who read it, if placed end to end, would have reached from Hyde Park Corner to about the top of Arlington Street. Was it worth the trouble?

Yes, I think so, for I had a great deal of fun writing it. I have had a great deal of fun – one-sided possibly – writing all my books. Dr Johnson once said that nobody but a blockhead ever wrote except for money. I should think it extremely improbable that anyone ever wrote anything simply for money. What makes a writer write is that he likes writing. Naturally, when he has written something, he wants to get as much for it as he can, but that is a very different thing from writing for money.

I should imagine that even the man who compiles a railway timetable is thinking much more what a lark it all is than of the cheque he is going to get when he turns in the completed script. Watch his eyes sparkle with an impish light as he puts a very small *a* against the line

$$4.51 \text{ arr. } 6.22$$

knowing that the reader will not notice it and turn to the bottom of the page, where it says

(*a*) On Mondays only

but will dash off with his suitcase and his golf clubs all merry and bright, arriving at the station in good time on the afternoon of Friday. Money is the last thing such a writer has in mind.

And how about the people who write letters to the papers saying they have heard the cuckoo, Doc? Are you telling me they do it for money? You're crazy, Johnson.

2

Although it is many years since I myself gave up writing letters to the papers, I still keep in close touch with the correspondence columns of the press, and it is a source of considerable pain to me to note today what appears to be a conspiracy of silence with regard to the cuckoo, better known possibly to some of my readers as the *Cuculus canorus*. I allude to the feathered friend which puzzled the poet Wordsworth so much. 'O Cuckoo! Shall I call thee bird or but a wandering voice?' he used to say, and I don't believe he ever did get straight about it.

In my young days the cuckoo was big stuff. Thousands hung upon its lightest word. The great thing, of course, was to be the first to hear it, for there was no surer way of getting your letter printed. The cuckoo always wintered in Africa – lucky to be able to afford it – returning to the English scene around the second week in April, and you never saw such excitement as there was from 9th April on, with all the cuckoo-hearers standing like greyhounds in the slips, one hand cupped to the right ear and the fountain-pen in the top left waistcoat pocket all ready for the letter to the editor at the first chirp.

Virtually all the men at the top of the profession – Verb Sap, Pro Bono Publico, Fiat Justitia and the like – had started their careers by hearing the first cuckoo and getting the story off to the *Daily Telegraph* while it was hot. It was the recognized *point d'appui* for the young writer.

'My boy,' I remember Fiat Justitia saying to me once after he had been kind enough to read some of my unpublished material, 'don't let editorial rejections discourage you. We have all been through it in our time. I see where you have gone wrong. These letters you have shown me are about social conditions and the political situation and things like that. You must not try to run before you can walk. Begin, like all the great masters, with the cuckoo. And be careful that it is a cuckoo. I knew a man who wrote to his daily paper saying he had heard the first reed-warbler, and the letter was suppressed because it would have given offence to certain powerful vested interests.'

I took his advice, and it was not long before editors were welcoming my contributions.

But how changed are conditions today. I quote from a letter in a recent issue of the *Observer*:

Sir,
If the hypothesis be accepted without undue dogmatism in the present rudimentary state of our knowledge that brain is merely the instrument of mind and not its source, the term soul and spirit could plausibly be regarded as redundant.

Pretty poor stuff. Not a word about hearing the cuckoo, which could have been br⌐ ⌐ht in perfectly neatly in a hundred ways. I should have handled it, I think, on something like the following lines:

Sir,
If the hypothesis be accepted without undue dogmatism in the present rudimentary state of our knowledge that brain is merely the instrument of mind and not its source, good luck to it, say I, and I hope it has a fine day for it. Be that as it may, however, I should like your readers to know that as early as the morning of 1st January

this year, while seeing the New Year in with some friends in Piccadilly, I distinctly heard the cuckoo. 'Hark!' I remember saying to the officer who was leading me off to Marlborough Street. 'The cuckoo!' Is this a record?

That, I fancy, is how Ruat Coelum and the others would have done it, but the letter which I have quoted is evidently the work of a beginner. Notice how he plunges at his subject like a man charging into a railway station refreshment room for a gin and tonic five minutes before his train leaves. Old hands like Verb Sap and Indignant Taxpayer would have begun:

Sir,
My attention has been drawn . . . .

Before I broke into the game I used to think of the men who had their attention drawn as unworldy dreamers living in some ivory tower, busy perhaps on a monumental history of the Ming dynasty or something of that sort and never seeing the papers. But when I became a correspondent myself and joined the well-known Fleet Street club, The Twelve Jolly Letter-Writers, I found I had been mistaken. Far from being dreamers, the 'My-attention-has-been-drawn' fellows were the big men of the profession, the top-notchers.

You started at the bottom of the ladder with:

Sir,
I heard the cuckoo yesterday . . . .

then after some years rose to a position where you said:

Sir,
The cuckoo is with us again, its liquid notes ringing through the countryside. Yesterday . . .

and finally, when the moment had come, you had your attention drawn.

There was, as I recollect it, no formal promotion from the ranks, no ceremony of initiation or anything like that. One just sensed when the time was ripe, like a barrister who takes silk.

I inadvertently caused something of a flutter in the club, I remember, soon after I got my AD, and was hauled over the coals by that splendid old veteran Mother of Six (Oswald-twistle).

'Gussie,' he said to me one morning – I was writing under the name of Disgusted Liberal in those days, 'I have a bone to pick with you. My attention has been drawn to a letter of yours in *The Times* in which you say that your attention has been called to something.'

'What's wrong with called?' I said. I was young and head-strong then.

'It is not done,' he replied coldly. 'Attentions are not called, they are drawn. Otherwise, why would Tennyson in his well-known poem have written:

> Tomorrow'll be the happiest day of all the glad new year,
> Of all the glad new year, mother, the maddest merriest day,
> For my attention has been drawn to a statement in
> the press that I'm to be Queen of the May, mother,
> I'm to be Queen of the May.

I never made that mistake again.

3

Returning to Dr Johnson, I am sorry that a momentary touch of irritation caused me to tick him off so harshly. I ought to have remembered that when he said that silly thing about writing for money he was not feeling quite himself. He was all hot and cross because of the Lord Chesterfield business. You probably remember the circumstances. He had wanted Lord Chesterfield to be his patron and had been turned down like a bedspread. No wonder he was in ugly mood.

In the days when I was hammering out stories for the pulp magazines and wondering where my next buckwheat cakes and coffee were coming from I often used to think how wonderful it would be if the patron system of the eighteenth century could be revived. (I alluded to it, if you remember, in the Foreword.) No blood, sweat and tears then. All you had to do was to run over the roster of the peerage and select your patron.

You wanted somebody fairly weak in the head, but practically all members of the peerage in those days were weak in the head and, there being no income tax or super tax then, they could fling you purses of gold without feeling it. Probably some kindly friend put you on to the right man.

'Try young Sangazure,' he said. 'I know the nurse who dropped him on his head when a baby. Give him the old oil and you can't miss. Don't forget to say "My Lord" and "Your lordship" all the time.'

I have never been quite clear as to what were the actual preliminaries. I imagine that you waited till your prospect had written a poem, as was bound to happen sooner or later, and then you hung around in his ante-room till you were eventually admitted to his presence. You found him lying on the sofa reading the eighteenth-century equivalent of *Reveille*, and when he said 'Yes?' or 'Well?' or 'Who on earth let *you* in?' you explain that you had merely come to look at him.

'No, don't move, my lord,' you said. 'And don't speak for a moment, my lord. Let me just gaze at your lordship.'

You wanted, you said, to feast your eyes on the noble brow from which had proceeded that *Ode to Spring*.

The effect was instantaneous.

'Oh, I say, really?' said the young peer, softening visibly and drawing a pattern on the carpet with his left toe. 'You liked the little thing?'

'*Liked it,* my lord! It made me feel like some watcher of the skies when a new planet swims into his ken. That bit at the beginning – "Er, Spring, you perfectly priceless old thing." I'll bet you – or, rather, I should say your lordship – didn't want that one back. However did your lordship do it?'

'Oh, just thought of it, don't you know, and sloshed it down, if you see what I mean.'

'Genius! Genius! Do you work regular hours, my lord, or does your lordship wait for inspiration?'

'Oh, well, sometimes one, as it were, and sometimes the other, so to speak. Just how it happens to pan out, you know. But tell me. You seem a knowledgeable sort of bloke. Do you write yourself by any chance? I mean, write and all that sort of rot, what?'

'Why, yes, my lord, I am a writer, my lord. Not in your

lordship's class, of course, but I do scribble a bit, my lord.'

'Make a good thing out of it?'

'So far no, my lord. You see, to get anywhere these days my lord, you have to have a patron, and patrons don't grow on every bush, my lord. How did that thing of your lordship's go? Ah, yes. "Oh Spring, oh Spring, oh glorious Spring, when cuckoos sing like anything." Your lordship certainly gave that section the works.'

'Goodish, you thought? I must say I didn't think it baddish myself. I say, look here, harking back to what you were saying a moment ago. How about me being your patron?'

'Your lordship's condescension overwhelms me.'

'Right ho, then, that's all fixed up. Tell my major-domo as you go out to fling you a purse of gold.'

4

Recently I have seemed to detect welcome signs indicating that the patron is coming back. I wrote an article the other day, in which I gave my telephone number.

'In the life of every man living in New York and subscribing to the New York telephone service' (I wrote) 'there comes a moment when he has to face a problem squarely and make a decision. Shall he – or alternatively shall he not – have his name in the book? There is no evading the issue. Either you are in the book or you are not. I am in myself. I suppose it was wanting to have something good to read in the long winter evenings that made me do it. For unquestionably it reads well.

Wodehouse, P. G. 1000 PkAv. BUtrfld 8–5029

Much better, it seems to me, than Wodak, Norma L. 404 E. 51. MUryhl 8–4376, which comes immediately before it, and Wodicka, Geo. D. 807 ColbsAv. MOnumnt 6–4933, which comes immediately after. Both are good enough in their way, but they are not

Wodehouse, P. G. 1000 PkAv. BUtrfld 8–5029

In moods of depression I often turn to the well-thumbed page, and it always puts new heart into me. 'Wodehouse,

P. G.,' I say to myself. '1000 PkAv.,' I say to myself. 'BUtrfld 8–5029,' I say to myself. 'Pretty good, pretty good.'

But – or as we fellows in the book say, BUt – there is just one objection to having your name listed – viz. that you thereby become a social outcast, scoffed at and despised by the swells who have private numbers, the inference being that you can't be very hot if you aren't important enough to keep your number a secret confined to a small circle of personalf riends.

Nevertheless, I shall continue to instruct the brass hats of the system to publish my name, address and telephone number. (Wodehouse, P. G. 1000 PkAv. BUtrfld 8–5029, in case you have forgotten.) A fig, if I may use the expression, for the snobs who will look down on me. What is good enough for Aaklus, Valbourg E., for the AAAAA–BEEEE Moving and Storage Company, for Zwowlow, Irving, for Zyttenfeld, Saml., and for the ZZYZZY Ztamp Zstudio Corpn is good enough for me.

Well, for weeks after the article appeared no day passed without two or three people ringing up to ask if that really was my telephone number. One of them rang up from Pasadena, California. He said – this seems almost inconceivable, but I am quoting him verbatim – that he thought my books were drivel and he wouldn't read another of them if you paid him, but he did enjoy my articles and would I like a coloured Russell Flint print of a nude sitting on the banks of the Loire. I said I would – you can't have too many nudes about the home, I always say – and it now hangs over my desk. And the point I am making is this. Whatever we may think of a man who does not appreciate my books, we must applaud what is indubitably the right spirit.

We authors live, of course, solely for our Art, but we can always do with a little something on the side, and here, unless I am mistaken, we have the patron system coming into its own again. It should, in my opinion, be encouraged.

If any other members of my public feel like subsidizing me, what I need particularly at the moment are:

> Golf balls
> Tobacco

A Rolls-Royce
Dog food suitable for
  (*a*) A foxhound
  (*b*) A Pekinese
  (*c*) Another Pekinese
Cat food suitable for
  A cat (she is particularly fond of peas)
and
Diamond necklace suitable for
  A wife

I could also do with a case of champagne and some warm winter woollies. And a few shares of United States Steel would not hurt.

SEVEN

Some Thoughts on Humorists

I

Well, time marched on, Winkler, and, pursuing the policy of writing a book, then another book, then another book, then another book and so on, while simultaneously short stories and musical comedies kept fluttering out of me like bats out of a barn, I was soon doing rather well as scriveners go. Twenty-one of my books were serialized in the *Saturday Evening Post*. For the second one they raised me to $5000, for the third to $7500, for the fourth to $10,000, for the fifth to $20,000. That was when I felt safe in becoming 'P. G. Wodehouse' again.

For the last twelve I got $40,000 per. Nice going, of course, and the stuff certainly came in handy, but I have always been alive to the fact that I am not one of the really big shots. Like Jeeves, I know my place, and that place is down at the far end of the table among the scurvy knaves and scullions.

I go in for what is known in the trade as 'light writing', and those who do that – humorists they are sometimes called – are looked down upon by the intelligentsia and sneered at. When I tell you that in a recent issue of the *New Yorker* I was referred to as 'that burbling pixie', you will see how far the evil has spread.

These things take their toll. You can't go calling a man a burbling pixie without lowering his morale. He frets. He refuses to eat his cereal. He goes about with his hands in his pockets and his lower lip jutting out, kicking stones. The next thing you know, he is writing thoughtful novels analysing social conditions, and you are short another humorist. With things going the way they are, it won't be long before the species dies out. Already what was once a full-throated chorus has faded into a few scattered chirps. You can still hear from the thicket the gay note of the Beachcomber, piping as the linnets do, but at any moment Lord Beaverbrook or somebody may be calling Beachcomber a burbling pixie and taking all the heart out of him, and then what will the harvest be?

These conditions are particularly noticeable in America. If as you walk along the streets of any city there you see a furtive-looking man who slinks past you like a cat in a strange alley which is momentarily expecting to receive a half-brick in the short ribs, don't be misled into thinking it is Baby-Face Schultz, the racketeer for whom the police of thirty states are spreading a dragnet. He is probably a humorist.

I recently edited an anthology of the writings of American humorists of today, and was glad to do so, for I felt that such publications ought to be encouraged. Bring out an anthology of their writings, and you revive the poor drooping untouchables like watered flowers. The pleasant surprise of finding that somebody thinks they are also God's creatures makes them feel that it is not such a bad little world after all, and they pour their dose of strychnine back into the bottle and go out into the sunlit street through the door instead of, as they had planned, through the seventh-storey window. Being asked for contributions to the book I have mentioned was probably the only nice thing that had happened to these lepers since 1937. I am told that Frank Sullivan, to name but one, went about Saratoga singing like a lark.

Three suggestions as to why 'light writing' has almost ceased to be have been made – one by myself, one by the late Russell Maloney and one by Wolcott Gibbs of the *New Yorker*. Here is mine for what it is worth.

It is, in my opinion, the attitude of the boys with whom they mingle in their early days that discourages all but the most determined humorists. Arriving at their public school, they find themselves placed in one of two classes, both unpopular. If they merely talk amusingly, they are silly asses. ('You *are* a silly ass' is the formula.) If their conversation takes a mordant and satirical turn, they are 'funny swine'. ('You think you're a funny swine, don't you?') And whichever they are, they are scorned and despised and lucky not to get kicked. At least, it was so in my day. I got by somehow, possibly because I weighed twelve stone three and could box, but most of my contemporary pixies fell by the wayside and have not exercised their sense of humour since 1899 or thereabouts.

Russell Maloney's theory is that a humorist has always been a sort of comic dwarf, and it is quite true that in the middle ages the well-bred and well-to-do thought nothing so funny as a man who was considerably shorter than they were, or at least cultivated a deceptive stoop. Anyone in those days who was fifty inches tall or less was *per se* a humorist. They gave him a conical cap and a stick with little bells attached to it and told him to caper about and amuse them. And as it was not a hard life and the pickings were pretty good, he fell in with their wishes.

Today what amuses people, says Mr Maloney, is the mental dwarf or neurotic – the man unable to cross the street un-escorted, cash a cheque at the bank or stay sober for several hours at a time, and the reason there are so few humorists nowadays is that it is virtually impossible to remain neurotic when you have only to smoke any one of a dozen brands of cigarette to be in glowing health both physically and mentally.

Wolcott Gibbs thinks that the shortage is due to the fact that the modern tendency is to greet the humorist, when he dares to let out a blast, with a double whammy from a baseball bat. In order to be a humorist, you must see the world out of focus, and today, when the world is really out of focus, people insist that you see it straight. Humour implies ridicule of estab-lished institutions, and they want to keep their faith in the established order intact. In the past ten years, says Gibbs, the humorist has become increasingly harried and defensive, increasingly certain that the minute he raises his foolish head the hot-eyed crew will be after him, denouncing him as a fiddler while Rome burns. Naturally after one or two ex-periences of this kind he learns sense and keeps quiet.

2

Gibbs, I think, is right. Humorists have been scared out of the business by the touchiness now prevailing in every section of the community. Wherever you look, on every shoulder there is a chip, in every eye a cold glitter warning you, if you know what is good for you, not to start anything.

'Never,' said one of the columnists the other day, 'have I heard such complaining as I have heard this last year. My last month's mail has contained outraged yelps on pieces I have written concerning dogs, diets, ulcers, cats and kings. I wrote a piece laughing at the modern tendency of singers to cry, and you would have thought I had assaulted womanhood.'

A few days before the heavyweight championship between Rocky Marciano and Roland La Starza, an Australian journalist who interviewed the latter was greatly struck by his replies to questions.

'Roland,' he wrote, 'is a very intelligent young man. He has brains. Though it may be,' he added, 'that I merely think he has because I have been talking so much of late to tennis players. Tennis players are just one cut mentally above the wallaby.'

I have never met a wallaby, so cannot say from personal knowledge how abundantly – or poorly – equipped such animals are with the little grey cells, but of one thing I am sure and that is that letters poured in on the writer from Friends of The Wallaby, the International League for Promoting Fair Play for Wallabies and so on, protesting hotly against the injustice of classing them lower in the intellectual scale than tennis players. Pointing out, no doubt, that, while the average run-of-the-mill wallaby is perhaps not an Einstein, it would never dream of bounding about the place shouting 'forty love' and similar ill-balanced observations.

So there we are, and if you ask me what is to be done about it, I have no solution to suggest. It is what the French would call an impasse. In fact, it is what the French do call an impasse. Only they say amh-parrse. Silly, of course, but you know what Frenchmen are. (And now to await the flood of strongly protesting letters from Faure, Pinay, Maurice Chevalier, Mendès-France, Oo-Là-Là and Indignant Parisienne.)

3

They say it is possible even today to be funny about porcupines and remain unscathed, but I very much doubt it. Just try it and see how quickly you find your letter-box full of communications beginning:

Sir,
With reference to your recent tasteless and uncalled-for comments on the porcupine . . . .

A writer in one of the papers was satirical the other day about oysters, and did he get jumped on! A letter half a column long next morning from Oyster Lover, full of the bitterest invective. And the same thing probably happened to the man who jocularly rebuked a trainer of performing fleas for his rashness in putting them through their paces while wearing a beard. Don't tell me there is not some league or society for the protection of bearded flea trainers, watching over their interests and defending them from ridicule.

There is certainly one watching over the interests of bearded swimming-pool attendants and evidently lobbying very vigorously, for it has just been ruled by the California State Labour Department that 'there is nothing inherently repulsive about a Vandyke beard.' It seems that a swimming-pool attendant in Los Angeles, who cultivated fungus of this type, was recently dismissed by his employer because the employer said, 'Shave that ghastly thing off. It depresses the customers,' and the swimming-pool attendant said he would be blowed if he would shave it off, and if the customers didn't like it let them eat cake. The State Labour Department (obviously under strong pressure from the League for the Protection of Bearded Swimming-Pool Attendants) held that the employer's order 'constituted an unwarranted infringement upon the attendant's privilege as an individual in a free community to present such an appearance as he wished so long as it did not affect his duties adversely or tend to injure the employer in his business or reputation'. And then they went on to say that there is nothing inherently repulsive about a Vandyke beard.

Perfectly absurd, of course. There is. It looks frightful. A really vintage Vandyke beard, such as this swimming-pool attendant appears to have worn, seems to destroy one's view of Man as Nature's last word. If Vandyke thought he looked nice with that shrubbery on his chin, he must have been cockeyed.

And if the League for the Protection of Bearded Swimming-Pool Attendants and the Executors of the late Vandyke start writing me wounding letters, so be it. My head, though bloody, if you will pardon the expression, will continue unbowed. We light writers have learned to expect that sort of thing.

'What we need in America,' said Robert Benchley in one of his thoughtful essays, 'is fewer bridges and more fun.'

And how right he was, as always. America has the Triborough Bridge, the George Washington Bridge, the 59th Street Bridge, auction bridge, contract bridge, Senator Bridges and Bridgehampton, Long Island, but where's the fun?

When I first came to New York, everyone was gay and lighthearted. Each morning and evening paper had its team of humorists turning out daily masterpieces in prose and verse. Magazines published funny short stories, publishers humorous books. It was the golden age, and I think it ought to be brought back. I want to see an A. P. Herbert on every street corner, an Alex Atkinson in every local. It needs only a little resolution on the part of the young writers and a touch of the old broadmindedness among editors.

And if any young writer with a gift for being funny has got the idea that there is something undignified and anti-social about making people laugh, let him read this from the *Talmud*, a book which, one may remind him, was written in an age just as grim as this one.

. . . And Elijah said to Berokah, 'These two will also share in the world to come.' Berokah then asked them, 'What is your occupation?' They replied, 'We are merrymakers. When we see a person who is downhearted, we cheer him up.'

These two were among the very select few who would inherit the kingdom of Heaven.

EIGHT
Lives of the Hunted

I

Until this golden age sets in, if it ever does, I shall have to resign myself to the obscurity which is the fate of light writers. Not that I mind it. There are compensations to being lumped in with the other outcasts under the general head of *canaille*.

People are always coming up to me in the street and saying, 'Hullo there, Wodehouse, don't you wish you were a celebrity?' and my invariable reply is, 'No, Smith or Stokes or Bevan' (if it happens to be Mr Aneurin Bevan) 'I do not.' Nothing would induce me to be a celebrity. If in a weak moment you let yourself become a prominent figure in the public eye these days, you are nothing but an Aunt Sally for all the bright young men in the country. Debunking the eminent is now a national sport.

It was not always so. There was a time when everyone looked up to celebrities and respected them. They had never had it so good. And then suddenly everything changed. Out like a cloud of mosquitoes came a horde of young men with fountain-pens and notebooks, dogging their footsteps and recording their every unguarded speech, till today you can tell a celebrity by the nervous way he keeps looking over his shoulder and jumping if anybody whistles at him.

The only celebrity I know of who is able to cope with the situation is Evelyn Waugh. It has probably not escaped the public's memory that a year or so ago the *Daily Express* rang him up at his Gloucestershire home and asked if their literary critic, Miss Nancy Spain, could come and interview him for a series they were running called 'A Cool Look at The Loved

Ones'. Mr Waugh, who was once on the *Express* and now regards it without much favour, said No, they jolly well couldn't. Nevertheless, Miss Spain duly appeared, accompanied by Lord Noel-Buxton, who seems to have come along for the ride. Mr Waugh – Waugh the Deliverer is what most celebrities call him now – ejected them with a firm hand and having escorted them to the front gate went back to the dinner which they had interrupted.

The episode so impressed me that I reached for my harp and burst into song about it.

THE VISITORS

My dear old dad, when I was a lad
    Planning my life's career,
Said 'Read for the bar, be a movie star
Or travel around in lands afar
    As a mining engineer,
But don't, whatever you do,' he hissed,
'Be a widely read, popular novelist.'
    And he went on to explain
That if you're an author, sure as fate,
Maybe early or maybe late,
Two jovial souls will come crashing the gate,
    Noel-Buxton and Nancy Spain.

Noel-Buxton and Nancy Spain, my lad,
    Noel-Buxton and Nancy Spain.
They're worse, he said, than a cold in the head
    Or lunch on an English train.
Some homes have beetles and some have mice,
Neither of which are very nice,
But an author's home has (he said this twice)
    Noel-Buxton and Nancy Spain.

Well, I said 'Indeed?' but I paid no heed
    To the warning words I quote,
For I hoped, if poss, to make lots of dross
And to be the choice of the old Book Soc.,
    So I wrote and wrote and wrote.
Each book I published touched the spot,
There wasn't a dud in all the lot,

And things looked right as rain,
Till as one day at my desk I sat
The front-door knocker went rat-a-tat,
And who was it waiting on the mat?
    Noel-Buxton and Nancy Spain.

So all you young men who hope with your pen
    To climb to the top of the tree,
Just pause and think, 'ere you dip in the ink,
That you may be standing upon the brink
    Of the thing that happened to me.
That stern, stark book you are writing now
May be good for a sale of fifty thou',
    But it's wisest to refrain.
For what will it boot though it brings to you
A car and a yacht and a page in *Who's Who*,
If it also brings, as it's sure to do,
    Noel-Buxton and Nancy Spain.

Noel-Buxton and Nancy Spain, my lads,
    Noel-Buxton and Nancy Spain.
They'll walk right in with a cheerful grin
    And, when they are in, remain.
I wouldn't much care to be stung by bees
Or bitten, let's say, by a Pekinese,
But far, far better are those than these,
    Noel-Buxton and Nancy Spain.

2

It was the *New Yorker* that started it all with its Profiles. It
had the idea that if you tracked down your celebrity, got him
talking and then went home and wrote a few thousand words
showing him up as a complete bird-brain, everybody – except
the celebrity – would get a hearty laugh out of it. They 'did'
Ernest Hemingway a year or two ago, sending a female reporter to spend the afternoon with him and write down every
word he uttered, with, of course, the jolliest results. If you
write down every word uttered by anyone over a period of
several hours, you are bound to hook an occasional fatuous
remark.

And it is not as if the celebrity got anything out of it, though there have been indications recently that better times are coming. The name of John Harrington is probably not familiar to my readers, so I will explain that he is the director of sports at a Chicago broadcasting station, and the other day he received a stunning blow. He is still walking around in circles, muttering to himself, and the mildest of the things he mutters is 'Bloodsuckers! Bloodsuckers!'

What happened was that he wanted to interview some members of the Kansas City Athletics baseball club and was informed by them that they would be charmed if he would do so, provided he unbelted $50 per member, cash in advance. No fifty fish, no interview. It was a new experience for him, and he is living it deeply and fully, like a character in a Russian novel.

Hats off, I say, to those Kansas City athletes. For years there has been too much of this thing of notebooked young men sidling up to the celebrated and getting away with all sorts of good stuff without paying a penny for it. The celebs were supposed to be compensated by a few kind words chucked in at the beginning.

'He looks like a debonair magician, quick and agile, in his fashionable suit of grey and elegant black patent-leather slippers.'

That was what the *Daily Express* said about Mr Cecil Beaton not long ago when he gave them an interview. A poor substitute for hard cash.

And it was an important interview, too, for in it Mr Beaton revealed for the first time the sensational facts in connection with his recent visit to the château where he has been staying in the wine country of France.

'Summer had come,' he said (Exclusive), 'and I found the atmosphere most stimulating. We had an amusing dish – a delightful creamy mixture of something I can't quite remember, but I recall truffles in it.'

All that free! The circulation of the *Express* shot up. Lord Beaverbrook was enabled to buy two more houses in Jamaica. The interviewer – and quite rightly, too, after landing such a scoop for the dear old paper – probably had her salary doubled, and was officially permitted to call Nancy Spain Nancy. But what did Mr Beaton get out of it? Not a thing except the passing gratification of seeing himself described as a debonair magician in black patent-leather slippers. Does that pay the rent? It does not. You can wear black patent-leather slippers till your eyes bubble, but the landlord still wants his so much per each week. High time those Kansas City boys put their foot down.

Though they were not the first to do it. Apparently you have to be a baseball player to stand up for your rights. I was reading the other day about an exchange of views which took place some years ago between Mr William ('Bill') Terry, at that time manager of the New York Giants, and a representative of the *New Yorker*, which wanted to do a Profile of him. (A *New Yorker* Profile takes up eighty-three pages in the middle of the magazine and goes on for months and months and months.)

'And where were you born, Mr Terry?' inquired the Profile hound, starting to get down to it.

A wary look came into Wm's face.

'Young fella,' he said, 'that information will cost you a lot of money.'

That ended the love feast. They had to fill up the eighty-three pages with one of those solid, thoughtful things of Edmund Wilson's.

Hats off, therefore, also to Bill Terry. But though I approve of this resolve on the part of the celebrated to get in on the ground floor and make a bit, I am not blind to the fact that there is a danger of the whole thing becoming more than a little sordid. At first, till a regular scale of prices is set up and agreed to by both contracting parties, one foresees a good deal of distasteful wrangling.

Let us say that you are a young fellow named Grover who had bowled twenty-two wides in an over, which had never been done by a clergyman's son on a Thursday in August at Dover. It will not be long before there is a ring at the bell, followed by the appearance of a gentleman in horn-rimmed spectacles.

'Good morning, Mr Grover. I am from *Time*. Two and

twenty wides in an over we understand you bowled last Thursday, and naturally anxious are all *Time* readers to hear——'

'How much?'

'£10?'

'Make it £20.'

'£15 call it, shall we?'

'Well, it depends. Are you going to refer to me as stumpy balding spectacled George Grover (28) no Laker he?'

'Certainly not. Something on the lines of a debonair magician, quick and agile, we were thinking of.'

'Yes, I like that.'

'Adding that not spoiled you has success.'

'Excellent. I don't mind knocking off ten bob for that.'

'Make it 12s. 6d.'

'No, not worth 12s. 6d. No money squanderer I.'

'Be it so. Now tell me, Mr Grover, your feelings can you describe when pouched in the gully was your twenty-second delivery?'

'I felt fine.'

'And may I say that for the sake of your wife and kiddies you did it?'

'Not for £15 you mayn't. We'd better go back to the £20 we were talking about.'

You see what I mean. Sordid. These negotiations are better left to one's agent. I have instructed mine to arrange for a flat payment of 10 guineas, to be upped, of course, if they want to know what I had for dinner at that amusing château in the wine country.

3

The name of the *Time* man in the foregoing scene was not mentioned, but I presume he was one of those appearing in a little poem which I jotted down just now on the back of an old envelope after brooding, as I so often brood, on the list in *Time* of its editors, managing editors, assistant managing editors, deputy assistant managing editors, contributing editors, corresponding editors, sympathetic encouraging editors and what not, which is my favourite reading. You will generally find me with my feet up on the mantelpiece, poring over his fascinating column, and it always inspires me to bigger and better things.

> I must confess that often I'm
> A prey to melancholy
> Because I do not work on *Time*.
> It must be jolly. Golly!
> No other human bliss but pales
> Beside the feeling that you're
> One of nine hundred – is it? – males
> And females of such stature.

> How very much I would enjoy
> To call Roy Alexander 'Roy'
> And have him say 'Hullo, my boy.'

> Not to mention mixing on terms of easy
> camaraderie with

> Edward O. Cerf
> Richard Oulahan, Jr.
> Bernadine Beerheide
> Virginie Lindsley Bennett
> Rodney Campbell
> Estelle Dembeck
> Old Uncle Fuerbringer and all.

> Alas, I never learned the knack
> (And on *Time*'s staff you need it)
> Of writing English front to back
> Till swims the mind to read it.
> Tried often I've my darnedest, knows
> Goodness, but with a shock I'd
> Discover that once more my prose
> Had failed to go all cockeyed.

> So though I wield a fluent pen,
> There'll never be a moment when
> I join that happy breed of men.

> And women, of course. I allude to (among others).

> Dorothea L. Grine
> Eldon Griffiths
> Hillis Mills

Joseph Purtell
Douglass Auchincloss
Lester Bernstein
Gilbert Cant
Edwin Copps
Henry Bradford Darrach, Jr.
Barker T. Hartshorn
Roger S. Hewlett
Jonathan Norton Leonard
F. Sydnor Trapnell
Danuta Reszke-Birk
Deirdre Read Ryan
Yi Ying Sung
Content Peckham
Quinera Sarita King
Old Uncle Fuerbringer and all,
O-old Uncle Fuerbringer and all.

A pity, but too late to alter it now.

NINE

Bridges, Snails and Meteorites

I

But though I fall short of the Luce standard and have turned out to be just one of the burbling pixies and as such more or less of a hissing and a by-word among the eggheads, I have never been sorry that I became a writer. Authorship has its up and downs, sometimes you are on the crest of the wave, at others in the whatever it is of a wave that isn't the crest – trough, that's the word I was groping for – but taking it by and large its advantages outweigh its defects. Certainly I have done much better at writing than I would have done in some of the other professions. I am thinking at the moment of the second-hand bridge business, snail-gathering and getting hit in the stomach by meteorites.

The secondhand bridge business attracts many because at first sight it seems a quick way of making easy money. You get anything from $125,000 for a used bridge, if in reasonably good condition, and one can always do with $125,000. But – and here is the catch – it is by no means everybody who wants a used bridge. You know how it is about buying bridges, sometimes people just aren't in the mood. You might have a good year when the bridges went briskly, but there would also be those long spells when nothing seems to go right. They were trying to sell one of the New York bridges the other day, and despite all the efforts of the auctioneers to sales-talk the customers into scaring the moths out of their wallets no one would bid a nickel for it.

It was a good bridge, too. It had four trusses and between the trusses three lanes for vehicular traffic, and was capable of carrying 100,000 vehicles and 500,000 pedestrians daily.

'Give it to your girl for Christmas and watch her face light up,' said the advertisements, but nothing doing. It went begging.

The fact is, bridges are always chancy things – unreliable. You never know what they are going to do next. This is exemplified by what occurred at the re-opening of the Harrison drawbridge over the Passaic river in New Jersey the other day.

The way these drawbridges work, in case you don't know, is as follows. A boat comes along and toots, you press a button, the bridge goes up, the boat goes through, you press another button, and the bridge comes down again, and so the long day wears on. And about as attractive a way of passing a drowsy summer afternoon as one could imagine. But in 1946, having gone up to allow a tanker to pass through, this Harrison bridge stayed up and remained that way for ten years. Then the Essex and Hudson Board of Freeholders, who never stand that sort of thing indefinitely, clubbed together and raised the money to have it put back into working order, and the big day for the re-opening ceremony was fixed.

The Mayor was there. There was a silver band. Speeches were made, the 'Star-Spangled Banner' sung, and school-children paraded in droves, many of them with clean faces. Somebody handed the Mayor the scissors to cut the ribbon, and at that moment, just as he was saying, 'I hereby declare that from now on everything is going to be like mother makes it,' a tanker tooted. Up went the bridge, stayed up and is still up. If they ever get it down again, I will let you know.

There is almost no industry fuller of pitfalls than bridge-selling. I knew a man in that line who heard one day that the inhabitants of Terra del Fuego were short of bridges. It was a long way to go, and it was no joke for him having to lug his bag of samples all those thousands of miles, but he stuck it out and arrived at journey's end with the muscles of his right arm pretty stiff and sore, but with a song in his heart as he thought of the business he was going to do. The natives seemed friendly, so he decided to stay the night, and in the morning he sent in his card to a high Terra del Fuegan official.

'They tell me that you people need bridges around here,' he said.

'Not bridges,' said the official. 'Breeches.'

2

The news in my daily paper that in certain parts of Wales the latest craze is snail-racing has turned my attention to these gasteropods after months and months during which I don't suppose I have given more than a passing thought to them.

As a writer I have always rather kept off snails, feeling that they lacked sustained dramatic interest. With a snail nothing much ever happens, and, of course, there is no sex angle. An informant on whom I can rely says they are 'sexless or at least ambivalent'. This means, broadly speaking, that there are no boy snails and no girl snails, so that if you want to write a novel with a strong snail interest, you are dished from the start. Obviously the snail-meets-snail, snail-loses-snail, snail gets-snail formula will not help you, and this discourages writers from the outset. Almost all we know of snails from English literature is Shakespeare's brief statement that they creep unwillingly to school.

But this snail-racing should mean a change for the better and give authors more of a chance. The way it works, I understand, is that each entrant pays a small fee and the owner of the first snail to pass the judges' box takes the lot. The runners have their owners' colours painted on their shells and 'are attracted to the winning-post by a pile of wet ivy leaves', with a delirious crowd, no doubt, shouting 'Come on, Steve' or words to that effect. Any competent author ought to be able to make something of this . . . the hero's fortunes depending on the big race, his snail Forked Lightning trained to the last ounce, the villain sneaking into Lightning's stable to nobble him by sprinkling him with salt, and the heroine foiling the scoundrel by removing the salt and substituting powdered sugar. There is surely a wealth of material here for something in the Nat Gould vein, and I shall probably have a go at it myself.

But when I spoke of snail-gathering as a walk in life and hinted that I did not look on it as one of the lucrative professions, I was not thinking so much of racing snails as of the ones you eat in France with garlic sauce. (If you do eat them. I wouldn't myself to please a dying grandfather.) These, I understand, flourish, if you can call it flourishing, mostly in Austria, and I was shocked to learn from a usually well-informed source that the Austrian boys who track them down are paid only sixty shillings for sixty pounds of them. (Schillings it should be really, of course, but I can't do the dialect.) Putting it more simply, they get one shilling (*schilling*) for each pound (*pcound*).

I don't know how many snails go to the pound, for it must vary a good deal according to their size and robustness. You get big beefy snails which go bullocking about all over the place – what are known in Austria as 'hearties' – and conversely you get wan wizened little snails which have stunted their growth with early cigarette smoking. Still, big or little, sixty pounds of them must take quite a bit of assembling, and I feel that what the Austrians call schnirkel-schnecke gatherers come under the head of sweated labour. But apparently Austrian fathers think differently.

'Well, Hans or Fritz or Wilhelm as the case may be,' says the Austrian father, addressing his Austrian son, 'the time has come for you to be deciding what you are going to do in the world. I myself made quite a good thing out of composing imitation Strauss waltzes, but the imitation Strauss waltz racket has gone blue on us in these rock 'n roll days, so what is it to be? The Army? The Bar? The Church? Forgery? Blackmail? Arson? Or do you see yourself making Viennese pastry?'

'Well, I'll tell you, Pop,' says the Austrian son. 'The thing I feel I have a call for is schnirkel-schnecke gathering.'

'Schnirkel-schnecke gathering, eh? Capital, Capital (*Das Kapital, das Kapital*),' says the Austrian father and pats him (we are speaking of the Austrian son) on the head and tells him to go to it and not to forget his old dad when he has cleaned up.

A misguided policy, it seems to me, because when the schnirkel-schneckes are sold to the French restaurant, the French restaurant gets about £840 11s. 5d. for the same amount of schnirkel-schneckes for which the schnirkel-schnecke gatherer, poor sap, got about £71 6s. 4d., leaving the latter down a matter of £769 5s. 1d. (check these figures).

Obviously what the boy ought to do is get a job in the French restaurant, marry the boss's daughter and become part proprietor.

3

I don't see that there is much real money, either, in getting hit in the stomach by meteorites.

Yes, I know what you are going to say. You are going to remind me of that episode in Tennessee last year. I had not forgotten it, but I think I can show that it in no way weakens my case.

Way down in Tennessee at a place called Wading River, Mrs Jane Elizabeth Baxter, who rented a bed-sitting-room at the house of a Mrs Birdie Tuttle, was lying on the sofa one afternoon when she was surprised – and at first none too well pleased – to see a meteorite come through the roof and hit her in the stomach. Reflecting, however, that there might be money in this, she applied to a neighbouring museum and learned with considerable gratification that it was prepared to offer $2750 spot cash for this visitant from outer space.

'Pretty soft,' said Mrs Baxter to Mrs Tuttle, and was stunned when the latter claimed that since she owned the premises on which the meteorite fell, it was rightfully hers. Mrs Baxter counterclaimed that she owned the stomach on which the meteorite fell, and an action resulted. I am glad to say that it was amicably settled out of court, and Mrs Baxter paid Mrs Tuttle $50. She then sold the meteorite to the museum for $2750, and that is all she has got out of the thing. She has reached a dead end.

That is why, if I had a son and he came to me and said, 'Father, I am concluding my military service in September and shall have to be thinking of making a living. How about this meteorite business?' I should discourage him.

'Don't be an ass, my boy,' I should say. 'It'll get you nowhere.'

He then, of course, brings up the Baxter–Tuttle case. He has read about it and been greatly impressed.

'But reflect,' he says. 'Reason it out. This Mrs Baxter got $2750 from the museum, so that even after slipping $50 to Mrs Tuttle she was $2700 ahead of the game. All that from one meteorite, mark you. A meteorite a day——'

'—keeps the doctor away. True. So far I am with you, but——'

'At $2700 per meteorite per person per day, that would be $985,500 a year – or in leap year $988,200. That's nice money.'

'Ah,' I reply, 'but have you considered, my boy, that whole days might pass without a single meteorite coming your way? There must be dozens of people who don't get hit in the stomach by a meteorite more than once or twice in a good season and are simply struggling along on a pittance.'

'I never thought of that,' says the lad, and he goes off and becomes an average adjuster and does well.

And meanwhile Mrs Jane Elizabeth Baxter, in the suit of chain-mail which she now habitually wears, is lying on her sofa at Balmoral, Eisenhower Road, Wading River, looking hopefully up at the ceiling. Good luck, Mrs Baxter. I think you are living in a fool's paradise, but nevertheless good luck.

And good luck, too, to Mrs Birdie Tuttle, who is down in the cellar, listening for the crash and waiting for her cut.

TEN

Crime, Does It Pay?

I

Of course, there are many other ways of making a living open to a writer who finds himself developing into a burbling pixie and decides to go straight and lead a new life. Some are attractive, some not, and as an instance of the latter one could scarcely do better than to cite the case of Patrolman Leroy Kidwell of the town of Sedalia, Missouri.

As I had the story from a correspondent on the spot, Television Station KDRO, whose headquarters are in Sedalia, was staging a money-raising drive for the polio fund, and got from one viewer the firm offer that he would pay $5 to see Patrolman Kidwell hit in the face with a custard pie. (My informant does not say so, but, reading between the lines, one receives the impression that this viewer had something against the zealous officer.)

With Station KDRO to think is to act. It routed Patrolman Kidwell out of bed and put it up to him.

'No, sir,' said Mr Kidwell firmly. 'Not for five bucks. But I'll do it for fifty.'

Scarcely had his words been relayed to the public when calls started pouring in, and when the pledges had reached $65, the patrolman expressed himself satisfied. He appeared on the screen, took the custard pie squarely between the eyes, wiped it off and went back to bed.

Now at first sight it might seem that Patrolman Kidwell had taken the initial step leading to ease and affluence. True, on this occasion the money went to the polio fund, but next time, one assumes, Mr Kidwell would pouch the takings. He would say to himself, 'This is a good thing. I will push it along.'

He was probably on the screen not more than about two minutes, and $65 for a couple of minutes' work is unquestionably good gravy. But only the vapid and irreflective would hold such an opinion long. Deeper thinkers would realize in a moment that this sort of thing, like getting hit in the stomach by meteorites, could never bring in a regular income over the years. These sudden successes are nearly always just a flash in the pan. It will probably be months before a group of citizens is again willing to pay out substantial money for the privilege of seeing custard pies thrown at Patrolman Kidwell. I shall be much surprised if a year from now he is not muttering to himself, as he walks his beat, 'Othello's occupation's gone.'

The prudent thing for anyone who wishes to provide for his old age is to find some steady job which will enable him to put by a certain something each week, so that every little bit added to what he has got makes just a little bit more, and one immediately thinks of crime, with its negligible overhead and freedom from income tax, as the solution.

Crime, especially in America, seems to be all the go these days. In New York the great thing is to stick up banks. Practically everyone you meet there is either on his way to stick up a bank or coming away from having done so. These institutions have a fascination for the criminal classes, attracting them much as catnip attracts cats. A young man went into a bank not long ago and asked to see the manager. Conducted into his office, he said he wanted a loan.

'Ah, yes,' said the manager. 'A loan, eh? Yes, yes, to be sure. And what is your occupation?'

'I stick up banks,' said the young man, producing a sawn-off shot-gun.

The manager handed over $1204 without security or argument.

Of course, you get your disappointments in this profession as in all others. Last week, a little group of enthusiasts set out to rob a bank, which involved a lot of tedious preliminary planning, not to mention the sinking of a good deal of capital in automatic pistols, tommy-guns and so on. They dashed up to the bank in their car, dashed up the steps and were about to dash through the door when they saw posted up on it the notice:

CLOSED WEDNESDAYS

And all the weary work to do over again. It was disheartening, they told one another, and they didn't care who heard them say so.

2

Nevertheless, though I fully appreciate that criminals, like all of us, have to take the rough with the smooth and cannot expect life to be roses, roses all the way, I do sometimes find myself wondering if I might not have done better on leaving the Hong Kong and Shanghai Bank to have bought a black mask and an ounce or two of trinitrotoluol and chanced my arm as a member of the underworld. When I see how well some of these underworld chaps are doing and think how little slogging brainwork their activities involve, it is hard not to feel that they are on the right lines.

Except for *Thank You, Jeeves*, which for some reason gave me no trouble at all and came gushing out like a geyser from the opening paragraph of Chapter One, I have never written a novel yet without doing 40,000 words or more and finding they were all wrong and going back and starting again, and this after filling 400 pages with notes, mostly delirious, before getting anything in the nature of a coherent scenario. A man like Charles Raynor (40) of 21 West 89th Street, New York, would raise his eyebrows at the idea of anyone expending so much energy, when all you need, if you want to put money in your purse, is to get acquainted with James Joyce in a bar and let Nature do the rest.

James Joyce – no, not the one you are thinking of – this one is a sailor who lives in Philadelphia and was recently awarded damages for losing a leg while working on his ship. When he met Charles Raynor, he had $21,000. This was speedily adjusted.

It was in a bar, as I have indicated, that Mr Joyce and Mr

Raynor got together, and after a few civilities had been exchanged, Mr Joyce told Mr Raynor what a lot of money he
had. On learning that what he had was only $21,000, Mr
Raynor expressed surprise that he should appear so satisfied.
Wouldn't he, he asked, like more? Why, yes, said Mr Joyce,
he was always in the market for a bit extra, but the problem
was how to get it. He could, of course, lose another leg, but
for some reason he shrank from that. He couldn't tell you
why, he just shrank.

Mr Raynor then said that it was a lucky day for Mr Joyce
when they met. It appeared that he, Mr Raynor, had a friend,
a Mr Spiller, who had invented a magic box that made $10
bills. Was Mr Joyce interested?

Yes, said Mr Joyce, he was. Interested was just the word.
It was of a box of this precise nature that he had often dreamed
when splicing the mainbrace and porting his helm on the seven
seas. He went with Mr Rayner to Mr Spiller's residence,
handed over a $10 bill, it was inserted in the box, there was
a buzzing sound, and out came the $10 bill together with a
second $10 bill. With a brief inquiry as to how long this had
been going on, Mr Joyce parted with $6200 for working
expenses, and the moment they had got it the Messrs Raynor
and Spiller parted from him.

I think these two men will go far. Indeed, the police say
they already have.

The methods of Betty Welsh (21) who is a gipsy were somewhat more elaborate, though she worked on similar lines.
Meeting Alice Barber, a dentist's receptionist, in the street,
she gave her a sharp look, asked if she might feel her pulse,
and, having done so, delivered the following diagnosis: 'Yes,
as I suspected, you have stomach trouble. Go home, light
nineteen candles and come back to me with $30 wrapped
round an egg.'

This seemed sound enough to Miss Barber. It was just the
sort of thing any good New York doctor would have recommended. She followed the instructions to the letter, but it
turned out that further treatment was required.

'No, not cured yet,' said Miss Welsh. 'Yours is a stubborn
case. We must try again. Go home, repeat the alphabet

backwards, and meet me here with a bottle of water, three potatoes and $40.'

But even this did not bring relief, and for a moment Miss Barber's medical adviser seemed nonplussed. Then she saw the way.

'Go to the jewellery store on 50th Street and First Avenue,' she said, 'get $500 worth of jewellery on credit and give it to me. That should do it.'

Unfortunately, Miss Barber told a boy-friend about it, and the boy-friend decided to take a second opinion. He called in the cops, and when Miss Barber and Miss Welsh arrived at the jeweller's, who should be waiting on the doorstep but Lieutenant Walter O'Connor and two gentlemanly patrolmen.

Interviewed later by the lieutenant, Miss Barber said, 'I had indigestion, so I thought I would give it a try.'

But while one respects practitioners like these and wishes them every success in their chosen careers, the world's worker one really admires is Robert Watson (45) of Hoboken, New Jersey, because he did down the income tax authorities – the dream of every redblooded man. He was recently convicted of having received seven illegitimate income tax refunds totalling $2500, and evidence was brought to show he was waiting for seventeen more government cheques averaging $400 each.

His method of procedure was to file a bogus return under a false name but a correct address, and then wait for the refund which he claimed. And he was just saying to himself 'Nice work, Bob.' At's the stuff to give 'em, Watson,' when Raymond del Tufto, Jr, United States Attorney for New Jersey, came down on him like a ton of bricks, and with the usual allowance for good behaviour we shall be seeing him again in about 1961.

3

I suppose that is really the objection to a life of crime, that the police are so infernally fussy. Over and over again they act in restraint of trade. Just before I left New York, I had a visit from the police. No, nothing I had done. I was as pure as the driven snow. What these policemen – there were two of them, a stout one and a thin one – wanted was to sell me a gadget designed to baffle the criminal classes. $8 was the price, but worth it, the stout one said, because the crime wave was becoming a regular tidal wave these days. Mounting higher every day, he said, and the thin one said 'Oftener than that' and gave it as his opinion that it was all these comic books that did it. They added fuel to its flames, he said.

The favourite trick of the criminal classes, they told me, is to come to your back door and knock on it and say they are from the grocer's, delivering groceries. When you let them in, they stick you up. The cagey thing, then, is not to let them in, and that was where you got your $8 worth out of this gadget. It is a round affair with a hole and a flap and you fix it to your back door, and when the criminal classes arrive and say they are from the grocer's, you hoik up the flap and look through the hole and say, 'Oh, you are, are you? Then where are the groceries, and why are you wearing a black mask and lugging round a whacking great gun?' Upon which, they slink off with horrid imprecations.

One can readily see where this sort of thing must lead. Back-door robberies will be stifled at the source, and those who want to turn a dishonest penny will have to do it by sticking up casual passers-by in the street, than which for a man at all inclined to shyness I can imagine nothing more embarrassing.

I know I should go all pink and flustered, if I had to do it. I can't see myself accosting a perfect stranger and saying, 'This is a stick-up.' It would sound so frightfully abrupt. I suppose the thing to do would be to lead up to it sort of.

'Oh – er – excuse me, I wonder if you could oblige me with a match? What a nuisance it is to run short of matches, is it not, when one wants to smoke. Though my doctor tells me I smoke far too much. Yours, too? Well, well, well. Dr Livingstone, I presume, ha, ha, ha. Dark here, isn't it? The evenings seem to be drawing in now, don't they? Christmas will be with us before we know where we are. Good night, sir, good night, and many thanks. Oh, by the way, there was one other thing. Might I trouble you to hand over your money and valuables?'

That would ease the strain a little, but nothing could ever make such a situation really agreeable. And suppose you happen to run across somebody deaf?

You say, 'This is a stick-up.'

He says, 'Huh?'

You say, 'A stick-up.'

He says, 'Huh?'

You say, 'A stick-up. A *stick*-up. S. for Samuel——'

He says, 'I'm afraid I couldn't tell you. I'm a stranger in these parts myself.'

Then what?

But the gravest objection to crime, to my mind, is the fatal tendency of the young criminal to get into a rut. Consider the case of the one whom for convenience sake we will call The Phantom.

I quote from my daily paper:

Lazarus Koplowitz lives at 60 Sixth Avenue, Brooklyn, where he operates a candy store. Four times in the last month he has been robbed by the same man, who appears at the same time of day – 3.15 p.m. – and threatens him with the same knife. The first time, on February 3, the unwelcome caller took $10 from Mr Koplowitz. On February 10 he took another $10, as also on February 17 and February 24. Police planted a detective in the rear for some days at the calling hour, then took him away. On March 3 the marauder came back and took a further $10.

I see no future for this Phantom. He has become the slave of a habit.

ELEVEN

Armadillos, Hurricanes and What Not

I

Winkler, my dear old chap, I really must apologize. Reading over these last chapters, I am shocked to see how I have been rambling. You asked me a lot of questions, and instead of answering them I went wandering off on to side issues like snails and bridges and meteorites and stick-up men and cuckoos, the last things in the world I should imagine your newspaper and radio public want to hear about. That is the curse with which we pixies are afflicted. We burble. I know we had a gentlemen's agreement that I was to survey mankind from China to Peru, but there are limits. From now on I will buckle down to it with a minimum of digressions, and as I see that you want information concerning my home life, I think I can scarcely do better than begin by telling you all about that.

As you rightly say, I am living in the country now. For seven years I had what is called a duplex penthouse apartment on the fourteenth floor of a building at 84th Street and Park Avenue, New York (BUTrfld 8–5029), but now I am permanently established in the little hamlet of Remsenburg, Long Island, oddly enough only a few miles from where I lived when I was first married forty-three years ago. Nice house now that we have got those two extra sun-parlours built on, and park-like grounds of about twelve acres. Why don't you come up and see me some time?

The household consists of self, wife, two Pekes, a cat and a foxhound, all of whom get along together like so many sailors on shore leave. The Pekes we brought with us, but Bill, the foxhound, and Poona, the cat, are strays who turned up from the great outdoors and seemed to be of the opinion that this was Journey's End. They were duly added to the strength.

Their origin is wrapped in obscurity. The fact of Poona being at a loose end and deciding to clock in and take pot-luck I can understand, for Long Island is full of stray cats walking through the wet woods waving their wild tails, but Bill is a dog of mystery. He is a foxhound of impeccable breed, obviously accustomed from birth to mixing with the smart hunting set – there are several packs on the island – and why he is not getting his nose down to it with the other foxhounds is more than I can tell you. I imagine that he just got fed up one day with all that Yoicks and Tally-ho stuff, and felt that the time had come to pull out and go into business for himself.

At any rate, he appeared in our garden one afternoon and sat down, and it was plain that he considered that his future career was up to us. He was in the last stages of starvation and so covered with swollen ticks that only the keenest eye could discern that there was a dog underneath. It took a vet working day and night to pull him round with injections of liver, for practically all the blood that had been inside him was now held in escrow by the ticks. It is agreeable to be able to record that his only worry today is having to watch his calories, for he is putting on weight terribly. A fox seeing him coming now, would laugh its head off.

For human society we rely mostly on Frances, our maid, who bowls over from Westhampton each morning in her green sports-model car, the Boltons, Guy and Mrs, a few other neighbours and the local children.

One of these dropped in for a chat the other day while I was watering the lawn.

'Hi!' he said.

'Hi to you,' I responded civilly.

'Wotcher doin'?'

'Watering.'

'Oops. Have you got a father?'

I said I had not.

'Have you got a mother?'

'No.'

'Have you got a sister?'

'No.'

'Have you got a brother?'

'No.'

'Have you got any candy?'

Crisp. That is the word I was trying to think of. The American child's dialogue is crisp.

Our garden is also a sort of country club for all the dogs within a radius of some miles. They look in for a bowl of milk and a biscuit most afternoons, and there is never any shortage of birds, squirrels, tortoises and rabbits. On a good day the place looks like a zoo. And while on the subject of rabbits, I see that the New York Heart Association has found a way of making rabbits' ears droop like those of a cocker spaniel. Their doctor Lewis Thomas has discovered that the trick can be done by injecting enzyme papain into the rabbit, and the Association is pretty pleased about it all. Too easily pleased, in my opinion. I mean, let's face it. After all the smoke has cleared away, Thomas, what have you got? A rabbit from whose ears all the starch has been removed. If you like that sort of rabbit, well and good, I have nothing to say, but I think invalids and nervous people should be warned in case they meet one unexpectedly.

We know, too, where, if we should want them, we can lay our hands on a few armadillos.

One morning not long ago the telephone-answering executive of the *New York Herald-Tribune* answered the telephone, and the caller said his name was Sidney A. Schwartz. He lived at Riverhead, which is seven miles from Remsenburg, where he kept bees.

'Ah, yes, bees,' said the *Herald-Tribune* man. 'And how are they all?'

'They're fine,' said Mr Schwartz, 'but what I rang up for was to ask if you would like to have ten armadillos.'

It was a strange and interesting story that he had to relate. What gave him the idea he could not say, but one afternoon as he was looking at his bees the thought flashed into his mind – Why bees? Why not armadillos?

He knew nothing of armadillos at that time except that nobody had ever claimed that they wrote the plays of Shakespeare, but he went out and bought a couple, and it so happened that they were of opposite sexes.

Well, you know what that means in armadillo circles, J. P. Love conquers all, as you might say. And when the union of two armadillos is blessed, the result is eight armadillos, sometimes more but never less. Came a day when armadillos began to sprout in every nook and cranny of the Schwartz home, and he was soon apprised of the drawbacks to this state of affairs. In addition to requiring large quantities of dog food, frozen horse meat, cod-liver oil and cream cheese, which dented the household budget considerably, armadillos – for reasons best known to themselves – sleep all day and come to life, like dramatic critics, only after dark. And unfortunately they are noisy and rowdy and seem to live for pleasure alone.

It was not long before *chez* Schwartz had become to all intents and purposes a night club, one of the more raffish kind, with armadillos, flushed with cream cheese, staggering about and shouting and yelling and generally starting a couple of fights before turning in for the day. It does not require much imagination to picture what it must be like with ten armadillos always around, two of them singing duets, the others forming quartettes and rendering 'Heart Of My Heart' in close harmony. Pandemonium is the word that springs to the lips.

And this is where I think that Mr Schwartz shows up in a very creditable light. Where a weaker man would have packed up and emigrated to Australia, he stayed put and rose on stepping-stones of his dead self to higher things. He had always wanted a Ph.D. degree, and here, he suddenly saw, was where he could get one. He would write a thesis on the nine-brand armadillo (*Dasypus novemcinctus*) and set his name ringing down the ages. He divided the young armadillos into two groups (it was no good trying to do anything with the father and mother, they were too soppy to register) and – I quote the *Herald-Tribune*:

One group he made to walk upon a treadmill to the extent of three miles a day. The other he allowed to lead completely sedentary lives, undisturbed by anything except the thoughts that normally disturb armadillos in the springtime. And at the end of some weeks he found that the armadillos which had led the strenuous life were happier than the armadillos which had lain slothful and passive.

And he got his Ph.D., showing that out of evil cometh good, and that has cheered him up quite a lot, but I must confess that I find the reasoning of his thesis shaky. How does he know that the athletic armadillos are happier than the other lot? They may be just putting a brave face on things and keeping a stiff upper lip. You can't go by an armadillo's surface manner. Many an apparently cheery armadillo without, you would say, a care in the world is really nursing a secret sorrow, sobbing into its pillow and asking itself what is the good of it all and how can it shake off this awful depression. I should require a lot more evidence than Mr Schwartz has submitted to convince me that the ones he thinks so chirpy are really sitting on top of the world with their hats on the side of their heads.

But what interests me chiefly in the story is not the *joie de vivre* or lack of *joie de vivre* of the armadillos but the Schwartz angle. If I say that my heart bleeds for him that is not putting it all too strongly. He has got his Ph.D., yes, and that, in a way, I suppose, is a happy ending, but he has also got all those armadillos, and more probably coming along every hour on the hour. The place must be a shambles.

So if I should get the armadillo urge and wish to add a few to the dogs, cats, squirrels, rabbits and tortoises in our garden, I have no doubt that Mr Schwartz would gladly let me have them at bargain rates. I must drop over there when I can spare time and study the situation at first hand. Taking care to go in the daytime, before the cod-liver oil corks have started to pop and the night revels have begun.

One does not want unpleasantness.

2

Of sport we have no lack in Remsenburg. Over at West-hampton, five miles away, there is a good golf course and the ocean to swim in, while if one prefers not to leave the home grounds, excellent mosquito-swatting can be found down by the water at the foot of our property. Over this I, of course, hold manorial rights. The only trouble is that the mosquito season is all too brief. It ends round about the beginning of September. After that nothing remains but the flies, and a hunter who has looked his mosquito in the eye and made it wilt finds but a tepid interest in flies. One likes a tang of peril with one's sport.

Have you ever reflected, Winkler, what a miserable, coddled creature, compared with a mosquito, a fly is? It takes three weeks to breed a new generation of flies, and even then the temperature has to be seventy degrees. A spell of cold weather and the fly simply turns its face to the wall and throws in the towel. How different with the mosquito. $2 million are spent yearly in efforts to keep mosquito eggs from hatching. Lamps, sprays and drenches without number are brought into action and oil in tons poured on the breeding grounds. And what happens? Do they quail? Do they falter? Not by a jugful. They come out in clouds, slapping their chests and whistling through their noses, many of them with stingers at both ends.

Science has now established that the only mosquitoes that sting are the females. The boy-friends like to stay at home doing their crossword puzzles. One pictures the male mosquito as a good-natured, easy-going sort of character, not unlike the late G. P. Huntley, and one can imagine him protesting feebly when the little woman starts out on a business trip.

'Oh, I say, dash it! Not *again*? Are you really going out at this time of night, old girl?'

'I work better at night.'

'Where are you off to now?'

'New York.'

'You mean Newark?'

(The scene of the conversation is the Jersey marshes, where mosquitoes collect in gangs.)

'No, I don't mean Newark. I mean New York.'

'You can't possibly go all the way to New York.'

'Pooh.'

'It's all very well to say Pooh. You know as well as I do that a mosquito can only fly 200 yards.'

'I can take the Holland Tunnel.'

'Costs 50¢.'

'Oh, you think of nothing but money,' says the female mosquito petulantly, and she strops her stinger on the doorstep and goes off and probably gets squashed. Rather sad, that, Winkler. Somebody's mother, you know. Still, we cannot allow ourselves to become sentimental about mosquitoes.

As an old hunter, I like the story of the general who, captured by the Chinese in Korea, relieved the monotony of imprisonment by swatting mosquitoes. His record was a 522-mosquito day in 1953, but his best all-over year was 1952, when he bagged 25,477. The secret of success, he says, is to wait till your quarry flattens itself against the wall. The simple creature does not realize that the wall is whitewashed, and falls a ready prey to the man who, not letting a twig snap beneath his feet, sneaks up behind it with a handsomely bound copy of *The History of the Communist Party in the Soviet Union.*

They say 1958 is going to be a good mosquito year. Let us hope so, for there are few more stirring sights than a mosquito hunt with the men in their red coats and the hounds baying and all that sort of thing.

Meet you in the Jersey marshes.

3

Compared with such centres as London, Paris or Las Vegas, I suppose one would say that life at Remsenburg was on the quite side. Or, for the matter of that, compared with Bad Axe, Michigan.

Bad Axe, Michigan, where it has been well said that there is always something doing, is the only place I ever heard of where you can get knocked down in the street by a flying cow. This was what happened the other day to Mrs Janet Whittaker of that town. She was sauntering along in a reverie, thinking of this and that, and suddenly this cow. It had been set in motion, apparently, by a passing car, and it hit Mrs Whittaker between the shoulder-blades. She was not greatly perturbed.

After a sharp 'Who threw that cow?' she speedily regained her poise. When you live in Bad Axe, Michigan, nothing surprises you very much.

But though, as I say, Remsenburg lacks some of the fiercer excitements of the places I have named, it is never dull. I have my work, and there are always the hurricanes.

The two hurricanes which dropped in last year on Long Island, Rhode Island and Nantucket have proved something which I have always suspected, and that is that there is a candour and frankness about the inhabitants of the eastern states of America which they don't have out west. Ask a Californian about the San Francisco earthquake and he will hotly deny that there ever was a San Francisco earthquake. 'What you probably have in mind,' he will say, 'is the San Francisco fire.' But we easterners are open and above-board. When we get a hurricane we call it a hurricane. Stop any Long Islander or Rhode Islander or Nantucketite in the street and say, 'I hear you had a hurricane the other day,' and his reply will be, 'You betcher.' He will not say, 'Are you alluding to last week's rather heavy fall of rain?' Californian papers, please copy.

Talking of Nantucket, one of New York's dramatic critics was caught there by the second hurricane. He gave it a bad notice. It apparently split into two when it got up there, and in his review in next day's paper he was rather severe about its lack of significant form and uncertain direction of interest. Still, he did admit that it was intense, vital and eruptive.

Our hurricanes were Carol and Edna. Dolly, their sister, a nice girl, went out to sea, but Carol gave us all she had got, and so eleven days later did Edna. Though Edna, when she arrived, did not have the same scope for self-expression. Carol had caught us unprepared, but we were ready for Edna. Baths had been filled with water, candles laid in. And all the trees which had not both feet on the ground had been uprooted by Carol, so that Edna's efforts were something of an anti-climax. Three days elapsed after Carol's visit before the electricity came on and enabled us to cook and have water, but with Edna we were in shape again next day.

I am sure you will want to know, Winkler, how I got on

under conditions which would have brought a startled 'Gor-blimey' to the lips of King Lear. I rose betimes, and when the fury of the elements had slackened off somewhat went for a refreshing dip in the bird-bath in the garden. What a lesson this teaches us, does it not, always to be kind to our feathered friends and never to neglect the filling of their tubs. There was a rich deposit of water in the bird-bath and I hopped about in it merrily. Then back to the house to a hearty break-fast – a slice of cake and a warm whisky and soda – and my day had begun. A sizeable tree had fallen across the drive, rendering it impossible to get the car out, so I walked hipperty-hipperty-hop two miles to the local store and bought bread, milk and cold viands. Before dinner I had another splash in the bird-bath. Bed at eight-thirty.

A thing about hurricanes which I can never understand is why Cape Hatteras affects them so emotionally. Everything is fine up to there – wind at five miles an hour, practically a dead calm – but the moment a hurricane sees Cape Hatteras it shies like a startled horse and starts blowing a steady 125 m.p.h. Hysteria, of course, but why?

The great thing to do when a hurricane comes clumping along and breaking all the trees in your garden – 'Can we knock this off our income tax?' are the words you heard on every side in those days – is to look for the silver lining and try to spot the good it has wrought as well as the bad. Thus, Hurricane Edna inadvertently settled a quarrel between two neighbours of mine by removing a tree that had been leaning from one neighbour's property into the other's. The latter had commanded the former to take the damn thing out of there, and the former had refused. Harsh words and black looks. Edna settled the dispute by lofting the tree into the road, a nice mashie shot.

Carol also put 260,000 telephones out of action. This was an excellent thing. There is far too much telephoning in America. It is a pleasant thought that for three days Vera (aged sixteen) was not able to ring up Clarice (fifteen and a half) and ask her if it was true that Jane had said what Alice had said she had said about what Louise had said about Genevieve. The father of many a family of growing girls, revelling in the unaccustomed peace, must have wondered why people made such a fuss about hurricanes.

Speaking of telephones and telephoning brings to my mind a little story which may be new to some of you present here tonight. While in New York not long ago, I was one of a bunch of the boys who were whooping it up in the Malemute saloon, and the conversation turned to the subject of poise on the stage, that indefinable quality that makes the great actor or actress able to carry on unruffled when things have gone wrong and the novice is losing his or her head. One of those present instanced the case of a female star, a veteran of the American theatre, who was playing a scene with a much younger actress when the stage manager, getting his cues mixed, rang the on-stage telephone at a moment when there was no place in the play's action for a phone call.

The novice sat there petrified, but not the star. Calmly she walked to the telephone, picked up the receiver and said 'Hullo?' while her co-worker looked on reverently, feeling 'What presence! What composure!' The star stood listening for a moment, then, turning to the young actress, held out the telephone and said, 'Here. It's for you.'

But, as you were just about to remind me, J.P., this has nothing to do with hurricanes, and it was of hurricanes that we were talking, was it not? I have little more to add on that subject except to say that there is talk now of Edna and Carol's younger sister, Flossie, being on her way to Cape Hatteras, and it is a relief to see that she is described in the papers as a 'small' hurricane. They can't come too small for me. My ideal hurricane is something dainty and petite, the sort of hurricane that tries to be cute and talks baby-talk.

TWELVE

Healthward Ho!

I

So much for the all-over picture of my home life, Winkler, but I imagine the question you are most anxious to have answered, as being of the greatest interest to your newspaper and radio public, is the one about health. Have I, you would like to know, a regimen?

I have indeed, old man. We septuagenarians must watch our health very closely if, like Old Man River, we want to keep rolling along, and the first essential, my medical adviser tells me, is to see that one does not put on too much weight. The less tonnage, the easier the heart can take it, and I am all in favour of letting my heart loaf a bit, always provided it understands that it must not stop beating.

My own weight varies a good deal from day to day, according to the weighing machine in my bathroom. The day before yesterday, for instance, it informed me – and I don't mind telling you, J.P., that it gave me something of a shock – that I weighed seventeen stone nine. I went without lunch and dined on a small biscuit and a stick of celery, and next day I was down to eleven stone one. This was most satisfactory and I was very pleased about it, but this morning I was up again to nineteen stone six, so I really don't know where I am or what the future holds. A knowledgeable friend says the machine needs adjusting. There may be something in this.

Still, as I say, the experience has given me quite a shock, and I think it will be safest if from now on I model my dietary arrangements on those of the young Lycidas of whom the poet Milton wrote in one of his less known passages:

. . . who, weighing fifteen-three,
Had given up potatoes, butter, beer,
Muffins and bread and all such plumping cheer
In timorous dread of swoll'n obesity,
Trusting he might become
More concave in the tum,
Less buxom and more lithe and debonair

and strive to avoid the bad example of his friend Thyrsis in the same poem:

Who sat him down, munching a piece of cake,
And shook his double chin and thus bespake:
'This banting is a fearsome thing, God wot!
All rot!
So come, thou goddess stout and holy,
To mortals known as Roly-Poly.
Come, too, ye sisters plump and arch
Glucose and Stearine and Starch.
Haste ye, nymphs, and bring with ye
Lots of sugar for my tea,
Lots of butter for my toast,
Of crumpets, too, a goodly host.'
With this he rose and puffed, as such men do.
Tomorrow to fresh foods and dainties new.

But though I emulate Lycidas, I shall still feel that Thyrsis has the right idea. This banting is, as he says, a fearsome thing, God wot, and I think if I had my life to live over again and were given the choice I would be a corpse in a mystery story. Corpses in mystery stories always manage in some mysterious way to do themselves extraordinarily well without ever putting on an ounce.

'I have concluded my autopsy,' says the police surgeon, 'and the contents of Sir Reginald's stomach, not counting the strychnine, are as follows:

Caviar Frais
Consommé aux Pommes d'Amour
Sylphides à la crême d'Écrevisses
Mignonette de Poulet Petit Duc
Point d'Asperges Aneurin Bevan

Suprême de Foie Gras au Champagne
Neige aux Perles des Alpes
Timbale de Ris de Veau Toulousiane
Le Plum Pudding
Friandises
Diablotins
Corbeille de Fruits Exotique

and, of course, lots of sherry, hock, Bollinger *extra sec* and liqueur brandy.'

And in Chapter One Sir Reginald is described as a stern, gaunt old man with the slender limbs and lean, racehorse slimness of the Witherington-Delancys. Makes one pretty wistful and envious, that.

2

I have always been a great reader of mystery stories or, as they now prefer to call themselves, novels of suspense, and I hold strong views on them, one of which is that the insertion into them of a love interest is a serious mistake. But the boys all seem to be doing that now. They aren't content with letting their detective detect, they will have him playing emotional scenes with the heroine.

Whoever first got the idea that anyone wants a girl messing about and getting in the way when the automatics are popping I am at a loss to imagine. Nobody appreciates more than myself the presence of girls in their proper place – in the paddock at Ascot, fine; at Lord's during the luncheon interval of the Eton and Harrow match, capital: if I went to a night club and found no girls there, I should be the first to complain: but what I do say is that you don't want them in Lascar Joe's underground den at Limehouse on a busy evening. Apart from anything else, Woman seems to me to lose her queenly dignity when she is being shoved into cupboards with a bag over her head. And if there is one thing certain, it is that sooner or later something of that sort will be happening to the heroine of a novel of suspense.

For, though beautiful, with large grey eyes and hair the

colour of ripe corn, the heroine of a novel of suspense is almost never a very intelligent girl. Indeed, it would scarcely be overstating it to say that her mentality is that of a retarded child of six. She may have escaped death a dozen times. She may know perfectly well that the Blackbird Gang is after her to secure the papers. The police may have warned her on no account to stir outside her house. But when a messenger calls at half-past two in the morning with an unsigned note that says 'Come at once', she just reaches for her hat and goes. The messenger is a one-eyed Chinaman with a pockmarked face and an evil grin, so she trusts him immediately and, having accompanied him to the closed car with steel shutters over the windows, bowls off in it to the ruined cottage in the swamp. And when the detective, at great risk and inconvenience to himself, comes to rescue her, she will have nothing to do with him because she has been told by a mulatto with half a nose that it was him who murdered her brother Joe.

What we all liked so much about Sherlock Holmes was his correct attitude in this matter of girls. True, he would sometimes permit them to call at Baker Street and tell him about the odd behaviour of their uncles or stepfathers . . . in a pinch he might even allow them to marry Watson . . . but once the story was under way they had to retire to the background and stay there. That was the spirit.

The obvious person, of course, to rid us of these pests is the villain or heavy, and in fairness to a willing worker it cannot be denied that he does his best. And yet for one reason or another he always fails. Even when he had got the girl chained up in the cellar under the wharf with the water pouring through the grating we never in our hearts really expect the happy ending. Experience has taught us that we cannot rely on this man. He has let us down too often and forfeited our confidence.

The trouble with the heavy in a novel of suspense is that he suffers from a fatal excess of ingenuity. When he was a boy, his parents must thoughtlessly have told him he was clever, and it has absolutely spoiled him for effective work.

The ordinary man, when circumstances compel him to murder a female acquaintance, borrows a revolver and a few cartridges and does the job in some odd five minutes of the day when he is not at the office. He does not bother about art or technique or scientific methods. He just goes and does it.

But the heavy cannot understand simplicity. It never occurs to him just to point a pistol at the heroine and fire it. If you told him the thing could be done that way, he would suspect you of pulling his leg. The only method he can imagine is to tie her to a chair, erect a tripod, place the revolver on it, tie a string to the trigger, pass the string along the wall till it rests on a hook, attach another string to it, pass this over a hook, tie a brick to the end of the second string and light a candle under it. He has got the thing reasoned out. The candle will burn the second string, the brick will fall, the weight will tighten the first string, thus pulling the trigger, and there you are.

And then of course somebody comes along and blows the candle out, and all the weary work to do over again.

The average heavy's natural impulse, if called upon to kill a fly, would be to saw through the supports of the floor, tie a string across the doorway, and then send the fly an anonymous letter telling it to come at once in order to hear of something to its advantage. The idea being that it would hurry to the room, trip over the string, fall through the floor and break its neck. This, to the heavy's mind, is not merely the simplest, it is the only way of killing flies. You could talk to him till you were hoarse, but you would never convince him that better results can be obtained through the medium of a rolled-up morning paper gripped by the football coupon. I have known a heavy to sit the heroine on a keg of gunpowder and expect it to be struck by lightning. You can't run a business that way.

It is a moot point and one, I think, that can never be really decided, whether American novels of suspense are worse than English novels of suspense or, as one might say, vice versa. My own opinion is that the American variety have it by a short head. English heavies sometimes have a glimmer of sanity, but American heavies never. They are always dressing up as gorillas or something. They seem unable to express and fulfil themselves without at least a false nose. It must be very difficult to bring one of them to the electric chair.

'But *why* in order to bump off deceased did you dress up as a gorilla?' asked counsel for the defence.

'Oh, I thought I would,' says the heavy.

'No special reason?'

'No, no special reason.'

'It just struck you as a good idea at the time?'

'That's right. It was how I saw the scene. I felt it, felt it *here*,' says the heavy slapping himself on the left side of the chest.

Counsel for the defence looks significantly at the jury, and the jury bring in a verdict of insane without leaving the box. The heavy goes to his asylum, and two months later is released as cured. Upon which, he dresses up as a Siberian wolf-hound and hurries off to rub out another citizen.

One is always seeing in the papers that some prominent person in Washington or elsewhere likes in his spare time to 'relax over a mystery story', presumably American, and I keep wondering how he manages it. The American mystery story calls for all that a man has of concentration and intelligence, if its tortuous ramifications are to be followed.

Not that you don't get some pretty testing stuff shot at you by English mystery writers from time to time. Passages, for instance, like:

'There's a reasonably good road through Slaidburn. It connects up Long Preston with Clitheroe; that is, it connects the arterial roads A 65 and A 59. It also connects with the railway junction at Holliford – that's the junction for your Kirkholm line. If you think it out, there's a circular route, so to speak. Kirkholm to Upper Gimmerdale by road, Gimmerdale to Slaidburn over the fells to Hawkshead and Crossdale, and Slaidburn back to Kirksdale by rail.'

'Aye, that's plain enough,' said Bord.

I am not saying that this does not tax the brain. It does, and one feels a rather awed respect for Bord, to whom it seemed plain enough. (I must get Bord to help me out with James Joyce some time.) But at least it is not pure padded cell, as are the activities of one and all in American mystery stories.

3

But to get back to the subject of health.

In addition to watching his diet the septuagenarian must, of course, have exercise, and there I am fortunately situated. In Remsenburg we enjoy a number of amenities such as fresh air, fresh eggs and an attractive waterfront on the Great South Bay, but we have not progressed on the path of civilization so far as to have postmen. I walk two miles to the post office every day to get the afternoon mail, accompanied by Poona the cat and Bill the foxhound, who generally packs up after the first furlong or so. (Someone tells me that this is always the way with foxhounds. They have to do so much bustling about in their younger days that when of riper years their inclination is to say, 'Ah the hell with it,' and just lie around in the sun. But Poona and I are made of sterner stuff, and we trudge the two miles there and two miles back singing a gipsy song. This keeps me in rare fettle.)

Also I still do my getting-up exercises before breakfast, as I have done since 1919 without missing a day, though it is an open secret that I now find a difficulty in touching my toes, and I catch – or try to catch – Poona the cat each night. We let her out at about ten p.m. for a breath of air, and once out she hears the call of the old wild life and decides to make a night of it. This means that, unless caught and returned to store, she will hit the high spots till five in the morning, when she will come and mew at my bedroom window, murdering sleep as effectively as ever Macbeth did. And I have the job of catching her.

When you are in your middle seventies you have passed your peak as a cat-catcher. There was a time – say between 1904 and 1910 – when it would have been child's play for me to outstrip the fleetest cat, but now the joints have stiffened a trifle and I am less quick off the mark. The spirit is willing, but the flesh doesn't seem to move as it did. The thing usually ends in a bitter 'All right, be a cad and *stay* out!' from me and a quiet smile from Poona. And then the reproachful mew outside my window as the clocks are striking five. And if I leave the fly-screen open so that she can come in through the window, she jumps on my bed and bites my toes. There seems no way of beating the game.

Still, things have brightened a good deal lately owing to Poona having been bitten in the foot by another cat – no doubt in some night-club brawl – and being able to operate only on three legs. One more such episode, and the thing, as I see it, will be in the bag. I may not be the sprinter I once was, but I feel confident of being able to overtake a cat walking on two hind legs.

Meanwhile, the exercise is doing me a world of good, for apart from the running there is the falling. Owing to the activities of hurricane Carol many of the trees on the estate are shored up with wire ropes, and any Harley Street physician will tell you there is nothing better for the liver than to trip over a wire rope when going all out after a receding cat and come down like a sack of coals. It amuses the cat, too.

That is about all I can tell you, J.P., with regard to my regimen for health, except that I make a practice of smoking all day and far into the night. Smoking, as everybody knows, toughens and fortifies the system. Tolstoy said it didn't, but I shall be dealing with Tolstoy in a moment and putting him in his place.

4

It can scarcely have escaped the notice of thinking men, I think, that the forces of darkness opposed to those of us who like a quiet smoke are gathering momentum daily and starting to throw their weight about more than somewhat. Each morning I read in the papers a long article by another of those doctors who are the spearhead of the movement. Tobacco, they say, hardens the arteries and lowers the temperature of the body extremities, and if you reply that you like your arteries hard and are all for having the temperature of your body extremities lowered, especially in the summer months, they bring up that cat again.

The cat to which I allude is not the cat Poona which I chase at night but the one that has two drops of nicotine placed on its tongue and instantly passes beyond the veil.

'Look,' they say. 'I place two drops of nicotine on the tongue of this cat. Now watch it wilt.'

I can't see the argument. Cats, as Charles Stuart Calverley once observed, may have had their goose cooked by tobacco juice, but, as he went on to point out, we're not as tabbies are. Must we deprive ourselves of all our modest pleasures just because indulgence in them would be harmful to some cat which is probably a perfect stranger?

Take a simple instance such as occurs every Saturday afternoon on the Rugby football field. A scrum is formed, the ball is heeled out, the scrum-half gathers it, and instantaneously two fourteen-stone forwards fling themselves on his person, grinding him into the mud. Are we to abolish Twickenham and Murrayfield because some sorry reasoner tells us that if the scrum-half had been a cat he would have been squashed flatter than a Dover sole? And no use trying to drive into these morons' heads that there is no recorded instance of a team lining up for the kick-off with a cat playing scrum-half. Really, one feels inclined at times to give it all up and not bother to argue.

To me, and to you, too, probably, Winkler, it is pitiful to think that that is how these men spend their lives, placing drops of nicotine on the tongues of cats day in, day out all the year round, except possibly on bank holidays. But if you tell them that, like that Phantom fellow, they have become slaves to a habit, and urge them to summon up their manhood and throw off the shackles, they just stare at you with fishy eyes and mumble that it can't be done. Of course it can be done. If they were to say to themselves, 'I will not start placing nicotine on cats' tongues till after lunch,' they would have made a beginning. After that it would be simple to knock off during the afternoon, and by degrees they would find that they could abstain altogether. The first cat of the day is the hard one to give up. Conquer the impulse for the after-breakfast cat, and the battle is half won.

But nothing will make them see this, and the result is that day by day in every way we smokers are being harder pressed. Like the troops of Midian, the enemy prowl and prowl around.

First it was James the Second, then Tolstoy, then all these doctors, and now – of all people – Miss Gloria Swanson, the idol of the silent screen, who not only has become a non-smoker herself but claims to have converted a San Francisco business man, a Massachusetts dress designer, a lady explorer, a television script-writer and a Chicago dentist.

'The joys of not smoking,' she says, 'are so much greater than the joys of smoking,' omitting, however, to mention what the former are. From the fact that she states that her disciples send her flowers, I should imagine that she belongs to the school of thought which holds that abstention from tobacco heightens the sense of smell. I don't want my sense of smell heightened. When I lived in New York, I often found myself wishing that I didn't smell the place as well as I did.

But I have no quarrel with Miss Swanson. We Wodehouses do not war upon the weaker sex. As far as Miss Swanson is concerned, an indulgent 'There, there, foolish little woman' about covers my attitude. The bird I am resolved to expose before the bar of world opinion is the late Count Leo N. Tolstoy.

For one reason and another I have not read Tolstoy in the original Russian, and it is possible that a faulty translation may have misled me, but what he is recorded as saying in his Essays, Letters and Miscellanies is that an excellent substitute for smoking may be found in twirling the fingers, and there rises before one's mental eye the picture of some big public dinner (decorations will be worn) at the moment when the toast of the Queen is being drunk.

'The Queen!'

'The Queen, God bless her!'

And then——

'Gentlemen, you may twirl your fingers.'

It wouldn't work. There would be a sense of something missing. And I don't see that it would be much better if you adopted Tolstoy's other suggestion – viz. playing on the dudka. But then what can you expect of a man who not only grew a long white beard but said that the reason we smoke is that we want to deaden our conscience, instancing the case of a Russian murderer of Czarist times who half-way through the assassination of his employer found himself losing the old pep?

'I could not finish the job,' he is quoted as saying, 'so I went from the bedroom into the dining-room, sat down there and smoked a cigarette.'

'Only when he had stupefied himself with tobacco,' says Tolstoy, 'did he feel sufficiently fortified to return to the bedroom and complete his crime.'

Stupefied with tobacco! On a single gasper! They must have been turning out powerful stuff in Russia under the old régime.

And, of course, our own manufacturers are turning out good and powerful stuff today, so let us avail ourselves of it. Smoke up, my hearties. Never mind Tolstoy. Ignore G. Swanson. Forget the cat. Think what it would mean if for want of our support the tobacco firms had to go out of business. There would be no more of those photographs of authors smoking pipes, and if authors were not photographed smoking pipes, how would we be able to know that they were manly and in the robust tradition of English literature?

A pipe placed on the tongue of an author makes all the difference.

THIRTEEN

Shaking a Head at New York

I

And now back to that questionnaire of yours, J.P., and let us see what else there is that you wanted to know. Ah, yes. Do I prefer living in the country to living in New York?

I do, definitely. I work better, look better and feel better. The cry goes round Remsenburg, 'Wodehouse has found his niche.'

Mark you, as a city slicker I was quite happy. I loved that duplex pnthse apt of mine. But residence in New York has disadvantages. For one thing, the telephone.

Having my name in the book, I got publicity of the right sort and my winter evening reading was all arranged for, but the trouble was that when people, curled up in the old armchair with the New York telephone directory, saw

Wodehouse, P. G. 1000 PkAv. BUtrfld 8–5029

it put ideas into their heads. Briefly, I had become, especially round Christmas-time, a sitting duck for every toucher on the island of Manhattan, and it was rarely that a morning passed without my hearing a breezy voice on the wire.

'Mr Wodehouse?'

'Speaking.'

'Is that Mr P. G. Wodehouse?'

'In person.'

'Well, well, well, well, well, well, well, *well*! How are you, P.G., how *are* you? Fine? Capital! No coughs, colds or rheumatic ailments? Splendid! That's wonderful. This is the Rev. Cyril Twombley. You won't know my name, but

I am one of your greatest fans and simply couldn't resist the urge to call you up and tell you how much I love your books. I think I've read every line you've written. Great stuff, P.G., great stuff. Jeeves, eh? Ha ha ha ha ha.'

Well, really, I would be saying by this time, this is extremely gratifying. An artist like myself is above any petty caring for praise or blame, of course, but still it is nice to feel that one's efforts are appreciated. Furthermore, though one is too spiritual to attach much weight to that, there does sort of flit into one's mind the thought that a man as enthusiastic as this will surely buy a copy of that book of ours that is coming out next month, which will mean 52½¢ in royalties in our kick, and may quite possibly give copies to friends. (Five friends? Ten friends? Better be on the safe side and call it five. Well, that is $2. 62 or thereabouts, and you can buy a lot of tobacco for $2. 62.)

But hark, he is proceeding.

'That was why I simply had to ring you up, P.G., old top. I just wanted to tell you what pleasure you have given me, and I am sure a great number of other people. Your sales must be enormous.'

'Oh, well. . . .'

'I'm sure they are, and they deserve to be, P.G., they deserve to be. You must be a millionaire by this time, eh, ha ha ha. And that brings me to another thing I was almost forgetting to mention. Our church is getting up a Christmas bazaar and looking about for contributions and we are hoping that you will. . . .'

In theory the unlisted subscriber avoids all this. If you try to get a number that is not in the book, Information tells you off good and proper.

'Sorrrrrrr-eeeeeeee, we are not allowahd to give out that numbah,' says Information, in a voice like an east wind sighing through the cracks in a broken heart.

The catch is, the unlisted boys tell me, that you keep giving it out yourself to casual acquaintances who write it down and give it to their casual acquaintances who write it down and give it to theirs, and pretty soon it is public property. I have an unlisted friend who, balancing his accounts after a certain period of time, found that his number was in the possession of twenty-three girls he no longer liked, fifty-six he had never liked, a former business associate who was suing him at the moment, a discarded masseur, three upholsterers who had made estimates for covering a sofa, and an unidentified alcoholic who rang up at regular intervals and always between the hours of three and four in the morning.

2

Almost as grave a drawback to life in New York as the ear-biting telephonist is the New York taxi-driver or hackie.

He is quite different from his opposite number in London, partly because his name, as stated on the card on the windscreen, is always something like Rostopchin or Prschebiszewsky but principally owing to his habit of bringing with him quips and cranks and wreathed smiles like the nymphs in 'L'Allegro'. Except for an occasional gruff grunter, all New York taxi-drivers are rapid-fire comedians, and they are given unlimited scope for their Bob Hopefulness by the fact that in American cabs there is no glass shutter separating them from the customer.

There are some who place the blame for this exuberance of theirs on the newspaper men who for years have been fostering the legend of the witty taxi-driver. 'They have been exalted as a group and called brilliant conversationalists so long,' says one soured commentator, 'that they have come to believe the stories they have read about themselves and so ham it up and babble nonsense over their shoulders whenever they have a passenger who will listen.'

It may be so, but myself I think it all dates back to the time when one of them, a man who liked his joke of a morning, chanced to drive Eddie Cantor one day and on the strength of his *bons mots* got enrolled on the comedian's staff of gag-writers. The word went round that fame and fortune awaited the hackie with a good comedy routine, and the boys buckled down to it seriously, with the result that, if you take a taxi nowadays, your ride is not so much a ride as an audition. The hackie's opening words are enough to warn you of the shape of things to come.

'I want to go to the Cunard-White Star pier,' you say.

'Okay. Don't be long,' he ripostes, quick as a flash.

'You know the way there, I suppose?'

'Garsh, yes, it ain't no secret.'

Then he settles down to it. A few gay observations on the weather and he is ready for the big yoks.

'Say, mister.'

'Hullo?'

'Your name ain't Crime by any chance, is it?'

'Crime?'

'C-r-i-m-e.'

'Oh, Crime? No. Why?'

'Just thinking of a feller I had in my crate the other day. We got talking and he said his name was George Crime.'

'Odd name.'

'What I thought. Well, sir, we got to where he wants to be took and he hops out and starts walking away. "Hi, brother," I say, "ain't you forgettin' something?" "Such as?" he says. "You ain't paid for your ride." "Why would I?" he says. "Haven't you ever heard that crime doesn't pay?" Hey, hey, hey.'

You laugh politely, but inwardly you are saying, 'Not so good, Prschebiszewsky.' The build-up a little too obvious and elaborate, you feel.

He continues.

'Say, Mister.'

'Hullo?'

English, ain't you? I see by the papers there's a lot of talk over there about this hydrogen bomb.'

'So I understand.'

'Same here. Fission. That's all they talk about. Now that's a funny thing. I can remember the time when fission was a thing you did in the creek with a hook and line. Hey, hey, hey.'

If the newspaper men really are responsible for this sort of thing, they have much to answer for. The only poor consolation one has is the reflection that if this had been taking place on the stage you would by this time have been hit over the head with a rolled-up umbrella.

Only once have I been able to stem the flow. My charioteer had opened brightly and confidently, getting a few well-spotted laughs at the expense of the police force and the street-cleaning system, and then he said, 'Say, mister.'

'Hullo?'

'English, ain't you? I see by the papers there's a lot of talk over there about this hydrogen bomb.'

'So I understand.'

'Don't talk about much else, they tell me. Now that's a funny thing. I can remember——'

'Yes,' I said. 'You know how it is in England. All that interests them is huntin', shootin' and fission.'

He gave a startled gasp, and silence fell, lasting till we had arrived at my destination. My better self had woken by now and I gave him a 50¢ tip, but there was no light in his sombre eyes as he took it. The unforgivable sin had been committed. He was feeling as Danny Kaye might feel if his supporting cast started hogging the comedy. As he drove away, his head was bowed and his air that of one who has been wounded in his finest feelings.

But cheer up, Rostopchin. Tomorrow is another day, Prschebiszewsky. There will be other English clients, and I know that that sparkle will be back in your eyes as you say, 'Say, mister.'

'Hullo.'

'English, ain't you? I see by the papers. . . .'

And so merrily on to the pay-off.

3

But worse than Rostopchin, worse than Prschebiszewsky, worse than the Rev. Cyril Twombley are the pigeons. One of the first things you notice if you live in New York is that there are far too many pigeons about. There are also far too many Puerto Ricans, if it comes to that, but it is the pigeons that thrust themselves on the eye and make you feel that what the place needs is a platoon of sportsmen with shotguns.

These birds are getting out of hand, and if steps are not taken a tense situation will develop. All over America there are restaurants called the Howard Johnson restaurants, owned and operated by a Mr Howard Johnson. There is one at 245 Broadway, just across from the City Hall, and the other day the lunchers there were interested to observe a pigeon enter and start to fill up at the counter in the window where there were open bins of pecans, walnuts, pistachios and jumbo cashews. Its tastes appeared to be catholic. It would hoist up a pistachio and a couple of walnuts and lower them into its interior and then waddle along and try the pecans and the jumbo cashews, and this went on for some twenty minutes and would probably have continued indefinitely had not Mr Benjamin Meltzer, manager of the establishment's ice-cream and nut department approached the bird from behind and enveloped it in a towel. He released it on to Broadway, and it flew away sluggishly, puffing a good deal, no doubt to get bicarbonate at the nearest drugstore.

'Tonight,' said Mr Meltzer, 'I got to clean out the window and put in new nuts, a three-hour job,' adding with some bitterness that he had worked in Howard Johnson's for six years and this was the first time he had had to wait on a pigeon. The bird, I need scarcely say, left without paying the bill.

This, as I see it, is just a beginning, the thin end of the wedge, as it were. Unless something is done and done promptly to put these birds in their place (preferably, as I say, with shot-guns) the *haut monde* of New York will soon be going to the Colony or Le Pavillon for lunch and finding that pigeons have booked all the best tables.

But don't get me wrong. I am not in any sense an ailuro-phobe. Down in Remsenburg many of my best friends are pigeons. I keep open garden for them and you will often find half a dozen or more moaning, if not in the immemorial elms at least in the maple tree I bought last week from the nursery garden at Patchogue. What I deprecate is the drift to the towns. A pigeon in the country, fine; but in New York it just takes up space which could be utilized for other purposes. There are about a thousand of them who hang round the 85th Street entrance to Central Park, sneering at passers-by and talking offensively out of the corners of their mouths. And you have to give them bread.

I tried not giving them bread, but I couldn't keep it up. My nerve failed me. I knew they would fix me somehow. There are a hundred things a gang of pigeons can do to get back at those who have incurred their displeasure – gargling on the window sill at five in the morning, scaring the daylights out of you by tapping on the pane with their beaks, swooping at your face, pecking at your ankles . . . I couldn't risk it. Appeasement, I felt, was the only course.

The situation, then, until I moved to the country, was, briefly, this. Each year by the sweat of my brow I won a certain amount of bread, and this bread I would naturally have liked to reserve for the use of what may be grouped under the head of 'my loved ones' – myself, my wife, my two Pekinese and, of course, any guests who might happen to drop in. But much of it had to go to support a mob of pigeons who had never done an honest stroke of work in their lives.

And they weren't even grateful. Stake a pigeon to a bit of bread, and not so much as a nod of thanks. The bird just pecks at it in a disgruntled sort of way.

'Bread!' it says to the other pigeons with a short laugh, and not a nice laugh, either. 'Stale bread! He wouldn't spring a nickel for a bag of peanuts, would he? Oh, no, not Wodehouse. Know what I heard someone call him the other day? Gaspard the Miser. We'll have to fix Wodehouse.'

'Shall we commence on him now?' says a second pigeon.

'Naw, we must wait,' says the first pigeon. 'We can't do nothing till Martin gets here.'

I have no doubt that if I had not fled the city and gone into hiding in Remsenburg, I should have been rubbed out by this time.

Up in Washington, I see by my paper, they are hoping to chase the pigeons away from the Treasury Department building by stringing electric wires where they roost. The idea being that after getting a few shocks they will go elsewhere. William W. Parsons, Assistant Secretary of the Treasury for Administration, told a House Appropriation Sub-committee he thought it would work.

I can just hear the 85th Street bunch chuckling when they read about it. No, Parsons, old man, it's no good, I'm afraid. You're just a dreamer chasing rainbows, Bill, old chap. If there is one thing life has taught me, it is that there is nothing you can do about pigeons. Either you have them or you don't. It is as simple as that.

FOURTEEN

Things Aren't the Same

I

What next, Winkler? Television? The motion pictures? Or shall it be the changes I notice now in my daily life? Suppose I tackle those first and get them out of the way.

By the time you have reached seventy-five you do find things quite a bit different from what they were when you were in your thirties. I have been a good deal impressed these last few years, for instance, by the kindlier attitude of New York taxi-drivers towards me – their attitude, I mean, towards Wodehouse the pedestrian. Where once, after nearly running me down, they would lean out sideways and yell 'Why dontcher look where yer goin', you crazy loon?' they now merely utter an indulgent, 'Watch it, grandpa.' Shows the passage of time, that, J.P. Silver threads among the gold, eh?

What other changes? Well, there is the income tax. Am I wrong, or isn't it a bit stiffer than it used to be? I seem to remember a time when, if one sold a story, one spent most of the proceeds on a slap-up dinner somewhere, but now it never seems to run to much more than a ham sandwich. I suppose income tax is necessary, but I feel it was a mistake to allow it to develop into such a popular craze.

Books, too. I find myself nowadays more and more out of tune with the modern novel. All that frank, outspoken stuff with those fearless four-letter words. It was a black day for literature, I often think, when the authorities started glazing the walls of public lavatories so that the surface would not take the mark of the pencil, for the result was that hundreds of young *littérateurs*, withheld from expressing themselves in the medium they would have preferred, began turning the stuff out in stiff-covered volumes at 12s. 6d., and more coming along all the time.

And even the purer-minded novelists are not wholly satisfactory. So many of them have such extraordinary ideas as to what constitutes age. 'He was a man not far from fifty, but still erect and able to cross the room under his own steam,' they write, or, 'Old though the Squire was, his forty-six years sat lightly upon him.' At seventy-five I have reached the stage when, picking up a novel and finding that a new character the author has introduced is sixty-eight, I say to myself, 'Ah, the young love interest.'

In real life, I must confess, I tend to become a bit impatient with these kids of sixty-eight. Noisy little brutes, rushing about all over the place yelling at one another. Want their heads smacking, if you ask me.

Another very marked change I notice in the senile Wodehouse is that I no longer have the party spirit. As a young man I used to enjoy parties, but now they have lost their zest and I prefer to stay at home with my novel of suspense. Why people continue to invite me I don't know. I am not very attractive to look at, and I contribute little or nothing to the gaiety, if that is the right word. Cornered at one of these affairs by some dazzling creature who looks brightly at me, expecting a stream of good things from my lips, I am apt to talk guardedly about the weather, with the result that before long I am left on one leg in a secluded corner of the room in the grip of that disagreeable feeling that nobody loves me. I am like the man who couldn't understand why he was shunned and thought he must have halitosis, only to discover that what kept people away from him was his unpleasant personality.

Trying to analyse my party-going self these days, I think the trouble is those paper hats. At a certain point at every American party everyone puts on paper hats and as the smiling hostess clamps mine on my brow, a sense of the underlying sadness of life sweeps over me. 'Man that is born of woman is of few days and full of trouble,' I say to myself. 'Ashes to ashes, dust to dust,' I say to myself, and, of course, this tends to prevent me being sparkling. The malaise is due, I think, principally to my spectacles. You can't wear spectacles and a paper hat and retain any illusion that you are a king among men. If hostesses would only skip the red tape and allow me to remain bareheaded I might be a social success and fascinate one and all.

And yet I don't know. Even given every advantage I think I should still remain the soggy mass of ineffectiveness which so repels my fellow-revellers and has caused so many women, parting from me, to say, 'Who *was* that frightful man?' The fact is, I no longer have the light touch. I am not bright. And brightness is what you want at parties. Take the case of Henry Biddle. Now there is a man whose technique strikes one as absolutely right.

Henry Biddle is a Texas oil man, and is being sued for $400,000 by a lady whom he encountered at a get-together in Bimini the other night. There was a misunderstanding, it appears, about the calypso band. Whether he wanted it to play one thing and she another, I couldn't tell you, but a sudden cloud fell on the party and it seemed to Henry that now was the time for all good men to come to the aid of it. You, Winkler, in such circumstances might have tried to help things along with an epigram or a funny story, I with one of those observations of mine on the weather, but Henry Biddle knew that this would not suffice. He hit the lady over the head with a bottle. This went well, and he hit her over the head with the bottle again. Somebody then hit him over the head with a bottle, and he stepped across to the bar, got more bottles and 'started throwing them in all directions'. The party had taken on a new lease of life.

It is possible that at this point you may be criticizing our hero's methods for a certain monotony, but you would be wronging him. The man was versatile, and this was not an end but a beginning. The hotel management, feeling that he had now livened things up sufficiently, ordered the band to intervene in the debate, and when the band advanced on him with knives, Henry ('Never at a loss') Biddle seized a fire-extinguisher and sprayed them with acid. The last seen of him before the constabulary arrived, he had backed into a corner and was swinging an electric fan around his head by its cord.

It is easy to see how this sort of thing must attract hostesses.

'Don't let me forget that charming Mr Biddle,' they say as they write their invitation lists. 'He always makes a party go so.' And they send him a special little note telling him to be sure to bring his fire-extinguisher.

Henry Biddle's tactics, of course, as he would be the first to admit, were not original. He was remembering the children's parties he used to attend as a tot where everything went, including gouging and biting. How clearly he recalled those happy, far-off binges. As if it had been yesterday he could see little Augustus beating little Gwendoline on her pink bow with a toy wheelbarrow to make her let go of the plush camel to which he had taken a fancy, while over yonder little Frank hammered the daylights out of little Alice, incensed because she had kicked him in the seat of his velvet knickerbockers.

'That's the stuff,' Henry Biddle said to himself, and reached buoyantly for his bottle.

All honour to him that after all these years he remains at heart a little child.

FIFTEEN

How I Became a Poet

I

We're getting along, Winkler, we're making progress. One by one I am ticking off the questions on your list, and now to decide on which of them to settle next like the butterfly I was speaking of, the one, you remember, that flitted from flower to flower. I think I will answer your query as to whether I have ever lectured or written poetry.

No, I have never lectured. If you are an author born in England, it is a thing that is expected of you, and I have received several offers to tour the United States and make an ass of myself like the rest of the boys, but I have met them with a firm *nolle prosequi* for I know my limitations. I have only the most rudimentary gift of speech, and after reading a book I bought the other day I know that I shall never be one of those silver-tongued orators. ·

The book was entitled *How to Become a Convincing Talker*, and almost from the first page I saw that talking convincingly must always be beyond my scope.

'Are you audible?' it asked me. 'Are you clear? Pleasant? Flexible? Vigorous? Well modulated? Appropriate in melody and tempo? Acceptable in pronunciation? Agreeable in laughter?' And the answer was No. I was husky, hoarse, muffled, thin, indistinct, glottal, monotonous, jumbled, unacceptable in pronunciation and disagreeable in laughter, and my melody and tempo, far from being appropriate, were about as inappropriate as could be imagined.

Could this be corrected? Yes, said the book, if I followed its instructions closely. I must lie on my back with a heavy book on my chest and – first in a whisper, then loudly – repeat a hundred times the words, 'Please sell me a box of mixed biscuits, a mixed biscuit box, also some short silk socks and shimmering satin sashes,' and after that rise, stand before the mirror, stretch all my muscles, raise myself on tiptoe, throw my head back and roll it from side to side and utter the word 'Li-yah' for from five to ten minutes, finally bringing the lips back into the position of the round O.

I gave it a miss. It would have cut into my time too much. After all, one had one's life to live, one's work to do. A nice thing it would be for the reading public if, just as they were expecting another book from me, they found that I hadn't touched a typewriter for six months because I had been spending all my time standing in front of a mirror bringing my lips back into the position of the round O. I decided then and there to abandon my dream of becoming a convincing talker.

I have my moments of regret, of course. The gift of convincing talk is one that often pays dividends. Thomas Lomonaco, to take a case at random, found it a very present help in time of trouble.

Thomas Lomonaco is a taxi-driver, and he was driving his taxi not long ago at Jamaica Avenue and 75th Street, Brooklyn, when he was hailed by Elmer Hinitz.

'Gimme about 50¢ worth,' said Elmer Hinitz.

At 80th Street he produced a switch-knife and, leaning forward, tapped Thomas Lomonaco on the shoulder.

'This is a stick-up,' he announced.

'You don't say?' said Mr Lomonaco, intrigued.

'Yay. Slip me your money, or I will expunge you.'

'I see your point,' said Mr Lomonaco humorously, eyeing the switch-knife. Then, becoming more serious, 'Yes, the meaning of your words has not escaped me, and let me say at once that I wholeheartedly sympathize with your desire to add to your savings with times as hard as they are in this disturbed post-war era. But your dreams of picking up a bit of easy money are rendered null and void by the fact that I have on my person at the moment no cash of any description. Would it soften your disappointment if I offered you one of my cigarettes? They are mild. They satisfy.'

Mr Hinitz accepted a cigarette and the conversation proceeded along agreeable lines and as far as 118th Street, when Mr Lomonaco said, 'Say, look. Have you ever seen our local police station?'

Mr Hinitz said he had not.

'Most picturesque. Sort of pseudo-Gothic. You'll like it,' Mr Lomonaco assured him. 'What say we drive there?'

And so convincing was his talk that Mr Hinitz immediately agreed. 'A good idea,' he said, and he is now in custody, held in $1000 bail.

To reporters Mr Lomonaco stated that this was the second time he had been stuck up while pursuing his profession. The other time was in Williamsburg, where a passenger threatened him with a pistol. Mr Lomonaco, the report runs, 'talked him out of the pistol'. Obviously a man who must have spent months, if not years, lying on the floor with a book on his chest, asking an invisible shop assistant to sell him mixed biscuit boxes, short silk socks and shimmering satin sashes.

How different is the story of the two explorers who were exploring in South America and chanced to meet one morning on a narrow mountain ledge high up in the Andes where there was not space for either of them to pass. Like all explorers, they were strong, silent men, and in any case would have hesitated to speak, never having been introduced, so for perhaps an hour they stood gazing at one another in silence. Then it occurred to one of the two that by leaping outwards putting a bit of finger-spin on himself he could jump round the other. This he proceeded to do, but by the worst of luck the same thought had occurred simultaneously to the other explorer, with the result that they collided in mid-air and perished in the precipice.

This would not have happened if they had been convincing talkers.

2

As a poet – a serious poet, that is to say – I developed late. When I was doing the 'By The Way' column on the *Globe*, I used to have to write a set of verses every morning between ten-thirty and twelve for seven years, but that was just frivolous light verse. It was only recently that I took to poetry in the true sense of the word.

They do ask the darndest questions on television in America. There is a thing on Sunday nights on one of the channels called 'Elder Wise Men', and the elderly sage they got hold of the other evening was John Hall Wheelock, the man who wrote a poem about having a black panther caged within his breast (than which I can imagine nothing more disturbing for anyone of settled habits and a liking for the quiet life).

'Tell me, Mr Wheelock,' said the interviewer, 'could you have helped being a poet?'

The implication being, one presumes, that he felt that Mr Wheelock hadn't *tried*. He could have pulled up in time if he had had the right stuff in him, but he adopted a weak policy of drift, and the next thing he knew he was writing about panthers caged within his breast.

'I don't believe I could,' said Mr Wheelock, and the interviewer frowned censoriously and became rather cold in his manner for the remainder of the conversation.

But I doubt that the thing is always deliberate. Many who become poets are more to be pitied than censured. What happens is that they are lured on to the downward path by the fatal fascination of the limerick form. It is so terribly easy to compose the first two lines of a limerick and, that done, the subject finds it impossible to stop. (Compare the case of the tiger cub which, at first satisfied with a bowl of milk, goes in strictly for blood after tasting its initial coolie.) And the difficulty in finding a last line discourages these men from sticking to limericks, which would be fairly harmless, so they take the easier way and write serious poetry. It was after they had scribbled down on the back of the bill of fare at the Mermaid Tavern:

> There was a young lady (Egyptian)
> Who merits a word of description

that Shakespeare, Bacon, Marlowe and the Earl of Oxford realized that the rhyme scheme was too tough and they were stuck.

'Bipshion?' suggested Bacon. (He would.)

'What do you mean, Bipshion?' said Marlowe irritably. He had a hangover that morning. 'There isn't such a word.'

'Hips on?'

'Doesn't rhyme.'

'I seem to have heard people talking of having conniption fits,' said Shakespeare diffidently. 'How about "And she suffered from fits (viz. conniption)"? Just a suggestion.'

'And as rotten a one as I ever heard,' snapped Marlowe.

'Oh, dash it all,' said the Earl of Oxford. (These peers express themselves strongly.) 'Let's turn it into a play.'

And they wrote *Antony and Cleopatra*.

A similar thing happened with Tennyson's

> There was a young fellow called Artie
> Who was always the life of the party.

This subsequently became *Idylls of the King*.

3

My own case is rather interesting. As I say, I had never written anything but light, frivolous verse, but I happened one Sunday morning to be skimming through my *New York Times* – for though well stricken in years, I can still lift my Sunday *New York Times* – and as I turned to the correspondence page of the book section I suddenly quivered in every limb. It was as though I had been slapped between the eyes with a wet fish.

The correspondence page of the book section of the Sunday *New York Times* consists of heated letters denouncing opinions expressed in letters of the previous week, and what had attracted my attention was one that began:

Sir,
I take issue with Miss U. S. Swisher . . . .

I would like my readers to try repeating those words to themselves. I think they will find that after a few minutes their haunting beauty grips them as it gripped me. I felt that only the finest poetry could do justice to the theme, and it seemed but an instant before I was at my desk, half-way through my first serious poem.

It ran as follows:

> The day, I recall, was a Spring one,
>   Not hot and oppressive, though warm,
> The sort of a day apt to bring one
>   Right up to the top of one's form.
> So when a kind friend and well-wisher
>   Said 'Don't just sit dreaming there, kid.
> Take issue with Miss U. S. Swisher,'
>   I replied, 'Yes, I will,' and I did.
>
> It made me feel just a bit saddish
>   To crush this poor (feminine) fish:
> A voice seemed to whisper, 'How caddish!'
>   But still I resolved to take ish.
> You can't be a competent isher
>   If chivalrous qualms make you wince.
> I took issue with Miss U. S. Swisher.
>   She's never been quite the same since.
>
> So though low in the world's estimation,
>   A bit of a wash-out, in short,
> I have always this one consolation;
>   I tell myself 'Courage, old sport!
> There are others more gifted and risher
>   And plenty more beautiful, *BUT*
> You took issue with Miss U. S. Swisher,
>   So you might be much more of a mutt.'

There it might have ended and I might have given up serious poetry and gone back to light verse, but a few days later, before the afflatus had had time to wear off, I happened upon an item in my morning paper which said that researchers at Michigan State University had discovered that hens are extremely sensitive to any form of discourtesy, and I was off again.

THE STORY OF OTIS

The tale of Otis Quackenbush is one I think you ought to hear,
So I'll relate it – and I'll try to keep it fairly short, too -- here.
To make a fortune he essayed, as many people do essay,
By raising fowls in Michigan, a section of the USA.

At first the venture prospered and the eggs were large and numerous.
'Hot diggety dog!' said Otis, who was always rather humorous,
'If things go on the way they are, I'll soon, I shouldn't wonder, wear,
To keep off chills, ten-dollar bills for spring and summer underwear.'
He spoke too soon. One afternoon the hens refused to lay for him,
Which meant of course a marked decrease in what's called take-
    home pay for him.
Inside each nest he tried his best to find an egg, but was it there?
Now to, now fro he searched, but no albuminous deposit there.
He clutched his head. 'This is,' he said, 'the darnedest thing I ever
    knew.
I'd hoped for stacks of income tax to give the Internal Revenue,
But now it seems those golden dreams, so roseate and fair withal,
Have got the axe. You can't pay tax if you have not the where-
    withal.'
And as, irate, he moaned his fate and started in to curse it, he
Met a friend named Hibbs, who was one of the nibs at Michigan
    University.
He told him the jam he was in. 'I am,' he said, and reticence threw
    aside,
'On the very verge of feeling an urge to end it all with suicide.'
Now Hibbs was a man who knew his hens, as one might say from
    A to Z,
And giving away this useful piece of friendly counsel gratis, said,
'The first and foremost memo every farmer has to stick in his
Notebook is this – there's nothing half so touchy as a chicken is.
Remember, then, that every hen, young, middle-aged or hoary'll
Be frightfully hurt if your manner's curt or in any way dictatorial.
And often in the summer months, when you're feeling dry and hot,
I've heard you speak quite brusquely when conversing with a
    Wyandotte.
Your clothes as well, they give an air of *laissez-faire* and messiness,
    And if there's one thing hens demand, it's chic and vogue and
dressiness.
    Those overalls you're wearing now. They're muddy. Do you roll
in it?
    And worse than that your old straw hat has got, I see, a hole in it.
    No wonder that these hens of yours are downing tools and packing
up.
Your speech and deportment are in urgent need of jacking up.'
And Otis said, 'By Jove, you're right!' A new expression lit his eyes.
He had far too much sense to take offence when a friend saw fit to
    criticize.

His upper lip grew stiff. The tip was just what he'd been hoping for.
'*Rem acu tetigisti* is,' he said, 'the phrase I'm groping for.
I see, old bean, just what you mean. The wounds that gashed my
   breast have healed.
My ways I'll mend and be a blend of Brummel and Lord Chesterfield.'
So now when Otis feeds his fowls, he wears – and very proper, too –
A morning coat, a monocle, striped trousers and a topper, too.
His mode of speech, too, once abrupt, he's disciplined until it is
Unlikely to shock a Plymouth Rock and wound its sensibilities.
He now has kegs of splendid eggs of extra special quality,
And all is gas and gaiters, not to mention joy and jollity.
If ever a farmer's heart was in a constant gentle glow, 'tis his.
It teaches us a lesson, this experience of Otis's.

After that there was no stopping me. From there to writing
'Excelsior' and 'The Boy Stood on the Burning Deck' was but a
step.

4

Hens, of course, are not pigs – no argument about that – but
the transition of thought between the two species is such an
easy one that I feel that this is the place to touch on the report
from Paradise, Nebraska, that the local agricultural school has
discovered that if pigs are given eight drinks of whisky a day
they 'acquire an optimistic view of life'. Mr John B. Fosdyke, a
member of the staff of the school, says they develop a strong
liking for these refreshers and 'get very cheerful.'

Does one or does one not shake the head? It all turns, it
seems to me, on what is implied in the word 'cheerful'.
Naturally, pig-lovers like their protégés to look on the bright
side – a pig that goes about wrapped in a Byronic gloom can
cast a shadow on the happiest farm – but one does not want
them getting over-familiar with strangers and telling long
stories without any point. And what of the morning after?
I can see a Paradise pig being irresistibly gay and amusing all
through Monday up to closing time, and on Tuesday sitting in
a corner with its head in its hands and merely grunting when
spoken to. There is no companion more depressing than a pig
with a really bad hangover.

Paradise, in my opinion, should watch its step.

SIXTEEN

Television

I

You ask me, Winkler, for my views on television.

Well, I have a set, but I very seldom switch it on. I have discovered a station on the wireless where they do nothing but play music, mostly grand opera, and I prefer of an evening to read my book and listen to that. Rather the quiet, home-body type, you would call me. When some Friday night there is a big fight on, you will always find me at the ringside, encouraging Sugar Ray Robinson or Carmen Basilio or whoever it may be with word and gesture, but apart from that television scarcely enters my life.

I know enough about industry, of course, to be able to understand the technical terms connected with it.

For example:

Intimate Show A comedy programme with no laughs.
Situation Comedy A programme that has the same story every week.
Satire Jokes which do not get laughs.
Fresh Humour Old sure-fire jokes told by a young comedian.
Literate Humour Old sure-fire jokes told by a young comedian with horn-rimmed spectacles.
Song Stylist A singer.
Internationally Famous Song Stylist A singer.
Singing Personality A lousy singer.
Long-term Contract A contract.
Seven-year Contract A contract for six weeks.
$10,000 a week salary $500.

But beyond this you might say that television is a sealed

book to me and one which I doubt if I shall ever open again except on Friday nights.

I am told by friends who follow all the programmes that by abstaining in this manner I miss a lot of good things. The other night, for instance, there appeared on the screen, demonstrating a mattress, a well-upholstered young woman who was introduced as Miss Foam Bedding of 1957 and was well worth more than a passing glance. (It 'is virtually impossible in America nowadays for a girl not to be Miss Something. A friend of a friend of mine is acquainted with a lady who has the job of putting imitation orange pips into tinned orange juice in order to create the illusion that the beverage has been freshly squeezed from the parent fruit. She is expecting any day to become Miss Ersatz Orange Pip of 1957.)

And then there was the man who was doing a cigarette commercial and fell into one of those sudden fits of dreaminess and abstraction which all of us experience now and then. He went through all the motions perfectly correctly. He drew in a mouthful of smoke, blew it out slowly, watching it curl over his head and smiled a smile of just the right degree of revolting-ness. Where he went wrong was in saying, 'Man, man! This is *real* coffee!' Might have happened to any of us, of course, but I think he was wise to enrol himself next day in the Dr Bruno Furst School of Memory and Concentration.

I sometimes think, looking back to the time when I was a viewer, that I could have endured television with more fortitude if they had not laughed so much all the time. Turning on the set after reading the morning paper was like coming out of the shadows into a world of sunshine.

American papers today go in exclusively for gloom. I never saw so many people viewing with concern and contemplating with the gravest apprehension as are writing now for the daily press of the country. Talk about looking on the dark side. The only ones who do not prophesy the collapse of civilization at 3.30 sharp (Eastern Standard Time) a week from Wednesday are those who make it Tuesday afternoon at 2.45. But twiddle that knob and everything is gaiety and happiness and the laughter of little children.

At least, one assumes that they are little children. On the

evidence submitted I would say their mental age was about six. Everybody is laughing on television these days. The studio audiences have, of course, been laughing themselves sick for years on the most flimsy provocation, but now the contagion has spread to the performers.

The other day John Crosby – not to be confused with Bing: Bing sings – John is the fellow who watches television for the New York *Herald-Tribune*, than which I can imagine no more appalling job – just think of *having* to watch television – you don't catch John Crosby singing – he groans a good deal, so that you may think he is singing, but . . . . Where was I? I seem to have lost the thread. Ah, yes, John Crosby. My reason for bringing him up was that he was complaining the other day about the time when Senator Margaret Chase Smith interviewed the Burmese Premier U Nu on television and U Nu was so doubled up with laughter throughout that you could scarcely follow what he was saying. It came out something like this:

'If aggression – ha, ha, ha – comes from a foe – ha, ha, ha – the United Nations are quite ready to pass resolutions condemning that foe, but – wait, folks, you ain't heard nothin' yet – when aggression comes from friends, they like – this is going to have you in stitches – they like to keep a little quiet – ha, ha, ha – or even if they are not quiet, they don't do full justice – ho, ho, ho.'

The whole punctuated with roars of merriment from the studio audience. No wonder John Crosby screams thinly and jumps six feet up in the air if you tap him unexpectedly on the shoulder. Just a bundle of nerves, our John.

The gruesome thing is that this is not always the laughter of a real studio audience. Frequently, it is tinned or bottled. They preserve it on sound tracks, often dating back for years, so that what you are getting is the mummified mirth of people who, in many cases, died way back in about 1946, and if that is not an eerie thought, what is? 'The voice I hear this passing night was heard in ancient days by emperor and clown,' as Keats put it, switching off the comedy programme.

Furthermore, somebody has invented what is known as a laugh machine which can produce completely artificial laughter. The man in charge of it keeps pressing a button at intervals during the cross-talk act, and the comedians love it.

Living-laughter studio audiences, as opposed to laugh machines and those indomitable wraiths who, in spite of having passed beyond the veil, are still in the highest spirits and always ready to do their bit, seem to be governed by some code of rules, probably unwritten and conveyed by word of mouth, for it is surely straining the probabilities a good deal to assume that a studio audience can read. It is a code subject to alteration without notice, and a certain amount of confusion sometimes results. Thus, in the United States it used to be obligatory to laugh whenever anyone on the television screen mentioned Brooklyn. If there was one credo rooted in the minds of the citizenry it was that the word Brooklyn was cachinnogenic. And now there has been a change of policy, and today you have to laugh at Texas.

Nobody knows why. It is just an order that has come down from the men higher up. It is perfectly permissible under the new rules to keep a straight face when somebody speaks of Flatbush or the Gowanus Canal, but a studio audience which fails to laugh at the story of the Texan who refused steak *aux champignons* because he did not like champagne poured over his steak soon finds itself purged. The secret police are knocking at its door before it knows where it is.

But there is a fine spirit stirring in America these days, I am glad to say. The people are on the march. The other day someone whipped out a revolver and shot his television set, and a week or so ago there was a still more impressive demonstration. Folks, let me lead by the hand into the Hall of Fame, Richard Wilton.

At one-thirty in the afternoon of what will no doubt be known as Wilton's Day and celebrated as a national festival, Richard Wilton (29), of 103 Baker Avenue, Brooklyn, entered the studio of the Columbia Broadcasting Company during the rehearsal of a television show, armed with an eight-inch carving knife.

'I hate all television!' he announced. 'I hate commentators. I hate the whole lousy bunch. There ought to be a law against television. I want to kill a TV operator.'

Having spoken these words, which must have touched a

responsive chord in many a bosom, this splendid fellow proceeded to stab a cameraman and to hit the producer on the
frontal bone with a carafe. And lest you purse your lips at
the latter statement, saying to yourselves, 'Hullo! What's
this? Did Wilton weaken?' I must explain that a carafe,
picked up on the set, was all he had to work with. After he
stabbed the cameraman, the knife broke. He had paid only
59¢ for it, not reflecting that you cannot get a really good
carving knife as cheap as that. If you are going to stab camera-
men, it is always wisest to go as high as a dollar.

It was as he was about to attack the director that the police
came in and scooped him up, a sad disappointment to the
better element. It appears that there is some law against
wiping out television directors with carafes, one of those strange
laws that get passed occasionally, nobody knows why.

Where Richard went wrong, in my opinion, was in confining
his activities to a rehearsal, for by doing so he missed the
studio audience. He should have bided his time till one of
these gangs had been assembled.

Where everything about television is so frightful, it is difficult
to say which is its most repulsive feature, but the majority of
connoisseurs would, I think, pick the studio audience. If it
would only stay quiet, nobody would have any complaint, but
it won't. It laughs like a congregation of hyenas at everything.
The other night on what was for some reason described as a
comedy programme a girl said to a man, 'You are selfish.'

To which he replied, 'How dare you call me a shellfish?'

The studio audience let out a bellow of mirth which was
audible as far downtown as the Battery, and all over America
strong men gritted their teeth and muttered, 'Wilton, thou
shouldst be living at this hour!'

But a time will come. In ninety days or whatever it is he will
be with us once more. Good hunting, Richard Wilton. And
don't make that mistake again of trying to do it on the cheap.
Avoid bargain prices. Even if it costs as much as $2, get a
good knife.

2

From the foregoing remarks you may have formed the impression that I dislike television. I would not go as far as to say that. Apart from thinking it the foulest, ghastliest, loathsomest nightmare ever inflicted by science on a suffering human race, and the programmes, except for those Friday-night fights, the most drivelling half-witted productions ever seen outside Guest Night at a home for the feeble-minded, I do not particularly object to it. As far as I am concerned, it can carry on, provided – I say provided – I have not to excite the derision of the mob by appearing on the screen myself.

But how often this happens. Every time I have a new book out, it comes again . . . the Finger. The telephone rings, and it is my publishers' publicity man informing me briskly that I am to appear on television next week – Monday 8.30, Sonny Booch's 'Strictly for Morons' half-hour; Tuesday, 9.15, Alonzo Todd's 'Park Your Brains in the Cloakroom'; and Thursday, 7.35, Genevieve Goole Pobsleigh's 'Life Among the Halfwits'.

You might suppose from all this that there is a great popular demand for me, that America wants Wodehouse and refuses to be put off with President Eisenhower and similar cheap substitutes, but this is not so. The explanation is that this publicity man thinks it will boost the sales of my book if I am seen by millions on the television screen, not realizing that the one way of slaying a book is to let the people get a look at the author.

Authors as a class are no oil-paintings. You have only to go to one of those literary dinners to test the truth of this. At such a binge you will see tall authors, short authors, stout authors, thin authors and authors of medium height and girth, but all of these authors without exception look like something that would be passed over with a disdainful jerk of the beak by the least fastidious buzzard in the Gobi desert. Only very rarely do we find one who has even the most rudimentary resemblance to anything part-human.

If they wanted to interview me on the radio, that would be different. I have an attractive voice, rich, mellow, with certain deep organ tones in it calculated to make quite a number of the cash customers dig up the $3.50. But it is fatal to let them see me.

Owing to my having become mentally arrested at an early age, I write the sort of books which people, not knowing the facts, assume to be the work of a cheerful, if backward, young fellow of about twenty-five. 'Well, well,' they tell one another, 'we might do worse than hear what this youngster has to say. Get the rising generation point of view, and all that.' And what happens? 'We have with us tonight Mr P. G. Wodehouse' . . . and on totters a spavined septuagenarian, his bald head coated with pancake flour to keep it from shining and his palsied limbs twitching feebly like those of a galvanized frog. Little wonder that when the half-yearly score sheet reaches me some months later I find that sales have been what publishers call 'slow' again. America's book-buyers have decided as one book-buyer to keep the money in the old oak chest, and I don't blame them. I wouldn't risk twopence on anyone who looks as I do on the television screen.

I have never understood this theory that you don't get the full flavour of a writer's work unless you see him. On every newspaper staff in America there are half a dozen columnists, and every day each of these columnists has his photograph at the head of his column. All wrong it seems to me. I mean, after you have seen these gifted – but not frightfully ornamental – men 300 or 400 days in succession you have had practically all you require and their spell wanes. It is a significant thing, I think, that the greatest of all columnists, Walter Winchell, who has led the field for a matter of twenty-five years, has never allowed his photograph to appear. And Walter is a good-looking man, too, not unlike what I was in my prime.

That is the maddening thing about this television business, that they are catching me too late. 'Oh, God, put back Thy universe and give me yesterday,' as the fellow said. Well, no, not yesterday perhaps, but say 1906 or thereabouts. I really was an eyeful then. Trim athletic figure, finely chiselled features and more hair on the top of my head than you could shake a stick at. I would have been perfectly willing to exhibit myself to America's millions then. But now I have definitely gone off quite a bit, and that is why, when this publicity man rings up, I have my answer ready, quick as a flash.

'Terribly sorry,' I say. 'I'm just off to the Coast.'

Heaven bless the Coast. It is the one safe refuge. Even press representatives or public relations lizards or whatever they call themselves know they can't get at you there. And these constant visits to the Coast are improving my prestige. 'Wodehouse always seems to be going to Hollywood,' people say. 'Yes,' reply the people these people are addressing, 'the demand for him in the studios is tremendous.' 'Odd one never sees his name on screen credits,' says the first people. 'Oh no,' (second people speaking). 'He writes under a number of pseudonyms. Makes a fortune, I understand.'

SEVENTEEN

The Girl in the Pink Bathing Suit

I

As a matter of fact, I have been to Hollywood, though not recently. I went there in 1930. I had a year's contract, and was required to do so little work in return for the money I received that I was able in the twelve months before I became a fugitive from the chain-gang to write a novel and nine short stories, besides brushing up my golf, getting an attractive sun-tan and perfecting my Australian crawl in the swimming-pool.

It is all sadly changed now, they tell me. Once a combination of Santa Claus and Good-Time Charlie, Hollywood has become a Scrooge. The dear old days are dead and the spirit of cheerful giving a thing of the past. But in 1930 the talkies had just started, and the slogan was Come one, come all, and the more the merrier. It was an era when only a man of exceptional ability and determination could keep from getting signed up by a studio in some capacity or other. I happened to be engaged as a writer, but I might quite as easily have been scooped in as a technical adviser or a vocal instructor. (At least I had a roof to my mouth, which many vocal instructors in Hollywood at that time had not.) The heartiness and hospitality reminded one of the Jolly Innkeeper (with entrance number in Act One) of the old-style comic opera.

One can understand it, of course. The advent of sound had made the manufacture of motion pictures an infinitely more complex affair than it had been up till then. In the silent days everything had been informal and casual, just a lot of great big happy schoolboys getting together for a bit of fun. Ike would have a strip of celluloid, Spike a camera his uncle had given him for Christmas, Mike would know a friend or two who liked dressing-up and having their photographs taken, and with these modest assets they would club together their pocket money and start the Finer and Supremer Films Corporation. And as for bothering about getting anyone to write them a story, it never occurred to them. They made it up themselves as they went along.

The talkies changed all that. It was no longer possible just to put on a toga, have someone press a button and call the result *The Grandeur that was Rome* or *In the Days of Nero*. A whole elaborate new organization was required. You had to have a studio Boss to boss the Producer, a Producer to produce the Supervisor, a Supervisor to supervise the sub-Supervisor, a sub-Supervisor to sub-supervise the Director, a Director to direct the Cameraman and an Assistant Director to assist the Director. And, above all, you had to get hold of someone to supply the words.

The result was a terrible shortage of authors in all the world's literary centres. New York till then had been full of them. You would see them frisking in perfect masses in any editorial office you happened to enter. Their sharp, excited yapping was one of the features of the first- or second-act interval of every new play that was produced. And in places like Greenwich Village you had to watch your step very carefully to avoid treading on them.

And then all of a sudden all you saw was an occasional isolated one being shooed out of a publisher's sanctum or sitting in a speak-easy sniffing at his press clippings. Time after time fanciers would come up to you with hard-luck stories.

'You know that novelist of mine with the flapping ears and the spots on his coat? Well, he's gone.'

'Gone?'

'Absolutely vanished. I left him on the steps of the club, and when I came out there were no signs of him.'

'Same here,' says another fancier. 'I had a brace of playwrights to whom I was greatly attached, and they've disappeared without a word.'

Well, of course, people took it for granted that the little fellows had strayed and had got run over, for authors are notoriously dreamy in traffic and, however carefully you train them, will persist in stopping in the middle of the street to jot down strong bits of dialogue. It was only gradually that the truth came out. They had all been decoyed away to Hollywood.

What generally happened was this. A couple of the big film executives – say Mr Louis B. Mayer and Mr Adolf Zukor – would sight their quarry in the street and track him down to some bohemian eating resort. Having watched him settle, they seat themselves at a table immediately behind him, and for a few moments there is silence, broken only by the sound of the author eating corned beef hash. Then Mr Mayer addresses Mr Zukor, raising his voice slightly.

'Whatever was the name of that girl?' he says.

'What girl?' asks Mr Zukor, cleverly taking his cue.

'That tall, blonde girl with the large blue eyes.'

'The one in the pink bathing suit?'

'That's right. With the freckle in the small of her back.'

'A freckle? A mole, I always understood.'

'No, it was a freckle, eye-witnesses tell me. Just over the base of the spinal cord. Well, anyway, what was her name?'

'Now what was it? Eulalie something? Clarice something? No, it's gone. But I'll find out for you when we get home. I know her intimately.'

Here they pause, but not for long. There is a sound of quick, emotional breathing. The author is standing beside them, a rapt expression on his face.

'Pardon me, gentlemen,' he says, 'for interrupting a private conversation, but I chanced to overhear you saying that you were intimately acquainted with a tall, blonde girl with large blue eyes, in the habit of wearing bathing suits of just the type I like best. It is for a girl of that description that I have been scouring the country for years. Where may she be found?'

'In God's Back Garden – Hollywood,' says Mr Zukor.

'Pity you can't meet her,' says Mr Mayer. 'You're just her type.'

'If you were by any chance an author,' says Mr Zukor,

'we could take you back with us tomorrow. Too bad you're not.'

'Prepare yourself for a surprise, gentlemen,' says the victim. 'I *am* an author. George Montague Breamworthy. "Powerfully devised situations" – *New York Times*. "Sheer, stark realism" – *New York Herald-Tribune*. "Whoops!" – *Women's Wear*.'

'In that case,' says Mr Mayer, producing a contract, 'sign here.'

'Where my thumb is,' says Mr Zukor.

The trap has snapped.

2

That was how they got me, and it was, I understand, the usual method of approach. But sometimes this plan failed, and then sterner methods were employed. The demand for authors in those early talkie days was so great that it led to the revival of the old press-gang. Nobody was safe even if he merely looked like an author.

While having a Malted Milk Greta Garbo with some of the old lags in the commissary one morning about half-way through my term of sentence, I was told of one very interesting case. It appeared that there was a man who had gone out West hoping to locate oil. One of those men without a thought in the world outside of oil, the last thing he had ever dreamed of doing was being an author. With the exception of letters and an occasional telegram of greeting to some relative at Christmas, he had never written anything in his life.

But by some curious chance it happened that his appearance was that of one capable of the highest feats in the way of literary expression. He had a domelike head, piercing eyes, and that cynical twist of the upper lip which generally means an epigram on the way. Still, as I say, he was not a writer, and no one could have been more surprised than he when, walking along a deserted street in Los Angeles, thinking of oil, he was suddenly set upon by masked men, chloroformed, and whisked away in a closed car. When he came to himself he was in a cell on the Perfector-Zizzbaum lot with paper and a sharpened pencil before him, and stern-featured men in felt hats and raincoats were waggling rubber hoses at him and telling him to get busy and turn out something with lots of sex in it, but not to much, because of Will Hays.

The story has a curious sequel. A philosopher at heart, he accepted the situation. He wrenched his mind away from oil and scribbled a few sentences that happened to occur to him. He found, as so many have found, that an author's is the easiest job in existence, and soon he was scratching away as briskly as you could wish. And that is how Noel Coward got his start.

But not every kidnapped author accepted his fate so equably. The majority endeavoured to escape. But it was useless. Even if the rigours of the pitiless California climate did not drive them back to shelter, capture was inevitable. When I was in Hollywood there was much indignation among the better element of the community over the pursuit of an unfortunate woman writer whom the harshness of her supervisor, a man of the name of Legree, had driven to desperation. As I got the story, they chased her across the ice with bloodhounds.

The whole affair was very unpleasant and shocked the soft-hearted greatly. So much so that a Mrs Harriet Beecher Stowe told me that if MGM would meet her terms for the movie, she intended to write a book about it which would stir the world.

'Boy,' she said to me, 'it will be a scorcher!'

I don't know if anything ever came of it.

3

I got away from Hollywood at the end of the year because the gaoler's daughter smuggled me in a file in a meat pie, but I was there long enough to realize what a terribly demoralizing place it is. The whole atmosphere there is one of insidious deceit and subterfuge. Nothing is what it affects to be. What looks like a tree is really a slab of wood backed with barrels. What appears on the screen as the towering palace of Haroun al-Raschid is actually a cardboard model occupying four feet by three of space. The languorous lagoon is simply a smelly tank with a stagehand named Ed wading about it in bathing trunks.

It is surely not difficult to imagine the effect of all this on a sensitive-minded author. Taught at his mother's knee to love the truth, he finds himself surrounded by people making fortunes by what can only be called chicanery. After a month or two in such an environment could you trust that author to count his golf shots correctly or to give his right sales figures?

And then there was – I am speaking of the old days. It is possible that modern enlightened thought has brought improvements – the inevitable sapping of his self-respect. At the time of which I am writing authors in Hollywood were kept in little hutches. In every studio there were rows and rows of these, each containing an author on a long contract at a weekly salary. You could see their anxious little faces peering out through the bars and hear them whining piteously to be taken for a walk. One had to be very callous not to be touched by such a spectacle.

I do not say that these authors were actually badly treated. In the best studios in those early talkie days kindness was the rule. Often you would see some high executive stop and give one of them a lettuce. And it was the same with the humaner type of director. In fact, between the directors and their authors there frequently existed a rather touching friendship. I remember one director telling a story which illustrates this.

One morning, he said, he was on his way to his office, preoccupied, as was his habit when planning out the day's work, when he felt a sudden tug at his coat-tails. He looked down and there was his pet author, Edgar Montrose (Book Society – Recommendation) Delamere. The little fellow had got him in a firm grip and was gazing up at him, in his eyes an almost human expression of warning.

Well, the director, not unnaturally, mistook this at first for mere playfulness, for it was often his kindly habit to romp with his little charges. Then something seemed to whisper to him that he was being withheld from some great peril. He remembered stories he had read as a boy – one of which he was even then directing for Rin-Tin-Tin – where faithful dogs dragged their masters back from the brink of precipices on dark nights, and, scarcely knowing why, he turned and went off to the commissary, and had a Strawberry and Vanilla Nut Sundae Mary Pickford.

It was well that he did. In his office, waiting to spring, there was lurking a foreign star with a bad case of temperament, whose bite might have been fatal. You may be sure that Edgar Montrose had a good meal that night.

But that was an isolated case. Not all directors were like this one. Too many of them crushed the spirit of the captives by incessant blue-pencilling of their dialogue, causing them to become listless and lose appetite. Destructive criticism is what kills an author. Cut his material too much, make him feel that he is not a Voice, give him the impression that his big scene is all wet, and you will soon see the sparkle die out of his eyes.

I don't know how conditions are today, but at that time there were authors who had been on salary for years in Hollywood without ever having a line of their work used. All they did was attend story conferences. There were other authors whom nobody had seen for years. It was like the Bastille. They just sat in some hutch away in a corner somewhere and grew white beards and languished. From time to time somebody would renew their contract, and then they were forgotten again.

As I say, it may be different now. After all, I am speaking of twenty-five years ago. But I do think it would be wise if author-fanciers exercised vigilance. You never know. The press-gang may still be in our midst.

So when you take your pet for a walk, keep an eye on him. If he goes sniffing after strange men, whistle him back.

And remember that the spring is the dangerous time. Around about the beginning of May, authors get restless and start dreaming about girls in abbreviated bathing suits. It is easy to detect the symptoms. The moment you hear yours muttering about the Golden West and God's Sunshine and Out There Beyond The Stifling City put sulphur in his absinthe and lock him up in the kitchenette.

EIGHTEEN

The Theatre

I

And now Ho for a chapter on the theatre and what I have done to put it on the map.

A dramatist friend of mine was telling me the other day that he had written his last play. He was embittered because the star for whom he had been waiting for two years backed out on obtaining a big television contract and another star for whom he had been waiting two years before that suddenly went off to Hollywood. And this after he had worked like a beaver rewriting his play to suit the views of the manager, the manager's wife, the principal backer and the principal backer's son, a boy of some fourteen summers named Harold, on whose judgement the principal backer placed great reliance.

Furthermore, he said, he could no longer face those out-of-town preliminary tours, with their 'Nobody comes to the theatre on Monday in these small towns. Wait till Tuesday.' 'Well, Tuesday, everyone knows, is a bad night everywhere. Wait till Wednesday,' and 'You can't get 'em into the theatre on a Wednesday. Wait till Thursday. Thursday will tell the story.' And always the manager at his elbow, chewing two inches of an unlighted cigar and muttering, 'Well, boy, there ain't no doubt but what it's going to need a lot of work.'

Myself, I have never regretted my flirtations with the drama. They cost me a lot of mental anguish, not to mention making me lose so much hair that nowadays I am often mistaken in a dim light for Yul Brynner, but one met such interesting people. I have encountered in the coulisses enough unforgettable characters to fix up the *Reader's Digest* for years and years. Most of these are enshrined in the pages of *Bring on the Girls*.

My first play was written in collaboration with a boy named Henry Cullimore when I was seven. I don't quite know what made us decide to do it, but we did so decide, and Henry said we would have to have a plot. 'What's a plot?' I asked. He didn't know. He had read or heard somewhere that a plot was a good thing to have, but as to what it was he confessed himself fogged. This naturally made us both feel a little dubious as to the outcome of our enterprise, but we agreed that there was nothing to do but carry on and hope that everything would pan out all right. (Chekhov used to do this.)

He – Henry Cullimore, not Chekhov – was the senior partner in the project. He was two or three years older than I was, which gave him an edge, and he had a fountain-pen. I mostly contributed moral support, pursuing the same method which I later found to answer so well when I teamed up with Guy Bolton. When Guy and I pitched in on a play, he would do the rough spadework – the writing – and I used to look in on him from time to time and say 'How are you getting on?' He would say, 'All right,' and I would say, 'Fine,' and go off and read Agatha Christie. Giving it the Wodehouse Touch, I used to call it. And so little by little and bit by bit the thing would get done.

This system worked capitally with all the Bolton–Wodehouse productions, and I believe it was the way Beaumont and Fletcher used to hammer out their combined efforts. ('How goeth it, my heart of gold?' 'Yarely, old mole. Well, fairly yarely.' 'Stick at it, boy. Hard work never hurt anyone.') But Henry Cullimore let me down. A broken reed, if ever there was one. He got as far as

ACT ONE

[*Enter Henry*]

HENRY: What's for breakfast? Ham and oatmeal?
      Very nice.

but there he stopped. He had shot his bolt.

How he was planning to go on if inspiration had not blown a fuse, I never discovered. I should imagine that the oatmeal would have proved to be poisoned – ('One of the barbiturate group, Inspector, unless I am greatly mistaken') – or a dead body would have dropped out of the closet where they kept the sugar.

The thing was never produced. A pity, for I think it would have been a great audience show.

Since then I have been mixed up in sixteen straight plays and twenty-two musical comedies as author, part author or just hanging on to the author in the capacity of Charles his friend. In virtually every theatrical enterprise there is a Charles his friend, drawing his weekly royalties. Nobody ever quite knows how he wriggled in, but there he is. Affability of manner has a good deal to do with it.

But though I attached myself to these straight plays, some of them the most outstanding flops in the history of the stage, my heart was never really in them. Musical comedy was my dish, the musical-comedy theatre my spiritual home. I would rather have written *Oklahoma!* than *Hamlet*. (Actually, as the records show, I wrote neither, but you get the idea.)

It was in 1904 that I burst on the theatrical scene with a lyric in a thing called *Sergeant Brue* at the Prince of Wales Theatre in London. In 1906 I got a job at £2 a week as a sort of utility lyricist at the Aldwych Theatre in the same town. This, as I have already recorded, involved writing some numbers with a young American composer named Jerome Kern, and when, a good many years later, I ran into him and Guy Bolton in New York, we got together and did those Princess Theatre shows. After that I worked with Victor Herbert, George Gershwin, Rudolf Friml, Sigmund Romberg, Vincent Youmans, Emmerich Kalman, Ivan Caryll, Franz Lehar and what seems to me now about a hundred other composers. For years scarcely a day passed whose low descending sun did not see me at my desk trying to find some rhyme for 'June' that would not be 'soon', 'moon', 'tune' or 'spoon'. (One bright young man suddenly thought of 'macaroon' and soared right away to the top of the profession.)

It is not to be wondered at, then, that when I can spare a moment of my valuable time, I find myself brooding on the New York musical-comedy theatre of today. The subject is one of compelling interest. What is going to happen to it? Can it last? If so, how much longer? Will there come a day when we reach out for it and find it isn't there? Are the rising costs of production ever going to stop rising? It is difficult enough to prize the required $250,000 out of the investing public now. What of tomorrow, when it will probably be half a million?

Have you ever tried to touch anyone for $250,000? It is by no means the same thing as asking for a fiver till Wednesday, old man. It takes doing. Howard Dietz, the lyrist, once wrote an opening chorus for a revue which was produced by a prominent Broadway producer called Max Gordon. It ran:

> What's all that cheering in the streets?
> What's all that cheering you're hearing in the streets?
> Max Gordon's raised the money,
> Max Gordon's raised the money . . .

and while joining in the cheering, one cannot help dropping a silent tear as one thinks of what Max must have gone through. And in his capacity of prominent Broadway manager, he presumably had to do it again and again and again.

How anyone who had once raised the money for a New York musical can bring himself to do it a second time is more than I can imagine. A few years ago a management decided that the moment had come to revive a show with which I had been connected somewhere around 1920 and asked me to look in at 'backers' audition'. I was there through the grim proceedings, and came away feeling like one of those can-you-spare-a-nickel-for-a-cup-of-coffee gentlemen of leisure who pop up through the sidewalk in front of you as you take your walks abroad in New York's seedier districts. My hat, quite a good one, seemed battered and shapeless, there were cracks in the uppers of my shoes, and an unwholesome growth of hair had sprouted on my cheeks, accompanied by a redness and swelling of the nose. I felt soiled. (There were headlines in all the papers – WODEHOUSE FEELS SOILED.)

A backers' audition is composed of cringing mendicants – the management, a pianist, some hired singers and some friends and supporters who are there to laugh and applaud –

and a little group of fat, rich men with tight lips and faces carved out of granite, whom you have assembled somehow and herded into a hotel suite. These are the backers, or it might be better to say you hope they are the backers, for while there is unquestionably gold in them thar heels, the problem is how to extract it.

Cigars, drinks and caviare have been provided, and the management proceeds to read the script, pausing at intervals to allow the hired singers to render the songs. The fat, rich men sit there with their eyes bulging, in a silence broken only by the champing of jaws and a musical gurgle as another whisky and soda goes down the gullet, and then, loaded to the Plimsoll mark with caviare, they file out, not having uttered a word.

And this goes on and on. In order to collect the money to produce *Oklahoma!* eighty-nine of these auditions had to be given. I imagine that it was not till about the sixty-third that somebody stirred in his chair and brought out a cheque-book. Perhaps one of the songs had touched his heart, reminding him of something his mother used to sing when he clustered about her knee, or possibly conscience whispered to him that as he was all that caviare ahead of the game, he ought to do something about it. So he wrote his cheque.

But for how much? $10,000? $20,000? Even if it was $50,000, it would only have scratched the surface. *Oklahoma!* was $20,000 short when it opened out of town, and would never have been brought into New York if S. N. Behrman, the playwright, had not come to the rescue.

However, let us suppose that somehow you have contrived to wheedle $250,000 out of the moneyed classes. What then? You are then faced with the prospect of having to play to $33,000 a week simply to break even. I was shown the weekly balance sheet of an apparently very prosperous Broadway musical comedy the other day. The gross box-office receipts were $36,442.90, which sounds fine, but after all expenses had been paid the profit on the week was $3697.83. I am no mathematician, but it looked to me as if they would have to go on doing about $37,000 a week for about a year and a half before the backers drew a cent. No wonder these prudent men are often inclined to settle for free cigars and caviare and not get mixed up in all that sordid business of paying out money.

That is why if you ever catch me in pensive mood, sitting with chin supported in the hand and the elbow on the knee, like Rodin's 'Thinker', you can be pretty sure that I am saying to myself, 'Whither the New York musical-comedy theatre?' or, possibly, 'The New York musical-comedy theatre . . . whither?' It is a question that constantly exercises me. I can't see what, as the years roll by and costs continue to rise, is going to happen to the bally thing.

2

It is the stagehand situation that causes a good deal of the present unrest. This situation – I am speaking of the stage-hand situation – is quite a situation. The trouble, briefly, is this. Stagehands cost money, and theatrical managers hate parting with money. The scene-shifters' union, on the other hand, is all for it. Blow the expense, says the scene-shifters' union. It likes to see money in handfuls scattered, always provided it is someone else's (or someone's else, as the case may be). This leads to strained relations, pique on both sides and the calling of some most unpleasant names. I have heard managers refer to the union as vampires, while the union, speaking of the managers, is far too prone to make nasty cracks about people who are so tight they could carry an armful of eels up six flights of stairs and never drop one of them.

Most plays nowadays are in one set, and a manager who puts on a one-set play feels that once this one set is in position he ought to be able to pay the scene-shifters off and kiss them good-bye. He sees no reason why he should have to pay a weekly wage to a gang of scene-shifters just for not shifting scenes. All he wants is an operative who will go over the set from time to time with a feather duster, to keep the moths from getting into it.

The union does not take this view. It holds that if the manager hasn't any scenes to shift he jolly well ought to have, and it insists on him employing the number of scene-shifters who would have been required to shift the scenes if there had been any scenes to shift, if you follow me. And as any attempt to brook the will of the union leads to a strike of stagehands, which leads to a strike of electricians, which leads to a strike of actors, box-office officials, gentlemanly ushers and the theatre cat, it gets its way. Thus we find Victor Borge, giving a two-hour solo performance on the piano at the Booth, obliged to supply eight stagehands. And a recent one-set comedy with three characters in it was attended nightly by no fewer than fifteen admirers and well-wishers. Some plays these last seasons have suffered from audience thinness, but no manager has ever run short of stagehands. They are there from the moment the curtain goes up, with their hair in a braid.

At a risk of becoming too technical, I must explain briefly how a troupe of stagehands with nothing to do is organized. There is, I need scarcely say, nothing haphazard about it. First – chosen by show of hands (stagehands) – comes the head man or Giant Sloth. His job is to hang upside down from a rafter. Next we have the Senior Lounger and the Junior Lounger, who lie on couches – Roman fashion – with chaplets of roses round their foreheads. Last come the rank and file, the twelve Lilies of the Field. It was because I was uncertain as to the duties of these that I looked in the other night at one of the theatres to get myself straight on the point, and was courteously received by the Junior Lounger, a Mr B. J. Wilberforce, who showed no annoyance at being interrupted while working on his crossword puzzle.

'I was wondering, Mr Wilberforce,' I said, when greetings and compliments had been exchanged, 'if you could tell me something about this situation?'

'What situation would that be?' he asked.

'The scene-shifter situation,' I said, and he frowned.

'We prefer not to be called scene-shifters,' he explained. 'There seems to us something a little vulgar about shifting scenes. It smacks too much of those elaborate musical productions, where, I am told, the boys often get quite hot and dusty. We of the élite like to think of ourselves as America's leisure class. Of course, when there is work to be done, we do it. Only the other night, for instance, the producer thought that it would brighten things up if an upstage chair were moved to a downstage position. We were called into conference, and long before the curtain rose for the evening's performance the thing was done. Superintended by the Giant Sloth, we Loungers – myself and my immediate superior, Cyril Muspratt – each grasped one side of the seat and that chair was moved, and it would have been the same if it had been two chairs. I am not saying it did not take it out of us. It did. But we do not spare ourselves when the call comes.'

'Still, it does not come often, I suppose? As a general rule, you have your leisure?'

'Oh, yes. We have lots of time to fool around in.'

'Never end a sentence with a preposition, Wilberforce,' I said warningly, and he blushed. I had spoken kindly, but you could see it stung.

At this moment somebody on the stage said in a loud voice, 'My God! My Wife!' – they were playing one of those Victorian farce revivals designed to catch the nostalgia trade – and he winced.

'All this noise!' he said. 'One realizes that actors have to make a living, but there is no need for a lot of racket and disturbance. It is most disagreeable for a man doing his crossword puzzle and trying to concentrate on a word in three letters beginning with E and signifying "large Australian bird" to be distracted by sudden sharp cries. Still, it might be worse. At the Bijou, where they are doing one of those gangster things, the Giant Sloth was often woken three or four times in an evening by pistol-shots. He had to complain about it, and now, I believe, the actors just say, "Bang, Bang!" in an undertone. Three letters beginning with E,' he mused.

I knew it could not be the Sun God Ra. Then suddenly I got it.

'Emu!'

'I beg your pardon?'

'That large Australian bird you were speaking of.'

'Of which you were speaking. Never end a sentence with a preposition, Wodehouse.'

It was my turn to blush, and my face was still suffused when we were joined by an impressive-looking man in slacks and a sleeveless vest. This proved to be Cyril Muspratt, the Senior Lounger.

'And do you, too, do crossword puzzles, Mr Muspratt?' I asked when introductions had been concluded.

He shook his head laughingly, looking bronzed and fit.

'I am more the dreamer type,' he said. 'I like to sit and think . . . well, anyway, sit. I read a good deal, too. What do you think of this bird Kafka?'

'What do you?'

'I asked you first,' he said with a touch of warmth, and sensing that tempers were rising I bade them good night and went on my way. So I still don't know how those Lilies of the Field fill in their time. Hide-and-seek, perhaps? The dark back of the theatre would be splendid for hide-and-seek. Or leap-frog? Perhaps they just catch up with their reading, like Mr Muspratt.

They tell a tale in Shubert Alley of a manager who walked one day on Forty-Fifth Street west of Broadway and paused to watch workmen razing the Avon Theatre.

'Gosh!' he said, much moved. 'They're using fewer men to tear down the building than we used to have to hire to strike a one-set show.'

And there, gentle reader, let us leave him.

3

But to a certain extent, I think, the troubles of the New York theatre must be attributed to the peculiar methods of the box-office officials. They seem to go out of their way to make it difficult for the public to buy seats. A lady living in Farmingdale, New Jersey, recently wrote to the box-office of one of the playhouses as follows:

Please send me four tickets at $4 for any Saturday evening. Cheque for $16 enclosed.

To which she received the reply:

There are no $2 seats on Saturday evenings.

She then wrote:

Please re-read my letter and cheque.

The theatre riposted:

There are no $2 seats on Saturday evenings.

Passions run hot in Farmingdale, NJ. The lady came back with a stinker:

I cannot understand what the difficulty is. Who on earth said anything about $2 seats? I wrote asking you for four seats at $4 each. I enclosed a cheque for $16. Four times four are sixteen. Nobody wants $2 seats, asked for them or sent a cheque for them. Please send me the tickets.

Did this rattle the box-office man? Did he blush and shuffle his feet? No, sir. His letter in reply read as follows:

There are no $2 seats on Saturday evenings.

NINETEEN

Christmas and Divorce

I

Looking back over what I have written, J.P., I see that I have not really covered that question you asked about the changes I notice now in the American scene. I spoke, you may remember, of the wonderful improvement there has been of late in American manners but I omitted to touch on those equally intriguing subjects, the recent upheaval in the world of divorce and the present swollen condition of the American Christmas. Both deserve more than a passing word.

The American Christmas is very different today from what it was when, a piefaced lad in my twenties, I first trod the sidewalks of New York. Then a simple festival, it now seems to have got elephantiasis or something. I don't want to do anyone an injustice, but the thought has sometimes crossed my mind that some of the big department stores are trying to make money out of Christmas. I cannot help thinking that to certain persons in New York – I name no names – Christmas is not just a season of homely goodwill but an opportunity to gouge the populace out of what little savings it has managed to accumulate in the past year. All those Santa Clauses you see. I feel they are there for a purpose.

Christmas in New York brings out the Santa Clauses like flies. Go into any big department store, and there is a Santa Claus sitting in a chair with children crawling all over him. 'Our humble heroes!' are the words that spring to my lips as I see them, for these stores are always superheated, and you cannot be a Santa Claus without padding yourself liberally about the middle. At the end of the day these devoted men must feel like Shadrach, Meshach and Abednego, and also probably not unlike King Herod, of whose forthright methods I have heard several of them speak with wistful admiration.

I interviewed one of them the other day in a restaurant whither he had gone in his brief time off to refresh himself with a quick wassail bowl.

'Don't you ever falter?' I asked.

He gave me a look.

'A Santa Claus who faltered,' he replied stiffly, 'would receive short shrift from his co-workers. Next morning at daybreak he would find himself in a hollow square of his fellow-Clauses, being formally stripped of his beard and stomach padding. We are a proud guild, we Santas, and we brook no weakness. Besides,' he went on, 'though the life of a department-store Santa Claus is admittedly fraught with peril, he can console himself with the reflection that he is by no means as badly off as the shock troops of the profession, the men who have to go into the offices. Take the case of a department-store Santa Claus in whose whiskers a child has deposited his semi-liquefied chewing-gum. A man who has had to comb chewing-gum – or for the matter of that milk chocolate – out of the undergrowth at the close of his working day becomes a graver, deeper man. He has seen life. And he knows he has got to go through it again tomorrow. But does he quail?'

'Doesn't he quail?'

'No, sir, he does not quail. He says to himself that what he is suffering is as nothing compared to what a man like, for instance, Butch Oberholtzer has to face. Butch is the Santa attached to a prominent monthly magazine, and it is his task to circulate among the advertisers during Christmas week and give them a hearty seasonal greeting from his employers. Well, you know what sort of condition the average advertiser is in during Christmas week, after those daily office parties. Let so much as a small fly stamp its feet suddenly on the ceiling and he leaps like a stricken blancmange. You can picture his emotions, then, when as he sits quivering in his chair a Santa Claus steals up behind him, slaps him on the back and shouts, "Merry Christmas, old boy, merry Christmas!" On several occasions Butch has escaped with his life by the merest hair's-breadth. I wonder if his luck can last?'

'Let us hope so,' I said soberly.

He shrugged his shoulders.

'Ah well,' he said, 'if the worst happens, it will be just one more grave among the hills.'

This man told me one thing that shocked me a good deal. For years I have been worrying myself sick, wondering why yaks' tails were imported into the United States from Tibet. I could not understand there being any popular demand for them. I know that if someone came up to me and said, 'Mr Wodehouse, I have long been a great admirer of your work and would like to do something by way of a small return for all the happy hours you have given me. Take this yak's tail, and make it a constant companion', I would thank him and giggle a little and say how frightfully good of him and it was just what I had been wanting, but I should most certainly try to lose the thing on my way home. And I would have supposed that a similar distaste for these objects prevailed almost universally.

I now have the facts. Yak's tails are used for making beards for department-store Santa Clauses, and I can never again feel quite the same about the department-store Santa Claus. His white beard, once venerable, now revolts me. Looking at it, I find a picture rising before my eyes of some unfortunate yak wandering about Tibet without a tail. You don't have to know much about the sensitive nature of the yak to realize what this must mean to the bereaved animal. It is bathed in confusion. It doesn't know which way to look.

But let us leave a distasteful subject and get on to the recent alarming slump in America's divorce rate.

2

In the realm of sport America has not been doing too well of late. The Davis Cup has gone to Australia again, and now the World Bridge Championship, played at the Hotel Claridge, Paris, is over, and the French team, headed by the Messieurs Pierre Ghestem and René Bacherich, are whooping and throwing their berets in the air, while Charles Goren, Lee Hazen and the other representatives of the United States sit huddled in a corner, telling one another that, after all, it is only a game.

The result apparently was against all the ruling of the form book, and I wish I knew more about Bridge, so that I could give you an expert analysis of the run of the play. All I have to go on is what Mr Hazen told an interviewer at the close of the proceedings.

'We in America,' said Mr Hazen, 'are used to playing with a conventional system. But the French have borrowed from the Viennese, the Swedish and the Norwegian.'

Well, naturally, an American who sits down to play Bridge with a Frenchman expects him to play *like* a Frenchman. It disconcerts him when the other suddenly tears off his whiskers and shouts, 'April fool! I'm a Norwegian!' He is bewildered and at a loss. He forgets what are trumps and even, if of a particularly nervous temperament, forgets that he is playing Bridge at all and keeps saying 'Snap!' every time a card is laid down. You can't win world tournaments that way.

Still more unsettling to the American team must have been the conditions under which the matches were played.

'The French system,' said Mr Hazen, 'is based on no interference.'

One sees what this means. When you play Bridge in France you do it in an atmosphere of cloistral calm, broken only by an occasional murmured 'Nice work, old man,' (*Joli travail, mon vieux*), 'At-a-boy!' (*Voilà le garçon*) and so on, and it would obviously take Americans, accustomed to the more boisterous ways of their native land, a long time to get used to this. Back home there was all the hurly-burly associated with the baseball arena, and without an audience shouting 'Take him out!' 'Who ever told you you could play Bridge, ya big stiff?' and the like, the American team was ill at ease and off its game.

Well, as they keep saying, it is only a pastime and these things cannot affect us finally, but any observer who is at all keen-eyed can see that Charles Goren and Lee Hazen are good and sore, as are their colleagues, and there has been some rather sharp criticism of Jeff Glick, the non-playing captain of the American team, for not having seen to it that the playing members had a few of those extra aces up their sleeves which make so much difference in a closely contested chukker.

However, Davis Cups and Bridge championships are not everything, and the downhearted were able to console themselves with the reflection that, whatever might happen on the tennis court or at the card-table, in one field of sport America still led the world. Her supremacy in the matter of Divorce remained unchallenged. Patriots pointed with pride at the figures, which showed that while thirteen in every thousand American ever-loving couples decided each year to give their chosen mates the old heave-ho, the best, the nearest competitor, Switzerland, could do was three.

'As long as we have Texas oil millionaires, Hollywood film stars and Tommy Manville,' people told one another, 'we're all right. Come the three corners of the world in arms, and we shall shock them.'

And, of course, at times they did, considerably.

But now the whole situation has changed. We learn from the New York *Daily Mirror* that, 'An amazing thing has been happening, little noticed, in our national life. Since 1946 there has been a forty per cent decline in the number of divorces.' Just like that. No preparation, no leading up to it, no attempt to break the thing gently. It is as if the *Mirror* had crept up behind America and struck her on the back of the head with a sock full of wet sand.

The paper omits to mention what is happening in Switzerland, but one assumes that the Swiss are still plugging along in the old dogged way and by this time may have got up to five per thousand or even six. For don't run away with the idea that the Swiss do nothing but yodel and make condensed milk. They have plenty of leisure, be well assured, for divorce actions. Probably at this very moment some citizen of the inland republic is in the witness-box showing the judge the bump on his head where the little woman hit him with the cuckoo clock. And America still sunk in complacency and over-confidence. It is the old story of the tortoise and the hare.

Well, the facts are out, but it is difficult to know where to place the blame. Certainly not on Hollywood. The spirit of the men (and the women) there is splendid. Every day one reads in the gossip columns another of those heart-warming announcements to the effect that Lotta Svelte and George Marsupial are holding hands and plan to merge as soon as the former can disentangle herself from Marcus Manleigh and the latter from Belinda Button, and one knows that George and Lotta are not going to let the side down. In due season she will be in court telling the judge that for a fortnight the marriage was a very happy one, but then George started reading the paper at breakfast and refusing to listen when she told him of the dream she had had last night, thus causing her deep mental agony. No, the heart of Hollywood is sound. So is that of the Texas oil men. And nobody can say that Tommy Manville is not trying.

It may be that it is the judges who are lacking in team spirit. A great deal must always depend on the judges. Some of them are all right. Not a word of complaint about the one in Hackensask, New Jersey, who recently granted Mrs Carmella Porretta a divorce because her husband, Salvatore, struck her with a buttered muffin. But what are we to say of the judge who, when Mrs Edna Hunt Tankersley applied to him for her twelfth divorce, callously informed her that as far as he was concerned she got her 'final final decree'? In other words, when this splendid woman, all eagerness to see America first, comes up for the thirteenth time, her industry and determination will be unrewarded. No Baker's dozen for Edna, unless, of course, she is shrewd enough to take her custom elsewhere.

Has this judge never reflected that it is just this sort of thing that discourages ambition and is going to hand the world's leadership to the Swiss on a plate with watercress round it? Can one be surprised that the Swiss, who pull together as one man in every patriotic movement, are steadily creeping up and likely to forge ahead at any moment?

A theory held by some to account for this distressing decline in the divorce rate in the United States is that the modern American husband, instead of getting a divorce, finds it cheaper to dissect his bride with the meat axe and deposit the debris in a sack in the Jersey marshes. I doubt it. One has heard, of course, of the man in Chicago named Young who once, when his nerves were unstrung, put his wife Josephine in the chopping machine and canned her and labelled her 'Tongue', but as a rule the American wife does not murder easy. A story now going the rounds bears this out, the story of the husband and wife in California.

For three or four days, it seems, the marriage between this young couple had been an ideally happy one, but then, as so often happens, the husband became restless and anxious for a change. A first he thought of divorce, and then he thought again and remembered that in California there is a community law which gives the sundered wife half the family property. And he was just reconciling himself to putting a new coat of paint on her and trying to make her do for another year, when an idea struck him.

Why not say it with rattlesnakes?

So he got a rattlesnake and put it in the pocket of his trousers and hung the trousers over a chair in the bedroom, and when his wife asked him for some money, he told her she would find his wallet in his trouser pocket.

'In the bedroom,' he said, and she went into the bedroom, whence her voice presently emerged.

'Which trousers?'

'The grey ones.'

'The ones hanging on the chair?'

'That's right.'

'Which pocket?'

'The hip pocket.'

'But I've looked there,' said his wife discontentedly, 'and all I could find was a rattlesnake.'

TWENTY

My Methods, Such As They Are

I

And now, to conclude, I see that you ask me to tell you what are my methods of work, and I am wondering if here your questionnaire has not slipped a cog and gone off the right lines. Are you sure your radio and newspaper public want to know?

I ask because I have never been able to make myself believe that anything about my methods of work can possibly be of interest to anyone. Sometimes on television I have been lured into describing them, and always I have had the feeling that somebody was going to interrupt with that line of Jack Benny's – 'There will now be a slight pause while everyone says "Who cares?"' I should have said that if there was one subject on which the world would prefer not to be informed, it was this.

Still, if you really think the boys and girls are anxious to get the inside facts, let's go.

I would like to say, as I have known other authors to say, that I am at my desk every morning at nine sharp, but something tells me I could never get away with it. The newspaper and radio public is a shrewd public, and it knows that no one is ever at his desk at nine. I do get to my desk, however, round about ten, and everything depends then on whether or not I put my feet up on it. If I do, I instantly fall into a reverie or coma, musing on ships and shoes and sealing wax and cabbages and kings. My mind drifts off into the past and, like the man in the Bab Ballads, I wonder how the playmates of my youth are getting on – McConnell, S. B. Walters, Paddy Byles and Robinson. This goes on for some time. Many of my deepest thoughts have come to me when I have my feet up on the desk, but I have never been able to fit one of them into any novel I have been writing.

If I avoid this snare, I pull chair up to typewriter, adjust the Peke which is lying on my lap, chirrup to the foxhound, throw a passing pleasantry to the cat and pitch in.

All the animal members of the household take a great interest in my literary work, and it is rare for me to begin the proceedings without a quorum. I sometimes think I could ·concentrate better in solitude, and I wish particularly that the cat would give me a word of warning before jumping on the back of my neck as I sit trying to find the *mot juste*, but I remind myself that conditions might be worse. I might be dictating my stuff.

How anybody can compose a story by word of mouth face to face with a bored-looking secretary with a notebook is more than I can imagine. Yet many authors think nothing of saying, 'Ready, Miss Spelvin? Take dictation. Quote No comma Sir Jasper Murgatroyd comma close quotes comma said no better make it hissed Evangeline comma quote I would not marry you if you were the last man on earth period close quotes Quote Well comma I'm not comma so the point does not arise comma close quotes replied Sir Jasper comma twirling his moustache cynically period And so the long day wore on period. End of chapter.'

If I had to do that sort of thing I should be feeling all the time that the girl was saying to herself as she took it down, 'Well comma this beats me period. How comma with homes for the feebleminded touting for custom on every side comma has a man like this succeeded in remaining at large as of even date mark of interrogation.'

Nor would I be more happy and at my ease with one of those machines where you talk into a mouthpiece and have your observations recorded on wax. I bought one of them once and started *Right Ho, Jeeves* on it. I didn't get beyond the first five lines.

Right Ho, Jeeves, as you may or may not know, Winkler, begins with the words:

'Jeeves,' I said, 'may I speak frankly?'

'Certainly, sir.'

'What I have to say may wound you.'

'Not at all, sir.'

'Well, then——'

and when I reached the 'Well, then——' I thought I would turn back and play the thing over to hear how it sounded.

There is only one adjective to describe how it sounded, the adjective 'awful'. Until that moment I had never realized that I had a voice like that of a very pompous headmaster addressing the young scholars in his charge from the pulpit in the school chapel, but if this machine was to be relied on, that was the sort of voice I had. There was a kind of foggy dreariness about it that chilled the spirits.

It stunned me. I had been hoping, if all went well, to make *Right Ho, Jeeves* an amusing book – gay, if you see what I mean – rollicking, if you still follow me, and debonair, and it was plain to me that a man with a voice like that could never come within several million light-miles of being gay and debonair. With him at the controls, the thing would develop into one of those dim tragedies of the grey underworld which we return to the library after a quick glance at Chapter One. I sold the machine next day, and felt like the Ancient Mariner when he got rid of the albatross.

2

My writing, if and when I get down to it, is a combination of longhand and typing. I generally rough out a paragraph or a piece of dialogue in pencil on a pad and then type an improved version. This always answers well unless while using the pad I put my feet up on the desk, for then comes the reverie of which I was speaking and the mind drifts off to other things.

I am fortunate as a writer in not being dependent on my surroundings. Some authors, I understand, can give of their best only if there is a vase of roses of the right shade on the right spot of their desk and away from their desk are unable to function. I have written quite happily on ocean liners during gales, with the typewriter falling into my lap at intervals, in hotel bedrooms, in woodsheds, in punts on lakes, in German internment camps and in the Inspecteurs room at the Palais de Justice in Paris at the time when the French Republic suspected me of being a danger to it. (Actually, I was very fond of the French Republic and would not have laid a finger on it if you had brought it to me asleep on a chair, but they did not know this.) I suppose it was those seven years when I was doing the 'By The Way' column on the *Globe* that gave me the useful knack of being able to work under any conditions.

Writing my stories – or at any rate rewriting them – I enjoy. It is the thinking them out that puts those dark circles under my eyes. You can't think out plots like mine without getting a suspicion from time to time that something has gone seriously wrong with the brain's two hemispheres and that broad band of transversely running fibres known as the *corpus callosum*. There always comes a moment in the concoction of a scenario when I pause and say to myself, 'Oh, what a noble mind is here o'erthrown.' If somebody like Sir Roderick Glossop could have read the notes I made for my last one – *Something Fishy* – 400 pages of them – he would have been on the telephone instructing two strong men to hurry along with the strait-waistcoat before he was half-way through. I append a few specimens:

Father an actor? This might lead to something.
(There is no father in the story.)

Make brother genial, like Bingo Little's bookie.
(There is no brother in the story.)

Crook tells hero and heroine about son.
(There is no crook in the story, either.)

Son hairdresser? Skating instructor?
(There is no son in the story.)

Can I work it so that somebody – who? – has told her father that she is working as a cook?

(This must have meant something to me at the time, but the mists have risen and the vision faded.)

Artist didn't paint picture himself, but knew who painted it. Artist then need not be artist.

(Who this artist is who has crept into the thing is a mystery to me. He never appears again.)

And finally a note which would certainly have aroused Sir Roderick Glossop's worst suspicions. Coming in the middle of a page with no hint as to why it is there, it runs thus:

An excellent hair lotion may be made of stewed prunes and isinglass.

The odd thing is that, just as I am feeling that I must get a proposer and seconder and have myself put up for Colney Hatch, something always clicks and the story straightens itself out, and after that, as in the case of Otis Quackenbush, all is gas and gaiters, not to mention joy and jollity. I shall have to rewrite every line in the book a dozen times, but once I get my scenario set, I know that it is simply a matter of plugging away at it.

To me a detailed scenario is, as they say, of the essence. Some writers will tell you that they just sit down and take pen in hand and let their characters carry on as they see fit. Not for me any procedure like that. I wouldn't trust my characters an inch. If I sat back and let them take charge, heaven knows what the result would be. They have to do just what the scenario tells them to, and no larks. It has always seemed to me that planning a story out and writing it are two separate things. If I were going to run a train, I would feel that the square thing to do was to provide the customers with railway lines and see that the points were in working order. Otherwise – or so I think – I would have my public shouting, as did the lady in Marie Lloyd's immortal song:

> Oh, mister porter,
> What shall I do?
> I want to go to Birmingham
> And they're taking me on to Crewe.

Anyone who reads a novel of mine can be assured that it will be as coherent as I can make it – which, I readily agree, is not saying much, and that, though he may not enjoy the journey, he will get to Birmingham all right.

3

Well, I think that about cleans the thing up, J.P., does it not? You will have gathered, in case you were worrying, that in my seventy-sixth year – I shall be seventy-six in October – 15th, if you were thinking of sending me some little present – I am still ticking over reasonably briskly. I eat well, sleep well and do not tremble when I see a job of work. In fact, if what you were trying to say in your letter was, 'Hullo there, Wodehouse, how *are* you?' my reply is that I'm fine. Touch of lumbago occasionally in the winter months and a little slow at getting after the dog next door when I see him with his head and shoulders in our garbage can, but otherwise all spooked up with zip and vinegar, as they say out west.

All the same, a letter like yours, with its emphasis on 'over seventy', does rather touch an exposed nerve. It makes one realize that one is not the bright-eyed youngster one had been considering oneself and that shades of the prison house are beginning, as one might put it, to close upon the growing boy. A rude awakening, of course, and one that must have come to my housemaster at school (who recently died at the age of ninety-six) when he said to a new boy on the first day of term:

'Wapshott? Wapshott? That name seems familiar. Wasn't your father in my form?'

'Yes, sir,' replied the stripling. '*And* my grandfather.'

Collapse of old party, as the expression is.

Index

(W) indicates a book or story by Wodehouse, or a show on which he worked.

Wain, John 525
Wallace, Edgar 271, 272, 369
Waller, Jack 320
Walls, Tom 131
Walpole, Hugh 294, 366–7
Wanger, Walter 332
Ward, Irene 361
Waugh, Alec (works) 247–8
Waugh, Evelyn (works) 379–80,
  394, 399, 546–7
Webb, Charlie (internee) 438–9,
  440
Webb, Clifton 173
Weller, Sam 131
Wells, H. G. 275, 301–2, 480
West, Mae 297
Wheaton, Anna 54, 60, 62, 65
White, T. H. (works) 389
White Feather, The (W) 261
Whoopee 211
Willard, John 14
Williams, Bert 9
Wilson, Harry Leon (works) 259
Winchell, Walter 614
Wodehouse, Armine 153, 477

Wodehouse, Ethel 63–6, 68, 83,
  89–90, 115, 180, 187, 196, 199,
  258, 267, 280, 285–7, 304, 307,
  354–5, 361, 377–8, 386, 389,
  408–10, 412
Wodehouse (senior) 11, 476
Woods, Al 269
Woollcott, Alexander 17, 216–18,
  222
Wordsworth, William 531
writing 479–81, 529–31, 640–5

Yellow Ticket, The 196
Youmans, Vincent 219, 224, 282,
  625
Young, Roland 333

Ziegfeld, Florenz 19, 27, 50, 51,
  54–5, 70, 74, 77, 115, 118–21,
  123, 127–32, 134–6, 148, 170,
  183, 206–13, 249, 270, 271,
  281–3, 289
Zimmerman, Freddie 49–50,
  129–30